AF560742

SOCIAL TRANSFORMATION IN NORTH-WESTERN INDIA

Social Transformation in North-Western India during the Twentieth Century

Edited by

CHETAN SINGH

INSTITUTE OF PUNJAB STUDIES
CHANDIGARH

MANOHAR
2010

First published 2010

ISBN 978-81-7304-838-8

Published by

Ajay Kumar Jain *for*
Manohar Publishers & Distributors
4753/23 Ansari Road, Daryaganj
New Delhi 110 002

Typeset at

Digigrafics
New Delhi 110 049

Printed at

Salasar Imaging Systems
Delhi 110 035

Contents

Preface

The Institute of Punjab Studies is an interdisciplinary forum for comprehensive studies of the people of north-western India in a broad historical and comparative perspective. The Institute organizes seminars and disseminates their proceedings through publications. The papers in this volume were presented at a seminar on social transformation held in September 2005 and have since been revised and updated. I am sure like our previous publications, the present volume would also be well-received.

Professor Chetan Singh has edited this volume with meticulous care and added a meaningful Introduction. Apart from the editor and the contributors themselves, my colleague Dr Sheena Pall helped in reading the proofs. She has also helped in the preparation of Glossary and Index. The Manohar Publishers have brought out this volume with their characteristic concern for quality. The Indian Council of Historical Research, New Delhi provided financial assistance for organizing this seminar. On behalf of the Institute of Punjab Studies I thank them all.

The quiet and sustained support of Professor G.S. Gosal, an eminent geographer and Chairman of the Institute, had been a source of encouragement. Professor J.S. Grewal, its Honorary Director, had been the moving spirit in the conceptualization and organization of the seminar. In the course of the seminar we were cheerfully helped by several of the colleagues at the Panjab University, particularly Dr Veena Sachdeva, Dr Reeta Grewal, Dr Sasha and Dr Sheena Pall. I am happy to acknowledge the help received from the Research Fellows of the Department of History, Panjab University, particularly Kuldip K. Grewal, Mohinder Singh, Charu Plaha, Vijay Lakshmi, Sonia Vig and Karamjit K. Malhotra. I am thankful to them all. I may also take this opportunity to acknowledge the lasting support received from the 'foreign friends' of the Institute for its programmes.

1 May 2009

INDU BANGA
Honorary Secretary

Introduction

CHETAN SINGH

It has never been easy for social scientists to explain even limited processes of social change with a great degree of certainty. How immensely more difficult it would be to describe large-scale social transformation over an entire region is something that needs no reiteration. The unlikelihood of social scientists ever agreeing on a single general theory of social change ensures that transformation in human societies would continue to be perceived, and studied, in many different ways. Naturally, this does not always contribute towards creating a complete and comprehensive picture. But it does enable the study of different dimensions of a particular phenomenon or, conversely, allow for the comparison of a single aspect of different developments. From the resulting multiplicity of viewpoints, it is possible that a functional understanding of social change emerges—an understanding which provides a broad, albeit uneven, platform for disputation and dialogue.

Any endeavour to understand social transformation would need to engage with history and mark a few periodic reference points. It would also need to identify ideas and institutions in which change is noticeable and, therefore, indicative of larger social transformation. From the point of view of contemporary India, the experience of colonialism represents a historical point of initial reference – a kind of inherited circumstance to which later developments are readily compared. Thereafter, the triumph of independence changed conditions dramatically as it extended the right of political participation to a previously marginalized population. It marks for Indian society and polity the commencement of a new chapter. For the north-western region, a third most obvious point of reference has been the Green

Revolution and its dramatic socio-economic consequences. It represents both the success and the failure of a development paradigm which has impacted enormously on the region.

The creation and consolidation of distinct identities has invariably been a part of social change. In fact, the 'idea' of identity and its articulation in various ways has always constituted an important part of the social dynamic of north-western India. Identity has sometimes been affirmed through religious ideology, at times by means of a heightened consciousness of caste, and at yet other times through a combination of both religion and caste. This, of course, does not encompass all the means by which identities were expressed. In independent India, assertions of identity have been made most effectively by communities participating in democratic politics. To the issue of identity may be added the notions of social justice (including social advancement) and equality. Apart from their acceptability as independent moral values, the adoption of these principles was intended to improve the social and economic condition of underprivileged social sections. The extent to which this has actually happened is a matter of debate. It would, indeed, be an important measure of social progress.

The exact nature of social change notwithstanding, the introduction of new technology over the past several decades has contributed undeniably to economic development. Not only has this increased production, it has also altered traditional social relationships. Growing literacy, greater mobility and improved avenues of employment are clearly evident even in the rural areas of north-western India. Contradictions and confrontations in society have become more overt, and the equations of political power are being rewritten. The modern Indian state and a changed polity have attempted to appropriate functions which were earlier the domain of institutions such as caste and community. Yet these traditional forms of social organization continue to assert their authority and seem, in fact, to have found a new relevance. The uneven nature of social transformation in contemporary India is quite apparent and represents a problem in itself.

The chapters included in this volume were presented at a seminar, 'Social Transformation in North Western India', organized by the Institute of Punjab Studies at the Panjab University, Chandigarh. They represent different academic disciplines, diverse interests and equally distinct points of view. If they appear at times to be incompatible, uneven and failing to fall into a pattern or a structured format—that is how they should be: truly representative of the region they seek to discuss.

Almost all social movements generate contradictions and a certain amount of internal debate. The resolution, or harmonization, of opposing positions remains an ongoing endeavour. In this process, there emerges, from time to time, a dominant and more acceptable opinion. This has equally been an essential part of the growth of Sikhism. One of the most significant historical developments in the region has been the emergence and dominance of the Khalsa. The establishment of the Lahore kingdom too is of particular importance in the history of the north-western region. However, for understanding developments that took place in the latter part of the twentieth century, the colonial period is almost defining in nature. The struggles of the Sikh community and its relationship with the colonial power are the focus of the first two articles of the volume. They touch upon the origins, as it were, of the transformation that occurred in the region in modern times. An attempt is made to explain the emergence of new social and political standpoints.

J. S. Grewal has traced the long-term consequences of the loss of political power by the old aristocracy in Punjab. He describes the impact that an expanding colonial power had on the economy and society of the region and particularly on the Sikhs. There was a noticeable and growing consciousness of distinct identities whose emergence can be traced to the colonial census system. Amidst the many social cross-currents in the region, the Singh Sabha Movement was perhaps the most successful. It represented and articulated the interests of the Sikhs as a distinct social entity – and thereafter as an explicit political entity. It seems that from the late nineteenth century onwards a combination of causes brought about a 'resurgence' among the Sikhs. This subsequently acquired a political form.

It is such a 'resurgence' that Veena Sachdeva examines with specific reference to the concept of sacred space 'as it emerged and grew in Sikhism'. Control over sacred space, especially Amritsar and the Harmandir Sahib, became a contentious political issue even during the reign of Ranjit Singh. Contrary to a proclaimed policy of refraining from controlling religious properties, the colonial government in Punjab took great interest in administering the Harmandir Sahib. This also meant, however, that not only was there a great deal of corruption, but also the affairs of the temple were not managed entirely in accordance with approved Sikh tenets. Brahmanical practices were quite evident on the temple premises, and it was felt necessary to put a stop to them. The region-wide struggle that ensued between the Sikh community and the British (and the old vested interests controlling the gurdwaras) is vividly described by Veena Sachdeva. It was finally in 1925 that the Shiromani Gurdwara Prabandhak Committee was recognized as the legal authority to manage and control Sikh gurdwaras.

A different social development underway at roughly the same time was the establishment of Sanatan Dharm institutions in the region. The objective of these was to popularize Sanskrit and encourage the study of the *Shastra*s and *Veda*s. Cow protection and an element of social reform too were part of their stated agenda. Sheena Pall examines the nature and functioning of these institutions. The Bharat Dharm Mahamandal, set up by Din Dayalu Sharma, became, for some time, the political instrument through which a clearly Brahmanical world-view was sought to be propagated. However, despite the support it received from the privileged sections of society—princes, aristocrats and businessmen—the Mahamandal had lost its effectiveness by the first few years of the twentieth century. From 1917 onwards, the Sanatan Dharm Pratinidhi Sabha (established in Lahore), along with many local *sabha*s, began to play a more active role. Dalits were approached and encouraged to adopt Brahmanical conventions. Orphanages were established with the purpose of preventing the conversion of Hindu children to another religion. An interesting observation that Sheena Pall makes is that more Sanatan Dharm Sabhas were established in areas with a large Muslim population than in overwhelming Hindu areas. This, it has been suggested, was a possible indicator of communal consciousness. Furthermore, imperfections in the census operations also caused distortions. Hindus who did not claim explicitly to belong to a specific religious sub-denomination were, by default, all clubbed into the category of Sanatan Dharmis. The latter, therefore, appeared to be far more numerous in the census than they may have been in reality. The census operations, and the classification criteria they adopted, had become obvious and important influences on the processes of identity formation and social transformation.

At the local level, colonial subjugation of the region was not simply a distant, impersonal development – it was a process which touched and changed individual lives. In many of his works, Bhishma Sahni has made penetrating observations about the everyday experiences of people and their changing world-view. Harish Sharma and Radha Sharma have chosen one such work – *Maiya Das ki Madi* – to illustrate the changes that took place in Punjabi society under colonial rule. These changes included the emergence of a new middle class and rapid commercialization in which an exploitative class of *sahukar*s became increasingly influential. Indebtedness among the peasantry led to land alienation. The old aristocracy, gripped by nostalgia, was reluctant to accept the growing importance of the trading community. Hopes of 'prosperity', ignited by the establishment of British rule, gave way to 'disillusionment'. Amidst these different trends, the relentless momentum of change is signified by the increasing importance of education as an instrument of rejuvenation – even regeneration. In the inspiring story of Rukmani who, in her search for an education, challenges patriarchy with silent determination and successfully confronts overwhelming odds, are seen the early and embryonic traces of nationalism. Creative writing and historical analysis are brought together by Harish Sharma and Radha Sharma as illustration and explanation of a society in 'transition'.

The relationship between the colonizer and the colonized was complex and multifaceted. Economic exploitation and political dominance were its most stark components. Western medicine was another significant, but subtle, element in this relationship. Therefore the assertion of the superiority of European medical knowledge became not only an instrument of British rule but also its justification. It was not without a struggle, however, that

Indian society made space in its mental world for Western medicine. What began as an effort to protect British troops from debilitating tropical diseases gradually became a policy which entered the larger domain of public health. The ensuing confrontation between Western medicine and indigenous practices and beliefs – especially centred on forced vaccination – forms the central theme of the subject explored by Sasha. Acceptance of Western medicine by educated classes in large towns was counterbalanced by the superstitions and rumours that became the basis of resistance in rural areas. Ever-present British racial prejudice was met by religious convictions, suspicion and notions of 'family honour'. It was only gradually, through increased sensitivity to social norms and a complementary change in attitudes on both sides, that Western medicine won greater acceptability. Through multiple strategies, and riding on the shoulders of colonial authority, it had established a foothold in the region by the mid-1920s.

Not all changes experienced by people belonging to the region occurred within its boundaries. There were distant linkages which could be part of a larger transformatory process. Common subjection to British colonialism seems to have bound the entire subcontinent ever more closely. Despite their essentially exploitative nature, the changes wrought by the colonial economy seemed to encourage extended mobility. They also offered opportunities of employment in new occupations. The Sikh diasporas that grew as a result of these changes forms the subject of the paper by Himadri Banerjee. He points to the interesting differences between the two Sikh diasporas – of Kolkata and of the Brahmaputra Valley – studied by him. For the Punjabi Sikhs of Calcutta (who were closely associated with Akali politics), intimate links with Punjab society and politics were crucial. These links not only formed the basis for their claiming superiority over the Bihari Sikhs but also provided the agenda for political action from time to time. By contrast the Sikhs in the Brahmaputra Valley pursued what Banerjee calls a 'politics of silence' regarding Akali politics in Punjab. Ramgarhias (artisan castes) formed an overwhelming majority in the Sikh diaspora of the Brahmaputra Valley. Migration to Assam had enabled the Ramgarhia Sikhs – working in railways, industry, plantations and construction – to become successful contractors. However, in Punjab their low social status remained unchanged. It was a reminder both of the pervasive nature of the caste system and of the predominance of the Jats in Sikh politics. Not surprisingly, then, the Sikh diaspora in Assam maintained a closer connection with the All-India Ramgarhia Movement. A more focused approach, directed towards improving the condition of the Ramgarhias, was adopted by the Sikhs of the Brahmaputra Valley. It is this immense social complexity amongst the Sikhs in eastern India that Himadri Banerjee has successfully highlighted.

If there is any aspect of social transformation in modern India that is explicitly associated with a large part of the north-western region, it is the wide-ranging changes that were brought in by the Green Revolution. The adoption of new crop varieties and farming techniques, and the harnessing of the productive power of a dynamic peasantry created a prosperous society. In popular imagination this was an exemplary story of successful agriculture-based development. The progress made, especially by Punjab, was indeed remarkable. But was this prosperity really as widespread as so many would like to believe? Assisted by the passage of time and with the benefit of hindsight, a new and more complete picture is slowly emerging. Without denying the benefit that it brought, it is perhaps time now to admit many of the flaws and follies of the Green Revolution. These have become even more obvious to scholars in recent times.

Sucha Singh Gill has dealt specifically with the long-term socio-economic trends traceable to the developments that took place in Punjab after the 1960s. His meticulous research exposes the hidden and ugly underbelly of an apparently affluent society. The poor peasant in Punjab paid a heavy price for the changes agrarian transformation engendered. Small and marginal land-holdings became economically viable because of the Green Revolution. With the passage of time, however, these were further subdivided amongst legal heirs, thereby resulting in small and marginal cultivators constituting more than 75 per cent of the total number of cultivators. This fragmentation of holdings altered the nature of tenancy relations. Prior to the Green Revolution, small peasants cultivated land which was obtained on lease from large landholders. At present, however, the position is reversed. The big cultivators now take land on lease, thus pushing out the poorer tenants. Traditional agriculture sustained by family labour has been replaced by a mechanized system depending increasingly on hired labour. Capital intensive agricultural practices and the exposure of agricultural produce to market fluctuations have enabled big farmers with adequate resources to take over land from poor and marginal farmers. Stagnant productivity and an escalating cost of production have marginalized the small peasantry. All these factors have combined to create what Gill describes as 'a phase of jobless growth'.

What were the social implications of such a development? This is the subject of the next chapter. On the basis of extensive fieldwork in Punjab, Manjit Singh has traced the impact the Green Revolution has had on the lives of the peasantry. From a subsistence-oriented 'moral economy' the shift has been towards money, market and conspicuous comsumption. Capitalist agriculture, Manjit Singh argues, has not only resulted in the disempowerment of the scheduled castes, but also ironically increased the incidence of bonded labour. This is a bondage rooted in indebtedness, and resulting in long hours of work and abysmally low wages for the indebted labourer. Numerous state schemes for rural development have failed to provide adequate support to the needy because the procedures for identifying the poor are inefficient and flawed.

A graphic yet nuanced description of the multidimensional change brought about by the Green Revolution is to be found in Kumool Abbi's chapter. Through her imaginative use of *Annadata* – a work by Baldev Singh – Abbi elaborates the diverse ways in which Punjabi society has been transformed. No longer do the Jat landed proprietors exercise complete control over the untouchable agricultural labourers who once worked on their fields. This reorientation of the relationship between the two also involves the complex issue of gender. Another indicator of changing times is the tightening grip of the business class, especially the middlemen (*aarhtiyas*), over the village economy – and particularly over the Jat peasantry. Growing commercialization has compelled farmers to learn to negotiate the uncertainties of the market. Many of them see this engagement with the market as a decline in social status. Failure to deal with altered socio-economic configurations in the region has seen some Jat peasant proprietors being reduced to the position of wage labourers. Abbi presents the cultural reflection of the souring of the dream of agrarian prosperity. Yet, there seems to be another, perhaps positive, dimension to social change in Punjab. With greater employment prospects in a growing economy, an increasing number of young women from villages have begun working in small towns. Economic independence and the corresponding freedom that this has been allowed to these women have enabled them to question male dominance – albeit in a limited manner. Quite expectedly, however, differing perceptions about the 'moral' costs that women pay for such change remain a palpable undercurrent.

Amidst descriptions of despondency in post-Green Revolution society, Kusum Chopra and Atiya Habeeb Kidwai point towards the emergence of a viable industrial alternative, which offers signs of hope. They stress the need for Punjab to develop industries in which it has a competitive advantage. The growth of traditional industries in Punjab from the Mughal period till recent times reveals that these have been employing an increasing number of people. An indicator of this is the diversified base of the urbanization process which is now no longer driven only by agricultural growth. The big cities of the region are growing ever more rapidly, and the total number of large cities has also increased. But this urban growth has not necessarily resulted in the decline of small towns. While industry is certainly beginning to get concentrated in the large cities, the smaller towns too have become more industrialized. Medium- and large-scale industries are now concentrated in the bigger cities while small scale industry has tended to prosper in small towns. Chopra and Kidwai argue that the two types of industries occupy different spaces. Small-scale industry is not threatened by the large industry, and hence there is less danger of unemployment.

An important measure of any process of social transformation in India is, quite evidently, the extent to which it alters the lives of the depressed section of society, especially the scheduled castes. In this context, some questions arise. To what extent have the underprivileged been active participants in the transformatory process? What opportunities has it afforded to them for a better future? Social change is usually a subtle ongoing process. Only occasionally has it been the result of a deliberately formulated policy or programme. It has perhaps always been the way of depressed and subordinated groups in India to weave through the interstices of the social order in search of a better social space. Over the long term many of them have succeeded remarkably. In the event of a constant denial of such a space, it is possible that for some social groups the attraction of an alternative route to social betterment or even an alternative social system became greater.

John Webster's study of the conversion of Dalits to Christianity in later-nineteenth-century Punjab seeks to examine the convoluted issue of the social mobility of the lower castes. Through a detailed review of major studies on conversion in Punjab, Webster discusses whether the conversion of a large number of people to Christianity can be considered a 'movement'. Furthermore, is it possible to see a broad 'pattern' in these conversions? He is inclined to regard the acceptance of Christianity by Dalits – especially Chuhras – in Punjab as a conversion movement. More importantly, however, he sees this movement as being situated in a specific Dalit context rather than as being the consequence of missionary activity. The Dalits saw the movement as being initiated by themselves in their own interest. For that reason, perhaps, Webster stresses the logical point that a conversion movement was possible wherever the earliest convert was himself a leader of his community. It was only after the process had started that the Christian mission came to play a more important organizing role in the movement. What provided an impetus to the movement was the 'demonstration effect of conversion'. It became apparent that conversion could open the way to literacy, landownership and a higher social status.

Finally, however, as the need arose for Christian missions in the region to consolidate their position – rather than expand their activities, the number of conversions declined. Undoubtedly the movement derived its strength from the Dalit search for dignity. Its 'rural and decentralized' nature reflected the Dalit social situation. Webster argues that the movement did 'not aim at transformation of a caste-based rural society'. Be that as it may, the conversions did prompt the Arya Samaj to look more closely at the Dalits and engage more seriously in their uplift.

The changing situation of another category of non-persons, that is widows, has been taken up by Reeta Grewal. She examines the demographic, legal and social position of widows in the rural and urban areas of the major sub-regions of north-western India under colonial rule. She analyses the census data on widows and accounts for their relatively low proportion in this region in political, economic, social and cultural terms. She looks at the nature of the widow's rights in the agrarian context, and the restrictions imposed on her in the Customary Law as recorded and formalized by the colonial state. The complexities and variations in the *karewa* (*chadar andazi*) form of marriage too are brought out. The author also discusses the Arya and Sanatanist prescriptions for the higher caste Hindu widows in an urban setting. Despite differences in their stance towards the problem of widows, the social reformers as well as the British administrators reinforced patriarchal controls over them. At the same time, this period saw the beginning of legislation concerning the widow's rights, growing social acceptance of her remarriage among the higher castes, and of her increasing access to education and gainful employment. The tendencies noticed in the early twentieth century not only expanded in the latter half of the century, there was also a qualitative change in the position of widows in independent India.

Surya Kant, in his chapter describing the socio-economic transformation of SCs in north-western India after Independence, presents a comprehensive picture for the whole region. The internal differentiation within the SCs of the region has always existed, and is reflected in their unequal socio-economic development. In order to understand the nature of the transformation, Surya Kant has adopted three primary indicators: literacy, urbanization and occupational diversification. An important point which emerges at the beginning is that the SCs in the north-western region constitute a larger percentage of its population than in the rest of the country. The number of castes and sub-castes constituting the SC population of India is indeed very large – and has been increasing. It must be mentioned, however, that basically 10 sub-castes (out of 1,221 in 2001) make up more than 50 per cent of the SC population of India. An overwhelming majority of the SC population lives in rural areas though there has been a gradual migration to urban centres.

In all three indicators of social change the SCs of the region trailed behind the non-SCs. But this is not the complete picture. It needs to be remembered that the baseline for SCs in the 1960s was much lower, and in this respect their progress has been relatively fast. This is supported by the statistics presented in the chapter, especially in the parameters of literacy, urbanization and occupational diversification. Urbanization, as a phenomenon however, varies considerably in each state of the north-western region. The urbanization indicator, therefore, varies correspondingly in different states. In brief, Surya Kant argues that despite the socio-economic development of the SCs in the region being lower than that of the non-SCs, the position of the former is much better compared to the overall position of the SCs in India.

Rural society in a rapidly changing environment is often paradoxical. Stereotypes are frequently challenged by diversities and differences persist despite the power of dominant trends. The image of the Punjab peasantry as being highly indebted, disenchanted with its prospects, addicted to liquor and opium and burdened by enormous unbearable demands of dowry is the one that has been most commonly presented. Even the issues of a declining sex ratio and patriarchy are regarded as typical of rural Punjab. It is Rajesh Gill's argument that the large macro-statistical landscape overwhelms the smaller picture that does sometimes tell a different and optimistic story.

Gill presents the case studies of two Punjab villages. The essay focuses on the nature of inter-caste relationships, the growing significance of panchayats, the changing occupations and the altered gender relationships. The literacy levels of the two villages vary, as does their caste structure. An element of caste segregation is apparent. Even the sex ratio (in the 0-6-year age group) in one of the villages is very low. At the outset, therefore, it appears that the familiar, dismal story is once again being repeated. But the emphasis of the article is on increasing prosperity, local autonomy and some element of hope. It is evident – as also indicated by some other contributions – that the democratic electoral system along with caste-based reservation in the panchayats has compelled the upper castes to treat the lower castes better. The latter now have a louder voice in village affairs. Many of the lower-caste residents have found government jobs or employment in industry. Neither of the villages has a liquor shop, gender and caste relations are becoming more flexible and patriarchy no longer remains unquestioned. Rajesh Gill has suggested that even against what appears to be a somewhat disheartening picture in Punjab, it is possible to find vibrant and increasingly prosperous village communities. There is, then, a need to recognize diversity and to adopt a more nuanced approach in our understanding of the region.

With regard to traditional institutions and organizations in rural India, such an approach becomes crucial for it is here that the confrontation between continuity and change comes clearly to the forefront. Even as society engages actively with modernity and is transformed, the forces of tradition are reluctant to loosen their grip. Perhaps the most assertive form of traditional control in north-western India is the *khap*s in Haryana. P.S. Verma has provided the historical background of the *khap* panchayats and described their organization and method of functioning. Even today, these *khap*s exert an enormous influence on a wide range of socio-political issues in Haryana. The fact that *khap*s are principally organized around caste *gotra*s clearly suggests that the caste factor weighs heavily upon the process of decision-making in rural Haryana. Apparently each *khap* is controlled by a dominant *gotra* and headed by a *pradhan*. Many of the minor caste groups are included by default in the *khap* panchayat of the dominant *gotra*. Verma points out that most of these *khap* panchayats are multi-village organizations and thus encompass a considerable extent of territory. In keeping with their traditional legitimacy, the *khap* panchayats have intervened in matters pertaining to virtually every aspect of village life. While issues of marriage, caste and social norms are of particular concern to the *khap*s, the resolution of inter-caste and inter-clan disputes also logically falls within their purview. Their exercise of customary authority does, on occasion, bring them into conflict with the administrative and legal institutions of the modern state. Even more importantly, *khap* panchayats have sometimes extended their support to explicitly political issues. Their political significance is further reinforced by the fact that *khap* panchayats – because of their organizational nature – have the ability to enforce their writ at the village level.

The traditional role of *khap* panchayats as institutions of social control was implicitly challenged in colonial times by the establishment of a judicial system which did not accord legal primacy to caste norms. After Independence, the importance given to panchayati raj institutions has tended to further erode the authority of caste-based *khap*s. A greater social and developmental role is now played by the modern state – a role which was once virtually the exclusive domain of the *khap* panchayats in Haryana. But the boundaries are still hazy. As long as caste remains an important consideration in politics, and the notion of *biradari* acts as the essential social adhesive, *khap*s will remain important mechanisms of political mobilization and control. Verma's paper brings out the complexities that permeate the confrontation between tradition and modernity in rural Haryana.

It is the universalization of literacy and education that possesses the enormous potential of questioning tradition and founding modernity. But the reverse is perhaps equally true. The recognition of the dialectical relationship between literacy and social transformation forms the starting point of the paper by Swarnjit Mehta and Simrat Kahlon. They clarify, at the outset, that literacy is both an indicator and an instrument of social transformation. The study examines literacy trends in three states of the north-western region over a forty-year period (1961–2001). An inter-state comparison between Punjab, Haryana and Himachal Pradesh forms the overall framework of this paper. The specific areas of comparison are female education, the rural-urban divide and literacy levels of the SC and ST populations. Literacy levels have been steadily improving in all states. But what stands out in the study is that the overall progress made by Himachal Pradesh has been far more impressive than that of Punjab and Haryana. Perhaps the fact that public spending on education has been by far the greatest in Himachal Pradesh is probably the single most important reason for its impressive performance. But certainly, many other factors – social and cultural – would have contributed to these variations in the three states.

One needs to then ask whether the position occupied by women in a particular society has a bearing on its becoming educated and progressive. Himachal Pradesh, for example, is situated fairly high on the Human Development Index. Is there reason to believe that this is, in some way, linked to a sex ratio and gender profile which is better than that of neighbouring Punjab and Haryana? Perhaps the numerous rights traditionally enjoyed by women in Himachal have made Himachal society more equitable. Questions and ideas such as these seem to have prompted Raj Mohini Sethi to take a closer look at the relationship between gender, property and reform in Himachal Pradesh. She emphasizes the fact that even though marriage customs in many parts of Himachal do not conform to Sanskritic principles, the proprietary and economic rights of widows and unmarried daughters are secure. Customary matrimonial practices and rules of inheritance, Sethi argues, gave considerable freedom to women in Himachal. This does not, of course, mean that there is no male dominance. It is suggested that both social and land reform carried out in Himachal Pradesh over a long period of time shows the mark of Brahmanical influence. This has tended to weaken the position of women and perpetuates patrilineal inheritance. In short, the processes of social transformation and modernization in Himachal Pradesh seem to have eroded the rights that were earlier assured to women by customary practice.

PART I

HISTORICAL PERSPECTIVES

CHAPTER 1

Sociocultural Transformation Among the Sikhs Under Colonial Rule

J.S. GREWAL

A study of social transformation among the Sikhs during the period of colonial rule ideally calls for a consideration of the colonial context, social cultural change among the Sikhs, their religious and social concerns, growth of political consciousness and reflection of their social consciousness in creative literature and the arts. Historians of the Sikhs have talked of Sikh resurgence in terms of rupture, re-formation and revival in relation to the earlier Sikh tradition.[1] They seem to agree, however, that the Khalsa tradition was revitalized during the period of colonial rule, and that this revitalization was accompanied by a certain degree of cultural reorientation. Only a few aspects of sociocultural transformation have been taken up for the present, and for the period of colonial rule up to about 1920.

> The Sikhs do not form a numerous sect, yet their strength is not to be estimated by tens of thousands, but by the unity and energy of religious fervour and warlike temperament. They will dare much, and they will endure much, for the mystic Khalsa or commonwealth.

These words are quoted by Harjot Oberoi from *A History of the Sikhs* (1849) by J.D. Cunningham who was one of the most informed individuals on the Sikh faith.[2] Cunningham had lived among the Sikhs for eight years (1837–45), and come into contact with all classes of men.[3] He was also more familiar with Sikh literature than all his European predecessors and contemporaries.[4]

One may agree with Oberoi that Cunningham provides credible testimony on Sikhism as a living faith in the 1840s. It must be added, however, that his testimony does not support the Sanatan Sikhism of Oberoi's conception.[5]

Cunningham was familiar with 'the Granth of the Tenth Master', called the *Dasam Granth*. In his view, it was only partly composed by Guru Gobind Singh. It was treated as a scripture, but Guruship was believed to have been vested only in the *Adi Granth*. Furthermore, the Sikhs did not regard even the most revered of their holy men as Gurus, because Guruship had been declared by Guru Gobind Singh 'to rest in the general body of the Khalsa'. Next in importance to the two *Granth*s were the *Var*s of Bhai Gurdas and the *Rahitnama*s of Bhai Nand Lal and Bhai Prahlad Singh. The former depicted Sikhism as a new dispensation and the Sikh Panth as a distinct entity; the latter underlined Sikh belief in the sovereignty of the Khalsa (*raj karega Khalsa*) and the vesting of Guruship in the *Adi Granth* as well as the Khalsa. The Khalsa were visible everywhere, not only in the literature held in high esteem by the Sikhs, but also on the ground. Cunningham had no doubt that the Sahajdhari Sikhs (the '*khulasa* Sikhs' of his predecessors) were almost unknown in the Punjab. They were seen in the cities of British India, but in the Punjab the warlike Singhs of the tenth king were predominant.[6]

There were 'elements of change within Sikhism'. 'Sikh sects' were already numerous. Cunningham lists at least eighteen denominations of the Sikhs in the 1840s. But his list contains several categories which, even according to him, were not 'sects'. In this category were Bedis, Trehans, Bhallas and Sodhis, the descendents, respectively, of Guru Nanak, Guru Angad, Guru Amar Das and Guru Ram Das. Of these Guru lineages, only the Sodhis sometimes claimed to be the Gurus. The Bhais and Gianis were simply the pious and learned Singhs. The Akalis and Nihangs were distinguished from the rest of the Khalsa by their asceticism and spirit of independence. The Nirmalas were known for administering the baptism of the double-edged sword. The Ranghretas, Ramdasis and Mazhabis were simply Singhs with an outcaste background. A few groups had been excommunicated by Guru Gobind Singh or the Khalsa, such as the Ram Raiyas, the Masandis and the Banda-Panthis. One is left with only the Suthra Shahis and the Udasis. The latter were proud of their association with the Sikhs and held the *Adi Granth* in reverence, but they were essentially a 'Hindu sect'. Cunningham is emphatic, therefore, that 'the great development of the tenets of Guru Gobind Singh has thrown other denominations into the shade'.[7]

The 'impress' of Guru Gobind Singh could be seen in the 'elevated and altered' constitution of the minds of the Singhs, as much as in the 'amplitude' of their physical frames. A living spirit possessed 'the whole Sikh people'. They were 'wholly different from other Indians' in their religious faith and worldly aspirations, and they were bound together by a 'community of inward sentiment, and outward object unknown elsewhere'. Their enthusiasm as converts to a 'new religion' was still fresh; their faith was 'still an active and living principle'. They continued 'to make converts'. With a firm faith in God, they felt convinced that 'sooner or later He will confound their enemies for His own glory'.[8]

The Singhs figure prominently among the topmost *jagirdar*s of the kingdom of Lahore. A dozen of them received revenues worth Rs. 1,000,000. On the whole, the Singhs got more than 60 per cent of the total revenue alienated by the state in favour of large *jagirdar*s. Of the remaining Rs. 5,000,000 given out in smaller *jagir*s, the Singhs had a lion's share. The Sikhs also received a very large share of the 'religious grants'. Foremost among them were the Sodhis, who got Rs. 500,000 a year. They were followed by the Bedis, who received Rs. 400,000. Together the Sodhis and Bedis received 45 per cent of the total revenue alienated by the state as *dharmarth*. The Golden Temple and many other gurdwaras had a fair share of the remaining Rs. 1,100,000. The Akalis too are mentioned as recipients of religious grants along with others. Cunningham leaves no doubt that the Singhs were active participants in the affairs of the kingdom of Lahore and formed the most important category of beneficiaries of its patronage. He does not give much detail, but a detailed study confirms his general impression.[9]

A little more than half of the nearly two scores of generals and commanders in the army of Lahore before the first Anglo-Sikh war were Sikhs. More significantly, all the Sikhs who joined the army were Khalsa Singhs. There was hardly any unit of cavalry, infantry and artillery that did not have Singh soldiers. Cunningham appreciated the 'manly deportment' of the Singh soldiers even after their defeat, which added 'luster to that valour which the victors had felt and generously extolled'. He refers to the Panchayats of Singhs from each battalion or company. Through them, Sikh people could intervene in the nomination, and in the removal, of their rulers on behalf of the Khalsa.[10]

Cunningham virtually equated the Sikh with the Singh. A careful reading of his *History* leaves little doubt that in estimating the number of 'Sikhs' he was actually counting the Singhs. His argument is something like this. The strength of the Sikh armies has been estimated to be 70,000 at the lowest and 250,000 at the highest. In his estimate, the Sikhs could muster about 125,000 'soldiers of their own faith'. Their families accounted for 625,000 to 750,000 Sikhs. However, not all Sikh families were represented in the army. Even those families that were represented did not spare all the brothers from agricultural work to join the army. He suggested, therefore, that the gross population of the Sikhs should range between 1,250,000 and 1,500,000. They were spread all over the central parts of the Punjab, with numerical dominance only in a small pocket in the protected Sikh states.[11]

There was a good deal of emphasis in Sikh literature on social equality. A good foundation was thus laid for 'the practical obliteration of all differences'. The erstwhile outcaste Chuhras and Chamars formed a part of the Khalsa Panth. Sometimes women too were initiated through the baptism of a single-edged dagger. All Sikhs partook of the sacred *parshad* in common. However, there was no injunction to change the traditional patterns of matrimony and commensality. Despite political and social differentiation, there was religious equality among the Khalsa in the 1840s.[12]

The subversion of Khalsa Raj in 1849 created a radically new situation. The loss of political power had immediate economic and social implications for the Khalsa and brought in its wake the problem of readjustment. The long-term policies of the new rulers created a new social and political environment and affected the Khalsa. New challenges had to be faced. The Khalsa tried to meet them in the light of their understanding of the past and their vision of the future. In order to be effective, they had to create new institutions.

As a part of the British empire, the Punjab came into closer contact with the rest of India and the rest of the world. This contact was facilitated by the new means of transportation and communication. Metalled roads, railways, post and telegraph and the press made the province a more compact unit. Not only could goods be imported or exported with greater ease, but new men and new ideas could also enter the Punjab. The ideas and programmes of the Brahmo Samaj, for instance, entered the Punjab in the wake of the Bengali babus in the new administration of the province. At a later stage, the ideas and programmes of Sir Syed Ahmad Khan came to influence the Punjabi Muslims. The Arya Samaj of Swami Dayanand found an equally congenial soil in the Punjab. Such developments could provide both a challenge and a point of reference for emulation for the Khalsa.

Colonial rulers were deeply interested in agrarian production. Revenue from land was still the major source of income. Periodic settlements of revenue in cash began to be made, involving the recording of rights in land. Irrigation through canals was even more efficacious for increasing agricultural production. A network of canals changed even the physical appearance of the province from the Jamuna to the Jhelum. External markets accelerated the process of commercialization and further increased agrarian production. This increase was reflected in the increased volume and value of trade. The development of the colonial economy spelt prosperity for the trading communities and large landholders, but it meant poverty and depression for the small peasant. This resulted in an increased number of tenants and the transfer of land to moneylenders. At the end of the nineteenth century, the Punjab Alienation of Land Act was passed to obviate the transfer of land from agriculturists to non-agriculturists. The major beneficiaries of this Act were the large landholders. The economic policies and measures of the colonial rulers thus had important implications for social change and affected the fortunes of various segments of the Punjabi society in different ways.

Change was equally true of the new administration. Not only

were the departments multiplied – with a lot of importance attached to revenue, police and justice – but also a large measure of bureaucratic rule was established in place of the *jagirdari* system. A new type of personnel was needed at the lower rungs of this administration. Import of personnel from Bengal and the United Provinces could serve this purpose in the beginning, but not for all time. Sooner than later Punjabis had to be inducted, thereby introducing a certain degree of competition amongst them. A new system of education was needed to produce suitable personnel. Urdu was introduced as the medium of education up to matriculation. English was introduced for higher education. The content of this new education was Western sciences, social studies and English literature. The educated Punjabis could, and did, cater to the needs of administration. New professions were thrown open by the new administration and the new system of education itself: law, medicine, engineering and teaching. New education also meant new ideas which could be disseminated through the print media. Journalism emerged as a new profession. Various segments of the Punjabi society were affected differently by new opportunities in services and professions.[13]

Census reports published by the administration, and the social categories used for classification, made the Punjabi people increasingly conscious of numbers and identities of various kinds. Classification in terms of religious communities proved to be important in different ways. Christian missionaries had begun to enter the Punjab with the advent of British rule. A large number of missions were established in the nineteenth century. The missionaries opened schools and eventually colleges. They also opened hospitals and established orphanages. But their primary objective was conversion. Optimistic about their success, they denounced all indigenous religious beliefs and practices as morally degrading. They condemned what they regarded as social evils arising out of discrimination on the basis of caste and gender. They were not unsuccessful in their evangelical objectives. Gradually at first, and then rapidly with the passage of time they gained converts, especially from amongst the lower castes and outcastes. The number of Christians in the Punjab increased from 4,000 in 1881 to about 300,000 in 1921.[14]

The activities of Christian missionaries obliged the leaders of the Punjabi society to set their own religious house in order. Re-evaluation of religious traditions, systematic formulation of religious beliefs and practice, propagation of ideas through the printing press and adoption of an educational system geared to socio-religious objectives became the common concerns of the Punjabis. Languages and scripts acquired a new kind of importance, and pivotal importance was given to religious scriptures. The Anglo-Vedic, Anglo-Islamic and Anglo-Sikh systems of education were the indigenous response to Christian schools and colleges, as well as to the government institutions in which no religious instruction was provided.

With the introduction of bureaucratic administration the decline of the former ruling class of the kingdom of Lahore was inevitable. Its members had earlier received *jagir*s for rendering services to the state. Their services were not needed anymore. Therefore, their *jagir*s had to be taken back. The *jagirdar*s who had resisted the British were generally given pensions for life. The others mostly retained a small part of their *jagir*s in perpetuity. The Khalsa *jagirdar*s suffered more than the others because of their larger number and greater opposition to the British. However, nearly all of them supported the British actively during the uprising of 1857–8 and received generous rewards. The Sikh aristocracy, as a class, was rehabilitated in the eyes of the British administrators and came to be treated as 'the natural leaders' of the Sikh people. At least half of the aristocratic families of the 1840s survived into the twentieth century by adjusting to the new situation and by making use of the new opportunities. Some new families also became 'families of note'. As a class, the Sikh aristocracy was next in importance to the ruling chiefs of the protected Sikh states like Patiala, Nabha, Jind, Faridkot and Kapurthala.

The religious grants given by the Sikh rulers were not entirely taken back by the British, even though they did not patronize religious institutions as a matter of policy. About three scores of gurdwaras continued to hold lands. A number of Sodhis and Bedis retained a part of their grants. The descendents of eminent Bhais and Gianis of the kingdom of Lahore too retained a part of their grants – like the families of Bhai Ram Singh, Bhai Gobind Ram and Bhai Gurmukh Singh. Some of the former grantees joined hands with the former *jagirdar*s to help the British administration control and manage the affairs of the Golden Temple. Regarding Amritsar as the possible source of Sikh resurgence, the Punjab administrators were anxious to keep the Golden Temple under close supervision. A 'simple magisterial and political control' was established over it by the administrative manual (*dastur al-aml*) of 1859, never to be relinquished till the Golden Temple was taken over by the 'high spirited' Khalsa in 1920.

The worst sufferers of the change from the Khalsa to the British Raj were the Singh soldiers. Many of them were retrenched after the Anglo-Sikh war of 1845–6. All of them were disbanded after the Anglo-Sikh war of 1848–9. The uprising of 1857–8, however, obliged the Punjab administrators to recruit some Sikhs afresh. Their performance in the service of empire proved to be amply satisfactory. From then on Sikhs began to be recruited in large numbers. During World War I, their absolute numbers in the Indian army were much smaller than the Punjabi Muslims', but their proportion in the Indian army – in proportion to their total population – was larger than that of any other religious community. There was a common assumption among the British that the Khalsa were distinguished from other Sikhs because of their martial spirit. Indeed, the Sikhs whom the British met in the battles of 1845–6 and 1848–9 were all Khalsa Singhs. Their martial prowess appeared to spring from their faith. The British army authorities insisted from the very beginning that all Sikhs joining the army should observe the Khalsa form. As in the army of Lahore earlier, so in the British Indian army now, all Sikh soldiers and officers were Khalsa Singhs.

The bulk of the Sikhs lived in the countryside as peasants, artisans and agricultural labourers. They were all affected by the agrarian policies of the British. The small Sikh landholders were prone to indebtedness, though perhaps less than their Muslim and Hindu counterparts. Many of them were reduced to the status of tenants. But the large landholders generally began to produce for the market. This was more true of the canal colonies, where Sikhs had got a large proportion of the land on account of their being good cultivators or good soldiers. Some members of the Sikh aristocracy also received large chunks of land as a reward for services rendered to the colonial rulers. The large landholders in general and the Sikhs in particular were the major beneficiaries of colonial rule in the countryside. In cities and towns, the Sikhs were mostly Khatris and Aroras. As part of the traditional trading communities, they were among the primary beneficiaries of colonial rule, but the number of the Sikhs amongst the Khatris and Aroras of the Punjab was rather small.

The percentage of agriculturists, artisans and traders and shopkeepers in the Sikh community did not change in any significant way. The agriculturists amounted to over 73 per cent in 1921. The Jatts alone accounted for more than 60 per cent of the Sikhs. The Khatris and Aroras were about 7 per cent – less than the Chuhras and Chamars. The Tarkhans, Nais, Jhiwars and other groups of the *jajmani* system represented nearly 12 per cent of the Sikhs.

However, all the Sikhs were not pursuing their traditional occupations. Many Khatri, Arora and Brahman Sikhs were in civil administration and in the professions of law, medicine, engineering, teaching and journalism. Many Jatt Sikhs were in the army and the police. This does not mean, however, that no agriculturist Sikhs were in civil administration or in other professions. Neither does it mean that there were no Khatris or Aroras in the army or the police. In fact, there were some Tarkhans, Kalals and Chuhras too in the army and some Labanas, Nais, Jhiwars and Chhimbas in the police. All the traditional segments of the Sikhs were represented in the professions too. However, the largest representation in the professions and in the civil services was that of the Khatris and Aroras. They were also the most educated amongst the Sikhs. But only about 10 per cent of the Sikhs were literate in the early decades of the twentieth century. Contrary to the general impression, the Sikhs were not given preference over others for civil employment. They held less than 8 per cent of the positions in various departments of the government. Even in the police, they held less than 9 per cent of the positions. One may add that in 1921 there were Jatt and Tarkhan Sikhs owning about a hundred factories. On the whole, a small but influential middle class was emerging among the Sikhs, to cooperate or 'compete' with 'the natural leaders' within the Sikh community, and to compete also with 'Hindus' and 'Muslims'.[15]

The demographic development of the period presents three striking features: the total number of Sikhs rose from about 2,000,000 in 1881 to more than 4,000,000 in 1931; the percentage of Singhs in the Sikh community rose to about 90; the Sikhs formed less than 14 per cent of the total population of the province. The early British administrators carried the impression that the Khalsa was decreasing in number after the loss of political power.[16] This is not borne out by the census returns of 1881, 1891 and 1901, when only the Singhs were taken into account in enumerating the Sikhs. In 1911, for the first time the census officials returned all those persons as Sikhs who claimed to be Sikhs, and there was the phenomenal increase of more than 37 per cent over the total of 1901. Even so, the percentage of non-Khalsa Sikhs was far smaller than that of the Singhs. Apart from the natural rate of increase, the increase in the percentage of Singhs was due to the increasing consciousness of Singh identity among the Sikhs and the conversion of non-Sikhs. This demographic change among the Sikhs underlined the importance of religious movements among them during the period of British rule.

N.G. Barrier, who pioneered the study of Sikhs under the British rule, makes two observations: one, that the spirit, and some personnel, of the Nirankari and Namdhari movements played a role in the early years of the Singh Sabha Movement; and two, that the Singh Sabha Movement 'marked a new chapter in the evolution of Sikhism'.[17] The first two movements had been initiated before the annexation of the Punjab as Sahajdhari movements in the north-west of the province. The Nirankari Movement, founded at Rawalpindi by Baba Dayal, remained confined to that region under his successors. Their following consisted of Khatri, Arora and Bhatia shopkeepers and traders. With their uncompromising belief in the Formless (Nirankar), which gave them the name Nirankari, they rejected belief in all the gods and goddesses of Hindu mythology and sacred literature.

They recognized the line of the ten Gurus from Guru Nanak to Guru Gobind Singh, and looked upon the *Adi Granth* as *Guru Granth Sahib*. The *hukamnama* of Baba Darbara Singh (1853–70) makes two things absolutely clear: one, that the Nirankaris had no use whatsoever for Brahmans; and, that *Guru Granth Sahib* was central to their ceremonies of birth, death and marriage. This *hukamnama* also refers to Baba Dayal as 'the true *guru*', not bracketed with any of the first ten Gurus or *Guru Granth Sahib*, but a guru nonetheless. He initiated both Singhs and non-Singhs to give guidance in the light of the Gurbani. The movement ignored the Khalsa tradition and its doctrine of Guru-Panth.[18]

The Namdhari Movement, initiated by Baba Balak Singh, was given a new orientation by Baba Ram Singh, a carpenter of Bhaini in district Ludhiana. He was in the army of Lahore when he came under the influence of Baba Balak Singh at Hazro in the early 1840s. Upon the latter's death in 1862, Baba Ram Singh inaugurated the 'Sant Khalsa' by administering the baptism of the double-edged sword to his followers. Their white dress and rosary proclaimed their spotless piety, but they wore *kachh, kesh, kara* and *kangha* and, in place of the *kirpan* they carried some simple weapon or merely a staff. They had no place for Brahmans in their rites or ceremonies. The popularity of Baba Ram Singh in the villages of the central districts made him potentially dangerous in the eyes of the British administrators who had gone through the trauma of 1857–8. He was allowed to visit Amritsar but was interned in his village before the middle of 1863. His following continued to grow, and was estimated to be more than 100,000 in the late 1860s. The 'Sant Khalsa' were spread over all the central districts, which had a Sikh population of good proportions. Despite their boycott of all things British, they were well organized in compact units under *suba*s (governors) who had their own secret means of communication. They earned the epithet *Kuka* because of the shrieks (*kuk*s) of individuals who became 'intoxicated' (*mastana*) during congregational hymn-singing (*kirtan*). The stauncher among the Sant Khalsa demonstrated their iconoclastic zeal by destroying idols and small structures erected over tombs and cremation spots. In 1866–7, a number of them were prosecuted and sentenced to imprisonment ranging from three months to two years.

Baba Ram Singh hated the beef-eating British for permitting cow-slaughter under their political domination. His hope of the return of Sikh rule was based on prophecies rather than on any political agenda. His followers did not do anything directly against the rulers but they killed some butchers. Eight of them were sentenced to death for killing butchers in Amritsar and Raikot. Baba Ram Singh was suspected of having encouraged them. His removal from Punjab was under consideration when a band of the Sant Khalsa struck – first at Malaud and then at Malerkotla – in the hope of getting arms to be used against more butchers. In the process, they killed ten persons. In turn, sixty-five of the Sant Khalsa were shot from cannons at Malerkotla by the deputy commissioner of Ludhiana and the commissioner of Ambala. Baba Ram Singh and his *suba*s were sent to distant jails. Baba Ram Singh remained in touch with his followers during his detention at Rangoon. In 1880, he was removed to Mergui where he died in 1885.

In his absence, but under the guidance of his younger brother Baba Hari Singh, the Sant Khalsa – generally called Namdharis and popularly known as Kukas – settled down to peaceful occupations. They abandoned their iconoclastic activity but not spiritual 'intoxication'. The Namdharis came to believe that Baba Ram Singh was the twelfth Guru in continuation with Guru Gobind Singh through Baba Balak Singh. This limited the scope of the doctrine of Guru-Panth and reduced the importance of the *Guru Granth* among the Namdharis. They set a lot of importance on ritual fire and Chandi literature. Their numbers began to dwindle, restricting the Namdhari following increasingly to carpenters. More even than their religious doctrines, their social background made them sectarian.[19]

An association called Sri Guru Sabha was founded at Amritsar in 1873, about a year after Baba Ram Singh was exiled. The immediate cause of its foundation was the announcement of the conversion of a few Sikh students to Christianity. Sardar Thakur Singh Sandhanwalia, on whose initiative the Singh Sabha was founded, became its first president. Its first secretary was Giani

Gian Singh of Amritsar (different from the celebrated author of the *Panth Prakash* and the *Tawarikh Guru Khalsa*). Nothing much is really known about the early activities of the Singh Sabha. In 1877, it petitioned the authorities of the Oriental College at Lahore to introduce Punjabi language and literature in its curriculum. The first publication of the Sabha is said to be an eighty page booklet entitled *Sri Gurpurab Parkash*, which was meant as a guide to help in celebrating the birth anniversaries of the Gurus. The most eminent individuals associated with the Sabha were Raja Bikram Singh of Faridkot, Kanwar Bikrama Singh of Kapurthala and Baba Khem Singh Bedi. In 1886–7, they were suspected by the British of sympathizing with Maharaja Duleep Singh whom Thakur Singh Sandhanwalia had persuaded to return to the Khalsa faith with the inducement that he could claim his heritage. Only in 1890 were the rules of the Singh Sabha published, laying down procedures for its functioning. By this time, Baba Khem Singh Bedi was its chief leader. He had the support of the government and the management of the Golden Temple.[20]

The second Singh Sabha was established at Lahore in 1879, on the initiative of Professor Gurmukh Singh and Bhai Harsa Singh, both teachers at the Oriental College. It was avowedly meant for propagating education and religion amongst the Sikhs. Its president, Diwan Buta Singh, was a publisher and its secretary was Professor Gurmukh Singh himself. Sardar Attar Singh, the former chief of Bhadaur, began to patronize the Sabha. After the mid-1880s, Jawahir Singh Kapur and Giani Ditt Singh abandoned the Arya Samaj to join the Singh Sabha. A number of periodicals – daily, weekly, fortnightly or monthly – were started by Professor Gurmukh Singh in the 1880s. The best-known and most influential amongst these was the *Khalsa Darbar*, which was edited by Giani Ditt Singh for a number of years till 1901. In 1886–7, the Lahore Singh Sabha demonstrated its loyalty to the British by telling the Sikhs to remain aloof from Maharaja Duleep Singh and his self-styled well wishers. In 1892, Professor Gurmukh Singh took the initiative to place the Sikh case before the Education Commission. The Sabha remained active only till the death of Professor Gurmukh Singh in 1898, and that of Giani Ditt Singh in 1901.

By 1901, more than a hundred other Singh Sabhas had been established in the Punjab. They were, almost a priori, in district towns like Rawalpindi, Lyallpur, Gurdaspur, Ludhiana, Jalandhar, Ambala, Ferozepur, Karnal, Montgomery, Hoshiarpur and Sialkot. But Singh Sabhas were not confined only to towns, like Dera Bab Nanak, Khanna, Ropar, Dipalpur, Pind Dadan Khan, Sahiwal, Wazirabad, Hargobindpur, Muktsar and Tarn Taran – they were found in villages, like Bilga, Badowal, Chamkaur Sahib, Khumano, Lidhran and Gujjarwal as well. Besides the Singh Sabhas in the state capitals like Patiala, Nabha, Sangrur, Faridkot and Kapurthala, there was an active Singh Sabha in Basaur village in the Patiala state. Since each Singh Sabha professed, in theory, to work for the entire Panth, some kind of coordination was needed. An early attempt in this direction was made in 1880, when a General Sabha was created at Amritsar for the Singh Sabhas of Lahore and Amritsar (and for others which might come up). In 1883, a resolution for starting a Sikh college was in fact passed in the General Sabha. It was soon reconstituted to form the Khalsa Diwan at Amritsar, with a patron, two vice-patrons, a president and a vice-president and two secretaries. More than thirty Singh Sabhas came to be affiliated to the Diwan. But there was a good deal of tension amongst its leaders, particularly between Professor Gurmukh Singh and Baba Khem Singh Bedi. The Diwan split in 1885, with the rump at Amritsar presided over by Baba Khem Singh Bedi. A Khalsa Diwan was set up at Lahore in 1886 with the support of thirty Singh Sabhas. The leading members of the Diwan set up the Khalsa College Establishment Committee in 1890. Donations from Sikh rulers and landed gentry were encouraging. However, the Sikh and non-Sikh opponents of the Lahore leaders succeeded in getting the site of the college shifted from Lahore to Amritsar. Before the close of the century, a school and a college were established at Amritsar to serve as models for Khalsa institutions elsewhere in the province.

The need for coordination was increasing, while the competence of the Khalsa Diwans at Amritsar and Lahore to meet this need was decreasing. The death of Professor Gurmukh Singh and Giani Ditt Singh accentuated the feeling among some new leaders that a common platform for the Panth was absolutely necessary. Largely on the initiative of Sardar Sunder Singh Majithia, the Chief Khalsa Diwan was established at Amritsar in 1902. Its president was Bhai Arjan Singh of Bagrian and its secretary Sardar Sunder Singh himself. This 'aristocratic' top might suggest a close link with the Amritsar Singh Sabha, but it would be erroneous to link it with either Amritsar or Lahore. In due course, the majority of the Singh Sabhas accepted the Chief Khalsa Diwan's lead to make it a representative body of the Panth. Its ideology was closer to that of the leaders of the Lahore Singh Sabha and the scope of its concerns was even wider. Directly or indirectly, the Chief Khalsa Diwan helped the foundation of several important organizations, notably the Sikh Educational Conference and the Punjab and Sind Bank. The *Khalsa Advocate* became its official organ.

There were several differences among the early leaders of the Amritsar and Lahore Singh Sabhas – social, ideational, personal and generational.[21] Their activities and attitudes can be appreciated in the light of these differences. Raja Bikram Singh of Faridkot patronized the Singh Sabha at Faridkot and financed Giani Badan Singh's annotation of the *Adi Granth* in reaction to Trumpp's work. Kanwar Bikrama Singh of Kapurthala, who patronized the Amritsar Sabha and Diwan, was instrumental in founding the Singh Sabha at Jalandhar and remained its president till his death in 1887. Thakur Singh Sandhanwalia was closely associated with the management of the Golden Temple and was able to persuade Maharaja Duleep Singh to return to the faith. For his activities in connection with Duleep Singh's return to the Punjab, Thakur Singh was exiled to Pondicherry where he died. These leaders belonged to the ruling houses and to old *jagirdar* families. Baba Khem Singh Bedi belonged to a Guru lineage which had become affluent and influential under the Khalsa Raj. Socially their equal, he was distinguished from the other leaders by his religious position. He deliberately imitated Guru Gobind Singh; his followers 'believed him to be an *avtar* whose mere touch would save them'. He used to distribute charms and his influence spread all over the north-west of the province. With consummate skill, he grew fabulously rich and had a number of supporters and protégés. He was knighted by the British government.

The only aristocrat to be directly associated with the Lahore Singh Sabha and Khalsa Diwan was Sir Attar Singh, the chief of Bhadaur, who had been made subordinate to the Maharaja of Patiala after 1857–8. He was well educated and had published several books in English before the Singh Sabha was founded at Lahore. He was appreciative of the work of Professor Gurmukh Singh first, and then that of Giani Ditt Singh. The moving spirit of the Lahore Sabha and Diwan was Professor Gurmukh Singh (whose father was a cook in the royal household of Kapurthala) who was patronized by Kanwar Bikrama Singh till he became a teacher at Oriental College, Lahore. Educated at Lahore, he actually belonged to a new generation, with new ideas and aspirations. He was joined by other like-minded young individuals, notably Jawahir Singh Kapur and Giani Ditt Singh. Jawahir Singh remained active in the support of Sikh education and in the cause of the Sikh educated class for employment in government services and their advancement in the new professions, generally arguing on the assumption of the 'distinctive character' of the Sikhs as 'a separate people'. Giani Ditt Singh proved to be the greatest publicist of the movement. He lectured and wrote on Sikh history and theology and highlighted the achievements of the Gurus and the Singh martyrs. Through this he sought to define the true Sikh doctrines and ritual practices, to denounce and ridicule popular belief in gods and goddesses, and to defend the movement against all its opponents, whether Sikh or non-Sikh.

The most persistent opponent of the Lahore Singh Sabha was Baba Khem Singh Bedi. In 1883 he had proposed that the Singh Sabha should be called 'Sikh Singh Sabha'. But he had to drop this motion because of strong opposition, presumably from the Lahore leaders and their supporters in the Khalsa Diwan. In 1885, Professor Gurmukh Singh demanded that Baba Khem Singh not sit on a cushion (*gadela*) in the presence of *Guru Granth Sahib*, and his demand was supported by an overwhelming majority. Bhagat Lakshman Singh, though baptized by Baba Khem Singh, looked upon the Lahore leaders alone as 'the pioneers of the Singh Sabha Movement'. He observed later that the Baba had never forgiven them for two reasons: they 'insulted' him by removing his *gaddi* cushions, and they never acknowledged him as 'the Guru of the Sikhs'.[22] After a sustained campaign to expel Gurmukh Singh from the Diwan – stopping him from addressing a congregation at Guru ka Bagh adjoining the Golden Temple, and threatening him with violence – Baba Khem Singh Bedi succeeded in getting him excommunicated in 1887 through a *hukamnama* issued by the manager of the Golden Temple. Bawa Udey Singh, a nephew of Baba Khem Singh, sued Giani Ditt Singh on the plea that he had ridiculed the Baba, among others, in the *Khalsa Akhbar* in 1887. In the process of litigation, the Khalsa Press and the *Khalsa Akhbar* had to close down for some time.

Avtar Singh Vahiria, the most articulate opponent of the Lahore leaders, was a staunch follower of Baba Khem Singh Bedi. He was secretary of the Rawalpindi Singh Sabha and editor of the *Sri Gurmat Prakashak*, both launched under the patronage of Baba Khem Singh. Avtar Singh published eight books relating to Sikh history, theology, religious practices and rituals. He expected a Sikh to give the same kind of allegiance to the descendents of the Sikh Gurus as a subject gave to the king. For him, Guru Nanak was an *avtar*, like Rama and Krishna. The *Veda*s and the *Purana*s were as authoritative as the Sikh scriptures. He subscribed to the ideal of *varnashrama*, involving the notions of purity and pollution. He stood for the worship of the Goddess, the Brahmanical rites of passage, the parity of *charan-pahul* with the baptism of the double-edged sword, and the parity of the Sahajdhari Sikh with the Khalsa Singh, both of whom were identified as 'Hindu'. In retrospect, Avtar Singh Vahiria liked to believe that he was trying to safeguard 'the ancient customs, rites and rituals of the Sikh community'. The inspiration for his basic ideas and attitudes came from his living guru, Baba Sir Khem Singh Bedi.[23]

The new generation of leaders were in sympathy with the ideas and objectives of the Lahore leaders. Bhai Takht Singh had actually studied at Oriental College, Lahore, and remained in close association with Professor Gurmukh Singh and Giani Ditt Singh. He was deeply interested in female education and founded the Sikh Kanya Mahavidyala at Ferozepur, which came to be regarded as the best institution for the education of Sikh girls over the decades. Bhai Mohan Singh Vaid, a leading member of the Singh Sabha of Tarn Taran, was an associate of Giani Ditt Singh. Like him, he played a leading role in defining Sikhism and propagating Khalsa rituals; he promoted the use of Punjabi in Gurmukhi script and the idea of a distinct Sikh (Singh) identity. Babu Teja Singh of the Bhasaur Singh Sabha and the Panch Khalsa Diwan was even more radical than the Lahore leaders in defining Sikhism and its scriptures, and in advocating Sikh *rahit* for women.[24]

Some of the Sikh writers generally associated with either Amritsar or Lahore are better understood as spokespersons of the Singh Sabha Movement in general. Giani Gian Singh was over fifty years old when the Amritsar Sabha was founded. His *Panth Prakash* (1880) was meant to be an improvement upon Ratan Singh Bhangu's work of the same title. His *Tawarikh Guru Khalsa*, in prose, was more comprehensive in its treatment of the subject. The appeal of his major works lay in the spirit in which they were written to celebrate the Khalsa tradition. Similarly, Giani Hazara Singh, who belonged to an old *giani* family of Amritsar, interpreted the *Var*s of Bhai Gurdas in a manner which made them eminently acceptable to the Khalsa Singhs. Bhai Vir Singh articulated ideas and concerns which place him much closer to the Lahore leaders than to any of the early leaders of the Amritsar Singh Sabha. The *Khalsa Samachar*, which he edited, is more of a continuation of the *Khalsa Akhbar* than a break with it.[25] In his novels too, Bhai Vir Singh valorized Khalsa ideology and Khalsa *rahit*.[26]

By far the most important writer of the Singh Sabha Movement was Bhai Kahn Singh of Nabha. Born in 1861, he was well acquainted with Sikh literature before he came into contact with Professor Gurmukh Singh and Giani Ditt Singh at Lahore in the early 1880s. His *magnum opus*, *Gurshabad Ratnakar Mahan Kosh*, was published in 1930 after a labour of fifteen years. It contains more than 64,000 entries which have a direct or indirect bearing on things related to Sikhism and Sikh history. His *Gurmat Martand*, published posthumously in 1962, contains two of his works which were published for the first time in the late 1890s: the *Gurmat Prabhakar* and the *Gurmat Sudhakar*. The former contained all the teachings of the Gurus, arranged in alphabetical order and supported by relevant quotations from the Gurbani.

The *Gurmat Sudhakar* was meant to identify the true teachings of the Guru in Sikh literature itself. Rejection of those elements that did not conform to the true teachings was implied in this approach. Apart from the compositions of Guru Gobind Singh, Bhai Gurdas and Bhai Nand Lal, more than a dozen major works of Sikh literature up to the time of Bhai Santokh Singh were used by Bhai Kahn Singh. The whole range of Sikh literature was used in his *Ham Hindu Nahin* (1898) to demonstrate that Sikh doctrines and Sikh religious practices were meant to be, and were, clearly different from those of the Hindus. In subsequent editions of this book, Bhai Kahn Singh developed the idea that the distinct identity of the Sikhs made them a distinct political entity.[27]

Another writer and publicist of this generation had a peculiar importance because of his choice of English as the medium of communication. Born in 1863, Bhagat Lakshman Singh was educated at Rawalpindi and Lahore before he took up teaching History and English at the Mission Collegiate School of Rawalpindi. There he received baptism from Baba Khem Singh Bedi and started the Khalsa Dharm-Parcharak Sabha. Reacting to attempts by the Arya Samaj writers, especially Bawa Chhajju Singh, to show that the Sikh Gurus were 'only Hindu reformers' who believed in the *Veda*s, he started the first Sikh English organ, *Khalsa*, in consultation with Bhai Jawahir Singh. He used this weekly to disseminate the view that 'the Sikh dispensation was an independent entity and not a subsidiary system, based on Hindu philosophy'. Guru Nanak and Guru Gobind Singh had themselves made it clear that this dispensation was based on divine revelation. Bhagat Lakshman Singh was a witness to the shaving of Sikh Rahtias by the leaders of the Wachhowali Arya Samaj, and he used the columns of the *Khalsa* to carry on propaganda work on behalf of the newly formed Khalsa Sudhar Sabha to counteract the Arya programme of *shuddhi*. Bhagat Lakshman Singh had no doubt whatsoever that 'it was Baba Nanak himself who conceived the idea of establishing a separate church' and that Guru Gobind Singh gave it 'a final and distinct shape'. The protagonists of the Singh Sabha Movement, in his view, had carried forward the work of the Gurus. The recognition of the Sikh community as an 'independent political entity' was a logical outcome of that movement. In retrospect, Bhagat Lakshman Singh reflected that – though independently of Bhai Kahn Singh of Nabha – he was preaching through the *Khalsa* the message of *Ham Hindu Nahin*. He wrote books on Guru Gobind Singh and the Sikh martyrs.[28]

With the support of scholars, creative writers and publicists as much as through their own lectures, writings and activities on the ground, the leaders of the Singh Sabha Movement were able to evolve a consensus. They were all agreed that the source of true Sikhism was the early Sikh tradition. This tradition was embodied in Sikh literature. By far the most important source of Sikh belief was the *Adi Granth*. Of equal importance were the genuine compositions of Guru Gobind Singh. The works of Bhai Gurdas and Bhai Nand Lal conformed to Gurbani and therefore these works were more important than the rest. The *Janamsakhi*s, the *Gurbilas* literature, and the *Rahitnama*s were useful in so far as they conformed to, and supplemented, the genuine Sikh tradition. On these assumptions Sikh ideology, Sikh history and the Sikh way of like could be systematized, revitalized and propagated through education and the print media.

Much that was un-Sikh in the lives of the contemporary Sikhs was to be discarded in the light of the Sikh tradition. The beliefs and practices of popular religion, which had nothing to do with Sikhism, were denounced and debunked. The cult of Sakhi Sarvar, Gugga Pir, Sitala and the like came under attack. The gods and goddesses of 'Hindu mythology' were categorically rejected. Belief in one God involved the rejection of other deities and their incarnations. Belief in the ten Gurus from Guru Nanak to Guru Gobind Singh, and in no other, involved the rejection of all personal gurus. The *Dasam Granth* was venerable because it contained the genuine compositions of Guru Gobind Singh. But Guruship was vested in the *Adi Granth* alone. The gurdwara, with congregational worship and community meal, was the most important Sikh institution. However, the gurdwaras of the Panth were controlled and managed by those who were alien to the Sikh tradition. This accounted for un-Sikh practices in the Sikh sacred spaces. An appeal made to the Sikh community and the British Government in 1887 highlights the importance of this concern. It points out that the management of the Golden

Temple was based neither on legislation nor on the principles of the Khalsa Panth. This implied that only the Khalsa were entitled to manage the affairs of the Golden Temple.

For the Sikh way of life it was necessary to first receive *pahul*, adopt the epithet Singh, carry a small *kirpan*, wear *kachh* and *kara*, maintain uncut hair (*kesh*) and *kangha*. This formulation of the '5ks' came handy in popularizing these old features of the Khalsa *rahit*. The ban on smoking and insistence on eating *jhatka* meat came from the same *Rahitnama* sources. Sikh rites of birth and death, and more so the rite of marriage, acquired great importance in the context of the need to shed all Brahmanical practices. There were precedents in theory and practice, but there was no uniformity in modes and no universality in application. The institution of marriage involved issues of property. Therefore it was seen as more important than the other rites of passage. This dimension of the institutions was highlighted by the death of Sardar Dyal Singh Majithia. His widow contested his will which alienated his ancestral property in favour of the Dyal Singh Trust. But the Chief Court decided in favour of the trustees. This gave great impetus to the demand for legal recognition of the Sikh rite of marriage. There was overwhelming support for the Anand Marriage Bill when it was passed in 1909 despite opposition articulated by some Sikhs and many Hindus.

The Anand Marriage Act has a direct bearing on Sikh identity. It may not be accidental that the leaders of the Chief Khalsa Diwan asked for separate electorates for the Sikhs for the first time in 1909 when separate electorates were created for Muslims. Political sanctity was imparted to separate electorates and larger than proportionate representation, called weightage, by the Lucknow Pact of 1916 between the Indian National Congress and the All-India Muslim League. A Sikh deputation met the governor-general in 1917 to plead for separate electorates for the Sikhs. This was conceded. The Act of 1919 provided ten seats for the Sikhs in the Provincial Council of fifty-eight seats. Sikh identity was legally and politically recognized as the culmination of the Singh Sabha Movement.

After the Act of 1919, politics became increasingly important for the people of the Punjab, as it did for people in the rest of

India. It dominated the life of the Sikhs too. However, it may be noted that the intellectual impetus provided by the Singh Sabha Movement was overshadowed, but not retarded, by politics. Not only did writers like Bhai Vir Singh and Bhai Kahn Singh continue to write in the twentieth century, new scholars and writers of great stature also appeared on the scene to study Sikh theology and Sikh history within the parameters of the Singh Sabha Movement. The most eminent among them were Professor Teja Singh, Bhai Jodh Singh and Professor Sahib Singh, all associated with the Khalsa College at Amritsar.

Sikhism was a living faith in the early nineteenth century, and Singh identity was the most dominant identity among the Sikhs. The doctrine of the *Guru Granth* was the primary doctrine, and the *Adi Granth* was regarded as the Guru. The *Dasam-Granth* was held in veneration as were the *Var*s of Bhai Gurdas and the *Rahitnama*s. The primary institution of the Sikhs was the gurdwara, with Harmandir Sahib as the most important place of Sikh pilgrimage, followed by Anandpur Sahib, Patna Sahib and Abchal Nagar (Nander). The doctrine of Guru Panth was not forgotten, but was overshadowed by the Sikh rulers who claimed to rule in the name of the Panth.

Before the end of Sikh rule at least two movements were gaining followers in their attempt to place the *Adi Granth* at the centre of Sikh religious and social life, with no role for Brahmanical rites and ceremonies in the lives of their followers: the Nirankaris and the Namdharis. During the late nineteenth century, the Nirankaris laid great emphasis on the Sikh ceremonies of birth, marriage and death. The Namdharis adopted the Singh identity in their anti-British stance. They treated the *Adi Granth* as their scripture, and the *Chand di Var* as a text of special importance. They began to treat Baba Ram Singh and his successors as personal Gurus. Consequently, the doctrine of *Guru-Panth* and *Guru Granth* were of little relevance to them. They did not establish any new educational institutions and thus had no access to Western science and social sciences or to English language and literature.

The Singh Sabhas were democratic and voluntary associations of Singhs who were concerned about the affairs of the Sikh community as a whole. Understandably, therefore, they came to coordinate their efforts through the Chief Khalsa Diwan. Other institutions like the Punjab and Sind Bank, Sikh Educational Conference and the Khalsa Tract Society were established to promote what they regarded as the collective interests of the Sikhs. They made effective use of the printing press and took to Anglo-Sikh education with great enthusiasm, establishing schools and colleges for boys and girls. They tried to promote Punjabi literature in Gurmukhi script. They were keen about the Khalsa *rahit* and acutely conscious of a distinct Sikh identity. They looked upon the *Adi Granth* as the Guru, the source of right belief and practice and the touchstone for separating truth from falsehood. They revived the doctrine of Guru Panth and demanded that no idols should be brought into the Golden Temple for worship, and that all the gurdwaras associated with their Gurus and Sikh martyrs should be managed and controlled by the representatives of the Khalsa Panth.

There was a great resurgence of the Sikhs in the late nineteenth century, swelling their numbers. It was articulated through religious, social and cultural activities. In the early decades of the twentieth century, this resurgence had begun to find political expression in diverse ways. Sikh identity was emerging as the basis of politics. On the whole, the Singh Sabha Movement provided a comprehensive interpretation of the earlier Sikh tradition and combined it with the adoption of a modern outlook, attitudes and institutions. The nature of its response to the colonial environment made it far more influential than the other Sikh movements.

NOTES

1. For a discussion of these views, see J.S. Grewal, *Historical Perspectives on Sikh Identity*, Patiala: Punjabi University, 1997.
2. Harjot Oberoi, *The Construction of Religious Boundaries: Culture, Identity and Diversity in the Sikh Tradition*, Delhi: Oxford University Press, 1994, pp. 215–16.
3. J.D. Cunningham, *A History of the Sikhs*, rpt, Delhi: S. Chand & Co., 1955, pp. xxxi-ii.
4. J.S. Grewal, *Contesting Interpretations of the Sikh Tradition,* Delhi: Manohar, 1998, pp. 23–35.

5. For Oberoi's conception of the Sanatan Sikh Tradition, see *The Construction of Religious Boundaries*, pp. 137–8.
6. Cunningham, *A History of the Sikhs*, pp. 81 n. 1, 321–47.
7. Ibid., pp. 81 n. 1, 347–9.
8. Ibid., pp. 11–12, 16, 75–6.
9. Ibid., pp. 383–6. Indu Banga, *Agrarian System of the Sikhs: Late Eighteenth and Early Nineteenth Century*, Delhi: Manohar, 1978.
10. Cunnigham, *A History of the Sikhs*, pp. 245, 289, 387–90.
11. Ibid., pp. 9, 311.
12. Ibid., pp. 313–18.
13. For the colonial context, see Kenneth Jones, *Arya Dharm: Hindu Consciousness in 19th Century Punjab*, New Delhi: Manohar, 1976; Richard Fox, *Lions of the Punjab: Culture in the Making*,. Berkeley: 1985; J.S. Grewal, *The Sikhs of the Punjab*, Cambridge: Cambridge University Press, 1990.
14. For Christian missionaries and the Punjabi response to their presence, John C.B. Webster, *The Christian Community and Change in Nineteenth Century North India*, Delhi: Macmillan, 1976.
15. For the effects of British rule on the Sikhs, and Sikh responses to colonial rule, J.S. Grewal, *The Sikhs of the Punjab*, pp. 135–40. See also Kenneth Jones, *Arya Dharm*; Ian J. Kerr, 'The British and the Administration of the Golden Temple in 1859', *The Panjab Past and Present*, 1976; Dolores Domin, *India: A Study in the Role of the Sikhs in 1857–58*, Berlin, 1977.
16. Cf. Oberoi, *The Construction of Religious Boundaries*, pp. 213–15. Early British administrators were thinking of the Singhs when they talked of decline. After 1857–8, the British army authorities insisted on the Singh form for the enlistment of Sikhs. All along, the British had equated the Sikh with the Singh.
17. N.G. Barrier, *The Sikhs and Their Literature*, Delhi: Manohar, 1970, pp. xxii-iv.
18. For the Nirankaris, John C.B. Webster, *The Nirankari Sikhs*, Delhi, 1979; J.S. Grewal, *The Sikhs of the Punjab*, pp. 140–1.
19. For the Namdharis, Ganda Singh, *Kukiyan di Vithia* (Punjabi), rpt Patiala: Punjabi University, 2000; J.S. Grewal, *The Sikhs of the Punjab*, pp. 141–4.
20. For factional information on Singh Sabhas and Khalsa Diwans, W.H. Mcleod, *Who is a Sikh? The Problem of Sikh Identity*, Oxford: The Clarendon Press, 1989; Oberoi, *The Construction of Religious Boundaries;* Grewal, *The Sikhs of the Punjab*, pp. 144–50.
21. For biographical information, Bhagat Lakshman Singh, *Autobiography*, ed. Ganda Singh, Calcutta: The Sikh Cultural Centre, 1965; Oberoi, *The Construction of Religious Boundaries*; Joginder Singh, *Sikh*

Leadership, Early 20th Century, Amritsar: Guru Nanak Dev University, 1999.

22. Lakshman Singh, *Autobiography*, p. 91.
23. Harjot Oberoi looks upon Avtar Singh Vahiria as the great defender of the Sanatan Sikh tradition, minimizing the significance of the nature of his connection with Baba Khem Singh Bedi. His publications reflected not so much the views and attitudes of any large number of Sikhs as of Baba Khem Singh Bedi. His bid to influence people seems to have met with little success.
24. N.G. Barrier, 'Sikh Politics and Religion: The Bhasaur Singh Sabha', in *Five Punjabi Centuries: Polity, Economy and Culture, 1500–1990*, ed. Indu Banga, Delhi: Manohar, 1997.
25. For a brief analysis of the contents of the *Khalsa Samachar*, Joginder Singh, 'Resurgence of Sikh Journalism', *Journal of Regional History*, Amritsar: Guru Nanak Dev University, 1982.
26. Harbans Singh, *Bhai Vir Singh*, Delhi: Sahitya Akademi, 1972.
27. Bhai Kahn Singh Nabha, *Ham Hindu Nahin* (Punjabi), 5th edn, rpt, Amritsar: Singh Brothers, 1995.
28. Lakshman Singh, *Autobiography*, pp. 137, 291–2.

CHAPTER 2

Sikh Resurgence and Control: The Golden Temple

VEENA SACHDEVA

The sanctity attached to the tank, the Harmandir and the town of Ramdaspur is reflected in the compositions of Guru Ram Das and Guru Arjan. The epithet *amritsar* (the pool of nectar) is used by Guru Ram Das as a metaphor for the True Guru whose utterance is truth. 'By bathing in this pool, even a crow turns into a swan. Blessed are they who, through the instruction of the Guru, have purified their hearts through the Name.'[1] In another verse, however, the epithet *amritsar* does not appear to be a metaphor:

A Sikh of the True Guru should rise at dawn and bathe in *amritsar*. He should repeat the Divine Name as instructed by the Guru so that all his sins are washed away. At sunrise he should sing *gurbani*, and remember the Name all the time. The Sikh who meditates on God with each breath and morsel is liked by the Guru.

This verse ends with Guru Ram Das saying that he seeks the dust of the feet of those Sikhs of the Guru who contemplate the Name and inspire others to do so. This verse evokes the image of Sikhs coming to the pool of nectar early in the morning for a sacred bath and participating in the *kirtan*. Guru Ram Das expresses his great regard for them.[2]

Guru Arjan leaves no doubt that *amritsar* is the pool of nectar dug by Guru Ram Das. He says that,

Evil thinking vanishes by meeting the *sadhu*; the sinful are purified; all the sins are washed away by bathing in the *sarovar* of Ram Das; sing the praises of God every day and meditate on him in association with *sadhs;* by meditating on the perfect Guru, all one's wishes are fulfilled.

The situation depicted in this verse is the same as that in the verse of Guru Ram Das, with the difference that the words 'Ramdas *sarovar*' are used in place of *amritsar*.[3] Guru Arjan looks upon the completion of the work on the tank as a result of God's grace. God himself has undertaken to fulfil the tasks of His devotees with His presence in their midst.

Beauteous is the spot and beauteous is the pool filled with nectar-like-water. With this are completed all objects and fulfilled all desires through God's grace; all impediments have vanished. This task has been accomplished by God as His own. Men are helpless without His grace. All praises to him who has created this pool. Bathing in this pool has the merit of pilgrimage to all sixty-eight sacred places, all charities and all rites.[4]

Guru Arjan explicitly refers to the Harmandir created for meditation on God:

The Sikhs sing the praises of God as *sants* and *bhagats;* through the praises of the Lord all their sins are washed away; the supreme *bani* in praise of God is the source of liberation; the eternal foundation of the Harmandir was laid at the happiest conjunction and through God's grace the task was accomplished.[5]

In another verse, Guru Arjan refers to the whole complex, the pool, the Harmandir and the garden. Here all wishes are fulfilled by chanting the praises of the Lord and meditating on Him. Through His grace, one is blessed in this world and the next.[6] About the town of Ramdaspur he says, 'I have seen all places but there is none like you. Founded by the Lord Himself, you are beauteous. Spread wide and thickly populated is the beautiful Ramdaspur. All sins are washed by bathing in Ramdas *sar*.[7]

In another verse, Guru Arjan says that God has given him refuge at His own feet. He has established his own rule (Ram-*raj*) in Ramdaspur. The praises of His being induce fear in the foes and they take flight.[8] In yet another verse, Guru Arjan depicts a situation which reminds one of his essential task in Ramdaspur:

I have established the *dharmsal* of truth, I search for the Sikhs of the Guru to wash their feet and waive the fan over them; I bow at their feet. Whosoever hears of the Guru, and comes to him, is given the boon of *nam*, *dan* and *isnan*. By boarding the true boat, the whole world has attained to liberation.

Guru Arjan goes on to add that the merciful God has now commended that none shall cause hurt to another and that humankind shall live in comfort under His mild rule (*halimi-raj*). Guru Arjan speaks what God has told him to speak.[9]

In a verse of Guru Arjan, which is sometimes used as evidence for the existence of traders and shops in Ramdaspur and for the absence of the tax collector, there are references to the founding of a town, its protective wall and its firm gates, its shops, *sahukars* and traders, who pay no *jizya*, fine or tax, its merchandise and the profits which come from trade. However, all these are metaphors. The *sahu*, in this town, is the true Guru and the Sikhs are his *banjaras*. They invest in the Name and obtain Truth as the profit. He who serves the Perfect Guru is admitted to this eternal city of Guru Nanak Dev.[10] Evidently, the city is a metaphor for the dispensation of Guru Nanak, which is significant in itself. However, it is possible that Guru Arjan's experience of the town of Ramdaspur provides the metaphors for the various features of an urban centre.

Bhai Gurdas refers to the throne, the court and the eternal rule of Guru Arjan. These metaphors are meant to underline the importance of what Guru Arjan had achieved. He filled the storehouse of Gurbani and remained absorbed in the Word in holy congregation. Sikh *sangats* came to him from all the four directions in countless numbers. The free kitchen (*langar*) of the *shabad* of the Guru ran ceaselessly. He taught millions how to remain detached in the midst of attachment (*maya vich udas*), thus creating millions of Janaks.[11] Just as the eternal city in the verse of Guru Arjan is the dispensation of Guru Nanak, so in the verses of Bhai Gurdas, the eternal rule of Guru Arjan is his success as the successor of Guru Nanak. Bhai Gurdas appears to assume that the Harmandir and Ramdaspur represent the centre of the Sikh world.

The sanctity of the *sarovar*, the Harmandir and Ramdaspur is assumed and reinforced in the verses of Guru Ramdas and Guru Arjan. These verses perpetuate the feeling of reverence and devotion among the Sikhs who read and recited these verses.

They are being read and recited every day by thousands of Sikhs, imparting the sense of sanctity to the Harmandir in the midst of *amritsar* as the heart of the city. Understandably, therefore, the Harmandir has been regarded as the most sacred place for the Sikhs from the time of Guru Arjan to the present day.

What made Ramdaspur even more important for the Sikhs was the activity of Guru Hargobind who is remembered as the master of *miri* and *piri*. The *var*s of Bhai Gurdas and the *Dabistan i-Mazahib* leave no doubt that Guru Hargobind conducted the spiritual and the temporal affairs of the Sikhs in a manner which is symbolized by the assumption of two swords. His lasting legacy in Ramdaspur was the Akal Takht (immortal throne) built in front of the Harmandir as the visible symbol of socio-political commitment.

Guru Hargobind did not live in Ramdaspur all his life. After fighting several battles with the officers of Emperor Shahjahan, he decided to establish his headquarters at Kiratpur. The control of the Harmandir passed into the hands of the Minas, the successors of Guru Arjan Dev's elder brother Prithi Chand, who claimed Guruship for themselves and did not acknowledge Guru Hargobind as the sixth Guru. The Harmandir appears to have remained under their control till the end of the seventeenth century.

Significantly, Ramdaspur was claimed by the Khalsa of Guru Gobind Singh, either during his lifetime or shortly after his death. Muhammad Qasim, who wrote his *Ibratnama* in 1723, was actually living in Lahore as a government accountant at the time of the fall of Sirhind in 1710. He refers to Ramdaspur as Chak Guru and to its large tank as *amritsar*. On Baisakhi day, the Sikhs would come in lakhs to this pleasant and charming place, which had tree-filled gardens. He goes on to add that a great multitude of Singhs gathered there at the fall of Sirhind and went on a rampage against the people of the neighbourhood 'the same way as at Sirhind'.[12] Though writing after the event, Muhammad Qasim was probably not mistaken about the synchronization of the fall of Sirhind and the occupation of Ramdaspur by the Khalsa.

Once again Ramdaspur became the rallying centre for the political activities of the Sikhs. The Akal Takht was revived for this purpose. The Mughal administrators could not tolerate this. Bhai Mani Singh, who was managing the affairs in Ramdaspur, was executed in 1734. For nearly a decade, Ramdaspur appears to have remained under the direct control of the Mughal *faujdar*s and *thanadar*s. One of them called Massa Ranghar started using the precincts of the Harmandir for staging performances by professional dancing girls. He was assassinated by Sukha Singh and Mahtab Singh for, in the eyes of the Khalsa, this act of blatant sacrilege of the Harmandir.[13]

After the death of Zakariya Khan, the Mughal governor of Lahore, the Khalsa killed the Mughal *faujdar* Jaspat Rai in an open battle. His brother, the Mughal *diwan* Lakhpat Rai, swore to destroy the Sikhs. Thousands of them were killed in a single campaign and the event is still remembered as a holocaust. Within two years, in 1748, however, the Khalsa built a mud fort called Ram Rauni, near the town of Ramdaspur, as a declaration of their decision that Ramdaspur, henceforth would be their headquarters. Between 1748 and 1764, Ramdaspur was besieged several times by Mughal and Afghan forces and the Harmandir was destroyed several times by the Afghans. Significantly, it was at this time that the Akal Takht became the symbol of the collective authority of the Khalsa and the locus of their general resolutions for defence or attack.[14]

In a *hukamnama* issued by the Khalsaji of Sat Sri Akal Purukh to the Sikhs of Patna, the Khalsa assume the Guru's position and ask for Rs. 125 to be sent to them besides *daswand*, *chaliha*, *kar*, *bhet* and *ardas*, or whatever belonged to the Guru. There is also a reference to the reconstruction of Sri Harmandir. This document bears a seal impression with the inscription *Akal Sahai Khalsa Ji.*[15] Ahmad Shah Abdali, the Afghan invader, defeated the Marathas in the battle of Panipat in 1761, but was himself defeated by the Khalsa on the bank of the river Chenab in 1764. The Khalsa passed a *gurmata* and occupied the entire *sarkar* of Sirhind. Confident in their success, they struck a coin at Lahore in 1765 as a declaration of their sovereignty. From 1748 to 1764, the Harmandir, the Akal Takht and Ramdaspur remained the centre of the political deliberations of the Khalsa and their campaigns. As early as 1769, Kesar Singh Chhibber looked upon Amritsar as *the sacred space* of the Sikhs.

In the collective consciousness of the Khalsa, Ramdaspur was more important than Lahore. Ram Sukh Rao refers to the role of Jassa Singh Ahluwalia in the reconstruction of the Harmandir with the support of the Sikh *sardars*. He used the services of Des Raj for this purpose. When it was pointed out to Jassa Singh that the whole place had been mortgaged to Sahib Singh of Naushehra, he made the payment due to Sahib Singh and started the work of construction.[16] Jassa Singh also appointed the functionaries of the Harmandir. With the offerings made to the Harmandir, he built the third storey of the Akal Bunga.[17] Revenues from land were granted to the various functionaries who worked under the administrative control of Jassa Singh.

A whole locality, Katra Guru, was established close to the Akal Bunga. All the income from this *katra* was given to the Harmandir. At one stage, Des Raj brought to the notice of Jassa Singh that he had spent Rs. 14 lakh on the work of re-construction, besides expenses incurred on the raw materials supplied from time to time.[18] It is interesting to note that according to Ram Sukh Rao, Jassa Singh Ahluwalia brought Kanwar Bhag Singh to the Akal Bunga so that Bhai Sadhu Singh could administer *pahul* to him.[19] Ram Sukh Rao gives the impression that with the consent of other Sikh rulers, Jassa Singh Ahluwalia took charge of the administration of the entire complex of the Harmandir as well as of the work of reconstruction. This was the position to which Ranjit Singh succeeded, presumably after the occupation of Amritsar in 1805.

The Sikh chiefs of the late eighteenth century contributed towards the development of the Harmandir. They built their *bungas* around the Harmandir, as well as about a dozen other *katras*, thus encouraging traders and craftsmen to reside in them. Some chiefs, like Jassa Singh Ahluwalia, Jassa Singh Ramgarhia, Mahan Singh Sukarchakia and Hari Singh Bhangi, built forts as well.[20] Thus a cluster of townships developed around Harmandir Sahib during the late eighteenth century. Nearly all Sikh chiefs gave *dharmarth* grants to their sacred shrine.[21] After Jassa Singh Ahluwalia's death, the affairs of the

Harmandir were managed by his successor Bhag Singh till Ranjit Singh took it over in the first decade of the nineteenth century.

Throughout his reign, Ranjit Singh paid as much attention to Amritsar as to his capital at Lahore. The fort of Gobindgarh was constructed in 1807. His frequent visits to Amritsar and the Harmandir are recorded in the *Events at the Court of Ranjit Singh* and the *Umdat ut-Tawarikh*. It appears that he began to treat Amritsar as his second capital, particularly after the construction of the Rambagh Palace. Whenever he visited Amritsar, he visited Harmandir Sahib too, especially on Diwali, Baisakhi, Maghi Sankrant, Nirjala Ekadshi, Massya, Holi and Dussehra.[22] Sometimes he visited the Harmandir before undertaking a campaign, and also after a successful campaign or conquest. The other occasions when he visited the Harmandir were the marriage of a prince or after his own recovery from illness. His first visit recorded in the *Umdat ut-Tawarikh* took place around Diwali day in 1809 when he distributed gold and silver and cows and horses among the people.[23] The last visit to the Darbar Sahib recorded in the *Umdat ut-Tawarikh* was in April 1838 when the Maharaja took Mackeson to the Harmandir and inspected the gold plating inside and outside.[24]

Many of the visits recorded by Sohan Lal Suri make for interesting reading. On the Baisakhi in 1814, for example, the Maharaja bathed in Sri Amritsar Sahib. Before making an offering of Rs. 5,000 at Sri Harmandir Sahib, he made donations (to Brahmans and other needy persons) of gold and silver, vessels of gold and silver, cows, horses, silken and woollen cloth.[25] After the conquest of Kashmir, the Maharaja visited Amritsar to express his gratitude. He offered Rs. 1,000 at Harmandir Sahib and the Akal Bunga and prayers were offered on his behalf.[26] During a visit to Amritsar in 1824, the Maharaja rode an elephant and inspected the construction of the city wall and its gates. He ordered the *jamadar*s in charge of the construction work to complete it as early as possible. He told Sardar Desa Singh Majithia to be strict in ensuring law and order in the city so that none oppressed another.[27]

During his visit to the Darbar Sahib in August 1835, the Maharaja issued an order for the preparation of a marble floor for the Darbar Sahib and its *parkarma*. Bhai Gurmukh Singh was ordered to send reliable persons to the suburbs of Jaipur to procure marble and to prepare the floor in perfect beauty and grace. This was at the time when the marriage of Prince Naunihal Singh had been fixed.[28] Some time later, the Maharaja gave Rs. 11,000 to Bhai Gurmukh Singh for the preparation of the floor of the *parkarma* of Darbar Sahib.[29] On 1 October 1835, the Maharaja visited Darbar Sahib and made the following offerings: a bejewelled gold umbrella, 500 gold coins for gold work, a carpet, one *rumala* and many other things for the *Granth Sahib*, besides an offering of Rs. 2,500 at the Harmandir and the Akal Bunga.[30]

On the Sankrant of Jeth (May) 1836, Ranjit Singh ordered all the princes and nobles and other eminent individuals associated with the State, to make offerings at Harmandirji. The Maharaja himself made an offering of Rs. 5,100. Others like Prince Kharak Singh, Kanwar Nau Nihal Singh, Kanwar Sher Singh, Mai Nakain Sahiba, Raja Hira Singh, Jamadar Khushal Singh, Sardar Tej Singh, and Raja-i-Kalan Raja Dhian Singh, made offerings of Rs. 1,100 each. Those who made offerings of Rs. 750 each were Raja Suchait Singh and Raja Gulab Singh. Sardar Dhanna Singh Malwai and Kashmira Singh made offerings of Rs. 500 each, while Bhai Ram Singh, Bhai Gobind Ram and Bhai Gurmukh Singh made offerings of Rs. 250 each. Many others also made offerings according to their rank.[31]

On the Sankrant of Baisakhi 1838, the Maharaja went to the Darbar Sahib and threw Rs. 25 into the tank before prostrating himself before Harmandirji and listening to the *Granth Sahib*. He made an offering and performed a circumambulation. He talked to a large number of people gathered there about the construction of the floor and the gold plating of the Harmandir. By way of *sankalp*, he gave away Rs. 5,000, an elephant with a silver seat, a horse with a gold saddle and eleven pitchers of gold. After that he made the following offerings: Rs. 1,100 at Harmandir, Rs. 500 at the Akal Bunga, Rs. 125 at the Jhanda Bunga, Rs. 100 each at Dukh Bhanjani, Baba Atal and Shahid Bunga. He also gave Rs. 100 to the *rababis*.[32]

There is hardly any doubt that the affairs of the Golden Temple complex were controlled and managed by Maharaja

Ranjit Singh. In the *Chiefs and Families of Note*, there is a reference to Sardar Desa Singh Majithia's appointment as the governor of the city of Amritsar and being given the charge of the Darbar Sahib. His son Sardar Lehna Singh later took over charge. This was regarded as 'a post of importance requiring great tact and judgement'.[33] In the early decades in particular, it was not always easy to manage the affairs at the Golden Temple. In April 1812, for example, it was submitted to the Maharaja that Akali Phula Singh claimed Rs. 1,000 out of the Rs. 1,100 presented as offerings to the Darbar Sahib on the occasion of Baisakhi. The Maharaja said that he would send for Akali Phula Singh and dismiss him. Later it was reported that Akali Phula Singh had arrived in Amritsar with his troops and started fighting with the Akalis of the Darbar Sahib with arrows and guns. Two or three men on both sides were killed and wounded. The Maharaja had to send his special horsemen to deal with the situation.[34] In January 1814, when Sardar Desa Singh Majithia was not in Amritsar, the Maharaja had to deal with the Akalis of Phula Singh and the other Akalis because of their dispute and claims for their share of income. He ordered that the Akalis of Phula Singh should take only the share that had been fixed for them, and should not claim anything more from the share of other Akalis. The Maharaja told them further that if they claimed more in the future, they would be turned out of Amritsar altogether. Nevertheless, the dispute went on for sometime before the Akalis of Phula Singh agreed to act in accordance with the order of the Maharaja.[35]

Maharaja Ranjit Singh used to give detailed instructions for the management of the Harmandir. A *sanad* to this effect, issued in 1837, addressed to Sardar Lehna Singh is reproduced below:

> You are requested to establish the following rule in the Akal Bunga and must be careful that it be not infringed. The offerings (*ardas*) and the proceeds (*jama*) of the *jagir* should be deposited in the same chest, and Sant Singh and both the Gurmukh Singhs should, on the first of Baisakh and at the Dipmala, open the said chest and dole out the collections as used to be done in the time of Desa Singh (Majithia) in the manner following: whenever there are hundred or fifty persons they ought to have their money allowances distributed to them

personally and individually, at which time four *mutsaddis* are to attend from Magh 1894 who are to keep the accounts of the receipts and disbursements.[36]

In order to control the Harmandir, the British started taking an interest in its affairs even before the annexation of the Punjab. In November 1847, Henry Lawrence, the British Resident at Lahore, ordered a reduction in the daily allowance to the Golden Temple from Rs. 11 to Rs. 3–12–0 as religious offerings from the State. In the same month, Lawrence approved the grant of a *jagir* valued at Rs. 700 to Bhai Makhan Singh, a *granthi* of the Golden Temple.[37] Sardar Lehna Singh Majithia continued to manage the affairs of the Golden Temple. In February 1848, however, Lehna Singh was replaced by Sardar Jodh Singh. The latter was an *adalati* (judicial officer) in Dera Baba Nanak and was transferred to Amritsar to take up the new position.[38]

After the annexation, the British rulers of the Punjab became the sole custodians of the Golden Temple. Sardar Jodh Singh was retained as its manager. He had supported the British during the Second Anglo-Sikh War. He was made extra assistant commissioner, and remained stationed at Amritsar till his retirement in 1862. In his capacity as extra assistant commissioner, Jodh Singh handled all cases, in the first instance, relating to the temple, while as manager he could fine *pujaris* for misconduct and exclude them from the temple for up to six months. He also supervised the temple finances.[39]

During the ten years from 1849 to 1859, the government directly managed the temple through a judicial officer of its own. At this time, a meagre amount of Rs. 4,000 per annum was being spent on the Golden Temple and Rs. 29,787 for the support of *granthis*, *pujaris*, *rababis* and other functionaries of the Golden Temple, the Akal Bunga, the Shahid Bunga, the Jhanda Bunga and the Baba Atal.[40] The provision of this amount of money from the land revenue of the state was in continuation of the earlier position of the Golden Temple. British willingness to continue this financial support sprang from their belief that it benefited the Raj politically because it provided a way to influence the important functionaries of the Temple, apart from gaining the gratitude of the Sikh community, which at least could be translated into a passive acceptance of British rule. From another perspective, the continued alienation of land revenue to the temple reflected British unwillingness to create discontent by ending a long-established practice in the Punjab of providing state support to religious institutions. At the same time, the British laid down new terms and conditions for the confirmation of *dharmarth* grants. Loyalty to the new regime and good behaviour were the necessary conditions. During the period of Sikh rule, grants could be made to the chief *granthi* of the Golden Temple by virtue of his sacred office. He shared these grants with other *granthi*s and also received the daily offerings to be divided among all the *pujari*s. In the new arrangement, it was proposed that a panchayat be formed to advise the chief *granthi* on the distribution of the income from grants and offerings among all the *granthi*s. After their death, their shares were to be determined forever by the district authorities, and each share was to be commuted into cash pension for life payable by the State treasury.[41] Furthermore, the entire octroi of the city had been dedicated to the Golden Temple. Initially, it was reduced to Rs. 50 per day. Gradually this amount was cut down till only 6 *paisa*s in a rupee were paid. This right too was finally taken away. Since the Sikhs were in a minority in the city, they had no representation on its municipal committee. However, the lighting expenses of the temple and the canal charges on the water supplied to the sacred tank continued to be paid out of municipal funds.[42]

In August 1858, the Punjab government issued a circular stating that its officials must not participate in the management of temples and mosques, thus implying that the people must manage their own religious institutions. The commissioner of Amritsar, R.N. Cust, initially tried to sever all connections with the Golden Temple and argued that the long-standing practice of supplying canal water free of tax to the temple tank should be discontinued. His superiors at Lahore – completely against their professed policy of religious neutrality – were absolutely keen on maintaining their hold over what they regarded as the key institution of the Sikhs. They labelled the Golden Temple 'as a special case to be dealt with caution and moderation'. They decided to convene a meeting of all interested parties, in September 1859, at the residence of Raja Tej Singh. The elite of the Sikh community attended the meeting: the Sikh chiefs, their representatives, principal shareholders, managers and officials of colleges and shrines. The deputy commissioner of Amritsar, Fredrick Cooper, was also present. It became clear that the British administrators were not ready to relinquish their control over the management of the Golden Temple. The only point open for discussion was the degree of control. An administration manual called *dastur al-aml* was prepared for the management of the Golden Temple. Some of the men connected with the Golden Temple were coerced into signing the document. The *dastur* provided that there would be a government appointed president called *sarbarah* to superintend the Darbar Sahib Management. The *sarbarah* was to be an extra assistant commissioner. He was to work for and control the temple according to the directions of an elected committee called the Golden Temple Committee. A *darogha* was appointed to help the *sarbarah*. The *pujari*s became the servants of the Golden Temple as well as the parties vested with rights to the temple and its establishments. They would continue to enjoy the temple's property and income. Most of them were allowed the right to occupancy during good behaviour. Their behaviour was to be judged by the *darogha* and extra assistant commissioner. Thus the Golden Temple virtually became an official concern to be run by the extra assistant commissioner as its *sarbarah*.[43] The higher officials in Lahore were pleased with the outcome. They accepted the need, indeed the desirability, for the British to continue to play a role in the affairs of the temple.

This arrangement, worked out in 1859, survived into the twentieth century, although the Committee became defunct in the 1880s. As the members died off, they were not replaced and the Committee finally became extinct in 1883. The British were of the view that since meetings of the Committee provided occasions for much wrangling, there was no practical advantage in retaining it. Finally, the entire control came to be vested in the *sarbarah* who received instructions from the deputy commissioner and was responsible only to the government.[44] The *pujari*s, who once had a respectable position and exercised some check on the administration, were gradually reduced to a lowly position. Many of them ceased to perform any duty in the temple. They adopted other professions such as shopkeeping and even assumed pretensions of leadership. But they continued to receive their share in the income of the Darbar Sahib. Some of them started sending their servants to do service in the temple. Those who attended their services turned dishonest because they were hardly paid anything. They began to steal coins thrown on the carpet before the Holy *Granth*. The priests bribed the ill-paid *darogha*, who was supposed to keep a watch over the money. He too began to share the loot. The *granthi*s tried in various ways to increase their income – so much so that the *karah parshad* offered by the pilgrims in the congregation was taken away to the houses of the magistrates and police officials or thrown to horses.[45]

The Government of India passed Act XX of 1863 to enable it to divest itself of the management of religious endowments. Clause 22 of this Act stated that:

> Except as provided in this Act, it shall not be lawful for any Government in India, or for any officer of any Government in his official character, to undertake or resume the superintendence of any land or other property granted for the support of, or otherwise belonging to, any mosque, temple, or other religious establishment, or to take any part in the management or appropriation of any endowment made for the maintenance of any such mosque, temple, or other superintendent thereof, or to be in any way concerned therewith.[46]

In the 1870s, the new commissioner of Amritsar, Perkins, was surprised to find that Act XX of 1863 was not being implemented and that there existed an official connection with the Golden Temple. His predecessor had exercised 'minute interference' in the affairs of the temple, and Perkins found himself being asked to even sanction certain religious ceremonies: the reading of the *Granth*, the distribution of alms by way of thanksgiving to the deity, the erection of a lightning conductor and making of an alms box for the Tarn Taran shrine.[47] Similarly, in 1882, the new lieutenant-governor, C.V. Aitchison, noted that the Golden Temple was the only religious institution in India over which it had been thought necessary to maintain direct control, whereas there was hardly anything unique to the Golden Temple to justify a special arrangement.[48] Despite these observations made by the officials, government control over the temple continued. Government not only appointed the manager, but also ensured that he acted in all ordinary matters in accordance with the advice and control of the deputy commissioner. The general committee was consulted only on special occasions. Ian J. Kerr points out that at no time in the half century following the annexation of the Punjab did the British withdraw from a direct and controlling role in the affairs of the Golden Temple: 'As far as the premier shrine of the Sikhs was concerned, Act XX of 1863 remained a dead letter'.[49]

British control over the Golden Temple resulted in its deterioration. The new rulers were not concerned with its upkeep or the maintenance of its sanctity. With the end of Sikh rule, state patronage to the Golden Temple came to an end. The income of the Golden Temple was now insufficient to meet its expenses. The Raja of Jind, who was commissioned to prepare a new paper, pointed this out but was told that the revenues of the temple were ample if economically managed.[50] In 1881, H.H. Cole, a European visitor, noted that 'the mosaics at the Golden Temple were suffering from dirt and neglect'. They were cracking. Cole recommended that these should be properly cleaned and 'kept from cracking by careful oiling'.[51] The deterioration was not merely physical. Another European observed curious sights on the pavement around the tank: 'Comb makers plying their trade, sellers of steel ornaments, *fakirs*, Hindu bathers, etc'.[52] J.C. Oman noticed 'a physician with the least possible quantity of clothing on his person applying a plaster to the head of a squalling infant'. At another place, he saw a woman sitting behind a covered volume, conversing with some members of her own sex, 'a *granthi* with a similar covered up book before him, was carrying a confidential conversation with a middle aged man, probably a shopkeeper'. As Oman passed, he heard 'it can be managed'. Thus, in the garb of religion, some persons 'lent themselves to the furtherance of the most immoral practices'; they arranged illicit relations as the temple afforded them greater facilities. All kinds of shops were opened in the premises and obscene booklets were being sold.

The precincts came to be used by *pundit*s and astrologers for the propagation of superstitious practices.[53]

On an earlier visit to the Golden Temple during the Diwali festival, Oman noticed the special treatment given to Europeans for whom several rows of seats were placed near the clock tower to watch the illumination of the temple. What even Oman found objectionable was the town band of musicians that was 'treating the European visitors to the popular English airs' and 'was out of keeping with the place and occasion'.[54] He was also struck by the manner of the policemen – 'representatives of the irresistible power of the *sarkar*' – who brought Oman and his family inside the Golden Temple with 'loud shouts, rigorous pushes to right and left, free use of official batons on the turbaned heads of their unoffending countrymen, who did not create even a smallest outward sign of irritation in the men so unceremoniously handled'.[55]

Matters of appointment could also sometimes become a problem. In all these matters, the major concern of the British was loyalty. If the official concerned was loyal, the British avoided making a change even if there were representations or complaints against him. In one such case, Bhai Jai Ram Singh, secretary of the Golden Temple Accounts Committee at Amritsar, lodged a complaint on 28 May 1902 that Jawala Singh, the *sarbarah*, had misappropriated nearly Rs. 90,000 from the income of the Golden Temple and also given *siropa*s to unauthorized persons. According to prevailing practice, the *siropa* given was to be 12 per cent of the offerings made by an individual. The complaint was that these persons had not given anything to the Golden Temple, and yet they had got *siropa*s of a total value of Rs. 415. The British administration did not take any action against the *sarbarah*, saying that he was a man of large private means, with lands in several villages and a pension holder of Kapurthala State. He was merely instructed to submit an abstract of the annual account to be published in future. About the *siropa*s given to the unauthorized persons, the British made it clear that since 'the amount involved in the *siropa*s, i.e. Rs. 415 was not large', no action could be taken. It is clear that the British were not very concerned about established rules and practices being followed. Bhai Jai Ram Singh who had filed the petition was the secretary of a 'self-constituted committee of no importance' that was bound to 'die a natural death'.[56] We learn from the same source that the lieutenant-governor approved of the orders passed by the deputy commissioner of Amritsar, adding that there was no need to take any further action.[57]

British officials started taking interest in the appointment of officials of the Golden Temple. In one case, they were of the view that a minor should not be appointed as a *granthi*. In another case, however, they approved the appointment of a minor, Fateh Singh. He was made a *granthi* after the death of Harnam Singh, despite the fact that a number of more eligible persons were available for the post.[58]

The atmosphere was vitiated further when idols began to be openly worshipped in the holy compound. J.C. Oman has given a detailed account of this development. He refers to a Brahman worshipping tiny images of Ganesha and Krishna, and another Brahman adoring the Sun. At the north-eastern corner of the tank, he noticed a temple of Shiva represented by a *lingam* four inches high with a bell on it. Oman refers to the *lingam* standing upon a substantial brick and marble platform at the foot of a spreading Banyan tree. He also noticed a little temple sacred to Devi. Proceeding further, he observed a Brahman engaged in worshipping a *Saligram* and a picture of the temple of Badri Narayan, while another was adoring a *Saligram* and a *tulsi* plant. Oman felt that the latter Brahman, 'appeared quite at home in the precincts of the Sikh temple, for he blew sundry loud blasts by means of a conch from which he managed to produce some three or four distinct notes'. For Oman, these noteworthy facts were something to think about.[59]

Oman was not the only author to notice idol worship in the *parkarma* of the Golden Temple. Other documentary evidence makes it clear that Brahmans used to come to the temple with images of gods. They would sit at the top of the stairs surrounding the tank with a piece of blanket or carpet spread out for people bathing in the *sarovar* to deposit their clothes and other articles for safe custody. Hindu pilgrims used to worship these images after bathing in the *sarovar*. On normal days, there were about twenty Brahmans, whereas during festivals there could be as many as thirty of them. These Brahmans were not confined to the *parkarma* alone. 'As a rule one of them used to officiate on the *har ke pauri*', the most sacred spot in the Harmandir, which was visited by one and all after paying homage to the *Granth Sahib*.[60] The majority of these Brahmans belonged to Himachal Pradesh. A few of them had come from places like Nurmahal, Shahbad, Sialkot and Peshawar.[61] It was in March 1899 that Jawala Singh, the *sarbarah* of the Golden Temple, concluded an agreement with about twenty Brahmans, besides the sweet-sellers, *kathawalas*, comb makers, etc. According to this agreement, the Brahmans and others were allowed to stay but were made to agree that they had no established rights and could be removed from the *parkarma* at anytime.[62]

In November 1904, Tikka Ripudaman Singh visited the Golden Temple on Diwali and noticed idols in the inner and outer *parkarma* of the temple. He wrote a letter to the lieutenant-governor pointing out that the Sikhs were not idol worshippers and that the *Granth Sahib* strongly prohibited idolatry. Therefore worshipping of idols in the Golden Temple should be stopped. He also expressed the view that the *sarbarah* of the Golden Temple was quite ignorant of the Sikh religion. Therefore, some orthodox Sikhs possessing force of character should be appointed to this most sacred and responsible post.[63] After receiving the letter, the lieutenant-governor asked R.E. Younghusband, commissioner of Lahore Division, to verify the facts through the deputy commissioner of Amritsar, C.M. King. The deputy commissioner visited the Golden Temple and confirmed the presence of about half a dozen or more idols arranged along the outer, but not in the inner *parkarma* of the temple. He also added that the idols had been there for 'at least 20 years'.[64] Younghusband, in his reply to the lieutenant-governor, emphasized that the worship of idols was hardly a matter in which government could interfere, and added that if the Sikhs felt strongly that these idols should be removed, they could bring pressure on the manager to remove them.[65] However, Sardar Arur Singh, the *sarbarah*, took action. On 1 May 1905, he issued a written order prohibiting the Brahmans from sitting on the *parkarma* of the Golden Temple with idols for worship. The Brahmans were also prohibited from cleaning vessels and other things of worship with ash and washing their clothes in the tank, besides spitting and rinsing their mouth in it. This order, however, did not prohibit them from bathing, doing *puja* or applying *tilak*.[66] The Brahmans obeyed the order and did not bring any idols to the Golden Temple on 2 May.[67]

A reaction against the order of Sardar Arur Singh began to take shape. The Sanatan Dharmi Hindus of Amritsar distributed an *ishtihar* announcing a meeting on 4 May 1905. A resolution was passed against the order of the manager. It was contended that Guru Nanak and other Sikh Gurus were Hindus, and did everything for the protection of the Hindus. This resolution encouraged the Brahmans to return to the Temple with their idols on 6 May. The manager then reported the matter to C.M. King, the deputy commissioner of Amritsar, through a *murasila*. Police help was sought to take action against the Brahmans, if necessary.[68] Another order was issued by the manager on 7 May. He himself approached the Brahmans to warn them not to bring idols into the Temple. This order of 7 May was finally implemented: idols were not brought to the *parkarma* thereafter.[69]

Though the order proved to be final, controversy on the issue of idols raged all over the Punjab for almost a year. Memorandums were presented to the lieutenant-governor. Some were opposed to the order while others appreciated it. The issue was debated in the press. Even the rulers of princely states took different positions. The agitation against the removal of the idols was led by Seth Radha Kishan of Amritsar. On 5 June 1905, he sent a memorandum to the lieutenant-governor with 13,000 signatures of Hindu and Sikh residents of Amritsar. It was argued that no 'representative bodies of the Hindu or orthodox Sikh communities, and no individuals entitled by their social and religious position to speak on behalf of their communities, were consulted by the said Sardar Arur Singh before taking action'. It was further contended that Brahmans had served in the Golden Temple ever since it became a place of pilgrimage. It was also said that the *sarbarah* had taken the side of the Tat Khalsa and that the order was not in accordance with the views of 'the great majority of the Sikhs'.[70] On the other hand, a number of letters were addressed to the lieutenant-governor from various parts of the Punjab appreciating the removal of idols. The Sri Guru Singh Sabha of Quetta, for example, appreciated the removal of idols on the plea that 'the idols were an unbearable reproach to the Sikh people'.[71] Similarly, the Sikhs of Rawalpindi held a meeting to approve of the action. The Hindu community of Shikarpur also offered their gratitude on the removal of idols.[72]

It is interesting to note here that opposing positions were taken by some of the Sikh rulers of the princely states. Raja Hira Singh of Nabha was not in favour of the removal of the idols. He thought that this action had resulted in disunion among Hindus and Sikhs. He stated his own position very clearly: 'I like equity and not oppression, and see all with one and the same eye without any distinction of caste or creed. Of course, God is one but there are various divisions and subdivisions among mankind, and it is the sacred duty of one to move within the circle he is born in'. Since he suspected Sardar Sunder Singh Majithia, Secretary of Khalsa College at Amritsar, of being involved in the Golden Temple affair, he refused to release the promised aid to the College.[73] On the other hand, Ṛaja Ranbir Singh of Jind and Bhai Kahn Singh of Nabha approved of the removal of the idols by saying that it was never a tradition, and hoped that others would not interfere in the affairs of Darbar Sahib.[74]

Subsequently, a widespread agitation started for control of the Golden Temple. In 1906, the *Khalsa Advocate* and the *Punjab* of Amritsar strongly urged that the rules governing the Golden Temple and other gurdwaras should be so altered as to remove certain patent evils. They emphasized that the positions of the *mahant*s and *pujari*s were never intended to be hereditary, and that these appointments should depend solely on the efficiency and good behaviour of the incumbents. They argued that the *jagir*s, or other property attached to a gurdwara, should not be considered as their personal property. The *sarbarah* should be an able and energetic Sikh, elected by the Panth. They urged that the old Committee of 1859, which had been abolished, should be restored.[75] In May 1907, the *Punjab* urged the formation of a Gurdwara Sambhal Committee or Committee for the Control of Gurdwaras.

What Harjot Oberoi refers to as the 'Rikabganj Movement' proved to be an important stage in the struggle for the control of the Golden Temple.[76] The architectural plans of the chief architect, charged with the mission of constructing a new capital in Delhi, needed to be accommodated at the cost of land owned by Gurdwara Rikabganj. The *mahant* of Rikabganj had sold land belonging to the gurdwara to the government for Rs. 39,133 without letting the public know anything about it. In May 1913, the British demolished the wall enclosing Gurdwara Rikabganj, which was 78 feet long on the north and 32 feet long on the east. Initially, the government's action went unnoticed because of the sparse Sikh population in Delhi and the fact that the gurdwara was located outside the city. But soon the news spread to the Punjab. There was a spate of telegrams, petitions and memoranda addressed to the viceroy, the lieutenant-governor of Punjab, and the commander-in-chief. Sikhs residing in Burma, China, Hong Kong and the United States sent telegrams asking for the reconstruction of the dismantled wall.[77] On 27 January 1914, Harchand Singh of Lyallpur visited the gurdwara. On his return to the Punjab, he issued a pamphlet in which he gave an eyewitness account of the gurdwara and its demolished wall. He concluded the pamphlet by saying that the Sikh public totally disapproved of a railing being put up instead of a wall and that by doing so the religious sentiments of the Sikhs would be hurt. In February 1914, a series of Diwans were held at Lyallpur, Lahore, Shimla, Amritsar, Ludhiana, Jalandhar, Tarn Taran, Rawalpindi, Patiala and Montgomery protesting against government action and asking it to rebuild the demolished wall at its own expense.[78]

The British sought the help of local collaborators like Raja Sir Daljit Singh to mobilize support for government policy. The latter contacted Sir Sundar Singh Majithia, secretary of the Chief Khalsa Diwan, who used all his resources to gather support for the government. He issued a pamphlet explaining the history of Gurdwara Rikabganj, the changes proposed by the government and the policy of the Chief Khalsa Diwan. The stand of the Chief Khalsa Diwan, and its approval of British policy, was opposed by the Sikhs. Protest meetings were held in Lahore, Patti, Ropar, Gojra, Khanna and Bhasaur. Maharaja Ripudaman Singh of Nabha proposed to finance the trip of Master Tara Singh to England to present the case of the Rikabganj wall to the British Parliament and the people. In March 1914, a monthly magazine, *Sikh Review*, was launched from Delhi under the patronage of Bhai Arjan Singh Bagrian, a friend of the Maharaja of Nabha. Sardar Sardul Singh Caveesher was appointed its editor.[79] When the movement was beginning to gain support in rural areas, the First World War broke out and weakened the agitation.[80]

After the war, the Central Sikh League was founded in Lahore on 30 March 1919. It was formally inaugurated in December 1919.[81] The leaders of the Central Sikh League demanded that the management of the Golden Temple should be handed over to an elected committee of Sikhs which would be responsible to the Panth. It bore no result. Thereafter, wherever the Sikhs gathered in their daily meetings, in the Singh Sabhas, or at the annual meetings of their Diwans, they put forth their demand that the Golden Temple, Nankana Sahib and Khalsa College be handed over to the Panth.[82] The government announced on 14 July 1920 that the question of the management of the Golden Temple at Amritsar had been under its consideration for some time, and that the elected representatives of the Sikh constituencies would be consulted after the elections. A committee would be selected to appoint a manager to check the accounts and to manage the affairs of the Golden Temple. The action proposed would be under the Religious Endowments Act of 1863 and government would stand aside from the management in future.[83] The Sikhs were not satisfied with these delaying tactics. The honouring of General Dyer by the *sarbarah* of the Golden Temple underlined the urgency of ending the *sarbarahi* system of gurdwara management. They organized public meetings, passed resolutions against official inaction and demanded the immediate resignation of the *sarbarah*. Having failed to forcibly pacify the Sikhs, the government decided to send the *sarbarah* on two months' leave. This did not satisfy the Sikhs either. They held a massive Diwan in Jallianwala Bagh and threatened to take out a mock funeral of the effigy of the *sarbarah* if he failed to resign by 29 August 1920. This threat so frightened the *sarbarah* that he appeared before the Diwan, begged forgiveness with folded hands, and announced that he had resigned. This incident was described in the confidential reports of the Punjab government as a 'decided victory for the party of reform'.[84]

The Sikhs now turned their attention to the issue of the reconstruction of the wall of Rikabganj Gurdwara. This issue, which had agitated the Sikhs for six years, had not yet been settled. Mota Singh, Harchand Singh and Teja Singh Samundari – who had initially played an important role in the Rikabganj movement – approached Sardul Singh Caveesher to take special measures to reconstruct the Rikabganj wall. On 2 September 1920, Sardul Singh made an appeal through a letter printed in the columns of the *Akali*, an upcoming newspaper of the Punjab, under the heading 'Wanted 100 martyrs to save the gurdwaras'. He sought martyrs who would be willing to sacrifice their lives to reconstruct the wall of Rikabganj Gurdwara in defiance of the British authorities. If government attempted to prevent the accomplishment of this noble task, the volunteers would lay down their lives. Within a fortnight Sardul Singh had received 700 offers. The method and mood of government changed. Before the band of martyrs, led by Sardul Singh, could reach Delhi to construct the demolished wall, the government reconstructed the wall at its own expense and published photographs of it in the newspapers to satisfy the people. On the whole, the Rikabganj movement 'had a considerable role in the rise of the Akali movement and its programme, organization and strategy'.[85]

Meanwhile, certain fresh developments at the Golden Temple and the Akal Takht brought these two shrines under the control of the reformers. A religious body in Amritsar called the Khalsa Brotherhood used to hold annual Diwans for the purpose of preaching equality among men and converting men and women of all castes to Sikhism. On 12 October 1920, a few low-caste men, baptized at the annual meeting of this society, were brought in a procession to the Golden Temple. However, the priests refused to offer prayers for them. The Sikhs insisted on the equal right of every Sikh to pray and also to offer and obtain *prasad* at the Temple. In the end, the Holy Book was opened and the following *vak* was read out:

Brother, He sends grace even to those who have no merit, and takes from them the true Guru's service, which is most noble, as it turns our hearts to the love of God. He Himself forgives and brings us into union with Himself. Brother, how worthless were we, and yet the perfect and the true enlightener took us on to His society. My dear, what a lot of sinners, He has forgiven by reason of His true word. How many He has ferried across the world-ocean in the Guru's safety bark. By the touch of the philosopher's stone, that is the Guru, base metal has become gold. Selfishness has departed and the Name has come to live in the heart. Our light has blended with His light and we have become one with Him.[86]

These words had a wonderful effect. The priests agreed to offer the prayers and accept sacred food from the converts.

However, the priests of the Akal Takht did not approve of this and fled from their posts. Since this throne of authority from which orders called *hukamnama*s were issued could not be left vacant, the reform party took up the challenge. Bhai Kartar Singh of Jhabbar called for twenty-five volunteers to take temporary charge of the ceremonies. Soon a provisional committee consisting of nine members with Sardar Sunder Singh Ramgarhia, the new *sarbarah*, as its head was formed. In order to counteract the move of the Akali leadership, the Punjab authorities announced a provisional committee of thirty-six members for the management of the Golden Temple, the Akal Takht and other nearby gurdwaras. The Akali leadership nevertheless went ahead with its original programme of forming a larger central organization under the name Shiromani Gurdwara Prabhandak Committee (SGPC). The thirty-six members of the official committee were also included in the new organization that now had 175 members.[87] It was responsible for launching a movement for liberating all gurdwaras. In this task, the Shiromani Committee was assisted by the Shiromani Akali Dal, formed at Amritsar in December 1920. These two organizations started a non-violent struggle against the government for the control of the gurdwaras.[88]

Chronologically, the first gurdwara to be reformed through agitation was Babe-di-Ber in Sialkot. A free kitchen, where food was distributed twice a day without any distinction of class or tribe or caste, was a great feature of this gurdwara.[89] The appointment of its *mahant* had always been subject to the approval of Sikh opinion. In 1918, on the death of Harnam Singh, his brother Gurcharan Singh, a minor, was nominated by his grandfather Prem Singh as successor under the guardianship of Gandạ Singh, an honorary magistrate. There was a wave of resentment amongst the Sikhs throughout the Punjab against this action. The Sikhs of the locality organized themselves and formed a *jatha*. They started holding weekly, and later daily, services in the gurdwara. Ganda Singh tried to obstruct them, but they succeeded in taking over control of the shrine and restarting the system of free *langar*, which had been stopped by the *mahant*. On 5 October 1920, the Sikhs held a big Diwan and elected a permanent committee of thirteen members for the control of the gurdwara.[90]

Another gurdwara to be thus liberated by the Sikhs was the Darbar Sahib at Tarn Taran. On 25 January 1921, a band of about forty Akalis took over the Darbar Sahib at Tarn Taran from its *mahant*s, but not before two Akalis had been killed and several others wounded by the *mahant*s' henchmen. In fact, a local *jatha* had been beaten up only a fortnight earlier. The *mahant*s were finally ejected and the SGPC appointed a managing committee. A bloodier event occurred at the birthplace of Guru Nanak. Over a hundred Sikhs entered the gurdwara at Nankana Sahib on 20 February 1921, without any intention yet of taking it over. They were attacked by the hired assassins of Mahant Narain Das. Most of them were killed or wounded, and burnt on the spot. The Akalis then arrived at Nankana Sahib in the thousands. The authorities arrested Mahant Narain Das and more than a score of his hired assassins. On 21 March 1921, the commissioner yielded to the strong pressure exerted by Sikh leaders. The keys of the gurdwara were handed over to a committee of seven members (with powers to co-opt Sardar Harbans Singh Atariwala as the president) to take charge of the gurdwara on behalf of the SGPC of Amritsar.[91]

In October 1921, the executive of the SGPC asked its secretary, Sunder Singh Ramgarhia – who was also the officially appointed Manager of the Golden Temple – to hand over its fifty-three keys to Baba Kharak Singh, president of the SGPC. Sunder Singh Ramgarhia sought the advice of the deputy commissioner who deputed his subordinate Lala Amar Nath to collect the keys from Sunder Singh Ramgarhia. The SGPC decided to hold protest meetings against this interference. The Akali protesters were arrested and awarded punishments. However, the number of protest meetings, arrests and punishments went on increasing till 17 January 1922, when all the Akali workers and leaders were released unconditionally and the keys of the Golden Temple were handed over to Baba Kharak Singh. The 'first decisive battle for India's freedom won' was the telegraphic message sent by Mahatma Gandhi to Baba Kharak Singh.[92]

The *mahant* of the gurdwara Guru Ka Bagh, near Ajnala in the Amritsar district, who had submitted to the Shiromani Committee nearly a year earlier, was encouraged by the administrators to treat the Akalis as trespassers. The Akalis accepted the challenge and launched a *morcha* which became the most famous in the Akali struggle for the control of gurdwaras. On 9 August 1922, five Akalis who had chopped wood from the land adjoining the gurdwara for the community kitchen (*langar*) were arrested and put on trial for theft. By 25 August, the number of Akalis arrested rose to over 200. Pickets were placed on the road to Guru Ka Bagh, and the gathering was declared to be an unlawful assembly. Akali volunteers continued to arrive in Amritsar, and bands of 50 to 100 and even 200 Akalis continued to march from the Akal Takht to the Guru Ka Bagh to suffer blows in passive resistance. By 19 October the number of Akalis arrested had risen to more than 2,450. On October 25, a *jatha* consisting entirely of army pensioners reached Guru Ka Bagh under the leadership of a retired subedar major. This development was deemed to have dangerous implications. The *mahant* was persuaded to sell the entire establishment to Sir Ganga Ram who, in turn, handed it over to the Akalis on 17 November 1922. In March 1923, more than 5,000 Akali volunteers were released from jails in appreciation of the role of the Akalis during a Hindu-Muslim riot in Amritsar. C.F. Andrews, who had visited the Guru Ka Bagh in September 1922, was shocked by the brutality and inhumanity of the British administrators and their henchmen. He admired the Akalis for their patient suffering without any sign of fear. In his eyes, the Guru Ka Bagh *morcha* was a new lesson in moral warfare.[93]

The last battle of 'the third Sikh war' was fought outside British territory in a neighbouring princely state. Maharaja

Ripudaman Singh of Nabha was forced to abdicate in favour of his minor son on 9 July 1923. Because of his sympathy for the Singh reformers, the SGPC decided on 4 August to take up his cause. Meetings were held in protest. In a meeting held at Jaito, in Nabha State, on 25 August, the action of the government was condemned. The organizers of the meeting were arrested. New leaders started an *akhand-path*. It was disrupted. The SGPC condemned the official action and resolved to restore the Sikh right to free worship.[94]

A decision was taken to send *jathas* from the Akal Takht to Jaito to complete the *akhand-path* as a matter of right. On 12 October 1923, the Shiromani Akali Dal and the SGPC were both declared as unlawful associations. All sixty members of the *morcha* committee were arrested and charged with treason against the King-Emperor. New members replaced the old ones and *jatha*s continued to reach Jaito. On 21 Feburary 1924, a special *jatha* of 500 Akalis was sent to mark the third anniversary of the Nankana Sahib massacre. Thirty thousand people witnessed its departure from the Golden Temple. The British administrators in Nabha decided to stop the *jatha* by firing at the Akalis. Three hundred volunteers were injured, and a hundred of them eventually died. Nevertheless, *jatha*s continued to march to Jaito till 101 *akhand-path*s were completed on 6 August 1925, and the right to free worship was firmly established.[95]

The Punjab governor, Malcolm Hailey, was now prepared to go a long way in conceding the demand with which the Akali movement had originally started. On 7 May 1925, a bill was introduced in the legislative council and adopted on 7 July. It received the assent of the governor-general in council on 28 July and came into force on 1 November 1925. This Act recognized the SGPC as the legal authority to manage and control Sikh gurdwaras.[96] The issue of control of the Golden Temple was finally settled in favour of the representatives of the Sikh community.

NOTES

1. For references to the *Adi Granth* the text given in the *Shabdarth* has been used. *Shabdarth Sri Guru Granth Sahib Ji*, Amritsar: Shiromani Gurudwara Prabandhak Committee, 1999 (cited hereafter as *Shabdarth*),

Pothi II, p. 493; Gurbachan Singh Talib, tr., *Sri Guru Granth Sahib*, Patiala: Punjabi University, vol. 2 (cited hereafter as Talib, *SGGS*), p. 1047.

2. *Shabdarth*, Pothi I, pp. 305–6; Talib, *SGGS*, vol. 1, p. 634.
3. Ibid., Pothi II, p. 624; Talib, *SGGS*, vol. 1, p. 1309.
4. Ibid., Pothi III, pp. 783–4; Talib, *SGGS*, vol. 3, pp. 1628–30.
5. Ibid., Pothi III, p. 781; Talib, *SGGS*, vol. 3, p. 1624.
6. Ibid., Pothi III, p. 782; Talib, *SGGS*, vol. 3, p. 1625.
7. Ibid., Pothi III, p. 1362; Talib, *SGGS*, vol. 3, pp. 2725–6.
8. Ibid., Pothi III, p. 817; Talib, *SGGS*, vol. 3, p. 1694.
9. Ibid., Pothi I, pp. 73–4; Talib, *SGGS*, vol. 1, p. 153.
10. Ibid., Pothi II, p. 430; Talib, *SGGS*, vol. 2, p. 911.
11. *Varan Bhai Gurdas*, *Var* 24, Pauri 19, 20. For the text, see Giani Hazara Singh and Vir Singh, *Varan Bhai Gurdas*, 17th edn, Amritsar: Wazir i-Hind Press, 1962; for the translation, see Bhai Jodh Singh, *Varan Bhai Gurdas*, vol. 2, Patiala: Vision and Vantura, 1998.
12. J.S. Grewal and Irfan Habib, eds., *Sikh History from Persian Sources*, New Delhi: Tulika/Indian History Congress, 2001, p. 118.
13. Teja Singh and Ganda Singh, *A Short History of The Sikhs (1469–1765)*, vol. 1, Patiala: Punjabi University, 1994, p. 119.
14. Ibid., pp. 127–73.
15. Ganda Singh ed., *Hukumname*, Patiala: Punjabi University, 1999, pp. 232–3.
16. Joginder Kaur, ed., *Fateh Singh Partap Prabhakar of Ram Sukh Rao*, published by editor, 1990, f. 64a.
17. Ibid., f. 63a.
18. Ibid., f. 64a.
19. Ibid., f. 63a.
20. *District Gazetteer Amritsar* (1892–93), p. 150; Ahmad Shah, *Tarikh-i-Hind* (the part translated by Gurbakhsh Singh as *Tarikh-i-Punjab*), Patiala: Punjabi University, 1972, p. 41; Veena Sachdeva, *Polity and Economy in the Punjab during the Late Eighteenth Century*, New Delhi: Manohar, 1993, p. 137.
21. *Foreign/Political Proceedings*, National Archives of India (NAI), New Delhi, 10 June 1853, no. 219, and 28 November 1856, no. 113; Indu Banga, *Agrarian System of the Sikhs*, New Delhi: Manohar, 1978, pp. 158–9.
22. H.L.O. Garrett and G.L. Chopra, eds., *Events at the Court of Ranjit Singh, 1810–1817*, Patiala: Languages Department Punjab, 1970, pp. 32, 53, 227, 237; Sohan Lal Suri, *Umdat ut-Tawarikh*, Daftar II, tr. Amarwant Singh and ed. J.S. Grewal and Indu Banga, Amritsar: Guru Nanak Dev University, 1985; pp. 106, 144, 147, 157, 175, 178, 191, 194, 212, 220, 229, 231, 241, 247, 260, 275, 316–17, 325, 337, 346, 348, 354, 363, 367, 376, 386, 395, 412; *Umdat ut-Tawarikh,* Daftar III, tr. V.S. Suri, New Delhi: S. Chand and Co.,

1961, pp. 201, 202, 204, 241, 242, 243, 247, 248, 289, 310–11, 419, 429.
23. Sohan Lal Suri, *Umdat*, Daftar II, p. 106.
24. Suri, *Umdat*, Daftar III, p. 429.
25. Suri, *Umdat*, Daftar II, p. 241.
26. Ibid., pp. 316–17.
27. Ibid., pp. 386–7.
28. Suri, *Umdat*, Daftar III, p. 242.
29. Ibid., p. 247.
30. Ibid., p. 248.
31. Ibid., p. 289.
32. Ibid., p. 419.
33. W.L. Conran and H.D. Craik, rvd., *Chiefs and Families of Note in the Punjab*, Lahore: Civil and Military Gazette Press, 1909, pp. 418–19.
34. Garrett and Chopra, *Events at the Court of Ranjit Singh*, pp. 38–9.
35. Ibid., p. 127.
36. As quoted by Indu Banga, *Agrarian System of the Sikhs*, p. 159.
37. *Political Diaries of Agent to the Governor General North-West Frontier and Resident at Lahore (1847–48)*, Allahabad: The Pioneer Press, 1909, p. 365.
38. Nazer Singh, 'Early British Attitude towards the Golden Temple', *Journal of Regional History*, vol. 3, Amritsar: Guru Nanak Dev University, 1982, p. 88.
39. Ian J. Kerr, 'British Relationships with the Golden Temple, 1849–90', *The Indian Economic and Social History Review*, vol. 21 (1), New Delhi: Sage, 1984, p. 141.
40. Ibid., pp. 141–2.
41. Ian J. Kerr, 'The British and the Administration of the Golden Temple in 1859', *Panjab Past and Present*, part II, no. 20, Patiala: Punjabi University, October 1976, p. 310; Nazer Singh, 'Early British Attitude towards the Golden Temple', pp. 89–90.
42. Teja Singh, *The Gurdwara Reform Movement and the Sikh Awakening*, Jullundur: Desh Sewak Book Agency, 1922, pp. 140–1.
43. Nazer Singh, 'Early British Attitude Towards the Golden Temple', pp. 91–3.
44. C.M. King, Deputy Commissioner, to Younghusband, Commissioner, Lahore, 17 June 1905, File no. 668/12, The Punjab Government Civil Secretariat, *Proceedings Home/Confidential File*, Punjab State Archives, Chandigarh, pp. 154–5.
45. Teja Singh, *The Gurdwara Reform Movement*, pp. 141–2.
46. Ian J. Kerr, 'British Relationship with the Golden Temple', p. 139.
47. Ibid., pp. 145–6.

48. Ibid., pp. 147–8.
49. Ibid., p. 149.
50. Ibid., p. 145.
51. H.H. Cole, *Preservation of National Monuments: Golden Temple at Amritsar*, Punjab, Lahore, 1884.
52. David Ross, *The Land of the Five Rivers and Sindh*, Patiala: Languages Department, Punjab, 1970, p. 193.
53. John Campbell Oman, *Cults, Customs and Superstitions of India*, 1908; rpt., Delhi: Vishal Publishers, 1972, p. 96; Teja Singh, *The Gurdwara Reform Movement,* pp. 142–3.
54. Oman, *Cults, Customs and Superstitions of India*, pp. 89–90.
55. Ibid., pp. 86–7.
56. R.E. Younghusband, Commissioner, Lahore, to A.H. Diack, Chief Secretary, Punjab, dated 16 August 1902, File no. 668/1, *Proceedings Home/Confidential File*, p. 19.
57. Ibid., p. 29.
58. File no. 669/12, Ibid., pp. 3–5. See also File no. 721/13, pp. 41–4.
59. Oman, *Cults, Customs and Superstitions of India*, p. 93.
60. Colonel Jawala Singh's agreement with the Brahmans, 31 March 1899, File no. 668/12, *Proceedings Home/Confidential File*, p. 196.
61. Ibid., pp. 247–8.
62. Ibid., pp. 195–7.
63. Tikka Ripudaman's letter dated 30 March 1905, ibid., p. 3.
64. C.M. King, Deputy Commissioner, Amritsar, to R.E. Younghusband, Commissioner, Lahore Division, 20 April 1905, ibid., p. 12.
65. R.E. Younghusband to A.H. Diack, 21 April 1905, ibid., p. 6.
66. Arur Singh's order dated 1 May 1905, ibid., pp. 229–30.
67. Report dated 6 May 1905, ibid., p. 233.
68. Murasila dated 6 May 1905, ibid., pp. 235–6.
69. Manager's order dated 7 May 1905, ibid., p. 240.
70. Memorandum to Denzil Ibbetson by Seth Radhakrishen, dated 5 June 1905, ibid., pp. 264–7.
71. Prem Singh, Secretary, Sri Guru Singh Sabha, Quetta, to the Lt.-Governor, Lahore, 12 May 1905, ibid., p. 65; Amar Singh, Deputy Inspector of Police, Quetta, to the Deputy Commissioner, Amritsar, 11 May 1905, ibid., p. 66. Also see pp. 72, 126, 169–71.
72. Telegram from Rawalpindi, dated 6 May 1905, ibid., p. 15; Letter from Shikarpur, dated 24 May 1905, ibid., p. 72
73. Ibid., pp. 154–8.
74. Raja of Jind's letter to Lt. Governor, dated 5 July 1905, ibid., p. 180; Kahn Singh's letter dated 13 May 1905, ibid., p. 126.
75. Mohinder Singh, *The Akali Movement*, Delhi: The Macmillan Company of India, 1978, p. 21.

76. Harjot Singh, 'From Gurdwara Rikabganj to the Viceregal Palace: A Study of Religious Protest', *The Panjab Past and Present*, vol. 14, no. I, Patiala: Punjabi University, April 1980, pp. 183–98.
77. Ibid., pp. 186–7. See also, Teja Singh, *Essays in Sikhism*, Lahore: University Press, 1941, p. 140.
78. Harjot Singh, 'From Gurdwara Rikabganj to the Viceregal Palace', *The Panjab Past and Present,* p. 187.
79. Ibid., pp. 189–90.
80. Teja Singh, *The Gurdwara Reform Movement*, pp. 143–5.
81. Joginder Singh, *Sikh Leadership*, Amritsar: Guru Nanak Dev University, 1999, pp. 7–8.
82. Teja Singh, *The Gurdwara Reform Movement*, p. 146.
83. Ibid., pp. 146–7.
84. Mohinder Singh, *The Akali Movement*, p. 21.
85. Harjot Singh, 'From Gurdwara Rikabganj to Viceregal Palace', *The Panjab Past and Present*, pp. 191–3.
86. Teja Singh, *The Gurdwara Reform Movement*, pp. 151–3.
87. Ibid., pp. 156–7.
88. J.S. Grewal, *The New Cambridge History of India*: *The Sikhs of the Punjab*, Cambridge: Cambridge University Press, 1994, p. 159.
89. Teja Singh, *The Gurdwara Reform Movement*, pp. 121–2.
90. Ibid., pp. 123–32.
91. Ibid., pp. 212–42; J.S. Grewal, *The Sikhs of the Punjab*, 1994, p. 159.
92. Teja Singh, *The Gurdwara Reform Movement*, pp. 342–67; J.S. Grewal, *The Sikhs of the Punjab*, pp. 159–60.
93. J.S. Grewal, *The Sikhs of the Punjab*, pp. 160–1.
94. Ibid., p. 161.
95. Ibid., pp. 161–2.
96. Ibid., p. 162.

CHAPTER 3

Sanatan Dharm Institutions in Colonial Punjab

SHEENA PALL

Kenneth W. Jones was the first scholar to take serious note of the Sanatan Dharm Movement and its institutions in colonial Punjab.[1] He refers to Pandit Shraddha Ram Phillauri who founded certain institutions, as the first protagonist of the 'Sanatanist cause'. In 1867–8 Phillauri founded a Hindu Sabha at Ludhiana to sustain *sanatana dharma,* setting up a Hindu school at the same time to teach Sanskrit and Persian. In 1880, he established Hari Gyan Mandir at Phillaur, with a school to teach the Vedas. He also founded the Hindu Dharm Prakashika Sabha for the defence of Hindu orthodoxy. These organizations remained 'uncoordinated' and without a 'central authority'.[2] By 1890 the Sanatanists had a network of local Sanatan Dharm Sabhas throughout the province.[3]

Jones took notice of the Bharat Dharm Mahamandal too. It was founded by Pandit Din Dayalu Sharma in 1887 for 'bringing together all leaders' of the Hindu community. Nine conferences of the Mahamandal were organized till 1902. Five of these were held in the Punjab: once each in Amritsar and Kapurthala, and three in Delhi. Jones points out that in 1902, Din Dayalu Sharma resigned from his position as secretary and withdrew from the Mahamandal. He was replaced by Swami Gyananand, and the headquarters of the Mahamandal were moved to Mathura first and then to Benares in 1903. With 950 branch societies affiliated to it from all over India, the Bharat Dharm Mahamandal emerged as an overarching organization, far more important than the local Sanatan Dharm Sabhas of the Punjab or the Hindu Dharm Sabhas of Bengal.[4]

Jones makes the general observation that Christian missionaries were the first to introduce new forms of religious organization and action in India as 'structured societies' with formal membership, written rules, and weekly meetings. They were strengthened by the British Indian government through 'laws granting legal recognition'. All other religious communities in India founded Sabhas, Anjumans, and Samajes, each with its own constitution and byelaws, publishing annual reports. These bodies purchased property, built places of worship, schools, orphanages, widow homes, reading rooms, homes for aged cows, dispensaries and hospitals. They also made use of the printing press to issue their own newspapers, journals, tracts and books. Funds were collected through innovative means, and the money collected was suitably utilized and invested.[5]

Independently of Jones, John Zavos observed that the Bharat Dharm Mahamandal emerged as a central organization for the network of Sanatan Dharm Sabhas which had been established in the Punjab and the North-Western Provinces by the late 1880s. According to Zavos, the programme of the Mahamandal included preserving Sanskrit manuscripts, improving old schools, opening new ones, and appointing learned Brahmans to lecture on orthodox Hindu religion and to refute the propaganda of 'modern Hindu sects'.[6]

The leaders of the Sanatan Dharm Movement looked upon the growing number of their institutions as a sign of its progress. Din Dayalu Sharma advertised with some satisfaction in 1889 that the number of Dharm Sabhas in India had risen from less than a hundred in 1887 to more than two hundred now. A decade later the number of Sabhas was nearly eight hundred.[7] The British administrators of the Punjab had already begun to take notice of the Sanatanist institutions. A list of the scientific, literary and charitable societies in the Punjab in 1889–90 included one Hindu Sabha, three Sanatan Dharm Sabhas and six Dharm Sabhas. These Sabhas had been founded mostly in the 1880s. The membership of these Sabhas ranged from 20 to 156; the main sources of their income were subscriptions and endowments.[8] The Hindu Sabha of Amritsar is stated to have been 'registered', presumably under the Societies Registration Act of 1860.[9]

Towards the end of the century, the official reports refer to 37 Sanatanist institutions in the British Punjab.[10] The earliest of these was founded at Simla in 1872. Fifteen institutions were supposed to have been founded in the 1880s and twenty-one more in the 1890s. In twelve districts there was no Sanatanist institution as yet. There was one institution each in twelve districts. In six districts were there two institutions each. In three districts there were three institutions each. Only in the district of Hissar were there four Sanatanist institutions. If one were to divide the Punjab into three zones for the pattern of the distribution of Sanatanist institutions, one would find an interesting correlation between the Hindu population and the number of institutions. In the western zone of eight districts there was one institution for about a lakh of Hindus. In the central zone of eleven districts there was one institution for about two lakh of Hindus. In the eastern zone of eight districts there was one institution for over two and a half lakh of Hindus. Thus, there is clear evidence of an inverse ratio between the Sanatanist institutions and the Hindu population in 1900.[11]

Almost two-thirds of the Sanatanist institutions around 1900 were Sanatan Dharm Sabhas with various names. The statements of scientific, literary and charitable societies in the Punjab in 1899–1900 mention the objectives as well as the names of many of these associations. For example, the S.H.K Sanatan Dharm Mandal of Hissar was meant to 'teach Sanskrit and other prescribed subjects and to support the principles of Sanatan Dharm'. The Sanatan Dharm Club in Hissar itself had the objective of 'diffusion of Sanatan Dharm'. The Mitt Hit Karin Sabha of Sohna was meant to 'preach the Manu Shastar' and to 'encourage the people for the learning of Sanskrit'. It was also the objective of this Sabha to 'persuade the persons to remove the bad customs in marriage ceremonies in India'. The Sanatan Dharm Sabha of Ambala Cantonment and the Sanatan Dharm Sabha of Ropar were meant to 'teach Vedas, etc.'. The aim of Sanatan Dharm Sabha of Jagadhri was diffusion of 'a better knowledge of the Shastras and the return to the old and purer forms of Hindu religion'. In the case of the Sanatan Dharm Sabha of Hoshiarpur, the objective mentioned explicitly is religious, social and moral reformation of the Hindus. The Sanatanist associations in Jullundur and Rahon, called Dharm Sabhas, aimed at the progress of Sanskrit language. The Sanatan Dharm Sabhas of Ludhiana and Ferozepore were meant to support and propagate the principles of Sanatan Dharm. Thus, collectively, the objectives of the Sanatanist institutions covered religious, social and cultural concerns. Important among these were the study of scriptural literature, the propagation of Sanskrit learning and the introduction of reform in social as well as religious matters. Concern for modern education is clearly stated in the objectives of the Sanatan Dharm Sabha of Lahore. Besides giving support to the principles of Sanatan Dharm and establishing a library of Sanskrit, religion, philosophy, science and literature, the objective of the Sabha was to establish a college to teach Sanskrit 'and other prescribed subjects'.[12]

Apart from these associations, the Sanatanists established a few institutions for the protection of cows as well as for education. The Gau Rakshni Sabha at Hissar was meant for the protection of infirm and unserviceable cows and oxen. This was also the objective of the Gau Rakshni Sabha at Bhiwani. The Sabha at Multan was called Gaushala Sabha but the objective was the same. The two educational institutions of the Sanatanist were in Lahore: a purely Sanskrit Pathshala and an Anglo-Sanskrit High School.[13]

The report provides some other information also on the Sanatanist institutions. The ones in Lahore, Amritsar, Simla, Jullundur, Hoshiarpur and Hissar were registered. The membership of the Sabhas ranged from 570 at Lahore to 10 at Ludhiana. The only Sabha to have female members was at Dera Ghazi Khan. The primary sources of income for these institutions were subscriptions and endowments. The subscription amount for each of the Sabhas at Hoshiarpur, Jullundur and Lahore was more than Rs. 2,000 but for the Sabha at Jalalpur the amount was only Rs. 11. The Sabha at Amritsar had an endowment of Rs. 4,500 and the Sabha at Gujranwala an endowment of Rs. 75. The subscription for the Gau Rakshani Sabha at Bhiwani was Rs. 4,000. The only institution to receive a grant from the government (Rs. 375 per month) was the Hindu Sabha of Amritsar.

By far the most important institution of the late nineteenth century was the Bharat Dharm Mahamandal, established in 1887 on the initiative of Din Dayalu Sharma (1863–1937). He had attended the annual session of the Indian National Congress at Calcutta in 1886. Notwithstanding his appreciation for the Congress as a political body of Indians, he felt unhappy that it had no interest in promoting 'Indian culture'. What was needed, really, was an all-India organization, concerned chiefly with Hindu culture. Pandit Madan Mohan Malaviya, whom he had met for the first time at the Congress, approved of Din Dayalu's vision and offered his support.[14]

On his return from Calcutta, Din Dayalu decided to give formal shape to an all-India Hindu organization. For this he had the support of some eminent individuals from the Kapurthala state: Diwan Ramjas, Diwan Mathura Das, Mishr Achchru Mal and Babu Hari Chand. He had also the support of Munshi Harsukh Rai, proprietor of the *Kohinoor.* A meeting of eminent Sanatan Dharmis of Kapurthala and Jullundur was called by Diwan Ramjas, the prime minister of Kapurthala, in April 1887. This meeting was followed by a conference at Hardwar on the occasion of Ganga Dashmi in May, when a large number of pilgrims would gather.[15]

To make arrangements for the conference at Hardwar, a Welcome Committee was constituted, with Din Dayalu as its secretary. He circulated the objectives of the conference for discussion. The basic purpose was to unite all the Sanatan Dharm Sabhas of India into a single organization. A central office could facilitate contact between different Sabhas and publish a monthly magazine to provide information on their activities. Uniform rules for all the Dharm Sabhas could be formulated. Annual conferences could be organized at sacred places to review, among other things, the activities of the central organization. An annual report could be published and circulated. Attached with the circular would be a questionnaire to elicit responses to matters relating to religion, society and culture.[16]

The conference was held from 29 to 31 May 1887. It was attended by aristocrats (*rais*), government officials and editors of periodicals from the Punjab and from places like Chunar, Patna and Calcutta. Resolutions were passed for the propagation of Sanatan Dharm based on *Shruti*, *Smriti* and the *Purana*s, to establish unity among the different sects of Hindus like the Shaivas and the Vaishnavas, and to uphold the *varnashrama-dharma*. It was also resolved that *pathshala*s should be set up for the propagation of Sanskrit and Hindi should be promoted as the language of education and administration. The government would be requested to introduce Hindi as the medium of instruction in government schools. It was at this conference that Din Dayalu proposed the name Bharat Dharm Mahamandal for the organization. It was unanimously accepted.[17]

The major concerns of the Bharat Dharm Mahamandal in the early years of its existence were organizational and educational. On 1 July 1893, Pandit Din Dayalu Sharma sent a circular letter to associations and individuals all over the country inviting their suggestions with regard to the establishment of a central office and a college. These suggestions were to be discussed at a conference at Delhi on 15 October 1893. There was good response to this circular letter from different parts of the country: Lahore, Amritsar, Shahpur, Gujranwala, Dera Ghazi Khan, Peshawar, Hoshiarpur, Rohtak, Hissar and the Mir State for example. Suggestions on these two issues were received by Pandit Din Dayalu even after the meeting. This correspondence provides useful insights into the thinking of the Sanatanists on these major issues in 1893.

It is clear that two regional *dharm mandal*s were already in existence: Sri Haryana Kurukshetra Dharm Mandal at Hissar and the Punjab Sanatan Dharm Mandal at Lahore. Each had a number of Sanatan Dharm Sabhas associated with it. The letter sent by the former is signed by a president, three vice-presidents and four secretaries, apart from Pandit Dev Dutt Sharma who signed as *updeshak*. In the case of the Punjab Sanatan Dharm Mandal, Lala Ishar Das is mentioned as president of the Karkun Committee and Pandit Gopi Nath as its secretary. The regional *mandal*s appear to have adopted formal constitutions. About the managing committee of the Bharat Dharm Mahamandal, it was generally suggested that it should represent different provinces of north India. Significantly, the south was not yet a part of their vision for the central organization. There was a suggestion that a subcommittee of the managing committee of the Bharat Dharm Mahamandal may consist of the trustees representing all the provinces, with a general trustee at the head office. There was also a suggestion that the Bharat Dharm Mahamandal may constitute a financial committee after its managing committee was in place. It was also suggested that the Bharat Dharm Mahamandal may have maharajas and rajas, and other rich or eminent individuals as its patrons. About where the head office of the Mahamandal should be located, there were several suggestions. Apart from Delhi or Lahore, it was suggested that the Mahamandal could have its head office at a place like Kashi or Hardwar.[18] It appears, however, that till the end of the century the Mahamandal did not have a permanent head office.[19] There was unanimity about the Mahamandal being registered.[20] At the conference of 2–4 November 1893, it was resolved to get the Mahamandal registered,[21] but even in 1902, it was still only being suggested that the Mahamandal should be got registered.[22]

There were several suggestions about the establishment of a college. One was to found a Sanskrit University for the country as a whole, with a number of colleges in different parts of the country. Even when no university was proposed it was suggested that there should be a Sanskrit college in each province, with a number of *pathshala*s at other places. Regarding the establishment of a single college, there were three suggestions: one that it may be at Delhi; two, that it may be located at Lahore where the Punjab Mandal had already resolved to establish a college; and three, that the college may be located at a sacred place like Kashi or Hardwar. The suggestions regarding the nature and character of the college also varied. One view was that it should be a Sanskrit college, having no Western type of education. The other was that it should have a balance between the Western and Sanskrit types of education. As Ganga Sahai of Rohtak put it, without English there was no employment and without Sanskrit there was no cultural heritage. The two in combination would produce true Hindus who would serve as a means for the progress of the people. There were a number of suggestions for the collection of funds ranging from respectable delegations being sent to the maharajas to the placing of *dan patar*s (donation boxes) at thousands of places in the country.

One significant suggestion was that individuals who were promoting traditional works of public welfare may be induced to divert their charitable resources to the new purposes envisaged by the Sanatanists.[23]

It may be added that Pandit Din Dayalu Sharma was in favour of a Sanskrit college. However, since there was no unanimity a committee of eleven members was appointed to identify the subjects to be taught in the proposed college. At the end of the conference, it was decided that all programmes of the Mahamandal should relate to Sanatan Dharm. Any support from those who did not subscribe to this *dharm*, need not be accepted. In fact, it was resolved that the primary objectives of the Mahamandal should be only three: to promote Sanatan Dharm on the basis of the Vedas and the Puranas, to promote Sanskrit learning, and to reform some of the prevalent practices.[24]

Between 1887 and 1902, nine conferences of the Mahamandal were held. After the first conference, representatives of the Shudras were also invited to these conferences. The notice for the second conference was issued in Hindi instead of Urdu.[25] The resolutions passed at these conferences are indicative of the concerns of the Sanatanists in the last decade of the nineteenth century: that the sixteen rituals (*solah sanskar*) should be performed in accordance with the Shastras; the condition of schools and *pathshala*s run by the Dharm Sabhas should be improved; religious instruction should be made compulsory in all schools and *pathshala*s and the question of religious instruction in government schools should be looked into; attention should be given to female education; the princely rulers of Rajputana and the Punjab should be requested to introduce Hindi in their *darbar*s; the custom of giving dowry to the daughter at the time of marriage should be discarded; the government should be approached to withdraw the Age of Consent Bill; and Guru Nanak Dev and Guru Gobind Singh and their followers should be regarded as Hindus.[26]

Dharm *prachar* was a major concern of the Mahamandal. Its learned *updeshak*s held discussions with others on the subjects of the Puranas, *avtar*s, idol worship, pilgrimage, *varnashrama-dharma*, *shraddha*, *tarpan*, widow remarriage, and consumption of meat and alcohol. The Sanatanist position on such issues was upheld on the authority of the Vedas and the Shastras. Numerous Dev Mandirs were set up under the control of the representatives of the local community. To encourage and appreciate the work of the *updeshak*s, titles and medals were instituted. Books were published and distributed to disseminate the Sanatanist message.[27] Separate teachers for religious instruction were preferred. The Mahamandal organized examinations in Sanskrit and rewarded deserving students. Schools and libraries were set up for the preservation and propagation of Sanskrit texts. The Devanagari Pracharini Sabha of Kashi was appreciated for promoting the cause of Devanagari.[28]

A number of chiefs associated themselves with the Mahamandal: Raja Shashishekreshwar Rai Bahadur of Tahirpur (Bengal); Maharaja Pratap Narayan Singh (of Ajudhya); Shri 108 Bal Krishan Lalji Maharaj of Kakroli; Maharaja Shri Lakshmishwar Singh of Darbhanga; the Maharaja of Nahan. Apart from the prestige, the chiefs provided financial help to the Mahamandal. Some of the chiefs came personally and presided over the sessions of the Mahamandal, while others sent their representatives to the conferences. The Maharaja of Kapurthala does not figure in the conferences of the Mahamandal but, as noted earlier, the administrators of Kapurthala state were actively involved with the establishment of the Mahamandal and its conferences.[29]

In the Punjab, a number of other important individuals were associated with the work of the Mahamandal. One such supporter of the Punjab Mandal was Sir Pratul Chandra Chatterjee, judge, Chief Court, Punjab.[30] Among the aristocrats from the Punjab to give support to the Mahamandal were Raja Harbans Singh of Sheikhupura, Lala Sant Ram and Rai Bahadur Gagarmal of Amritsar, and Diwan Bhagwan Das Dahreewale and Rai Bahadur Mela Ram of Lahore. Two other supporters to figure in the records are Seth Lakshman Das of Mathura and Rai Bahadur Lala Shri Krishandasji Gurwale of Delhi. Quite often these aristocrats were elected as presidents of the local organizing committees, which were responsible for collecting funds and making arrangements for the conferences of the Mahamandal at different places. Sometimes lectures and conferences were also held in their private halls, residences and gardens.[31]

Contemporary comments on the Mahamandal are not without interest. A report in *The Tribune* refers to a special meeting of the Bharat Dharm Mahamandal held at Delhi in 1891. This meeting was attended by the Maharaja of Kishangarh:

> Several Pundits chanted Vedic mantras and received the Maharaja with blessings and a heavy shower of flowers. The leading Hindu *reisis* of Delhi were present. Pundit Din Dyal Sharma, General Secretary in a brief address explained the objects [*sic*] of the Mahamandal and expressed his thanks to the Maharaja for attending the meeting of the Mahamandal. The meeting concluded with cheers for the Empress Victoria and His Highness the Maharaja who was very much delighted at what he saw and expressed sympathy with the Mahamandal movement.[32]

Towards the end of the century, the Maharaja of Darbhanga was emerging as a prominent patron of the Mahamandal. He paid all the expenses for its conference in 1900. The Maharaja was praised in Sanskrit by Pandit Rameshar Das of Benares for his liberal financial and personal support. Many prominent personalities attended the conference, like the diwan of the Gwalior state, Raja Partab Singh of Faizabad, Lachhman Das, a banker of Mathura, Pandit Gopi Nath, secretary of the Bharat Dharm Mahamandal, Lahore and editor of the *Akhbar-i Am*, Pandit Birwa Nand of Bombay, Pandit Chunni Lal, secretary Prem Sagar Sabha, Lahore, Pandit Sham Das of Lahore, Babu Hari Chand of Kapurthala state, and numerous other pandits from Agra, Karnal, Hissar, Gurgaon, Hardwar, Karachi, Rohtak, Ambala and Benares.[33]

Commenting on the activity of the Bharat Dharm Mahamandal as early as 1890, *The Tribune* observed that it had been 'conspicuously successful' in its efforts at Hindu revival in the Punjab, and other places. Hundreds of branch societies had been founded in cities and towns for the 'protection of the ancient Hindu religion, the preservation of the religious rites in their integrity and the diffusion of sacred learning'. Sanskrit schools had been opened under the auspices of the Chief Branch Societies, where 'instruction of high standard' in the Vedas and Shastras was imparted. Libraries had also been attached to the schools, where every one could read and examine the Vedas,

Shastras, Puranas and other religious books. Many new books were written by the Pandits of the Society to refute arguments advanced against the ancient religious systems 'in a masterly style'.[34]

A vernacular periodical expressed the opinion that 'this religious movement will do the work of more than a thousand National Congresses'. The Congress was destined to be cast into the shade by the Mahamandal and 'in time to be obliterated'.[35] However, the *Mahratta* of Poona, only hoped that the Mahamandal would succeed in uniting people of diverse religious beliefs just as the Indian National Congress had created 'unity of sentiments and opinions' in political matters throughout the country.[36]

There were others who looked upon the work of the Mahamandal as a reaction to the Arya Samaj. According to the *Indian Mirror*, its founders never intended it to be 'a connecting link between different sects of Hindus'. Nor were they inspired by liberal and philanthropic motives to make the Indians 'a homogeneous nation in every respect'. The followers of the Mahamandal were '*pucca* conservative Hindus, following *Puranic* doctrines, now known as Sanatan Dharma'. Their chief objective was to undo the work of Swami Dayanand, the founder of the Arya Samaj, and to strengthen only 'the followers of the *Puranic* doctrines'. Similarly, the *Hindu* asserted that the object of the originators of the Mahamandal was 'not so much to purge Hindu society of its grievous defects', or to unite Hindus of all persuasions, as to present 'a temporary and apparently formidable front to the Arya Samajes'. The work of the Mahamandal was seen to be 'a destructive one in the main'.[37]

At the beginning of the twentieth century the Sanatanist leaders of the Punjab lost their importance in the Bharat Dharm Mahamandal. Swami Gyananand was running a society in Mathura which translated Bengali books into Hindi for publication. He had the support of the maharajas of Rajasthan, a few aristocrats, and several members of the Theosophical Society. After a meeting between Pandit Din Dayalu and Swami Gyananand this society was merged with the Mahamandal in March 1901. Swami Gyananand set up a separate office of the Mahamandal at Mathura. Without the knowledge of Pandit

Din Dayalu but on his behalf, Swami Gyananand proposed a new set of rules and procedures for the Mahamandal to be considered in a meeting held at Mathura on 28–30 March 1902. No representative, even of the most important Sabhas of the Punjab was invited. Against the advice of the maharaja of Darbhanga who was the general president of the Mahamandal and the considered view of Pandit Din Dayalu Sharma, the new rules were formulated. Immediately after the meeting, Din Dayalu sent his resignation to the Maharaja of Darbhanga. Thereafter he did not associate himself with the Mahamandal. After 1902, the Bharat Dharm Mahamandal became increasingly ineffective in the Punjab.[38]

A conference of Sanatan Dharmis of the Punjab was held at Lahore in 1917 to organize the Sanatanists. An association called the Sanatan Dharm Pratinidhi Sabha Punjab was established at Lahore. The Pratinidhi Sabha began to set up local Sabhas, high schools and *pathshala*s. However, this work does not appear to have gone far. A Sanatan Dharm Conference was held at Sargodha in 1923 to rejuvenate the Pratinidhi Sabha. Pandit Din Dayalu Sharma presided over this conference. Elections were held all afresh and Malik Mathura Dass was elected its president while Goswami Ganesh Dutt was elected its general secretary. As the latter belonged to Lyallpur, the office of the Pratinidhi Sabha was set up there.[39]

Significantly, the number of Sabhas increased from 110 to over 200 in 1923. A conference of the Pratinidhi Sabha was convened at Rawalpindi in November 1924. Nearly 1,500 delegates attended this conference and Pandit Madan Mohan Malaviya presided over it. In November 1925, Maharajadhiraj Rana Dholpur was the general president of a conference of the Pratinidhi Sabha held at Lahore on the invitation of Rai Bahadur Ram Saran Dass and Principal Raghuwar Dayal. This conference was attended by about 8,000 delegates. The maharaja of Patiala, the raja of Mandi, governor of the Punjab, Sir Malcolm Hailey, and Chief Justice Sir Shadi Lal came for this conference. For the conference of the Pratinidhi Sabha at Multan, held in December 1926, Maharajadhiraj of Alwar was the general president and nearly 20,000 delegates attended. The maharaja of Alwar and the maharaja of Darbhanga gave generous donations.[40]

The annual report of the Pratinidhi Sabha Punjab for the year 1928 gives some idea of its constitution. Apart from a number of patrons, the Sabha had a general president, a president, a vice-president, a general secretary, a secretary, an accountant and an auditor. It had nine departments, each managed by a secretary (*mantri*). Another important office was that of the *dalpati* who headed the Mahabir Dal. The patrons of the Sabha consisted of chiefs, aristocrats, government officials and heads of religious institutions. Like the office-bearers, they were elected at the annual meeting of the Pratinidhi Sabha, held generally in March. The Pratinidhi Sabha had a core committee (*atrang*) and an executive committee (*karyakarini*) to conduct its activities in accordance with its rules and regulations (*neeyamawali*).[41]

The work of the departments of the Pratinidhi Sabha related to administration (*karyalaya*), propaganda (*prachar*), education (*siksha*), temple reform (*mandir sudhar*), publicity (*samachar*), religious learning (*vidhat*), the youth, Dalits (*antyajodhar*), and the Mahabir Dal.[42] The nine departments were not of equal importance, neither is there adequate information on all of them. About the 'youth societies', all that is known is that they were established in order to influence the Hindu youth in Sanatanist ways.

The primary function of the administrative department was to coordinate the activities of the Pratinidhi Sabha. It assigned duties to individuals for *prachar* and other kinds of work. Meetings of the various committees were called and their recommendations were sought to be implemented. The department communicated with associated Sabhas and tried to meet their requirements. It was responsible for the collection of funds and their proper use; a detailed account of income and expenditure was maintained to be properly audited. In addition, one finds the department approaching the law courts to protect the rights of Sanatanist individuals and institutions. Protests were made by the department against any bill or proposal if it appeared to hurt the interests or the religious sentiments of the Sanatanists.[43]

The department for *prachar* had six branch offices, one each at Ambala, Amritsar, Ferozepore, Rawalpindi, Mianwali and Multan. Whenever the programme in a particular area extended over a period of time, temporary branch offices were set up for easy accessibility for *pracharaks*. The object of *prachar* was to make Hindus aware of their ancient religion and to overcome the shortcomings in their social and religious life. They were aware that the purpose of their *prachar* was to obviate the influence of the radical reformers. Sanatanist *pracharaks* went to other provinces and the Indian states and even to other countries, like Afghanistan, Malaya, British East Africa and Fiji, where Hindus were settled. To reach larger numbers the *pracharaks* used occasions like fairs and festivals and spread their message through the modes of *kathas*, *kirtans*, lectures and *bhajans*.[44]

The department for the reform of temples made efforts to revive old temples, construct new ones and protect them. Important among the new temples constructed was the Lakshmi Narayan Temple midst the Durgiana *sarovar* in Amritsar in 1924. Though the donation came from Seth Nathushahji Rangwale, the temple was managed by a registered committee. Its president was a member of the Punjab Legislative Council, Lala Keshav Lal. Generally with regard to disagreements about temples, the Pratinidhi Sabha was of the view that they should not be taken to the courts. Instead, they should be resolved in Sanatan Dharm Panchayats.[45]

The primary objective of the department for the betterment of Dalits was to obviate their conversion to other religions, like Christianity and Islam. Significantly, the report mentions Ad-Dharm as a rival faith.[46] The Dalits were also warned against those who tried to win them over by offering money, food, and other kinds of inducements. The department had its own *updeshaks* and *bhajniks* for *prachar* among Dalits. They were not supposed to have any contact with other *updeshaks* and *bhajniks*. Separate temples were constructed for the Dalits. Wherever they had difficulties of access to water, wells were dug for them. Separate *pathshalas* were set up for their children. The Dalits were advised to keep their hair in a topknot (*choti*), observe fasts, perform marriage and death rituals according to Brahmanical conventions, and to abstain from drinking alcohol, eating meat and gambling.[47]

The publicity department of the Pratinidhi Sabha reported the activities of the Sabhas, conferences and celebrations. It advertised the programmes of *prachar*. Allegations of opponents were refuted and their excesses were highlighted. For the propagation of Sanatanist ideas and objectives, articles were published in various newspapers and periodicals, either in their own, like the *Bhism* and the *Akhbar-i Am* in Lahore, the *Sanatan Dharm Pracharak* in Amritsar, the *Mahabir* in Delhi, the *Jagrit* in Lyallpur and the *Bharatmitra* in Calcutta, or in others like the *Sudarshan,* the *Hindu Herald* and *The Tribune* in Lahore, the *Hindu Sansar* in Delhi and the *Bangbasi* in Calcutta. It was the function of the department to keep the government informed of the needs and demands of the Pratinidhi Sabha.[48]

The function of the Vidhat Parishad was to organize discussions on important or controversial subjects by learned scholars. A major objective of such meetings and seminars was to refute the criticism of opponents regarding the sacred scriptures. As an essential part of this concern, books related to *Shruti, Smriti* and the Puranas were edited and published. Books by other scholars were approved for use in *prachar*. Books for religious instruction in Sanatan Dharm schools and *pathshala*s were also prepared. Sanatanist scholars sought to create awareness among the common people about religious fasts, festivals and rituals through their books and essays. Since ritual was all-important, the correct time and date of festivals and fasts were advertised in newspapers.[49]

The Pratinidhi Sabha attached great importance to *katha* and the observance of festivals. *Katha*s were organized in more than two hundred towns with the help of the local Sanatan Dharm Sabhas. The themes taken up for *katha* were selected from the Vedas, Shastras and Puranas. Apart from *katha vachak*s, the *pujari*s of *mandir*s, religious instructors of schools, and *pracharak*s performed *katha* in local temples and halls. The local Sabhas were asked to celebrate festivals in accordance with the Shastras as interpreted by the Sabha. *Pracharak*s were sent overseas to organize festivals like the Basant Panchmi, Holi, Nirjala Ekadashi, Vyas Puja, Shivratri, Deepmala, Ram Navami, Gita Jayanti and Janmashtami. *Rakhi*s made of *mauli* were recommended for use on Raksha Bandhan. The birth anniversaries of figures like Shivaji and Maharana Pratap were celebrated. Vir Bairagi (Banda Bahadur) began to be treated as a Hindu martyr.[50]

The Pratinidhi Sabha developed an interest in fairs. Among the places mentioned are Katas Raj, Ram Chautra, Chintpurni, Ram Tirath and Chiniot. The fair at Kurukshetra held at the time of the solar eclipse was the most important.[51] During these fairs, lectures were delivered by *updeshaks*, *bhajniks* and learned scholars of the Sabha. They participated in *shastrarth* as well. Generally the discussions were about rituals like the *shraddha,* the practice of idol worship, the belief in avatars, the status of the Puranas and the *Ramayana,* and the position of Brahmans in the *varna* order. The *Satyarath Prakash* also was a subject of debate.[52]

The workers of the Pratinidhi Sabha clashed with the Arya Samajists during the course of *prachar* at several places in the districts of Hissar, Rohtak, Sialkot and Jhelum. They had skirmishes with the Akalis at Attock, Rawalpindi, Kohat, Sialkot and Lyallpur. It is important to note that the Akalis were opposed to the Sanatanist claim that the ten Gurus of the Sikhs were Sanatan Dharmis and that they had given the *updesh* of Sanatan Dharm from the Darbar Sahib. There was also a dispute about a place which, according to the Akalis, was a gurdwara. The Sanatanists clashed with the Muslims over a slaughterhouse and the conversion of Chamars to Islam in the districts of Gurgaon, Sheikhupura and Ferozepore. Significantly, the Sanatanists had a confrontation with Ramdas, the Vaishnava *mahant* of Pindori, who claimed to be a Sanatan Dharmi.[53]

Like the Christian missionaries and the Arya Samajis, the Pratinidhi Sabha set up orphanages for destitute Hindu children. The basic concern was to prevent their conversion to another faith. There were orphanages at Lahore, Delhi and Kasur, each with a separate committee. The children at the orphanages were taught Sanskrit, Hindi, Urdu and Mahajani along with religious instruction. Special attention was given to providing a technical skill to help them find employment. They were trained in certain crafts like carpentry, tailoring, dyeing, iron work, photography, calligraphy and carpet weaving. A report of the number of male and female children in the orphanage, their age, and the nature of their education was published annually. Orphanages had their own *bhajan mandalis* and a band. The accounts of the orphanages were audited. A weekly entitled *Mahabir* was also issued.[54]

Widow homes were set up to provide food, clothing and proper accommodation. They were also provided with a monthly stipend. The main objective was to make widows financially independent by teaching them to sew and stitch. Each Sabha was asked to help at least four widows.[55]

The concerns of the Pratinidhi Sabha are reflected in some of the resolutions passed in the conference at Kurukshetra. Besides founding new Sabhas, Mahabir Dals and an orphanage for Hindu boys at Lahore, the conference resolved to establish a Rishikul Brahmacharyashram at Kurukshetra. The practice of collecting money by placing idols of gods on the roadside was condemned. The Sanatan Dharmis were requested to get the Mandir Sudhar Bill passed in the Punjab Legislative Assembly.[56]

The Pratinidhi Sabha sent petitions and deputations to the government and, depending upon the importance of the issue, mobilized support for their position. Proposals were sent to the Punjab government with a request to declare Ram Navami a holiday in government offices. The government was also requested to conduct an investigation into the Malakpur and Softa riots and to punish the culprits. Permission was sought from the chief commissioners to continue *nagar kirtan* in the Sheikhupura district and to prevent the demolition of a *mandir* in Peshawar. The deputy commissioner was requested for permission to carry out the procession of 'Ved Bhagwan' at Hazara, which had been stopped earlier. Through the good offices of the North Western Railway, a tract on the historical and religious importance of Kurukshetra was published and distributed on the occasion of the solar eclipse. Deputations were sent to the governor protesting against the opening of a cow slaughterhouse in Fazilka.[57] The government was requested to issue orders to the jail authorities that Hindu prisoners admitted to a jail should not be obliged to remove their sacred thread.[58] The deputy commissioner of Lahore was requested to declare a holiday for Hindus on account of Nirjala Ekadashi.[59]

The Gaur Bill and the Sharda Bill, which were meant to provide for divorce and widow remarriage among Hindus, were opposed on the grounds that they interfered with the religious customs of the Hindus. In order to make the government aware of the feelings of the Hindus, meetings were called, advertisements and tracts were distributed and representations were sent to the government. The Pratinidhi Sabha sent its representatives to attend the All Party Convention that was held at Calcutta.[60]

A large number of institutions associated with the Punjab Pratinidhi Sabha in Sind, the N.W.F. Province, Kashmir, Balochistan, the British Punjab, the princely states, Delhi and the United Provinces are mentioned in its report of 1928. Table 3.1 is prepared on the basis of the report, but only for the institutions located in the British Punjab.

The core institution of the Sanatanists was the Sabha.[61] The Sabhas were rather unevenly spread over the province. The Shahpur district had twenty-six Sabhas but Rohtak had only one. Gujrat had twenty-five Sabhas and Gurgaon only three. Ten districts had up to ten Sabhas each, sixteen districts up to twenty Sabhas each, and three had more than twenty each. The number of Sabhas in a district was not necessarily proportionate to its Hindu population. The district of Rawalpindi, for example, with a Hindu population of 56,174 had 18 Sabhas, but the district of Lahore with a Hindu population of 2,08,543 had 14. In the district of Karnal, which had a population of 4,57,137, the number of Sabhas was no more than 5. Significantly, there was an inverse ratio between the number of Sabhas and the number of Hindus in these three districts. These districts were in fact representative of three zones. In the western districts of Shahpur, Gujrat, Mianwali, Jhelum, Rawalpindi, Multan, Muzzafargarh, Attock and Dera Ghazi Khan there were 158 Sabhas for a Hindu population of 6,16,319. In the central districts of Sheikhupura, Hoshiarpur, Jullundur, Sialkot, Gurdaspur, Lahore, Gujranwala, Jhang, Lyallpur, Ferozepore, Amritsar and Montgomery, the number of Sabhas was also 158 but the population was 19,10,475. In the eastern districts of Kangra, Ambala, Karnal, Hissar, Simla, Ludhiana, Gurgaon and Rohtak there were no more than 47 Sabhas though the Hindu population

TABLE 3.1: SANATAN DHARM INSTITUTIONS IN THE BRITISH PUNJAB (1928)

Districts	*SDS*	*MD*	*Educational Institutions*						*O*	*Total*
			C	*HS*	*MS*	*PS*	*PP*	*D*		
Shahpur	26	11		1	1	2	6		3	50
Gujrat	25	24		5	5	5	7		3	74
Mianwali	21	9				1	4		3	38
Jhelum	20	8		1	1	1	6		4	41
Rawalpindi	18	3		1	4	4	3		4	37
Multan	14	9		1	1	1	6		3	35
Muzzafargarh	13	6					1		1	21
Attock	11	5		1	1	1	6		3	28
Dera Ghazi Khan	10	3		1	2	2	4		3	25
Sheikhupura	19	6					1		2	28
Hoshiarpur	18	13		3	9	9	5			57
Jullundur	17	16			2	2	4	1	1	43
Sialkot	17	10							2	29
Gurdaspur	14	13			1	1		1	1	31
Lahore	14	6	1	1	1	2	4		10	39
Gujranwala	12	1		2	2	2	2		1	22
Jhang	12	9			1	1	5		2	30
Lyallpur	11	9		1	1	1	5		6	34
Ferozepore	9	8		1	3	3	6		1	31
Amritsar	8	18		1	2	2	2		2	35
Montgomery	7	4					2		2	15
Kangra	13	3		2	3	3	2		1	27
Ambala	12	6							1	19
Karnal	5	2		1	1	1				10
Hissar	5	2					1			8
Simla	5	2		1	2	2	1		1	14
Ludhiana	3	5		1	1	1			1	12
Gurgaon	3	4								7
Rohtak	1			1	1	1				4
	363	215	1	26	45	48	83	2	61	844

Source: Report of Sanatan Dharm Pratinidhi Sabha Punjab, 1928.

Notes: SDS – Sanatan Dharm Sabha, MD – Mahabir Dal, C – College, HS – High School, MS – Middle School, PS - Primary School, PP – Putri Pathshala, D – Dalit School, O – Others.

was 29,00,000.[62] One can see that the inverse ratio holds good not just for a few districts but actually for three large and contiguous zones. This pattern does not appear to be accidental. The number of Sanatan Dharm Sabhas corresponded directly to the increasing proportion of Muslims in a zone. It was perhaps a reflection of communal consciousness.

The reports of three conferences of the Sabhas held in 1928 in Gujar Khan in the Rawalpindi district, Dinanagar in the Gurdaspur district and Moga in the Ferozepore district reflect their concerns. The conference at Gujar Khan expressed its concerns about establishing widow homes and propagating the importance of their duties; teaching Hindi and Sanskrit to the children; giving support to the orphanage at Delhi and the educational institutions of the Sanatanist, especially the Sanatan Dharm College at Lahore; taking the children to the temple twice daily for religious education; giving all possible support to the Sanatan Dharm School at Gujar Khan; establishing an *akhara* in all towns and villages where Hindu youth may enhance its physical strength through exercises of all kinds; ensuring that the pending Mandir Sudhar Bill was passed; and fixing the marriageable age for girls at twelve and boys at eighteen.[63]

At Dinanagar the issues discussed were ways to ensure that the pending Mandir Sudhar Bill was passed; that the bill introduced by Gaur providing for divorce among Hindus was not passed; that the ruler of Mandi abrogated the provision of widow remarriage; that cow slaughter was not legally allowed in Fazilka; that the Raghunath Mandir of Peshawar was not demolished; that vanaspati ghee was not imported; that the Municipality of Hardwar rescinded its decision to ban the sale of the *Gita* and any exposition of Sanatan Dharm from the platform near the Brahmkund.[64]

The conference at Moga was convened to ensure that regular *katha* and *kirtan* were organized in all temples and that all festivals were celebrated and the number of Mahabir Dals in the Malwa region was increased; that adequate support was given to widows and they were taught crafts in order to make them economically independent, that Stri Satsangs were organized to inculcate the principles of widowhood; that the Dalits were treated well and their physical, psychological and economic condition was improved, that *pathshalas* were opened for them, that they were taught handicrafts and provision of adequate drinking water was made for them, that the Mandir Sudhar Bill was passed, that Brahmachary ashrams were established outside every town, that a girl below the age of twelve, a boy below the age of eighteen and a man above the age of forty were not allowed to marry, that a person who was not a genuine Sanatan Dharmi was not associated with the Mahant Harnam Das Trust, that two rupees were given for charitable purposes to the Sanatan Dharm Pratinidhi Sabha on the occasion of a marriage, that all Hindu children were given education in Hindi and Sanskrit, the ideas and practices of Sanatan Dharm in the Malwa region were propagated, and that the birth anniversary of Bhagwan Ram (Ram Naumi) was declared a public holiday.[65]

It is obvious that the concerns of the local Sabhas were not necessarily local. In fact, the local Sabhas were expected to help some of the most important institutions of the Sanatanists. Many of the concerns expressed at these conferences were common to all or two of them. Though all the issues brought up at the conferences did not include every possible concern of the Sanatanists, altogether they are quite comprehensive. They relate not only to the spheres of religion and culture but also to matters social, economic and political.

Significantly, Mahabir Dals were founded in the Punjab in 1923 by Goswami Ganesh Dutt.[66] The primary function of the workers (*sevaks*) of the Dals was service to the Hindu community. The choice of Mahabir as the name for the organization was deliberate as Hanuman was regarded as the ideal devotee of Ram. Dedicated young men were encouraged to join the Dals. They were instructed to lead a disciplined life of celibacy (*brahmacharya*), just like Hanuman. Regular chanting of Hanuman Chalisa in the temple of Mahabir was a part of their daily routine. They were also to abstain from consumption of meat, alcohol and intoxicants. A rigorous routine of physical exercise included wrestling. They were trained also in the art of fencing for the use of the *lathi*. It was the duty of the *sevaks* to serve and protect the young and the old, especially women and the sick. They made all the arrangements required for festivals, fairs, celebrations and processions. They took care of the women and children lost at the fairs and restored them to their families. When a fire broke out or a house collapsed, as well as during epidemics and famines, the *sevak*s rendered various kinds of services. Their role during riots was even more crucial.[67]

The report of 1928 contains information on the Punjab Mahabir Dal and its activity as a department of the Pratinidhi Sabha. The Dal held general meetings to discuss all important issues. It had a set of rules and regulations which could be amended. Committees were formed for implementation of the decisions taken. The Punjab Mahabir Dal was created primarily for the protection of religion and for community service. Till the verdict of the court, the *sevak*s of the Dal protected the Raghunath Temple of Peshawar. The Dalpati of the Mahabir Dal protested against the permission given to the Muslims to open a cow slaughterhouse in Fazilka. The general secretary of the Punjab Mahabir Dal sent a telegram to the commissioner of Rawalpindi requesting permission to restart the procession of the Vedas in Hazara which had been stopped. The general secretary and Dalpati of the Punjab Mahabir Dal attended the All Party Convention held at Calcutta to discuss the future political action in India. The Mahabir Dal decided to publish an appeal for the Pandit Banshi Ram Memorial Fund. A training camp at Amritsar was organized to train the *sevak*s in the art of using the *lathi* as a weapon. This camp was attended by twenty-five *sevak*s from different towns.[68]

The Punjab Mahabir Dal collaborated with the local Dals on various occasions. The report mentions six religious fairs at Bachoki Gosaiya, Ram Tirath, Kurukshetra, Ram Chautra, Katas Raj and Chintpurni for which the Punjab Mahabir Dal and the *sevak*s of the local Dals worked jointly. The Dal *sevak*s from different towns would arrive at the site of the fair to make necessary arrangements. Their number ranged from sixty-five to nine hundred, depending on the nature and importance of the occasion. The Dalpati of the Punjab Mahabir Dal would reach the site a few weeks earlier and make arrangements for the *sevak*s' boarding and lodging. He organized the workers into groups and work was allocated to each group for the smooth conduct of the programme. The workers took special care to protect the women at *ghat*s and temples during the fair. It was their job to rescue pilgrims from drowning at the *ghat*s and from accidental fires. They set up free kitchens for the poor. Lost children were reunited with their parents and lost baggage was returned to the owners. Sick and injured pilgrims were provided with medical aid. The Mahabir Dal set up temporary dispensaries of both modern and traditional medicine for the convenience of pilgrims. The last rites of unclaimed corpses during epidemics were performed by the *sevak*s. They caught thieves, miscreants, drunkards and troublemakers and handed them over to the police. The *sevak*s also prevented people from gambling. They made arrangements for food and organized lectures for the *pracharak*s. After the fair, the *sevak*s purchased train tickets for the old and women and also helped them to board the trains. The work done by the *sevak*s and the Punjab Mahabir Dal was often appreciated by government officials.[69]

The local Mahabir Dals functioned in their own right. In 1947 the secretary of the Mahabir Dal of Jagadhri requested the minister of finance to improve the condition of road leading to the fair, and of the transport facilities for the convenience of the pilgrims. He also asked for the provision of clean drinking water at religious fairs. A petition was sent to the government to pass the Mandir Sudhar Bill in the Punjab Legislative Assembly.[70] The Mahabir Dals of the Gurdaspur district organized a conference at Dinanagar. Their concerns were reflected in the resolutions passed: the Punjab Mahabir Dal was requested to organize a training camp for the workers in the Gurdaspur district; an appeal was made to support the Pandit Banshi Ram Memorial Fund; and the efforts of the Pratinidhi Sabha for temple reform were praised.[71]

In 1928 there were 215 Dals in the Punjab. More than a score of these were founded in 1928 itself. The distribution of Mahabir Dals reflects the same inverse ratio between their number and the number of Hindus in the three zones. There were 78 Dals in the western zone, 113 in the central zone, and 24 in the eastern zone. In keeping with this pattern, Gujrat had 24 Dals while Karnal had only 2.

The educational institutions of the Sanatanists were not uniform in character. There was only one college in the Punjab, the Sanatan Dharm College at Lahore, established by Pandit

Din Dayalu Sharma in 1916–17.[72] It was affiliated to the Punjab University for B.A. courses in English, Sanskrit, Persian, History, Economics, Philosophy and Mathematics, and M.A. courses in Sanskrit and Economics in 1918.[73]

The total number of high schools was twenty-six but there was no high school in eleven districts. In the rest, the number varied from one to five. Only one district had five high schools. The number of high schools in the western zone was eleven, in the central zone it was nine, and in the eastern zone six. The students of class ten had to pass the certificate examination held by the Punjab University. There were forty-five middle schools in all, but eight districts had no middle school. The Hoshiarpur district alone had nine middle schools. None of the other districts had more than five. The subjects taught were English, Mathematics, Science, History, Geography, Sanskrit, Hindi, Persian, Drawing, Physiology and Hygiene.[74] In all the educational institutions of the Sanatanists religious instruction (*dharm siksha*) was compulsory. This was a corollary of Pandit Din Dayalu's conviction that 'knowledge of religion was the very essence of education'.[75]

Apart from the Anglo-Sanskrit institutions for boys, the Sanatanists established a number of *Putri Pathshala*s for girls. The *Putri Pathshala*s were up to the primary level and laid emphasis on religious instruction. The medium of instruction was Hindi.[76] In 1928 there were eighty-three such *pathshala*s in all but seven districts. In the rest, the number varied from one to seven. Six districts had more than five *pathshala*s each. The number of *Putri Pathshala*s in the western zone was forty-three, in the central zone thirty-six, and in the eastern zone only four. It must be added that there were two separate primary schools for the children of Dalits in which they were taught Hindi and Urdu.[77] The inverse ratio remained remarkable for all the educational institutions. In all, there were 154 high schools, middle schools and *Putri Pathshala*s in the Punjab. Their number in the western districts was 69, in the central districts 67, and in the eastern districts 18. The broad pattern of inverse proportion is clearly visible.

The pattern of inverse proportion was true for the Sanatan Dharm Sabhas, Mahabir Dals and the educational institutions put together. In the western zone, which had 11.37 per cent of the total Hindu population of the British Punjab, the number of these institutions was 305. In the central zone which had 32.26 per cent of the total Hindu population, the number of institutions was 338. The eastern zone, which had 53.35 per cent of the total Hindu population, had 89 Sanatanist institutions.[78]

Among the remaining sixty-one institutions, twenty-seven were called Sanatan Dharm Yuvak Sabhas, but there is no information about their purpose or activities. The Stri Satsangs were twenty-two in number and their objective was to protect women and widows from the corrupting influence of *dharmnashini* societies which encouraged widows to remarry despite its prohibition in the Shastras. These *satsang*s were generally conducted by the headmistresses of the *Putri Pathshala*s and *updeshika*s. At times even *katha vachak*s were invited. *Katha*s from sacred scriptures like *Shrimat Bhagwat, Bhagwat Gita*, *Yog Vashisht, Atam Purana, Ramayana* and *Mahabharata* were held. The *satsang*s were organ-ized in the afternoons when the women were free from house-hold activities. All women joined in the singing of hymns. Money collected as offerings in these *satsang*s was utilized to give monthly help to widows and orphans.[79] The names of the remaining institutions are suggestive of their nature: Rai Bahadur Lala Hari Chand Vishnu Narayan Trust at Lahore,[80] Sanatan Dharm Balak Sudhar Sabha at Lahore, Krishan Kumar Sabha at Shahpur, Sanatan Dharm Vidhyarthi Sabha in Lahore, Sanatan Dharm Pracharini Sabha at Lyallpur, two orphanages at Lahore, one widow home at Rawalpindi, and Gaushala Sabhas at Lahore, Ferozepore, Ludhiana and Muzaffargarh.

The attitude of the Indian princes towards the Sanatanists is important in several ways. Farquhar observed that the Bharat Dharm Mahamandal was supported by 'numerous ruling princes'.[81] Jones states that the Mahamandal was sustained by the 'members of the ruling Hindu aristocracy' who donated generously for its projects.[82] The rulers of the princely states of the Punjab supported the activities of the Sanatanists in the British Punjab. During the minority of Maharaja Jagatjit Singh of Kapurthala, Diwan Ramjas and Diwan Mathura Dass attended the first and second sessions of the Bharat Dharm Mahamandal held at Hardwar and Vrindavan in 1887 and 1889 respectively.

Even after the end of the minority administration in 1890, Diwan Ramjas was elected president of the fifth session of the Mahamandal held at Delhi in 1893. The state of Kapurthala hosted and generously aided the seventh session of the Mahamandal in 1897.[83]

That the princely patronage of the Sanatanist continued into the twentieth century is evident from contemporary evidence. Maharaja Jagatjit Singh of Kapurthala responded to the requests of the Sanatan Dharm Pahar Prant Conference held at Hoshiarpur in 1926. All articles like *durrie*s, *kanat*s and tents required for setting up the *pandal* for the conference came from Kapurthala, besides a generous donation.[84] The maharaja of Patiala and the raja of Mandi attended the conference of the Punjab Sanatan Dharm Pratinidhi Sabha held at Lahore in 1925.[85] In 1939, the maharaja of Patiala agreed to become the general president of the Pratinidhi Sabha.[86] He extended his patronage to the Punjab Mahabir Dal in 1945.[87] Even after 1947, he made liberal donations to the Punjab Pratinidhi Sabha at New Delhi.[88] A building constructed by the Pratinidhi Sabha at Lahore was named Bhupinder Bhawan in recognition of the support from the maharaja of Patiala.[89] According to Sanatanist sources, a conference of the Pratinidhi Sabha was held at Baijnath and presided over by the raja of Guler; the raja of Mandi graced the occasion with his presence. The rajas of Chamba, Saanghdhi and Lambagram aided the Pratinidhi Sabha for the promotion of education and health care in Kangra.[90]

The Pratinidhi Sabha was allowed to pursue its activities in the princely states. Pandit Din Dayalu is said to have attended the *raj tilak* ceremony of Maharaja Bhupinder Singh and blessed him. He was invited to Patiala and Nabha to hold discussions and give lectures.[91] *Updeshak*s and *bhajnik*s were sent to Patiala, Faridkot, Kapurthala, Bahawalpur, Chamba, Mandi and Suket for *prachar*. Festivals were celebrated in accordance with the Shastras by the *pracharaks* at Nabha, Faridkot and Jind. Stri Satsangs were organized at Bahawalpur. *Shastrarth* was held at Jind. The *prachar* in Patiala was disrupted due to a clash between the Sanatanists and the Aryas. A petition was sent to the ruler of Mandi to do away with the recently passed laws permitting civil marriage and widow remarriage among Hindus. The ruler of Mirpur was requested to grant permission to conduct *aarti* in the Mahabir Temple, which had been temporarily closed due to a court case.[92]

Local Sanatan Dharm Sabhas were registered within the Patiala territories. The Sanatan Dharm Sabha of Sherpur, for example, was registered under 'religious and charitable societies' after it was ensured that it had no connection whatever with any political movement.[93] The Sanatan Dharm Sabha of Patiala received regular donations on behalf of the Ram Lila Committee for the performance of *Ram Charitra* in Patiala.[94] The Sanatan Dharm Sanskrit English High School of Patiala and the Sanatan Dharm High School of Bhatinda (Bathinda) regularly received grant-in-aid from the education department of the Patiala state.[95] Out of the twelve schools that received grant-in-aid, the Sanatan Dharm High School of Patiala received the largest sum. This school was also granted a strip of *nazool* land by the Ijlas-i-Khas for the construction of new classrooms and a boarding house. In 1935, Maharaja Bhupinder Singh deputed a prince to lay the foundation of the school's new blocks.[96] As may be expected, the Sanatan Dharm schools had to function according to the rules of the Patiala state in order to get grant-in-aid.[97]

In *The Tribune* of 5 August 1893, there is a reference to a religious debate at Nabha under the auspices of Raja Hira Singh, between the best representatives of the Arya Samaj and the Sanatan Dharm Sabha.[98] The Shri Sanatan Dharma Sabha of Nabha state was founded in 1893 either before or after this debate. In 1898, a *sahukar* of the city of Nabha, Lala Pala Mal Agarwal, donated a house and a few shops to the Sabha for its use by way of *dharmarth*. After his death, a close relative, Ghayo Mal, began to use the yard of the building for his purposes and also to interfere with the work of the Sabha. Its members approached Raja Hira Singh in 1905 with the will of the donor. Ghayo Mal was told by Raja Hira Singh that he had no right to keep the keys of that building. Ghayo Mal appealed and the key was given to him on the condition that he would keep the building open at all times for the use of the Sabha, give Rs. 200 a year to the Sabha and would not use the place for his own business. He accepted the conditions but did not honour them. In the summer of 1918 he handed over the keys to the members of the Sabha but moved the criminal court against them. The case was dismissed. He appealed to the high court but the judge, Sardar Bachan Singh, dismissed the appeal. Ghayo Mal asked for a review in the Judicial Council. His plea was rejected by D.M. Narsingh Rao on 21 January 1919, upholding the decisions of the lower courts. In 1921 Ghayo Mal fell from the roof of the building and died. There was no dispute till 1925 when the sons of Ghayo Mal went to the court of the district magistrate, Sardar Chhajju Singh, the *nazim* of Nabha, who dismissed the case in early 1926, finding no truth in their contention that the place was not being used for charitable purposes, and at the same time appreciating the work being done by the Sabha. Ghayo Mal's sons went to the court of the chief judicial officer, Sardar Narain Singh Gill, who dismissed their appeal in 1927. The decision of these courts was upheld by the assistant administrator of Nabha, Sardar Gurdial Singh, and also by the administrator of Nabha, Diwan Gyan Nath. Thus, for more than two decades, the ruler of Nabha, the diwan of Nabha, the courts of Nabha, and the administrators of Nabha supported the Shri Sanatan Dharma Sabha of Nabha against persistent opponents who appear to have possessed considerable influence and material means. The Sabha too appears to have been increasing its resources. In 1913, it was able to purchase another house from the widow of a local Khatri.[99]

It is not clear whether or not the Shri Sanatan Dharma Sabha of Nabha was a registered body. In its annual report of 1928 it is stated that its rules required the publication of an annual report. It had been holding its annual sessions rather regularly. In 1926, the Sabha held its thirty-fourth annual session. A procession called the *nagar kirtan* was taken out, with the 'Ved Bhagwan' riding on an elephant accompanied by horsemen bearing silver sticks. Senior police officers of the state were there in uniform, on horseback, to look after all the arrangements. Learned pandits of the town recited the Vedas while walking barefoot in the procession. The *sevak*s of the Mahabir Dal sang *bhajans*. There were other groups of singers as well. The procession wound through the streets and lanes of the city for three hours in the evening, receiving homage from the people.

For four days the lecturers and *bhajnik* of the Sanatan Dharm Pratinidhi Sabha, Lyallpur (now Lahore), addressed the people in the gorgeous *pandal* of the Sabha which was actually set up by the state. The British Administrator Nabha, Wilson Johnston, and his *naib*, Sardar Gurdial Singh, participated in the proceedings in the presence of the state officials. During the year, the Sabha had organized *prachar* and celebrated festivals like the Basant Panchmi. It was reported that tracts produced by the Sabha were distributed, and the reading room of the Sabha remained open. On Sundays, a *katha* of *Shrimad Bhagvat* was performed. Minor repairs of the building of the Sabha were carried out.[100]

The year 1927 was rather dismal by comparison for various reasons. One was litigation. Another was the Kumbh Mela at Hardwar. Consequently, the Basant Panchmi festival was treated as the annual session of the Sabha. The usual activity of *prachar* remained lacklustre and no funds could be collected. The income of the Sabha was only about Rs. 230, whereas in 1926 it had been nearly Rs. 590. However, the Sabha hoped to do better in 1928.[101]

In 1926 the Shri Sanatan Dharma Sabha of Nabha was running a free Hindi *pathshala* in which the mahajani accounting system and Hindi language were taught to more than forty students in three classes. The members of the executive committee of the Sanatan Dharma Sabha of Nabha requested for a grant of Rs. 500 a year to turn this institution into a free primary school on a sound and good footing for which the estimated expenditure per year was Rs. 1,140. They proposed to have three trained teachers and a *chaprasi* for the proposed Sanatan Dharm Free Primary School. The Nabha state had its own rules for giving grant-in-aid. The institutions were told that if they were given a grant by the state, their school would have to be open to inspection by the inspecting officers of the state and the continuance of the grant would depend on the work of the teachers being satisfactory. This was acceptable to the Sanatan Dharma Sabha, and its president informed the director of education that the school would be open to all communities. Early in 1927, the director of education was informed by the state authorities that he was authorized to make provision to the extent of Rs. 420 as grant-in-aid for the primary school to be established by the Sanatan Dharma Sabha of Nabha.[102]

The Shri Sanatan Dharma Sabha of Nabha had a duly constituted working committee with a president, a vice-president, and a general secretary. The general secretary, Hari Das 'Sabir', was a *hakim* and a poet who wrote in Urdu but who was also familiar with Persian poetry. It may be safe to presume that he personally drafted all kinds of representations and reports on behalf of the Sabha. Early in 1928 one finds the Sabha writing to Rai Bahadur Gyan Nath, the administrator of Nabha, in support of an earlier request made by the Mahabir Dal of Nabha about repairs of the outer *parikrama* of the old Hanuman Mandir which thronged with men and women, the old and the young on Tuesdays. The *pujari*s of the mandir also looked to the Sabha for help. A few days later one finds Hari Das 'Sabir' requesting Diwan Gyan Nath to preside over the annual session of the Sabha, mentioning that the Sabha had been founded thirty-five years ago and the rulers of Nabha (Maharaja Hira Singh and Maharaja Ripudaman Singh) had taken the trouble of attending the sessions of the Sabha from time to time. The present administration had also helped the Sabha in every way; two years earlier, Wilson Johnston had come to the annual session of the Sabha; Sardar Gurdial Singh and other eminent officials of the state had also associated themselves with the work of the Sabha. Diwan Gyan Nath agreed to preside over the annual session. However, it was postponed because of the excessive heat and the unpreparedness of the All-India Sanatan Dharm Pratinidhi Sabha of Lahore to participate. On 4 June 1928, the Sanatan Dharma Sabha of Nabha celebrated the birthday of King-Emperor George V with the praises of God, the greatness of Raj-Bhakti, and the blessings of the British Raj. An appropriate resolution was passed appreciating among other things the freedom to propagate one's religion. Hari Das 'Sabir' recited a congratulatory poem.[103]

In 1930 the Shri Sanatan Dharma Sabha submitted a petition to the president of the Council of Regency requesting that free electricity be provided to the Mahabir Temple and the building of the Sabha. The Choudharies of Nabha and the members of the working committee of the Sabha jointly stated that the Sabha owned a building of its own which was open to use by the Hindu public for marriages and *katha*s as well as for lodging travellers. This building as well as the Hanuman Temple had electric lighting arrangements but had no funds to pay the bills. However their request was declined because the state did not give this concession to any organization.[104]

Eight years later, when Diwan Gyan Nath was president of the Council of Regency, Sardar Gurdial Singh, the home member, wrote to him that the Sanatan Dharma Sabha of Nabha had constructed a large hall in their Sabha mandir by raising donations from the public. The members of its managing committee had applied for a grant from the state because the hall was still to be plastered and doors and windows had to be fixed up. This building was used by the public for marriage parties and to accommodate religious preachers who visited the town. There was some savings from the provisions made for *dharmarth* and a sum of Rs. 400 could be granted to the Sabha. The president wanted to know if such grants had been given in the past to other religious or charitable institutions. It was submitted by the home member that the Gurdwara of Baba Ajpal Singh of Nabha had received several thousand rupees for improvements and the Jama Masjid of Nabha had received a grant for the completion of tile flooring. On 23 June 1936, the Council resolved to grant Rs. 400 to the Shri Sanatan Dharma Sabha. By this time, the Sabha was over four decades old with a creditable record.[105]

It is interesting to note that Raja Hira Singh patronized not only the Sanatan Dharma Sabha of Nabha but also a Gaushala which was established in 1907. It was managed by the choudharies of the town. In 1912, it was shifted to Bazidpur Bir, about 7 miles distant from Nabha. It continued to function during the rest of Raja Hira Singh's reign and also under his successor Maharaja Ripudaman Singh. In 1924, a public meeting was held and twenty-four members were nominated to the management committee, to be subsequently elected annually. In the beginning Raja Hira Singh used to support the Gaushala with funds from the state treasury. To make the institution financially independent, he created permanent sources of income for it like a fee of Rs. 2 for marriages throughout his territory except the Bawal area; 1 per cent of the octroi of the city of Nabha; *choudhriat* due to the choudhries of the city; income from the *bhunga* and the *masool phatak*. By 1927 the Gaushala had more than Rs. 1 lakh. It was decided to create a trust and use the interest accruing from it for the upkeep of the Gaushala. At the same time the Gaushala continued to receive 1 per cent from the octroi, money given in charity, subscriptions from members and income from the sale of milk, calves and manure, etc. It had two branches now, one serving as a *pinjrapole* and the other as a dairy run on modern lines. The rules and regulations of the Gaushala of Nabha as approved by the state administration were published in 1931. The Gaushala had a general committee, a managing committee, and a working committee. The functions of the president, the vice-president, the secretary, assistant secretary and treasurer were clearly defined.[106]

In 1927, the Gaushala Committee decided to celebrate the Gopalastami festival and the Gaushala anniversary. In this connection it was decided to invite Lala Diali Ram, a former director of education in Patiala, and the president of the Sanatan Dharm Sabha of Patiala, Goswami Jiwan Das, an *updeshak* of the Sanatan Dharm Pratinidhi Sabha of Lahore, and Pandit Bishambar Datt, another *updeshak* of the Pratinidhi Sabha. The choice of these speakers is suggestive of the links between the members of the Gaushala Committee and some of the known leaders of the Sanatan Dharm Sabha.[107] The annual report of the Gaushala for 1933 refers to visitors to the Gaushala from Ferozepore city, Kaithal, Amritsar, Jaito and Raikot to see its functioning: they appreciated the work being done by the Gaushala. It is interesting to note that a young student from the state was specifically sent to the agricultural college at Lyallpur for a formal course in dairy farming. The idea was to entrust the dairy of the Gaushala to this trained person. The budget of the Gaushala was more than Rs. 10,500 and it had Rs. 1,20,000 deposited in the bank with a 5 per cent interest.[108] Early in 1940 the Council of Regency decided to grant 6 *bigha*s of state land in front of the Gaushala building for the Gaushala dairy farm, where the Gaushala Committee proposed to construct a cowshed and a shed for bulls and enclose the rest of the land with a proper fence. This land was given on a nominal lease of Re. 1 a year.[109] Subsequently, the Gaushala Committee appears to have requested the president of the Council of Regency for Rs. 8,000 as donation and 100 *bigha*s of land in Bazidpur Bir for producing green fodder. There is no evidence, however, that these requests were granted.[110]

The policies of the princely states were not the same for all organizations. In 1926, the secretary of the Arya Pratinidhi Sabha, Punjab, protested against the prohibition on celebrating the anniversary of the Arya Samaj in Faridkot state. He added that the authorities were prejudiced against the Arya Samaj because the Sanatan Dharm Sabhas, among other bodies of a similar character, received assistance and patronage from the state.[111] This appears to be true for all states. They were not sympathetic to radical reforms like that of the Arya Samajists. The Sanatanist institutions in the states appear to have received much larger patronage than the institutions of the Arya Samaj.

In 1928, there were 70 Sanatanist institutions in the princely states. This number was much smaller than the number of Sanatanist institutions in the British Punjab. In the first place, the Hindu population of the British Punjab (54,17,186 in 1931) was much larger than the Hindu population in the princely states (18,02,700 in 1931).[112] Nevertheless, whereas in the British Punjab there was one institution for 6,012 Hindus, in the princely states there was one institution for 25,752 Hindus. Thus, even in terms of proportions, the British Punjab had four times more Sanatanist institutions than the princely states. What is far more important is that the number of Sanatanist institutions in the princely states of Patiala, Nabha, Jind, Mandi, Nahan and Chamba was comparable with the eastern zone of the British Punjab in which they were located. Therefore, the difference is zonal rather than between state and British territory.

Finally, for both the princely states and the British Punjab, the census figures for the Sanatan Dharmis are misleading.[113] Some categories of Hindus were not enumerated among the Sanatan Dharmis, but once they were accounted for, the rest of the Hindu population was treated as Sanatan Dharmi. Just as the Hindus, in general, were treated as a residual category in the total population, so also were the Sanatan Dharmis treated as a residual category among the Hindus. Actually, the number of Hindus who were influenced by the Sanatan Dharm ideology, or supported its institutions, was evidently much smaller. This distinction has generally been ignored by the historians.

NOTES

1. Writing on the modern religious movements in India in 1914, J.N. Farquhar had no idea of the Sanatan Dharm Movement in the Punjab. Under the subheading of caste organizations, he takes up the Bharat Dharma Mahamandala for discussion. According to him the Bharat Dharma Mahamandala was formed in 1902 in Mathura, from where its headquarters were moved to Benares in 1905. The Mahamandal also had a provincial office at Lahore. J.N. Farquhar, *Modern Religious Movements in India*, New Delhi: Munshiram Manoharlal, 1977, pp. 317, 318. Nearly fifty years later, Charles S. Heimsath, writing on Indian Nationalism and Hindu social reform, stated that Pandit Din Dayalu Sharma from the Punjab founded the Sanatan Dharma Sabha in 1895 in Delhi and Hardwar. Charles S. Heimsath, *Indian Nationalism and Hindu Social Reform*, Bombay: Oxford University Press, 1964, p. 318.
2. Kenneth W. Jones, *Socio-Religious Reform Movements in British India: The New Cambridge History of India*, III, I, Cambridge: Cambridge University Press, 1999 (rpt.), 1st edn., 1994, pp. 107, 108; *Arya Dharm: Hindu Consciousness in 19th Century Punjab*, New Delhi: Manohar, 1989 (rpt.), 1st edn., 1976, p. 28. Shraddha Ram Phillauri laid 'the foundation for later Sanatanist movements'.
3. Jones, *Arya Dharm*, p. 111.
4. Jones, *Socio-Religious Reform Movements*, pp. 78, 79, 80, 81, 217.
5. Ibid., p. 215.
6. John Zavos, 'Patterns of Organisation in Turn of the Century Hinduism: An Examination with Reference to Punjab', *International Journal of Punjab Studies*, vol. 7 (1) January–June 2000, Coventry, p. 40.
7. Harihar Swaroop Sharma, *Vyakhyan Wachaspati Pandit Din Dayalu Sharma: Smarak Granth*, New Delhi: Dev Publishing House, 1985 (henceforth *Smarak Granth*), pp. 33, 93. For information on Pandit Din Dayalu Sharma, see Sheena Pall, 'Din Dayalu Sharma: The Formative Phase of the Sanatan Dharma Movement in late Nineteenth Century North India', *Indian History Congress Proceedings*, 63rd Session, Kolkata: Calcutta University (2003: 1012–20).

8. *Report on the Administration of the Punjab and its Dependencies for 1889–90,* Lahore: Printed at the Punjab Government Press, Appendix: Statement of Scientific and Literary and Charitable Societies in the Punjab, 1889–90.
9. The Societies Registrations Act of 1860 gave legal recognition to associations and also provided a framework for their functions. The following societies could be registered under this Act: charitable societies; the military orphan funds or societies established at the several presidencies of India; societies established for the promotion of science, literature or the fine arts; for instruction, the diffusion of useful knowledge (the diffusion of political education), the foundation or maintenance of libraries or reading rooms for general use among the members or open to the public, or public museums and galleries of paintings and other works of art; collections of natural history; mechanical and philosophical inventions, instruments and designs. This Act also permitted registration of societies for charitable purposes. A religious society could also be called a charitable society for a religious purpose. It could also be a charitable purpose and a religious society might legally be registered under the provisions of this Act. For registration the Memorandum of Association contained the name of the society; objects of the society; names, addresses, occupations of the governors, councils, directors 'committee' or other governing bodies to whom, by the rules of the society, the management of its affairs was entrusted; and a copy of the rules and regulations of the society. A society could own property and run educational institutions. An individual could be admitted as a member of a society in accordance with its rules and regulations. Members had to pay a subscription and were entitled to vote. V.R. Manohar and W.W. Chitaley, *The A.I.R. Manual, Civil and Criminal*, vol. 31, Nagpur: All India Reporter Limited, Congressnagar, 1979 (4th edn.) (1st edn. 1946), pp. 764–814.
10. *Report on the Administration of the Punjab and its Dependencies for 1899–1900,* Lahore: Printed at the Punjab Government Press, Appendix: 'Statement of Scientific and Literary and Charitable Societies in the Punjab, 1898–9', 1899–1900.
11. *Census of India,1901, Imperial Tables I-VIII, X-XV, XVII and XVIII for the Punjab with the Native States under the control of the Punjab Government and for the North West Frontier Province*, Table VI, Religion. The western zone included the districts of Shahpur, Gujrat, Mianwali, Jhelum, Rawalpindi, Multan, Muzzafargarh and Dera Ghazi Khan. The central zone included the districts of Hoshiarpur, Jullundur, Sialkot, Gurdaspur, Lahore, Gujranwala, Jhang, Lyallpur, Ferozepore, Amritsar, and Montgomery. The eastern zone included the districts of

Kangra, Ambala, Karnal, Hissar, Simla, Ludhiana, Gurgaon and Rohtak.
12. *Report on the Administration of the Punjab and its Dependencies for 1899–1900.*
13. Ibid.
14. *Smarak Granth*, p. 23.
15. Ibid., pp. 23, 24.
16. Ibid., pp. 24, 25, 30.
17. Ibid., pp. 31, 32.
18. Nehru Memorial Museum and Library, New Delhi, Pandit Din Dayalu Papers, Private Correspondence, Most of these letters are in Urdu but some are in Hindi.
19. Pandit Harihar Swaroop says that the head office of the Mahamandal should remain in Delhi itself but elsewhere he says that it was shifted to Lahore. Furthermore, the Punjab Mandal was merged with the Mahamandal at Lahore in 1897. *Smarak Granth*, pp. 89, 112.
20. Pandit Din Dayalu Papers.
21. *Smarak Granth*, p. 89.
22. Ibid., p. 190.
23. Pandit Din Dayalu Papers.
24. *Smarak Granth*, pp. 88–9.
25. Ibid., pp. 24, 33, 34.
26. Ibid., pp. 45, 88, 111, 154, 158, 159, 160. In March 1891, both the Indian Penal Code and the Criminal Procedure Code were amended to raise the age of consent to twelve for married and unmarried girls; sexual intercourse with girls below that age was punishable with up to ten years in prison and/or transportation for life. Janaki Nair, *Women and Law in Colonial India: A Social History*, New Delhi: Kali for Women, 1996, p. 75.
27. *Smarak Granth*, pp. 32, 33, 41, 42, 145, 151, 159.
28. Ibid., pp. 59, 144, 159.
29. Ibid., pp. 24, 44, 46, 54, 60, 62, 63, 92, 111, 157. Among them were Diwans Ramjas, Mathura Das, Babu Hari Chand (judicial assistant) from the judiciary, and Misr Achchru Mal from accounts.
30. Ibid., p. 112.
31. Ibid., pp. 32, 35, 93, 112, 142, 143, 152.
32. Nehru Memorial Museum and Library, New Delhi, *The Tribune*, 29 October 1891, p. 4, microfilm no. 7.
33. National Archives of India, New Delhi, Internal B, nos. 112/114, 1902, Foreign Department Proceedings, proposed deputation of the Bharat Dharam Mahamandal Society to the King's coronation, p. 6.
34. Ibid., p. 14.
35. Ibid., p. 10.
36. Ibid., p. 9.

37. Ibid., p. 13.
38. *Smarak Granth*, pp. 185, 186, 189, 190.
39. *Annual Report of Shri Sanatan Dharm Pratinidhi Sabha Punjab*, Lahore: Goswami Ganesh Dutt, 1928, pp. 2, 3.
40. Ibid., pp. 3, 4, 5, 6, 7.
41. Ibid., pp. 15, 16, 17, 19, 20.
42. Ibid., p. 18.
43. Ibid., pp. 19, 20. The main sources of income were donations and special deputations for collection of funds: they accounted for over 60 per cent of the total income. Among the other sources were funds received from the Sabhas on different accounts, charity received on the occasion of marriages and *katha*s, and fees from educational institutions. About 60 per cent of the total expenditure was on salaries, travelling allowances, and publicity. Among the other items of expenditure were the running of a central office and sub-offices, free kitchens (*langar*), stipends given to widows, deputations sent for *prachar*, activities of Mahabir Dal, and work for the Dalits, pp. 161, 162.
44. Ibid., pp. 30, 31, 32, 41, 42, 43, 47, 49, 56.
45. Ibid., pp. 4, 133, 134. The *mahurat* of the Durgiana *sarovar* was done at Amritsar by Pandit Madan Mohan Malaviya in 1924. A Temple Reform Bill was prepared by Professor Gulshan Rai to be presented in the Council for approval by the government.
46. For Ad Dharm see Mark Juergensmeyer, 'Ad Dharm', in *Precolonial and Colonial Punjab: Society, Economy, Politics and Culture*, ed. Reeta Grewal and Sheena Pall, New Delhi: Manohar, 2005, pp. 393–408.
47. *Annual Report of Shri Sanatan Dharm Pratinidhi Sabha Punjab*, pp. 135, 136.
48. Ibid., pp. 143, 144.
49. Ibid., pp. 145, 146.
50. Ibid., pp. 43–6, 47, 48.
51. Ibid., pp. 48–56.
52. Ibid., pp. 57, 74, 75, 76, 77, 79. The *shastrarth*s on the themes of *Arya Samaj Nastik Samaj Hai* and mention of *Gauwadh* in the Vedas were not held as the Arya Samajist contestants failed to appear at the last moment.
53. Ibid., pp. 78, 79, 80, 81, 82. For Mahant Ram Das, see *The Mughal and Sikh Rulers and the Vaishnavas of Pindori: A Historical Interpretation of 52 Persian Documents*, ed. B.N. Goswamy and J.S. Grewal, Simla: Indian Institute of Advanced Study, 1969, pp. 20, 21, 68.
54. *Annual Report of Shri Sanatan Dharm Pratinidhi Sabha Punjab*, pp. 90, 91, 92, 93.

55. Ibid., pp. 64, 94.
56. Ibid., pp. 69–70.
57. Ibid., pp. 21, 22, 23–4, 25. Punjab State Archives, Chandigarh, File no. 57, 1928, Punjab Government Civil Secretariat, Home-Jails, B. Proceedings, request of certain Sabhas in the Punjab to declare Ram Navmi as a public holiday, pp. 1, 2, 9, 13, 14, 20, 33, 36.
58. Punjab State Archives, Chandigarh, File no. 153, 1921, Punjab Government Civil Secretariat, Home-Jails, B. Proceedings, application of the Secretary Sanatan Dharm Sabha Lahore praying that Hindu prisoners may be allowed to wear the sacred thread while confined in jails in the Punjab, pp. 1–2.
59. Punjab State Archives, Chandigarh, File no. 242, 1937, Punjab Government Civil Secretariat, Home-Jails, B. Proceedings, request of the Sanatan Pratinidhi Sabha, Punjab and the Sanatan Dharm Sabha, Lahore, that Saturday the 19th June 1937, be granted a holiday for Hindus on account of Nirjala Ekadashi, p. 2.
60. *Annual Report of Shri Sanatan Dharm Pratinidhi Sabha Punjab*, pp. 22, 27.
61. It is important to point out that the category of the Sanatan Dharm Sabhas also included the Dharm Sabhas of Jullundur and Amritsar, the Hindu Sabhas of Ludhiana and Rawalpindi and the Sanatan Dharm Brahman Sabhas of Lahore, Hoshiarpur and Simla.
62. *Census of India, 1931, vol. XVII, Punjab, Part I, Report*, 1933, p. 317.
63. *Annual Report of Shri Sanatan Dharm Pratinidhi Sabha Punjab*, pp. 60, 61, 62.
64. Ibid., pp. 66, 67, 68.
65. Ibid., pp. 62, 63, 64, 65.
66. Ibid., p. 3. For social tensions leading to riots in the Punjab in the 1920s, see Prem Raman Uprety, Chap. 8, 'Anatomy of Communal Riots', in *Religion and Politics in Punjab in the 1920s*, New Delhi: Sterling Publishers, 1980, pp. 134–74.
67. *Annual Report of Shri Sanatan Dharm Pratinidhi Sabha Punjab*, pp. 110, 111.
68. Ibid., pp. 111, 112.
69. Ibid., pp. 113, 114, 115.
70. Punjab State Archives, Chandigarh, File no. 121, 1947, Punjab Government Civil Secretariat, Home-General, C. Proceedings, request from the Honorary Secretary S.D. Mahabir Dal, Jagadhri for the Mandir Sudhar Bill to be passed in the next session of the Punjab Legislative Assembly, pp. 3, 4.
71. *Annual Report of Shri Sanatan Dharm Pratinidhi Sabha Punjab*, p. 115.

72. Bhagwati Prasad Madhav, ed., *Goswami Ganesh Dutt: Smriti Granth*, New Delhi: Sri Sanatan Dharm Pratinidhi Sabha Punjab, 1969 (henceforth *Smriti Granth*), p. 294. With the initiative of Din Dayalu Sharma, the Hindu College at Delhi was established on 15 May 1899. *Smarak Granth*, pp. 122–5.
73. Punjab State Archives, Chandigarh, Part A, nos. 10–11, 19–20, 1918, Home Education Proceedings, Punjab, Affiliation of Sanatan Dharm College, Lahore, pp. 15, 33.
74. *Annual Report of Shri Sanatan Dharm Pratinidhi Sabha Punjab*, pp. 124, 125.
75. *Smarak Granth*, p. 317.
76. *Smriti Granth*, pp. 155, 263–4.
77. *Annual Report of Shri Sanatan Dharm Pratinidhi Sabha Punjab*, pp. 136, 140.
78. *Census of India, 1931, vol. XVII, Punjab*, p. 317.
79. *Annual Report of Shri Sanatan Dharm Pratinidhi Sabha Punjab*, pp. 82, 83, 84. *Smriti Granth*, p. 292.
80. This trust provided monthly financial assistance to orphans and widows. It is interesting to note that the list of recipients included Muslims. This trust also ran a Rai Bahadur Hari Chand Dharmarth Ayurvedic Aushadhalaya at Hardwar. *Annual Report of Shri Sanatan Dharm Pratinidhi Sabha Punjab*, pp. 95, 96.
81. J.N. Farquhar, *Modern Religious Movements in India*, p. 319.
82. Jones, *Socio-Religious Reform Movements in British India*, pp. 79, 82.
83. *Smarak Granth*, pp. 32, 35, 87, 111.
84. Punjab State Archives, Patiala, File no. c/2–1–26, 1926, Kapurthala State, Sadr Office, Conference of the Shri Sanatan Dharm Doaba Pahar Prant, Hoshiarpur, pp. 13, 22, 33.
85. *Annual Report of Shri Sanatan Dharm Pratinidhi Sabha Punjab*, p. 5.
86. Punjab State Archives, Patiala, case no. 7vi/a-14, 1939, His Highness' Govt., Patiala, Finance Donation, His Highness' subscription for General Presidentship of the Sanatan Dharm Pratinidhi Sabha Punjab, p. 13.
87. Punjab State Archives, Patiala, case no. 6471 F, 1945, His Highness' Govt., Patiala, Deodhi Mualla Office, regarding detailing of military band for Sanatan Dharm Mahabir Dal Lahore, p. 5.
88. Punjab State Archives, Patiala, File no. 1252 A, 1948, Finance Donation, Patiala, Additional grant of Rs. 10,000 and 5,000 to Honorary Secretary, Indian Olympic Association Patna and Goswami Ganesh Datt, Secretary, Sanatan Dharm Sabha Delhi respectively, p. 2.
89. *Smriti Granth*, p. 312.
90. Ibid., pp. 307–8.

91. *Smarak Granth*, pp. 145–6, 147, 276.
92. *Annual Report of Shri Sanatan Dharm Pratinidhi Sabha Punjab*, pp. 21, 24, 36, 37, 40, 48, 74, 78, 89.
93. Punjab State Archives, Patiala, case no. 6 of 1985 (1928), His Highness' Govt., Patiala, Home Department, Registration of Sanatan Dharam Sabha at Sherpore, p. 5.
94. Punjab State Archives, Patiala, case no. 2678 F, 1938, His Highness' Govt., Patiala, Deodhi Mualla Office, regarding a donation of Rs. 150 contributed to the President Shri Sanatan Dharm Sabha, Patiala for celebrating Ram Lila, pp. 8, 9.
95. Punjab State Archives, Patiala, File nos. 1301 of 2.3.45, 5969/1297 AR 200 of 1944 and 8004–91 of 1935, His Highness' Govt., Patiala, Finance Grant and Relief, Regarding award of grants-in-aid to the denominational schools in the state.
96. Punjab State Archives, Patiala, case no. I.V. IV. N-135 of 1992 (1935), His Highness' Govt., Patiala, Ijlas-i-Khas, Grant of land in front of Sanatan Dharm High School in Tohba Mool Chand to Sanatan Dharm High School, Patiala, speech delivered by H.H. Shri Yuvraj Bahadur, pp. 3, 19.
97. Punjab State Archives, Patiala, case no. 167/I-AR, 1944, His Highness' Govt., Patiala, Finance Grant and Relief, regarding award of grant-in-aid to denominational schools, p. 1. Article 17 of the rules for grant-in-aid required that grants were awarded only to those teachers who held certificates from the Punjab Education Department. For example, the grant of a particular teacher was discontinued because he held a B.T. degree of the Hindu University Benares.
98. Nehru Memorial Museum & Library, New Delhi, *The Tribune*, 5 August 1893, p. 4, microfilm no. 9.
99. Punjab State Archives, Patiala, File no. 4130/E, 1928, Office of the Administrator, Nabha State, cutting from the *Sudarshan*, Lahore.
100. Ibid., Annual Reports published in the *Sudarshan*, Lahore.
101. Ibid.
102. Punjab State Archives, Patiala, File no. 2963/E, 1927, Office of the Administrator, Nabha State, papers regarding the state grant-in-aid towards the maintenance of a free primary school by the Sanatan Dharam Sabha, Nabha.
103. Punjab State Archives, Patiala, File no. 4130/E, 1928, Office of the Administrator, Nabha State, Representations of Shri Sanatan Dharma Sabha, dated 29 Chet and 2, 3, 16 Baisakh and 24 Jaith, Sammat 1985.
104. Punjab State Archives, Patiala, File no. 6262E, 1931, Office of the President Council of Regency, Nabha State, Petition from Choudhries

of Sanatan Dharam Sabha Nabha regarding free supply of electricity to the temple.

105. Punjab State Archives, Patiala, File no. 4130/E, 1928, Office of the Administrator, Nabha State, note of the home member to the President of the Council of Regency, dated 29 April 1936, his note of 6 May 1936 and resolution number 39 of the Council passed on 20–3 June 1936.
106. Punjab State Archives, Patiala, File no. 3566E, 1927, Office of the President, Council of Regency, Nabha State, Rules and Regulations of the Gaushala of Nabha, 1931.
107. Ibid., letter of the President of the Gaushala Committee to the Chief Police Officer of Nabha, 26 October 1927.
108. Ibid., report of the President Gaushala, Nabha, 1933.
109. Ibid., resolution no. 58 passed by the Council of Regency in their meeting of 3/6 January 1940.
110. Ibid., notes on dispatch no.7763 and no. 9920, p. 3.
111. Punjab State Archives, Patiala, File no. 5, 1926, Faridkot Government, Council of Administration, File regarding activities of Arya Samajists, etc., p. 1.
112. *Census of India, 1931, vol. XVII, Punjab*, p. 317.
113. According to the census of 1931, the number of Sanatan Dharmis in the British Punjab was 53,84,202 and in the princely states 21,83, 533. Ibid., p. 95.

CHAPTER 4

Reflections on Punjabi Society in Transition in Bhishm Sahni's Novel *Maiya Das ki Madi*

HARISH C. SHARMA AND RADHA SHARMA

Historical events have always attracted the attention of the creative imagination of novelists, poets and short story writers. Bhishm Sahni's novel *Maiya Das ki Madi*, the subject of the present paper, is exceptional. It deals with a time period stretching from the middle of the nineteenth to the onset of the twentieth century. The novel was first published in 1988, and its new edition appeared in 1992.[1] It is a novel in a class by itself. To deal with an event, and to deal with a process are two different things. And further, to deal with a process in a narrative – as Bhishm Sahni has done – is an onerous task. Urban life in India, as well as in the Punjab, was undergoing changes of several kinds during the second half of the nineteenth century.[2] The novel deals with the changing historical situation in the urban society of the Punjab after its annexation to the British empire in the middle of the nineteenth century. It is a commentary with observations on the behaviour, attitudes, rites, and rituals, issues related to women, caste and classes and clan and kinship relationships and the changing urban landscape in the Punjab. There is telling commentary on the new administration and administrative practices, innovations in the means of communications, emergence of the middle classes, processes of increasing commercialization, and their impact on the trading classes as well as the peasantry. This refers, particularly to the comparison of the mechanism of assessment and collection of land revenue between the pre-British and the British period.[3] The comment on how the investments made in India were the source of exploitation and 'Drain' is significant for the understanding of the instrument of exploitation during the Raj even for a layman.[4] These changes had created both tensions and paradoxes not known before.[5] The novel, thus, is a wide spectrum of the social, economic, religious and political life of the people of the Punjab struggling to grapple with a fast-changing world which was moving towards the twentieth century.

Bhishm Sahni, in his novel, chose to deploy his creative skills to reconstruct the historical past of the society of the Punjab with a *qasba*, or small town, as a referent. In his narrative, Sahni has created real people in a recognizable historical setting which has been a rare component of historical narrative in India.[6] From the description in the narrative, the *qasba* referred to in the novel seems to be located in the district of Jhelum, now in Pakistani Punjab. This novel, therefore, can be understood as a reflection of the changing social and political life of the people of western Punjab in particular. The novel opens a new window on history and literature, together with an authentic style which leaves a powerful impact on the mind of the reader.

The novel is situated in the period that followed the annexation of the Punjab to the British empire. The annexation had exposed the Punjab to all the influences that had been sweeping the rest of the subcontinent since the early nineteenth century. Innovations – consequent upon the establishment of the British rule – in political, administrative, economic, social and cultural spheres affected the lives of the people in myriad ways. The last quarter of the nineteenth and early years of the twentieth centuries was a period of transition, or the initial phase of social transformation in the Punjab. The traditional order, with feudal characteristics, was gradually fading out, and in the wake of the changes new social classes were emerging. New modes of transportation opened up a new world and education brought in new ideas and manners of expression. The railways, roads, cantonments, civil line bungalows and church buildings changed the landscape of the towns of the Punjab.[7] A new wave of social and religious reform among all the communities of the Punjab was an offshoot of a new education based on the recommendations of the Woods Despatch of 1854 and the emergence of the middle classes. These movements drew their authority from the scriptures and ancient practices and used them as weapons to reform society. The reformers initiated a process of regeneration and revitalization of sociocultural norms and practices.[8] In the process, the protagonists of the movements invited confrontation not only with the orthodox leadership but also with the multitude of the lesser educated who looked upon any attempt to change cultural practices with fear and suspicion. The time period covered by the novelist is, in this sense, a complete period. It begins with the end of medieval era of the history of the Punjab, that is, with the end of the Khalsa Raj and the beginning of the British Raj. The annexation of the Punjab by the British had raised hopes and aspirations. The novel ends with the beginning of disillusionment with the 'prosperity brought about by the Raj'.

The point of the novel around which the entire narrative is woven is that the people of the Punjab accepted colonial rule in the initial stages. They are portrayed as being euphoric about it. As the colonial policies unfolded, the initial euphoria turned first into indifference and then into resentment against British rule, which was articulated through rebellious expressions. These changes have been portrayed through the owners and residents of a mansion or *madi* situated in the centre of the *qasba*. Dewan Maiya Das, the protagonist of the novel, and the successive generations living in the *madi* were the remnants of the old order. Maiya Das refused to readjust to the political changes. He was a *sahukar* and a loyal functionary of the Lahore *darbar*. His loyalty to the *darbar* was absolute. During the days of Anglo-Sikh wars – *laam ke dino mein* – he had credited all his wealth to the Lahore *darbar*.[9] The annexation rendered him without wealth or power, leaving him a shadow of the 'glorious' past.[10] He did not readjust to the changed political reality that the Punjab had become a part of *sarkar-i-inglishia*. He now had no role in the day-to-day developments of the *qasba*. With the establishment of the new administration (*amaldari*) with a new ethos, people were losing their respect for the practices of the old order. The new administration had its own dynamics. It did not function with reference to the past practices. It had its own presumptions, predilections and pressures.

For the Dewan, it was paradoxical that the subject people had accepted the reality. In the name of tradition, the feeling was '*jo bhi hakim-i-waqt hai, wohi sir ka sahib hai, usi ke samne sir navao, usi ki namak halali karo*'.[11] Opinions were divided over this. One opinion said this represented traditional wisdom: '*yeh niti hai mere bhai, prachin kal se chali aa rahi hai*'.[12] Wisdom lay in submitting to the changed political reality quickly. Others said that it was not wise to do so. It was treachery: '*yeh niti nahin ghaddari hai*'.[13] The former opinion had more takers than the latter.

The new administration gradually began to make an impact. A new building with yellow limewash (*pili kothi*) had come up just on the outskirts of the town.[14] It was an addition to the landscape. This was the office of the *tahsildar*. The deputy commissioner too held his court in this building. New laws and regulations were introduced and new settlements established. The new settlement was beyond the comprehension of most people. Dewan Maiya Das too was not sure of what was happening around: '*jo parampara baap-dada ke zamane se chali aa rahi hai, use tora kaise ja sakta hai!*'[15]

He was curious as to how centuries-old practices and customs could be replaced with new ones? This curiosity was not without foundation. Never before in Indian history had the state intervened in the social lives and economic relationships of the people as effectively as the British did. His understanding of the situation was that

> The village patwari earlier estimated the harvest and the share of revenue that each cultivator was supposed to pay to the village headman (*mukhia*). The remittance to the headman was in the form of grains or a share of the produce. The headman then converted the kind into cash by selling the grain in the market or to the *sahukar* in the village and remitted the amount to the treasury at each harvest. Earlier, the entire village was assessed collectively. Now, the entire land will be divided among all the cultivators (as per their ancestral shares). The principle of collective ownership will not be operative. Each cultivator will now pay his share separately. Each cultivator would pay revenue in cash based on individual assessment (*takhmina*). Earlier the revenue was assessed on the standing crop or the share of the state was apportioned on the harvesting floor, that is, out of the actual produce.

The estimates now will be on the basis of the measurement of land, classification of soil, method of irrigation and the average revenues paid previously. The assessment based on this principle will be fixed. Earlier the revenue was paid after the harvest. Now the payment will have to be made before the harvest. Earlier the entire village paid the revenue collectively. [*Pahle khet kat jane par lagan diya jata tha, ab katai se pahle hi lagan ka bhugtan karna hoga. Pahle sara gaon mil kar sanjhi bhugtan karta tha, ab har hal jotne wala kisan apni-apni zamin ka khud bhugtan karega*].[16]

Each cultivator would now be responsible for the remittance to the treasury. The fixed revenue would be paid every year: '*har saal utna hi lagan dena hoga, na kam na jyada, yeh nahin ke fasal acchi nahih hui to lagan kam ho jayega*'.[17] Those unable to make payment on time could go to *sahukar*s, borrow from them on interest, and remit the tax. In the event of consecutive poor harvests for two or three years, the cultivators could keep on borrowing. What interest would be charged (*byaj kitna hoga?*). The *sahukar*s would decide the rate of interest to be charged from debtors. In case of disputes, the state had established law courts: 'Be careful the law will favour the creditors rather than the debtors.'[18] Maiya Das did not believe that the new *amaldari* would last long: '*nai amaldari jyada der tak nahin chalne wali*'.[19]

The peasants coming to the town to make purchases had to sell their surplus grains to get some cash which they spent in the shop of the *sahukar*. In a short span of time *sahukar*s had opened several shops. The provision to mortgage lands with the *sahukar*s now had legal sanction. This benefited the *sahukar*s the most. In contrast with the policy of the pre-British state wherein creditors were discouraged from ousting the debtors from their lands, debtors could now easily be ousted by alienating land in favour of the creditors.[20] Thus had begun a vicious circle. Even junior officers like the *qanungo*s had become more influential than the *kardar*s of earlier times.

Bhishm Sahni reflects upon the emergence of the trading middle classes. The *sahukar*s did not confine their activities to the business of moneylending. The introduction of the railways had facilitated the influx of imported cloth and other glittering articles of artificial jewellery and cosmetics. The *sahukar*s with surplus money began to invest in trading as well. This process is depicted through the characters of Lala Gobind Ram and Malik Mansa Ram.[21] Mansa Ram was a servant (*gumashta*) of Lala Gobind Ram. He visited Jhelum city frequently to buy goods of various descriptions, including chintz made in the textile mills of Britain. He consequently rose to become an affluent man in the town. He was now Malik Mansa Ram. He could, with his newly acquired wealth, compete with the *jagirdar*s of the town. Gobind Ram and Mansa Ram had no qualms about their dealings with poor peasants. Peasants would approach them to sell grains for some cash to buy essential items for their households. These newly emerged traders would buy the grains at less than the prevailing price on the condition that in return the peasant buy all his necessities only from their shop. Goods were then sold to the peasants at prices higher than those prevailing in the market. The cash would then, after circulation, come back to the traders and *sahukar*s. For Dewan Maiya Das, the protagonist of the traditional morality, it was painful to come to terms with the unscrupulous practices of these upstarts. He pointed out to Gobind Ram, '*seth yeh to thugee hai*'. Gobind Ram replied, '*thugee nahin dewan ji, yeh vyapar hai*'![22] A sense of defeat overcame Maiya Das and he realized that times had changed and old values had vanished. This kind of profiteering had not been a part of traditional trading practices. Dewan Maiya Das died a vanquished person.

Dewan Dhanpat, a usurper, was a nephew of Dewan Maiya Das born out of an illicit relationship of Maiya Das's younger brother. He and his sons quickly adapted themselves to the new conditions. They prospered and enjoyed all the benefits of power, and dominated the life of the town for a few decades.

Dhanpat was wily and cunning. He knew how to take advantage of the changing reality.[23] He virtually behaved as the 'ruler' of the town. Of his three sons, Kalla, the eldest, was mentally retarded, the second son, Manjhla, was a lecherous ruffian and the third, and youngest, Hakumat Rai, after completing his studies in *Vilayat* had become a barrister. He hoped to be awarded the title of Rai Bahadur for his services to the *sarkar*. Lekh Raj, was the ousted legal heir to the *madi*. He had taken active part during the Anglo-Sikh wars in the defence of the Khalsa Raj. He represents the emerging nationalist sentiment in its embryonic form. There are portrayals of many other characters who represented the emerging upper middle class of traders and professionals. The character that draws our attention most is Rukmani – nicknamed Rukmi – the wife of Kalla. Bhishm Sahni has addressed issues regarding the condition of women through her character.

Rukmani was married to Kalla under mysterious circumstances when she was thirteen years of age. She was cut off from the world outside the *madi*, and took some time to come to terms with her new life. As she grew up, she began to understand the ways of the world. In the process she turned out to be the image of a woman who had the extraordinary elasticity and adaptability to survive under adverse conditions. She accepted Kalla as her destiny with all sincerity. She withstood all provocations and tolerated the lecherous taunts of Manjhla and his ruffian friends. She resolved to live in the world on her own terms. As a step towards asserting herself and to give expression to her identity, she decided to join the girls' school that was about to be established by a *vanprasthi*, an Arya Samaj preacher or *pracharak*.[24]

The opening of a school for the education of girls in the town can be contextualized in the larger perspective of the reform movements and their programme of women's education. The Arya Samaj was founded in the Punjab in 1877.[25] In a short period a vast section of the educated urban middle class had come under its influence. The movement regarded the condition of women to be a matter which was an integral to its programme. In fact, all the movements among Hindus and Sikhs that arose in the Punjab towards the end of the nineteenth century had incorporated 'upliftment of women' and 'women emancipation' with greater emphasis on their education.[26] The Arya Samaj philosophy of social reconstruction had a well-defined place for women with special emphasis on their right to education. It prescribed for women elementary knowledge of grammar, religion and religious texts, medicine, arithmetic and all that would enable them to become good wives and mothers. Arya Samajis had begun to open girl's schools during the early 1880s.[27] In Amritsar, Jalandhar and Lahore, girls' schools were opened in 1885.[28] Initially the response was not encouraging but with the passage of time it gained momentum. By the end of the nineteenth century, girls' schools were opened not only in Ferozepur, Moga and Kapurthala, but also small towns like Patti and Bagha-purana.[29] The opening of a school for girls by a *vanprasthi*, an Arya Samaj *pracharak*, in the *qasba* of the *madi* is therefore understandable.

The decision of Rukmani was a signal to break away from the shackles of a patriarchal superiority. She went to get herself enrolled in the school wrapped in a white sheet, unusual for a woman of her age. This was a significant symbol – unbinding of herself from all those relations which had no meaning for her. No one in the brotherhood and the *qasba* had protested when she was being married to Kalla.[30] It was therefore not necessary to seek permission from anyone including Dewan Dhanpat, the patriarch. When she went to school to enrol herself, the *vanprasthi* asked her if she had the permission of her people?[31] She replied, 'Whom do I ask?' He further enquired if the people of the household objected. She replied even more firmly by saying, '*ji main parhungi*'.[32] It soon became the talk of the town that '*madi walon ki bahu*' had enrolled herself in the school. The ladies would now be going to school with their faces uncovered! The times had changed!

Dewan Dhanpat did feel insecure in the new situation, though he did not think it wise to oppose the new reality. He felt himself duty-bound not to obstruct the process.[33] He was conscious that the *sarkar* was opening schools all over and Christian missionaries had also opened a Mission school in the town. Therefore, any act of obstruction would not be seen with favour by *sarkar-i-inglishia*. He therefore chose to feign indifference to this development. He expressed his displeasure when Manjhla and his ruffians beat up the *vanprasthi*.[34] This did not deter the *vanprasthi* and Rukmani from their resolve. Manjhla had claimed 'moral ground' for their opposition to Rukmani going to school. He tried to gather the support of the people of the town by arguing that women going to school was an act of shamelessness. Women of *respectable* families were not allowed to move out of their homes with their faces uncovered: '*ham yeh besharmi nahin hone denge*'.[35] The *pracharak* would be exploiting the daughters and the *bahus*. He warned both Kalla and Rukmani and the *Vanprasthi* of dire consequences if she dared to move out of the house. The expressions were: '*agar teri gharwali ne ghar ke baahar pair rakha to mujhse bura koi na hoga, apne ghar ki aurton ko ham beparda nahin hone denge, main taangen cheer kar rakh doonga*'. He warned the *vanprasthi* sternly: '*harami budha agar madi ke pas phir kabhi nazar aaya to taange tor doonga*'.[36] The reaction of the people of the town was rather mixed. Some of them went to the extent of equating the girl's school with a brothel: '*yahan ham kanjarkhana nahin banane denge*'.[37] All these reactions came from men. The only woman to respond to the men's reaction was Bhagsudi, a widow who had the courage to question the right of Manjhla and his cohort to disallow Rukmani from going to school. She protested and dared Manjhla to harm Rukmani.[38] She was the only one in the town who dared to rise and question the high and mighty. Still, a large section of the population of the town remained silent, if not indifferent. The reaction of Lekh Raj was, however, the most eloquent. He declared with great enthusiasm that a new life had been infused in the town, and it was the dawn of a new era: '*kasba jee utha hai! andhere me diya jal utha hai!*'.[39]

It was the response of a revolutionary. He paid the price for his revolutionary ideas by losing his freedom. Dhanpat had him arrested on the false charge of trying to incite rebellion against the state.[40] Dhanpat, otherwise, had felt constrained to stop the opening of the school – those who supported the move could certainly be eliminated. By getting Lekh Raj eliminated, the legitimate heir to the property of Dewan Maiya Das, Dewan Dhanpat achieved the twin objectives of performing service to the British Raj and to himself.

There were initially varied responses – retrogressive, indifferent and positive – to the women's education initiative that started with just a few girl students. As the years passed, the movement gained momentum and the school began to run successfully. The old *vanprasthi* was succeeded by Rukmani as the head teacher of the school. She was now, more respectfully, called Rukmani Devi.[41]

The school was up to only the fourth standard, beyond which women were not supposed to be educated. The Arya Samaj

Movement in its early years could not transgress these basically patriarchal values that did not visualize the role of women outside the four walls of the house. Lala Lajpat Rai, Lala Sunder Das and Lala Dev Raj, the propagators of women education, did not perceive the objective of educating women beyond a particular limit. Sunder Das held that 'the character of girls education should be different from that of boys in many essential respects'.[42] The idea of educating women was centred on the requirements of patriarchy. The reformers, in fact, strove to educate women and improve their status in proportion to their own raised status as new professionals, public servants and traders.[43]

There is another point which emerges in the narrative. The old *jagirdari* class could not appreciate the rise of the affluent class of traders and businessmen. They still considered themselves as part of the ruling class and thus belonging to the highest strata in the social order. To preserve this status was essential to their survival. Dhanpat's decision to marry his son to the daughter of Malik Mansa Ram, the affluent trader of the town, was the result of this mindset. Mansa Ram had earned a fortune by trading in imported goods of all description, and had also opened a *mandawa*.[44] Dhanpat considered him to be an upstart and felt it was necessary to never allow Mansa Ram to regard himself as his equal. In matrimonial relations, the family of a bride was always at the receiving end in relation to that of the bridegroom.

The introduction of the railways in 1862 – and other means of communications and transportation – had changed the landscape of the Punjab.[45] Within a few decades, all the towns of the Punjab were connected with the metropolitan centres: Bombay, Calcutta and Madras and Karachi. This development opened a new window and enabled people to move out of small towns to see the new world. The movement of people now became much faster and more comfortable. They were happy with this change and expressed their joy and gratitude to the British in folk songs like, for instance:

Shava shava ve firangia amar hoe tera raj
Shava shava ve karmawalia ve tu sabhna da sartaj.[46]

This euphoria, however, did not last long. Towards the end of the century, euphoria was replaced first by recession, and then by resurgence. The new middle class began to understand the exploitative character of the Raj. The demand for more political rights, articulated first by the Indian Association and then by the Indian National Congress, began to gain momentum. The partition of Bengal in 1905 and the disturbances over the increase in water rates in 1907 contributed towards the emergence of a new leadership from amongst the newly emerged middle class. This leadership had the courage to challenge the authority of the natural leaders on the one hand and the Raj on the other. And now the singing of *shava shava* was no longer in the air. The rise of political movements was based on new perceptions about the nature and character of the Raj. The resurgence in the sphere of social and religious reforms had changed the lives of the people in many ways, and had made them more politically conscious than ever before.[47]

The struggle for the freedom of the country from foreign rule had begun. The leaders of the various movements found expression at two levels. First, they sought to reshape the traditional social order and customs, and second, they began to struggle against colonial values and ideology which were essentially exploitative in nature. The atmosphere now resounded with a new song: '*asaan te saiyaan saada karam kama de, saada ghulami kolon des chhuda de*'.[48] A new era in the lives of the people of the Punjab had begun.

NOTES

1. Bhishm Sahni, *Maiya Das ki Madi*, 1st pub. 1988; rpt., New Delhi: Raj Kamal Prakashan, 1992, hereafter referred to as *Madi*.
2. See also, Prakash Tandon, *Punjabi Century (1857–1947)*, London: Chatto and Windus, 1961.
3. *Madi*, pp. 150–1.
4. Bhishm Sahni re-enacts a meeting supposedly of the shareholders of the company who were given to understand that all investments made in India were treated as debited to the Indian account. The shareholders, therefore, were entitled to not only dividends on profits but also the interests that accrued to the account. The principal amount was also to be ultimately withdrawn, ibid., p. 201.

5. Meenakshi Mukherjee, 'Reality and Realism: Indian Women as Protagonists in Four Nineteenth Century Novels', in *Social Transformation and Creative Imagination*, ed. Sudhir Chandra, New Delhi: Allied Publishers, 1984, pp. 201–2.
6. Ibid., p. 201.
7. For corroboration see, Reeta Grewal, 'Urban Revolution Under Colonial Rule', in Indu Banga, ed., *Five Punjabi Centuries: Polity, Economy and Culture 1500–1990*, New Delhi: Manohar, 1997, pp. 438–54.
8. See J.S. Grewal, *The Sikhs of the Punjab*, Cambridge: Cambridge University Press, 1990, pp. 128–56.
9. *Madi*, p. 121.
10. Ibid., p. 150.
11. Ibid., p. 145.
12. Ibid., p. 144.
13. Ibid., pp. 145–6.
14. Ibid., p. 147.
15. Ibid., p. 150.
16. Ibid., pp. 150–1.
17. Ibid., p. 151.
18. Ibid., p. 151.
19. Ibid., p. 150.
20. Ibid., p. 151. This was in contrast to the practices of the pre-British period. The state under Maharaja Ranjit Singh exercised a check over the moneylenders by issuing orders that the creditors would not attach bullocks, fodder and other implements of the cultivators in execution of decrees. The state ensured that the land was not abused and it remained under cultivation. Radha Sharma, *Peasantry and the State: Early Nineteenth Century Punjab*, Delhi: K.K. Publishers, 2000, p. 176.
21. *Madi*, p. 152.
22. Ibid., p. 153.
23. He was the first one in the *qasba* to present himself before the new officer to express his loyalty to the British. He assured the officer that the ruler was next to god for him: '*hakim-i-waqt uska parmeshar hota hai*', ibid., 167.
24. Ibid., pp. 219–20.
25. Swami Dayanand arrived in Lahore in April 1877 and the first meeting of the Lahore Arya Samaj was held on 24 July 1877. Kenneth W. Jones, *Arya Dharm: Hindu Consciousness in 19th Century Punjab*, New Delhi: Manohar, 1976, p. 37.
26. *Satyarth Prakash*, 7th edn., Delhi: Arsh Sahitya Prachar Trust, 1972, p. 98.
27. Jones, *Arya Dharm*, p. 87.

28. Ibid., pp. 87–8.
29. Ibid., p. 88.
30. *Madi*, p. 265.
31. Ibid., p. 265–6.
32. Ibid., p. 266.
33. Ibid., p. 283.
34. Ibid., p. 282.
35. Ibid., pp. 281–2.
36. Ibid., pp. 238–9.
37. Ibid., pp. 261–2.
38. Ibid., pp. 239–41.
39. Ibid., p. 287.
40. Ibid., p. 285
41. Ibid., pp. 281–2, 302–3.
42. Dev Raj (Lala), *Pathshala ki Kanya*, 1st pub. 1894, 2nd edn., Lahore: np, 1903, pp. 1–8.
43. Radha Sharma, 'The Women Question and the Socio-Religious Reform in the Punjab: Late 19th and Early 20th Century', *Proceedings of the Punjab History Conference*, Patiala: Punjabi University, 1994.
44. *Madi*, p. 194.
45. On 10 April 1862, the first railway line between Amritsar and Lahore was opened to public traffic in the Punjab. *Punjab Administration Report, 1862*, pp. 74–5. See also G.S. Khosla, 'The Growth of Railway System in the Punjab', *The Punjab Past and Present: Essays in Honour of Dr Ganda Singh*, Patiala: Punjabi University, 1976.
46. *Madi*, p. 208.
47. For the political, social and cultural developments in the Punjab during the colonial period see articles in Indu Banga, ed., *Five Punjabi Centuries, Polity, Economy and Culture, c. 1500–1990*, New Delhi: Manohar, 1997; Reeta Grewal and Sheena Pall, eds., *Pre-Colonial and Colonial Punjab: Society, Economy, Politics and Culture: Essays for Indu Banga*, New Delhi: Manohar, 2005.
48. Ibid., p. 333.

CHAPTER 5

Changing Attitudes towards Medicine in Colonial Punjab

SASHA

The introduction of Western medicine in India gives insights into the complexity of relationships between the colonizers and the colonized. Western medicine was a 'tool of the empire' through which the supremacy of the West was pronounced. The process of penetration of Western medicine opened a window to the different sections of Indian society. The medical doctor was the most visible representative of European knowledge, and *doctory ilaj* came to be intricately linked with colonialism. The penetration of Western medicine shaped the attitudes of different classes.

In the nineteenth century, when the British annexed the Punjab, a new concept regarding the State's responsibility for the protection of the health and well-being of its people was emerging in Britain.[1] These new concerns of the State were gradually seen in India also. Initially, however, the public health policy in India emerged out of the concern for improving the health of British troops in India. Hospitals for the troops and medical institutions meant exclusively for Europeans were established in the early decades of the nineteenth century. By William Bentinck's time, government intervention in matters of health and sanitation had begun to be advocated.[2] With the takeover of the Empire by the Crown in 1858, the sphere of public health policy incorporated the general public as well.[3]

Western medicine was the key component of colonial public health policy. A formal decision to introduce its teaching was taken in 1835. This led to the marginalization of traditional medical systems. Indigenous practitioners began losing aristocratic patronage and public support among the emerging middle classes. The local *hakims* and *vaids* were trained in the rudiments of Western medicine to cater to the health needs of potential recruits to the army. This arrangement continued till 1889, when the indigenous practitioners were excluded from government medical service under an all-India shift to a policy which clearly favoured Western medicine.[4]

Western medical institutions were introduced in the Punjab in the first year of annexation. There were hospitals for the troops and those that were meant exclusively for Europeans. The missionaries set up hospitals and dispensaries mainly for the natives. In 1849, the government established civil hospitals at Amritsar, Jalandhar, Multan and Sialkot. In the 1850s, government dispensaries came up at many places including Rawalpindi, Peshawar, Amritsar, Bannu, Hazara, Sialkot, Dera Ismail Khan and Dera Ghazi Khan.[5] During the first three decades, the government dispensaries were classified on the basis of their financial resources. In 1879, medical institutions were reclassified on the basis of the number of beds.[6]

In 1886, medical institutions were broadly categorized as 'government' and 'aided' hospitals and dispensaries. Medical institutions that had not less than forty beds and not less than twenty in-door patients daily now came to be defined as hospitals. Government hospitals were of two kinds – provincial hospitals, which were controlled and supported by the provincial government, and local hospitals, which were controlled and funded by municipal committees and district boards. Below them were three grades of dispensaries. The 'aided' medical institutions included private charitable hospitals and dispensaries, which received grants from public funds.[7]

A hierarchy of medical personnel was also set up. Hospitals were placed under the inspector general of prisons until 1880, when, the civil medical department was organized. This department was now placed under an inspector general of civil hospitals. The civil surgeon was the chief medical officer who supervised the functioning of the dispensaries of the district. He also supervised the work carried out by the assistant surgeons and hospital assistants. The subassistant surgeons looked after medical institutions at the subdivisional headquarters. Hospital assistants looked after the functioning of the minor hospitals and dispensaries in different towns. The deputy commissioner at the district level and assistant commissioner, *tahsildar*s and *naib tahsildar*s at the *tahsil* level worked in association with the medical staff.[8] The services of pensioned subordinates and missionary doctors were also used.[9]

The establishment of this Western system also resulted in new forms of diagnosis and treatment of diseases. To treat diseases – malaria, smallpox, cholera and the plague – which were the most common, the British adopted measures which revolved around the body rather than the disease. They acted on the assumption that Indians had insanitary habits which required constant surveillance and isolation. Consequently, administrators laid stress on cordoning, quarantine and disinfection of the dwellings and personal belongings of the sick. The afflicted were segregated in tents and huts till they recovered or expired. Their attendants and relatives were isolated separately. Disinfection and fumigation of their dwellings and household articles was carried out to prevent the spread of the disease. However, the measures became focused and specific as the aetiology of different diseases became clear with the passage of time. Thereafter, the British dispensed quinine, conducted vaccinations and inoculations and made improvements in the drainage systems and water supply.

The people nevertheless had limited access to medical facilities. This was due to the fact that public health policy was accorded low priority as compared to other social concerns. At the end of 1866 there were 69 dispensaries in the Punjab. Their number rose to 267 in 1898 and by the end of 1919 it had risen to 504.[10] Despite an increase in their numbers in 1912, there was only one dispensary for every 43,000 inhabitants,[11] and by the end of 1919 there was one dispensary for every 40,000 persons.[12] The sanitary commissioner attributed this to lack of funds and admitted that medical facilities for the public were insufficient: 'In parts of the Punjab, the medical needs of the people are insufficiently met owing to the scantiness of the dispensaries in proportion to the population'.[13]

Meanwhile, the indigenous population had recourse to the

indigenous systems of medicine that continued to exist. To treat various diseases, the physicians practised Ayurvedic and Unani systems of medicine. The Ayurvedic system represented a codified body of medical knowledge and theory and was based on the three medical texts of ancient India, namely, the *Caraka Samhita, Sushruta Samhita* and *Astanga Samhita*.[14] The Unani or the Tibb system that had developed in Arabia and Persia and came to India after the Turkish conquest was based on medical concepts developed in Egypt and Greece.[15] The two systems laid emphasis on the co-relation between the elementary forms of nature and conditions of health and disease.[16] Disease was considered as a natural process and the symptoms were regarded as reactions of the body to the disease. Ecology and the patient were more prominent than the clinical and laboratory approach of Western medicine. The similarity in the method of diagnosis and training led to the coexistence of the Ayurvedic and Unani systems of medicine. The two systems accommodated each other. Some essentials from the Ayurvedic system, especially the use of botanical products, were incorporated in the Unani system following which the two became fairly integrated.[17]

Along with the Ayurvedic and Unani systems, people tended to combine practices of a psychological nature with medicines and some procedures to obtain relief from various disorders. There were large local and subregional variations in these. Generally, there was a very thin line of distinction between medicinal and non-medicinal remedies.

Traditional remedies for the treatment of various diseases were extensive. Belief in the curative properties of herbs and plants was widespread. To cure fever – in the area to the south of the Sutlej – a purgative, made by boiling a mixture of senna, cassia, fennel, rose leaves, figs and tamarind, was given to the patient.[18] The treatment of smallpox revolved around cleansing of the blood as the disease was believed to be due to the blood sucked in by the child 'in utero'. For this, *ludhrak* – that had earlier been rubbed in rosewater – was given to the patient. Pearls, in the form of powder, were applied externally to the pustules. Milk was given along with *munaqqa* (dry grapes) to bring out the pocks. When the disease matured, roasted gram was given to cause desiccation.[19] Cauterization was carried out by the barber to cure the plague. For this, the milky juice of *ak* (wild bush) was collected in a cup of wheaten dough and applied over the buboe which was then cauterized.[20] Early British records also refer to variolation as a procedure for reducing the intensity of smallpox. In 1873, about eighty variolators from different social backgrounds were reported to be working.[21]

The belief in 'remedies' of a non-medicinal nature was fairly widespread, albeit its forms and expressions varied considerably. These included the use of charms, repetition of certain religious *mantras* (hymns) and giving opprobrious names to the patient to expel the disease. People believed in obtaining cures from different diseases through various psychological practices. In Bannu district, the patient was often wrapped in the warm skin of a newly killed sheep and placed in a closet, the apertures of which were tightly closed, in the belief that this was a cure for fevers. This process was repeated every three days till the patient either died or recovered.[22] To cure smallpox, Hindus fed their uninfected children with milk and rice and washed their hands with water. This was then sprinkled over the sick child with the repetition of *chuto*, meaning 'release', which signified expulsion of the disease.[23] They also poured water at the feet of the goddess to cool her hot power, while the Muslims soaked their sick child's clothes in water and threw the water at the root of a tree to cool *kudrat* (nature).[24] The Hindus gave opprobrious names to their children and dressed them in rags to prevent them from contracting smallpox.[25] People drank water in which red-hot iron had been plunged to obtain relief from cholera.[26] In Ludhiana district, opium was given to the sick as a cure for cholera.[27]

Charms were often used to cure epidemics. In certain areas of the Punjab, the patient was made to stare at a charm written on a *pipal* leaf till he recovered from fever.[28] The Muslims of Gurdaspur district believed that looking at Allah's name written on the patient's nail would bring relief. The Hindus, on the other hand, tied an amulet on a coloured piece of thread knotted five or seven times and hung it around the neck of the patient.[29]

Cure was also sought by transferring the disease. To transfer fever, a winnowing fan, liqour, a fowl and a pot containing two or three human images made of flour were taken to the village boundary where the comestibles were eaten and the winnowing fan was left behind so as to pass on the disease.[30] In the plains of the Punjab, to transfer smallpox, a pot filled with flowers and rice was buried in a pathway and covered with a flat stone. It was believed that whosoever touched it would contract the disease bringing relief to the original sufferer. This was known as *chalauwa*. Another measure included placing a pile of earth containing scabs or scales from the body of a smallpox patient, decorating it with flowers in the middle of the road. Whosoever touched it was expected to get the disease in place of the patient.[31] The disease was also sought to be transferred to poor children by giving them copper coins which had been touched by children suffering from smallpox.[32] Cholera too was sought to be cured by transference. The villagers of central Punjab would force a Chamar to sit on bullocks and drive him out of the village in the belief that the disease would go with him.[33] Plague was believed to be transferred from one village to another by placing old winnowing fans in a line on public roads or joint boundaries of the villages.[34]

At the same time a general belief involved the worship of the associated deity to cure and prevent the diseases. Smallpox was believed to be caused by the goddess Sitala, who was worshipped to obtain a cure.[35] In addition to the smaller *mand*s (places where Sitala Mata is worshipped) in villages where the deity was worshipped, there were seven principal shrines of the deity in the Punjab region at Patri, Kabri, Biholi, Suva, Bidhlun, Birdhana and Gurgaon. People visited these shrines to seek protection and to appease the goddess.

Fairs were held at the principal shrines. The worship was performed on the seventh day of the month of *Chet* called *sil*. Only women and children worshipped the goddess. Her image was taken to the town daily on a donkey from her temple and brought back in the evening. Fowls, pigs, goats, coconuts were offered and were later eaten by the sweepers. An adult, upon recovering from smallpox, would free a pig from captivity.[36] At Gurgaon, an annual fair was held which was attended by about 30,000 pilgrims.[37] Fairs were held at Jawahari on 7th *Chet*, in Sonepat and Narela twice a year on the 21st of *Chet* and *Asuj* and in Narhaula from the 28th to the 30th *Chet*.[38]

Cholera, like smallpox, was attributed to divine intervention. In the Punjab, Mari was considered to be the goddess of cholera. To obtain a cure, Mari was propitiated by making an offering of pumpkin, a male buffalo, a cock and a he-goat, all of which were to be decapitated with a single blow before her altar. Hindu women propitiated the goddess by participating in a *puja* and dancing frantically in a circle.[39]

These indigenous customs and practices were looked down upon by the British. They considered such practices unscientific, irrational and irrelevant. It was believed that such practices resulted in spreading the diseases rather than curing them. The practice of holding annual fairs was also looked down upon. Fairs and pilgrimages were considered as sources of infection and the pilgrims the chief agents for spreading the infection.

Indigenous medical practices too were criticized by the British. The 'obnoxious' practice of variolation was believed to be behind the spread of smallpox.[40] Variolation was considered as infectious as the disease itself because it induced the disease in its full intensity.[41] The epidemics at Kangra, Hoshiarpur, Jalandhar and Gujrat in 1873 were attributed in particular to the practice of variolation.[42] Elsewhere, variolation was said to be behind the outbreak of smallpox in 1886 at Peshawar, Dera Ismail Khan, Shahpur and Jhelum.[43] The 1887 epidemic at Bannu was also attributed to the arrival of the variolators.[44] The district administrators also considered social customs like sitting next to a sick or dying person to be responsible for the spread of the plague. The infection was particularly conveyed by the women who touched with their *chadar* (a sheet used as a veil) the wounds formed by opening of the buboes by the Chamars.[45]

The British condemned the indigenous practices and were at the same time insensitive to the social and religious susceptibilities of the people. The vaccinators were often coercive, incompetent and callous while carrying out the vaccine operations.[46] They performed a large number of operations in a limited time without any regard to the 'convenience and religious observances' of the people.[47] In an attempt to vaccinate a large number of children in a day, often the vaccinators carried out their work negligently. In Hazara, buffalo lymph was taken on the fifth day instead of the sixth due to which people complained of inflammations and vesicular eruptions.[48] Some children died after they were improperly vaccinated.[49]

The British implemented these measures forcibly. The vaccinators in connivance with the *lambardar*s and *zaildar*s, forcibly collected and vaccinated children without the consent of their parents. Women were dragged out of their homes and children snatched from their arms. The beards of the men were also pulled for not bringing the children out of their homes to be vaccinated.[50] In many cases, the mother, along with the 'vacciniferous' child, was dragged for days and made to travel for miles and forced to witness the pain of her child while the lymph was being extracted. This continued till either the arm of the child became inflamed or the child became feverish.[51]

The administrators were often indifferent to the economic hardships their measures entailed. During the cholera epidemic at Mianwali in 1876, no remission of land revenue was given in the autumn crop.[52] In the areas around Kohat cantonment and Dera Ghazi Khan, where rice cultivation and cultivation of high-grade crops was prohibited to prevent outbreaks of malaria, no compensation was given to the villagers even though it had been promised.[53] The colonial authorities generally believed that measures to combat the plague left the 'agricultural pursuits' unaffected and that the people were in a position to pay the land revenue. No remission in land revenue was granted to farmers in the worst and longest affected Jalandhar division. In 1898, they were only given a few days' respite in the payment of revenue of the *rabi* (spring).[54]

As may be expected, the insensitive attitude of the British resulted in varying responses from the local population to Western medicine. The response of different sections of the people to the new medical practices would depend on the extent to which they were involved and affected, and the manner in which the representatives of the state dealt with them. Some sections of the society collaborated with the British and voluntarily carried out the requisite measures. In other cases, attitudes ranged from sullen acceptance to active resistance.

In urban areas, leading men voluntarily accepted Western medicine and cooperated with the authorities. 'Leading men of influence' were selected in consultation with the deputy commissioner to assist the medical staff in the implementation of different measures. The importance of such practices was explained to them and they were asked to popularize the new medical practices. In the first decade of the twentieth century, several individuals cooperated with the authorities in stamping out epidemics.[55] For instance, the 'leading men' of Lahore bought a desiccator for the neighbourhood.[56] Rai Bahadur Lala Kishen Das of Delhi placed four of his gardens at the disposal of the public for use during evacuation.[57] Also, the *imam* of Jama Masjid and Hakim Abdul Majid helped to allay the panic caused by the plague.[58] At Denga, Attar Singh, a doctor, visited every house during the influenza epidemic, giving solace and consolation and did not charge any fees. The 'leading men' of Denga opened a milk shop, where milk was given free to the poor and at half price to others.[59]

The educated middle classes, comprising doctors, lawyers, teachers and journalists, acted as intermediaries between the colonial state and the masses. They made use of the press and appealed to their fellow countrymen to adopt Western medicine. *The Tribune* exhorted the people to devise means to combat the plague, adopt precautionary measures and observe the rules of hygiene. It called upon the educated to give the necessary advice to their ignorant brethren and to remove their misunderstandings regarding the preventive measures.[60] The educated middle class made use of the press to appeal to the British to take adequate relief measures. During the malaria epidemic in 1908, an appeal was made in the *Khalsa Advocate* to the lieutenant-governor to organize relief measures.[61] In 1910, the residents of Amritsar appealed to health officers and engineers to take timely precautions, like clearing drains, to prevent disastrous outbreaks.[62] During the influenza epidemic in 1918, the *Khalsa Advocate* again appealed to the lieutenant-governor to arrange medical relief for the helpless village folk.[63]

At the same time, the educated middle classes were generally restrained in expressing their resentment against the handling of epidemics. It was mostly voiced through the lodging of complaints with the authorities. In Moga, a complaint was made against a native doctor in connection with the plague operations.[64]

In Jalandhar, higher authorities were approached against the 'arbitrary' orders of the cantonment magistrate to disinfect the houses by burning dry grass in them.[65] The newspapers were rather stringent in voicing their criticism of the inadequacy of eradication measures. The *Khalsa Advocate* condemned the mode of vaccination and pleaded for its discontinuation: [66]

> Vaccination is useless and there is no excuse for continuing it. In many cases, leprosy spreads through vaccination. Children die in great agony. The whole business of inoculation is quackery. How long the people will continue to submit to this infamous treatment, I cannot say, but in their ignorance they are the prey of Government supported quacks who make a living by putting poison in the blood of the people. The whole thing is horrible and disgusting for words.

The racialism built into the preventive measures also came in for criticism. The practice of asking several questions during medical examination at Tara Devi station, situated just short of Simla, was seen as imbued with racialism. *The Tribune* wrote accusingly that, 'The Government of India's administration is infected with the colour pest.' Further, 'within an area of twenty miles of the Imperial headquarters, an educated Indian was treated as a menial.'[67]

Resistance to the eradication measures also came from those people who were directly affected by them. Indigenous practitioners were against Western science which treated the body as an isolated clinical object. There was a strong dislike for and anger against Western science being a superior form of medical science. The Western system was criticized on the grounds that it only removed and destroyed the germs and did not understand the reason for the production of those germs. Several instances of resistance were noticed. In Amritsar, in 1875, during the cholera epidemic a native practitioner of traditional medicine incited the Kashmiris against getting themselves inspected because his private practice 'got affected by the medicines administered by the administration'.[68] In the early 1880s, in Delhi, a native Christian, Udey Ram, prevented the vaccinator from vaccinating the Chamars.[69] Some sections of the society like Brahman priests, keepers of Sitala temples, *mullah*s and variolators felt that vaccinators deprived them of their livelihood. They tried to prevent the vaccinators from doing their job.[70]

Resistance against vaccination was even stronger. The caste Hindus resisted vaccination on the plea that the vaccines contained substances which were not permitted by their religion. The Khatris of Rahon sent a petition to the deputy commissioner saying that the prophylactic serum contained animal matter the use of which was forbidden by their religion.[71] A strong reluctance was reported from Gurgaon, Lahore, Gujrat, Muzaffargarh and Dera Ismail Khan districts for the same reason.[72] The upper-caste Hindus also opposed vaccination on the grounds of caste. In the arm-to-arm vaccination, lymph was often taken from sweepers' children and injected into children of higher castes. Often vaccinators themselves belonged to a lower caste. Thus, in Ludhiana, of the 611 persons vaccinated only 54 were Hindus.[73] In Delhi, Lala Hardhyan Singh and Lala Kishan Chand, both members of the municipal committee, and Lala Ram Kishan Das, an honorary magistrate, did not get the children in their respective families vaccinated.[74]

The articulation of resentment in the urban areas, however, was rather subdued and restrained compared to the reactions of the trading classes in the small towns and of the peasantry and rural artisans whose livelihoods were threatened equally by the diseases and the preventive measures.

In the small towns people connived with the lower government functionaries to avoid the new medical treatment. In Rohtak district, some bribed the vaccinators to let their children remain unvaccinated.[75] In Palwal, members of municipal committees bribed vaccinators not to carry out any vaccinations in their *mohalla*s.[76] To escape vaccinations residents of Ludhiana bribed the registration writer to not register births.[77] In Karnal, the wealthier people paid money to the vaccinator to go away and not vaccinate the children.[78] In Simal Mazra, in Garhshankar district, the *lambardar*s allowed plague victims to be secretly buried.[79]

The people often showed reluctance to adopt new medicinal practices. At Garhshankar, the Sayyids objected to the house-to-house inspection by the Muhammadan *dhais*.[80] During the cholera epidemic, the Muhammadans of Khanpur strongly objected to the disinfection of bedding and articles by steam or sunlight on the grounds that they were *Namazi*s and their religion did not permit such practices.[81] Inhabitants of Kalka were so opposed to desiccation and disinfecting that they prevented even the affected houses from being treated.[82] Several Hindus and Jains were opposed to the extermination of rats on religious grounds. They either buried the baits laid by the district administrators or released the rats caught in the traps. The Jains established rat hospitals to protect them. In one such hospital 8,000 rats were found.[83] In Sialkot district, the Jains, locally called Bhabras, did not permit rat extermination in their houses.[84] During the malaria epidemic of 1910 in Gurdaspur district, instead of taking the quinine given by the quinine distribution society, the people gave it to their cattle or put it in ponds and dung heaps.[85]

In fact, there was a general reluctance to cooperate with the plague measures. At Khan Khanan, the people preferred to die in their own village rather than move into the camps.[86] The residents of Paragpur were 'obstructive and impertinent' while refusing to go to the camps; they moved into the camp only after the arrest of a couple of men.[87] The people in Sialkot district refused to evacuate their houses for fear of theft.[88] At Patiala, the *jagirdar*s and *sardar*s decided against evacuation and it was only after a great deal of persuasion that they agreed to move out.[89] Even by 1907 the attitudes of the people had not changed much and they were not willing to evacuate on any 'considerable scale'.[90]

In the towns, people actively opposed the measures and their resentment was directed against the subordinate staff. In the initial stages, it was directed against the vaccinators. In 1891, in Rohtak, the vaccinators were assaulted on the grounds that they had unnecessarily vaccinated many children.[91] After the outbreak of the plague and in reaction to the coercive measures of the administration and medical officers the people took out processions, threatened government functionaries, hurled abuses at them and at times even assaulted them physically. The prime targets of these angry reactions were the subordinate staff dealing with the plague measures.

During the plague epidemic, residents of Garhshankar held a demonstration in the bazaar to protest against house-to-house 'inspections' by the Muhammadan *dhai*s and the arrest of some men.[92] At Hajipur, hospital assistants were threatened with violence when they came to dispose of the remains of a victim.[93] The residents of Sihowal and Darya Nangal violently threatened the *naib tahsildar*;[94] at Kathgarh, a person actually attacked the *naib tahsildar*, but the *chaukidar* who was ordered to arrest the culprit refused to do so.[95] Subordinate medical staff at Hajipur complained of assaults and abuses by the Chamars who had been asked to carry the baggage of nurses.[96] In Banga circle, hospital assistants and compounders were accused of bribery, extortion and ill treatment: abuses were hurled at them, and some of them were even attacked.[97]

In rural areas, the general disapproval of the people towards the measures found expression in rumours. The rumours revolved around the vaccinations and plague eradication measures, both of which were carried out with coercion. Regarding vaccination, it was believed by some that the government was marking children because it was looking for people fit enough to be slaves.[98] Another rumour that found easy acceptance was that the British wanted to cut short the growth of the nation by injuring the nerves of virility and making the children impotent. They also believed that the British were taking out blood to prepare a blood mummy. Some even believed that the government was trying to find a child who had milk in his veins, as such a child would be the Imam Mahdi whom the British were trying to kill.[99] Some thought that by vaccinating people, the government was collecting a certain quantity of human blood for propitiating a deity.[100] Vaccinations were also seen as a means of spreading Christianity! [101]

A rumour which found easy credence was that, to arrest the plague the government was resorting to poisoning the afflicted persons.[102] Medical subordinates were believed to be administering pills of a suspicious nature and a certain hospital assistant had actually died after consuming his own pill.[103] The authorities were said to be interested in killing a large number of people simply because Queen Victoria had died. The inoculators were said to be moving around villages carrying needles filled with the plague poison to spread the disease. Native officers, like assistant surgeons and *naib tahsildar*s, were suspected of spreading the disease by distributing poisoned sweets or by poisoning village wells.[104] Credence was also given to the idea that male members of the family were being killed by the plague poison so as to secure their female relations for the enjoyment of officials. *The Tribune* reports another widespread rumour that people were being poisoned as the king required money; if they died leaving behind no heir, the property would be escheated to the king. It seems that rumours were more prevalent in areas where the measures were forced upon the people and mistrust of the local administration was high.[105]

The rural population often concealed the sick. During the cholera epidemic in 1872, patients were concealed because of the fear of quarantine.[106] In 1875, people concealed the sick in Amritsar district due to their resentment against cleaning operations.[107] Concealment of cholera cases continued till the third decade of the twentieth century. This tendency was rather pronounced among rail passengers going to Simla because of the stringent measures. Sometimes, in trains, children suffering from cholera were hidden under the seats or in toilets. [108] There was also utmost dislike for the arm-to-arm vaccination of children who were concealed in their homes till the vaccinator had left the area.[109] One such instance was reported from a village in Jhang district, where the women locked themselves in along with their children.[110] In Lahore district, children afflicted with smallpox were concealed precisely when the vesicles were ripe and they were required to be brought for inspection.[111] The fear of segregation was generally behind the concealment of plague cases. In Khan Khanan, for instance, even after evacuation Dr James discovered eleven more cases.[112] In Sadhowal village, constable Sadr Din discovered graves of people who had been secretly buried after succumbing to the plague.[113] Villagers buried corpses even within their houses; in Sheikhupura, the body of a person who had died of the plague was found hidden in a stack of *chari* (fodder).[114]

Temporary migrations were another means of avoiding Western medical practices. During the vaccination season, people in Jhang and Lahore districts migrated to other places and returned only after the vaccinator had left the village.[115] Widespread exodus during the plague epidemic was fairly common. There was considerable movement of panic stricken people from Jalandhar to other areas.[116] Only about half the population was left behind at Eminabad.[117] In Singhoi, in Jhelum *tahsil*, people deserted the village and all shops were closed: 'scarcely is a Emam seen there' reported *The Tribune*.[118]

Western medicine provided a window to the prevalent social prejudices. In their handling of women, the attitude of the British was no different. They showed scant regard for social susceptibilities and the general disregard for women's health got highlighted. Local British administrators not only adopted a very rigid attitude, they also allowed subordinate native functionaries to implement preventive measures with force, which not infrequently resulted in the maltreatment of women.

Initially, rural women were vaccinated at a central place, often the *maidan* of a village. Sometimes they had to walk for several miles to the vaccination venue, and wait there for several hours with a 'crowd of men'.[119] Moreover, male vaccinators, whose touch was considered polluting, carried out the vaccinations.[120] In 1884, house-to-house vaccination was started. Vaccinators, accompanied as they were by a *tahsil* or a municipal *chaprasi* or a policeman, generally adopted an overbearing attitude.[121] They often came when no male member of the house was present, and this was construed as an invasion of domestic privacy.[122] In 1885, female vaccinators were employed in Delhi to vaccinate women;[123] but it was only in 1910 that the system of house-to-house vaccination gained acceptability in most of the district headquarters.[124] Also, women were forcibly evacuated to the cholera camps and it was admittedly 'most repugnant to the feelings of the people'.[125] Although British administrators reported that female hospital assistants and *dhai*s looked after women during the plague epidemic, the situation on the ground was different at many places. At Ambala, for instance, there were no *dhai*s to look after the requirements of women in the camps.[126] Some regard to their privacy was shown only in the camps where women and children were accommodated separately in huts which were marked off by bamboo screens (*sirki*).[127]

However, on their return to the village, women were roll-called every day and 'passed under the personal observation' of the *tahsildar* and the hospital assistant accompanying him. The medical officer then examined them, along with men, in the village ground. To make critical diagnoses, the male doctors had to search for bodily signs of the plague by examining the armpits, neck and thighs of women. For instance, in March 1897, at Kalka, Jackson, a European plague medical officer, made women uncover their faces in the course of the medical examination.[128] In another instance at Jandiala, the civil surgeon examined a woman from Khatkar Kalan who was suffering from fever. He examined a gland in her right groin and reported that it was of a size of 'an almond', following which she was moved to a shed. Her attendants were not allowed to accompany her; the house she came from was dug up and whitewashed. Commenting on this the civil surgeon of Hoshiarpur wrote, 'she was so nervous and terrified that her one desire was to be left alone, and allowed to go back to her own home'.[129] It was only at a few places that upper-class women observing *purdah* were examined in their homes by *dhai*s.[130] However, appeals in *The Tribune* asking for the medical examination of women of all classes only by *dhai*s were turned down by the administration.[131]

The corpses of women were inspected by medical officers and male subordinate staff for signs of the plague. Surgeon Captain C.H. James recorded that he himself inspected the body of Nihali, wife of a Lohar (blacksmith), at Kumam village in Banga circle, and found enlarged glands and other signs of the disease.[132] In Aur circle, corpse inspections were carried out in several villages. The bodies of women were inspected by Medical Officer Clerk at Palewal, Medical Officer Davis and Hospital Assistant Asa Ram at Mukandpur, and Hospital Assistant Jawahir Singh at Rahpa.[133]

Plague inoculations were carried out by male medical officers who inoculated both women and men in the village ground.[134] Only women observing *purdah* were inoculated in their own or their friends' houses. They covered their arms with muslin and extended them through a small hole in the curtain for inoculation by the assistant surgeon.[135] The Khatris of Rahon, the Rajputs of Garhshankar, and the Sayyids of Saloh were refused permission to get their women inoculated by a lady doctor.[136]

Compared to the natives, however, the British were more enlightened, yet their attitudes were conditioned as much by patriarchal notions current in their own milieu as by the notions of the relative worth of women in rural Punjab. A much smaller proportion of the resources allocated for health care in the colonial Punjab appears to have been spent specifically on and for women.[137] In terms of relative access to medical facilities, out of 2,755 beds for indoor patients in 1886, only 823 were for women.[138] In 1911, only 25 dispensaries in the province catered to women patients; of these only 7 were run by the government.[139] This insensitivity towards the general welfare of women's health and a disregard for their religious susceptibilities resulted in fewer women opting for Western medicine.

The insensitive handling of women coupled with limited access to medical facilities also brought to the forefront the attitude of the indigenous population. The upper classes brought in the question of 'honour' and 'custom'. The elite among both Hindus and Muslims forbade their women to get inoculated. The Rajputs believed that exposing their women violated the *purdah* and would make it difficult for their daughters to get married. The Sayyids believed that their religion forbade the inoculation of women by men. As a result, women benefited much less from the inoculation drive. Only 28 per cent of the women in a village in Banga and only 38 per cent in another village is Hoshiarpur district could avail themselves of this preventive measure.[140]

The prejudice attached to vaccination and revaccination was one of the major obstacles in the path of preventive measures.[141] Women regarded a visit to the temple of goddess Sitala as being 'far more efficacious' than vaccination.[142] An assistant surgeon, Ram Kishen, was of the opinion that Hindu women were opposed to vaccination due to their upbringing, which made them timid and averse to any kind of surgical intervention.[143] The women also felt discouraged by the manner in which vaccination was carried out. Often they were dragged out of their homes.[144] The vaccinators were overbearing and unmindful of their domestic privacy. A vaccinator's visit was considered as alarming as 'a visit of a tiger or beast of prey'.[145]

Considerations of family honour prevented infected women from getting themselves treated in hospitals and dispensaries.

Compared to men, fewer women received treatment in government hospitals and dispensaries. From 1875 to 1885, of the total number of people going to dispensaries the percentage of males varied between 70 and 75 per cent, while the corresponding figures for women were 25 to 30 per cent. The situation improved marginally in the next ten years when the proportion of women going to dispensaries increased by about 5 per cent. There was no substantial improvement in the situation at the beginning of the twentieth century as the number of women availing themselves of medical facilities continued to be considerably lower than that of the men. Of the total number of patients treated in dispensaries in 1901–2, 54.1 per cent were males, whereas the remaining 45.9 per cent probably included more male children than females, both young and adult.[146]

A gradual change in the attitude of both the indigenous population and the British took place. This became evident in the second decade of the twentieth century. Till then, the local population had been reluctant to adopt Western medical practices. The forcible implementation of Western medical practices resulted in the outbreak of riots. These riots, along with the limited acceptability of Western practices, brought about a change in the attitude of the British.

Efforts were made to popularize Western medicine. For this, various experimental measures were undertaken which included replacing the cow calf lymph with other forms of lymph. In 1890, buffalo, donkey, sheep and goat lymph were also used for making the vaccine.[147] In 1896, calf lymph preserved in vaseline was used. Further changes were made in the vaccine in 1904 when glycerinated lymph treated with chloroform was used.[148]

Changes were also made in the administrative machinery. To make vaccinators acceptable to the people, municipal committees were asked in 1874 to choose local persons of 'good character' as vaccinators.[149] In 1881, persons with 'some standing' were given training and employed as vaccinators.[150] In 1891, the *tahsildars* and *naib tahsildars* were asked to inquire about the conduct of the vaccinators from the people and the difficulties they faced during vaccination operations.[151] Consequently, in early twentieth century, persons of high castes were trained as vaccinators. Under dyarchy and provincial autonomy, measures were introduced to make vaccination operations more effective. By 1925, the scheme to employ female vaccinators to vaccinate women observing *purdah* was put into operation in greater parts of the Punjab.[152] Also, in 1944, a scheme for training women in girls' schools run by local bodies and the government was started. These teachers wielded influence with the local people and could vaccinate women in their homes.[153]

The services of indigenous practitioners were also utilized. *Vaid*s and *hakim*s assisted in the maintenance of the camps and hospitals.[154] In early 1907, the secretary to the government of Punjab proposed to employ them in local bodies and municipal committees.[155] Subsequently, in July 1907, district and local bodies and municipal committees started employing *hakim*s and *vaid*s to carry out functions like the distribution of medicines.[156]

The services of various other agencies, both religious and non-religious, were also utilized. The Arya Samaj in Jalandhar explained the necessity and importance of preventive measures to the traders and asked them to cooperate with the authorities.[157] The relief committee of the Punjab Brahmo Samaj supplied medicines and carried out the work of disinfecting.[158] The Punjab Hindu Sabha issued pamphlets in the vernacular giving directions regarding the implementation of the plague measures. People like Pandit Sundar Mal at Lahore devoted their time and energy in treating patients.[159] In 1933, assistance from 2,875 Boy Scouts was sought.[160] Hoardings in the vernacular were set up at various places highlighting the benefits of Western medicine. Public announcements were made and pamphlets in the vernacular were also issued. In 1934, the Red Cross Society helped in transporting people and providing relief material in the form of temporary kitchens, first-aid, milk, clothing and shelter.[161] In 1935, in Gujranwala district, the honorary health lecturer of the Red Cross society delivered 622 lectures with the help of a magic lantern.[162]

As a result of these measures, a considerable change took place. There was a substantial increase in the number of people going to medical institutions and the number of vaccinations also increased. By the mid-1920s, when the process of penetration by Western medicine had become less aggressive and covered larger areas, it became acceptable and popular and the indigenous and Western systems began to coexist peacefully.

NOTES

1. John V. Pickstone, 'Dearth, Dirt and Fever Epidemics: Rewriting the History of British Public Health, 1780–1850', in *Epidemics and Ideas: Essays on the Historical Perception of Pestilence*, ed. Terence Ranger and Paul Slack, Cambridge: Cambridge University Press, 1995, pp. 138–42.
2. Anil Kumar, *Medicine and the Raj: British Medical Policy in India, 1835–1911*, New Delhi: Sage, 1998, pp. 88–9.
3. Anand Gauba, *Amritsar: A Study in Urban History (1840–1947)*, Jalandhar: ABS Publications, 1988, pp. 161–2; Mark Harrison, *Public Heath in British India: Anglo Indian Preventive Medicine, 1859–1914*, New Delhi: Cambridge University Press, 1994, pp. 61, 231–4.
4. Anil Kumar, *Medicine and the Raj*, pp. 45–8, 216–18.
5. Based on the gazetteers of the districts of Amritsar, Jalandhar, Ambala, Delhi, Dera Ghazi Khan, Multan, Rawalpindi, Bannu, Peshawar and Sialkot.
6. *Punjab Government Civil Secretariat Proceedings, Home* (cited hereafter as *Proceedings, Home*), August 1879, sr. no. 11, p. 765.
7. *Punjab Government Civil Secretariat Proceedings, Home: Medical and Sanitary* (cited hereafter as *Proceedings, Home: Medical and Sanitary*) May 1886, sr. no. 21, pp. 48–50.
8. *Imperial Gazetteer, Provincial Series, Punjab*, vol. 1, pp. 98–9, 144–5.
9. Anil Kumar, *Medicine and the Raj*, p. 99.
10. *Proceedings, Home: Medical and Sanitary*, July 1902, nos. 16–17, p. 1. Also, *Proceedings, Home: Medical and Sanitary*, September 1920, no. 96, p. 29.
11. *Proceedings, Home: Medical and Sanitary*, July 1913, nos. 60–2, p. 1.
12. *Proceedings, Home: Medical and Sanitary*, September 1920, no. 96, p. 29.
13. *Proceedings, Home: Medical and Sanitary*, July 1902, nos. 16–17, p. 1.
14. Debiprasad Chattopadhyaya, *Science and Society in Ancient India*, Calcutta: Research India Publications, 1977, pp. 19–20. Also, Priya Vratt Sharma, ed., *History of Medicine in India* (*From Antiquity to 1000 AD*), New Delhi: INSA, 1992.
15. Asoke K. Bagchi, *Medicine in Medieval India*, New Delhi: Konark, 1997, pp. 70–1.

16. Poonam Bala, *Imperialism and Medicine in Bengal*, New Delhi: Sage, 1991, p. 33.
17. Bagchi, *Medicine in Medieval India*, p. 72. Also, Bala, *Imperialism and Medicine in Bengal*, pp. 33–4.
18. *Gazetteer of Ludhiana District*, 1904, p. 46.
19. *Gazetteer of Attock District*, 1907, p. 264.
20. *Gazetteer of Ludhiana District*, 1904, p. 46.
21. *Proceedings, Home: Medical and Sanitary*, October 1873, no. 5, p. 815. The inoculators kept dry crusts from pustules mixed with a few grains of rice in a box. Smallpox was induced by inserting the mixture into a wound made near the base of the thumb. This was kept for six hours. Dietary restrictions were imposed. For six days, cold water was poured over the patients' head. This was discontinued for three days when the eruptions began. Pustules were opened and pus drained off. Amongst the Muslims, the Sayyads and Mullahs performed inoculations. Rajputs and Nais acted as inoculators amongst the Hindus of all areas barring south-east Punjab where the Hindus did not protect themselves for fear of offending the goddess. *Imperial Gazetteer of India, Provincial Series, Punjab*, vol. 1, Calcutta: Superintendent of Government Printing, 1908, p. 146. Also, David Arnold, *Colonizing the Body: State Medicine and Epidemic Disease in the Nineteenth Century India*, New Delhi: Oxford University Press, 1993, pp. 127–8.
22. *Gazetteer of Bannu District*, 1883–4, p. 14.
23. J. Abbott, *Indian Ritual and Belief: The Keys to Power* (cited hereafter as *Indian Ritual and Belief)*, New Delhi: Manohar, 1984, pp. 37–8.
24. Ibid., p. 8.
25. William Crooke, *An Introduction to the Popular Religion and Folklore of Northern India*, Allahabad: Government Press, NWP and Oudh, 1894, pp. 86–7.
26. Abbott, *Indian Ritual and Belief*, p. 221.
27. *Gazetteer of Ludhiana District*, 1904, p. 46.
28. *Gazetteer of Attock District*, 1907, pp. 264–6.
29. *Gazetteer of Gurdaspur District*, 1914, p. 62.
30. Abbott, *Indian Ritual and Belief*, p. 388.
31. Crooke, *Popular Religion and Folklore*, pp. 106–7. In hill areas, a stake was driven into the earth where four roads met and certain drugs and grains buried close by. It was believed that any person touching the stake would contract the disease.
32. Abbott, *Indian Ritual and Belief*, p. 170.
33. Crooke, *Popular Religion and Folklore*, p. 110.
34. Abbott, *Indian Ritual and Belief*, p. 388.
35. Crooke, *Popular Religion and Folklore*, p. 78.
36. *Gazetteer of Karnal District*, 1918, pp. 72–3.
37. *Gazetteer of Gurgaon District*, 1883–4, p. 44.

38. *Gazetteer of Delhi District,* 1883–4, pp. 57–9. Also, *Gazetteer of Delhi District*, 1912, p. 98.
39. Crooke, *Popular Religion and Folklore*, pp. 41–2.
40. *Proceedings, Home: Medical and Sanitary,* October 1880, no. 12, p. 541.
41. *Proceedings, Home: Medical and Sanitary*, December 1879, no. 11, pp. 6–7.
42. *Proceedings, Home,* October 1873, no. 5, pp. 814–15.
43. *Proceedings, Home: Medical and Sanitary*, June 1887, no. 23, p. 56.
44. *Proceedings, Home: Medical and Sanitary*, July 1887, no. 24, p. 83.
45. Major E. Inglis, *Plague in Jullundur and Hoshiarpur, 1897–8*, Lahore: Punjab Government Press, 1998, p. 15.
46. *Proceedings, Home: Medical and Sanitary*, November 1878, no. 10, p. 941. Also, *Proceedings, Home: Medical and Sanitary*, December 1879, no. 11, p. 7.
47. *Proceedings, Home: Medical and Sanitary*, February 1881, no. 13, pp. 82–3.
48. *Proceedings, Home: Medical and Sanitary*, February 1890, no. 28, pp. 9–10. Also, *Proceedings, Home: Medical and Sanitary*, January 1896, no. 40, pp. 1–6. Instances of poor vaccine operations were also reported from Khangarh in Muzaffargarh district, Satrad Kalan village in Hissar district, and villages in the districts of Gurgaon, Hissar, Karnal, Jalandhar, and Montgomery.
49. *Proceedings, Home,* April 1874, no. 6, p. 185. Also, *Proceedings, Home: Medical and Sanitary,* December 1884, no. 18, pp. 140–1. The sanitary commissioner himself wrote that he rarely found a good cicatrix in the children. The vaccinators hurriedly carried out vaccinations to show the largest number of operations to please the authorities.
50. *Proceedings, Home: Medical and Sanitary*, February 1881, no. 13, pp. 82–3. If the people resisted, the *chapras*is and vaccinators used force against them.
51. *Proceedings, Home: Medical and Sanitary*, December 1884, no. 18, p. 141.
52. *Proceedings, Home*, October 1876, no. 8, p. 661.
53. *Proceedings, Home: Medical and Sanitary*, September 1894, no. 37, pp. 163–4. Also, *Proceedings, Home: Medical and Sanitary*, May 1896, no. 40, p. 71.
54. *Proceedings, Home: Medical and Sanitary*, June 1898, no. 149, p. 2.
55. *Proceedings, Home: Medical and Sanitary*, December 1907, nos. 6–9, pp. 1–2.
56. *The Tribune*, 24 March 1904, pp. 2–3.
57. *The Tribune*, 17 April 1907, p. 3.

58. Narayani Gupta, *Delhi: Between Two Empires 1803–1931: Society, Government and Urban Growth*, New Delhi: Oxford University Press, 1981, p. 138.
59. *Khalsa Advocate*, 5 November 1918.
60. *The Tribune*, 28 April 1907, p. 3.
61. *Khalsa Advocate*, 7 November 1908.
62. *Khalsa Advocate*, 14 September 1910.
63. *Khalsa Advocate*, 27 October 1918.
64. *The Tribune*, 30 April 1901, pp. 3–4.
65. *Proceedings, Home: Medical and Sanitary*, July 1911, nos. 16–18, pp. 1–3. Also, *The Tribune*, 19 May 1911.
66. *Khalsa Advocate*, 9 September 1908.
67. *The Tribune*, 10 May 1917, p. 5.
68. *Proceedings, Home:* June 1876, no. 8, p. 337.
69. *Proceedings, Home: Medical and Sanitary*, July 1884, no. 18, p. 89.
70. *Proceedings, Home: Medical and Sanitary*, February 1881, no. 13, pp. 81–2.
71. Captain E. Wilkinson, *Report on the Inoculation in Jullundur and Hoshiarpur Districts of the Punjab October 1899–September 1900*, (cited hereafter as *Inoculation in Jullundur and Hoshiarpur 1899–1900*), Lahore: Punjab Government Press, 1901, pp. 50–1.
72. *Proceedings, Home: Medical and Sanitary,* July 1890, no. 29, pp. 40–1.
73. *Proceedings, Home*, August 1874, no. 6, p. 378. Also, *Proceedings, Home: Medical and Sanitary*, December 1879, no. 11, p. 7.
74. *Proceedings, Home: Medical and Sanitary*, December 1884, no. 18, pp. 144–5.
75. *Proceedings, Home*, April 1874, no. 6, p. 185.
76. *Proceedings, Home: Medical and Sanitary*, October 1880, no. 12, p. 540.
77. *Proceedings, Home: Medical and Sanitary*, June 1880, no. 12, pp. 342–3.
78. *Proceedings, Home: Medical and Sanitary*, July 1891, no. 30, p. 59.
79. *Proceedings, Home: Medical and Sanitary*, April 1898, no. 280B, p. 5.
80. *Proceedings, Home: Medical and Sanitary*, June 1898, no. 149, pp. 2–5.
81. *Proceedings, Home: Medical and Sanitary*, September 1897, no. 44, pp. 634a–634i.
82. *Proceedings, Home: Medical and Sanitary*, May 1904, nos. 42–3, p. 2.
83. *Proceedings, Home: Medical and Sanitary*, October 1907, no. 70, p. 75.
84. *Gazetteer of Sialkot District*, 1920, p. 31.

85. *Gazetteer of Gurdaspur District*, 1914, p. 197.
86. *Proceedings, Home: Medical and Sanitary*, April 1898, no. 273B, p. 10.
87. *Proceedings, Home: Medical and Sanitary*, June 1898, no. 148, p. 3.
88. *Gazetteer of Sialkot District*, 1920, p. 31.
89. *Proceedings, Home: Medical and Sanitary*, May 1901, no. 94B, pp. 1–3.
90. *Proceedings, Home: Medical and Sanitary*, July 1908, nos. 10–11, pp. 2–3.
91. *Proceedings, Home: Medical and Sanitary*, July 1891, no. 30, p. 42.
92. *Proceedings, Home: Medical and Sanitary*, June 1898, no. 149, p. 5.
93. *Proceedings, Home: Medical and Sanitary*, June 1898, nos. 154–5, pp. 1–2.
94. *Proceedings, Home: Medical and Sanitary*, May 1901, nos. 111–23, pp. 3–4.
95. Inglis, *Plague in Jullundur and Hoshiarpur, 1897–8*, p. 146.
96. *Proceedings, Home: Medical and Sanitary*, June 1898, nos. 154–5, pp. 1–2.
97. Inglis, *Plague in Jullundur and Hoshiarpur, 1897–8*, p. 53.
98. *Proceedings, Home: Medical and Sanitary*, December 1879, no. 11, pp. 6–7.
99. *Proceedings, Home: Medical and Sanitary*, February 1881, no. 13, p. 84.
100. *Proceedings, Home: Medical and Sanitary*, December 1879, no. 11, pp. 6–7.
101. *Proceedings, Home: Medical and Sanitary*, February 1881, no. 13, p. 84.
102. *Proceedings, Medical and Sanitary*, June 1898, nos. 122–26B, p. 1.
103. *The Tribune*, 14 May 1901, p. 3.
104. *Proceedings, Home: Medical and Sanitary*, June 1901, nos. 99–100, pp. 2–3.
105. *The Tribune*, 14 May 1901, p. 3.
106. J.M. Cunningham, *Report of the Cholera Epidemic of 1872 in Northern India*, Calcutta: Superintendent of Government Printing, 1873 (cited hereafter as *Cholera Epidemic of 1872*), pp. 4–5.
107. *Proceedings, Home*, June 1876, no. 8, p. 337.
108. *Proceedings, B, Home: Public Health*, 1931, no. 10, p. 29.
109. *Proceedings, Home: Medical and Sanitary*, June 1880, no. 12, pp. 342–3.
110. *Proceedings, Home: Medical and Sanitary*, February 1881, no. 13, p. 83.
111. *Proceedings, Home: Medical and Sanitary*, July 1884, no. 18, p. 92.

112. *Proceedings, Home: Medical and Sanitary*, April 1898, no. 273B, p. 9.
113. *Proceedings, Home: Medical and Sanitary*, June 1898, no. 149, p. 3.
114. *Proceedings, Home: Medical and Sanitary*, April 1898, no. 276B, p. 20. Also, Inglis, *Plague in Jullundur and Hoshiarpur, 1897–8*, p. 81. In another village, Dhahan, in Banga circle, an infected corpse was found locked up in a room.
115. *Proceedings, Home: Medical and Sanitary*, February 1881, no. 13, p. 83. Also, *Proceedings, Home: Medical and Sanitary*, July 1884, no. 18, p. 92; *Gazetteer of Hissar District and Loharu State*, 1904, p. 313. Such instances of people leaving their homes till the tour of the vaccinator was over were also reported from Hansi and Bhiwani in Hissar districts.
116. *The Tribune*, 24 February 1902, p. 5.
117. *The Tribune*, 9 April 1903, p. 5. Also, *Gazetteer of Hissar District and Loharu State*, 1904, p. 52.
118. *The Tribune*, 21 April 1904, p. 5.
119. *Proceedings, Home: Medical and Sanitary*, February 1881, no. 13, pp. 82–3.
120. *Proceedings, Home: Medical and Sanitary*, December 1881, no. 13, p. 83.
121. *Proceedings, Home: Medical and Sanitary*, December 1884, no. 18, pp. 140–1.
122. *Proceedings, Home: Medical and Sanitary*, December 1884, no. 18, pp. 140–1.
123. *Proceedings, Home: Medical and Sanitary*, December 1884, no. 18, pp. 140–1. For vaccinating women, the assistance of the medical mission was sought.
124. *Proceedings, Home: Medical and Sanitary*, August 1910, no. 76, p. 233.
125. Cunningham, *Report on the Cholera Epidemic of 1872*, p. 29.
126. *Proceedings, Home: Medical and Sanitary*, May 1898, nos. 16–51B, p. 5.
127. Inglis, *Plague in Jullundur and Hoshiarpur, 1897–8*, pp. 20–7.
128. *Proceedings, Home: Medical and Sanitary*, April 1897, no. 43, p. 376.
129. *Proceedings, Home: Medical and Sanitary*, January 1898, no. 45, pp. 18(2)-18(3).
130. *Proceedings, Home: Medical and Sanitary*, January 1898, no. 45, p. 20.
131. *The Tribune*, 23 April 1901, p. 5.
132. Inglis, *Plague in Jullundur and Hoshiarpur, 1897–8*, p. 137.
133. Ibid., pp. 137–9.
134. Ibid., p. 20.

135. Captain E. Wilkinson, *Report on Inoculation in Jullundur and Hoshiarpur Districts of the Punjab, October 1899–September 1900*, Lahore: Punjab Government Press, 1901, pp. 47–9.
136. Ibid., pp. 50–1.
137. *Proceedings, Home: Medical and Sanitary*, May 1887, no. 23, pp. 43–4. Also, *Proceedings, Home: Medical and Sanitary*, July 1889, no. 27, p. 283; *Proceedings, Home: Medical and Sanitary*, July 1894, no. 37, pp. 145–6.
138. *Proceedings, Home: Medical and Sanitary*, May 1887, no. 23, pp. 43–4.
139. *Proceedings, Home: Medical and Sanitary*, July 1912, no. 80, p. 80.
140. Wilkinson, *Inoculation in Jullundur and Hoshiarpur*, pp. vi-vii.
141. *Report on the Administration of the Punjab and its Dependencies for the Year 1905–06*, Lahore: Punjab Government Civil Secretariat Press, 1907, p. 50.
142. *Proceedings, Home: Medical and Sanitary*, August 1908, no. 72.
143. *Proceedings, Home: Medical and Sanitary*, July 1884, no. 18, pp. 92–3.
144. *Proceedings, Home: Medical and Sanitary*, February 1881, no. 13, p. 83.
145. *Proceedings, Home: Medical and Sanitary*, December 1884, no. 18, pp. 140–1.
146. *Proceedings, Home: Medical and Sanitary*, July 1903, nos. 46–7, p. 1.
147. *Proceedings, Home: Medical and Sanitary*, July 1891, no. 30, p. 42.
148. *Proceedings, Home: Medical and Sanitary*, July 1907, no. 70, p. 52.
149. *Proceedings, Home*, April 1874, no. 6, p. 186.
150. *Proceedings, Home: Medical and Sanitary*, February 1881, no. 13, pp. 84–5. For this purpose, Sayyids, Mullahs, Brahmans and variolators were employed as vaccinators. No person belonging to a low caste was employed.
151. *Proceedings, Home: Medical and Sanitary*, July 1891, no. 30, p. 60.
152. *Report on the Administration of the Punjab and its Dependencies for the Year 1925–6*, Lahore: Punjab Government Civil Secretariat Press, p. 111.
153. *Proceedings, B, Home: Public Health*, 1944, no. 76, p. 5.
154. *Proceedings, Home: Medical and Sanitary*, September 1898, nos. 121–9, pp. 2–3.
155. *Proceedings, Home: Medical and Sanitary*, May 1907, nos. 28–32, pp. 1–3.

156. *Proceedings, Home: Medical and Sanitary*, July 1907, nos. 32–5, p. 1. Also, *Gazetteer of Attock District*, 1907, p. 261. For instance, the district boards of Tallaganj and Pindigheb in Attock district employed *hakims* to distribute medicines during outbreaks of epidemics.
157. *Proceedings, Home: Medical and Sanitary*, June 1901, nos. 99–100, pp. 2–5.
158. *The Tribune*, 19 April 1907, p. 5.
159. Ibid., 30 April 1907, p. 5.
160. *Proceedings, B, Home: Public Health*, 1936, no. 178, p. 43.
161. *Proceedings, B, Home: Public Health*, 1934, no. 36, pp. 31–9. In addition to camps in schools and tents, the Red Cross also set up two health centres—one at Wazirabad and the other at Gujranwala. Its women health visitors visited the sick and administered medicines.
162. *Gazetteer of Gujranwala District*, 1935, p. 335.

CHAPTER 6

Home Away from Home: Punjabi-Sikhs in Eastern India

HIMADRI BANERJEE

Many of the unfortunate experiences of the closing decades of twentieth century in Punjab often complicate the reading of the Sikh past. Perhaps these led to a deep but imperceptible ethnic divide in some quarters of Punjab, Haryana and Delhi. It affected a sizeable section of north Indians and its message had sometimes crossed the geographical limits of the country. Contemporary Indian political developments not only stimulated deep reactions among the Sikh diasporic population, but also paved the way for the introduction of a few important faculty positions in some of the prestigious universities of North America.[1]

The rigorous scrutiny of the Sikh sacred sources in some of these academic institutions across the Atlantic, however, has been seen as 'deliberate attacks' upon the community's religious beliefs and historical traditions, and have evoked mixed reactions in its ranks.[2] All these ongoing debates among the Sikhs on the varied spectrum of studies of Sikhism in the West help to locate a paradigm shift in Sikh studies. The present has considerably encouraged a wider review of the Sikh past beyond the territorial limits of Punjab in the near future.

Authorities on Sikhism in India continue to miss some of the important areas of the Panthic encounters at the all-India level. Numerous Sikh settlements grew up in different parts of India over the last few centuries. Compared to the total Sikh population, these are minuscule units and their significance cannot be determined in terms of their small demographic size.[3] They offer an interesting opportunity of appreciating how the message of Sikh Gurus has been kept alive in a predominantly non-Sikh milieu.

The varied history of these settlements has so far received only casual attention. Thus the Assamese-Sikh past of the Brahmaputra Valley still stands beyond any scholarly scrutiny.[4] We are yet to have any professional historian studying the history of the Dakhani Sikhs of the erstwhile princely state of Hyderabad.[5] The reconstruction of the three-hundred-year long history of the Bihari-Sikhs has almost been a mere bureaucratic endeavour.[6] Again the legacy of the medieval Nanakpanthi-Udasi tradition in the sacred space of Puri is an illusive domain for the Sikh settlers of Cuttack, Bhubaneswar and Sambalpur of the post-Independence decades![7] Even the story of the smouldering caste rivalry in Shillong's Sikh world around Bara Bazaar and Police Bazaar is largely unknown beyond the Khasi Hills.[8] It is not certain when and how these fragmented Sikh pasts can be incorporated within the arena of Sikh studies. Their inclusion would be a welcome addition to one's wider understanding of the history of the Sikhs of Punjab.

This chapter is broadly divided into four sections. After a brief introduction, the history of the Calcutta Sikhs is discussed in the next section. There an attempt has been made to show how numerous factors contributed to the growth of the Sikh population in the city, the reasons for its closer ties with the politics and culture of Punjab and its resultant impact on the Sikh settlement of the locality. The next section outlines the Ramgarhia past of upper Assam. Here the discussion has been initiated with a brief reference to the causes of Ramgarhia domination in Assam and their 'politics of silence' regarding contemporary Akali politics in Punjab. Also analysed are their contributions to the wider Ramgarhia Movement of Punjab. Finally, the concluding section seeks to examine the nature of relationship between the Sikh world of Punjab and that of eastern India. It also attempts to argue whether the relationship offers any pointers regarding the hierarchy and stratification in the contemporary Sikh world.

SOURCES AND METHOD

My area of research is the history of the Sikhs and Sikhism of eastern India under colonial rule. I therefore need to specify its relevance and significance in this volume which aims to outline some of the major trends of social transformation in northwestern India, especially those of the Sikh world of the last five hundred years. I seek to review some of the main issues to which the Sikhs of eastern India had often responded and the way in which they contributed to the changing socio-political developments in far away Punjab. In this context I would also like to explore whether their interactions had left behind any permanent imprint upon the community. For this I would be referring to those Sikhs whose mother tongue is Punjabi and who (generally) follow the dress code, food habits, rituals and lifestyle of their brethren from Punjab. Their settlements are situated in distant places—some are separated by more than 1,000 miles. Many of the residents have permanent ties with Punjab, regard it as their home and visit it at regular intervals. Thus any major political development of Punjab was bound to have some immediate repercussions upon them. In a sense, they constitute a 'petite Punjab' away from Punjab, though they are less than 1 per cent of the total Sikh population.[9]

Any attempt at reconstructing their past would, however, be incomplete if the role of the colonial state as well as its crucial relationship with these groups is not reviewed simultaneously. It is imperative because the Sikhs of Punjab have been projected as the defenders of the British administration since the post-Mutiny years. Thus the intervention of the British Raj at different levels of the regional politics and economy would constitute another important area of my enquiry. Broadly speaking, I have brought under scrutiny the first five decades of the twentieth century when the struggle for freedom created another interesting space for interactions between the Sikhs of Punjab and their fellow religionists in eastern Indian provinces, thereby extending the scope of the Sikh past beyond Punjab. Finally, in this study Punjab refers to the undivided Land of the Five Rivers till 1947 while the focus on eastern India would be confined to the two specific areas of Sikh settlements, viz., the city of Calcutta (now Kolkata) and the Brahmaputra Valley.

The territorial limits of my enquiry are partly determined by the nature and extent of the availability of relevant source materials. Secondly, the reconstruction of the history of two different Sikh settlements in the widely separated tracts of eastern India is likely to offer a micro-level distinctiveness to the local Sikh world outside Punjab. Thirdly, in their selection special importance has been attached to the complex and varied human profile of these two areas, which may provide an additional opportunity for analysing certain unique forms and levels of interactions between the Sikh world of Punjab and its counterpart in eastern India.

Let us first review the Calcutta-Sikh scenario. Here one would be encountering a few well-known features of Jat 'preponderance' in the Sikh Panth which many senior British civilians and modern social scientists have often come across in the Manjha-Malwa-Doaba districts of Punjab. They emphasize the close linkage of the Jats with the rural Sikh identity as well as the twentieth-century politics of the Akalis. All these have made Sikhism and 'Jatism' almost two sides of a common social experience and religious belief system. It was discernible not only in Punjab but also in Calcutta.[10] There were other Sikh groups like the Khatris, Ramgarhias and Ahluwalias who added to the demographic heterogeneity of the metropolis. Many of them enthusiastically responded to the different Akali programmes beginning with the Gurdwara Reforms Movement (1920s) that survived beyond the tragic days of the Operation Blue Star (1984). In most cases the Jats had been in the forefront of these movements and generally maintained their leadership throughout the period.

In the same period the Brahmaputra Valley Sikhs had a distinct past as well as a different demographic composition. The steady immigration of the Ramgarhias, an artisan community from rural Punjab, began with the gradual economic transformation of the region under colonial rule. With their hereditary expertise in manufacturing different indigenous machineries associated with agriculture and their ability to keep these tools in working condition made them an important human factor in the industrialization of Assam through key sectors like oil, coal, tea, timber and the railways. Their technical skill coupled with managerial proficiency and hard labour in different industrial organizations initially run and controlled by European agencies offered them important employment opportunities. Here they worked under conditions very different from what they had experienced in their native villages in Punjab.[11] Similarly the nature of their jobs as well as employment opportunities also differed significantly from the Sikhs of the Calcutta metropolis. These two dissimilar situations in two widely separated Sikh settlements of eastern India – one in a big city with enough demographic plurality and the other confined to a particular caste group (i.e. Ramgarhias) scattered in small isolated pockets over five hundred miles in the Assam Valley from Guwahati to Digboi – may add a few interesting dimensions to the enquiry.

My study of the Calcutta Sikhs is based on the British Intelligence Branch records preserved in the West Bengal State Archives, newspapers reports, printed Punjabi sources and personal reminiscences of a number of older Sikhs of Calcutta. The different categories of sources often supplement each other and offer an interesting profile of the Calcutta Sikhs of this period. Of these, again, the different governmental agencies generally offered the most comprehensive and detailed account on the varied nature of the Sikh political activities in the city. Yet these sources did not provide adequate information on the contemporary Sikh cultural agendas. I had to depend on some other non-official sources in this regard.

Assam government records, however, miss much of the richness of their Bengal counterparts. They hardly throw any significant light on the Ramgarhia settlements of the Assam Valley. I, therefore, have to depend primarily on a few written and oral testimonies of the community of a later date. A sizeable portion of the sources was collected during my different trips to Guwahati, Jorhat, Tezpur, Dibrugarh and Digboi.[12] It was my privilege that the informants from the Ramgarhia community maintained their contact long after my visits to those places. Later, even some of the descendants of the first group of the Ramgarhia pioneers contacted me over the telephone and wrote letters. They communicated their families' past blending it with many interesting details of their ties with Punjab. Some others sent me a few souvenirs brought out on the occasion of the annual meetings of local Sikh bodies. One even mailed me a few scattered pages of a caste journal carrying interesting information on the activities of their eastern Indian brethren in Assam. Such sources often carry personal bias and therefore need to be cross-checked with other materials, if possible.

I also had the privilege of consulting many of the old files of *The Ramgarhia Gazette* published regularly from Simla since 1922.[13] Besides, other categories of private papers, like diaries, last testaments and account books of one or two Ramgarhia families would occasionally figure in the enquiry. A few of them refer to their important links with the Ramgarhia Educational Institutions at Phagwara and therefore offer some meaningful insights to the investigation. While reviewing these varied sources, I have also made a quick survey of some of the relevant diaspora writings on the Sikhs to evaluate if these patterns of Sikh dispersal within India provide any indication of the bigger migration experiences of the second half of the twentieth century.[14]

THE SIKHS OF CALCUTTA

It is widely assumed that the Sikh perception of British rule underwent a paradigm shift during the last phase of the Singh Sabha movement in the early years of the twentieth century.[15] Contemporary Punjabi rural society had other causes of complaint against the Raj. It began with the Chenab Canal Colony agitation of the Punjab peasantry (1907) and soon its leadership was taken up by a section of the urban middle class. They were no less dissatisfied with the colonial politics restricting their employment, electoral and political opportunities. It is not certain if the message of Swadeshi and Boycott from Bengal provided an additional stimulus to the politics of *nai hawa* (new wave) under Denzil Ibbetson, the lieutenant-governor of Punjab (1907–8). Later on the province continued to witness the ravages of World War I: price rise, demobilization, the radical voice of the Ghadar, the havoc of influenza, the Rowlatt Satyagraha, the Jallianwalla Bagh massacre and, above all, the call for the Non-Cooperation Movement and the consequent Akali struggle for gurdwara reforms. These developments turned Punjab into a major battleground for the national struggle.[16] They paved the way for a wider cooperation with the radical politics of Bengal.

Even prior to these developments, the Sikhs had numerous

links with the city. Maharaja Ranjit Singh's *vakil*s as well as a few displaced nobles of the Khalsa *darbar* occasionally visited the place owing to its growing political importance. Sikh soldiers serving the colonial army were present here in the post-Mutiny years. During his brief stay in the British-Indian capital, Maharaja Duleep Singh met a few of them (1861) who had just returned after the Second Anglo-Chinese War. Actually these soldiers were often in and out of the city in connection with the different military expeditions of the British Raj. Traders from Punjab visited Calcutta as the railways significantly reduced the distance between the two wings of the empire. In the early years of the twentieth century, the metropolis witnessed the introduction of the modern surface communication system. It sent important signals to many Sikhs interested in owning or driving different types of automobiles.

Here the domination of the Jat Sikh bus and taxi drivers-cum-owners was evident right from the beginning. Even the big industrial organizations, commercial warehouses, factories, among others, employed Sikhs as security guards and *darwan*s. Besides, the railways, by engaging a number of Sikh technical hands in its different workshops in and around the city, namely, Kharagpur and Kanchrapara in the early years of the twentieth century, added to the local demographic heterogeneity. These Sikhs were possibly the Ramgarhias. Closely following them were a number of Punjabi hoteliers and automobile spare-parts dealers in the city. They were most likely Jats, but the presence of Khatris cannot altogether be ruled out.[17] They added colour and complexity to the local Sikh demography. The rise of Calcutta as the most important port of embarkation for emigration to the different Far-East and South-East Asian countries sometimes served as an additional stimulus to the growing Sikh presence in eastern India.[18]

These developments made Calcutta an important centre of Sikh activity in eastern India. Immigrants did not always miss the older ties with their place of birth. Many of them maintained regular contact through personal visits, letters, remittances or meeting friends who had recently returned from Punjab. Already the Ghadarite encounter at Budge Budge (1914) had placed Calcutta on the twentieth-century political map of the Sikhs.[19]

Later on, many Ghadarites embraced Marxist ideology, participating in the Communist Movement and establishing closer links with their counterparts in Bengal. Contemporary British Intelligence records offer many interesting phases of their interactions. Names like Baba Gurdit Singh, Genda Singh and Balwant Singh Pardeshi frequently figure in their proceedings.[20] There were even proposals of sending a few important Communist leaders from Bengal to Punjab for a political dialogue between the two distant parts of the British-Indian Empire.[21] A few others established closer ties with the Kirti Kishan Party and the Naujawan Sabha of Punjab (1933) while others joined the ranks of the Peasants and Workers Party.

The Gurdwara Reforms Movement of the 1920s deepened some of these connections and offered the city its most enduring link with the Sikh politics of Punjab. Non-violent Akali resistance to the Raj had already received the support of the Congress leadership at the national level. The struggle, therefore, had an increasing influence on the Calcutta Sikh politics of the 1920s. Besides sending *satyagrahis* for some of the major *morchas* (campaigns) in Punjab, local Sikhs raised a *shahidi* (martyr) fund, distributed leaflets depicting the political sacrifices of the Akalis, highlighted British police repression on their *jathas* (groups) and held *diwans* (religious meetings) in the gurdwaras at Ballygunge (Bakul Bagan Road) or Jagat Sudhar (Kalighat). The meetings were sometimes addressed by important nationalist leaders like Subhas Chandra Bose and Jatindra Mohan Sengupta and even resulted in processions on some major streets of the city.[22] Whenever any senior Sikh leader with some Shiromani Gurdwara Prabandhak Committee (SGPC) or Congress link came to Calcutta, he was given a hearty welcome at the railway station. Later he was taken to the local gurdwara for a comfortable stay in the city. Generally he addressed the local *sangat* (religious assembly) and was then given a rousing send-off. The meetings were widely publicized beforehand so that they were well attended. Sometimes *ragis* (musicians) from Punjab arrived in the city on their way to Burma and beyond for their fund-raising campaigns. They too did not miss out on the usual Sikh hospitality of the city.

Akali politics increasingly radicalized the Sikhs of Calcutta. A few of them had occasionally encountered police harassment in the streets of the metropolis in the 1910s. The new political developments in Punjab prompted them to form a Bengal unit of the Akali Dal and rally under its banner. It spearheaded many of the major protest marches against the Raj. Contemporary British intelligence sources portrayed it as a movement of the 'lower class Sikhs' of bus and taxi drivers-cum-owners. Soon the ranks of the protestors were swelled by others, many of whom were *darwans* (security personnel). The message of the Akali struggle emboldened them to set up links with the wider transport trade union politics of the city. Later on they formed the Bengal Khalsa Bus Syndicate for 'improving' and 'safeguarding' the interests of Sikh 'drivers, conductors, cleaners and owners of buses, taxis and similar vehicles' against the 'alleged *zulm* (oppression) of the Police'.[23] They became more and more restive and critical of the government in the different *diwans* of the gurdwaras. Their supporters raised funds 'for propaganda work and test cases against the police'. Sometimes their demonstrations became violent. Protestors went down the streets and took the path of open resistance against the British Raj. In response to the call to boycott the Simon Commission (1928), they kept their buses and taxis off the roads on the day of the strike. Their radical politics reached a new height during the days of the Civil Disobedience Movement in the early 1930s.

The growing dominance of the Akalis and the presence of an increasing Punjabi-Sikh population had other long-term implications. They made the local populace increasingly aware of the significance of gurdwaras in the life and politics of the Sikhs. The institution was nothing new to the city. The Calcuttans knew of the 'native' Bihari-Sikhs and their gurdwaras around Bara Bazaar in central Calcutta. Prior to the movement of the Akalis, there had been occasional tussles for the control of the Bada Sikh Sangat.[24] Their struggle, however, had never been as complex or long drawn as the local Akalis had made it since the 1920s. In the course of the next two decades, the mercury of the Akali politics sometimes rose high, but it never led to any major bloody outburst.

Of the different early twentieth-century gurdwaras in Calcutta, the Punjabi-Sikhs controlled two of them since their foundation.

Both of them were closely linked with their expanding settlements in Bhowanipur, Garcha, Paddapukur and Kalighat in south Calcutta. One was on the Bakulbagan Road marking almost the northernmost limit of their habitation while the other still stands near the Rashbehari Avenue under the management of Sri Guru Singh Sabha, Calcutta.[25] During those days, the gurdwaras provided a platform for holding regular meetings and for mobilizing public opinion in support of different Akali political programmes. It is likely that the different Akali game plans against the management of the Bada Sikh Sangat were first elaborated here, but no one ever came forward to forcibly take possession of it.[26]

The Akalis had a long list of complaints against the management board of the Bada Sikh Sangat controlled by the Bihari-Sikhs (representing a different ethnic Sikh group from them at the local level). The board was accused of gross violations of certain Sikh rituals (for example, the continuation of Hindu practices like *arati* or prayer with oil lamp), the misappropriation of *golak* (gurdwara funds), the mortgaging of gurdwara property to outsiders, the long and costly legal battles by its executive body, etc. All these led to a steady deterioration in the regular *langar* (common kitchen) service and the normal residential facility extended to Sikh immigrants on their way to South-East Asia or Australia. Perhaps, the most important source of their irritation was the board's close connection with the authorities of the Patna Harimandir which held a different political opinion from that of the SGPC, Amritsar.[27] The presence of a few non-Khalsa members in its management board perhaps made matters even worse.

Against this background came the Punjab Sikh Gurdwaras and Shrines Act of 1925 (Act VIII of 1925) virtually giving the Akalis of Punjab firm control over the different gurdwaras within the territorial limits of Punjab. In Bengal, however, it did not offer them any similar legal authority over the management of the Bada Sikh Sangat.[28] This intensified the frustration of the local Akalis. In the past few years, they had gradually realized that the running of the Bada Sikh Sangat was not all a bed of roses. Except for its 'historic' association with the name of the founder of the Sikh Panth, it had virtually lost all its old grandeur, organizational infrastructure and financial assets. Infighting among its board members discouraged devotees from assembling there on the days of Baisakhi. Even the SGPC believed that control of the gurdwara was more a financial liability than anything else.

A section of the existing board members appealed to the SGPC for its immediate intervention as they found it impossible to negotiate the chronic debt burden of the gurdwara. The local Akalis endorsed the proposal. This, however, put the apex Sikh body in a very difficult situation. Neither could it ignore the appeal of the local *sangat* nor did it have enough legal endorsement under the Punjab Act of VIII of 1925 to take over the management of the gurdwara. Besides, the huge debt burden heightened its dilemma. Considering the prevalent Sikh euphoria about it, a section of the local Akalis were ready to come forward and extend moral support to the SGPC taking over of this financially crippled and a faction-ridden gurdwara, far away from its headquarters.[29]

The ineffectiveness of the Punjab Act VIII of 1925 in eastern India, however, provided the SGPC, disgruntled forces in the management board of the Bada Sikh Sangat and the colonial administration with a convenient escape route. Local anti-SGPC elements in the management board were never happy with the dominance of the Akalis for the latter had tried to introduce many corrective measures affecting their position in the *sangat*. Similarly, [the pro-SGPC local Akalis] found it extremely difficult to increase the income of the gurdwara so that its huge deficit could be made good within a short span of time. Finally, the local administration was no less apprehensive of the activities of the SGPC in a territory not legally endorsed under the Act VIII of 1925.

It seemed that all three contending parties were in no mood to continue the existing arrangement in the Bada Sikh Sangat. The Calcutta High Court also struck down the agreement. It reshuffled the management board of the gurdwara and handed it over to a High Court-appointed Receiver (1927?). He was Sir Sunder Singh Majithia (1872–1941), a moderate Sikh member of the Punjab legislative council with close links with the Punjab administration as well as the important Akali leaders of the period.[30] The SGPC agreed to the new settlement. This may have been due partly to its weak legal position in eastern India and partly to the presence of a centrist Sikh leader like Majithia as the head of the new trust board. Perhaps the appointment of a Receiver of the High Court also relieved the SGPC of a burden which was quite unpleasant.

The functioning of the new board was, however, beset with numerous difficulties. Initially, it had promised to offer the local Punjabi-Sikhs some control over the gurdwara administration. Majithia was not readily available in Calcutta owing to his numerous commitments to Punjab politics. The day-to-day functioning of the board, however, could hardly satisfy the local Akalis. It could not even keep a check on the financial irregularities of the gurdwara fund. The Bengal government also realized that the board needed an immediate overhauling so that it could withstand the scathing Akali criticism. It was seriously in search of an amicable solution which would not only neutralize the local Akalis but also put an end to the long-standing financial mismanagement and the chronic administrative disorder in the Bada Sikh Sangat Trust Board. It was therefore looking for an honest Sikh who would try to restore the pristine glory of the Bada Sikh Sangat.

During these years the government had also developed a better understanding of the Sikh situation of Calcutta. It had realized that all Calcutta Sikhs, including their Akali protagonists, had different political ideologies and plan of actions. They were not always in favour of the radical politics of the early 1920s. The different secret official reports of the late 1920s and early 1930s increasingly emphasized the presence of a growing division in the Akali ranks. The old position of Baba Gurdit Singh had steadily come under serious challenge. He had already been imprisoned for his aggressive speeches in different Sunday gurdwara meetings. This had a temporary 'sobering effect' upon him. The local-level Congress leadership also found it difficult to go along with his different aggressive political postures. In Niranjan Singh Talib of the newspaper *Daily Desh-Darpan* published at the Kavi Press (1933), they perhaps found a convenient political face [to] negotiate whenever necessary with the local Sikh world. Similarly, Raghbir Singh Bir (1896–1974), with his moderate strategy, provided an alternative to the radical politics of the Baba. After his departure from Lahore, Bir had been active in Calcutta Akali politics since 1922/3. He had successfully opposed Gurdit Singh's leadership in the Khalsa Bus Syndicate (1928) resulting in a major split in the organization.[31] This might have partly affected Akali militancy in the city. These fissures in the Akali ranks offered the local administration an opportunity for manoeuvring with the different shades of the Akalis.

The Bengal government identified a small creamy layer among the Sikhs of Calcutta. Many of them had been certain beneficiaries of British rule. A section of them had friendly relations with the moderate Sikh leadership of Punjab and Calcutta. The local administration thought of making the best use of these complex affable ties in the reorganization of the Bada Sikh Sangat management board, although any definite documentary evidence pointing out the different stages of these behind-the-scene negotiations is not available.[32] Finally, one High Court (Calcutta) ruling of 1932 pulled out a big surprise. It suggested the name of Laddha Singh Bedi (1878–1939) as the sole trustee of the Bada Sikh Sangat.[33]

As a descendant of Guru Nanak's family, Baba Laddha Singh Bedi was widely venerated in Calcutta and Punjab. Bedi had been in the city for nearly thirty years and was known for his enthusiastic support of the cause of Sikh education and religion. He was equally regarded for his 'sound' business acumen which helped him to make a fortune from the coalmines in Ranigunj (Burdwan district) and railway construction works, till then a closed preserve of British loyalists.[34] Bedi had never been part of any political activity of the Akalis though they had generally respected him as a devout Sikh. His pious Sikh image steadily grew in the late 1920s and contributed much to his elevation as the president of the management board of the Jagat Sudhar Gurdwara (Kalighat) in 1930. He continued to be regarded as the most presentable Sikh personality not only by the larger sections of the Calcutta Sikhs but also the British administration resulting in his nomination for president of the new Trustee Board of the Bada Sikh Sangat in the mid-1932.[35]

With Bedi at the helm of administration of the Bada Sikh

Sangat (February 1933), certain significant changes started taking place. Soon the board, with the prior approval of the High Court, introduced certain modifications in its size, administrative procedures and election schedule. Within a period of another four years (April 1937), it could confidently announce 'the repayment of all its debts', but also pride itself for holding elections as per the directives of the High Court, Calcutta. Simultaneously, it initiated a vigorous policy of damage control with regard to the different daily services of the gurdwara as well as its fund management. Thus, before his death in 1939, Bedi had once again set the Bada Sikh Sangat back on track. The Board had successfully accommodated the local Akalis while curtailing their radical politics. Its creditors had also got back their respective dues. Even the Bengal government had every reason to be happy with the performance of the Trustee Board: it had celebrated Baisakhi with its usual festivity, and also restored the practices of keeping the *sangat* open for pilgrims and immigrants on their way to the different countries beyond India.[36]

These achievements of the Trustee Board were, no doubt, partly Baba Laddha Singh's personal success story. His individual charisma as a member of Guru Nanak's *jati*, his wide acceptability among the different levels of the colonial bureaucracy, and above all, the massive financial support he received to make good the deficit of the Bada Sikh Sangat contributed much to its change for the better. After the Baba's death, his son succeeded him (December 1939), who, however, made no secret of his financial inability to run the show (1941). Actually Baba's death took place at a very crucial time. He had already witnessed the beginning of World War II as well as the renewal of the radical politics of the nationalists in Bengal. With his passing away, the Bada Sikh Sangat not only resumed legal battles on different minor local issues, but also opened newer avenues of confrontational politics with the nationalists in Calcutta city.[37]

In the early 1940s, the local government, however, expressed deep satisfaction with the functioning of the Bada Sikh Sangat. The Board was reported to be firmly 'under the control of well-meaning rich Sikhs' who could successfully keep the different 'subversive' forces under their control. Even Gurdwara Jagat Sudhar, the next important gurdwara of the city, became more or less free from the influence of the Akalis. There were two major national and international developments which largely relieved the government of the radical Sikh politics of the city. One was the progress of the Second World War and the Shiromani Akali Dal's decision to extend necessary 'support' to the 'war efforts' of the British Raj in Punjab that had virtually made the Akalis an inactive and 'moribund' force in the city. Also, during these years the powerful Bus Syndicate had lost much of its earlier political cohesion.

The sudden lull in Akali political activity in the city brings to light its intimate links with the Sikh politics of Punjab. A few radical Sikhs, with their close ties with the local Communist leadership, might have occasionally taken out protest marches in the city, but the predominant section of the Akalis either remained dormant or kept themselves away from the [radical] political activities of the city. They were increasingly concerned with the partition of Punjab and its unfortunate implications for the Sikhs. The British administration also used different coercive tactics to restrain those Calcutta Sikh politicians who had close links with the nationalist politics of the Congress. Many of them were sent to prison. The newspaper, *Daily Desh-Darpan*, was declared politically 'offensive' and was forcefully withdrawn from circulation. Taken as a whole, Sikh politics in Calcutta in the early 1940s became increasingly quiet. It did not even dare to disturb the colonial administration because moderate leaders like Raghbir Singh and his associates more or less then dominated the local scene.

The uneasy silence, however, underlined that something serious was in the pipeline of the Sikhs. The growing reality of the partition of Punjab and the beginning of a long chain of communal riots resulted in a definite change in their political mood. The failure of the Akalis to resist the partition of Punjab generated anger and frustration. It found expression in their active participation in the Calcutta communal riots of August 1946. A few sources have referred to the Hindu-Sikh collaboration against the Muslims during the days of the communal holocaust in the city.[38] Sometimes these Sikhs had been aggressive even with the weaker Bihari-Sikhs who represented a small segment of the local Sikh population. Taking advantage of the tumultuous situation of the city, one of their gurdwaras in central Calcutta was first desecrated and then forcefully taken over by the Punjabi-Sikhs.[39] The aggressors had been looking forward to such an opportunity since the days of the Gurdwara Reforms Movement (1920–6), but had failed due to the strong presence of the colonial administration. During these days the Akalis had also failed to rally adequate public support in their favour. But in mid-1946 there had been a radical shift in the old scenario. In the midst of a general communal unrest and mass slaughter, the Punjabi-Sikhs achieved their target.[40] Here the Akali movement of the 1920s perhaps broke some of the previous rules of its game for it had now to play on a different turf.

In the midst of all these political developments, a gradual change was taking place in the social profile of the Sikh community in Calcutta. In the early years of the twentieth century, the community initially consisted of men from the transport world. They required not only adequate space for parking their vehicles, but also ready cash for running their business. These factors generally discouraged them from spending on a larger sum on renting residential spaces in the densely populated areas of central Calcutta. On the other hand, the sparsely inhabited southern localities around Bhowanipur offered the new migrants greater opportunity to rent additional space for their residence, kitchen and garage at a lower price. In an all-male domain, many could stay together at a minimum cost, sharing the living room, kitchen and toilet.

The Bakulbagan gurdwara came up very close to the Punjabi-Sikh settlement in Bhowanipur-Paddapukur area. It was situated on a road of the same name in a locality predominantly inhabited by men from the transport world. Many of them were drivers while others worked round the clock to keep their taxis or buses in perfect running condition. It is likely that the space around the Bakulbagan Road leading to Paddapukur Park constituted an important core area of the Punjabi-Sikh settlement in south Calcutta. Later on, it pushed steadily towards the south till it had reached the Hazra Park–Kalighat area.

In the early 1930s, the Calcutta Sikhs were no longer a community of first-generation male migrants working hard for their daily living. As the businesses of some of them flourished, they had to spend a larger part of their time away from home, moving from place to place, supervising their respective trades with adequate expertise and seriousness. Some tried setting up a small office to monitor their business from a central place. They naturally felt the need to appoint one or two subordinates to supervise their trade at different points. The commercial success of Inder Singh Mahajan as a hotelier or Raghbir Singh Bir as the owner of nearly forty taxis within a decade may be dated back to this period. Both of them gradually transferred a part of their profits from one trade to another, the second being very different from the first one.[41] Thus Mahajan opened a cloth store while Bir, a poet, entered the print world, joining the *Daily Desh-Darpan* in the late 1930s.

There were many such success stories during the same decade.[42] Their rise underlined the growing differentiation among the Calcutta Sikhs. Perhaps many of them eventually felt the need to bring their women folk from Punjab. The presence of women led to the growth of individual households, the cooking of Punjabi food, as well as the presence of guests on festive occasions. This in turn resulted in the steady rise of newer demands at the family level (gradual change in the consumption pattern) and a consequent increase in the cost of living.[43] Many community kitchens thus gave way to nuclear family hearths with younger couples. (These experiences facilitated the development of a small domesticity facilitating women's participation at the different levels of family life, which was steadily growing distinct from the male dominated public space where the varying waves of Punjab politics as well as the growing demands of everyday life often ruled the roost.)

With the consequent birth of a new generation, many of whom were born outside Punjab, the Calcutta-Sikh population steadily transformed itself from an 'immigrant to a minority community'. It looked forward to additional space for uninterrupted religious instructions and newer educational facilities in the city. After long deliberations and debates, a new gurdwara as well as a Khalsa School came up in their core settlement area in south Calcutta. The gurdwara offered the community a religious place as well as 'a social centre for education and the elderly'. It was named Gurdwara Jagat Sudhar (Kalighat) and remained under the supervision of the Sri Guru Singh Sabha, Calcutta (1930).[44]

The Khalsa School was established in 1935. It was expected to provide the younger generation the best secular training commensurate with the Sikh religious traditions. Thus living far away from their place of birth, the Calcutta Sikhs still sought to keep the community responsive to its cultural roots and religious education.[45] The extent of the success of these attempts, however, needs to be debated. Their gurdwaras had sometimes been accused of perpetuating group rivalry and political intrigue among the seniors (belonging to different Akali factions), while the Khalsa School came to be denounced as the epicentre of numerous disruptive forces affecting the students in their teens. Nonetheless, these two institutions produced a few front-ranking Sikh leaders who played an important role in the Akali politics in Punjab in the post-Independence decades.[46]

Although the bulk of the early Calcutta Sikhs were bus drivers, taxi owners, hoteliers, contractors and security personnel, a small section of them also made some significant contributions to the enrichment of Punjabi literature and press. They were primarily the product of the Ghadarite and Akali struggles.[47] The political climate of the city brought them closer to some of these experiences. It is likely that they had already been working as a group in Bhowanipur area (1919). On *gurpurab*s (1922) they read out patriotic poems and distributed printed tracts, leaflets, etc.[48] It is likely that these were not printed in Calcutta. The great success of the Punjabi print world would have to wait a few more years till the arrival of Munsha Singh Dukhi (1890–1971) in the city from Punjab.[49] Dukhi had intimate links with the Ghadarite revolutionaries. This led to his imprisonment during World War I. After his release from British jails, he came to Calcutta (1920). As a man of radical politics, he decided to write the poetry of protest so that his mother tongue could become a popular vehicle for nationalist expression. During his eleven years of stay (1920–31), he devoted much of his time and energy to the publication of a literary journal and the setting up a Punjabi press in the city. These initiatives not only earned him a permanent place in the development of Punjabi literature but also brought into the limelight some of the significant linkages that the Sikhs of Calcutta had with Punjab.

A sizeable part of the creative writings of Dukhi had a close relation with the different Akali *morchas* of the 1920s. In 1925 his first collection of poems entitled *Prem Gatha* was published. It highlighted the sacrifices of the Akalis at Nankana Sahib, Guru-ka-Bagh and Jaito. Perhaps the long absence from the place of his birth made him even more sensitive to the sacrifices of the Akalis. With regular feedbacks from Punjab, he tried to internalize these sufferings and sought to convey his understanding in the language of the common man. His poems might not be of great poetic height, but the sincerity of his emotions made them valuable. He also translated two novels (1927 and 1928), one from Bengali (*Anandamath*) and the other from English (*Uncle Tom's Cabin*). Dukhi selected these two classics from two different literatures because both of them conveyed the message of protest and revolt, which had been the main thrust of his writings.[50]

Dukhi had also been toying with the idea of setting up a formal literary group where he could work with others for the development and enrichment of the Punjabi language in Calcutta. It led to the formation of the Kavi Kuthia literary group (1922). Here he established contacts with other budding poets of his generation, one of them being Saudagar Singh Bhikhari (1898–1992), a Ramgarhia Sikh who had recently returned from his brief East African sojourn. Bhikhari remained in the city till the mid-1950s and actively participated in different ongoing literary experiments. Dukhi's lifelong friendship with Bhikhari yielded many enduring results. One of them was the publication of a monthly literary magazine *Kavi* (1923). The Calcutta chapter, however, reflects a fruitful relationship with the magazine's Punjab counterparts and it received regular contributions from many of the front-ranking litterateurs of the province. Initially, the *Kavi* was printed in Punjab and copies were later on taken to Calcutta for sale and distribution. This proved to be costly and inconvenient and was therefore quickly abandoned. In 1927 a new Punjabi press was set up in Calcutta for the publication of the *Kavi*.[51] It carried the message of protest, nationalism and revolution to the wider Punjabi world. The British, however, were quick to take action. The press was seized and publication was stopped with immediate effect (1931).

This also led to an abrupt end of the Dukhi-Bhikhari phase of Punjabi literary experiments in Calcutta. It is uncertain whether the closure of the press was partly due to demise a deterioration of the relationship between them. But the British police assault quickened its demise. During its brief period of existence in the city, the press could claim some significant achievements. It successfully laid the foundation of a literary platform which was the first of its kind outside Punjab. It brought together other Punjabi poets, journalists, short-story writers and critics of different shades under a common banner. A few of them mailed their contributions directly from Punjab. They were not all Sikhs. This fact underlines the significance of the mother tongue (Punjabi) conveyed through the medium of print culture. Its message could cut across religious affiliations and the physical distance that separated Punjab from Bengal. Further, when communal political considerations had already made deep inroads into the Indian political scenario, in Bengal the Punjabi language continued to seek its roots in a common cultural heritage beyond narrow religious affiliations.

These literary experiments steadily crossed the limits of Calcutta and made them an integral part of the wider Punjabi cultural milieu. They highlight an interesting cultural space of the Calcutta Sikh often missed by the historians of Bengal and even of Punjab. The local Sikh milieu was no doubt dominated by men from the world of surface transport and the radical Akalis around gurdwaras, but it did not fail to produce an important literary group with a regular Punjab linkage. The *Kavi* might have temporarily stopped publication, but the succeeding generation of poets and journalists continued to carry forward its incomplete task which had its beginning with the publication of a new Punjabi nationalist daily from Calcutta. This was the *Daily Desh-Darpan* (1933) and its founding editor was Niranjan Singh Talib. Since then the management of the newspaper, as well as its ideology and the area of focus, has changed many times, but it continues even today as an interesting mouthpiece of the local Punjabi world.[52] In the post-

Independence years, it competes with another daily of tabloid size since the early 1960s – the *Navi-Parbhat* – which seeks to establish newer channels of political contacts with Punjab. Their varied political ideals as well as conflicting economic interests at the local level have often created more of a cacophony with very little permanent impact on the contemporary Punjab scenario.

THE RAMGARHIA SIKHS OF ASSAM

In the first quarter of the twentieth century, Assam drew a few hundred Ramgarhias from the districts of Gurdaspur and Amritsar despite the constraints like heavy monsoon rain, autumnal floods, damp climate and malaria fever. Of all the Sikh caste groups in Assam, they were the most numerous. They gradually settled down in different places from Guwahati to Margarita – a distance of more than 500 km. Their numbers steadily increased as the century rolled on. In this sense the Assam Sikh demographic profile differs significantly from the one in Calcutta.

The Ramgarhias primarily represented a composite artisan-caste group including carpenters, blacksmiths and some others. As *kamin*s (village artisans) they were long associated with the agrarian society of Punjab rendering respective caste services to rural folk and in return receiving (customary) wages at the end of the harvest.[53] As the rural social fabric experienced numerous dislocations from the last quarter of the nineteenth century onwards, the artisans showed signs of unrest and often came into conflict with the zamindars. With agrarian tensions in the background, many Ramgarhias abandoned their ancestral caste callings. The Punjab Land Alienation Act (Act XIII of 1900) debarred them from purchasing lands in rural society. It also precipitated their migration beyond the villages and in their search for other employment opportunities in the wider world.[54] Late-nineteenth-century colonial penetration led to the introduction of the railways, oil explorations, coal mining, tea cultivation and other allied economic developments in the Brahmaputra Valley and beyond. These changes encouraged many Ramgarhias to migrate in that direction.[55] *The Census of 1901* suggests that a few Sikhs had already been serving the railways in Assam.[56] Their Ramgarhia identity, however, cannot be specifically established. Later evidence, however, refers to a small Punjabi settlement near the Guwahati Railway Station. The station master was a Ramgarhia Sikh. It was perhaps through his benevolence that a few of his caste fellows managed to stay in the railway colony. It is not clear whether all his neighbours were Ramgarhias. Reviews of other sources indicate that such a situation possibly prevailed in Guwahati. The Ramgarhias laid the foundation of the first gurdwara in Guwahati in the early years of the twentieth century.[57]

The Ramgarhias were 'largely reliant on their own skill and understanding with a premium on inventiveness'. Many of them initially took up jobs laying railways lines. As they steadily pushed beyond Guwahati in the post-World War I years, they also trickled down to places in upper Assam. One such position was Mariani in central Assam which steadily grew as a railway junction and important commercial centre catering to the needs of the nearby tea gardens. Situated on the main railway line connecting Guwahati with the different tea, coal and oil producing centres of upper Assam, Mariani's heterogeneous demographic profile, with a sprinkling of Sikhs, is also mentioned in Assamese writing.[58] An unpublished diary of Charan Singh Matharu, a nonagenarian Ramgarhia, mentions[59] that many Sikh passengers usually boarded the train or alighted in Mariani after the long journey from Punjab.[60] During the post-World War I period, a large number of Ramgarhias steadily migrated to the town following the introduction of the railways in upper Assam. The same source further suggests that this was largely possible due to the personal initiative of a Ramgarhia Permanent Weigh Inspector of the region. He offered employment as well as contracts to many of his caste men from Gurdaspur district. Two of his beneficiaries were the brothers Sohan Singh and Tahel Singh who later became contractors and invited their own kinsmen from Amritsar and Gurdaspur districts. The new Ramgarhia migrants were encouraged to settle in and around Jorhat, which had been growing as an important business centre. Many of them also worked in the brisk constructions works of these two brothers. Thus kinship and caste affiliations played a significant role in the proliferation of Ramgarhia settlements in the Valley.

Their employment in the different oil fields of upper Assam is likely to have been begun even earlier. In Digboi, oil was found in the last decade of the nineteenth century. In other parts of the undivided North Lakhimpur district, coal was discovered even earlier. The railways also helped to intensify the growth of the tea and plywood industries in the neighbourhoods of Dibrugarh, Makum and Moranhat of the same district.[61] Newer employment opportunities like the strategic military construction works, road construction, maintenance of small smelting shops for iron fabrications, developments of coolie lines, repairing of tea processing machineries, driving or cleaning of automobiles, etc., kept a good number of Ramgarhias active. Early-twenty-first century oral testimonies, as well as the records of the Digboi oil factory, indirectly attest to the fact that a sizeable number of civil and military contracts were regularly bagged by two Ramgarhias whose closeness to the local officials and the completion of their assigned jobs within the stipulated time perhaps contributed to their success.[62] One of these contractors was Sunder Singh whose name was long associated with a residential locality in Digboi town while the second one was Mohan Singh Hadiabadi (1889–1964), widely known for his pioneering contributions in the development of the Ramgarhia educational institutions at Phagwara (Punjab) and to the All-India Ramgarhia Movement of the first half of the twentieth century.[63]

The Ramgarhias were found working in other sectors of the industrial and plantation economy as well. They served the transport sector as the Jats did not join in larger numbers during the pre-Independence years.[64] They were equally successful as private contractors and entrepreneurs of small engineering works. Contemporary sources outlining their early experiences (and the volume of income) in upper Assam are not available. Local Assamese sources either ignore them owing to their minuscule numbers or refer to them as mere outsiders engrafted upon the local society. These projections are likely to miss the human face of their problems.[65]

In the absence of written sources, one has to depend on the reminiscences of the later-day Ramgarhias. There are two interesting written testimonies from persons of two different generations – one (Balbir Singh Hanspal) referring to his grandfather's time (beginning with 1913) in Guwahati and the other (Wassan Singh) recalling his younger days in Jorhat nearly seventy years ago (late 1920s onwards). Balbir Singh Hanspal, an engineering graduate from the Assam Engineering Coilege (1966), writes about his grandfather Kissen Singh (1882–1945?), his father Mohinder Singh (1917–73) and also himself (1938) with detailed documents in support of his statements. He refers (euphorically) to his grandfather's struggling days as a bus driver beginning in 1913 under a British company, then the setting up of his own transport service (1917/18), and finally of his becoming a government contractor and purchasing a plot of land for his family in Guwahati (1926).

> Unlike other Ramgarhia migrants in Guwahati, it was the British people who brought him [Kissen Singh] to Assam for their work. He used to drive their buses between Guwahati and Shillong. At that time it took about two days to reach Shillong. In those days there were only five Ramgarhia families at Guwahati. By profession they were all drivers, but later on they became *thekedars* [contractors]. . . . He sent his son for higher education to Rurki from where he did his diploma in Civil Engineering. He joined hands with his father and developed the business to a large scale. . . . My grandfather left for Punjab in the year 1941 and died there in the year 1942 (approximately) at the age of 45 years. . . . I was born in 1938 in the village of Marar (Gurdaspur district) . . . I continue to live on the same land purchased by my grandfather in Guwahati. [66]

There is a good deal of confidence in the testimony of Balbir Singh. He looked back to the past when his grandfather had to work very hard to earn his livelihood, but he also seemed to be aware of the long chain of success the family experienced later on. Unlike his grandfather, he does not always seek his roots in Punjab where he was born, but regards Assam as his home.

Almost similar are the feelings of Wassan Singh Bamrah of Jorhat. A close relative of Rais Sohan Singh Matharu, he was born in 1916 in the Khujala village of Gurdaspur district. He came to Jorhat in 1928 along with senior members of his village and other relatives of the neighborhood[67] and decided to stay on in Assam. His testimony needs to be viewed with a note of caution. On certain points, it suffers from incompleteness and exaggeration owing to his old age. Otherwise Wassan Singh's oral testimony has a freshness of its own and one can almost visualize the conditions at his place of work nearly eighty years ago (2005):

> During those initial years of stay, busy work schedule generally compelled us to live as close to our place of work as possible. Still I had to walk a long distance to attend my regular duty. I could purchase a bicycle after ten years of work. Then domestic life was all a male affair. Here the younger ones usually prepared food in a common kitchen and washed the utensils and clothes of the seniors. All were huddled together in a common mess and led a struggling life. We had long working hours. Our wage rates also varied from four to one anna according to the age and efficiency of a worker. The seniors used to lead us in our place of work. We accepted their leadership without any question.

Wassan Singh's testimony carries the impression of a rigorous and disciplined life. It also suggests that he and his compatriots had come to Assam to earn as much money as possible within the minimum possible time without offending the sentiments of their supervisors. They generally worked in a group and helped their caste associates as and when needed. In recent years Wassan Singh has also built his own house. He is nearly ninety years of age and does not want to go back to his place of birth in Punjab.

Balbir Singh of Guwahati or Wassan Singh of Jorhat do not represent the contemporary minority voice of the community. There are similar testimonies of the descendants of Hukam Singh Bassan of Makum Junction, Sundar Singh Bamrah of Mariani, Tehal Singh of Jorhat, Nicka Singh of Panitola, Ganga Singh Babrah of Dibrugarh, Man Mohan Singh Hanspal of Tezpur and Mula Singh of Nagaon.[68] Their forefathers came to Assam in the 1920s and worked in different parts of the Brahmaputra Valley, and now the third or fourth generations are all permanently settled in that part of India. They are mostly engaged in their own business and they frequently move from one part of Assam to another communicating with the local people in their mother tongue. Even the younger Ramgarhia daughters can speak Assamese, Punjabi, Hindi and English. They are in touch with Punjabi culture through food, dress, lifestyle, etc., and visit Punjab on special occasions like the marriage or death of a near one or for certain other pressing needs. These visits are generally short and of a temporary nature and do not imply any plan of permanent settlement there because the visitors have already developed many long-term social and economic interests in Assam.[69]

Their decision to stay on in Assam was not taken overnight. Many of them wanted to return after earning a considerable sum within the shortest possible time. To many of them this desire was as good as a faith and persisted over the years. In this sense it must have taken them a long time before finally deciding to settle permanently in Assam. It was again an outcome of numerous factors. On several earlier occasions they had faced personal hardships and tragedies. Another important reason was their hazardous working conditions in Assam. Factors like the physical distance between Punjab and Assam, the exaggerated notion of the unhealthy climate of the Brahmaputra Valley and the scattered nature of their settlements in different parts of upper Assam might have served as an initial deterrent. A few of the early immigrants even went back if one is to go by the written testimony of Charan Singh Matharu.[70] However many others braved the early difficulties and agreed to negotiate the challenges of the north-east. Assam was a comparatively sparsely populated area. Efficient mechanics as well as a strong labour force was in universal demand. A higher wage prospect as well as an opportunity of showing their traditional skill and expertise to a newer audience must have encouraged many Ramgarhias to move to the Assam Valley. Their ranks were also swelled by a few who could not go to East Africa[71] due to personal constraints. After a few years, they steadily earned the admiration of the local colonial officials, British planters and other Indian contractors for their hard work, skilled performance and industrious character.

With this goodwill in their favour, many of the Ramgarhia *thekedars* were hopeful of bagging bigger contracts in the near future. In this way began the successful careers of two Ramgarhia contractors of undivided Assam. One was Rais Sohan Singh of Jorhat while the other was Rai Bahadur Nagina Singh of Shillong. Private letters of these two Ramgarhias show how their close contact with the local colonial world facilitated their steady rise and growing financial success.[72] Their customary skill in maintaining different agricultural implements, so long confined to the village level, found a wider outlet in Assam. Far away from their native place and their families, the heavy pressure of work may have turned a few of them into 'workaholics'.

There is reason to believe that the Ramgarhias gradually negotiated many of the challenges at their places of work in the Assam Valley. Sometimes these challenges again led to newer tensions in the social framework of Punjab. Perhaps one needs to look back to the rural society of Punjab of the same period for a better understanding of the situation. The low social status of the Ramgarhias in their place of birth, the impossibility of purchasing new agricultural lands owing to serious legal disability, the increasing conflict with the zamindars for recovering their customary village dues, the bitter experiences of some of the immigrants in the villages who had already worked in Assam, etc., made matters extremely uncomfortable.

On the other hand, their external Khalsa symbols offered them a convenient opportunity of presenting themselves as Sikhs in Assam. It often pushed their 'disdained' artisan or *goli-kara* social stigma to the background. In this sense, they were possibly working with an additional sense of social equality on the railway lines, oil drilling sectors or tea gardens, which was almost impossible to attain in the rural society of Punjab. The growing job opportunities in Assam and the stricter work schedule must have gradually pulled them out of their customary rural social hierarchy with the Jats at its apex. As a section of the Ramgarhias from Assam tried to carry back their newly acquired social baggage to their native villages in Punjab, the Jat landowners, who were also the 'managers of the (lower caste) workforce', may have sometimes felt threatened. They gradually sensed the need to 'resist it, with force if necessary.'[73]

With these conflicting experiences, some Ramgarhias began to seriously think of taking their families with them into Assam. Many of their kinsmen in the Brahmaputra Valley were already expressing similar thoughts, perhaps for different reasons. Local pressure of work, declining contact with the family at home, increasing income opportunities in Assam, etc., must have precipitated their decision and goaded them to action. A sizeable section of the economically well-off married members perhaps first thought of bringing their families from Punjab. In Assam they were needed to take over the charge of their larger households which sometimes included one or two persons not related by blood. Many others followed suit.

Their enthusiasm for returning to their ancestral villages in Punjab, which had so long been dominant in their minds, was therefore indefinitely pushed to the background. The return of these natives became almost a myth and no longer troubled them seriously. With the growing presence of the other sex, it ceased to remain exclusively a male world. Separate individual households steadily grew up and added interesting social profiles to the local Ramgarhia world. Field reports for the present study from Mariani, Jorhat, Dibrugarh and Digboi suggest that by the late 1930s individual households of the married Ramgarhia families were no longer a rare sight. In the course of another decade, the new generation of Ramgarhias was almost ready to follow its predecessors. Many of the younger generation got employment, thanks to their father's long and good track records. Many others managed to carve out a separate space of their own which their predecessors could never have contemplated. These 'New Adults' – Ramgarhias of the post-Independence decades – generally did not talk of returning to Punjab.[74] Occasional cataclysmic events like the Sikh carnage of 1984 threw up many frustrating experiences in northern India, but Assam had been comparatively free from them. This strengthened their aspiration to acquire a larger social space in contemporary Assamese society which their predecessors never had in the 1920s.

Everywhere the spread of Sikhism is intimately associated with the foundation of gurdwaras. They offered the community a place for common worship. The twentieth-century Ramgarhia experiences in the Brahmaputra Valley had been no exception. In the initial years of the twenty-first century, the Valley has nearly thirty gurdwaras, one each in smaller towns like Mariani and Golaghat while the comparatively larger urban centres like Jorhat and Digboi have more than one. During my last visit to Guwahati (November 2005), the provincial capital reported at least eight gurdwaras in different parts of the city. The most important gurdwara is the Sri Guru Singh Sabha situated in Fancy Bazaar which is the commercial centre of the city.

Founded more than one hundred years ago, the Sri Guru Singh Sabha had long been an important centre of Ramgarhia power in the Assam Valley. In the past their control had been even more decisive. Sixty years ago, no non-Ramgarhia could ever aspire to be a member of its executive body. A Guwahati based second-generation Khatri M. (Mehta) Lal Singh had to suppress his caste identity for a considerable number of years to be a member of the management board run by the Ramgarhias. He had to lie low till the initiation of some significant changes in the gurdwara management board in 1942.[75]

With such firm caste control in the background, the 'Sikh Temple' at Fancy Bazaar area was formally inaugurated in 1909. It was called the Guwahati Ramgarhia Sabha from the days of its foundation. Soon other gurdwaras came up in four other places of upper Assam, namely, Mariani, Digboi, Tinsukia and Jorhat, under a similar Ramgarhia patronage. They were all known as the Ramgarhia gurdwaras. Of these four again, the gurdwara at Mariana came first owing to the city's growing commercial importance (1922). It was founded on a piece of land given by the railways and remained the headquarters of Ramgarhia activity in Assam till it was taken over by their caste brethren in Jorhat (1937). It regularly celebrated *gurpurab*s, maintained intimate links with the All-India Ramgarhia Sabha (situated in Simla, then in Punjab) by sending annual subscriptions for its mouthpiece *The Ramgarhia Gazette*.[76] In 1926 another important Ramgarhia gurdwara sprang up in the Digboi Oil Refinery area. In spite of its distance from the Mariani–Jorhat road map, Mohan Singh Hadiabadi brought it within the *All-India Ramgarhia Directory*. It was followed by a new gurdwara at Tinsukia (1936), a prosperous commercial centre in upper Assam. The gurdwara in Jorhat rose comparatively late owing to the presence of an older one in the nearby Mariani. The local affluent Ramgarhias took over the leadership of the community in Assam and made it an integral part of the wider Ramgarhia movement with its intimate links with Punjab.

Dibrugarh had always been an important centre of tea, timber and oil exploration. The existence of a Sri Guru Singh Sabha was reported even before the close of the nineteenth century. It was founded by a group of Sikh soldiers who were there for a brief period. In the later years, as the number of the Ramgarhias steadily increased in the town, the Sabha's managerial control gradually passed into their hands. They had to agree to the continuation of its old name. In the late 1940s, a national school was set up in the compound of the gurdwara. It was perhaps a sequel to the local leadership's increasing closeness with the local Congress politics.[77] Later on, newer gurdwaras came up in Sadiya (1950) and a few other places.

The Ramgarhias thus managed to have a network of gurdwaras in the Assam Valley. These institutions celebrated *gurpurab*s and other community festivals round the year and strengthened the Ramgarhia identity at the lower level. The immigrants also felt the need to set up an apex body at the provincial level because it was destined to offer them their own channel of communication with the All-India Ramgarhia Sabha (Punjab). A three-tier caste podium evolved out of it,[78] conveying to its members the different plans and programmes of the all-India body through the provincial unit and vice versa. Its organizational mouthpiece, *The Ramgarhia Gazette*, faithfully served the purpose that the senior caste leaders of their community had been contemplating at the national level.

It seems likely that the Ramgarhias had already learnt the significance of exercising control over their gurdwaras from the Akalis. These religious institutions gave them an effective organizational support for conveying the message of the Ramgarhia identity and funding its mobilization. These gurdwaras continued to remain essentially a platform for caste mobilization extending service and loyalty to the all-Indian leadership in its commitment to give the community a modern look, a new identity as well as a place of honour within the larger Sikh society.

The history of the Ramgarhias in Assam would perhaps be incomplete without a reference to their close interaction with the All-India Ramgarhia Movement. As mentioned earlier, their growing financial success as well as exposure to the problems of the wider world beyond Punjab brought about a significant change in their perception and assessment of some of the major social issues of rural Punjab. An occasional visit there made many of them conscious of the yawning gap between their actual social status in the villages and the newer (also higher) one they had been aspiring for but had been persistently denied by the dominant social group (i.e. the Jats) in Punjab.[79] The first quarter of the twentieth century had already witnessed an interesting phase of community mobilization among the Ramgarhias in Amritsar, Tarn Taran, Simla and a few other places.[80] It was initially a movement of an educated few trying to grapple with some of the larger needs and aspirations of the community. The leadership of the late 1920s, therefore, found it convenient to stick to some of its old mobilization techniques like bringing out a newspaper in the vernacular and occasionally sending off a *pracharak* (missionary) to communicate the message of the movement to the wider sections of the community. The elitist nature of the early Ramgarhia movement was responsible for its being confined to the educated few, i.e. government officials, pleaders, schoolteachers, etc. Incidentally, these were the years of the Akali struggle and the mass move-ments of the Congress led by Gandhi. The existing Ramgarhia leadership learnt from the great success of these two movements and felt the need to address some of the basic problems of the dominant sections of the community.

One such area had been the introduction of primary education on a larger scale for the members of the community. It had a special appeal for the technically skilled and financially successful Ramgarhias. Their legal disability to hold a piece of land in rural society as well as their access to hereditary technical skills encouraged them to look beyond the limits of the village. With their growing material success outside Punjab, many of them increasingly felt the need of some basic educational facilities of the time. Not having these facilities had put the community in innumerable difficulties not only in Punjab, but also in Assam and East Africa. On the other hand, a minimum control over these would give the community a larger control and manoeuvrability in any modern society.

Mohan Singh Hadiabadi from Assam had been one of the early associates of the new identity movement of the Ramgarhias. His initial career as a small-scale contractor in Burma and

Assam, spreading over a decade, as well as his frequent travels between his different workplaces in Assam and the new centres of Ramgarhia Movement in Punjab, perhaps gave him some insights into these problems. Generally speaking, his fellow Ramgarhias of Assam were also aware of it. Their celebration of *gurpurab* in the different Ramgarhia gurdwaras like Jorhat and Mariani and the weekly arrival of *The Ramgarhia Gazette* had made them aware of the significance of the movement. They sent regular subscriptions to the Ramgarhia Central Board, Punjab, remitting money in advance to ensure the receipt of the copies of the gazette. As early as 1927, they had successfully set up the Assam Ramgarhia Sabha with Rais Sohan Singh of Jorhat[81] as its president and received another *pracharak* from Punjab with much fanfare and enthusiasm.

These developments in Assam underlined the close link between the new movement and its Assam rank and file. Like many of his contemporaries in the early 1920s, Mohan Singh Hadiabadi had struggled hard in the Brahmaputra Valley. His intimate knowledge of their problems proved useful when he later joined the Ramgarhia Movement in Punjab. Even after his initial financial success and participation in the movement, he continued visiting his places of work in Assam. He never lost touch with the movement in Assam and tried to maintain contact through its front-ranking leaders Sohan Singh of Jorhat and Sundar Singh of Mariani.[82] Through their patronage and encouragement, the different Ramgarhia gurdwaras of Assam carried the message of the movement to different parts of the Valley.

Mohan Singh, with a few of his close associates, planned to set up a small primary school at Phagwara (1929). This underlined his deep commitment to the cause of education, which, in his opinion, was the key to [the Ramgarhia] modernity and progress in the twentieth century. In this sense, Hadiabadi was 'a person bending a tradition to his vision, leaving the tradition behind in [a] somewhat modified form'.[83] His emphasis on education made the movement sufficiently popular and secured the (patronage) and support of a wide section of the community. During his lifetime, it grew steadily into a massive educational foundation in Punjab.

After Hadiabadi, the mantle formally fell upon his son-in-law,

Mela Singh Bhugal who also had his initial training in Assam. His association with the movement possibly goes back to the late-1930s. These two personalities from the Brahmaputra Valley not only offered the community a newer space away from the anti-colonial politics of the Akalis, but also added fresh perspectives to its search for all-India recognition of the Ramgarhia power in the post-Independence years. Its increasing tilt in favour of different streams of technical education in Punjab provided the community with newer pastures beyond the social dictates of the Jats. Unlike many other contemporary movements, it was no longer restricted to the narrow limits of some caste reforms. Hadiabadi's emphasis on modern education as an essential ingredient of the Ramgarhia mobilization made him an important pointer of 'modernity' in the rural society of Punjab. In this sense, Hadiabadi did not 'just plug in' the movement, but went considerably beyond. He gave it a new lease of life and unravelled its latent potential. The message of the new Ramgarhia movement thus owed a great deal to Assam. Besides sending two of its powerful leaders, the movement remitted much needed seed money and gave new direction to the community's progress. The local Ramgarhias felt emboldened and proudly identified themselves with the ideology and programme of the central leadership. Their enthusiasm, however, proved to be short-lived. A series of rapid political developments in the Brahmaputra Valley in the early 1940s made matters extremely grave for the community. A chain of events steadily unfolded the social vulnerability of this minuscule immigrant community even though it had participated to the development of Assam. It also raised grave doubts about the community's continued and uninterrupted existence in the north-east.

The process began with the outbreak of World War II along the Indo-Burmese frontier. It resulted in large-scale migration from Burma to Assam (which also included a few of their caste fellows). Around the same time there had been an influx of a large number of hard-working Muslim peasantry from the densely populated districts of north-eastern Bengal to the sparsely inhabited *char* lands (river banks) of the lower Brahmaputra Valley. It stimulated a steady rise in the mercury of the Muslim League politics which in turn generated an alarm among a section of the Assamese Hindu population that they were being steadily 'submerged' by such 'outsiders'.[84]

Such bitter venom against all non-Assamese had alarmed even the indigenous Assamese-Sikhs who had been there for more than two centuries. The latter's bid for an all-Assam body with 'a son of the soil' status made matters worse for the Ramgarhias of the region. It not only fractured the imagined unity among the Sikhs in the Valley but also stimulated newer areas of friction among them. Further, the political fallout of the Government of India Act of 1935 adversely affected the constitutional position of Assam within the future Indian federal set-up. These numerous developments along with the rising tempo of the nationalist movement complicated the regional scenario. Even the community's long managerial control over the Guwahati Ramgarhia Sabha was seriously threatened (1942).[85]

In their hour of crisis and isolation, the Ramgarhias of Assam showed sufficient political maturity and organizational strength. They looked to their apex body for necessary moral support and strength. An immediate outcome of it was the enthusiastic response of the central leadership to the cause of the local Ramgarhias. It emboldened the provincial leadership to formulate its battle strategy. After two years of groundwork in Punjab and Assam, the annual session of the All-India Ramgarhia Sabha took place in April 1945 at Jorhat.[86] A few noted all-India leaders (Mohan Singh Hadiabadi in particular) came all the way from Punjab to grace the occasion. All understood that the smooth functioning of the Assam Ramgarhia Sabha was always significant for making the movement a success at the all-India level. There is very little doubt that the reciprocity of interests between the Assam Ramgarhia Sabha and its central board brought the needs of the periphery (i.e. Assam) centre stage and encouraged the national leaders to undertake more than 1,000-mile journey for a cause which they recognized to be justified. It underlined the organizational flexibility of the movement, thereby signalling to other Ramgarhia boards – at places like Jamshedpur (Bihar), Kanpur (United Provinces) and Kharagpur (Bengal Presidency) – the need to strengthen their fraternal ties with the central leadership. They would then also be able to look to the core in similar times of difficulty and crisis. It was a unity based essentially on caste and kinship, which continued to play an important role in the early-twentieth-century politics of mobilization for power.

The new Sabha was no less significant for the local leadership. The new office-bearers, headed by Sohan Singh (also a member of the Assam legislative council), did not fail to reap as much profit as it could out of this celebration. While extending a rousing reception to the central leaders at the different stages of the celebration, the Sabha consolidated its power over the community residing in Assam. *The Ramgarhia Gazette* gave a graphic description of many of the developments. It acknowledged that the provincial body felt immensely happy about these developments because they gave the local leadership moral dignity and prestige, salvaged it from its beleaguered position and legitimized its power over the local gurdwaras. As the sole mouthpiece of the community in the Valley, the Assam Ramgarhia Sabha even demanded the framing of certain rules for the betterment of the working conditions of the Ramgarhias of the tea gardens and factories run under private management. It was the new voice of the Ramgarhia Sabha demanding protection of the interests of the community at the local level.[87] There was certainly a new boldness and confidence which the prospect of freedom from British rule had brought to its rank in Assam.

AN OVERVIEW

This chapter seeks to point out how some major movements in Punjab had evoked interesting responses from the Sikhs of eastern India. It also underlines the fact that the Sikhs residing in the Brahmaputra Valley as well as in Calcutta remained in regular touch with many contemporary Punjab experiences. They tried to make certain meaningful contributions to these developments. The news of any significant rise in the political mercury in Punjab was generally conveyed to eastern India and it sometimes drove the local Sikhs to action owing to their varied Punjabi ties and compulsions. Such developments took place even beyond the realm of politics. The Calcutta-based literary movement around the Kavi Kuthia also sought to make certain interesting contributions to the enrichment of the Punjabi language. It envisaged an effective link between the literary personalities of two distant parts of India. All these experiences suggest that the Sikh world of Punjab did not remain isolated and insular from the rest of the Punjabi-Sikh community residing in different parts of India. On the other hand, the latter often regarded the former as its epicentre of power and looked to it for necessary guidance and leadership. Their interaction therefore, remained extremely complex, often multilayered and highly sensitive. Many of these levels of communication persist even today. The conflicting fallout of Operation Blue Star as well as the Sikh carnage of 1984 in different urban centres outside Punjab is a grim reminder of such links.

The anti-colonial struggle of the Akalis as well as the mobilization of the Ramgarhia community offered the local Sikhs two major areas of interaction with their Punjabi brethren. The local Sikh world neither followed any well-defined plan nor had any uniform pattern of interaction – rather there had been a certain amount of plurality and variety in their response. The Akali struggle for gurdwara reforms, which occupied centre stage in the Jat dominated Sikh politics, produced deep reverberations in the Calcutta metropolis. The city's political climate was deeply surcharged with the spirit of the Congress-led nationalist struggle and of the embryonic Leftist radicalism. It offered the Akalis a convenient area of action and made them a lively political force in the streets of Calcutta. They not only sent *satyagrahis* to Punjab but also formed the Khalsa bus syndicate to protect the interests of Sikh drivers, owners, cleaners and mechanics who constituted the predominant section of the local Sikh population. Their involvement in Sikh politics added a subaltern bias to the Akali protest marches in the city, where religion and national politics joined hands and also changed places on many occasions.

As early as the 1920s, the local Akali leadership managed to forge a meaningful understanding with the nationalist leadership in the city. It survived the tumultuous days of the Quit India Movement (1942) and the Calcutta riots of 1946. This was something unique because we do not have any similar developments in other parts of eastern India. Even in Punjab, the Akalis, during their days of anti-colonial struggle, maintained enough space for their own political initiative and kept the local Congress leadership at arm's length. In Calcutta, Sikh politics, however, broadly followed the Congress leadership and agreed to play second fiddle to it owing to its minority position in the local situation. Political pragmatism dictated the Akali strategy and gave it a new political credibility in this region.

The situation in Assam differed considerably from the Calcutta scenario. In the Brahmaputra Valley the Ramgarhias maintained links with their home province in a different way from that of the Akalis. They broadly followed the plans and programmes of their Punjab leadership for mobilization and elaborated the same before the rank and file of the community. Like their central leaders, in Assam the Ramgarhia patriarchs were primarily concerned with the identity of the community and therefore drifted away from the anti-colonial Akali politics. It also partly explains why the message of the contemporary Akali struggle did not reach the Valley in a big way. The Ramgarhias had, however, learnt the significance of gurdwaras in the mobilization of the community and used these religious places in communicating the ideology of their central leaders from Punjab. The nature of their politics no doubt differed from that of the Akalis, but their pattern of mobilization through their community-controlled gurdwaras was largely based on that of the Akalis of the same period.

The eastern Indian Sikh world also underlines that it was spacious enough to accommodate both the Akali struggle as well as the articulation of the Ramgarhia community. It is likely that these two distinct types of Sikh politics emanated from different forms of social aspirations of these two communities. Further, the prevailing tensions and rivalry in the rural society of Punjab strengthened the Ramgarhia identity and helped the community to rally under a well-defined programme. The community again looked to the patronage of the colonial power for its success. The Ramgarhia leadership of Assam clearly understood its restricted goal at this level and relentlessly pursued it. It was also aware of the need of maintaining a cordial relationship with the English or their representatives working as tea planters, railway officials, contractors, senior-level supervisors in oil and coal companies, etc. The Ramgarhias' early migration from Punjab, their subsequent settling and continuance in the Valley were largely dependent upon colonial patronage. Probably that is why they never tried to oppose those who represented, or appropriated, the symbols and powers of the British Raj at the local level.

The eastern Indian Punjabi-Sikh world has, however, at least one distinctive characteristic of its own which deserves special attention. It had to encounter two distinct indigenous categories of miniscule Sikh groups of eastern India, namely, the Bihari-Sikhs of Calcutta and the Assamese-Sikhs of the four Nagaon villages in Assam. The Jat–Ramgarhia divide among the Punjabi-Sikhs, which had predominantly figured in the rural society of Punjab, was often set aside when they had to negotiate with either of these two eastern Indian native Sikh groups. The Punjabi-Sikhs universally regarded themselves as a socially superior group of Sikhs and maintained a sharp line of demarcation from their native Sikh brethren. The former never regarded the latter as their social equals, universally decried their gurdwara management, their rituals, and posed themselves as the torch-bearers of the Great Tradition of Sikhism emanating from Punjab. They felt that these indigenous forms of Sikhism represented heterodoxy and therefore needed to be set aside and condemned as firmly as possible. It was therefore nothing unusual that they had never dreamt of having a *roti-beti* relationship with these indigenous Sikhs. On the contrary, the Punjabi-speaking Sikhs even made serious attempts to capture one or two gurdwaras of the Bihari-Sikhs in Calcutta. It possibly added another dimension to the gurdwara movement of the period. In a way, such developments led to further intensification of tension and rivalry. They also highlighted a greater stratification and hierarchy in the eastern Indian Sikh world.

NOTES

1. Joseph T. O'Connell, 'Sikh Studies in North America: A Field Guide', in *Studying the Sikhs: Issues for North America,* ed. John Stratton Hawley and Gurinder Singh Mann, New York: State University of New York Press, 1993, pp. 113–28.

2. N. Gerald Barrier's essay provides an outline of this academic encounter in the West. See his 'Tradition and Sikh Identity in the Modern World', *International Journal of Punjab Studies*, vol. 2 (no.1), January–June 1995, pp. 103–22. Hew McLeod's writings raised much controversy in the Sikh world. He has narrated the experiences of these years in his autobiography. W.H. McLeod, *Discovering the Sikhs: Autobiography of a Historian*, New Delhi: Permanent Black, 2004, pp. 98–192. For the Sikh point of view, see Bachittar Singh Giani, *Planned Attack on Aad Sri Guru Granth Sahib: Academics or Blasphemy*, Chandigarh: International Centre of Sikh Studies, 1994.
3. The scholarly indifference about these Sikhs may be due to three major reasons. In the first place, they constitute less than 1 per cent of the total Sikh population. Their demographic insignificance compared to their scattered presence in different parts of India perhaps largely explains the silence of the academicians regarding them. Secondly, these Sikhs, in contrast to their Punjabi counterparts, represent a weaker economic group. Hence their contributions to the development of the society and economy of Punjab are believed to be equally insignificant. Finally, these settlements of the non-Punjabi-speaking native Sikhs generally stand beyond the scope of influence of the Sikh Gurdwaras Act of 1925. The SGPC, which otherwise plays a very crucial role in the contemporary Sikh life of Punjab, finds very little interest in the different activities of these Sikhs of the eastern region.
4. They represent a hyphenated Sikh community of a little over 4,000 population. Their history goes back to the activities of a small section of *barkandaze*s (mercenary soldiers) who had been raiding lower Assam in the last quarter of the eighteenth century. The local Sikhs reject this version of history. According to them, Maharaja Ranjit Singh dispatched a contingent of 500 Sikh soldiers from Punjab to Assam in response to an appeal by the Ahom King Chandrakanta Singh in the first quarter of the nineteenth century. They came to fight the Burmese invaders and were defeated. With most of their compatriots dead in the battlefield, those Sikhs who remained alive did not go back to Punjab. They stayed on in this region marrying Assamese women. The Assamese-Sikhs trace their origin to those Sikh soldiers from Punjab. For details, see L.P. Singh, 'The Assamese Sikh Community of Assam', *Nanaksar Smritigrantha*, Nagaon: The Organization Committee, 1994, pp. 39–40. This claim of the Assamese-Sikhs is not, however, borne out by any contemporary document. For a detailed discussion, see the present author's *The Other Sikhs: A View from Eastern India*, New Delhi: Manohar, 2003, p. 61. Except for an anthropological study of Birinchi Kumar Medhi ('The Assamese-Sikhs: A Study of their Social Relations in a Rural Setting', unpublished Ph.D. thesis, 1989 Gauhati University),

there has so far been very little attempt to reconstruct the Assamese-Sikh past.

5. The Dakhani Sikhs also claim that they were either the descendants of those Sikhs who had settled here since the days of Guru Gobind Singh or of the soldiers sent by Ranjit Singh in defence of the Nizam's kingdom in the 1830s. A.H. Bingley, *The Sikhs*, Patiala: Languages Department, rpt. 1971, pp. 67–8; *Encyclopaedia of Sikhism*, vol. I, Patiala: Punjabi University, 1992, pp. 488–9; Nanak Singh Nishter, *Sikhs in Present Context*, New Delhi: Sanbun, 2000, p. 81. For a different view, see Karen Leonard, *Social History of an Indian Caste: The Kayasths of Hyderabad*, Hyderabad: Orient Longman, 1994, pp. 58–61.
6. The history of the Bihari-Sikhs has figured predominantly in the writings of the British administrator-historians. These are some of their significant writings. Charles Wilkins, 'The Sikhs and their College at Patna [1781]', in *The Early European Accounts of the Sikhs and History of Origin and Progress of the Sikhs*, ed. Ganda Singh, New Delhi: Today & Tomorrow's Printers & Publishers, 1974, pp. 207–11; V.H. Jackson, ed., *Journal of Francis Buchanan (Afterwards Hamilton) Kept During the Survey of the Districts of Patna and Gaya in 1811–12*, Patna: Superintendent, Government Printing, Bihar and Orissa, 1925, pp. 73, 171–2, 183–5; *Census of India, 1901*, Report, vol. V, part II, pp. 244–6; S.A. Askari, 'Some Records Relating to the Sikhs in Bihar', Draft Report of the Regional Records Survey Committee, Bihar (1960–61), pp. 58–66 (unpublished paper seen courtesy of Professor Kirpal Singh, Punjabi University, Patiala); L.S.S. O'Malley, 'The Agraharis of Sasaram', *Journal of Asiatic Society of Bengal*, 1904, vol. LXXVI, part III, pp. 35–43; Ved Prakash, *The Sikhs in Bihar*, Patna: Janaki Prakashan, 1981.
7. For details see the present author's 'Sikhism in Jagannath Tradition: From the World of the Nanakpanthis to the World of the Khalsa', in Tony Ballantyne, ed., *Textures of the Sikh Past: New Historical Perspectives*, New Delhi: Oxford University Press, 2007, pp. 218–56.
8. Jayanta Sarkar, 'Sweepers of Shillong', in *Cultural Profile of Shillong*, ed. B.B. Goswami, Calcutta: Anthropological Survey of India, 1979, pp. 116–32; S.S. Dutta Choudhury, 'Sikh', in *People of India: Meghalaya*, ed. K.S. Singh et al., Calcutta: Seagull Books, 1994, pp. 174–80; B. Dutta Roy, 'History of Shillong', in *The Shillong Times: Golden Jubilee Souvenir*, ed. Manas Chaudhuri, Shillong: Shillong Times, 1995, p. 21; I.S. Jasnal, 'Assam cho Wasade Punjabi te Unha da Sabhiyachar', *International Journal for Punjabi Research and Literature*, vol. 2, 1995, pp. 46–7.
9. The calculation is based on the census statistics of 2001. See Gopal Krishan, 'Sikh Spatial Distribution', in *Five Centuries of Sikh Tradition:*

Ideology, Society, Politics and Culture, ed. Reeta Grewal and Sheena Pall, New Delhi: Manohar, 2005, pp. 246–51. He has been working on this aspect of the Sikh demography over the last three decades. Even his latest research more or less confirms his earlier findings of 1971. See his 'Distribution of the Sikhs Outside the Punjab', *The Indian Geographical Journal*, vol. XLVI, nos. 1–2, 1971. The study does not refer to the different territorial and ethnic divisions among the Sikhs. He is also silent on the native Sikhs who constitute an important section of the eastern Indian Sikh population. For a brief history of these native Sikhs, present author's Presidential Address, 'The Other Sikhs: Sikhs and Sikhism in Eastern India', Modern Section, *Indian History Congress*, Sixty-Sixth Session, Visva-Bharati, Santiniketan, 2006.

10. For the distinctiveness of the Sikh Jats, see Denzil Ibbetson, *The Panjab Castes*, Patiala: Languages Department Punjab, rpt. 1970, pp. 118–19; W.H. McLeod, *The Evolution of the Sikh Community*: New Delhi: Oxford University Press, 1975, pp. 95–101; Arthur Helweg, *Sikhs in England*, New Delhi: Oxford University Press, 1986, pp. 13–21, 49. The Jat hegemony in Calcutta does not necessarily negate the presence of the other Sikh caste groups like the Khatris, Aroras and Ramgarhias. Here too the contemptuous term *Bhapa* is widely used for those trading groups who have come from western Punjab. Similarly, the active presence of the Ramgarhia Sabha is conveyed through its annual meeting as well as the publication of souvenirs on that occasion. I have seen some of these volumes through the courtesy of the Sabha. It has its permanent office at 8, Camac Street (10th floor), Calcutta–700012.
11. Ramgarhias represent a composite caste of Sikh Tarkhans (carpenters), Lohars (ironsmiths), Raj (masons), etc. They are an enterprising, hard-working group of men, who constitute the lower social rank in the rural society of Punjab. They have been contemptuously described as members of a *kati-vadhi biradari*—that is, men of a community whose members often hurt themselves in the course of their occupational work. Satish Saberwal, *The Mobile Men: Limits to Social Change in Urban Punjab,* New Delhi: Vikas Publishing House, 1976, pp. 86–91, 99. For their status and position as one of the *kamins* (artisans) in the rural society of Punjab, see the present author's *Agrarian Society of the Punjab (1849–1901)*, New Delhi: Manohar, 1982, pp. 175–200. For a popular account of the Ramgarhia community, see Bakhshi Singh Adil, *Sampuran Ramgarhia Itihas*, Amritsar: Nawin Prakashan, 1991.
12. In connection with my research, I visited Guwahati in January 2002 and August 2002, Jorhat in October 2003, Tezpur in December 2004, and Digboi and Dibrugarh in February 2005.

13. I have consulted these files of *The Ramgarhia Gazette* (1922–68) preserved in the custody of Gurbachan Singh Shembhi, General Secretary, Shri Guru Singh Sabha, Shimla (June 2005). I am thankful to him for giving me the necessary access in this regard. I am also grateful to Gurbachan Singh, President, All India Ramgarhia Association, Chandigarh, for introducing me to the local Ramgarhia community of Shimla.
14. For a detailed bibliography on Sikh migration to the West and other parts of the world, see W.H. McLeod, *Historical Dictionary of Sikhism*, Lanham: The Scarecrow Press, 1995, pp. 313–18. Also see his 'Forty Years of Sikh Migration', in *Exploring Sikhism: Aspects of Sikh Identity, Culture, and Thought*, ed. idem, New Delhi: Oxford University Press, 2000, pp. 237–53; Darshan Singh Tatla, *The Sikh Diaspora: The Search for Statehood*, Seattle: University of Washington Press, 1999.
15. The Singh Sabha Movement of the late nineteenth century sought to achieve a communal identity of the Sikhs separate from that of the Hindus. It was led by a group of educated Sikh middle-class men with moderation and loyalty towards British rule. The sentiments about the English underwent a significant change in later years, when the movement's leadership passed into the hands of a radical section known for its more orthodox and stringent views in matters like governmental intervention on different Sikh rituals, its definition and scope in the everyday life of the community. The new Sikh leadership came to be called the Tat Khalsa or True Khalsa. For the history of these years, see Harjot Oberoi, *The Reconstruction of Religious Boundaries: Culture, Identity and Diversity in the Sikh Traditions*, New Delhi: Oxford University Press, 1994.
16. For the history of the contemporary political situation in Punjab, see Norman G. Barrier, 'The Punjab Disturbances of 1907: The Response of the British Government in India to Agrarian Unrest', *The Punjab Past and Present*, vol. VIII, part II, October 1974, pp. 444–76; Mohinder Singh, *The Akali Movement*, New Delhi: National Institute of Panjab Studies, rpt. 1997; K.L. Tuteja, *Sikh Politics, 1920–40*, Kurukshetra: Vishal Publications, 1984.
17. Nowadays, most of the owners of automobile spare parts shops are from the different subgroups of the Khatri/Arora community. Generally speaking, these shops are found either around the most congested part of Dalhousie Square or in the vicinity of Bhowanipur area in the southern part of the city. Perhaps this was not the case during the early decades of twentieth century when many Jats also took up the same profession in the city. This is primarily based on my field survey in the Mango Lane (Dalhousie Square) area. A sizeable number of them were from the Potohar region of western Punjab. I had once or

twice visited some of these shops on the occasion of Baisakhi with Captain Bhag Singh (the former editor of *The Sikh Review*) who was also from the same area of Punjab. This point has also been confirmed by Jagmohan Singh, General Secretary, Dumdum Gurdwara (12 November 2004) and Lakhbir Singh Nirdosh, a well-known Punjabi poet who also had his shop here till the early 1990s (23 September 2004). Among the early hoteliers of the city, one may refer to the name of the late Inder Singh Mahajan. He came to the city around 1920 and established Amritsar Restaurant (then known as Amritsar Hindu Hotel) in 1925 in Moti Sil Street, near Metro Cinema. Later on he also set up a cloth shop Mahajan Shop in Bhowanipur area of which I came to know from his son's (Kulwant Singh) testimony sent via e-mail (8 January 2004).

18. A significant number of Sikhs migrated to Malaya, Fiji and a few other South Pacific countries through the port of Calcutta. The researches of Hew McLeod, Verne Dusenbery, Karnail S. Sandhu underline the point. During the early decades of the twentieth century in Malaya, they came to be called 'Bengalees' for they had earlier all come there from a port in Bengal (i.e. Calcutta). I owe this information to Professor Verne A. Dusenbery; Karnail Singh Sandhu, *Indians in Malaya: Some Aspects of their Immigration and Settlement,* Cambridge: Cambridge University Press, 1969, pp. 124–5. A sizeable number of migrants going to Canada left India through Calcutta. Archana B. Verma, *The Making of Little Punjab in Canada: Patterns of Immigration,* New Delhi: Sage, 2002, p. 100.
19. Budge Budge is close to Calcutta. For other details of the movement, see Harish K. Puri, *The Ghadar Movement: Ideology Organization & Strategy,* Amritsar: Guru Nanak Dev University, 1983; Hugh Johnston, *The Voyage of the Komagata Maru*, New Delhi: Oxford University Press, 1979.
20. Baba Gurdit Singh (1860–1950?) was perhaps one of the most well-known figures of the Kamagata Maru episode (1914). In Calcutta, he was convicted several times for delivering seditious speeches which were sympathetic towards the Indian revolutionaries. Another front-ranking personality was Balwant Singh Pardeshi (1886–1960?) of the Communist Party of India. He was also a member of the Kirti Kishan Party and maintained contact with the Ghadarites. He was expelled from Bengal in 1932 and again in 1940. According to one report of the Intelligence Branch, nearly 1,000 Sikhs, chiefly taxi drivers and *darwans*, were present to see him off at Howrah Station. Calcutta police continued to maintain a separate file on Balwant Singh Pardeshi till 1960. For details, see File no. 204/1911 under the title 'The Recent Development in Sikh Politics: Leading Personages in Sikh Politics', Appendix A; File no. 435/88 under the title 'Singh Balwant

Sardar (Pardeshi), s/o Late S. Narain Singh of Bala Chak Amritsar, Punjab of 105, Bakul Bagan Road, Calcutta and of Wasu, Guzrut, of 8/A, Ramamoy Road, Calcutta, Nanakana Shaheb, Sheikupura, Punjab'. Fauja Singh, ed., *Who's Who: Punjab Freedom Fighters*, vol. I, Patiala: Punjabi University, 1972, pp. lxxiv-lxxv, 130.

21. A section of the paragraph is primarily based on a survey of the British Intelligence Branch records (Bengal) relating to Sikh activities in Calcutta in the 1920s and 1930s. Of the Calcutta Sikh *satyagrahi*s who went to participate in the Akali struggle in Punjab, many senior Calcutta Sikhs told me about Nirmal Singh Ajaib. One of them was the Late Kartar Singh Kanjla of Kalighat (15 April 1997). I have also borrowed from Shallu Chawla, 'The Freedom Movement in the Erstwhile Princely States of East Punjab, 1920–1947', unpublished Ph.D. thesis, Punjabi University, 2002, p. 121. Again File no. 289/27 also refers to the close connection of the Bengal revolutionaries with their Punjab counterparts.
22. A group of 100 Akali Sikhs from Bengal reached Amritsar on 19 June 1924, participated in the Jaito Satyagrah, and suffered imprisonment for nearly 14 months. See the *Akali* (Amritsar), 20 August 1926, quoted in the Calcutta Police Abstracts (Special Branch), 26 August 1925. For a critical reaction, see *The Statesman*, 24 August 1924. Again on 27 September 1931, another group of Akali volunteers was proposed 'to be sent to Daska, Hoshiarpur'. Report on the Political Situation and Labour Unrest for the seven days ending 3 October 1931. Intelligence Branch, C.I.D. Bengal. On the collection of subscriptions for the Akali cause in Punjab, the Calcutta Police (Intelligent Branch) had numerous files. References here are to two of them. For the state of Nabha, see Report on the Political Situation and Labour Unrest for the period ending 10 April 1924; 15 May 1924; 29 May 1924 and 12 June 1924. Regarding the collection of subscriptions for the Shahidganj Gurdwara Movement, an Akali Dal deputation from Punjab came to Calcutta and 'remitted a sum of Rs. 10,000.00' to Amritsar. For details, see Intelligence Branch File no. 109/26 under the title 'Connection of Bengal Revolutionaries with the Punjab and vice-versa'. Thirdly, on the Calcutta Sikhs' holding of Diwans, the British Intelligence Branch provides perhaps the most regular and detailed information. Almost every Diwan held at the Bada Sangat Gurdwara (Bara Bazaar), Ballygunge Gurdwara (Bakul Bagan Road) and Jagat Sudhar (Rashbehari Avenue/Kalighat) was regularly recorded in different files. These are too numerous to be mentioned separately. Finally, regarding the participation and address by the Congress leaders, see Report on the Political Situation and Labour Unrest for the Period ending 4 January 1928; 12 February 1930; 5 September 1931. Also see Sisir Kumar Bose and Birendra

Nath Sinha, eds., *Netaji: A Pictorial Biography,* Calcutta: Ananda Publishers, 1979. About the different Sikh processions on the streets of Calcutta, even the Bengali press did not fail to record the important issues. See *Ananda Bazaar Patrika*, 25 Bhadra 1329 BS; *Masik Basumati*, Baisakh 1330 BS.

23. Note on the Akali Dal and SGPC, extract from Weekly Report (I.B.), Bengal, 27 April 1922; Report on the Progress of the Non-Cooperation Movement and Labour Unrest for the Week ending 6 September 1923; Report on the Political Situation and Labour Unrest for the Period ending 15 February 1928; Tanika Sarkar, *Bengal Politics, 1928–34: The Politics of Protest*, New Delhi: Oxford University Press, 1987, pp. 16, 36, 95.
24. For the Bihari-Sikhs of Calcutta, see the present author's essay 'The Agraharis: A Minority Group within the Larger Sikh Community', in Himadri Banerjee etal., *Calcutta Mosaic*, New Delhi, 2009, pp. 163–93. The Bada Sikh Sangat is the oldest gurdwara in Calcutta, founded in 1790 by a Bihari-Sikh. The local Sikhs claim that it is associated with the memory of Guru Nanak's visit to the region. They regard it as a historic gurdwara. It witnessed serious tussles for power from the 1860s onwards leading to legal intervention by the High Court, Calcutta, in 1870. For details, see Suit no. 91 of 1870 in the High Court of Judicature at Fort William in Bengal—Ordinary Original Civil Jurisdiction. For a popular account of the different Calcutta gurdwaras, see Dalip Singh, *Kalkatta Sathit Itihasak Gudware ate Panthak Jathedandiya da Sankhep Itihas,* Calcutta: The Author, 2000. It offers a distinct Punjabi-Sikh bias in the reconstruction of the history of the Calcutta gurdwaras. The author has deliberately ignored the pioneering role of the Bihari-Sikhs in the foundation of some of the older gurdwaras of the city.
25. It is likely that the space around the Bakulbagan Road leading to Paddapukur area in the north and then turning a little south-eastward as far as the Hazra Park perhaps remained an important core area of the early Punjabi-Sikh settlement in south Calcutta. I had the opportunity of visiting these places on many occasions. There I came across some of the descendants of the older Sikh families of the city. On many occasions I met Kartar Singh Kanjla, Manjit Singh Calcutta and Meher Singh Garib. Meher Singh's father, Iswar Singh, was long associated with the early Akali Dal politics in Calcutta in the pre-Independence days. Manjit Singh later became the education minister of Punjab. Kanjla was respected for his links with the freedom struggle. I had also tried to identify the Bakulbagan Gurdwara earlier situated on the plot number 105 of the same road. The area continued to be dominated by motor mechanics, garage owners, taxi drivers, etc. The entire space has now been taken over by the local Bengalis. I have so

far not been able to locate the gurdwara premises on the Bakulbagan Road. Perhaps it has ceased to exist.

26. Contemporary British Intelligence Branch files suggest that many Sunday *diwans* of the Bakulbagan Gurdwara witnessed serious verbal accusations against the Bada Sikh Sangat management board. Later on, similar developments were reported from the Jagat Sudhar Gurdwara at Kalighat in the 1930s. The opposition, however, never took a violent turn as had been claimed by a section of the members of the Bada Sikh Sangat management board in their complaints to the police. They tried their best to prevent any possible extension of the SGPC influence over the board. *Daily Desh-Darpan,* 13 April 1941, p. 21.

27. The following report of the Commissioner of Police, Calcutta, provides a succinct description of the situation:

    A green leaflet in Gurumukhi over the signature of Gurdit Singh, Hardyal Singh Sodi and 25 other Sikh leaders of Calcutta, printed at the Kavi Press, has appeared. It explains that the Bada Sikh Sangat has been hopelessly mismanaged during the last two or three months by the Receiver appointed by the High Court; it alleges that the Receiver has spent nothing towards the worship of the Granth Saheb, the wages of servants and feeding of guests; and it urges the Sikh community to be prepared to lay down their lives to save the Sangat from the *Mohunt's goondas* A Diwan was held at 105, Bakulbagan Road, on the 11th, at which about 350 Sikhs were present, Balwant Singh presiding. Gurdit Singh referred in his speech to the mis-management of the Bada Sikh Sangat.

    Intelligence Branch, C.I.D., Bengal, Report on the Political Situation and Labour Unrest for the period ending 21 November 1928.

28. For the impact of the Akali Movement, see Mohinder Singh, *The Akali Movement,* pp. 137–50. The Act was effective within the limits of Punjab. The rest of India was virtually left out of it. The Bada Sikh Sangat management board later exploited the legal lacuna of the Act and sought to dislodge the SGPC from there.

29. *The Daily Desh-Darpan*, 15 April 1941 (a special issue devoted to the Bada Sikh Sangat), pp. 10–32, provides a brief history of the administration of the gurdwara from 1920–41. The paragraph relies on the information furnished in it.

30. For a brief life sketch of Sundar Singh Majithia, see N. Iqbal Singh, 'Sardar Bahadur Sir Sundar Singh Majithia', in *Encyclopaedia of Sikhism*, vol. IV, Patiala: Punjabi University, 1998, pp. 281–3.

31. Intelligence Branch, C.I.D., Bengal, Report on the Political Situation and Labour Unrest for the Period Ending 14 March 1928, 6 June

1928, 5 September 1928. Also see *The Daily Desh-Darpan*, 15 April 1941, pp. 19–32.

32. It is not certain whether the High Court had reviewed any list of names acceptable to the local Sikhs. It is possible that the intervention of some senior Akali leaders may have tilted the balance in favour of Baba Laddha Singh Bedi. He was possibly a good friend of Raghbir Singh Bir (a moderate Akali leader, respected for his honesty by the local government). He was equally known to Niranjan Singh Talib (editor of *Daliy Desh-Darpan* and a local-level Congress leader). His appointment as the sole Trustee of the Bada Sikh Sangat by the High Court at Calcutta, was quite acceptable to both the major Sikh political groups of the city. My discussion is primarily based on a conversation with Saran Singh (28 November 2005), a widely respected senior Sikh citizen of Calcutta. He is also the son-in-law of Raghbir Singh Bir and the editor of *The Sikh Review*, Calcutta, and Jaswant Singh, son of Raghbir Singh Bir (21 February 2006).
33. Suit no. 1213 of 1932 dated 25.7.32 quoted in the *Daily Desh-Darpan*, 13 April 1941, p. 24.
34. For a brief career of Bedi in Calcutta, see his obituary published in *the Amrita Bazar Patrika*, 9 January 1940.
35. Even today many senior Calcutta Sikhs remember the rich contributions of Baba Laddha Singh Bedi to the welfare of the community. His dilapidated palatial Bedi-Manzil, once situated near the Rabindra Sarobar, Calcutta, still remains a source of nostalgia for many of them. He used to extend generous support and protection to any newcomer Sikh in Calcutta in the 1930s. I heard about Baba Laddha Singh Bedi from Jaswant Singh (16 June 2000), former secretary, Patna Harimandir Sahib, Patna, and Bhupinder Singh Sarna, ed., *Daily Desh-Darpan* (25 August 2002).
36. This paragraph is based on the report of *Daily Desh-Darpan*, 15 April 1941, pp. 19–32.
37. During these years, the Badi Sikh Sangat Board even launched a suit against the staging of a Bengali play entitled *Punjab-Keshari Ranjit Singha*. It was a high-pitched drama of patriotism narrated within the framework of a Bengali *jatra*. The dramatist was accused of 'demeaning the noble character of Maharaja Ranjit Singh' on the Calcutta public stage. There was also a rumour of violent Sikh demonstrations on the opening day of its performance. All these shrewd moves of the Bada Sikh Sangat Trustee Board definitely put the nationalist Sikhs on the defensive. In their hour of crisis, they appealed to the SGPC and urged its immediate intervention. A delegation from Calcutta also met the SGPC at Amritsar and sought its blessings. The SGPC intervened and endorsed the staging of the drama. It was an instant

success at the prestigious Star Theatre, Calcutta. Banerjee, *The Other Sikhs*, vol. I, pp. 205–7.

38. Suranjan Das, *Communal Riots in Bengal, 1905–47*, Delhi, 1991, pp. 91, 167, 182; Mijanur Rahman, *Krishno Sholoi*, Calcutta: Biswakosh Parishad, 1412 BS, p. 76.
39. As a result of the Punjabi-Sikhs' intra-communal offensive against the Bihari-Sikhs, the Munilal Singh Sangat situated on the Mahatma Gandhi Road was forcefully occupied by the former. There had even been an attempt to introduce a major structural change in the gurdwara building, but it was prevented by the timely intervention of the High Court at Calcutta. The gurdwara is till there with its incomplete structure. This part of the information was furnished by Santokh Singh, manager, Bada Sikh Sangat (24 July 2001).
40. Oral testimony, Jaswant Singh (16 June 2000). Personal communication Kulwant Singh (8 January 2004).
41. This year is mentioned on the foundation stone of the Sri Guru Singh Sabha. It has been placed just at the entry point of the Jagat Sudhar Gurdwara.
42. For Inder Singh Mahajan, see the personal communication of Kulwant Singh (10 January 2004). For Raghubir Singh Bir, see n. 32.
43. Kulwant Singh in the same communication (10 January 2004) referred to the presence of three 'prominent hoteliers' of the 'Jaggu Bazar area' in the 1930s. 'Their names were Gyan Singh, at the corner of Jaggu Bazaar itself, Juwand Singh of Shan Khalsa Hotel and near to this on Asutosh Mukherjee Road itself was the hotel of Ishwer Singh Garib who had sometimes been the President of the Bengal Akali Dal.' Coming to the world of automobile, I mention that well in the 1930s, there was a petrol pump by Sardar Labh Singh it was situated a little away from the Ballygunge Railway Station towards the Rash Behari Avenue.
44. A survey of the different advertisements published in the *Daily Desh-Darpan* in the late 1930s and early 1940s would suggest that there had been an increasing emphasis on the Punjabi lifestyle in these sources. In a few cases I came across some interesting references to Punjabi medicines, sweetmeats, pickles and *desi-ghee*, and their target readers were obviously Punjabi-Sikh consumers. *Daily Desh-Darpan*, 17 January 1937, 29 December 1938, 26 November 1939 and 14 November 1940.
45. This part of the paragraph is primarily based on my numerous visits to these places. I also had the privilege of talking to Gyani Gurcharan Singh who had served the Jagat Sudhar Gurdwara for more than thirty years. I gathered much interesting information from Hardev Singh Grewal who had sometimes served in *Daily Desh-Darpan*. Also see Arthur Helweg, *Sikhs in England*, New Delhi: Oxford University Press, 1986.

46. I have before me the names of at least three successful Sikh leaders who had their initial training in politics in the different Calcutta gurdwaras. They are Niranjan Singh Talib, Manjit Singh Calcutta and Surjit Singh Minhas. The first two had at some time been cabinet ministers in the Government of Punjab while the third one had served as Speaker in the Punjab Vidhan Sabha.
47. Already the spirit of revolt of the Ghadarites as well as the voice of protest of the Gandhian *satyagrahi*s and Akali *jatha*s had stimulated a good number of nationalist Punjabi writings. Thus, long after the Singh Sabha days, the mother tongue of the Punjabis witnessed another important turning point. It increasingly became the vehicle of popular imagination and an instrument of everyday mobilization. Contemporary Punjabi poets like Gurmukh Singh Musafir and others carried the message of the struggle and sufferings of the Akalis in the language of the people. For details, see Sant Singh Sekhon and Kartar Singh Duggal, *A History of Punjabi Literature*, New Delhi: Sahitya Akademi, 1992, pp. 132, 138–47, 242, 250–1.
48. British records suggest that similar poetic gatherings continued to take place in the Bakulbagan Gurdwara as late as 1929. Intelligence Branch, C.I.D., Bengal, Report on the Political Situation and Labour Unrest to the period ending 19 June 1929. Also see Saudagar Singh Bhikhari, 'Karam ate Kalam da Mujjasam', in *Karam ate Kalam da Wanjara*, idem, Amritsar: Bhikhari Yadgari Foundation, n.d. pp. 36–7.
49. For Dukhi's life, see Swaran Singh Sanehi, *Munsha Singh Dukhi: Jiwan te Rachna*, Patiala: Punjabi University, 1990. Dukhi himself provided an outline of his life in his *Saheedi Rut*, Phagwara: Principal Bikramjit Singh, 2004, pp. 24–5. I am grateful to Bikramjit Singh for sending me a copy of it.
50. Saudagar Singh Bhikhari, 'Sahitya da Prayojan ate Anubad di Mahattawa', idem, pp. 62–7.
51. Dukhi is also credited with the publication of two other weekly literary magazines. These are *Syndicate* and *Sanjhiwal*, Sanehi, *Munsha Singh Dukhi*, pp. 127–8; Parminder Singh, 'Munsha Singh Dukhi', *Jan Sahit*, January–February 1978, pp. 116–22. Dukhi's connection with the local Punjabi literary world continued even afterwards. *Daily Desh-Darpan* and *The Ramgarhia Gazette* published many of his poems in the 1930s.
52. Hardev Singh Grewal, 'Punjabi Sahit nun Bangal di Dan', *Jan Sahit*, January–February 1978, p. 123.
53. On the Ramgarhia position in the wider Sikh society, see W.H. McLeod, 'Caste in the Sikh Panth', in W.H. McLeod, ed., *The Evolution of the Sikh Community*, New Delhi: Oxford University Press, 1975, pp. 93, 101–2; 'Ahluwalias and Ramgarhias: Two Sikh Castes' in McLeod, ed., *Exploring Sikhism: Aspects of Sikh Identity,*

Culture, and Thought, New Delhi: Oxford University Press, 2000, pp. 216–36.

54. Annual Report on the Punjab Land Alienation of Land Act XIII of 1900, quoted in present author's *Agrarian Society of the Punjab, 1849–1901*, pp. 92, 102; Saberwal, *The Mobile Men: Limits to Social Change in Urban Punjab* [ref. p. 169 n. 11], pp. 85–105; Harish C. Sharma, *The Artisans of the Punjab: A Study of Social Change in Historical Perspective, 1849–1947*, New Delhi: Manohar, 1996, pp. 110–18.
55. Priyam Goswami, *Assam in the Nineteenth Century: Industrialization and Colonial Penetration*, Guwahati: Spectrum Publications, 1999, p. 216. That country had already been known to them since the late nineteenth century. H.S. Virk (formerly of the GNDU, Amritsar), in a personal communication (24 May 2005) has enriched my understanding regarding the position of the Sikhs in Burma under colonial rule.
56. *Census of India, 1901*, vol. IV, Assam, part I, Report, p. 33.
57. Case No. 1 of 1950, Gauhati High Court, Form No. (2), Form of Deposition dated 2 January 1952, in the Commissioner's Court, English translation (seen through the courtesy of Dr T.N. Singh, former judge, Gauhati High Court; *The Assam Tribune*, 22 April 1990; Kudeswar Hazarika, *Itihasar Chhan-Poharat Purani Guwahati*, Guwahati: Saraighat Prakashan, 2002, pp. 215–17; Dipankar Banerjee, 'An Oasis of Devotion', *Heritage Guwahati*, Guwahati: Kamrup District Administration, 2004, p. 65. Professor S.S. Sagar's unpublished autobiography also refers to the presence of the Ramgarhias in the Guwahati region in the early years of the twentieth century. Diary perused through the courtesy of the author.
58. Mariani is situated around 15 km. south of Jorhat, on the main railway line connecting Guwahati with Dibrugarh. In the first quarter of the twentieth century, Mariani was a part of the old Sibsagar district. There is a wonderful description of the old Mariani Railway Station and of an adjoining motor garage possibly run by a Sikh mechanic in a novel written against the background of the developing tea industry in the locality. See Rasna Barua, *Seuji Patar Kahini*, Nalbari: Journal Emporium, 1959, pp. 75–81.
59. Written note by Charan Singh (28 October 2004), a widely respected man in the local Ramgarhia community, who died recently (2005). He came to Jorhat in the early 1920s.
60. One learns that in the 1920s, the journey from Punjab to Guwahati took five days from the written testimony of Surjit Singh (6 July 2005). He has long been associated with the North-East India Sikh Pratinidhi Board, the apex body of the Assam gurdwaras, and resides in Guwahati.

61. Dibrugarh has been an important centre of tea trade since the late nineteenth century. It is situated at a distance of 480 km. from Guwahati. Makum is positioned around 40 km. east of Dibrugarh while Moranhat is located approximately 35 km. south of Dibrugarh.
62. Coal and oil were found in Digboi long before the end of the nineteenth century. It was then 'a small camp in the jungle' and gradually became a very important early centre of the East India Company's colonial penetration in the north-east of India. For its early history, see P.C. Barua, *The Saga of Assam Oil: From Nahorpung to Numlaigarh (1825–1999)*, Guwahati: Spectrum Publications, 1999. Sundar Singh was an efficient *mistri* (technician) of the Digboi Oil Company. His name was associated with a part of the Refinery Settlement Area. It was called Sundar Singh Basti. In 1945, when a Kali temple was constructed in the same area, its old name gradually fell into disuse. Dwijendrachandra Debasarma, *Saru Saru Manuhar Saru Saru Katha*, Tinsukia: Print & Book Centre, 2000, p. 126. The author of the book had long been a member of parliament from upper Assam.
63. Mohan Singh Hadiabadi's early connection with Assam had been described thus:

    GSR [Gurdial Singh Rehill] said that Mohan Singh's Fa.[Father], who had earlier been well off, later had bad times—even drove a tonga for a while; died leaving Mohan Singh a debt of Rs.10,000. For a while Mohan S. [Singh] was so poor he didn't have a bed, but always read newspapers, so his sons say that he would sleep on the newspaper he had read; this was said by a young man visiting GSR. 'Historical Notes on the Ramgarhias: Record of Interviews with Sardar Gurdial Singh Rehill', unpublished manuscript prepared by Satish Saberwal (September 1969).

    I have tried to get further information regarding Hadiabadi's early days in Assam. Neither the Ramgarhia Educational Foundation, Satnampura (Ludhiana) nor *The Ramgarhia Gazette* throws much definite light on this particular phase of his life. It is likely that this part of his life story has been deliberately left out by his contemporaries. Absence of information has encouraged the spread of numerous anecdotes about Hadiabadi's early life. On the other hand, there are numerous references to the manifold 'heroic' successes during the later part of his life in the different issues of *The Ramgarhia Gazette*. He was even hailed as the second Jassa Singh Ramgarhia. For details see, 25 March 1943, 23 September 1954, 17 January 1963 of *The Ramgarhia Gazette*.
64. Compared to Calcutta, the Jats did not migrate in larger numbers to the Assam Valley. It may be largely due to the bad condition of macadamized roads and the lack of adequate infrastructural facilities

required for the growth of a modern transport system in the region.

65. This is even partly true with regard to the much acclaimed Mulk Raj Anand's novel *Two Leaves and a Bud*, New Delhi: Arnold-Heinemann, 1983. It was first published as early as 1937 and has been generally regarded as a classic of the Indian-English genre. On page 111, the reader will meet Hamir Singh, a heartless and corrupt Sikh *chaprasi* (menial staff) of the tea garden, though his caste identity has not been mentioned. The character fails to capture the real face of humanity though it is quite a living one.
66. Written testimony of Balbir Singh Hanspal (28 March 2005).
67. Written testimony of Wassan Singh (19 March 2005).
68. Written statements of Hardyial Singh (February 2005), Jagjit Singh Bamrah (12 April 2004), Dewan Singh (8 October 2004), Jagjit Singh (20 September 2005) and Ajit Singh (10 June 2004). I have personally collected the testimony of Man Mohan Singh Hanspal (29 December 2003), while that of Mula Singh was communicated by his son Devinder Singh (5 March 2005).
69. I had the privilege of meeting many of my Ramgarhia friends of Assam in their houses and gurdwaras. I travelled with them in the different areas of Digboi, Dibrugarh, Tezpur, Jorhat and Guwahati. I am in touch with them by telephone as well as through postal communications. On the basis of my four-year long intensive contact with them, I feel that a sizeable section of the Ramgarhias have almost become sons of the soil. They maintain some relations with Punjab, but they do not feel inclined to go back there.
70. His written statement (28 October 2004).
71. They were mostly given jobs laying railways in Kenya and Uganda. For the history of the Ramgarhia migration to East Africa, see J.S. Mangat, *A History of the Asians in East Africa, c. 1886 to 1945*, Oxford: Clarendon Press, 1969, pp. 67, 70–89. Many of them later migrated to Britain for different reasons. For their history in Britain, see Parminder Bhachu, *Twice Migrants: East African Sikh Settlers in Britain*, London: Tavistock Publications, 1985.
72. I had the privilege of working with the family papers of Rais Sohan Singh of Jorhat. I have come across more than fifteen certificates issued by different district-level British officials and senior tea planters recording their personal happiness and satisfaction with the different construction works of Sohan Singh. These were issued over a period of nearly twenty years from 1912 to 1932. A number of certificates were similarly issued to Kushal Singh of Jorhat. I had also the opportunity of seeing a few letters and certificates issued to Nagina Singh of Shillong, the present capital of Meghalaya. Till 1972 Shillong was the capital of undivided Assam. Balbir Singh Hanspal, grandson of Sundar Singh Hanspal, also mailed me a few certificates issued

by different British officials in the early 1920s (written testimony, 28 March 2005).

73. These are from the writings of Satish Saberwal. His pioneering researches on the Ramgarhias offer us many interesting insights into the changing Ramgarhia-Jat caste equation of early-twentieth-century rural Punjab. For details, see his *Mobile Men*, pp. 86–109; 'Status and Entrepreneurship: The Ramgarhia Case', in *Dimensions of Social Change in India*, ed. M.N. Srinivas, S. Seshaih and V.S. Parthasarathy, Bombay: Allied Publishers, 1977, pp. 157–68.

74. These are borrowed from the researches of Arthur Helweg, op.cit., pp. 131–51.

75. M. Lal Singh (1902?–61) was a well-known personality in the Sikh politics of Assam. Born in Gujranwala, he came to Assam with his father Keshar Singh in early twentieth century and got his education in a local school in Guwahati. He was a Khatri by caste, but remained a member of the executive committee of the local gurdwara. He perhaps suppressed his Khatri caste identity so that he could maintain his good relationship with the locally dominant Ramgarhias. He married his daughter to a locally powerful Assamese-Sikh family. He carried on his enterprising trading ventures and became a rich man. As the Assamese-Sikhs began to have a dominant voice in the local politics, he came closer to the Assam Sikh Association and asked for special quota protection for them in the provincial administration. Finally, the Assam government agreed to grant them a special status. He was on good terms with the Congress politicians of Assam and tried to enter the Assam council politics. As he became increasingly powerful in the local politics, he decided to challenge the Ramgarhia domination in Guwahati Gurdwara in the 1940s. Finally, a compromise formula was evolved. As a result, the old name of the Gauhati Gurdwara was changed by deleting its old Ramgarhia link from it. I came to know about Lal Singh's career from his son Dr Thir Narayan Singh, former judge, Gauhati High Court, and Iqbal Kaur, daughter of Lal Singh, presently residing in the Faujdarry Patti, Nagaon.

76. The foundation of a gurdwara at Mariana is closely associated with the name of Sunder Singh Bamrah (written testimony of Devinder Singh Bamrah, 1 May 2005). His contribution is also respectfully remembered by Inder Singh, a senior Ramgarhia Sikh of nearly ninety years of age (father of Devinder Singh Bamrah) from Mariani. The gurdwara generally maintained its regular link with the central body of the Ramgarhias in Punjab. *The Ramgarhia Gazette* frequently referred to the different activities held in the gurdwara over a period of two decades (23 March 1927 to 9 November 1947). For a brief history of *The Ramgarhia Gazette*, see Saberwal, *The Mobile Men*, pp. 94–5.

77. According to Maheswar Neog, the gurdwara was established in 1911–12. For details, see his *Pabitra Assom*, Guwahati: Lawyer' Book Stall, 1969, p. 36. There are, however, reports of the celebration of a *gurpurab* in 1899. This was probably a gurdwara founded within the limits of the military area. There were, however, attempts at setting up a Ramgarhia Sabha in 1944 (*The Ramgarhia Gazette*, 4 July 1944), but it continued to maintain its old name (*The Ramgarhia Gazette*, 15 May 1947). Dibrugarh has always been an important concentration point of the Ramgarhias, but it had also shared some important interesting experiences of the national struggle. Here one needs to remember the sacrifices of Bairam Singh during the days of the Civil Disobedience Movement (*Tindiniya Assamiya*, 16 August 1930). He suffered arrest and imprisonment. He was a Jat and not a member of the dominant Ramgarhia community. I got much interesting information about the local Ramgarhia world during my meeting with Resham Singh, a prominent member of the Assam Pratinidhi Board (23 and 24 February 2005).
78. The three-tier caste podium is represented by the local gurdwara at the lowest level, followed by the provincial unit in the middle and at its top stood the all-India body of the Ramgarhias in Punjab.
79. Except for Saberwal's study, I do not have any other source pointing out the unfortunate experiences of the Ramgarhias in the villages. It underlined that the Jats were in no mood to agree to the higher social position claimed by the Ramgarhias. For details, see Saberwal, *The Mobile Men*, pp. 103–4.
80. Ibid., pp. 92–102.
81. Rais Sohan Singh's private papers are carefully preserved by his son Ajit Singh (October 2004). These sources point out that he had already been working as a *mistri* (a lower level technical staff) in 1911. In the course of another fifteen years, he established himself as a first-class contractor in Assam. In 1927 he was more or less recognized as an important Ramgarhia local leader. He was actively associated with the movement from the mid-1920s and devoted a considerable amount of time and energy to its success in Assam. Later he became Chairman, Jorhat Municipality and Member, Assam Legislative Council. He also served as Chairman, Reception Committee, Assam Ramgarhia Conference, which had its first meeting in Jorhat (1945). He died in 1957. His private papers point to his close relationships with the wider Ramgarhia world beyond Assam.
82. Personal communication of Satish Saberwal (6 July 2005).
83. It is difficult to suggest when Hadiabadi finally left Assam. He had a big landed estate and other categories of immovable properties in Digboi, Makum Junction and a few other places in Assam and beyond (in Madhya Pradesh and Punjab). In the early 1940s, he appointed a

few salaried employees to supervise his construction business in Assam. He came regularly to Assam in the early 1930s, less often in the late 1930s owing to his growing involvement in the Ramgarhia Movement in Punjab. His will (registered in the Court of District Judge, Lakhimpur, Dibrugarh district on 16 March 1968) shows that his savings bank account (Index no. 25) at Imperial Bank, Dibrugarh, was in effective operation till 1935. It also suggests that his other bank accounts were frequently operated from Punjab. This year may be taken as the rough dividing line of his career in Assam. During these years he also became an important architect of the Ramgarhia movement and his speeches as well as visits to different places figured in *The Ramgarhia Gazette*. In the late 1930s, there are only two references to his visit to Assam (28 February (?) 1937 and 31 December 1939). A reading of the old files of *The Ramgarhia Gazette* gives an insight to his deep links with Assam till his end in 1964.

84. The question of the entry of 'foreigners' had often played an important role in Assamese politics. It remained something like the 'other' in the development of Assamese nationalism from the late nineteenth century onwards. For a general description of the situation in Assam, see H.K. Barpujari, 'North-East India: The Problems and Politics Since 1947', General President's Address, *Indian History Congress*, Fifty-Sixth Session, Calcutta, 1995.
85. For the trouble in the Guwahati Gurdwara and its judicial settlement, see *The Ramgarhia Gazette*, 4 June 1942.
86. Ibid., 14 August 1946, 6 June 1944 and 13 June 1946.
87. For the numerous demands of the Assam Ramgarhia Sabha, see *The Ramgarhia Gazette*, 22 May 1947.

PART II

ECONOMIC TRENDS AND THE PEASANTRY

CHAPTER 7

Agrarian Transformation and Marginalization of the Poor Peasantry in Punjab

SUCHA SINGH GILL

Punjab state has experienced tremendous progress in agricultural development in the post-Independence era, especially after the mid-1960s. This has been reflected in terms of the considerable increase in the per hectare yield in wheat and paddy as well as in total production. The per hectare yield of wheat increased from 901 kg. in 1950–1 to 4,332 kg. in 1998–9, and that of rice from 892 kg. per hectare to 3,152 kg. per hectare during this period. The net sown area increased from 35.37 lakh hectares in 1950–1 to 42.03 lakh hectares in 1998–9 but the gross sown area has increased from 41.62 lakh hectares to 77.39 lakh hectares during this period. The cropping intensity has increased from 118 in 1950–1 to 184 in 1998–9. The percentage of cultivated area irrigated increased from 56 in 1950–1 to 96 in 1998–9. The total production of food grains produced in the state increased from 19.9 lakh tonnes in 1950–1 to 226.9 lakh tonnes in 1998–9. At present the state is producing more than 10 per cent of the total food grains of the country. The massive quantitative changes in the major indicators of agricultural development and increase in productivity have been accompanied by qualitative changes in agrarian relations. These changes have serious implications for the poor cultivators/peasants. This chapter is an attempt to capture these changes and highlight their impact on the poor peasants of the state.

CHANGES IN DISTRIBUTION OF LANDHOLDINGS

Green revolution technology brought a tremendous increase in the per acre yield and made small and marginal holdings viable. The technological change was accompanied by an increase in the number of holdings in the state. This was largely due to the subdivision of the holdings among the legal heirs of succeeding generations. The number of operational holdings was reported as 13.75 lakh in 1970–1 (*Agricultural Census*, 1973) and was estimated by NSSO as 17.56 lakh in 1991–2 and 18.44 lakh in 2003. This increase in the number of operational holdings has brought a sharp change in the structure of landholdings in the state. The marginal holdings (one hectare and below) constituted 11.71 per cent of the total holdings in 1970–1 and cultivated 1.46 per cent of the cultivated area. The proportion of these holdings has increased and become very high. This increased to 59.02 per cent in 1981–2, 63.22 per cent in 1991–2 and marginally declined to 62 per cent in 2003. But the area cultivated has increased at a slow pace under marginal holdings. This has increased from 1.46 per cent in 1970–1 to 3.91 per cent in 1981–2, 6.2 per cent in 1991–2 and 6.52 per cent in 2003. The small farmers (cultivating between 1 and 2 hectares) constituted 19.06 per cent of the total holdings in 1970–1 and cultivated 7.09 per cent of the total area in the state. The proportion of the small farmers declined to 10.39 per cent in 1981–2, but increased to 11.92 per cent in 1991–2 and 13.66 per cent in 2003. The small and marginal cultivators together constituted less than 21 per cent of the total cultivators, and cultivated 8.55 per cent of the area under cultivation in 1970–1, and accounted for 75.66 per cent of the total cultivators in 2003 and cultivated only 20.52 per cent of the total area under cultivation. The semi-medium (cultivating land between 2 and 4 hectares) cultivators were 32.70 per cent of the total cultivators in 1970–1, but their proportion had diminished to 13.95 per cent in 1981–2, 13.85 per cent in 1991–2 and 13.40 per cent in 2003. The area cultivated by semi-medium cultivators declined marginally from 24.80 per cent in 1970–1 to 21.76 per cent in 1981–2, but subsequently increased to 26.72 per cent in 1991–2, and almost stayed at that level in 2003 (26.19 per cent). The medium cultivators cultivating land between 4 and 10 hectares accounted from 30.51 per cent of the total cultivators in 1970–1, but their proportion declined to 14.15 per cent in 1981–2, 9.82 per cent in 1991–2 and 9.23 per cent in 2003. The medium cultivators operated 45.05 per cent of the total cultivated area in 1970–1, this increased to 45.85 per cent in 1981–2 but declined in the subsequent years to 40.55 per cent in 1991–2 and 38.75 per cent in 2003. The share of the large cultivators, each operating above 10 hectares, stood at 6.02 per cent in 1970–1, declined to 2.48 per cent in 1981–2, 1.69 per cent in 1991–2 and marginally increased to 1.70 per cent in 2003. Their share in the cultivated area declined from 22.12 per cent of the total in 1970–1 to 19.58 per cent in 1981–2, 15.79 per cent in 1991–2 and 14.55 per cent in 2003 (Table 7.1). The data of the distribution of operational landholdings and area operated by different size classes of holdings during the last three decades or more brings out that there was a sharp increase in the proportion of marginal holdings between 1970–1 and 1981–2, and that later there was a continuation of this trend between 1981–2 and 1991–2 and rise in the share of small farmers from 1981–2 to 2003. These two categories of cultivators can be clubbed together as poor peasantry.

The rise in share of land cultivated by poor peasantry has not been at the rate commensurate with the rise in the proportion of their number. In the case of other category of cultivators, viz., semi-medium, medium and large, the decline in the share of number of cultivators was sharp between 1970–1 and 1981–2 and slow between 1981–2 and 2003. But the proportion of land operated by them has declined at a slow pace. In year 2003, the proportion of medium and large cultivators was 10.93 per cent, while the land operated by them was 53.30 per cent; as compared to this, their share in number was 36.53 per cent while they operated 67.17 per cent of the operated area in 1970–1. Thus, the average size of these holdings in relation to small and marginal holdings has gone up, making differentiations among the peasantry quite visible. Three-fourths of the peasantry is visibly poor, 10.73 per cent is rich and 13.40 per cent falls in between.

TABLE 7.1: CHANGES IN PERCENTAGE DISTRIBUTION OF OPERATIONAL HOLDINGS AND AREA OPERATED BY DIFFERENT SIZE CLASSES IN PUNJAB

Size/class of holdings (in hectares)	1970–1		1981–2		1991–2		2003	
	No.	Area	No.	Area	No.	Area	No.	Area
Marginal (0–1)	11.71	1.46	59.02	3.91	63.22	6.20	62.00	6.52
Small (1–2)	19.06	7.09	10.39	8.90	11.92	10.74	13.66	14.06
Semi-Medium (2–4)	32.70	24.80	13.96	21.76	13.85	26.72	13.40	26.19
Medium (4–10)	30.51	45.05	14.15	45.85	9.82	40.55	9.23	38.75
Large (10 and above)	6.02	22.12	2.48	19.58	1.69	15.79	1.70	14.55
All size classes	100.00	100.00	100.00	100.00	100.00	100.00	100.00	100.00

Source: NSS, 26th, 37th, 48th and 59th rounds.

CHANGES IN TENANCY RELATIONS

On the eve of India's Independence a major part of the land in Punjab was under tenant cultivation. Land revenue records indicate that land under tenant cultivation was 48.6 per cent in 1947 and 48.2 per cent in 1952.[1] This is also confirmed by a field report of three villages in Punjab, according to which the area under tenant cultivation was between 37 and 50 per cent in 1952.[2] The 8th round of the National Sample Survey estimated that in 1953–4, the extent of land under tenant cultivation was 40.42 per cent in Punjab (including Delhi and Himachal Pradesh) and 37.71 per cent in PEPSU. The Farm Management Survey data related to Ferozepur district showed that the percentage of operated area under tenancy was 37 in 1954–5.[3] Thus it can be safely assumed that at the time of enacting of the land reforms legislations in Punjab and PEPSU, nearly 40 per cent of the operated area was under tenancy. Of the total leased-out area, 49.52 per cent in Punjab, and 32.83 per cent in PEPSU, was leased out by non-cultivating landowners. The remaining area was leased out by cultivating owners (Table 7.2).

Tenancy was of two kinds: (a) occupancy and (b) at will. In Punjab, occupancy tenants with inheritable rights cultivated 7 to 10 per cent of the cultivated area and tenants-at-will cultivated between 30 and 40 per cent of the area in 1952.[4] According to the report of the PEPSU government in 1952, there were 6,16,799 acres under occupancy tenants and 10,46,532 acres under tenants-at-will.[5] Thus the major part of the tenanted area was under tenant-at-will with no security of tenure.

The tenants were further of two types: (a) pure tenants and (b) owner-cum-tenants. Pure tenants did not own any land, whereas owner-cum-tenants leased-in land to increase the size of their holdings (Tables 7.2 and 7.3 show the percentage distribution of land leased out and leased in). In Punjab, 19.51 per cent and in PEPSU, 16.90 per cent of the households were of pure tenants and 35.99 and 35.85 per cent respectively, were of the owners-cum-tenants. They were leasing in land from both non-cultivating owners and cultivating owners. In Punjab, non-cultivating owners' contribution was the largest in leasing out land and accounted for nearly 50 per cent, followed by cultivating

TABLE 7.2: PERCENTAGE DISTRIBUTION OF AREA LEASED OUT, 1950–1 TO 1953–4

Livelihood class	Percentage of Estimated Households	Percentage of Area Leased Out			
		1950–1	1951–2	1952–3	1953–4
Punjab					
1. Cultivating owners	35.99	37.08	35.64	36.45	38.10
2. Non-owning cultivators	19.51	5.65	5.63	5.49	6.97
3. Non-cultivating owners	3.54	50.67	52.07	50.62	49.52
4. Others	40.96	6.60	6.66	7.44	5.41
Total	100.00	100.00	100.00	100.00	100.00
PEPSU					
1. Cultivating owners	35.85	52.93	53.93	53.65	50.38
2. Non-owning cultivators	16.90	2.92	2.77	2.79	3.14
3. Non-cultivating owners	7.27	30.77	30.35	30.53	32.88
4. Others	39.98	14.08	12.95	13.03	13.60
Total	100.00	100.00	100.00	100.00	100.00

Source: NSS, 8th round.

TABLE 7.3: PERCENTAGE DISTRIBUTION OF AREA LEASED OUT, 1950–1 TO 1953–4

Livelihood class	Percentage of Estimated Households	Percentage of Area Leased Out			
		1950–1	1951–2	1952–3	1953–4
Punjab					
1. Cultivating owners	35.99	21.87	23.56	27.13	23.07
2. Non-owning cultivators	19.51	65.00	63.86	61.43	63.70
3. Non-cultivating owners	3.54	0.28	0.27	0.18	0.18
4. Others	40.96	12.85	12.31	11.26	8.05
Total	100.00	100.00	100.00	100.00	100.00
PEPSU					
1. Cultivating owners	35.85	57.52	60.37	61.13	54.17
2. Non-owning cultivators	16.90	36.98	32.66	31.16	39.74
3. Non-cultivating owners	7.27	–	–	0.71	0.58
4. Others	39.98	5.50	6.97	7.00	0.50
Total	100.00	100.00	100.00	100.00	100.00

Source: NSS, 8th round.

owners whose contribution varied between 35.64 and 38.10 per cent of the total leased-out area.

Most of the land under tenancy was without any formal contract. Informal contracts accounted for more than 70 per cent of the land. Sharecropping was the most important method of payment of rent. Under this system, landlord and tenant shared the crop on a 50:50 basis. Besides, the tenants were to render services of various kinds to landlords. (The distribution of land leased in under different types of contracts is shown in Table 7.4.)

Land, which is a major source of income, an indicator of one's position in rural society, was concentrated in a few hands. In Punjab 35.51 per cent and in PEPSU 41.52 per cent of the households were without land. Farmers owning 5 acres or less constituted 35.04 per cent in Punjab and 20.82 per cent in PEPSU of the total rural households. Their share of land was 10.80 and 5.46 per cent in Punjab and PEPSU respectively. At the top, the percentage of farmers who owned more than 30 acres of land was 2.74 in Punjab and 3.91 in PEPSU. Their share of land was respectively 30.60 per cent and 28.30 per cent.

Land relations in Punjab, as they prevailed at the time of enactment of the land reforms legislation, were broadly pre-capitalist in nature and not conducive to capitalist progress. The large area under tenancy was being cultivated by tenants who did not have enough surpluses to invest in the improvement of land and introduce modern methods of cultivation. At the same time, the tenants had no interest in improving the land as they did not enjoy security of tenure. The widespread fragmentation of landholdings also discouraged the peasant cultivators from investing in the digging of wells or installation of tube wells. The big landowners, who did not cultivate themselves, were primarily interested in rent and a large number of them also resorted to moneylending. The combination of land rent and usury as a mode of exploitation of the poor tenant cultivators, along with the existence of an equally large number of self-cultivators, displayed a mixture of tenure systems. This was accompanied by a primitive mode of cultivation based on bullock power carried on largely in rain-fed areas with inadequate

TABLE 7.4: PERCENTAGE DISTRIBUTION OF AREA LEASED IN: ACCORDING TO TYPE OF LEASE, 1950–1 TO 1953–4

Type of lease		Percentage of area			
		1950–1	1951–2	1952–3	1953–4
Punjab	1. With formal contracts:				
	1.1 Cash rent	3.60	3.28	4.85	6.95
	1.2 Fixed crop rent	0.85	0.82	1.09	1.31
	1.3 Proportionate crop rent	18.24	20.05	18.47	17.99
	2. Without formal contracts:				
	2.1 Cash rent	10.81	10.82	9.95	5.26
	2.2 Fixed crop rent	2.31	3.04	2.71	3.04
	2.3 Proportionate crop rent	27.75	26.75	31.42	37.10
	3. Other types	14.14	13.17	12.75	13.17
	4. Unspecified	22.30	21.57	18.76	15.18
	Total	100.00	100.00	100.00	100.00
PEPSU	1. With formal contracts:				
	1.1 Cash rent	24.37	17.69	18.56	15.77
	1.2 Fixed crop rent	–	–	–	–
	1.3 Proportionate crop rent	0.91	0.93	5.43	11.16
	2. Without formal contracts:				
	2.1 Cash rent	–	1.80	0.01	2.07
	2.2 Fixed crop rent	–	–	–	0.03
	2.3 Proportionate crop rent	10.64	13.20	14.55	11.82
	3. Other types	15.49	15.62	18.69	16.52
	4. Unspecified	48.59	50.76	42.76	42.63
	Total	100.00	100.00	100.00	100.00

Source: NSS, 8th round.

irrigation networks. Some scholars later characterized these relations as a semi-feudal mode of production in Indian agriculture.[6] The existence of this mode of production promoted neither economic growth nor equitable distribution of income and wealth. The capitalist transformation of the economy demanded changes in these obsolete relations of production so that they could no longer block the expansion of the forces of production. The land reforms measures were intended to transform these pre-capitalist/semi-feudal land relations into a capitalist one.

Over a period of time, especially after 1970–1, there has been a change in the pattern of tenancy. Earlier it was the big landowners of who mainly leased out their land to small and marginal owners of land but in the post-green revolution period, it is the relatively big cultivators, who are better endowed with resources, who lease in land. The proportion of tenant holdings with wholly or partly leased-in land in 1981–2 stood at 21.3 per cent in Punjab but declined in 15.9 per cent in 1991–2 and increased to 12.6 per cent in 2003. The area under tenancy, however, increased from 16.1 per cent in 1981–2 to 18.8 per cent in 1991–2. This implies that the size of tenant holdings has gone up. The 48th round of the NSS has brought out the fact that as the size of holdings increases the percentage of leased-in land also increases. Table 7.5 shows that in the small holdings the share of leased-in land was 11.70 per cent in 1991–2 while for semi-medium holdings this share was 15.01 per cent. This

TABLE 7.5: PERCENTAGE OF AREA OWNED AND LEASED-IN BY SIZE/CLASS OF HOLDINGS IN PUNJAB, 1991–2

Size class of operation holding (hectares)	Owned area	Leased-in area
0.002–0.2	85.21	13.22
0.21–0.5	85.61	14.38
0.51–1.0	81.31	18.68
1.01–2.0	88.29	11.70
2.01–4.0	84.52	15.01
4.01–10.0	79.19	20.41
10.01 and above	72.99	26.71

Source: NSS, 48th round.

share was 20.41 per cent for medium holdings and 26.71 per cent for the large holdings. It is evident that large owners of land lease in more land from the non-cultivators many of whom are small owners.

NSS data further brings out that sharecropping as a mode of rent payment has been replaced by the fixed-rent system. Cash rent payment has emerged as the dominant mode of tenancy in Punjab. 49.17 per cent of the land leased on rent in 1991–2 was under fixed-money rent, followed by fixed-produce rent over 18.24 per cent of the total land leased in the state. The share of the produce, as a mode of rent payment, has been reduced to an insignificant amount, accounting for 11.31 per cent of the land leased in the state. The cash-rent system has been further strengthened in recent years. Table 7.6 shows that fixed-money rent payment increases as the size of holdings rises. It was at 22.36 to 41.54 per cent of land leased in by marginal cultivators but rose to 40.61 per cent of the land leased in by small farmers, 49.54 per cent of land leased in by semi-medium farmers and 70.63 per cent of land leased in by medium farmers and 64.24 per cent of the land leased in by large farmers. Thus, the nature of tenancy has been transformed from sharecropping in 1950s to the fixed-rent system dominated by cash payment in the 1990s and after. It has been further transformed from leasing in land by poor farmers – to supplement subsistence farming as a mode of living – to leasing in land by relatively big farmers to add to their holdings for achieving better utilization of machinery (capital) for profit/income-raising commercial farming. This type of tenancy is characterized as 'reverse tenancy' in literature and is capitalist in nature. This tenancy has the potential to crowd out the small and poor tenants from the business of the land-lease market. The results of NSS data are supported by several studies conducted by individual scholars.[7]

LABOUR USE PATTERN AND MODE OF CULTIVATION

On the eve of Independence, though the area under tenancy was large in Punjab (and PEPSU), the state was dominated by peasant proprietors. These peasants cultivated their land largely with family labour and the bullocks owned by them. The share of

TABLE 7.6: PERCENTAGE DISTRIBUTION OF AREA LEASED-IN: BY TERMS OF LEASE FOR BROAD SIZE/CLASS OF OPERATIONAL HOLDINGS IN PUNJAB, 1991–2

Size class of holdings (in hectares)	Fixed money rent	Fixed produce rent	Share of production	Share of produce with other terms	From relatives with no specified terms	Other terms	Not reporting	Total
0.002–0.2	31.82	29.60	–	19.29	–	–	19.29	100
0.21–0.5	41.54	–	20.6	–	–	–	38.40	100
0.51–1.0	22.36	52.06	18.73	–	–	–	6.85	100
1.01–2.0	40.61	10.46	10.36	–	18.01	–	20.57	100
2.01–4.0	49.54	17.12	12.50	–	10.41	0.40	10.03	100
4.01–10.0	70.63	6.66	11.45	–	6.01	–	5.25	100
10.01 and above	64.24	7.38	11.55	–	8.06	–	8.77	100
All sizes	49.17	18.24	11.31	2.50	6.94	0.09	11.75	100

Source: NSS, 48th round.

hired labour was a small component of the total labour used in the state. Hired labour was largely paid in kind, and a sizeable part of it was in the form of sharecropping under the *seree/sanjhi* system. There has been a significant change in the demand for labour and in the labour utilization pattern. These changes are the consequence of technological changes on the one hand, and changes in agrarian relations on the other hand. Technological changes have been experienced in the form of mechanization of agriculture – signified by the extensive use of tractors, electric motors, diesel engines and other mechanical inputs such as combine harvesters, threshers, chemical inputs such as fertilizers, insecticides, weedicides, HYV seeds, etc. The extensive use of agricultural machinery has led to an increase in cropping intensity from 126 in 1960–1 to 181.4 in 1980–1 and 186 in 2000–1. This has transformed Punjab's agriculture from nearly single crop per year to nearly double crop. This increased the demand for labour per hectare. But increased mechanization also led to the substitution of capital for labour as well as animal power. The net effect on demand for labour was the outcome of both negative and positive effects of labour substitution by machinery and growing cropping intensity in the state. Starting with the green revolution, the demand for labour per hectare per net sown area, increased from 108.76 man-days in 1971–2 to 119.8 in 1985–6. Although the demand for labour per hectare of cropped area declined during this period, the demand per hectare of net sown area increased due to the fast increase in cropping intensity. In the post-1985–6 period, the fall in demand in per hectare cropped area continued but the cropping intensity grew at a very slow rate, leading to a decline in the demand for labour even in absolute terms.

The impact of mechanization on labour demand had greater negative effects in the state. Technological changes in agriculture were accompanied by changes in the share of family and hired labour. Even up to 1971–2, family labour of the peasants was a major component of the total labour used in the agriculture of the state. Family labour accounted for 55.1 per cent of the total labour used in the Punjab agriculture, while hired labour accounted for 44.9 per cent of the labour. This proportion changed in favour of hired labour in the subsequent period.

Hired labour constituted 63.1 per cent of the total labour used in the state while the share of family labour declined to 36.9 per cent in 1985–6. Although the share of family labour improved in the later years, hired labour has remained the dominant labour in Punjab agriculture. The share of family labour stood at 43.2 per cent while that of hired labour was 55.14 per cent in 1995–6 (Table 7.7).

There are differences in the share of family and hired labour over different size classes. The share of hired labour rises with the rise in the size of operational holdings. In the present mode of cultivation, with double crop per year, even the small and marginal cultivators depend on hired labour during the busy season. The agriculture of the state is dominated by hired labour, which has replaced family labour. This has converted a majority of the farmers into supervisors/managers who depend on hired labour for agricultural operations. In fact, man-days per hectare cropped area are declining with the extensive use of agricultural machinery and other inputs. In the 1950s, a tractor (symbol of mechanization) was rarely visible. It has now become all-pervasive. The number of tractors was less than 5,000 (4,935) in 1961, but increased to 41,185 in 1972 and 3,30,000 in

TABLE 7.7: CHANGING LABOUR UTILIZATION IN PUNJAB AGRICULTURE: MAN-DAYS

Year	Family labour per cropped hectare	Hired labour per cropped hectare	Total per cropped hectare	Total demand thousand man-days	Labour demand per hectare of net cropped area
1971–2	42.69	34.76	77.45	4,33,324	108.76
	(55.1)	(44.9)	(100)		
1985–6	25.93	44.32	70.25	5,02,850	119.80
	(36.9)	(63.1)	(100)		
1995–6	23.82	33.33	55.14	4,24,861	102.20
	(43.2)	(56.8)	(100)		

Source: R.S. Sidhu and S.S. Johl, 'Three Decades of Intensive Agriculture in Punjab: Socio-Economic and Environment Consequences', in *Future of Punjab Agriculture*, ed. S.S. Johl and S.K. Ray, Chandigarh: CRRID, 2002.

Note: Figures in parentheses are percentages.

1995–6. Similarly, tractor-driven tillers, disc harrows, seed and fertilizer drills, spray pumps, harvester combines and threshers had not appeared on the agricultural scene in 1961. Their number would be counted in lakhs in 1996 (Table 7.8). The wooden plough and wooden carts, which had dominated agriculture, also disappeared from the scene. Animal power has been replaced by diesel and electric power. The 59th round of the NSS has shown that machinery operated by electricity/diesel/petrol/kerosene has almost replaced animal power in ploughing activity in Punjab, accounting for 97.5 per cent of the energy used. The share of animal power was merely 2.5 per cent in 2003.

In irrigation, harvesting and threshing of crops, electricity/diesel/petrol/kerosene account for 100 per cent of the energy used and animal power plays no role (Table 7.9). This indicates that where ploughing, irrigation, harvesting and threshing are concerned, agricultural operations are now completely mechanized. Therefore, for agricultural operations, farmers either own mechanical agricultural inputs or have to depend on custom hiring of tractors, combines, threshers and tube wells. It is a well-known fact that it is very difficult for small and marginal farmers to own all these instruments and machinery. Therefore,

TABLE 7.8: AGRICULTURAL MACHINERY IN PUNJAB

Machinery/Implement	1961	1972	1996
Tractor	4,935	41,185	3,30,000
Tillers	–	–	2,28,000
Disc harrows (tractor drawn)	–	–	2,48,000
Seed-cum-fertilizer drill	–	–	1,35,000
Spray pumps	–	–	5,10,000
Tractor-drawn combines	–	–	46,000
Self-propelled combines	–	–	23,000
Threshers	–	–	3,05,000
Cane-crushers (bullock operated)	73,691	91,991	–
Cane-crushers (power operated)	1,566	9,500	35,000
Tube wells	13,548	3,28,450	8,75,000
Wooden ploughs	6,73,835	6,53,642	–
Carts	2,83,575	3,02,761	–

Source: Statistical Abstract of Punjab 1978 and Agricultural Statistics of Punjab, 2000.

TABLE 7.9: PERCENTAGE DISTRIBUTION OF FARMERS' HOUSEHOLDS OF DIFFERENT SIZE/CLASSES OF OPERATIONAL HOLDINGS: BY PRIMARY SOURCE OF ENERGY FOR AGRICULTURAL ACTIVITIES IN PUNJAB, 2003

Size of land-holdings (in hectares)	Ploughing		Irrigation		Harvesting and threshing	
	Electricity/ diesel/ petrol/ kerosene	Animal power	Electricity/ diesel/ petrol/ kerosene	Animal power	Electricity/ diesel/ petrol/ kerosene	Animal power
0.01–0.4	93.6	6.4	100	0	100	0
0.41–1.0	94.8	5.2	100	0	100	0
1.01–2.0	97.9	2.1	100	0	100	0
2.01–4.0	99.2	0.8	100	0	100	0
4.01–10.0	100.0	0.0	100	0	100	0
1.01 and above	100.0	0.0	100	0	100	0
All sizes	97.5	2.5	100	0	100	0

Source: NSS, 59th round.

they depend on the big and rich farmers for some of the operations, and pay for the custom hiring of machinery at agreed rates. There is a well-established practice and market for custom hiring of tractors, reapers, combines, threshers and tube wells. In every village/area, the rates for the use the of various agricultural machines are public knowledge and are fixed from time to time on the basis of energy costs and competition among the suppliers. Agricultural operations in the state have become capital intensive, involving a lot of investment in agricultural machinery and requiring a large amount of working capital for each crop for inputs such as fertilizers, insecticides, weedicides, pesticides, etc., and for hiring labour during the busy season. The cost of such operations is crowding out the poor farmers from the lease market as well as in agricultural operations. Besides, agriculture has become highly commercialized. More than 50 per cent of the wheat, 74 per cent of the paddy and nearly all of the cotton and sugar cane production was sold in the market in the triennium ending 1997–8. Similarly, most of the input required, such as energy, seeds, chemical inputs, implements/machinery and labour, is purchased from the market. The high linkages to the market and capital-intensive operations have made agriculture a business which is subject to market and weather risks. These risks make agriculture a difficult proposition for resource-poor farmers. Farmers who are well endowed with resources in terms of landholding size, ownership of agricultural machinery and access to working capital can overcome these risks with risk insurance and management. They can use this as an opportunity to take over land from the resource-poor farmers by way of land leasing in, mortgage of the land from the poor, or finally, by purchase of land. All three processes are active in the rural areas of Punjab, but the land-lease market is a more active process in the present situation.

MARGINALIZATION OF PEASANTRY

The green revolution technology increased the income of the farmers by increasing the per acre yield/productivity, which was accompanied by a rise in cropping intensity. This was supplemented by favourable prices of agriculture products, mainly wheat and paddy. A record level of income per acre was achieved during 1977–8 and 1978–9. In the subsequent years, especially in the early 1980s, per acre income began to stagnate.[8] But in the decade of the 1990s, per acre income began to decline, indicating the exhausting impact of the green revolution technology.[9]

The stagnating productivity of the major crops, accompanied by a fast rise in the cost of cultivation compared to the slow rise in prices has adversely affected farming and farmers in the state. But farming activities of the poor peasants have been hit very hard affecting their viability. Punjab Agriculture University has worked out that, 'the income condition of the farmers owning 2 hectares of land is unsatisfactory and the economic condition of farmers owning less than 1 hectare is the worst and cannot be improved with the existing technology and cropping system'.[10] The 59th round of the NSS has estimated that there are 18,44,200 farmers in Punjab. An estimated 62.00 per cent of these are marginal farmers, each operating less than one hectare of land.

Another 13.66 per cent are small farmers, each cultivating less than 5 acres (1–2 hectare) of land. These farmers are facing a viability crisis and many of them want to abandon cultivation. It is reported that 36.9 per cent of the farmers in Punjab want to abandon agriculture. The social and economic processes are working against small and marginal farmers: 75.66 per cent of the total farmers (small and marginal) are facing the heat of a viability crisis. Farmers, who find crop production non-viable are shifting to dairying/livestock for their livelihood. The 48th round of the NSS stated in 1991–2, that 42.17 per cent of the total farmers in the state were mainly engaged in dairying/livestock, and 54.02 per cent in crop production. The size class distribution of the farmers shows that the operators of tiny plots – less than 0.002 hectares – do not engage in crop production, but 81.47 per cent are engaged in dairying activity. The farmers operating land between 0.002 and 0.20 hectares (less than 0.5 acres) were also mainly engaged in dairying. Among them 82.68 per cent were mainly dairying/livestock producers, and 11.32 per cent were engaged in crop production. The farmers operating land between 0.21 and 0.50 hectare, and all size classes above this, were mainly crop producers to the extent of 95.12 to 98.18 per cent. In the case of large holdings – each operating an area of above 10 hectares – no one was engaged in dairying/livestock production as the main activity. Thus, dairying/livestock production was the principal/main activity of farmers operating less than half an acre of land. The marginal farmers, operating land between 0.51 and 1.00 hectare, were mainly crop producers in 1991–2. The other farmers were mainly crop producers, with a very small proportion of them being engaged in dairying (Table 7.10).

The data reveals that as the size of the holding increases, the proportion of the holding mainly used for dairying declines and becomes zero at the large size of 10 hectares and above. The 59th round of the NSS highlight (Table 7.11) that out of the 18,44,200 operational holdings estimated during 2003, the number of operational holdings with one acre (0.40 hectare) or less land under cultivation was 9,30,400 (50.45 per cent). These holdings are of a tiny size, and are incapable of giving farmers sufficient income from crop production. Therefore, the farmers

TABLE 7.10: PER CENT DISTRIBUTION OF OPERATIONAL HOLDINGS: BY MAIN USE IN PUNJAB, 1991–2

Size class (in hectares)	Crop production	Horticulture orchards	Plantation	Livestock/ dairying	All including others
Less than 0.002	–	–	–	81.41	100
0.002–0.2	11.32	0.43	–	82.68	100
0.21–0.5	96.91	–	–	3.09	100
0.51–1.0	98.18	–	–	1.83	100
1.01–2.0	95.12	–	0.73	4.15	100
2.01–4.0	97.49	–	0.60	1.69	100
4.01–10.0	98.08	0.93	0.57	0.49	100
10.01 and above	97.15	1.36	1.50	–	100
All sizes	54.02	0.32	0.25	42.17	100

Source: NSS, 48th round.

TABLE 7.11 SIZE/CLASS DISTRIBUTION OF FARMERS AND AREA UNDER DAIRYING IN PUNJAB, 2003

Size class (in hectares)	Number of farmers	Area under dairying (in hectares)
1	2	3
With <0.01	54,800 (2.97)	2,133.23 (97.93)
0.01–0.40	8,75,600 (47.48)	2,107.12 (7.11)
0.41–1.00	2,13,100 (11.55)	2,080.02 (1.61)
1.01–2.00	2,51,900 (13.66)	3,558.21 (1.14)
2.01–4.00	2,47,300 (13.40)	5,326.10 (10.82)
4.01–10.00	1,70,200 (9.23)	5,863.17 (0.61)
10.00+	31,400 (1.70)	1,443.13 (0.40)
All classes	18,44,200 (100.00)	22,310.98 (0.90)

Source: NSS, 59th round.

Note: (i) Figures in parentheses in column 2 are percentages of total holdings; (ii) figures in parentheses in column 3 are percentages of the total area under operational holdings.

depend considerably on dairying as the major source of income. Farmers operating less than a quarter of an acre (0.01 hectare) numbered 54,800 (2.97 per cent of the total) and used 97.93 per cent of their land for dairying. Farmers operating land between a quarter of an acre and one acre (0.01–0.4 hectare) numbered 8,75,600 (47.48 per cent) and used 7.12 per cent of their land for dairying. As the size of holdings becomes between 1 and 2.5 acres (0.40–1 hectare), the proportion of the operated area used for dairying falls to 1.61 per cent. This falls further to 1.14 per cent for small farmers, 0.82 per cent for semi-medium holdings, 0.61 per cent for medium holdings and 0.40 per cent for large holdings (Table 7.11).

Table 7.11 indicates that the largest number of farmers depending on dairying as a major source of income is concentrated in the tiny-sized holdings below 1 acre in size or up to 0.40 hectare. In 2003, out of a total 18,03,300 farmers, in the *rabi* season, 10,23,200 (56.74 per cent) were engaged in cultivation, while 17,67,800 were engaged in dairying as a major or subsidiary activity (Table 7.12). If it is assumed that all farmers engaged in cultivation are also engaged in dairying as a subsidiary/part-time activity, then the number of farmers engaged in dairying, as a major activity, turns out to be 7,44,600 or 41.30 per cent. Most of those farmers who are operating tiny

TABLE 7.12: DISTRIBUTION OF FARMERS IN AGRICULTURAL AND ALLIED ACTIVITIES IN PUNJAB, 2003 (*RABI* SEASON)

Type of activity	No.	Percentage
Cultivation	10,23,200	56.74
Orchards	8,700	0.48
Dairying	17,67,800	98.03
Sheep and Goat	8,000	0.44
Piggery	300	0.02
Poultry/Duckery	6,800	0.38
Beekeeping	400	0.02
Other than animal farming	5,400	0.30
Total	18,03,300	100.00

Source: NSS, 59th round.

holdings are pushed out of cultivation. In 1991–2, 6,62,828 (42.17 per cent) of the farmers in Punjab were engaged in dairying as a main activity, and 8,49,036 (54.02 per cent) were engaged in cultivation. Thus, a large proportion of the farmers, whose operational holdings are not viable in cultivation, have shifted to dairying and allied activities. Thus, the number of cultivators in Punjab, reported in 2003 by NSS data, was 10,23,200; which is closer to the number of cultivators (i.e. 9,97,370) reported by agricultural census data in 2000–1.

The capacity of agriculture is not sufficient to absorb the number of farmers engaged in agricultural and allied activities. A large number of farmers are trapped in agriculture, despite their desire to get out. The 59th round of NSS emphasizes that 36.9 per cent of the farmers in Punjab do not like this profession and are continuing with it out of compulsion for want of alternative job opportunities. Out of the 6,80,509 farmers who do not like agriculture, 5,44,039 (79.95 per cent) reported it as not profitable and a risky proposition. A large proportion among them are deep in debt and some of them have even committed suicide. A major part of the loans taken by tiny cultivators is for non-productive purposes, while only a small proportion is for productive purposes. The share of non-productive loans in 2003, of holding sizes below a quarter of an acre (below 0.01 hectare), was 88.6 per cent. For holding-sizes of a quarter of an acre to one acre (0.01–0.4 hectare) it was 75.5 per cent. For all other categories, productive loans ranged between 57.9 and 82.9 per cent, while they ranged between 11.4 per cent for the lowest sized holdings and 24.5 per cent for second lowest sized holdings.

CONCLUSION

The process of agricultural development in Punjab has led to changes in the structure of the operational landholdings. There has been a shift in the proportion of these holdings, leading to a decline in the share of the medium and semi-medium class from 63.21 per cent in 1970–1 to 22.63 per cent in 2003. There was an increase in the share of marginal holdings from 11.71 per cent in 1970–1 to 62.0 per cent in 2003. This is not accompanied by a corresponding shift in the area under cultivation, resulting in a large proportion of holdings in the marginal category being tiny holdings below one acre. These holdings number 9,30,400, which is 50.45 per cent of the total farm holdings in the state, and they constitute 81.36 per cent of the total marginal holdings. The marginal and small holdings put together constitute the poor peasantry in the state and account for 75.66 per cent of the total operational holdings. This has been described as the marginalization of the peasantry. These two categories of peasantry operate 20.52 per cent of the total area in the state.

Tenancy relations have been transformed in the last fifty years or more. In the 1950s, it was the big, non-cultivating owners who leased out their land to non-owner cultivators/tenants and to small owner-cum-tenant cultivators. The rent was mainly fixed in terms of a share of the produce, and the share was traditionally fixed at one-half. At present, the land is being leased in largely by relatively well-off and large cultivators, and the rent is fixed in cash. The leasing out is being done by small owners of land to the large cultivators. Due to the mechanization of agriculture, and its character being transformed into commercial cultivation, the small tenants are being crowded out of cultivation. This type of tenancy is labelled as reverse tenancy, which is capitalist in nature. In fact, the capitalist mode of production has become dominant in the state. Agriculture is being organized predominantly by hired labour, and cultivators largely perform a supervisory role. The cultivation is capital intensive, requiring a large investment in agricultural machinery and implements, and also a large amount of working capital. This has also made agriculture a risky business due to marketing, investment and crop risk problems. This has created a viability crisis for small and marginal farmers.

A large number of tiny, marginal and also some small farmers are being crowded out of crop cultivation. The majority of these farmers are shifting to an option that is closer to their known skills, i.e. livestock rearing/dairying. At present, dairying is the major activity of more than 40 per cent of the farmers. Most of the tiny farmers who are largely engaged in dairying find it very difficult to eke out a living. They are resorting to non-productive loans largely for the consumption of the family: to meet the expenditure of social ceremonies and medical treatment. Although they are trapped in agriculture, they do not want to continue in it. A large proportion of the farmers who do not like cultivation belong to the marginal and tiny farmer category. The proportion of farmers in the state who do not like farming is 36.9 per cent and 79.95 per cent among them find it non-profitable and risky and therefore dislike the profession. The majority of the farmers not only belong to the categories of tiny, marginal and small farmers; but they also lack the education and skills to adopt non-farm employment. In the state, 44.0 per cent of the members of farmer households, aged 7 years and above, are illiterate, 6.5 per cent are literate but have education below the primary level, and 15.2 per cent have education up to the primary level. A vast majority of the farmers who are illiterate, or semi-literate, belong to the category of poor farmers (marginal and small). Thus a majority of the resource-poor farmers are facing a viability crisis, and are entrapped in a profession that they do not like. Such farmers lack resources, education and skills to shift to other occupations. The capitalist mode of individualized farming is throwing them on the margins as dairy farmers. But their low level of income and their high indebtedness for non-productive purposes cannot permit them to survive as farmers. Many of them are being pushed out of farming in a phase of jobless growth. This is bound to generate a crisis of a large magnitude and tragedy for the marginalized peasantry.

NOTES

1. B.D. Talib, 'Agrarian Tension and Peasant Movements in Punjab', in *Agrarian Struggle in India After Independence*, ed. A.R. Desai, New Delhi: Oxford University Press, 1986.
2. Wolf Ladejinsky, 'Field Observations in Punjab', in *Selected Papers of Wolf Ladejnsky*, ed. L.J. Walinsky, New Delhi: Oxford University Press, 1977.
3. Pranab Bardhan, 'Variations in Extent and Forms of Agricultural Tenancy-I: An Analysis of Indian Data across Regions and Overtime', *Economic and Political Weekly*, vol. 2 (37), 1976.
4. Ladejinsky, 'Field Observations in Punjab'.

5. Government of PEPSU, 'Land Reforms in PEPSU', *Indian Journal of Agricultural Economics*, vol. 8 (1), 1953.
6. Amit Bhaduri, 'A Study of Agricultural Backwardness under Conditions of Semi-feudalism', *Economic Journal*, vol. 86 (320), 1973; Pradhan H. Prasad, 'Reactionary Role of Usurer's Capital in Rural India', *Economic and Political Weekly*, vol. 9 (32–4), 1974.
7. J.S. Brar and S.S. Gill, 'Tenancy Reversal and Operational Enclosures: A Study of Doaba Region', in S.S. Gill, ed., *Intervention for Agrarian Capitalist Transformation in Punjab and Haryana,* vol. 6 of *Land Reforms in India*, New Delhi: Sage, 2001; I.S. Chatha, J. Singh, and S.S. Grewal, 'Land Lease Market: Its Impact on Operational Holdings', *Indian Journal of Agricultural Economics*, vol. 41 (4), October–December 1986; Sandeep Kaur, 'Credit Market in Punjab: A Study of District Sangrur', Punjabi University, Patiala, Department of Economics, M.Phil. dissertation, 2005; H.S. Sidhu, 'Production Conditions in Contemporary Punjab Agriculture', *Journal of Punjab Studies*, vol. 13 (1), 2006; Iqbal Singh, 'Reverse Tenancy in Punjab Agriculture: Impact of Technological Change', *Economic and Political Weekly*, vol. 24 (24), 25 June 1989; R.P. Singh, and S.S. Grewal, 'Tenancy Pattern in Post-Green Revolution Punjab', in *Intervention for Agrarian Capitalist Transformation in Punjab and Haryana*, vol. 6 of *Land Reforms in India*, ed. S.S. Gill, New Delhi: Sage, 2001.
8. Report of the Expert Committee, *Diversification of Agriculture in Punjab*, Chandigarh: Government of Punjab, 1986.
9. R.S. Sidhu, and S.S. Johl, 'Three Decades of Intensive Agriculture in Punjab: Socio-Economic and Environment Consequences', in S.S. Johl and S.K. Ray, eds., *Future of Punjab Agriculture*, Chandigarh: CRRID, 2002; R.S. Ghuman, 'World Trade Organization and Indian Agriculture with Special Reference to Punjab: Crisis and Challenges', in S.S. Johl and S.K. Ray, eds., *Future of Punjab Agriculture*, Chandigarh: CRRID, 2002.
10. Punjab Agriculture University, *Proceedings of Brain Storming Meeting on Farmers and Farming in Punjab*, Ludhiana, 1998.

BIBLIOGRAPHY

Bardhan, Pranab, 'Variations in Extent and Forms of Agricultural Tenancy-I: An Analysis of Indian Data across Regions and Over Time', *Economic and Political Weekly*, vol. 2 (37), 1976.

Bhaduri, Amit, 'A Study of Agricultural Backwardness under Conditions of Semi-feudalism', *Economic Journal*, vol. 86 (320), 1973.

Brar, J.S. and S.S. Gill, 'Tenancy Reversal and Operational Enclosures: A Study of Doaba Region', in S.S. Gill, ed., *Intervention for Agrarian*

Capitalist Transformation in Punjab and Haryana, vol. 6 of *Land Reforms in India*, New Delhi: Sage, 2001.

Chatha, I.S., J. Singh and S.S. Grewal, 'Land Lease Market: Its Impact on Operational Holdings', *Indian Journal of Agricultural Economics*, vol. 41 (4), October–December 1986.

Directorate of Agriculture, *Agriculture Census of Punjab, 1970–1*, Chandigarh: Government of Punjab, 1973.

Economic Advisor, *Statistical Abstract of Punjab 1978 and 2000*, Chandigarh: Government of Punjab, 1979 and 2001.

Ghuman, R.S., 'World Trade Organization and Indian Agriculture with Special Reference to Punjab: Crisis and Challenges', in S.S. Johl and S.K. Ray, eds., *Future of Punjab Agriculture*, Chandigarh: CRRID, 2002.

Government of PEPSU, 'Land Reforms in PEPSU', *Indian Journal of Agricultural Economics*, vol. 8 (1), 1953.

Kaur, Sandeep, 'Credit Market in Punjab: A Study of District Sangrur', Punjabi University, Patiala, Department of Economics, M.Phil. dissertation, 2005.

Ladejinsky, Wolf, 'Field Observations in Punjab', in *Selected Papers of Wolf Ladejnsky*, ed. L.J. Walinsky, New Delhi: Oxford University Press, 1977.

National Sample Survey, 8th Round, 48th Round and 59th Round, New Delhi: Government of India, 1958, 1982, 1993, 2005.

Punjab Agriculture University, *Proceedings of Brain Storming Meeting on Farmers and Farming in Punjab*, Ludhiana, 1998.

Prasad, Pradhan H., 'Reactionary Role of Usurer's Capital in Rural India', *Economic and Political Weekly*, vol. 9 (32–4), 1974.

Report of the Expert Committee, *Diversification of Agriculture in Punjab*, Chandigarh: Government of Punjab, 1986.

Sidhu, H.S., 'Production Conditions in Contemporary Punjab Agriculture', *Journal of Punjab Studies*, vol. 13 (1), 2005.

Sidhu, R.S. and S.S. Johl, 'Three Decades of Intensive Agriculture in Punjab: Socio-Economic and Environment Consequences', in Johl and Ray, *Future of Punjab Agriculture*, Chandigarh: CRRID, 2002.

Singh, Iqbal, 'Reverse Tenancy in Punjab Agriculture: Impact of Technological Change', *Economic and Political Weekly*, vol. 24 (24), 25 June 1989.

Singh, R.P. and S.S. Grewal, 'Tenancy Pattern in Post-Green Revolution Punjab', in *Intervention for Agrarian Capitalist Transformation in Punjab and Haryana*, vol. 6 of *Land Reforms in India*, ed. S.S. Gill, New Delhi: Sage, 2001.

Talib, B.D., 'Agrarian Tension and Peasant Movements in Punjab', in A.R. Desai, ed., *Agrarian Struggle in India After Independence*, New Delhi: Oxford University Press, 1986.

CHAPTER 8

Social Transformation in Rural Punjab since the Green Revolution: A Study of the Rural Poor

MANJIT SINGH

INTRODUCTION

This chapter is based on empirical studies conducted between 2002–5. Though it is not grounded in any theoretical structure, which is the normal practice, it throws light on the ground reality that can be used by other scholars working in the area. It unfolds the impact of development in Punjab on the rural poor through seven steps. In step one, the condition of the Punjab peasantry immediately prior to the onset of the green revolution is discussed. I have tried to present a holistic picture of the Punjab peasants in their own perception. This portrayal is also important in order to have an idea of what the market economy does to an organically linked peasantry. The second lists factors that facilitated the unleashing of the Green Revolution in Punjab. Among many such factors, the important ones – social, economic, political, natural, and cultural – numbering eighteen have been listed. What the Green Revolution took away from the peasantry of Punjab, and what it introduced into agriculture, is discussed in section three under the heading 'political economy of the green revolution'. How the traditional organic linkage between nature, culture and economy was ruptured to pave the way for the mechanization of rural life and economy is discussed in this section. It is shown that not all the apprehensions expressed at the beginning of the Green Revolution turned out to be true. However, the general outcome of the penetration of money and market economy into Punjab agriculture is certainly worse than what was anticipated at the outset. Section four provides a glimpse of the marginalization of the Dalits in rural Punjab. Though caste-based social discrimination in Punjab was not very different from the rest of the country, the economic deprivation, in the form of loss of both employment and land, became acute due to the intensification of the mechanization and modernization of agriculture. The gulf between the rural rich and poor has widened.

Section five deals with the most interesting aspect of the impact of the Green Revolution on labour, that is, generation of 'profit' by engaging bonded labour. It only proves that the social forms of all the three steps involved in the extended reproduction of agrarian capital, namely, the relations of production, distribution and consumption, are relatively autonomous. It is not necessary that the relations of production would automatically put in line the relations of distribution and consumption. The roles of social structure, social movements and culture are crucial in shaping the balance between all the three steps of social relations of production, distribution and consumption. Thus the use of bonded labour for the production of profit in a capitalist agriculture was anathema neither in history nor in Punjab during the Green Revolution. This is true even today. Section six shows, on the basis of empirical research, that more than 55 per cent of the indebted rural labourers are in debt to such an extent that it is difficult for them to come out of the debt trap. It should be a serious concern of the policy planners. The final section of the chapter throws light on the effectiveness of the rural development schemes that focus on the generation of rural employment, asset-building for the poor and providing houses to the Dalits living below the poverty line. It is found that the rate of underdevelopment is much faster than the efforts to bring the poor out of their poverty. The overall picture is one in which the poor are being pushed to the margins in rural Punjab.

CONDITIONS OF THE PEASANTRY DURING THE MID-1960s

The agriculture of Punjab during the 1960s was largely targeted towards meeting the needs of the cultivating families, as there was only a negligible penetration of the market. It was nature-friendly and eco-friendly agriculture. Though economic production was at a lower level, it was sustainable in all respects. As Gandhi said, nature could meet the needs of the people but not the greed. The traditional form of agriculture of the early 1960s was need-based agriculture. There was no question of unemployment as there was more work than the supply of labour power. Moreover, the availability of work and employment was spread relatively more evenly over the year. The simple reason for the even distribution of employment was the varied times of agricultural operation for the multiple cropping system. The traditional cropping pattern included vegetables, pulse crops (*mash*, *moong*, lentil and gram), oil seeds (mustard, *tarameera*, linseed, sesamum), jute crops like sunhemp, cotton, sugar cane, maize, wheat, etc. All these crops have different timings for sowing, caring, maturity and harvesting, leading to the guarantee of supply of work throughout the year. In fact, agriculture was a way of life and not a sheer means of economic sustenance. In the social division of labour within the village, not only was manpower given a due share of labour, but even animal power was accounted for. In fact, there was a complete harmony of relations between human beings, agriculture, and animal beings. The term 'animal being', is deliberately used here as animals were part of the organization of labour at the family level. Just as human children and elderly persons were cared for in order to sustain the relatively stable reproduction of life, so were the domestic animals cared for whether they were economically useful or useless. The peasantry[1] looked at all the means of production as a form of an organic unity. For the peasantry, land is as important as human progeny or domestic animals. The peasants would regard the land as adorable as their own son, and so was the attitude towards milk produced by animals. They were never considered as commodities for sale.

The subsistence peasant economy left hardly any surplus with the peasants. The life of scarcities precluded the possibility of expansion of the commodity market. The *biradri* form of community living was the defence of the peasantry against a life of perpetual scarcities and uncertainties. The peasantry were scared of the moneylenders and abstained from taking loans which often resulted in their losing their land to the moneylenders. At a time of crisis in an individual household, such as the loss of draught animals, milch animals, and failure of crops due to bad weather, the entire peasant community would stand by the victim and would extend their meagre resources to help him out. In the process, the prevailing social relations, epitomized by caste and class affiliation, were recreated on a continuous basis. Both from land and animals as much energy/potential was exploited as could be recuperated through the traditional agricultural practices.

The lack of supply of electric power, and the virtual absence of modern means of communication and transport, including metalled roads, further cemented the bond of interdependence between the land, domestic animals and human beings. The need for irrigation water was met either by the bullock-driven Persian-wheels or by canals which were further supplemented in parts of Punjab by rain water. A large number of cattle in this state were maintained for both milk production and draught purposes. They also supplied farmyard manure, which is important for organic agriculture. The very limited access to literacy in the rural areas forced the peasantry to depend upon their traditional knowledge of agriculture. In other words, a life of general scarcities forced the peasants to depend more on their own cooperation, collective strength and the bounties of nature.

The peasant economy is also a moral economy, whereby the means are as, if not more, important as the ends. In this sense the riches amassed through immoral means were decried and were not approved of by the community. Since the moral code was community-centred, individual interests could not overshadow collective interests. It was in accordance with this moral code that economic and social reproduction was sustained through cooperation rather than competition. If at all there was any competition, it was intra-community competition, located in communitarian moral ethics. Concepts like sympathy, empathy, selfless free service and mercy were central to the sustenance of community life.

The cultural life of the people, including traditional sports, folk music and other activities pertaining to material and non-material culture, was sustained through an 'on the job training to the future generation'. The daily praxis, whether for the sake of material production or cultural production, was not mediated by any instrumental rationality; it was carried out in its true meanings sans the mediation by profitability. Life was easy and simple to understand, as the words carried their intrinsic meanings – what they stood for. In other words, the symbolic system, the backbone of cultural life, performed its function of communication and not otherwise. Though life was full of uncertainties and scarcities, the strength to withstand all these difficulties was far greater than the burden of difficulties, as they were shared by the community as whole. The impact of distress, therefore, was not as severe for an individual then as it is today. The simple reason is that any gain or loss within the community was collective as the gap between the individual and the collective was the barest minimum.

WHAT ACCOUNTED FOR THE GREEN REVOLUTION?

Punjab, the land of five rivers, successfully ushered in the green revolution during the late 1960s. Some of the important favourable factors – natural, social, economic, political, administrative and infrastructural – which facilitated the Green Revolution have been enumerated below:

1. Fertile alluvial soil, rich with organic material;
2. Relatively even topography, facilitating the use of all the desirable inputs, such as, machinery, surface irrigation, etc.;
3. Traditionally high underground water aquifer maintained by the sufficient precipitation of rainfall as well as continuous flow of rivers in this region;
4. Favourable natural climate, flora and fauna;
5. Social composition, whereby Jat peasants were self-cultivating, primarily with the help of family labour, supported by the agricultural labour under the *jajmani* system;
6. Weaker development of social structure responsible for the perpetuation of the landlord castes/classes that could have acted as pillars of feudalism;
7. The *rayatwari* system of land settlement in parts of Punjab;

8. Inheritance of canal irrigation network from the British;
9. Strong peasant movements, particularly in the erstwhile feudal estates; immediately after Independence and, consequently, implementation of first phase of land reforms;
10. Successful implementation of land consolidation, leading to the enhancement of scope for modernization of agriculture;
11. Inheritance of rail and road links at the time of independence, which soon grew into an extensive network of metalled roads to facilitate trade in agriculture;
12. State policy whereby electric power was made available for agricultural development and the latest technology was spread through state departments and Panjab Agricultural University, Ludhiana;
13. Role of abundant supply of local labour at cheap wage rates. One of the reasons for the availability of surplus labour was the extensive landlessness among the Scheduled Castes (SC) in this region. Also the lack of social movement among the agricultural labourers provided a handle for the landowning farmers to squeeze them to the hilt;
14. Concentration and mutual reinforcement of multiple sources of power, viz., economic, political, social, cultural and religious, in the hands of a single dominant caste called Jat Sikh;
15. Early exposure of the peasantry of Punjab to the world at large, both as soldiers working in the British army and as emigrant workers;
16. Relatively less stringent caste disabilities, including untouchability, often attributed to the strong influence of Sufism in the Sikh religion;
17. Some immediate factors such as the challenge from the left militant movement (Naxalite movement), pressure on the Indian economy due to the import of food grains, and a favourable global political balance of power acted as a catalyst to give the initial boost to the green revolution;
18. The role of Panjab Agricultural University in the adaptation of quality seeds and dissemination of the information among the peasants through various means of extension education.

THE POLITICAL ECONOMY OF THE GREEN REVOLUTION

The 'naturalized' bond between the peasantry and the means of production was slowly ruptured with the penetration of money and market economy towards the late 1960s. Soon the content of the closed village economy changed radically, though the outer shell still remains in a fossilized form. There was an initial reluctance to accept the new market-friendly package, which was soon overcome by the success story of early farmers. In the national division of agriculture labour, Punjab and Haryana were encouraged to be the national granaries. First came the chemical fertilizers along with the tube wells operated by electric power which gave the initial boost to the agricultural production. Slowly the high-yielding varieties (HYV) of different crops, one after the other, were introduced into the cropping pattern of Punjab. The Mexican dwarf wheat varieties that initiated the Green Revolution in Punjab quite suddenly more than doubled the wheat yield. The extraction of higher yields, though of lower quality, soon exhausted the fertility of the land and required more and more supplementation of nutrients through chemical fertilizers. The peasants were becoming dependent on the market, both for the seed as well as for fertilizers. Another immediate impact of chemical fertilizers on the land was the destruction of the natural micro-flora of the soil, leading to the total dependence of the soil on chemical fertilizers; that is, the intrinsic bio-cycle of recuperation of fertility within the soil was broken, making space for the entry of market-driven chemical fertilizers and new seeds.

Since the HYV were introduced to the age-old ecology from outside, they were more prone to disease and needed much more care. They also came under attack from new diseases in the form of microbes (bacteria, fungus, etc.) and from new types of insect/pests. And so appeared the new varieties of weeds for which the local farmers did not have any solution. The lure of the high yields ushered in by the magic seeds wore down the initial resistance of the peasants to change over to the new pattern of agriculture. The boost to the agricultural economy came not only from the chemical fertilizers and added potential of new seeds but also from the latent fertility of soil that had not been utilized fully till then.

Thus began the Green Revolution. Within a short period of five to ten years the peasants of Punjab generated so much surplus that they did not know what to do with it. With the increase in production and profitability there was also an increase in the proportionate rate of consumption of liquor. The expenditure on conspicuous consumption, such as dowry and other durable consumer goods, acquired new proportions which could not have been imagined in the past. Part of the surplus was also used for productive purposes such as buying machinery including tractors, threshers, tube wells and other tools/implements. Within a short span of ten years, by the late 1970s, the Punjab peasantry had already transformed into farmers[2] of different sizes. The binding of Punjab agriculture to the market from both the ends, that is, input and output, transformed the very spirit of agriculture right from within. Agriculture was no more a way of life. It was reduced to the instrumental use for profit-making by an individual, often at the cost of community life. The very cord of the moral economy that bound the peasantry together as a community slowly vanished. The new binding force of the market, paradoxically, bound the economy together but atomized the rural society to individuals pursuing individual goals at the cost of the collective.

The cancerous expansion of the market to the rural areas left no corner untouched in the social, political and economic space. The mutual dependence of the peasants was snapped and was transferred to the market instead. Old models do not wither away so soon, however. Though the reality of economic relations changed very fast, it was not as straightforward as it appears from theoretical formulations. In other words, social relations woven through culture display much more resilience compared to economic relations. Even for rational economic production, primordial relations – such as bonded labour, *corvee* (unpaid labour), forced labour, debt bondage and caste relations – are used even today. It is for the same reason that, in the heart of the Green Revolution, bonded labour is engaged in agriculture even today.

The one-to-one relation, in a given mode of production, between production, distribution and consumption, as envisioned in theory, never existed in practice. It is always found in a modified form, in various degrees, as per the contingencies of the given space and time. Moreover, there is relative autonomy of all the three steps involved in a given mode of production. An agricultural commodity can be produced for profit – essentially a capitalist end – by using slave, bonded or any other form of unfree labour. The surplus thus accruing in the form of 'profit' would not essentially be profit as understood under capitalist relations of production. Rather it would be 'profit +', which means more than profit. The discrepancies noticed at the level of production and distribution of surplus, under the predominantly capitalist relations of production, become more glaring at the level of consumption. Here culture influences the pattern of consumption, which often carries hangovers from the feudal past. That is what happened in the case of the surplus generated from capitalist agriculture in Punjab during the 1970s and 1980s. The expanded capitalist production provided an opportunity to the farmers of Punjab for enhanced conspicuous consumption in the form of lavish expenditure on dowry, marriage ceremony, and liquor consumption. Slowly it also gave impetus to over-mechanization, particularly tractorization, which started eating into the initial gains from the green revolution. By the mid-1980s, the greenery of the Green Revolution had already started to fade.

RAMIFICATIONS OF THE GREEN REVOLUTION IN THE SOCIAL SECTOR

Disempowerment of the Already Powerless: The Scheduled Castes

There are thirty-nine SCs in Punjab, and in 1991 they constituted 28.3 per cent of the total population in the state. By 2001, the proportion of SCs increased to 28.85 per cent. This may not be entirely due to the natural demographic growth. A large number of SCs are also moving in from other neighbouring states. The state has the highest proportion of SCs, but as far as their empowerment is concerned, it hardly matches the image of immense prosperity that the state projects to the rest of the country. Some of the following facts throw light on the ground realities faced by the SCs in Punjab.

According to the 1991 census, among the SCs, there were less than 5 per cent cultivators but 60 per cent agricultural labourers. SCs shared 4.82 per cent of the number of operational holdings and 2.34 per cent of the total area under cultivation. The overall literacy in the state was 58.5 per cent but that of the SCs was only 41.09 per cent. The literacy gap between the overall literacy rate and that of SCs was the fourth highest among the states of India, as per the 1991 census. This gap is relatively smaller even in poor states like Madhya Pradesh. In fact, in Assam and Arunachal Pradesh, SCs are more educated than the overall average of the population. It is to the credit of Punjab that there are 3,368 villages (26.89 per cent) in Punjab where more than 40 per cent of the population is SC. Also there are 33 towns with a SC population of 30 per cent and above. From the above figures it can clearly be seen that Punjab has a long way to go to ameliorate the condition of the most deprived sections of rural society. Engaging child labour, bonded labour and coerced labour does not match the image it generally projects outside to the rest of the country.

Not all SCs in Punjab are equally marginalized. Of the 39 SCs, 12 'Most Depressed Scheduled Castes' (MDSC) constitute 13.23 per cent of the total SC population of Punjab, as per the 1991 census. If one looks at the social and economic conditions of the MDSC, it would appear that one is not talking about the post-Green Revolution Punjab but of medieval Punjab. The following facts are revealing. Among the MDSC, 85.4 per cent are living below the poverty line. Out of the total number of children above six years of age, 48.4 per cent work as labourers. The literacy rate among the 12 MDSCs is only 20.4 per cent. The current literacy rate is not only low, there is no hope in the near future of spreading literacy among them. Child enrolment in school (6–14 years age group) is only 24.8 per cent. Freedom does not mean much to these most deprived SCs. Only 10 per cent of them own houses (7.8 per cent *katcha* and 2.4 per cent *pukka*).

The global development experience has shown that abundance amidst misery is not sustainable. A skewed distribution of resources leads to financial crises even within the parameters of a liberal model of development. That is why the active intervention of the state to leash the 'free hand of the market' becomes indispensable as a guarantee for averting any political or social crisis. What is true of global capitalist relations is even more true of the inter-sectoral relations of an economy. The 'natural' limitations of agriculture render it non-competitive in the face of secondary, tertiary and IT sectors of the economy.

Further, within agriculture, the forward march of global capital breaks away from its cycle of extended reproduction those sections of society first that are at the margins. In the case of rural Punjab, agricultural labourers, largely constituted by the Dalit population – who are trying to find a foothold in the rural non-farm sector – are the first casualty. It is easier to face economic hardship than the social legitimization of it through the heavy hand of caste ideology. It is interesting to note how the tribal-like caste organizations, arranged in hierarchy, are used to defend the material and non-material gains of the people in power. And the state is fully aware of this fact. True to its structural limitations, the state would find a solution to the unequal distribution of resources by creating separate ministries for the purpose. However, it is yet to be conceded that to remedy the wrongs of history by giving special attention to the Dalit people is not a matter of charity but the legitimate debt society owes to them.

BONDED LABOUR IN PUNJAB

Understanding of Bondage by the District Administration

The research team for this study visited headquarters of both districts to inform the district authorities about the survey on bonded labour. The fieldworkers were successful in contacting the deputy commissioners of the respective districts, who further instructed the appropriate departments to coordinate with the team and provide necessary help and guidance. Extended meetings were held at both Jalandhar and Bathinda district headquarters. At both meetings, all the officers, from the senior most to the junior-level ones, were sure that there was not a single bonded labourer in their district. 'How do you know?'

was our immediate next question everywhere. With equal ease and confidence, the most common response was that since no complaints had been received from their officers from the department concerned, it was obvious that the district was free of bonded labourers. The team's next question was, 'What do you mean by bondage?' The uniform answer was 'If a labourer is not allowed to move around freely, and is made to work under surveillance, and at the slightest defiance he can be assaulted by the employer, he is clearly a bonded labourer.'

The notion of bondage at the level of the officers is what they have received from the history books about the chattel slavery or indentured labour of British times. A little deeper quizzing revealed that most of them were not aware about the detailed defining characteristics of bondage explained in the Bonded Labour System (Abolition) Act, 1976. Or else, they were not in agreement with the definition of bondage given by the Act, and instead were going by their own vague notions of it. This position, partly determined by the 'convenience' and path of 'least resistance', and partly by the bias of their own social position *vis-à-vis* the labourers, was the safest for their own self-interest.

More serious probing revealed that nowhere vigilance committees were constituted, and if they were there, they were only on paper. No meetings were held on the question of identification of bonded labour. One deputy commissioner suggested that the issue not be highlighted as it might cost dear to the political bosses in the state and the administration within the district. Like most of the employers, the district authorities did not consider debt-bondage, the most common modern form of bondage, as the defining variable of bondage. Generally, the attitude of the district authorities was either evasive or of brushing the issue under the carpet. In Jalandhar district the deputy commissioner flatly refused to recognize the prevalence of any bondage in his district. In order to fortify his position he also rejected the claims of bondage made by some of the NGOs. And thus he announced his verdict: 'There is no need for such a survey.' However, when asked for the basis of his certification of 'No Bondage' he did not know how to respond. The team explained at length the statutory meanings of bondage and, finally, he conceded that there was a need for such a survey for the identification of bondage. Not only did he develop an appreciation for the commitment of the team, he also immediately arranged other help for the visiting team.

The above details have been narrated not to accuse anyone who is part of the system, but to apprise the state officials that there is a gap between those who are victims of the bonded labour system and those who are part of the system responsible for identifying them and releasing and rehabilitating them.

Study of Bonded Labour in Bathinda and Jalandhar

In the search for bonded labourers in agriculture the team visited 37 villages in Jalandhar and 28 villages in Bathinda districts. Data was collected from 898 households in which it was found that nearly 90 per cent were attached labourers. In Jalandhar, there were hardly any local attached labourers, in contrast to Bathinda, where attached agricultural labourers were in large number. Migrant attached labourers in Jalandhar work for wages from Rs. 600 to 1,600 per month, depending on the skill and age of the worker. Some of them are supplied by the labour supplying agencies that maintain records of each and every labourer supplied by them.

According to the present survey estimates, there are still nearly one lakh attached labourers in Punjab, and not less than one-third of them are migrants. The condition of local attached labourers from Bathinda is deplorable. They are still trapped in the old *siri* system that stands extinct under the Bonded Labour System (Abolition) Act, 1976. There was not a single attached agricultural labourer who was not in debt. The most common practice found was that an attached labourer would borrow the entire amount of annual wage in advance, over and above the amount of debt which he has to pay to his previous employer, before he could join with the new one. It was found that the amount of debt advance ranged from Rs. 20,000 to 40,000. They start at an early age at the command of their parents whose only thought is of getting rid of their perpetual state of debt bondage. Now as adult labourers, their experience shows that it is not easy to come out of the debt trap. During the fifty years of their labour they were not paid regular wages and survived on hopes. Despite foregoing their regular wages, the debt amount increased by 87 per cent over the original amount of debt advance. This is a situation of debt trap and the labourers have lost all hope of coming out of this perpetual state of indebtedness. Moreover, the accounts are maintained by the employers, and the labourers being illiterate, cannot remember the amount of the advance debt taken by them. They have to accept whatever they are told by the employer at the end of every year. They are not free to change their employer unless they arrange cash to clear the outstanding debt. The only source is the subsequent employer, and thus the chain of debt keeps on extending over their whole life. It was found that there is a lot of difference between the wages promised and the wages actually paid. A large number of the labourers have not even been promised the minimum wage, leave alone the payment of minimum wage (see Appendix for the comparative wage rates in Punjab and Haryana). Even those labourers who were paid the first wage as per the rate promised to them, were later kept on hope. According to the Bonded Labour System (Abolition) Act, 1976, most of these labourers fall under the definition of bonded labourers.

In Bathinda it was found that there were four such labourers who had to sell their houses in order to clear their huge amounts of debt. In two cases, the houses of attached labourers were attached and in one case a buffalo was attached to recover the debts. This was a clear violation of the Code of Civil Procedure. Farmers treat attached labourers as day and night labourers. Consequently, if any labourer is absent from work he is fined at double the rate of his/her normal wage. The code has also been interpreted (though wrongly) that the attached labourers need not be given any paid leave. Even in the event of illness, a labourer has to bear not only all medical expenses, but also pay a fine for the days he remained absent from work. The team found labourers who had been physically assaulted by landlords and coerced to perform illegal acts such as stealing government wood. There was a labourer who was not allowed to attend the funeral of his relative. One of the labourers had also attempted suicide.

On the basis of these observations this study has estimated that most of the attached labourers, often fall into the trap of debt bondage and nearly three-fourths of them hail from a single caste, namely, Mazhabi Sikh. Most of them are called *siri/ sanjhi* (local name for attached agricultural labour), and these labour tenures are also named as forced labour in the Bonded Labour Act, 1976. The bondage is primarily perpetuated through the heavy advance of debt on which a usurious compound rate of interest, often ranging from 24 per cent to 60 per cent, is charged. Once indebted, it is difficult for the labourer to come out of the debt-trap. The labourers are indebted not only to the farmers, even the commission agents in the grain markets use the weapon of debt to squeeze them white.

Though there are not many cases where physical coercion is involved to keep labourers in bondage, the fact remains that most of them are born into debt and die in debt. Four such labourers had met with accidents while working in the fields. Two of them inhaled insecticide/pesticide while spraying crops and the other two received physical injuries – one hurt his back-bone when he fell from an electric pole and the other fractured his leg while repairing a tube well inside the well. In none of these cases were the labourers compensated. The brother of a deceased labourer is now working to clear the debt.

Children in the age group of 8–10 years are also working for the same employer for whom the father works so that some relief from debt is secured. They are promised Rs. 2,000–4,000 per annum as wages. They hardly receive any of this amount, because their wages are adjusted against the interest of the pre-existing heavy debt accumulated by their parents. It is sad but true that women labourers from the same families clean the cattle sheds of the farmers in lieu of the interest amount of the debt advanced, which might initially have been only Rs. 3,000–5,000.

In rural areas there are no definite daily working hours. The working day is stretched according to the demand for labour, contingencies of the very nature of the labour process, timings of the supply of electricity used for irrigation or the amount of influence the employer commands over the labourer due to his vulnerability on various accounts. The data presented in Table 8.1 clearly shows that half the labourers work for more than 18 hours a day. There were only 2 per cent of workers whose daily working hours fell within the statutory limit of 8 hours. Further, it can also be observed that attached labourers work much longer hours compared to casual labourers. Out of the total attached labourers, 79 per cent work for more than 15 hours a day. Among the attached labourers more than 55 per cent work for more than 18 hours a day. This itself is indicative of the element of bondage involved in the attachment. Among the casual labourers, on the other hand, there were only 7.6 per cent labourers who worked for more than 18 hours a day. Certainly it is indicative of the use of freedom of choice by the casual labourers which is missing in the case of attached labourers. One of the most important sources of bondage is provided within the terms and conditions of attachment as circulated in the official *Gazette* notification on minimum wage. It is clearly mentioned in the *Gazette* that attached agricultural worker means 'whole time worker', which means that he is always at the beck and call of his 'master'.

The number of daily working hours is also analysed in the light of the annual income of attached and casual labourers. (Table 8.2). On the whole, it can be seen that 17 per cent such labourers earn not more than Rs. 12,000 a year. It can be said

TABLE 8.1: NUMBER OF DAILY WORKING HOURS OF WORKERS ENGAGED IN DIFFERENT OCCUPATIONS

Daily no. of working hours	No. of workers working as		Total no. of workers
	Attached labour	Casual labour	
Up to 8	4	14	18
9–12	121	65	186
13–14	48	4	52
15–18	189	2	191
18–24	444	7	451
Total	806	92	898

Source: Survey conducted in June 2004.

TABLE 8.2: WAGES PAID TO AGRICULTURAL LABOUR AT THE TIME OF SURVEY (JUNE 2004)

Annual wage income (Rs.)	No. of workers working as		Total no. of workers
	Attached labour	Casual labour	
Up to 6,000	17	4	21
6,001–12,000	110	22	132
12,001–18,000	523	55	578
18,001–24,000	154	9	163
24,001+	2	2	4
Total	806	92	898

that these are the really poorly paid agricultural labourers. The most startling figure is of labourers whose income falls between Rs. 12,000 and 18,000 per annum. The percentage of these workers is 64.37. If one analyses the annual income from wages in the light of the long hours of work, it can be safely concluded that the status of all these workers is closer to that of bonded labourers. There were only 18.6 per cent labourers whose annual income was beyond Rs. 18,000 per annum. On the face of it, it seems that all labourers earning more than Rs. 18,000 per annum are receiving at least the statutory minimum wage prescribed by the labour department. However, the fact remains that all these labourers who earn more than Rs. 18,000 per annum also work for 16–18 hours a day. If one were to strictly follow the statutory provisions, then the overtime rate should be double the normal wage rate. This means the rate of exploitation, particularly of attached agricultural labourers, is extremely high – which is unacceptable in an agriculturally prosperous state like Punjab as evident from Table 8.2.

Table 8.3 is a comparative statement of the actual annual wage paid to an attached agricultural labourer and the difference between the monthly wage adjusted to an 8-hour day and the Statutory Minimum Wage. It can be seen that in the case of both attached agricultural labourers and casual labourers, the average wage received with unlimited number of hours of work is still marginally below the Statutory Minimum Wage. But if the

TABLE 8.3: COMPARATIVE STATEMENT OF ACTUAL ANNUAL WAGE AND THE DIFFERENCE BETWEEN THE ADJUSTED WAGE TO 8-HOUR DAY AND THE STATUTORY MINIMUM WAGE

Nature of work	Average monthly wage income (Rs.)	Average daily working hours	Av. monthly income for 8-hour day	Statutory minimum wage w.e.f. 1–3–04	Difference between the col. 4 & 5
1	2	3	4	5	6
Attached Labour	1427	14.23	802	1410	-608
Casual Labour	1425	11.67	976	1410	-434

working hours are adjusted to an 8-hour day, the respective deficit in the payment of minimum wage enhances to Rs. 608 per month and Rs. 434 per month. It is a clear indication that the prosperity of Punjab agriculture is to some extent at the cost of the life and property of rural labour.

INDEBTEDNESS OF RURAL LABOUR

The amount of debt outstanding against different types of rural labourers is another indicator of debt dependence that may ultimately lead to debt bondage. It is interesting to note that the extent of indebtedness of labourers and the prosperity of agriculture are directly proportionate to each other. That is, the better the agriculture, the higher the amount of debt. This is perfectly true of the indebtedness of rural labour in Punjab. More than 55 per cent of indebted rural labourers are indebted to such an extent that it is difficult for them to come out of the debt-trap. The debt amount of these households is more than Rs. 20,000 each. In fact, there are nearly 30 per cent of indebted households whose outstanding debt is more than Rs. 50,000 each, and who are clear cases of debt bondage. The most common amount of debt was expected to be in the range of Rs. 10,000 to 20,000, but there were only 24 per cent of households whose debt was in this range. Of the total indebted households, nearly 20 per cent are those whose debt amount to less than

Rs. 10,000. A higher amount of debt was found among the attached labourers as compared to the casual labourers. In fact, the very 'attachment' of agricultural labourers to their employer is cemented by the high pressure of debt burden on the former. Other independent studies of attached labourers in south Punjab also show that there is a strong tendency among attached labourers to degenerate into debt bondage.

The sociology of debt provides a glimpse of the social dimension of indebtedness and bondage. Of the total number of indebted households, 84 per cent are SCs, 2 per cent are STs, 10.7 per cent fall under the category of backward classes, and only 3 per cent of indebted households belong to the general castes. The data shows that all households indebted to the employer belong to the SCs. Also, of the 166 households that are indebted to moneylenders, 78.9 per cent belong to the SCs. This clearly shows that multiple deprivation/disabilities combine in the SCs and make them potentially vulnerable to bondage.

STATE AND RURAL DEVELOPMENT

Rural development depends on some of the following fundamental aspects of development, namely, health, education, drinking water, housing, employment and infrastructural development. In order to address these parameters of development a large number of rural development schemes have been launched. Their major focus are the rural poor, more particularly the SCs/STs and women. Some of the important rural development schemes related to the empowerment of Dalits and women are meant to them sufficient employment and sources of livelihood. Here three schemes related to employment have been evaluated, namely, Swarnjayanti Gram Swarozgar Yojana (SGSY), Employment Assurance Scheme (EAS), and Jawahar Gram Samridhi Yojana (JGSY). There are also housing schemes meant to provide shelter to those who are 'homeless'. The schemes evaluated in this category are Indira Awas Yojana (IAY), the Pradhan Mantri Gramodaya Yojana (PMGY) and the Credit-cum-Subsidy Scheme for Rural Housing (CCSRH). Among the schemes meant to attract number of children whose parents do not wish to send them to school, the midday meal scheme is one which encourages children to attend school and also helps in retaining them there. The present study deals with the various major developmental schemes mentioned above.

In order to get feedback from the field, a detailed study in Ludhiana district of Punjab was conducted during 2002–3. The survey area included four blocks of Ludhiana district, namely, Ludhiana-I (Block-I), Pakhowal (Block-II), Ludhiana-II (Block-III) and Machhiwara (Block-IV). A sample of 800 households was taken. They were constituted by 194 non-beneficiaries of the development schemes of the government and 606 beneficiaries. The results are presented in this section. It is worth mentioning here that Block-I and Block-II are the most developed and Block-III and Block-IV the least developed parts of the district. A sample of 200 respondents from each block has been studied, which includes both beneficiaries and non-beneficiaries of the developmental schemes of the Ministry of Rural Development. Though it is not easy to summarize all the findings of the study which are so diverse, an attempt has nevertheless been made to give a brief account of the findings that flow from the field experience and also from the quantitative data.

A large number of rural workers are part of the informal sector of the economy. The sociology of work throws light on the relation between the casualization of work and caste affiliation. Casualization of work is inversely proportionate to the status of caste, that is, the largest number of casual labourers hail from the SCs who are busy in the non-agricultural sector. The type of agriculture that has evolved in Punjab has narrowed down the employment opportunities for labourers, and most of the rural labourers work in the non-farm sector. The employment of labour in agriculture, limiting to less than 3 per cent, is shockingly low. Unless some immediate steps are taken to provide alternative employment opportunities, rampant rural unemployment may turn into a serious social crisis. Though the traditional gender-specific division of family labour, where man is the breadwinner and woman the housekeeper, has not yet been broken, there is a direct positive impact of the rural development schemes on the generation of employment opportunities for women. The overall impact of the various developmental schemes seems to be positive, but it is not as significant as it was expected to be.

The number and frequency of child workers is lower among the non-beneficiary households. This is not due to their preference for school but is, in fact, for want of sufficient employment opportunities for their children. A regional analysis of the employment of children among the beneficiary households reveals that the major concentration, particularly of male child workers, is among the backward blocks. This is also true of the non-beneficiary households. One can, therefore conclude that under-development induces child labour. It can, therefore, be concluded that the removal of social and economic disparities from society can partly solve the problem of child labour.

The overall data shows that 97.52 per cent of the households among the beneficiaries and 98.45 per cent among the non-beneficiaries are landless. In Blocks-I, II and III, among the non-beneficiaries, there is not even a single household owning agricultural land. Among the beneficiary households, 71.88 per cent belonging to the general castes are landless. On the other hand, 99.61 per cent of the SC households are landless. This means that almost 100 per cent of SC households are landless. It is interesting to note that nearly 14 per cent of the non-beneficiary households earn, on an average, more than Rs. 50,000 per annum and yet they still possess yellow cards denoting that they remain below the poverty line. Of the beneficiary households, 16 per cent were earning more than Rs. 40,000 per annum, indicating that there is an improvement in their average annual income with the implementation of the various developmental schemes. There is a definite upward economic mobility among the small minority of lower castes such as the OBC-II and SCs.

The most interesting fact that emerges from the data is that 84.27 per cent of the SCs and 71.11 per cent of the OBC-II are landless labourers. The sex ratio found from the sample is quite close to the latest Census 2001 figures of Punjab state. Interestingly, in the age group of less than five years, there are more female than male children among the lower castes; after the mid-20s, the gender proportion of population is either even or females are in a majority. Sociological analysis reveals that nearly four-fifths of the population among the general castes is literate while among the SCs it is only three-fifths. Similarly, 68.85 per cent of the females belonging to the general castes are literate, while this percentage for the SC females is only 52.04 per cent. The sample survey further shows that the frequency of child labour is inversely proportionate to the economic status of the rural poor.

Scheme-wise analysis shows that dairy farming and small businesses are the two most popular activities among the SGSY beneficiaries. About 80 per cent of the total loans distributed were utilized for these two activities. After a study of loan repayment the overall picture that emerges clearly shows that four-fifths of the beneficiaries are repaying loans on a regular monthly basis. It was also found that the households availing the schemes are financially so weak that small-scale gains from a limited scheme are not enough to pull them out of their current poverty. It suggests that the extremely poor households are perpetually in debt and are in need of bigger doses of financial help in order to achieve the viability of the schemes. Of the total beneficiaries who had repaid their due loans, 61.54 per cent could successfully generate income from these schemes and return the loans. However, there are also some limitations in the SGSY scheme. For instance, there are fake beneficiaries who corner the gains in connivance with various officials. Selection of the beneficiaries is also influenced by the local politicians, particularly of the existing ruling party. Banks also need to be instructed to cooperate with the poor potential beneficiaries and not harass them on one or the other pretext.

EAS and JGSY are two schemes for generating employment, particularly for the scheduled caste, and Below Poverty Line (BPL) households. The purpose of these two schemes is to generate employment through building assets for the village as a whole. Though under EAS there is some amount of grant which serves the purpose in a limited way, the amount earmarked under JGSY is so meagre that this scheme is simply ineffective. It was surprising to find that the average wage-rate paid to the labourers is far below the prevailing Statutory Minimum

Wage, recommended by the state department. The rate of wage-payment under EAS is worse. The JGSY is being implemented through contractors, which is entirely against the spirit of the scheme. Panchayats were found to be abdicating their responsibilities and had instead left the asset-building to contractors who often engage labourers at a wage-rate far below the prescribed minimum wage. In some villages instead of manual labour, an excavating machine, owned by one local minister, was being used to desilt ponds. However, the vouchers slowed that labourers were doing the work.

The house-construction scheme for the BPL households in the rural areas under IAY and PMGY is one of the most successful schemes of the Ministry. However, the amount sanctioned under IAY and PMGY is often insufficient to meet construction needs, and the beneficiaries invariably have to add some amount from their own pockets. This suggests that, taking into account the rising prices of the building material, there is a need to enhance the amount of financial assistance by at least 25 per cent. Toilets are part of house construction. There is a separate amount of Rs. 2,500 for toilet construction which is not enough for the completion of the prescribed toilet.

CONCLUSION

The Green Revolution gave a serious blow to the age-old social bond among the rural people of Punjab. It is not only the commodification of economy, rather the entire life has been commodified under the impulse of money and market economy. The liberal market has expedited the polarising effects. In order to hold on to the social and economic space, the severly affected farmers tend to transfer their burden onto the labourers. Engaging bonded labour in agriculture is one outcome of this 'struggle for survival'. Rampant illiteracy among the labouring poor, landlessness and their marginalized social status together make them vulnerable and prone to bondage. All the developmental schemes to empower the rural poor have only limited impact. Many of such schemes remain entangled in the maze of bureaucracy. Therefore, there is an urgent need to take steps towards an all inclusive growth.

NOTES

1. There is a clear distinction between the categories of peasant and farmer as they are historical categories. The peasantry largely belongs to the pre-capitalist form of social relations of production whereby economic, social, political, cultural and spiritual relations are intertwined in a definite mould. That is, social and cultural relations are no less important than the relatively 'vegetating' economic relations. Peasantry produces from the land to meet the economic needs that are defined by the existing social, cultural and political relations; and together they mirror each other. For instance the means of production such as land, cattle and workers are revered like deities and protected against the seductive pull of the market. The Punjab peasantry equates selling of milk or of land with the selling of their son in the family. Barren lands are not disposed of for better income, and the attitude was similar towards old cattle which have lost economic utility. For the same reason, the elderly in the family are not considered a burden; rather they are respected as wise persons whose experience is used for the collective good of the family. In a nutshell, the peasantry live in a 'naturalized' web of social relations where social and cultural relations were as important as economic relations. In other words, in the *weltanschauung* of peasantry, ends do not determine the means nor are they divorced from each other. The morality of means is crucial to the economic ends, which is fundamental to the continuous reproduction of a stable social system matching the overall nature of the prevalent milieu.
2. In the present study a demarcation is made between the peasant and the farmer on the basis of their level of integration into the money and market economy of the type of capitalist farming. The peasantry reproduces collective life unmediated by the market and looks at agriculture as the source of life, not as a means of profit. On the other hand, the farmers treat land, labour, machinery and also animals as a means to make profit for personal use.

APPENDIX

COMPARATIVE STATEMENT OF THE STATUTORY MINIMUM WAGE OF AGRICULTURAL LABOUR IN PUNJAB AND HARYANA

Category of Workers	Minimum Wage Rate in Punjab as on 1–3–2004	Minimum Wage Rate in Haryana as on 1–1–2004	Difference Between Punjab & Haryana
Casual agricultural labour	Rs. 80.93 (with food)	Rs. 83.31 (with food)	Rs. –2.38
	Rs. 90.63 (without food)	Rs. 87.31 (without food)	Rs. +3.32
Attached agricultural labour (whole-time servant)	Rs. 16,923.95 per annum (with food)	Rs. 30,450.00 per annum (with food)	Rs. –13,526.05
Projections of daily casual wage (with food) × 365	Rs. 29,539	Rs. 30,408	Rs. –869
Difference between the actual and projected minimum wage of attached agri. labour	Rs. –12,615	Rs. +42	

The comparative statement of the statutory minimum wage in agriculture in Punjab and Haryana is revealing. There are two different wage rates for casual agricultural labour, one with food and the other without food. In Punjab the daily wage of a casual agricultural labourer is Rs. 80.93 (with food) which is Rs. 2.38 less than in the neighbouring state of Haryana. In fact, it should have been the other way round as the state of Punjab is agriculturally more prosperous than Haryana and the cost of living of a Punjabi agricultural labourer is also not lower than his counterpart's in Haryana. However, as far as the wage rate of a casual labourer without food is concerned, the Punjab government prescribes Rs. 3.32 more to labourers in agriculture, compared to Haryana. In other words, Haryana compensates with only Rs. 5 towards food whereas Punjab provides little less than Rs. 10 a day for food to the labourer. In this calculation Punjab has shown better heart for its labourers than its neighbour.

The most shocking difference in wage rates between Punjab and Haryana is in that of the attached agricultural labourer who is also mentioned as a 'whole-time servant'. The statutory minimum wage in Punjab is only 56 per cent of the wage rate prescribed in the state of Haryana. How these calculations are done in Punjab and Haryana only the respective departments of labour can explain, but from the labourer's point of view, at least, the wage rate of an attached labourer in Punjab should not in any way be less than in Haryana.

The survey went into the internal logic of the statutory minimum wage payment to labourers. For instance, in the notification of minimum wage to be paid to attached agricultural labourers in both Green Revolution states, it is clearly mentioned that *attached agricultural labourers are whole-time servants*. This means that they are always at the beck and call of their master. There is no paid holiday for them, as if they are machines and need no rest. If they have to go on leave, they must either produce a substitute labourer or else bear a wage deduction at double the rate of their wage for that working day. The reason for imposing a fine on leave is that the market rate of a casual wage labourer is always almost double that of the wage paid to an attached labourer for a day. This is also clear from the logic of the statutory minimum wage regulations in Punjab. That is, the statutory minimum wage rate of a casual agricultural labourer is Rs. 80.93 (with food) whereas the daily earning of an attached agricultural labourer happens to be Rs. 46.37 which is 57.3 per cent of the prevailing minimum wage of a casual agricultural labourer. Therefore, it is not that the employer is devising his own non-market mechanism for fleecing the labourers. The very structure of statutory minimum wage regulations provides the ground for employers to impose fines on the agricultural labourers.

The real question that arises regarding the statutory minimum wage of attached labourers in Punjab is that when a labourer is a 'whole-time servant' and sells all his 24 hours a day for 365 days to the employer, what is the logic for prescribing his daily wage only at the rate of 57.3 per cent of the prevailing statutory minimum wage of the casual agricultural labourer. There is an element of bondage in the officially sanctioned statutory minimum wage of attached labour on two accounts: One is that a human being is officially being asked to be a 'whole-time servant' of his employer, with no provision for rest time or any earned holiday, including weekend holiday. International labour standards and laws apart, by no stretch of imagination can the state officially sanction the selling of the entire labour power of a labourer for a year to an employer, sans a single holiday. Two, not only is the basic human freedom of recreation, cultural and physical, denied to an attached agricultural labourer, he is also officially 'forced' to work at 57 per cent of the prevailing customary or statutory minimum wage for similar work.

For comparative purposes, for this study the daily wage (with food) of a casual agricultural labourer was multiplied by 365 days of a year, as there is no holiday prescribed or actually availed of by the labourer, to arrive at the figures presented in the table in this Appendix. It is interesting to note that the Haryana government has prescribed in the statutory minimum wage Rs. 42 more than the projected wages that were arrived at for this study by considering the entire annual earnings of a casual labourer. On the other hand, from the comparable figures for Punjab, one can find that the Punjab government has prescribed Rs. 12,615 less than the projected amount. How can there be such a wide gap between the two states of Punjab and Haryana in the officially sanctioned minimum wage for attached agricultural labour? This raises the fundamental question of the very *procedure* of arriving at the 'sacrosanct' figures of minimum wage rates.

CHAPTER 9

The Green Revolution, Globalization and the Punjab Peasantry: Some Cultural Dimensions of Change

KUMOŎL ABBI

The economic success of Punjab's Green Revolution and the socio-economic crisis that a later phase of dwindling productivity has generated during the 1990s, have both received a good deal of attention and analysis. Issues like environmental degradation, decline in productivity, the need for crop diversification to overcome the problems created by over-reliance on rice–wheat cultivation, the growing gap between crop-yield and employment generation, problems of marketing and the failure of procurement prices to keep up with the rising costs of inputs of labour, fragmentation of holdings and severe limits on extending the area of production, the tragedy of certain farmers committing suicide, etc., have all been matters of considerable debate, scholarly, political and journalistic.[1]

However, the cultural aspect of the change that has since come about – partly because of the green revolution and the related mechanization and capital intensive nature of agriculture, and partly by the communication revolution represented by the extension of radio, television, telephone coverage, computerization, economic liberalization and the growing exposure to globalization – has failed to receive the requisite scholarly attention, particularly amongst sociologists and anthropologists. There have been some village studies, some studies of selected aspects of socio-economic changes, within which cultural aspects have received piecemeal attention. However, a systematic study, specifically devoted to cultural change, is conspicuous by its absence.[2]

This chapter seeks to undo this neglect by drawing on the novel *Annadata* by Baldev Singh,[3] and by attempting to specifically deal with certain important aspects of cultural change which rural Punjab, particularly the Jat peasantry, has been undergoing, especially since the late 1990s. As the novel is at present available only in Punjabi, I shall attempt to highlight the important points of the narrative and present an approximate translation in English of the relevant extracts, phrases and words.

As the title of the novel – *Annadata* (Food Provider) – suggests, the writer sees the Jat peasant as the person who has been bearing the proud responsibility, as well as the backbreaking burden, of providing food to the nation. The writer has a keen eye and a sympathetic understanding of how recent developments in the life-situation of the peasant, as the food provider to the nation, have placed him in an unenviable predicament.

Both economically and culturally, the peasant is exposed to pressures which threaten his familiar way of life and the complex ways in which he faces and negotiates the day-to-day challenges. The challenges he is faced with, as the author contends, relate, apart from his economic survival and the dominant position in the village politics and caste hierarchy, to issues concerning status, appropriate honour and shame. The proper conduct of women, especially in relation to education outside employment, contacts with classmates and fellow workers, particularly of lower castes, are matters of concern, as are issues relating to occupational training for diversifying into areas other than agriculture. The author is nostalgic about how things were earlier.[4] He particularly sees adolescent girls and young married women; the underhand ways of *aarhtiya*s and petty government officials; and upwardly mobile, educated lower castes; exploitative sadhus; prosperous Jats (for their consumerist class related lifestyle, expensive dowries, palatial houses and other ostentatious practices, demeaning poor caste fellows in comparison) as problematic aspects of the contemporary social world of the medium-, small- and marginal-level Jat farmer with whom the author is particularly concerned.

Whether or not this novel is emblematic of a particular conjuncture in Punjabi rural society, wherein agriculture has lost its sheen, both as an ideal occupation and as pre-eminent contributor to the Punjab economy, is a highly complex issue and perhaps best avoided.

Besides caste, class, gender and other markers of social difference, issues of disciplinary, ideological or personal perspectives are involved. For it is almost a truism that facts of economic and social situation are neither transparent nor do they imprint themselves directly on the mind. They are always mediated by conventions of reading, writing and scholarly enquiry. So is the case with Singh's novel. It articulates a certain Jat-centric, masculinist perspective, and has a widespread caste and community resonance wherein the world of the Punjab peasantry – particularly of the less prosperous Jats – suffers from a sad state of drift. For the purpose of analysis certain themes that form an important aspect of the discourse of the novel have been identified here.

The novel is centered on the family of Wasakha Singh, which is facing the painful transition of being reduced to a small, or even marginal level of landholding. Of his two sons the younger, Sardool, has already claimed his own share of the family land and property and moved out to set up a separate household nearby. Wasakha Singh, having reached the evening of his life, has handed over the effective management of the family and farm to his elder son, Wazir. As a sign of retirement, he has moved into the enclosure where livestock is tethered. The novel primarily revolves around Wazir, his family, their struggles to survive, their changing fortunes and those of their neighbours and kin (including Sardool and his children).

At the beginning of the novel, the family is struggling to survive. Wazir is at the *mandi* waiting for his turn to sell his produce. He and his wife Gian Kaur have three sons. The eldest, Bhagtu, is missing after an unsuccessful attempt to emigrate abroad. The second, Rajpal, is a graduate but after failing to get a salaried job he has resumed farming and is very active in union politics. The third, Guran, attempts to move out of farming and dreams of a career as a folk singer. There is also a young unmarried daughter who lives with the family, and has been withdrawn from college after failing in the ten plus two examination.

The novel begins ominously on a dark, quiet night, when Wasakha Singh comes out of his enclosure and, with his walking stick, knocks at the family door (p. 6).

Gian Kaur gets up startled, 'Babaji, what are you doing here at this time?'
'*Jhoti adingi jandi hai bhai.* The buffalo is in heat. Tell the boy to take her out.'
'I will tell them', Gian Kaur replies.

The supposed similarity of overpowering animal lust provides the author with a key metaphor to establish equivalence between a young woman and a young female buffalo (*jhoti*) in heat. It is this metaphor that colours much of the novel's characterization of women protagonists, especially young women who are viewed as deviating from caste and status, appropriate sexual modesty and restraint. A silent or, at times, clearly culturally pointed reproach seems to be directed not only at such culturally disapproved behaviour as elopement and pre-marital or extramarital affairs, but also at women's active search for academic or professional identities and meaningful extra-domestic or public roles. Related to this is the portrayal of men's helplessness in the face of such conduct. This has serious implications for status maintenance in the village and for men's struggle to uphold their masculine image and family honour.

JAT–CHAMAR SEXUAL INTIMACY: THE INCREDIBLE BECOMING CREDIBLE

A most crucial event marking the progression of the narrative is the disappearance one morning of Wazir's daughter Bhupi. The search for her brings to the surface a significant aspect of the village social relations. What was once perhaps unthinkable has come within the realm of possibility. Bhupi is suspected to have eloped with Kewal, a Chamar boy, the younger brother of Ruldu, the family's own *siri*.[5] The village folk though incredulous take it as a sign of changing times; yet the narrative stops short of making the possibility a fact.

The Chamar boy returns home, only to declare that Bhupi has been taken away by some unknown powerful persons. The futile search for Bhupi continues, but she is never found. His inability to cope with both personal and impersonal hostile forces creates in Wazir an overwhelming feeling of helplessness. In a moment of despondency and destructive introspection, he opts out of life's futile struggle.

The real consequences of Bhupi's disappearance hits Gian Kaur as she gets a clue from Dalipo (p. 77):

Saying something to herself, Dalipo turned. Then she stopped suddenly, as if remembering something, and turned again and asked, 'Where did you send your girl Bhupi so early?'

Gian Kaur's legs trembled, but she stabilized herself, 'Where did you meet Bhupi?'

'My brother was not well. He had acute stomach ache. I was walking towards the pond where I thought I saw Bhupi. I called out, but she did not reply. At that moment, somebody came from the *Chamaran da vehra* on a cycle; he appeared to be Kishna's son. She sat on his cycle and went towards the city.'

This information was not easy to reconcile (p. 85):

Gian Kaur went and sat on the other *manja*. What if what Dalipo had said turned out to be true? Bhupi and Kewal . . . the thought made her tremble. Horrible thoughts troubled her, and seemed to crawl inside her . . . hope that *harami* does not play with the honour of the girl . . . what if there are four or five people . . . ? On the face of it he did not look like such a swine. He always addressed Bhupi as 'Behanji, behanji'. Where could they have gone? Don't know what my daughter will be undergoing . . . ? Quietly, she sobbed. Afraid of Rajpal, she could not even weep openly.

Rajpal too stayed awake. He did not possess the energy to hear and see anything. He could not even meet the gaze of his mother. 'A boy like Kewal, our servant, who lived on our *jhoothi* rotis! How could he trap her? Something is wrong somewhere. Hope Bhupi did not take the initiative. In college, too, because of her activities, and on the advice of her friends I had her name struck off the rolls. Hope Bhupi is not taking revenge on me . . . .'

The news had spread and everyone in the village seemed to know about it. But fearing Rajpal's aggressive temperament, people could not openly relish the incident. They tried to grapple with the story and to piece it together . . . (pp. 87, 89, 90):

This was the topic of discussion in the village *sath*.[6] The daughter of the Dhillon's and Kishna Chamar's son! Some were surprised while others were worried:

'It's really Kalyug.'

'These are all the colours of God, keep on watching.'

'Those who lived off us have even started eyeing our sisters and daughters.'

Ram Singh who was sitting in the *sath* was very upset by the episode. 'It had to happen, now it could only happen like that,' he was about to say, when someone remarked:

'Have you not read Waris Shah: Love does not look at caste nor does it look at age?'

'How can we forget—daughter of the Jats and son of the Chamars? The one who has done this deed will have to pay for it: shoes for shoes, abuses for abuses, and girl for girl', commented Ghukkar.

Saran Singh interjected, 'I don't understand one thing. If the girl had to blacken her face, then why not with a *khandani* (respectable) boy?'

'What do you mean? Even Kishna Chamar has a *khandani marhi*,' Ghukkar again teased.

'The girl appeared very wise to me, but she never cast her eyes down while passing by,' said Saran Singh. 'The girl would jump about like a *jhoti*. She had some trouble with the masters in her school as well. She even looked Rajpal straight in the eye. Even this ordinary man's legs trembled when he saw her,' he spat out with excitement.

'Still, what has happened is unfortunate. We all have sisters and daughters. Now whether if their daughter returns within an hour, or does not come back for a month, she has already been branded. Everyone will say she has spent a night with the son of a Chamar,' Taya Nihala spoke wisely.

'Don't worry,' Ghukkar responded, 'nothing will happen, people will forget about it and in a few days, it will be history.'

'If the girl had been married off at the right time this problem would never have arisen,' Ram Singh genuinely sympathized with Wasakha Singh's family.

'What do you think is the truth, Ram Singh?' Saran started the conversation again.

'God knows. At the moment they are all rumours. I have heard that college-going boys and girls go to many *mela*s together and come back after a couple of days.'

'Kishna's Kewal studies in college, I accept, but this *Kanjar*'s sister has been out of college for almost two years,' Ghukkar said viciously. 'It may have been an old association.' (p. 92)

The news of Bhupi's disappearance hurts the pride of the old patriarch Wasakha Singh (pp. 100–11, 148):

'It will be better if I get sick and die. What is the point of living now? What more does one have to bear now? What happened?' Wasakha Singh asked Gian Kaur sympathetically.

'I don't know. The day before yesterday she had gone off to sleep quite comfortably. She had spent the day normally. No one could imagine that she had any evil intentions. When, Babaji, you came to tell me about the buffalo, I checked then and she was fast asleep. When I got up early in the morning she was nowhere to be seen. I thought she had perhaps gone out for a while. But it is almost two days now and not a word about her. As if the earth has swallowed her!'

She picked up the dishes and sat near Babaji. 'Dalipo Budhi had come. She was saying that she had seen our girl standing near the Dabwalla pond just before daybreak. She sat behind Kishna Chamar's son's bicycle and went in the direction of the city.'

'Kewal, the one who is Ruldu's younger brother?' Wasakha Singh asked surprised.

'Yes, Babaji'.

'Kishna Chamar's son?' He again asked.

Gian Kaur did not reply, she only sighed.

'May this rotten woman burn in hell,' Wasakha Singh cursed her helplessly. 'In all this there is another thing which is corroding me. Sardool [his younger brother] did not ask even once about Bhupi. How did all this transpire? Are these blood relations? She is your real niece, like your daughter. It is okay, don't talk to each other, don't exchange gifts with each other, but when such a calamity strikes, be one and stand together . . . before the world.'

The helplessness and inability is also reflected in the dialogue between Wazir Singh and Wasakha Singh (pp. 148–50):

'Why don't you rest at home?'

'I was grateful when the rice was sold. All I wanted to do was to go home and enjoy a refreshing bath and change into clean clothes. When I reached home it was an entirely different lamentation going on. I just could not bear the whole thing, Bapu. I just collapsed in the *vehra*, losing consciousness. Bhagtu's mother told me they threw water on me and massaged my feet. Only then did I come back to my senses. I just wanted to meet you.

'Where are Rajpal and Guran?'

'I have not seen either of them'. Wazir came and sat near Bapu on the tyre. Then controlling himself he spoke, 'Bapu, what are these times we are facing?'

Wasakha Singh could not answer. What could he say? He sympathetically put his hand on Wazir's shoulder and lowered his gaze, a spontaneous sigh enveloping him. The father and son sat together for a long time, silently consoling each other.

'If I had known, why would I have gone to the *mandi*'? Wazir broke his silence. 'Rajpal would have himself dealt with the buying and selling. Now we have lost everything. I just feel like consuming something and dying. How will I face the world? I don't even feel like going out of the house. . . .' Wazir began to cry.

Wasakha tried to reassure him, 'Nothing will be solved if you cry. Keep yourself strong. Let's discuss with Rajpal and inform the police. At least we will find out the whereabouts of the girl. She could not have been consumed by the earth abruptly.'

Wazir suddenly got up.

'What happened?' Wasakha Singh asked worried.

'I have to go,' he wiped his tears.

'Where to? The *mandi*?'

'What is left for us in the *mandi*? They have taken the paddy. Aarhtiya Lekhi Ram was saying that with this even my past debts will not be cleared. Half the amount is still outstanding. By the time of the next wheat harvest it will be double. Just washed my hands off the whole thing and came away. At home I was struck by Bhupi's boulder . . . Bapu, I feel what has happened has happened for the good. If she had been found dead in a pond or well, that would have been even better. How would we have married her off? If we had the capacity to marry her off and meet the demands of the others, we would have married her off four years back. All this would never have happened. If the head is covered, the feet become bare. If the feet are covered, one is left with nothing. Wazir walked out of the enclosure without listening to another word from Wasakha Singh.

The suspected elopement also has inimical implications for the hierarchical, *seri* relations between Wasakha Singh's family and Kishna Chamar (p. 150):

When Kishna, having crossed the threshold, stood in the *vehra*; his legs were trembling. An unknown fear gripped him. Seeing his weeping face, Gian Kaur came out of her house, but his apologetic expression and way of crying restrained her from uttering any bitter words.

Having taking off his shoes outside, Kishna was standing barefoot, his hands folded reverently, as a devotee waits outside a gurdwara. As Gian Kaur came out, he moved forward, touched her feet with both hands and placed the hands on his forehead. He did not say anything at all. Gian Kaur kept staring at him. Sensing her anger, Kishna was petrified – as if anticipating an impending catastrophe. He again bent towards Gian Kaur's feet and began to cry.

Gian Kaur stood impassive, silently watching him. She thought, deep inside he is as pained as us, or maybe he is just pretending. Even otherwise these people are habitually more prone to tears. If they don't do that, who would extend sympathy to them? I am sure he knows where Kewal has gone with the girl. Now no one is at home; neither Rajpal nor his father. Maybe that's why he is here.

'No one is at home,' she muttered.

'It is not my fault, Bibi,' Kishna stood with folded hands.

It appeared to Gian Kaur as if he had understood the turmoil of her inner self. She felt surprised, but did not utter a word. Kishna felt scared of her silence, not knowing what she would say. What would she do? A really terrible thing has happened. How do I say it?

'I don't know anything about it, Bibi. This worry has not let us sleep the whole night. I don't understand why fate has willed it to happen. If you say so, I will go to the *thana* and file a report.' Kishna stopped speaking and wiped his tears.

'No need to go to the *thana*,' Gian Kaur responded immediately. She thought to herself: that would be disastrous. Those who do not know would also come to know. Tomorrow we have to marry off the girl as well. It is not easy to keep such a thing a secret for long.

'Whatever you command, Bibi. I am your indebted slave. If you make me stand in the sun, I will do that too. Our Kewal has made a mistake. You may even cut off his head, I will not protest. This bad blood has beaten to dust the good deeds of his ancestors. We always thought of your house as our shelter and came here without hesitation. But how do we face you now? It is this thought that has been troubling me all the time, Bibi.' He began to wipe his tears again.

She spoke authoritatively, 'Stop displaying your tears. Go find out. Search for your son. Listen to another thing. Don't go doing *ba ba* around the whole village? You know Rajpal's anger. . . .'

'All right Bibiji, I will immediately send Ruldu to enquire from relations and even go myself.' So saying, Kishna turned away.

As he came out of the house, he felt as if he had committed a theft and yet come out of the *thana* without a beating. He heaved a sigh of relief. He had found it difficult to breathe before Gian Kaur.

Walking towards home, he thought: 'Where could those *Kanjar*s have gone? What did the girl see in Kewal? The elders are so right when they say that love is blind, and I feel even deaf. Sardarni has not given up her pride. She said, "Don't go around doing *ba ba* everywhere". These Jats, even if they lie under you, they don't give up their upmanship. This is all due to the grace of Bhagat Ravidas that ours is a boy. If people around come to know then let them. The boy has nothing to lose. After a few months we will say with pride: "Our boy has taken a *jattan di kudi*," which is no mean achievement. Then he thought: it is a bad thing to have happened. After all, she is a daughter of the village. It is a matter of the *izzat* of the entire village. But who thinks about it these days? Gian Kaur says don't do *ba ba*. Why should I do it? Does she have any control over her daughter? What did she see? Not caring about *khandan*, caste or *biradari*. The caste factor is the main thing after all. Our Kewal is no less than any Jat boy. He is more educated than any other boy in the village. I have bent my back providing him an education—now this crisis! If something disastrous transpires it will be the end of us. Hope wherever they are, they remain safe and sound. . . .'

That momentary outburst notwithstanding, Kishna is a very gentle and God-fearing man. He has always remained indebted to Wasakha Singh. Though Ruldu sometimes clashes with Rajpal or his father Wazir – and suggests to his father that he work as a *siri* with another Jat – Kishna has no malice towards this family. His motto is: if you partake of someone's salt, be loyal till the last breath. He was even keen for Kewal to become a *siri*. But Kewal refused to give up his studies.

One day, Kewal passed a remark on his father's blind devotion: 'Now that they are left with just five *killa*s,[7] and have, on top of it, bought a tractor, you want to send me as a *siri*! I fear that soon they might just refuse Ruldu. Moreover, Bapu, if both of us are there, what will they do to pass the time? One thing is possible; we will work on the lands and set them to work sewing *jutti*s.' Kewal laughed all by himself. Kishna got angry and told Kewal not to speak like that. (p. 154)

It was a matter of pride among the Chamar households that Kewal had studied more than the Jat boys, though their own boys, too, dropped out of school rather early. Some left studies after class five, or at the most, went to work after failing in the tenth standard. Many of Kewal's mates were working as *siris* with the Jats. Some worked for daily wages in the city, while some sewed *juttis* with their fathers or brothers (pp. 80–1, 173–4, 179).

After the news of Kewal's return, Rajpal made the self-degrading journey to Kishna's home. The journey, though a short one, was a journey of loss of pride and honour. On the extreme corner were the houses of the Chamars. Wasakha Singh would tell them, that his father had himself brought Kishna's father from Vadda Pind. He had given him a place to stay free of cost. Every harvest Kishna's father managed to collect enough for a year, while he was helped out during the festivals.

Now there were almost twenty-eight to thirty houses. Earlier, Kishna was Wasakha Singh's *siri*. In his free time, he would even sew *juttis*. Now Kishna's eldest son was a *siri* with Wazir. For two generations, these houses had come to each others aid. Adjoining these houses of the Chamars was a stinking pond. The open drains linked to it gave out a strange odour which permeates the entire atmosphere. When the brave ones of the village passed the way, they usually kept a hand over their nose. The various *galis* of these houses were full of puddles and slush.

It was almost dark when Rajpal, dodging the swarm of mosquitoes circling around his head as well as the slush and keeping a hand on his nose, arrived outside Kishna's door. On Kewal's request, the door was closed and kept shut. He wanted to sit and think at leisure. What had happened? Where had they taken Bhupi? How come she had an association with boys of that kind? When did she get so close to them? They all seemed to be strangers. Maybe some boys of the college were also a part of the group. But no one came in front of him. Whenever, he saw Bhupi, Kewal had often felt a strange excitement building up within him. But he was sensible, he knew she was a forbidden fruit for him. Both of them were divided by the walls of caste and class. His brother was working as a *siri* at their place. Before that it was his father who had worked as a *siri*, and before that his grandfather. Maybe even Bhupi, in her heart, did not give him more status than the younger brother of their *siri*.

Kewal sat thinking in the *kothri* in shocked surprise. The entire village must have assumed Bhupi had eloped with him. Maybe behind his back they would be saying, '*Kutta Chamar, Jatti kad ke lai gaya*'. Even Rajpal must be thinking along similar lines. 'What if he sends me to the police? If he does not believe me, then what happens?

How did those fellows know about Rajpal? One was even abusing him. That only means they had been meeting Rajpal before as well. They could not have taken Bhupi by force; she has gone of her own accord. Don't know where she could be now? What will I tell Rajpal?

What side would it be? I don't know for how long I kept running in the fields. Which turning led to the road? But they will not be waiting there till now' . . . . Then he again thought – it has been four days since I went to college. What will my friends be thinking? Maybe the same rumours have carried over there . . . everyone in college knew Bhupi.[1]

As it was daybreak, the news had spread like wildfire that the 'Chamar boy, Kewal, had returned home.'

It is Gian Kaur's clinical analysis of the socio-economic situation of the family to Bhagtu, her wayward son, that makes the conditions for Bhupi's departure (p. 179):

'How did it all happen?' asked Bhagtu of Gian Kaur.

'What can I say son, when luck does not favour you? We have never harmed anyone. After you left home, Rajpal completed his B.A. He was pushed around for almost a year, but where does one get jobs these days? Rajpal came to his father and said, "Bapu, I will work on the land." Your father was shocked. "If you wanted to mingle with mud then why did you waste studying for fourteen years." He was right son. Your father wanted his son to be an officer, but these are the privileges of the strong. What could your father do? Rajpal, himself, began to go to the fields. Then he became obsessed like you: "I want to own a tractor. If land is less, we will lease it in . . ." You know, son, the circumstances in which we sent you. Where would the tractor have come from? What was required was a wad of notes. Your father was scared. If he said "no", then, like you, he too would have left home. Parents are scared of so many things. After consulting Babaji, the two *killa*s – mortgaged at the time of your leaving – were sold and the tractor was brought home. We even acquired a trolley. But it was not easy to pay the instalments for the tractor in five *killa*. We ploughed other's lands; even carried loads. But one day, while unloading, the tractor became hot. Don't know what it was, but Rajpal had to get five thousand rupees from the *aarhtiya* to get it repaired.

Then almost a year after we purchased the tractor, one day the bank people came. They said, "Pay up your instalments, otherwise we will take away the tractor." Rajpal requested that he be given a month's time. The sarpanch became the guarantor. But how could he collect the notes in a month? The bank people came again. This time the police came too. Rajpal went into hiding; the tractor was parked in someone else's home. They picked up your father. The next day, the sarpanch freed him on bail and gave an undertaking: "The amount due to the bank will be returned this month." Then Rajpal went and sold the tractor in the *mandi* at Kotakapura. Shera purchased the trolley. Don't know who purchased the ploughs? Rajpal also purchased an old scooter.'

'Here it is', Gian Kaur pointed towards a scooter lying in the *vehra*.

'What else, Bebe?'

'What else son? Two more *killa* were lost. One old tyre of the tractor is lying in the enclosure. Your Baba sits on it to reflect: "The boys tried very hard, but destiny has played truant with us." Now your Baba has stopped coming out. Even earlier he had to be called to the *sath*. This Bhupi episode has really hit him hard.'

'You should have just married her off, Bebe.'

'To whom? Wherever we negotiated, someone asked for a motorcycle or a Maruti. We don't even have the capacity to buy a bicycle. You know everything.'

'When did you make Bhupi leave college?' Bhagtu asked suddenly.

'It was Rajpal who insisted that she leave college. She really protested against it. She said, "Has he won any gold medals himself that he is asking me to leave?" Then she kept on insisting that she wanted to work in a PCO in the city. They would pay about five hundred rupees a month. Your Chacha Sardool's Mito is working in the city. I don't know what it is called PCA . . . PCA. . . .'

At times Wazir feels like throwing away the bandage on his eye, go to the fields and sow the wheat or have it sown. All his life he had been doing it himself, but now – *navian guddian nave patole*. In pursuit of a tractor, first the oxen were sold, then the plough; even the yoke for the oxen became useless – *balan ban gaaye*. Now that he was left without the tractor, the ox and the plough, he has to look to strange hands to plough the fields. Seeing the brick houses, even the mud ones were demolished. Wazir heaves a sigh he feels hedged in from all sides. The impending debt of Lekhi Ram Aarhtiya makes him evaluate his situation (p. 155):

'Did you meet Lakhi Ram Aarhtiya?' he asked Rajpal quietly.

'No Bapu, just did not get the time.'

'Lekhi was saying even my previous accounts will not be cleared'.

'The accounts of these sister-fuckers would not be cleared for a whole lifetime. Every season they put up a sheller, or buy a plot or open a finance company. They squeeze the Jat like sugar cane in a *ghalari*. Let me be free from here then I will gherao them too,' said Rajpal angrily.

After a short pause, Rajpal again continued, 'Baba used to tell us: "We used to have eighty acres." How much is left now? Where have they gone? This Lekhi Ram Aarhtiya used to sell vegetables in the village on his bicycle. Then, by my reckoning, his children should have been begging around . . . but they have six *aarhat* shops, two shellers, a *karkhana* shelling *sarson ka tel*. Where did it all come from; did it fall from the sky? This has been made by squeezing the blood of the Jat.'

This triumph of the Chamars, too, hurt the pride of the Jats, who see themselves being looked down upon. Kewal, being summoned to the police station, restores some semblance of pride (pp. 107–8):

It is evening. The usual people are gathered in the village *sath*: Ram Singh, Taya, Nihala, Narain Singh and Sajjan Singh. Ghukkar, of course, is always there. Even the passersby linger on to catch the gossip. Today also the *sath* is crowded.

'Baba Ram Singh, they have taken away our Ranjha', Ghukkar was the first to inform everyone.

'Who has taken which Ranjha away'? said Ram Singh in surprise.

'They, *begane put* (strangers), have taken him away. Now when he gets a beating, he will know what it means to fall in love'.

'Taya Singha, the police came in the afternoon. They have taken away Kishna's son Kewal. Got it'?

'Of course I have got it. But why are you holding up your tail like a squirrel?'

'It is a matter so right for holding one's tail up. The Chamars who strutted, "*Bai hum ne jatton ki kudi kaddi hai*" (We have taken away the girl of the Jats.)—now, after the coming of the police, are hiding their tails in their underwear.'

Listening to Ghukkar, Naraina burst out laughing.

'*Oai*, why don't you behave and tell what happened properly', said Ram Singh.

Ghukkar became composed and said seriously, 'Baba, the police came today. Rajpal was with them. He must have brought them along. I got in among the crowds. As the *thanedar* entered, he immediately told Kewal, "Come on, get up." Kishna pleaded with folded hands: "*Mai baap*, he is not well. He has been badly injured." When his mother came forward, a policeman pushed her away. Then the *sipahi*s got hold of Ranjha", threw him in the car and drove off . . . rode off leaving behind a crying Kishna, his wife and Ruldu. When a tearful Kishna pleaded with people: "Come with me to the *thana,* otherwise they will beat Kewal to death", everyone began to slink away.'

However, Kewal's arrest is not so simply forgotten. It leads to an uproar, and Rajpal has to accept the changing times (pp. 247, 264):

The thing which Rajpal most feared actually happened. The matter reached the court from the *thana* and finally the press. Some journalists tried to get hold of Bhupi's photograph. Rajpal braced himself for this eventuality. What could he do? The village people and relatives knew already, now even the distant acquaintances will know. What did it matter now? One thing that kept bothering Rajpal was the possibility that Kewal actually did not know where Bhupi had gone: 'I have a feeling Kewal does not know at all. This police can even force the stone to talk; could be an innocent is taking the beating.'

Rajpal wanted to express his sympathy to Kewal. He wanted to say, 'It is all the fault of that *sala thanedar*. I had tried to explain to him many times, "What is the need to bring Kewal to the *thana*." He did not agree. Even now I did not create any hurdle in your getting bail. Otherwise, how would you have been out so quickly? I did not even go to the court on the date set for the hearing. If my lawyer had argued the case, then you would have had to cool your heels in the jail for another two months.' He had many more things to say. But Kewal's hostile response changed his mind. He said to himself, 'Let the Chamar go to hell; *sala* shows his sullenness . . .'.

The bitterness between the families also affects Ruldu's working at the farm as *siri* (p. 260). He remains stone-faced while working in the fields these days. He knows that the knots of suspicion can never be undone. He has to somehow manage with Rajpal till the harvest. He had made this promise to the sarpanch. At night, when he comes back and looks at Kewal, he feels troubled. He seethes with anger inside, and abuses Rajpal.

Ram Singh and Nihala – while visiting Wasakha to sympathize

with him about the lack of news regarding the whereabouts of Bhupi – start talking about old times when even bad characters showed respect for their village sisters or daughters:

'Ram Singh, you know very well how even the robbers avoided robbing a village if they came to know that a daughter of the village was married there. They left their loot right there, and instead gave a *shagun* to the girl. Now, as you can see, not to speak of the neighbouring areas, your own village boys behave so badly.'

At this point, Roop Chand Aarhtiya's arrival from the town surprises everyone. After the usual greetings, a routine enquiry about the state of his business elicits an earful from him about how hard if was for him to earn a living as hardly any customer turns up to shop these days:

'You are not the only one suffering such a plight. The Jat, too, is caught in this vicious, squeeze,' Baba Ram Singh spoke up. 'The lands are shrinking, reduced to just one and a half to two *killa*s each. How does one sow enough crops in these? Even if we sow the seeds, how does one meet the needs of the family? The debts are never returned. Tractors bought for three lakhs are sold for peanuts. . . . See how crowded is the *tractoran di mandi*. It appears as if the tractors of the entire country are being sold there! Even the animal *mandi* at Jagraon is not able to gather so many animals. You can see from here itself, Roop Chand. If the Jat does not have money, then how will your goods be sold? We, too, are suffering and you are suffering too.'

Wazir, carrying the burden of this existence, has to accept Bhagtu's decision to become a *sadhu* and renounce the world. Guran's decision to seek a new life troubles him because he demands a share in the meagre land left. But the impending marriage of the sarpanch's son really breaks his heart, as he compares the destiny of the sarpanch's son with that of Rajpal, who struggled so hard to succeed but ultimately lost out, with not even the prospect of a wedding before him. The news of Bhupi being seen in a truck somewhere in UP shatters the wall of composure he has created around himself. The *aarhtiya*'s visit makes him cave in completely (pp. 343–4):

Wazir was in deep thought. How will I pay off the *aarhtiya*'s loan? He has converted seven or eight thousand to eighteen. How much will be the output of wheat? I fear there will be not enough to eat. How will we meet the household needs? Lekhi Ram will come again. It is good we sold the tractor trolley and were able to return the bank loan. Rajpal told me that five or six thousand rupees were still outstanding. I had thought I have three boys; farming would not be difficult at all. We could add another five or seven *killa*s. But we seem to have lost everything. I feel this house has been ruined. I can't visualize what the future will be. Lekhi Ram says it is an outstanding amount of eighteen thousand rupees, which cannot be paid off in one's lifetime. The interest will multiply every month. Should we sell the *jhoti*, or the buffalo, or perhaps the space of the enclosure? One animal can be easily accommodated in the *vehra*. But how will we look after the animal? Would we sow fodder or our crops? Guran and Bhagtu will take their share and separate. Rajpal, too, shall work as a labourer like Gill's Desu. Will this *jattan da put* accept it?

Lost in thought, Wazir lies down on a loose *manja*. As he closes his eyes, he once again sees Lekhi Ram. He is insulting Wazir before the entire village, threatening to take him to the *thana*. Then he sees the police coming in a big hurry. They have caught hold of him and Rajpal. They are both being dragged away. Then he begins to see Bhupi. Three or four boys are pulling her away, while she is calling out for help. He is running after them. But he cannot keep pace. As he tries to run, his feet seem to fall backwards. On one side, it is Lekhi Ram looking daggers at him, and on the other, it is the police. Bhupi is standing alone at a distance. . . . Then Bhagtu comes in front of him. . . . On one side, wearing earrings, Guran is dancing. People are laughing heartily. Gian Kaur is still remonstrating with herself. The police are dragging him and Rajpal away. Wasakha is looking back at his days of glory.

Wazir Singh did not realize when he got up from the *manja*, when he picked up the spray and swallowed it. (p. 345)

DASAUNDHA SINGH GILL: A SOCIALLY AND MORALLY DOWNWARD JOURNEY

The protagonist, Dasaundha Singh Gill (later nicknamed Desu), has much Jat pride, but neither sufficient land nor finance, nor any special skill or enterprise to maintain a dignified social existence as a marginal farmer. He even lacks the reputed Jat capacity for continuous hard work and a willingness to stake all to defend family honour. He too is a victim of circumstances which have made the small farmers' struggle for survival a battle against heavy odds. But in this case, behind the facade of bravado, the will to fight seems corroded from within – making the struggle look more farcical than tragic. Desu manages to survive, but at the cost of his family honour which makes him and his wife a butt of sexually snide remarks at the village *sath*. The text initially shows Dasaundha Singh Gill as a village dandy (p. 172):

When he walked past in his pleated kurta and *chaddara*, and wearing a pointed *jutti*, then one felt like glancing at him from afar. But the spike in his pointed *jutti* did not last for long. When Bheero was married here, the house reflected prosperity. The younger brother, Labh, had completed his tenth and roamed aimlessly. There was a prospect of his becoming a peon in the school and he asked his brother to help.

Desu replied with irritation, 'You, a son of the Gills, would now clean up the school like the Chamars! You would offer water to the school teachers, and stand before them with folded hands! Won't you feel ashamed?'

But Labh persisted and he managed to get the job of a peon in a high school near the village. He would go on his bicycle in the morning, carrying his tiffin-box, and return in the evening.

Dasaundha Singh was very annoyed about the whole thing: 'Why did he take up the job of a peon? It is better to consume poison and die rather than suffer this ignominy.' He shared this feeling with many in the village.

A number of Jat households came to look at Labh as a possible match, but when they came to know that Labh worked as a peon they backed out. Finally, a lesser household found him acceptable. About six months after the wedding, Dasaundha Singh portioned his assets. He was then left with just his share of two and a half acres of family land. Even their mother went towards Labh's *chulah*.

Unlike Desu, Labh is realistic about his prospects and clear about his priorities (p. 272).

Labh himself could not do farming. What could he manage in two and a half *killa*s? Dasaundha had not even given him the farming instruments in the family partition. Labh gave the land to Baba Narain's family on a half crop-sharing basis.

Time moved on. Since the peon, Labh Singh, was a matriculate, the government department promoted him to the rank of a clerk. He bought a scooter. He pulled down the *kutcha* house he inherited and constructed two *pukka* rooms, a boundry wall and an iron gate. Outside the house was a huge nameplate with 'Labh Singh Gill' written on it.

On the other hand, Dasaundha Singh's condition deteriorated. He could not work on the land properly. He had not given Labh the oxen, the plough and the other instruments, but as he lacked initiative and enterprise, what good were the instruments to him? The first thing Dasaundha Singh did was to sell his buffalo. Bheero had strongly protested,

'Why are you selling it? It will maintain the prosperity of the house. I will look after my buffalo, even if I have to go out to get the grass to feed it.'

'From where will you get the grass? Now the *bahu* of the Gills will go and cut grass, like the *kamins*?'

'I have no hesitation in doing my own work. Why be ashamed of the effort of one's hand? At least we can sell enough milk to run the household. The children will be looked after, and I'll pass my time.'

'I have to sow the new seeds, pay for the water and purchase the manure. From where will I bring currency notes? If you don't have four quintals of grains, how will you feed the children?'

Both were right in their own way.

Dasaundha Singh had sown wheat on two *killa*s of land, but for one reason or the other he could not tend the crop regularly to ensure proper growth. Sometimes it was not watered on time and at after times it rained out of time. He blamed everything on his bad luck. Over the next three years, Dasaundha Singh first mortgaged part of his land, following which he had to sell it. First people removed the word 'Gill' from his name. Then, as time elapsed, 'Singh' was also cut out. Later even 'Dasaundha' got gradually shortened to 'Desu'.

Times became very tough for Desu, and it was only the fear of losing the roof over his head that made him come out of his slumber (p. 277):

One day Desu made a resolution. He picked up his bicycle, without mudguards, and took it to the cycle repair man. To his wife Bheero he only said, 'Make two *roti*s for me in the morning. I have to go for work.'

The next day, he wrapped himself in a *khes*, took his cycle and rode to the city. The spokes of the bike screeched without grease, sometimes the pedals came in the way. Desu felt irritated and swore at the bike. By the time he reached the city, he was exhausted. He went and stood near a group of Bhaiyas[8] at the labour chowk. He covered his face with his *khes*. If he bumped into a Mazhabi or Chamar of the village, it would be disastrous! They would go back to the village and mock at him: 'The Gill's Desu, was standing in line with the daily wagers.'

When a scooter or car stopped, the crowd of Bhaiyas would scramble for selection. By about eight-thirty, the rush had sorted out. A few old labourers were left. Desu was still standing at the side. Then one man on a scooter stopped near him.

'Will you come?' he asked Desu. It was his first day. Desu's heart skipped a beat. What kind of work will it be? He was still debating whether to say yes or no, when two Bhaiyas came and stood next him.

'Hey, Bhaiyas', the man on the scooter hailed, 'will you come too?'

'Yes, of course. What will you pay?'

'The usual daily wage'.

'Okay, tell us the address,' the Bhaiyas said.

The deal was struck. The *scooterwala* gave the address and drove away. When Desu and the Bhaiyas reached the employer's home, he was a shocked to see there the *mistri* (mason) of Vadda Pind, Karnail Singh, savouring a cup of tea. Overcoming his first instinct to go back he went ahead bravely, prepared for the consequences, and parked his bicycle.

'How are you Gilla?' The *mistri* asked in a mocking tone.

That's how it sounded to Desu. He did not reply then. He thought to himself, 'If one has to dance in public, why brother to put on a veil.'

The employer began to explain the work to him. Desu had to remain with the *mistri* on the terrace, while the Bhaiyas brought the bricks from the ground.

After a while they all got to work. In about half an hour, the *mistri* and Desu got into a scuffle.

The employer came, upstairs to them in a hurry and asked, 'What happened.'

'Put this Gill Sahib on some other work. I will manage with the Bhaiyas,' said the *mistri*, setting in place a brick. 'He does not know anything about tools and keeps handing me the wrong ones. If I ask for a glass of water, he says, "Go down and drink it."' The mason stood up leaving his work.

'I will leave, let the *mistri* work,' said *Desu* starting to wash his hands.

The employer got a bit worried about finding another labourer. He came close to Desu and said, 'You come downstairs, we will send the Bhaiyas here.'

The employer sent the Bhaiyas upstairs to work with the *mistri*. Desu, however, moved to pick up his bike in order to leave, but the employer stopped him.

'Come on, get back to your work. Work at least for half a day,' said the employer glancing at the unfinished work.

'I have not asked for money,' Desu protested.

'You need not go to the *mistri*. Work at the cutting downstairs. Come, leave the bike. I will get some more tea.'

Desu sat down on the side, and the employer went inside to ask for tea and came back to stand near Desu.

'Do you know the *mistri*?'

'Yes, that is why this *sala* is showing off. He comes from the village next to ours.'

'Why is he troubling you?'

'How can this *sala* trouble me? I know their family – their misdeeds – inside out. That is why this *sala* is afraid of being found out. Their entire lives they have served as *sepi* with the Jats: sometimes begging for fodder, sometimes for wheat straw. Now he thinks he is being modern, insulting me. Don't I know it? Thinks I am a simpleton. Now *Baoji*, I too have become a daily wager. Would I accept his superiority? Does he think he can put down the Jats this way? *Sala* boasts that Jats are working as daily wagers under them. *Sala*, has forgotten when he used to come to our fields to sharpen our sickles. Now he says: "Wash the glass and bring me water to drink." Ha! Serving him drink will be my. . . .'

At this point the housewife brought the tea. Soon after that, Desu got busy preparing the mud. He worked very hard and prepared the mud to a smooth paste in about half an hour, for which the Bhaiyas had spent two hours without accomplishing much. By the afternoon he became very tired. Not being a regular daily wager, he did not know the art of conserving his energy by working slowly, as the Bhaiyas did. The owner was pleased with his work and asked him to come the next day. But Desu received the day's wage and decided not to return.

Later, Desu started going to town regularly, sometimes he got work, sometimes not. There was strong competition from the Bhaiyas who kept coming to Punjab in large numbers. They undercut the locals in wages, but did not work as hard as them. This situation was doubly unsatisfactory for Desu. It hurt his Jat pride to line up with the Bhaiyas as a daily wager, and the work – despite being exhausting and at times quite humiliating – failed to meet his day-to-day subsistence needs. This state of helplessness and want pushed him still further towards moral and social degradation.

It is the prelude to Lohri (p. 319):

There was excitement among the people to go to Muktsar, which would give them an enjoyable outing and an opportunity to seek the Guru's blessings. As the sun went down, the fog set in. For a couple of days the sun had been playing hide and seek. After being just feebly visible during the afternoon, it would hide in the fog. People go indoors early in the evening. Even Bheero had retreated inside with her two little children. There was no wood to light the *chulah* and no *atta* (flour) to cook the food. Desu had not yet returned from the city. It is only on his return could one hope for something to eat.

After a long wait, when it was pitch dark, Desu entered the home. Placing his cycle next to the wall, he removed the empty bag from the handle and flung it away viciously. Bheero understood, and with a sinking feeling she said, 'No work again today'.

'In which well do I drown myself? *Sala* city *wallahs*; they sort out the labour as if they are buying an animal at *pashuan di mandi*. I kept on waiting in the cold till the evening like a sheep dog.' Hunger, fatigue, cold and anger do not let Desu speak more. He had thought riding back, I'll ask Bheero to make me some tea, if some tea leaves or jaggery are available. But seeing the cold *chulah* he understood. He just went inside and lay down on the loosened *manji*, pulling up a dirty *chaddar*. Bheero, too, lay down on the adjoining *manji*, along with the two children and sighed, 'The children also went to sleep hungry.'

Desu could not speak. He pushed aside the quilt and sat up, placing his head on his knees. He sat there for a very long time, as if he had slipped into sleep. After what seemed like ages, he slowly lifted his head and spoke in a deathly voice, 'You could have gone to Babaji's *samadh*.' He did not have the guts to glance at Bheero's *manja*.

Bheero did hear it, but she pretended not to. The fog in the night became intense.

Bheero – around thirty years in age, dark complexioned, sharp featured and a mother of two children. She thought for a long time about what Desu had said. Surely he knew . . . the price one would have to pay for going to the *samadh*.[9] What could he do if she refused to go? But the kids, being hungry, would wake up in the middle of the night and ask for food. He too would will go to sleep hungry, and without sleep how will he work?

For how long would the neighbours help? She could not even ask her Labh *devar* with whom they had no interaction. Removing a corner of the quilt she glanced at Desu, who sat with his head locked between his knees. If this man were worth anything, why would she have to go knocking at other's doors? A sigh escaped her. Then she got up and covered herself with the dirty *khes*. Saying softly to Desu, 'Keep the lamp burning. Don't latch the door from inside,' she slipped out. The cold icy winds dashing against her body, she stopped for a while at the turning of the *gali*. Because of the darkness, cold and fog, she was in two minds. Then the hunger of the children and Desu's hunger propelled her, and she began to walk towards the Baba's *samadh*.

The decision was morally repugnant and personally distasteful to Bheero. Besides, her honour and dignity as a woman was crucially involved. Several times she almost turned back . . . (p. 326):

'Bheero, go in now. Baba will now have *bhog*.'

Bheero pushed aside the excited hands of Bhagtu, and asked him entreatingly to let her leave that day: 'I will come again sometime.'

'When you come again, we will see. This is for now. Why get cursed by Baba for nothing? Gift of the body is the purest gift. Money is impure and collected by cheating. The body is ours. It can be purified by taking a bath. Go in now. Baba will be angry if you are late.'

Bheero kept silent, not moving.

'If you like, you can have another peg of liquor. It will make your mind strong.'

Bheero made up her mind fast, 'Let me then have a bit more, Baba.' Soon after, she put the glass near the fire and reluctantly walked in towards Baba's *samadh*.

When Bheero – carrying a *dolu* (bucket) of *dal* and *rotis* – pushed open the door with trembling hands, almost half the night had elapsed. She placed the bucket of *dal* and the *rotis* on a ledge in the room and latched the door. The cold wind passing through the open crevices seemed to pierce her body. Seeing the children still asleep, she called Desu, 'Come on, eat up.' Getting into the warm quilt made her tremble, and she firmly clung to her children for warmth.

Desu sat up on his *manja,* pulled the quilt over his shoulders and stole a glance at the bucket of *dal* and *rotis*. Bheero felt very irritated: 'Now he can't even get up and eat?'

'You could have got a sip of liquor?' said Desu, looking like a scared cat.

'Come, you God's creature, *rab deyan bandeya*. Get up and see for yourself,' said Beero bitterly. She wanted to tell him some nasty truths and to keep abusing him. But all she could say with utmost contempt was, '*Sala*, passing for a man.' Then she quietly covered her face.

CITY PUBLIC SPACES AND WOMEN'S ERODING HONOUR CONSTRAINTS

Another important aspect of the discourse relates to the movement of women, especially younger women, from the private domestic world in villages to public spaces in the city, in particular, those functional spaces that link the city business, transport and other public activities with the outer world of villages, towns and other cities. Meeto (Gurpreet Kaur, Wasakha Singh's younger son's younger daughter) and her friend Kanto represent two such women who regularly commute to the city for work by bus or tempo. In fact, the text first introduces Kanto early in the morning waiting for Meeto at the village tempo stand to take a tempo together to the city. Before starting work at their respective PCOs the two usually have tea together, either at Meeto's place of work or at Kanto's, depending on which one they reach first. This gives them the opportunity to exchange gossip and plan the day's shared activities such as shopping or socializing.

Apart from their common village backgrounds, Meeto and Kanto's circle of working women friends and acquaintances has many things in common. They have a similar higher secondary or undergraduate-level college education, which distinguishes them from the ordinary illiterate or primary- or middle-level school dropout girls. In addition, they have similar low-level, tertiary jobs such as PCO attendants, receptionists, salesgirls, telephone operators, etc. Further, they and their circle have similar urbanized consumerist tastes in clothes, cosmetics, ornaments, dress accessories, entertainment and socializing. For the village youth, particularly the girls, these represent glamour, urban modernity, freedom from needless social restrictions including earning a living and choice of mates. There is, however, a frequent mismatch between the generally low levels of incomes and their consumerist tastes. Besides, there may be pressures or unconcealed expectations to help augment the family income or to meet emergency needs. Thus, through example, persuasion or social pressure by peers, many of them may start dating, acquire indulgent boyfriends, well-off patrons and even slide into sexually entertaining clients on a commercial basis.

The text leaves little doubt that Meeto and Kanto have already developed the social connections and skills necessary for providing clandestine sexual services to a limited selection of persons. The PCOs, where they are formally employed, serve as contact points and respectable covers for carrying on the more lucrative and morally dubious sexual dealings on the side. Further, the text also points to the financial benefit their families derive from their additional income, and how the incremental flow of benefits induces the families to overlook the possible sources of that income and makes them complicit in the resulting loss of their social dignity and honour (p. 218).

It was Bhupi's friend Kanto who had befriended Meeto, and gradually arranged a job for her in the city. First it was at a photostat machine. Later she negotiated with a PCO and got her a job there. In the years that passed, Meeto and Kanto deepened their bonds with each other. The two were a topic of discussion in the village, and gossiping about them in the village *sath* acquired new dimensions. Gradually, the two transformed in terms of dress and fashion: sometimes a short-hemmed *kameez*, sometimes a fully pleated salwar, sometimes tight hems and at other times loose ones. The village girls became aware of changing trends from these two. The ones who regularly went to the city would be surprised: 'They earn only seven hundred rupees but how do they spend so much?'

Their day in the city begins with successfully negotiating the complicated web of relationships they have created around themselves (pp. 220–3):

Deepa came back after taking a round. Meeto was surrounded by clients. The cabin was overcrowded. Some were grumbling and coming out. The sound of bus horns was piercing the ears. . . . A young man walked into the cabin. Deepa pressed Meeto's hand as a silent sign to her to look around. As she glanced back, Meeto looked pleased and gratified; it was Pritam standing behind her.

'I was about to dial your number.'

'Really!'

'Swear on you.'

'Ask Deepa, I just mentioned your name.'

'What is your programme?'

'There are many.'

'Come on, let's go.'

'I have to go to a friend's wedding at one. Till then I am all yours,' Meeto put on an act of surrender.

'So you have learnt the tricks of the trade,' Pritam laughed. He looked at his watch and said, 'Come let's go.'

The encounter with Pritam Canadawallah takes her to the bazaar and to a hotel. After coming back she describes to Deepa her time with Pritam (p. 225):

When Meeto entered the PCO, Deepa was herself ringing up someone. Three others were standing in the PCO cabin. Meeto was looking very tired and desperately in need of a cup of tea. There was no place to sit. Deepa got up, glanced towards the three and said, 'Today it would not be possible to go. . . .'

As Meeto sat down, she hit Deepa on her waist, 'Three in one.'

'My *jutti*,' said Deepa glancing at her shoe.

Meeto yawned hard and Deepa looked at her in surprise.

Meeto understood and then spoke up, 'What can I do *yaar*? *Saala* insisted so much. I had to take half a peg. I enjoyed it then, but now my body seems to be breaking in pieces.'

'What all did you wrangle out of him?' Deepa asked.

'He gave me a suit, of course, not to forget the food. In a drunken stupor he even muttered that he wanted to marry me.' Meeto laughed a tired laugh.

'Hari has still not come. *Saala* said he would come in the afternoon,' observed Deepa, looking worried and disappointed. 'Now it is almost two. Come on, order for some tea, bitch,' Deepa said with a hint of jealousy.

'If you had come with me, you could have savoured roast chicken . . . *Shahi paneer*, not to forget the whisky.'

'Your tea will suffice for now.'

As Meeto was handing over a slip for two cups of tea, Deepa asked her to tell the boy to get the special one. (p. 231)

Meeto's final act of complete exposure to the outside world is the message Deepa communicates to her about the summons from the SHO, Shukla (p. 231):

'What was he asking about me'? asked Meeto, worried about herself. 'What had he to say?'

'Well, he has the list of everyone's names. He will call everyone; you as well as Kanto. He was even asking about Bhupi.'

While describing Meeto's home environment, the emphasis

remains on how her parents, especially her father Sardool, remains aloof from village activities and maintains a somewhat distinctive and urban-centred lifestyle (p. 290):

Sardool was always well-dressed. He kept a radio at home. Now they say people can even see a television antenna on his terrace. Meeto's interaction with the city has made them decorate the home beautifully. They have a huge gate, regardless of the fact that no tractor or trolley passes through it. He leaves the gate ajar, puts out a *moorha*, switches on the radio and sits listening to Radio Jalandhar or Lahore.

Another aspect, which attracts much criticism and even malicious gossip, is the licentiousness of Meeto in the city and her father's indifference to get her married. Sardool's insensitiveness to village gossip is seen as a mark of his lack of shame and sense of honour.

His wife fights with him every day over the issue of Meeto's marriage being put off. Sardool does not ask anyone nor does he bother to look for a match for Meeto. When he is not present in the *sath*, one can usually hear severe criticism of him. He is contemptuously called a pimp living on his daughter's income.

Sardool's character is well summed up by Ram Singh:

'Wazir is a good man, he got the cataract much before his time. This Sardool is hale and hearty; he prefers to be blind. Can't he see his full-grown daughter? How she prances about in the city? Just marry her off, let her do whatever she wants in her in-law's house.'

The father's permissive or complicit behaviour, and the daughter's continuous use of the city as a sexual playground, finally provides the village gossips with another absorbing topic:

The whole village is discussing Sardool's daughter, Meeto. She has recently got an abortion done. The news, having reached the perspective in-laws, caused them to cancel the impending marriage. (p. 356)

FROM *MANDI* TO *APNI MANDI*

The two concepts *mandi* (market) and *apni mandi* (our market) seem indexical of the transition that Punjab farmers – particularly small and marginal farmers – have experienced. This transition was from an initial green revolution-linked prosperity induced by assured procurement prices for wheat and paddy and keen market-demand, to the later stage of growing impoverishment due to the rising costs of labour, machinery and other inputs. There was stagnation in productivity, and a slackness of demand which lead to a glut in the market. Procurement agencies and *aarthiya*s looked with bored indifference at the grain heaps brought to the *mandi*s. The novel, while describing the increasing economic misery of small and marginal farmers, brings out some of it's significant social and cultural consequences—other than those already analysed in the earlier sections of this paper.

First, however, a word about the transition to *apni mandi*. Before the transition, the farmer is a producer of grain and sells it wholesale in the market through his own *aarhtiya*s with whom he has multifaceted relations other than selling grains. These include the purchase of inputs and taking credit to meet social, ceremonial and personal emergency needs. The transition to *apni mandi* attests to his loss of land through partition or sale leaving a drastically reduced area for cultivation. He reduces, or altogether gives up, the production of grain and instead starts cultivating vegetables and fruits which he takes to the market for retail sale. This yields greater profit, but puts him in the demeaning company of the much despised peddlers or Bhaiyas, thereby causing a loss of social and self-esteem.

The novel begins with Wazir Singh, the main protagonist, sitting on his *manji* to protect a mound of wheat he has brought to the *mandi* for sale. Wazir is yet to recover from a cataract operation. With his eye still bandaged with a green bandage, he can only dimly see with his good eye, which too, he keeps mostly closed for the fear of dust. The severe visual impairment seems to symbolize his incapacity to assess, and respond adequately to, the rapidly changing world around him (p. 7):

> Wazir is waiting alone. Everywhere there is a scramble, anger and helplessness. The government and non-government agencies have not so far entered the *mandi* to procure paddy. For almost a month the farmers have been sitting on their harvests protecting them. They have to prepare the fields for the next harvest. So many family responsibilities have been held up, pending the sale of paddy. They have struggled very hard from the sowing to taking the harvest to the *mandi*. They have taken loans, borrowed much money. . . . The farmers are restless.

The weather, too, is undependable. It was cloudy in the morning, but it cleared up towards the afternoon; and then the clouds came back in the evening. What if it rains or a storm comes? The thought worries the farmers guarding their harvests.

Sitting on his mound of paddy, Wazir is surprised, 'Today no *roti* has come from home.' Neither Rajpal, nor Guran have come home nor have they sent *roti* through the neighbours. It is almost sunset. Bodha Singh, sitting on the next mound, had offered to share his *roti* in the afternoon. But Wazir had refused casually, 'My *roti* will also be here soon.'

But the *roti* did not come. Nor was a message sent to him. Now this long wait has killed his hunger. He begins to adjust the green bandage on his left eye. It was only four days ago that he, and many others of the village, had got themselves operated on at the free eye camp held at the village primary school. This way it was easier for the people at home. Going to the city hospital is not without its problems. Moreover, private doctors charge enormous fees.

Wazir tries to lift the green bandage and attempts to look around. The afternoon appears to have long passed. Even the sun was about to set. If not the *roti*, at least they could have sent the tea. If Rajpal has not returned from Chandigarh, at least Guran is at home. Ruldu is there, too. What about the numerous neighbours?

While Wazir is getting restless, the other farmers protecting their mounds are venting their anger on the government and the *aarhtiya*s . . . (p. 27). As evening draws near, small groups will be formed on the mounds of paddy. One can hear soulful songs on some of the mounds. Sometimes, even abuses being exchanged are heard. Some people will drink themselves silly and lose control. They will all say, 'Were there no liquor, the Jat would die of worry and longing. . . .' The endless wait for Wazir continues till the next day.

Sitting on his mound of paddy, perched on his *manja*, Wazir Singh is looking at the wide expanse of paddy around him. The eye that has been operated upon is sometimes intensely painful. The manure and the dust in the *mandi* also cause irritation. Because of the cataract, he has cloudy vision. Only when someone comes close is he able to recognize that person. The farmers are sitting in groups. There has been a rumour since last night: 'The paddy will be sold today.'

Wazir remembers the days when they were sowing the paddy with such enthusiasm; then watering it and spraying it. He has seen the harvest sprout like his own children. Now? Such indifference. He watches the heaps of paddy, dotted till the horizon and thinks, 'Where will the government keep so much of paddy? The paddy procured last year must be rotting in goverment godowns. This is what Rajpal would tell us. . . .' Wazir's thoughts now turned to Rajpal, 'Has Rajpal returned from Chandigarh? Don't know? No one has come from home. Someone left some *rotis* last night. He could have woken me up as well.'

'They say the paddy will be sold today.'

'That's what I heard. Good if it is sold. Now we have to prepare the fields for the wheat,' Wazir sighed.

A little later Wazir, feeling unhappy, is again lost in thought and begins to reflect (pp. 27, 31): 'Why didn't Rajpal come? He knows I have undergone an operation. He will have to run around, have the rate determined and get the paddy weighed. Yesterday two houses with push got their mounds weighed. Mahla was right, this way you may even sit here for a month, no one would care. . . . In those days where was all this paddy? If the wheat had the *chhole* (gram) mixed with it, it had to be sold for less, otherwise *chhole* had to sieved out. Bapu would give *makki* (corn) and take one and a half times wheat during the wheat season. Now *makki* and *chhole* have become rarities. No one sows them anymore. Earlier, the city dwellers would come to the village to pick up *chuliyan*. Now it is the villagers who go to the city to buy vegetable: sometimes *saag*, sometimes *kaddu*, sometimes *chuliya*. The youngsters would not even know the meaning of *holan* (barbecued green grass pods). Except for the Jat, this is a season for everyone – the cattle, birds, insects and the two-legged animals are in everyway trying to grab his produce.

Bapu would make me and Sardool catch, in our hands, the droppings of the oxen before it touched the ground, to show respect to the god of food who would otherwise be insulted and angry. Now you can see the stray cattle moving around leaving their droppings, the pigs and dogs, too, are moving around. And the *Annadata* lies discarded, thrown in the dirt and dust. When the *Annadata* is treated with such disrespect, it is inevitable that the Jat should suffer ignominy.

There appears to be a commotion in the *mandi* . . . (p. 32):

The sacks of weighed paddy are being stacked. The people with trolleys, trucks, and bag-handlers are in their element. The farmers who have not yet been able to sell their paddy are hanging around the inspectors with a worried look. The moist paddy is being spread out in the sun. The owners of this paddy are sad. They are looking with longing at the paddy being piled up in sacks. They wonder when their paddy will be sold and packed in gunny bags. The clever ones, and those with access, have even got there moist paddy weighed.

The accountants of the *aarhtiyas* have opened the old account books (*bahi khatas*) and have started fiddling with figures. The employees of the Kheti Bari Vikas Bank, the sahkari bank, are on the lookout for clients. The farmer is fully trapped in the system. The shopkeepers in the city are waiting hopefully – it is almost the Diwali, Dussehra and wedding season. It is during such times that shopkeepers make their earnings for the year. These days even they are looking sad. They say, 'If the Jats don't have money, with what hope will they visit the bazaar'

After Wazir committed suicide, the family of Wasakha Singh underwent many changes. The son and wife of Bhagtu – who had renounced the world and broken off all worldly relationships – came back to live with the family. The woman, Malkit, married her former husband's younger brother, Rajpal, on whom the main responsibility of supporting the family and managing land fell. The *siri* Ruldu, had left and Rajpal arranged with the Bhaiyas to have the wheat crop harvested. The inherited family land also became drastically reduced. One *killa* was first lost for the repayment of an old debt incurred when Bhagtu made an unsuccessful attempt to emigrate abroad (pp. 357–8):

'Rajpal, son, don't plough the *killa* near the motor. I have it now.'

'You have it!' said Rajpal surprised.

'Yes! I have it', said Shera with conviction.

'Is your brain alright, *chacha*?'

'Yes, it is alright. That is why I have come to tell you that this *killa* was mortgaged to me. The interest multiplied, but I kept quiet out of respect for your father. He later sold it to me.'

'How could he have sold it without anyone knowing about it? Mortgaging or selling a *killa* of land makes a Jat's stomach churn inside out.'

'I kept quiet, Rajpal, for I wanted to talk only when you had harvested the crop and left the field vacant. I have the sale papers. You can see them if you like.'

When Rajpal asked his mother about his father selling the *killa* of land; she just said, 'He may have done it. What else could he have done? There was no saving from paddy. Then wheat had to be sown, fertilizers and insecticide had to be bought. Ruldu had to be paid . . . you also have been taking money from time to time. You didn't think then from where the father was bringing money to give.'

Then Bhagtu, despite his declared renunciation of the world

and family relations, takes over the *killa* of land next to the *samadh*, and encloses it to extend the land area of the *samadh*. Guran has brought out an audio-cassette on his own, and the posters of his cassette are posted in villages and at bus-stands in various towns. Further, he has sold his share of land to the sarpanch. In a way, Guran, too, like Bhagtu, has broken off all relations with the family. After the *bhog* ceremony of Wazir – but for a few days spent to dispose of the produce of land – he has not visited the village again.

Rajpal is now left with four *canals* of land. What would he do with it, and what can he produce on it? This he is finding difficult to understand. The abandoned well and the dilapidated shack covering the motor are still in his possession. Standing outside the shack, he is thinking:

'I have enough land for sowing fodder for the cattle, but how can I meet the needs of the family? Lekhi Ram manipulated the loan account to eighteen thousand rupees. How can that be cleared?'

While Rajpal was in this predicament, a partial way out was suggested to him by a Bhaiya who asked him to let him have his land to grow vegetables on a sharecropping basis. He and his three companions would provide the labour (sow, water, watch, and in every way look after the growing vegetables, and even take them to the market for sale) and take a half share of the produce. The other half would be Rajpal's in return for providing the land. Rajpal told him he would give his reply the next day.

Meanwhile, he started thinking: 'It is not possible to grow any grain crop in four *canals*. If I am able to earn two or three thousand rupees in every season, then it will be all right. The family needs can be met with that. I can also look for some job. I am not alone now. Chona and his mother are also there to be looked after. Then there are Babaji and my mother. Chona has to be sent to school and expenses will be incurred on his clothes and books. I think I should first consult Babaji'.

Meanwhile, disturbed over her husband's death and the worsening family situation, Gian Kaur began to have mental fits which underlined the urgency of reorganizing the family and farm set-up (pp. 363–4):

Wasakha Singh sat pensively on the *manja*: 'Rajpal, I think we should sell the cattle. Now your mother is in no position to look after them. We can buy the milk for tea.'

'Babaji, we should sell the buffalo, but keep the *jhoti* which will soon start lactating. I will look after it myself,' said Malkit Kaur.'

'What would we feed her with? There is nothing in sight yet.'

'I am sure I can feed her well. If you bring her into the courtyard, it will be easier for me to look after her. Then we won't need the enclosure either. You, too, come here. It will be easier to give you tea when you need it. Moreover, the mother's state of mind cannot be depended upon.'

Thus the buffalo and the enclosure were sold, and Wasakha Singh moved inside the house.

Rajpal's arrangement with the Bhaiyas – whereby each side received a half share of the produce – continues and they grow a variety of seasonal vegetables. But his Jat prejudice about selling vegetables still persists, and he lets the Bhaiyas handle the selling part.

One day, because of an emergency, he has to take two baskets of pumpkins to the *mandi* himself. On his return with empty baskets, he sees a Bhaiya sitting near a pile of green onions which he has cut and washed.

The Bhaiya says to him, 'Sardar, in fifteen or twenty days, the *tinda*s will be ready. They will fetch a high price; about twenty rupees a kilogram. If we sell in the *apni mandi*, we stand to gain.'

Rajpal thinks: These Bhaiyas have changed so much now. They have become very clever. But voicing his reservations, he says, 'It is the Baurias[10] who sell vegetables there.'

'So what? Bauria is also a human being,' says the Bhaiya. 'Sardar, I, too, was a Jat of my area, now here I work as a labourer.'

Though Rajpal does not respond to the Bhaiya, he starts to think: If I do the selling myself how much will I gain? I do need the money badly. 'Bring the empty baskets to the house', he tells the Bhaiya, and goes back home.

The prospect of making good money to reduce his financial hardship proves too tempting for Rajpal to ignore. The very next morning, swallowing his Jat pride, he himself takes his vegetable to the *apni mandi* to sell. The text gives a view of him sitting in the company of many vegetable sellers, mostly Baurias and Bhaiyas.

Rajpal Singh Dhillon is also sitting there in line with a basket of *tindas* and *kaddus*. He has also beside him a pile of raw onions. Likewise, someone else is selling cauliflower, some others brinjals, and still others potatoes. Rajpal is thinking: Who would know? Like me, someone among them may be a Gill, a Sandhu or a Brar Jat.

NOTES

1. Vandana Shiva, *The Violence of the Green Revolution: Third World Agriculture, Ecology and Politics*, London: Zed Books, 1991; G.S. Bhalla and G.K. Chaddha, *Green Revolution and the Small Peasant: A Study of Income Distribution among Punjab Cultivators*, New Delhi: Concept Publishing Co., 1983; G.K. Chaddha, *The State and Rural Economic Transformation: The Case of Punjab, 1950–85*, New Delhi: Sage, 1986; S.S. Gill, 'Contradictions of Punjab Model of Growth', *Economic and Political Weekly*, 15 October 1988; S.S. Johl, *Future of Agriculture in Punjab*, Chandigarh: Centre for Research in Rural and Industrial Development, 1988; H.S. Shergill, *Rural Credit and Indebtedness in Punjab*, Chandigarh: Institute for Development and Communication, monograph series, vol. 4, 1998; Pramod Kumar, and S.L. Sharma, Coordinators, *Suicides in Rural Punjab*, Chandigarh: Institute for Development and Communication, monograph series, vol. 5, 1998; K.G. Iyer and M.S. Manick, *Indebtedness, Impoverishment and Suicides in Rural Punjab*, Delhi: Indian Publishers Distributors, 2000.
2. B.L. Abbi and Kesar Singh, *Post-green Revolution Rural Punjab: Profile of Economic and Socio-cultural Change (1965–95)*, Chandigarh: Centre for Research in Rural and Industrial Development, 1997; P.S. Judge, 'Emerging Trends in the Caste Structure of Punjab', *The Administrator*, vol. XLII, January–March 1997, pp. 55–6; S.S. Jodhka, 'Caste and Untouchability in Rural Punjab', *Economic and Political Weekly*, vol. 37 (19), 11 May 2002, pp. 1813–23; Harish K. Puri, 'Scheduled Castes in the Sikh Community: A Historical Perspective', *Economic and Political Weekly*, vol. 38 (26), 28 June–4 July 2003, pp. 2693–2701.
3. Baldev Singh, *Annadata*, Ludhiana: Chetna Prakashan, 2004. The page numbers mentioned in the text refer to this particular publication. As *Annadata* is in Punjabi language and script, the responsibility for this English translation is entirely mine.
4. That is, before the productivity of the green revolution reached a plateau, and then subsequently declined from the early 1990s onwards, thus adversely affecting the farming community – especially the Jats who dominated rural Punjabi society.
5. *Siri*: is an agricultural labourer mainly on long-term contract basis.

6. *Sath*: is a common village gathering place set aside for formal gatherings or for the village males to sit around and gossip.
7. *A killa*: is a measure of land, about an acre, but varying in different parts of Punjab.
8. Bhaiya is a general term used in Punjab to refer to migrant Hindi-speaking labourers from Uttar Pradesh and Bihar.
9. *A samadh* is a shrine of a deified local male, elder/martyr/saint with a reputation for having *karamat* (mystical power) to confer boons on devotees.
10. Bauria/Bawaria is a Punjabi Scheduled Caste, today working mainly as landless agricultural labourers. They are mostly found in the districts of Ferozepur, Bathinda, Ludhiana and Sangrur.

BIBLIOGRAPHY

Abbi, B.L. and Kesar Singh, *Post-green Revolution Rural Punjab: Profile of Economic and Socio-cultural Change (1965–95)*, Chandigarh: Centre for Research in Rural and Industrial Development, 1997.

Bhalla, G.S. and G.K. Chaddha, *Green Revolution and the Small Peasant: A Study of Income Distribution among Punjab Cultivators*, New Delhi: Concept Publishing Co., 1983.

Chaddha, G.K., *The State and Rural Economic Transformation: The Case of Punjab 1950–85*, New Delhi: Sage, 1986.

Darling, Malcolm Lyall, *The Punjab Peasant in Prosperity and Debt*, London: Oxford University Press, 1947.

Dutta, Nonica, *Forming an Identity: A Social History of the Jats*, New Delhi: Oxford University Press, 1999.

Fox, Richard G., *Lions of the Punjab*, Delhi: Low Price Publications, 1990.

Gill, S.S., 'Contradictions of Punjab Model of Growth', *Economic and Political Weekly*, 15 October 1988, p. 2167.

Gupta, Dipankar, 'Whither the Indian Village? Culture and Agriculture in 'Rural India', *Economic and Political Weekly*, 19 February 2005.

Iyer, K.G. and M.S. Manick, *Indebtness, Impoverishment and Suicides in Rural Punjab*, Delhi: Indian Publishers & Distributors, 2000.

Izmirlian, Harry Jr., *Structure and Strategy in Sikh Society*, New Delhi: Manohar, 1979.

Jodhka S.S., 'Crisis, Crisis, Crisis . . . Rural Indebtedness and Farmer's Suicides in the Post-green Revolution Punjab', *International Journal of Punjab Studies*, New Delhi: Sage, 1999, pp. 117–25.

———, 'Caste and Untouchability in Rural Punjab', *Economic and Political Weekly*, vol. 37 (19), 11 May 2002, pp. 1813–23.

Johl, S.S., *Future of Agriculture in Punjab*, Chandigarh: Centre for Research in Rural and Industrial Development, 1988.

Judge, P.S., 'Emerging Trends in the Caste Structure of Punjab', *The Administrator*, vol. XLII, January–March 1997, pp. 55–6.

Juergensmeyer, M., *Religious Rebels in the Punjab: The Social Vision of Untouchables*, Delhi: Ajanta Publications, 1988.

Kaur, Ravinder, 'Jat Sikhs: A Question of Identity', *Contributions to Indian Sociology*, n.s., vol. 20 (2), July–December 1986, pp. 221–40.

Kessinger, Tom G., *Vilayatpur 1848–1968: Social and Economic Change in a North Indian Village*, Berkeley: University of California Press, 1974.

Kumar, Pramod and S.L. Sharma, Coordinators, *Suicides in Rural Punjab* Chandigarh: Institute for Development and Communication, monograph series, vol. 5, 1998.

Leaf, Murray J., 'The Green Revolution in a Punjab Village: 1965–1978', *Pacific Affairs*, 1980, pp. 617–25.

Louis, Prakash, 'Caste Tensions in Punjab: Talhan and Beyond', *Economic and Political Weekly*, vol. 38, no. 28, 12–18, July 2003, pp. 2923–6.

Marenco, Ethne K., *The Transformation of Sikh Society*, New Delhi: Heritage Publishers, 1976.

Pettigrew, Joyce, *Robber Noblemen: A Study of the Political System of the Sikh Jats*, London: Routledge and Kegan Paul, 1975.

Puri, Harish K., 'Scheduled Castes in the Sikh Community: A Historical Perspective', *Economic and Political Weekly*, vol. 38 (26), 28 June–4 July 2003, pp. 2693–2701.

Sharma, M.L. and T.M. Dak, eds., *Green Revolution and Social Change*, Delhi: Ajanta Publications, 1989.

Shergill, H.S., *Rural Credit and Indebtedness in Punjab*, Chandigarh: Institute for Development and Communication, monograph series, vol. 4, 1998.

Shiva, Vandana, *The Violence of the Green Revolution: Third World Agriculture, Ecology and Politics*, London: Zed Books, 1991.

Sidhu, R.S. and S.S. Johl, 'Three Decades of Intensive Agriculture in Punjab: Socio-Economic and Environmental Consequences', in *Man and Development*, Chandigarh: CRRID, 2001.

Simmons, Colin and Salinder Supri, 'Participation in Rural Non-farm Activity in India: A Case Study of Cultivating Households of Jalandhar District Punjab', *International Journal of Punjab Studies*, vol. 2, 1995, pp. 13–153.

Singh, Baldev, *Annadata*, Ludhiana: Chetna Publications, 2004.

Singh, Gurharpal, *Ethnic Conflict in India: A Case Study of Punjab*, New Delhi: Macmillan India, 2000.

Singh, Sukhdev and P.S. Jammu, 'Untouchability in Rural Punjab: An Analysis', *IASSI Quarterly*, vol. 13 (4), 1995.

Smith, M.W., 'Social Structure in the Punjab', in *India's Villages*, ed. M.N. Srinivas, London: Asia Publishing House, 1955.

CHAPTER 10

The Industrial Base of Punjab: Linkages with Urban Structure

KUSUM CHOPRA AND ATIYA HABEEB KIDWAI

Post-Green Revolution Punjab's development is said to be a tale of 'Tiring Lands and Retiring Peasantry'. This should not happen to one of post-Independence India's success stories. Like all good stories, this too should have a happy ending. The pathos and the failures of post-Green Revolution Punjab should become a thing of the past and be forgotten. After all Punjab is India's 'Hero Number One' of yesteryears. One would like to see a resurgent Punjab walk to a shining horizon and live happily ever after. For this to happen there has to be a twist in Punjab's story.

One may ask, what can the twist in the story be? The globalized answer is simple: leave behind the tired rural lands and hope that they will recoup; and leave behind the retiring peasantry and let them rest. Move on to places where the action of the twenty-first century is – get urban, get global. It is the age of the 'yuppies', the young and upwardly mobile; in Punjab it should be the age of the 'puppies' – Punjabi and upwardly mobile.

Gone are the days of the Green Revolution when Punjab's charisma lay in its villages and it was said with much conviction, that the state had prospered without creating stark regional disparities because it did not have an overpowering metropolitan city. The country should be aware that Punjab is set to become 'metropolitan', in both economic and sociocultural terms and it may also have cities and regions which will be bypassed and become redundant if the state does not intervene.

Doing anything in Punjab is easier than it is in most other parts of the country because the state today has

- infrastructure ratings twice as high as the national average;
- the highest per capita consumption of power in the country;
- the highest road length per square kilometre of area;
- the highest number of banks and vehicles per thousand population;
- the highest number of small-scale industries per capita;
- double the national average of net small savings;
- per capita incomes in the state are among the highest at current prices and this income is more evenly distributed creating a large middle class; and,
- it is getting urban at a faster rate than witnessed in many parts of the country.

In this chapter it is argued that given this base, Punjab should concentrate on the development of a combination of 'new' industries, the structure of which is divorced from the past, but for which the state has substantial comparative advantages. This sounds paradoxical because the industrial base of Punjab and its industrial needs have historically been quite diversified though mostly 'local' and unchanging. Without a natural resource endowment, it could not specialize in first-generation mineral and metal-based heavy industries with strong backward and forward linkages important for further industrialization. The national-level industrial specialization in Punjab has been historically limited to a few industries such as the bicycle industry, hosiery, sewing machines, sports goods, the spatial location of which in the state cannot be explained by the classic factors of industrial location.

To substantiate this argument the discussion here will focus on the industrial base of Punjab during the three important periods of Punjab's history, namely, (i) the Mughal period, (ii) the colonial period, and (iii) the post-Independence period.

THE MUGHAL PERIOD

During the Mughal rule the major urban centres between Delhi and Lahore were the entrepôts along the Grand Trunk Road, the main transport artery of northern India. All these nodes, listed in Table 10.1, have continued to exist and are still important. The economic base of these centres was determined by trade and the requirements of the marching armies along the route on which they are located. Some of these centres were known for their indigenous industries and handcrafted products while others organized trade with Afghanistan and China. Table 10.1 shows some of the main products of these towns as well as of their hinterlands which formed their production base and their trade.

TABLE 10.1: TOWNS IN PUNJAB ALONG GRAND TRUNK ROAD AND THEIR INDUSTRIAL PRODUCTS DURING THE MUGHAL PERIOD

Towns	Industrial Products	Hinterland Products
1. Delhi	Calico, chintz, rupee mint (1595) and rupee mint (Aurangzeb)	
2. Narela	Indigo	
3. Sonepat		Wheat, sugar, rice, sugar-refined candied
4. Ganaur		
5. Samalkha		
6. Panipat	Calico, muslin, cords, knives	Mango (Kairana)
7. Gharaunda		
8. Sarai Pul		
9. Karnal		
10. Tirawri		
11. Thanesar	Woven fabrics	
12. Shahabad		
13. Ambala		Calico (Samana)
14. Aluwah		
15. Sarhind	Chintz, red muslin, rupee mint (Aurangzeb), copper mint 1595	Mango, roses (Pinjaur)
16. Khanna		
17. Lashkar Khan		
18. Doraha		
19. Ludhiana		Calico (Machhiwara)
20. Phillaur		
21. Nurmahal		
22. Nakodar		Cavalry horses (Jalandhar), muslin, calico, striped muslin, gold brocades (Bajwara)

23. Sultanpur	Chintz, quilts	
24. Govindwal		Cavalry horses
25. Naurangabad		
26. Nuruddin		
27. Sarai Amanat		
28. Lahore	Fine calico, striped silk, shawls, satin embroidery, coarse woollen stuff, felts, carpets, swords, leather, bows and arrows, sugar and candied sugar, rupee mint 1595, rupee mint (Aurangzeb)	Grapes, melon water, melon, mango, peach, fig, mulberry, quince

Source: Based on the information given in Map 4b in Irfan Habib, *An Atlas of the Mughal Empire*, New Delhi: Oxford University Press, 1982.

THE COLONIAL PERIOD

Towards the end of the nineteenth century the types of industrial goods that Punjab produced were much more diversified and spatially dispersed than they were during the Mughal period (see Tables 10.2 and 10.3). Yet the basic character of industrialization did not change very much. Industries still remained small scale, catered to local demand and prospered through the patronage of the royalty. A few products were also exported. The regional specialization in industrial products remained more or less the same though many more urban centres had begun producing these as well as a diversified array of goods. There was a very limited development of the 'modern' manufacturing sector which was confined mainly to the production of bicycles, sugar and woollen and cotton textiles. The demand for many of the goods produced by this sector was generated by the royalty in the small and numerous princely states of undivided Punjab and the neighbouring Himalayan region which mostly depended on imports of industrial consumer goods from Punjab. There was also a significant demand from agricultural households for farm implements and related wood and metal products which were produced locally. The British presence was conducive to the growth of some specialized local industry too as it encouraged the exports of luxury goods like jewellery, shawls, *pashms* to Europe. The newly developed hill stations also generated demand for goods like furniture, metal products and construction material.

TABLE 10.2: INDIGENOUS CRAFT INDUSTRY IN URBAN PUNJAB (*c.*1900)

Indigenous craft product	Articles produced with town location
Woollen goods	*Pashm* shawls (Amritsar, Ludhiana, Dera Nanak)[1]
	Blankets/rugs/*alwans*/serge (Ludhiana, Bassi, Pathankot)
	Cloth (Delhi) Stockings, gloves (Ludhiana)
	Coarse blankets (Dhariwal, Dina Nagar)
	Carpets (Amritsar, Majitha)
Cotton goods	Coarse cloth (Ludhiana, Bassi, Rahon)
	Pagris, khes, chautahis (Sunam)
	Quilts (Sultanpur in Kapurthala)
	Curtains (Sultanpur in Kapurthala – exported)
Silks	Weaving (Amritsar, Patiala, Jalandhar, Batala)[2]
	Pure silk fabric (Samana)
	Silk mixed with cotton
	Netted fabric of silk and silk with cotton
	Gabrun, susi (Amloh, Bassi, Batala, Nur Mahal)
Carpets and rugs	Woollen carpets (Amritsar)[3]
	Namdas, cotton carpets (Delhi, Amloh, Batala)
	Durrees (Nabha, Banur)
Jewellery/ornaments	Gold/silver ornaments (Nabha, Amritsar)[4]
Traditional embroidery	*Phulkari* (Ludhiana, Dina Nagar)
	Gold/silver embroidery (Delhi, Patiala, Sangrur)
	Turban embroidery (Ludhiana)
Gold and silver lace/braid	*Gota kinari* (Nabha – exported, Jalandhar, Rahon)

Iron works	Agricultural implements
	Blacksmithy (Delhi, Tarn Taran, Rupnagar)
	Tinsmiths, nickel platers (Delhi)
	Iron and bent-wire furniture (Delhi)
	Iron jars (Nakodar)
Brass and copper	Domestic utensils (Bhadaur, Nabha, Bassi)[5]
Metal and bell metal	Bell metal cups (Bhadaur, Phagwara)
Pottery and earthenware	Tiles (Jalandhar)
	Paper pottery (Urmur Tanda)
	Clay toys (Nabha)
	Chilm, hookah, surahi (Barnala, Nakodar)
Glass	Bottles, mirrors, lamp chimneys (Hoshiarpur)
	Coloured cups and tumblers (Dasua)
Wood Products	Carvings (Amritsar, Batala, Delhi)
	Furniture (Kartarpur, Sangrur – English style)[6]
	Doors/doorways
	Legs for beds (Narnaul, Samana)
	Cartwheels (Bassi)
	Wooden cotton presses (Tarn Taran)
Inlaid work	Inlaid furniture and utility goods (Hoshiarpur, Mansa)
Lacquer work	Ornamented wood (Ferozpur, Kharar)
Ivory carving	Billiard balls (Ludhiana, Delhi, Jagraon)
Paper and fibres	Bags, ropes, baskets[7]
	Bookbinders (Delhi – many employed)
	Printing presses (Delhi)
Leather goods	Boots, saddles, harness (Delhi, Sangrur, Dina Nagar)
	Tanning (Delhi)
	Native shoes (Ludhiana)
	Well gear (Sangrur)
Chemical goods	Soap makers (Batala)
	Oil presses (Delhi, Ludhiana)
	Breweries and distilleries (Delhi)
Consumer items	*Izarband* (latticed string to tie *pyjamas*) (Patiala)
	Cotton turbans (Batala)

Source: *District and State Gazetteers of the Undivided Punjab (1904–1930)*, Delhi: Low Price Publications (1993 reproduced edition); *Imperial Gazetteer of India (1910), Provincial Series, Punjab*, vols. 1 and 2, New Delhi: Atlantic Publishers and Distributors, 1991.

TABLE 10.3: MANUFACTURING INDUSTRY IN URBAN PUNJAB (*c.*1900)

Manufacturing industry	Articles produced with town location
Cotton	114 steam factories for ginning and pressing cotton in 1904 compared to 12 in 1891. In 1891 there were 6 cotton weaving and spinning mills in Delhi and 42 distributed between Amritsar, Nabha, Malerkotla, Khanna, Ferozpur.
Woollen	Only one mill in the province in Dhariwal employing 908 workers in 1904. It produced broadcloth, blankets, greatcoats, serge, flannel, tweeds, *lois*, shawls, travelling rugs, knitting yarn, caps, socks, gloves.[8]
Breweries	8 breweries and 6 distilleries in the Province (mainly in Delhi)
Ice factories	15 ice factories
Indigo	The number of factories decreased from 27 to 12
Iron foundries	None reported in Indian Punjab.
Iron and wire works	Bicycles (Delhi)
	Gunsmiths (Delhi)
	Foundry (Rupnagar, Jalandhar)
	Railway wagons (Delhi)
Paper mills	Paper mills (Delhi)
Food products	Flour mills (Delhi, Jalandhar, Ludhiana, Khanna)
	Sugar factories and refineries (Delhi, Sujanpur, Shri Govindpur, Machchiwara)
	Forage press (Amritsar)
Instruments, workshops	Survey instruments (Malerkotla) Municipal supplies (Amritsar), Arsenal (Ferozepur)

Source: As in Table 10.2.

THE POST-INDEPENDENCE PERIOD

The British government had developed the agriculturally prosperous western areas of undivided Punjab as the food basket of the country through large-scale investments in irrigation in the early twentieth century. These areas went to Pakistan after the Partition of the country. Hence in the post-partition period, the thrust of the Indian government was on developing Punjab's agricultural potential through substantial investments on agricultural infrastructure, technology, extension work and research. This was instrumental in ushering in the Green Revolution in the state in the mid-1960s.

The growth of Punjab's economy subsequently was very significant and this is reflected in its per capita income which has, almost uninterrupted, remained amongst the highest among the states of India. Some of the states that invested heavily in developing their industrial potential are, however, now catching up, as is indicated in Table 10.4. While growth in Maharashtra and Gujarat has resulted from an extension of their manufacturing base, the engine of growth for most of the south Indian states has been the IT industry.

TABLE 10.4: PER CAPITA INCOME IN THE MAJOR STATES OF INDIA (AT CONSTANT PRICES OF 1993–4)

State	1993–4 (in Rs.)	Ranks	2002–3 (in Rs.)	Ranks
1. Andhra Pradesh	7,416	8	10,633	9
2. Assam	5,715	12	6,220	12
3. Bihar	3,037	15	4,048	15
4. Gujarat	9,796	4	13,715	4
5. Haryana	11,079	3	14,757	3
6. Karnataka	7,838	7	11,799	6
7. Kerala	7,938	6	11,389	7
8. Madhya Pradesh	6,584	10	7,038	11
9. Maharashtra	12,183	2	15,484	1
10. Orissa	4,896	14	5,836	13
11. Punjab	12,710	1	15,264	2
12. Rajasthan	6,182	11	7,608	10
13. Tamil Nadu	8,955	5	12,839	5
14. Uttar Pradesh	5,066	13	5,610	14
15. West Bengal	6,756	9	10,952	8
India		7,690		10,964

Source: *Statistical Abstract of Punjab, 2004*, Publication No. 905, Chandigarh: Economic Adviser to Government, Punjab, pp. 140–1.

The growth of the industrial sector in Punjab has been largely based on a diversified small-scale sector which has been in existence since the colonial period. There has, however, been a limited growth of a large-scale manufacturing sector, which has had a constricting effect on the overall industrial output in the state, as indicated in Table 10.5. It is interesting to note that while Gujarat's share in the industrial output of India is three times its share in the population of the country and Maharashtra's is twice its share in population, Punjab stands much lower, implying that the contribution of factory production in the state is not very significant.

TABLE 10.5: SHARE OF POPULATION AND OF TOTAL OUTPUT OF REGISTERED FACTORIES IN THE MAJOR STATES OF INDIA (2001)

State	Percentage share in population	Percentage share in total output of registered working factories
1. Andhra Pradesh	7.41	6.64
2. Assam	2.59	0.83
3. Bihar	8.07	0.70
4. Gujarat	4.93	15.33
5. Haryana	2.06	4.73
6. Karnataka	5.14	5.73
7. Kerala	3.09	2.49
8. Madhya Pradesh	5.87	3.97
9. Maharashtra	9.42	18.83
10. Orissa	3.58	1.40
11. Punjab	2.37	3.95
12. Rajasthan	5.49	3.24
13. Tamil Nadu	6.07	9.80
14. Uttar Pradesh	16.16	6.97
15. West Bengal	7.79	4.56
16. Others	10.83	9.96
India	100.00	100.00

Source: *Statistical Abstract of Punjab, 2004*, Publication No. 905, Chandigarh: Economic Adviser to Government, Punjab, pp. 96–7 and 424–7.

In terms of the contribution of the different sectors in the economy in Punjab, in the Net State Domestic Product (NSDP) the share of the agricultural sector, though still dominant, has gradually declined between 1973 and 2003, the shares of the secondary and tertiary sectors have increased by 5 and 10 percentage points respectively but the growth rate of manufacturing slowed down in the 1990s and, the contribution of finance and the real estate business has increased significantly though it is lower than in several other states such as Gujarat and Maharashtra (see Table 10.6).

The surplus generated from the agricultural sector over the years in Punjab has been ploughed back into agricultural modernization or it has been invested in industries in the nearby urban areas in the agriculturally prosperous regions. Though the number of industries has increased, the industrial character of the state has not changed substantially because it still mainly caters to the demand generated by a prosperous agricultural hinterland. There has been a marked degree of rural-urban interaction and integration which has led to a relatively higher growth of medium- and small-size industries which are invariably located in medium- and small-size towns. In the mid-1970s, 99.29 per cent of all industrial units were small-scale with 68.30 per cent of the total employment under small, medium and large units. However, since the capital investment in the medium and large industrial units is usually very substantial, the share of the fixed investment of small-scale units in the total manufacturing sector was only 43.91 per cent resulting in a total output of Rs. 567.57 crore in 1975–6, which formed about 60 per cent of the total industrial output. During the last three decades, the number of medium- and large-scale industrial units consistently increased from 144 in 1975–6 to 620 in 1997–8 but it subsequently declined to 553 in 2002–3. Some of these industries could not survive the competition in the post-liberalization period. This has been a matter of concern. On the other hand, as indicated in Table 10.7, small-scale industries have consistently increased in their numbers and in their employment over the years.

Table 10.7 indicates that the share of the small-scale industries in industrial employment has been increasing during the last three decades and was between 70 and 80 per cent. Their share

TABLE 10.6: SECTORAL SHARES IN NET STATE DOMESTIC PRODUCT AT CONSTANT PRICES (1973, 1983, 1993, 2003) #

Sectors	Punjab				Gujarat*	Maharashtra*
	1973	1983	1993	2003–4	1986	1986
1. Agriculture and livestock	55.66	49.25	47.89	39.89	29.08	22.55
2. Forestry, logging, fishing, mining.	0.22	0.29	0.34	0.72	2.07	1.31
A. Primary Total	55.88	49.54	48.23	40.61	31.15	23.86
3. Manufacturing	9.18	11.82	14.4	15.07	19.03	29.46
4. Construction	6.28	4.7	4.48	6.17	4.17	4.08
5. Electricity, gas, water	0.79	1.11	0.94	0.69	2.29	2.13
B. Secondary Total	16.25	17.63	19.82	21.93	25.49	35.67
6. Transport, storage, communication	3.67	4.48	2.45	4.94	8.87	7.76
7. Trade, hotels, restaurants	13.67	16.54	13.1	13.65	15.17	14.07
8. Finance and real estate	3.28	3.83	7.76	10.04	8.08	9.44
9. Administrative, sanitary, community, & personal services	7.25	7.98	8.64	8.83	11.24	9.19
C. Tertiary Total	27.87	32.83	31.95	37.46	43.36	40.47
Total NSDP (a+b+c)	100	100	100	100	100	100
Total NSDP (Rs. in millions)	1,53,332	2,61,840	2,70,676	3,75,823	3,22,468	7,11,814

Note: #1973, 1983 NSDP is at constant prices of 1971; # 1993–4, 2003–4 estimates are at constant prices of 1993–4
*Two most developed states.

TABLE 10.7: SHARE OF SMALL-SCALE INDUSTRIAL UNITS IN INDUSTRIAL EMPLOYMENT, INVESTMENT, OUTPUT AND EXPORTS IN PUNJAB (1966–7 TO 2004–5)

Years	Total no. of units ('000)	% share of small units	Employment in all units('000)	% share of small units	Fixed invest. (Rs. crores)	Share of small units	Total industrial output (Rs. crores)	Share of small units	Total exports (Rs. crores)	Share of small units
1966–7	8.15	98.53	98.74	56.72	163.57	36.68	293.00	68.26	–	–
1975–6	20.42	99.29	199.63	68.30	349.25	43.91	952.48	59.59	75.63	62.99
1980–1	43.57	99.48	374.64	70.70	1,059.54	31.35	2,259.51	49.50	162.13	52.54
1990–1	160.74	99.77	856.16	78.12	5,352.58	25.20	11,213.53	36.12	769.12	65.49
2000–1	201.23	99.69	1,127.27	79.63	20,544.14	20.00	44,901.50	40.81	4,014.96	56.39
2004–5	204.67	99.71	1,183.60	79.00	25,800.00	20.93	57,000.00	46.49	10,728.94	57.79

Source: Directorate of Industries, Government of Punjab, Chandigarh.

in total industrial production reduced from 68 to 36 per cent between 1966–7 and 1990–1, indicating a lower output growth compared to medium and large industries. This trend seems to have continued till the end of the 1990s. Thereafter, with some reduction in the number of medium- and large-scale industries, the share of small industries in total industrial output increased again in 2004–5.

The largest number of small-scale units is in repair services, metal and leather products, hosiery and garments. Output per invested rupee and per employed worker is high in industries like transport equipment, basic metals, hosiery, leather products and in miscellaneous industries. Employment is relatively higher in industries like basic metals, cotton and woollen textiles, food products rubber and plastics which have more fixed capital. Medium and large-scale industries like cotton/woollen/synthetic textiles, followed by food and beverages, basic metals, chemical products and transport equipment are relatively more numerous. Employment, output and investment are also high in these industries.[9]

On the basis of the four parameters mentioned in Table 10.7, viz., number of industrial units, employment, fixed investment and industrial production in the two groups of 'small', 'medium and large' industries, the districts of Punjab have been clubbed into three categories defined on the basis of values of these parameters. In Category One these values are relatively higher; in Category Two the values are of the middle order; and, in Category Three they are relatively lower (Table 10.8).

TABLE 10.8: CATEGORIES OF DISTRICTS

Categories	Small-scale industries	Medium- and large-scale industries
One	Amritsar, Jalandhar, Ludhiana	Ludhiana, Patiala, Rupnagar
Two	Patiala, Sangrur, Faridkot, Gurdaspur	Amritsar, Jalandhar, Kapurthala, Hoshiarpur, Sangrur
Three	Ferozepur, Hoshiarpur, Kapurthala, Bathinda, Rupnagar	Bathinda, Faridkot, Ferozepur, Gurdaspur

Source: Directorate of Industries, Government of Punjab, Chandigarh.

In Tables (10.9 and 10.10) the district-level data on the four parameters mentioned above have been classified according to the three categories mentioned in Table 10.8, in order to get an overview of the last three decades.

From Tables 10.9 and 10.10 the following conclusions can be drawn:

- The shares of the three districts listed in Category One has ranged between 50 and 70 per cent between 1977–8 and 1999–2000 in the total number, total employment, total investment and total industrial production in both the designated industrial size classes. The share of Category Two has been around 20 to 40 per cent, the remaining being the share of Category Three.
- A clear trend is seen in small-scale industries where, in Category One, shares of the given four parameters have declined between 1977–8 and 1999–2000. The other two categories have improved their shares indicating a dispersal of these industries to the relatively lagging districts in the state.
- The medium and large industries, on the other hand, show an opposite trend where proportions under each head except in fixed investment in Category One have increased in the same period, while they have declined in the other two categories. The share of fixed investment in recent years is seen to grow in these two categories with a larger concentration in Category Two. There is, therefore, a clear indication that medium and large industries have a tendency to concentrate in Category One districts. In recent years some of these industries have been seen to shift their base in other districts, especially in those falling in Category Two, which include districts like Amritsar, Jalandhar, Sangrur, Kapurthala and Hoshiarpur.
- Output per worker in small-scale industries was the lowest in Category One districts in 1977–8 because of the large number of workers employed in traditional industries in old towns. With a low capital base their productivity levels were low. While substantial growth in investment and production was seen in Category Two and Three districts

TABLE 10.9: SHARE OF EACH CATEGORY IN TOTAL NUMBER, EMPLOYMENT, FIXED INVESTMENT AND PRODUCTION IN INDUSTRIES

(*Rs. in crores*)

Small-scale Industries								
Category	Number		Employment		Fixed investment		Production	
	1977–8	1999–2000	1977–8	1999–2000	1977–8	1999–2000	1977–8	1999–2000
One	58.77	50.83	69.68	60.42	63.09	49.69	58.83	57.84
Two	27.52	28.52	19.93	24.07	26.95	30.74	27.90	28.43
Three	13.71	20.65.	10.39	15.51	9.96	19.57	13.27	13.73
	100.00	100.00	100.00	100.00	100.00	100.00	100.00	100.00
Total	24,281	1,99,071	1,63,134	8,83,005	194.72	3,793.67	701.50	16,610.85

Medium- and Large-scale Industries								
Category	Number		Employment		Fixed investment		Production	
	1977–8	1998–9	1977–8	1998–9	1977–8	1998–9	1977–8	1998–9
One	53.14	57.31	47.69	54.57	69.60	53.45	59.93	62.99
Two	33.71	31.89	38.92	35.75	23.15	37.63	28.17	26.36
Three	13.15	10.80	13.38	9.69	7.25	8.93	11.90	10.65
	100.00	100.00	100.00	100.00	100.00	100.00	100.00	100.00
Total	175	602	77,971	2,27,929	309.94	14,038.54	607.48	25,375.60

Source: Directorate of Industries, Government of Punjab, Chandigarh.

TABLE 10.10: OUTPUT PER WORKER AND CAPITAL-OUTPUT, EMPLOYMENT-INVESTMENT RATIOS IN SMALL, MEDIUM AND LARGE INDUSTRIES

Category	Output per worker (Rs. lakhs)		Capital-output ratio		Employment-investment (Rs. lakhs) ratio	
	Small-scale Industries					
	1977–8	1999–2000	1977–8	1999–2000	1977–8	1999–2000
One	0.36	1.80	0.2976	0.1961	9.25	2.83
Two	0.60	2.22	0.2681	0.2469	6.19	1.82
Three	0.55	1.67	0.2083	0.3257	8.74	1.84
Total	0.43	1.88	0.2778	0.2283	8.38	2.33
	Medium- and Large-Scale Industries					
Category	Output per worker (Rs. lakhs)		Capital-output ratio		Employment-investment (Rs. lakhs) ratio	
	1977–8	1998–9	1977–8	1998–9	1977–8	1998–9
One	0.98	12.85	0.5917	0.4695	1.72	0.17
Two	0.56	8.21	0.4202	0.7874	4.23	0.15
Three	0.69	12.24	0.3106	0.4630	4.64	0.18
Total	0.78	11.13	0.5102	0.5525	2.52	0.16

Source: Directorate of Industries, Government of Punjab, Chandigarh.

in small-scale industries between 1977–8 and 1999–2000, medium and large industries had high growth in these parameters in Category One followed by Category Two districts.

- Though more capital is now being invested in small and large industries compared to earlier years, the growth rate of employment is far lower than that of fixed investment and of production. Employment generated per invested rupee has gone down rapidly in both industry groups. However, the level of employment generated in small industries is relatively higher compared to the large industries. Per worker output has improved in both the industry groups with substantial absolute gains in medium and large industries.

The post-Green Revolution period did see a perceptible change in the industrial structure of Punjab, though the importance of the traditional industries did not decline. In terms of number of units, employment, fixed investment and production, the textile (especially hosiery and garments) industry, the food and beverages industry, basic metals, machinery and equipment, metal products, rubber-plastics, chemical and products, transport equipment, are still the most dominant in terms of employment in all the industry groups, i.e. large/medium and small scale. The growth rate of production has been the highest in the manufacture of automobile parts, sugar, rice-shellers, cycles, cycle parts and hand tools. Most of these are older industries. Employment growth rates have been the highest in older industries like rice-shellers, automobile parts, hand tools and sugar. Industrial exports from the state have also been significant in the older industries such as readymade garments and hosiery, cycle and cycle parts, yarn, textiles and hand tools.

Table 10.11 gives a district-wise list of the dominant industries in Punjab. One can see that most of these industries in districts away from the main transport arteries are linked to the demand pattern of the immediate hinterland, while those on main arteries or directly connected to the highway transport network, cater to the demands outside the state.

Though some internationally well-known Indian and foreign companies have come to Punjab,[10] the new-generation industries have, by and large, bypassed the state. This has slowed down

TABLE 10.11: DISTRICT-WISE DOMINANT INDUSTRIES IN PUNJAB (1971 AND 2001)

Districts	Dominant industries in the districts – 1971#	Dominant industries in the districts – 2001*
1. Amritsar	Woollen and cotton cloth, agricultural implements, brass utensils	Textiles, food and beverages, machinery and equipment
2. Bathinda	Agricultural implements, cotton ginning and bales, mustard oil	Food and beverages, machinery and agricultural equipment, chemical products, basic metals
3. Faridkot	Agricultural implements, thread yarn, snuff	Paper and products, food and beverages, machinery and equipments, non-metallic products
4. Firozepur	Agricultural implements, cotton ginning and cloth, enamel wire	Food and beverages, machinery and motor repair, wood products, motor vehicle repair
5. Gurdaspur	Woollen products, engineering and electrical goods	Textiles, food and beverages, non-metallic mineral products, machinery and equipment, wood products
6. Hoshiarpur	Raisins, turpentine and pine oil, shoes, jams and pickles, wood products	Food and beverages, non-metallic mineral products, textiles, chemical products, basic metal, wood products
7. Jalandhar	Motor spare parts and electric goods, pump sets, furniture, carpets	Basic metal and metal products, non-metallic mineral products, rubber, leather and plastic products, furniture, transport equipment, motor vehicle workshops
8. Kapurthala	Leather and rubber goods, textiles,	Transport equipment, food and beverages,

	generators, railway wagons	textiles, machinery and equipment, motor vehicle workshops
9. Ludhiana	Vanaspati, hosiery goods, soap	Textiles, food and beverages, basic metals, metal products, rubber and plastic products, machinery and equipment, paper products, transport equipment
10. Patiala	Rolling bars, centrifugal pumps, cycle parts, biscuits	Food and beverages, basic metals, chemicals, motor vehicle workshops, transport equipment
11. Sangrur	Iron bars, cycle parts, sugar, shellers	Food and beverages, textiles, paper and products, chemicals and products, basic metals, machinery and equipment, metal products
12. Rupnagar	Locks, calcium ammonium nitrite, conduit pipes, sugar	Radio–T.V. manufacture, electrical machinery, basic metals, chemicals and products, motor vehicle workshops

Source: # Census of India, 1971 Town Directory; * Statistical Abstract of Punjab, 2004.

industrial growth in the current decade. To counter this, and to attract fresh investments in this sector, 24 industrial estates with all the infrastructural facilities have been set up in the state at 18 locations.[11]

INDUSTRY-URBAN LINKAGES

Urbanization in Punjab is slowly getting hinged to a diversified array of development processes and is undergoing a change as it is no longer driven only by agricultural growth. As shown in an earlier paper, Punjab's urbanization had the following characteristics:[12]

- *Pre-Green Revolution period*: process of urbanization slow, regionally less disparate, hinged to agricultural development and administration. The urban base consisted of a large number of small towns.
- *Green Revolution period*: process of urbanization gradual, regionally less disparate than in many other states in the country, hinged to agricultural growth. A large number of medium-sized *mandi* (trading) towns emerged consequent to the growth in agricultural production.
- *Post-Green Revolution period*: process of urbanization faster, more regionally disparate, hinged to both agricultural as well as industrial development and based on the growth of the larger towns.

It is interesting to note the changes in the class-wise distribution of the urban population in Punjab in the three decades between 1971 and 2001. In 1971, apart from the share of cities with a population of more than 1,00,000 (lakh plus cities), which has always been the highest, one finds that the share of the other size classes followed a normal distribution. However, in 1991 and 2001, the distribution got skewed as a larger share of urban population got concentrated in the larger cities (Table 10.12). The number of these cities also increased.

There has been a slow transition in Punjab from a concentration of population in small towns at the beginning of the twentieth century to a shift of population to relatively larger towns. But now this change is becoming more apparent and Punjab's level of urbanization is higher at nearly 34 per cent than that of the rest of the country, at 28 per cent.

A metropolitan city, Ludhiana, emerged on the map of Punjab for the first time in the census of 1991. Ludhiana's population increased almost one and a half times and today it stands at about 1.5 million. In the 2001 census, Amritsar also acquired the status of a metropolitan city and it is likely that in the next decade Jalandhar too may become a metropolis. The number of

TABLE 10.12: SHARE OF TOWNS IN DIFFERENT SIZE CLASSES* IN TOTAL URBAN POPULATION AND IN TOTAL NUMBER OF TOWNS IN PUNJAB (1901–2001)

Class	1901		1951		1961		1971		1981		1991		2001	
	% share of urban pop.	No.	% share of urban pop.	No.	% share of urban pop.	No.	% share of urban pop.	No.	% share of urban pop.	No.	% share of urban pop.	No.	% share of urban pop.	No.
I	18.4	1	39.06	1	38.45	4	41.50	4	46.38	7	54.16	10	58.27	14
II	13.8	2	6.25	2	10.18	5	13.64	7	14.39	10	19.91	18	15.91	18
III	16.6	4	31.23	17	28.26	23	21.18	21	20.24	27	12.92	24	13.10	36
IV	21.75	14	16.99	20	10.49	20	13.58	32	11.28	36	10.82	45	9.81	54
V	24.4	32	13.08	29	10.15	32	6.68	28	6.50	40	1:72	14	2.58	28
VI	4.8	10	5.00	25	2.45	19	1.45	12	1.21	14	0.47	6	0.34	7
Total	100	63	100	96	100	103	100	103	100	134	100	117	100	157

Notes: * *The Census of India* classifies towns into six size classes on the basis of their population as follows: Class I >100,000; Class II 50,999–99,999; Class III 20,000–49,999; Class IV 10,000–19,999; Class V 5,000–9,999; Class VI <5000.

Source: *Census of India*, *Series 20, Punjab, Part II A and II B, General Population Tables* and *Primary Census Abstract, 1991* and *Census of India 2001.*

TABLE 10.13: FUNCTIONAL TYPOLOGY OF TOWNS BASED ON MOST DOMINANT FUNCTION 1971 AND 1991 (IN BRACKETS)

Districts	Agriculture	Industry	Trade and Commerce	Transport	Other Services	Total Number of Towns	% Urban Workforce 1971	% Female Workers in Urban Workforce 1971
	I & II	V-a & V-b	VII	VIII	IX			
1. Amritsar	2 (4)	2 (1)	1 (2)	0 (0)	2 (2)	7 (9)	28.10	4.37
2. Bhatinda	4 (4)	0 (0)	7 (6)	0 (0)	0 (1)	11 (11)	29.84	4.43
3. Faridkot	0 (2)[13]	0 (0)	6 (4)	0 (0)	1 (3)	7 (9)	28.76	3.60
4. Ferozepur	2 (3)	1 (0)	3 (3)	0 (0)	3 (3)	9 (9)	27.94	4.28
5. Gurdaspur	1 (3)	2 (1)	3 (4)	0 (0)	4 (4)	10 (12)	26.13	3.94
6. Hoshiarpur	2 (3)	0 (0)	4 (4)	0 (0)	3 (2)[14]	9 (9)	27.13	5.20
7. Jalandhar	2 (3)	3 (2)	4 (4)	0 (0)	2 (4)	11 (13)	26.76	5.06
8. Kapurthala	0 (0)	1 (1)	0 (0)	0 (0)	2 (2)	3 (3)	28.31	5.00
9. Ludhiana	1 (4)[15]	1 (1)	4 (4)	0 (0)	0 (1)	6 (10)	29.96	3.90
10. Patiala	2 (2)	2 (1)	2 (7)	0 (0)	5 (2)	11 (12)	27.94	5.84
11. Rupnagar	2 (0)	1 (1)	0 (1)	0 (0)	4 (6)	7 (8)	27.74	5.27
12. Sangrur	6 (3)	1 (0)	4 (8)	0 (0)	1 (1)	12 (12)	28.12	3.65
Total	24 (31)	14 (8)	38 (47)	0 (0)	27 (31)	103 (117)		
% 1971	23.30	13.59	36.90		26.21			
% 1991	26.50	6.84	40.17	0.00	26.50			

Notes: Cantonments are excluded.
Categories I–IX are categories of industrial classification as given in the census.

towns with one lakh plus population has also grown from 9 in 1991 to 14 in 2001.

Considering the fact that the pattern of both urbanization and industrialization is changing in Punjab, and this change replicates a pattern associated with economic growth, one should assess the inherited functional classification of Punjab towns in terms of the new developments.

Surprisingly about half the towns in Punjab in 1991 were functionally either predominantly agricultural (26.5 per cent) or predominantly engaged in other services (26.50 per cent). A majority of the towns were in trade and commerce (40.17). Only about 7 per cent of the towns were predominantly manufacturing. The share of manufacturing towns, in fact, declined from 13.59 per cent in 1971 to 6.84 per cent in 1991 because the villages which acquired the status of new towns were largely agricultural and changed the proportions in their favour. The proportions in all other functional types remained, more or less, the same over the two Green Revolution decades. This indicates that industry in Punjab is highly concentrated in a few urban centres which mainly cluster around the larger cities, namely, Amritsar, Ludhiana, Jalandhar, Patiala, Sangrur, and in towns in the vicinity of Chandigarh because of better access to industrial infrastructure and technology. For similar reasons many other district headquarters – and some nearby towns – have also seen an upswing in industrial activity.

In terms of growth rates the industrial towns can be classified into the following categories as seen is Table 10.14.

This indicates that though industrialization is an important factor in triggering the process of urbanization, it alone cannot ensure urban growth. In cases such as that of Punjab, it has to be supplemented by the simultaneous growth of trade, commerce and services.

The overall impact of new trends in urban and industrial growth has been positive in terms of per capita income growth in Punjab, as has been discussed earlier. The middle class has consequently enlarged; a globalized lifestyle has emerged among them, creating new consumer-demand patterns and linked jobs. Urban areas may therefore hope to have a more resilient job market. These hopes may, however, be negated if the rural areas

TABLE 10.14: TOWNS WITH MORE AND LESS THAN AVERAGE ANNUAL GROWTH RATE FOR PUNJAB AND THEIR MOST DOMINANT FUNCTIONS

	1961–71	Towns	1981–91
Above average: Ludhiana Khanna, Hoshiarpur, Rupnagar, Sirhind, Adampur, Batala, Barnala, Phagwara, Pathankot, Dera Bassi	Three most dominant functions were a combination of manufacturing, trade and commerce and services	Ludhiana, Gobindgarh, Malout, Qadian, Patran, Bhowanigarh, Sultanpur, Shahkot, Mohali, Barnala, Ahmadgarh	Three most dominant functions were a manufacturing, trade and commerce and services
Below average Jalalabad, Kurali	Three most dominant functions were a combination of agriculture, trade and commerce and services	Patti, Machhiwara	Three most dominant functions were a combination of trade and commerce and services and agriculture

do not simultaneously experience the benefits of a growth consequent to globalization. The above trends can have adverse repercussions on the urban centres in which manufacturing has a significant presence. The comparative advantage of medium- and large-scale units, in terms of productivity gains, usually has a tendency to elbow out small-scale units, resulting in falling employment. With the existing diversified base of small-scale industries in the small and medium towns of the state, Punjab should ensure that this threat does not become real. It is necessary to further strengthen the backward and forward linkages of these units with the rural economy, not only to sustain the small and medium towns, but also to absorb the surplus generated by the farm sector, to process agricultural produce and to provide employment to the manpower released from the rural areas. Since larger units usually have a tendency to locate in larger urban centres, they will further metropolitanize the state. How a metropolis-centred growth can be used to advantage in the changed socio-economic scenario of Punjab, is for the planners to now decide if the story of Punjab has to have a happy ending.

NOTES

1. *Pashm* imported from Kashmir, Kulu, Bashahr.
2. Raw material mainly imported from China, associated arts developed, e.g. *phulkari*s and embroidery on items of daily use.
3. Fine carpets were also manufactured using *pashm*.
4. Workers in the jewellery industry outnumbered those in iron and steel. Amritsar alone produced superior jewellery worth two million pounds sterling.
5. Copper largely obtained from Kabul.
6. Made in four styles, early Hindu, Muhammadan, Sikh and European (made in cantonments).
7. Made everywhere, especially in jails, the paper industry declined due to competition from mill-made paper.
8. The native *shawl* weaving industry and the manufacture of *pattu* and blankets were not affected by foreign imports. Most of the produce was exported abroad or to other Provinces. Raw wool was imported from Australia.
9. Directorate of Industries, Government of Punjab, Chandigarh.

10. Such as Ranbaxy (medicines), Hero Cycles, Avon Cycles, Punjab Tractor Ltd. (Swaraj tractors and combine harvester), Oswal Woollen Mills (Monte Carlo, Casablanca), Oswal Knit India Ltd. (Pringle), JCT Textiles, DCM (Ctv picture tube, steel rope, castings), Birla_VXL (OCM) (woollen fabric), JIL (Maltova, Viva, range of wines and liquor) Gujarat Ambuja (cement), Godrej (washing machines), ACC (cement), SIEL (chemicals, vanaspati), Abhishek (denim), SmithKline and Beecham, Pepsico, Nestle, GEC.
11. Amritsar, Batala, Bhatinda, Dhandari Kalan (near Ludhiana), Goindwal Sahib (near Amritsar), Hoshiarpur, Jalandhar, Khanna (near Ludhiana), Kotkapura (near Bathinda), Ludhiana, Moga (near Ludhiana), Nabha (near Patiala), Nawanshahar, Rajpura, Mohali, Derabassi and Chalanon (near Chandigarh), Tarn Taran (near Amritsar).
12. Kusum Chopra, Atiya Habeeb Kidwai and Subhash Marcus, 'Urbanization Process in the Undivided Punjab', in *Five Thousand Years of Urbanization: The Punjab Region*, ed. Reeta Grewal, New Delhi: Manohar, 2005, pp. 175–98.
13. Badnikalan and Bagapurana: new towns.
14. Talwara: predominant function is construction because of the dam construction.
15. Three out of four are new towns.

BIBLIOGRAPHY

Census of India, series 20, Punjab, Part II A and II B, General Population Tables and Primary Census Abstract, 1991 and *Census of India*, 2001.

Chopra, Kusum, Atiya Habeeb Kidwai and Subhash Marcus, 'Urbanization Process in the Undivided Punjab', in Reeta Grewal, ed., *Five Thousand Years of Urbanization: The Punjab Region*, New Delhi: Manohar, 2005, pp. 175–98.

District and State Gazetteers of the Undivided Punjab (1904–1930), Delhi: Low Price Publications (1993 rpt. edn.).

Habib, Irfan, *An Atlas of the Mughal Empire*, New Delhi: Oxford University Press, 1982.

Imperial Gazetteer of India (1910), Provincial Series, Punjab, vols. 1 and 2, New Delhi: Atlantic Publishers and Distributors, 1991 (rpt.).

Statistical Abstract of Punjab, 2004, Publication No. 905, Chandigarh: Economic Adviser to Government, Punjab, pp. 140–1.

PART III

SOCIAL TRANSFORMATION

CHAPTER 11

Large-Scale Conversions to Christianity in Late Nineteenth-Century Punjab as an Early Dalit Movement

JOHN C.B. WEBSTER

In the late nineteenth century, Dalits in several parts of India converted to Christianity in very large numbers. This was true of the Pulayas in Travancore, of the Madigas and then of the Malas in what is now Andhra Pradesh, of the Paraiyas in what is now Tamil Nadu, of the Chuhras in the Punjab and of the Bhangis in Uttar Pradesh. Dalits in Karnataka, Maharashtra and Gujarat also converted to Christianity in significant but smaller numbers. In writing my history of the Dalit Christians back in 1992, I not only described these as conversion *movements*, but also saw a broad pattern to them. In this chapter, both of those premises will be examined more closely with reference to the Punjab. The first section reviews some of the major studies of the Dalit conversion movement in the Punjab in order to determine the best approach to examining these premises, given the nature of the sources available. In the second section that approach is applied to the source materials in order to flesh out those premises in greater detail. The concluding section offers some reflections on the significance of the findings.

The Chuhra conversion movement in the Punjab has, by general consensus, been traced back to the conversion of a thirty-year-old man named Ditt in June 1873. Ditt was illiterate and lame, a dealer in hides and skins who lived in the village of Shahabdike, located in the eastern part of Sialkot district. Ditt first heard the Christian message from Nattu, the son of a landlord in a neighbouring village, who had recently converted. When he had learnt enough to decide that he too wanted to become a Christian, he walked the thirty miles to Sialkot, accompanied by Nattu who introduced him to the Rev. Samuel Martin, the United Presbyterian missionary stationed there. After examining him over a period of days, Martin baptized Ditt who then returned to his village. Ditt came back to Sialkot in August bringing his wife, daughter and two neighbours to be baptized. The following February he returned again with four men whom he had prepared for baptism, one of whom, Kaka, became an active voluntary evangelist.

There is no record of these events in the annual reports for 1873 or 1874 of the Sialkot Mission submitted to the General Assembly of the United Presbyterian Church of North America. They first appear in the history of the mission published by its founder, the Rev. Andrew Gordon, in 1886. Gordon drew at some length on the story of Ditt, indicating how he and those whom he had brought for baptism shared their new Christian faith with friends and neighbours, urging them to become Christians as well.[1] Gordon also made the point that an unnamed Chuhra, later identified by others as Karm Bakhsh, initiated a similar movement in Gujranwala district,[2] while another was led by Chaughatta from Awanka, a village near Dinanagar in Gurdaspur district,[3] both of which were independent of each other, as well as of the earlier and larger movement initiated by Ditt. Gordon confined his narrative account to what were still the beginnings of the movement, and all subsequent histories are totally dependent upon Gordon for information on the opening stages of this conversion movement.

Frederick and Margaret Stock's *Peoples Movements in the Punjab*, published in 1975, is the first full-length study of this Chuhra conversion movement. It is a United Presbyterian denominational history like Gordon's, but is at the same time an attempt to draw more universally applicable lessons and principles for evangelism, church planting, and church growth from the United Presbyterian experience with the Chuhra movement. Despite the title, the Stocks do not explain why they employed the term, 'movement', as a label for all the conversions among the Chuhras, although some of the features of what they do describe suggest that the term was not inappropriate. There are some serious critical problems with this book, especially in making connections between mission theory and evidence, but it does trace the movement's growth, with highs and lows over the decades, and what the mission did to help or hinder it from its inception with Ditt on into the post-Independence period in Pakistan.[4]

The Christian Community and Change in Nineteenth Century North India (Webster 1976), was a case study of the Lodiana (later Punjab) Mission of the Presbyterian Church in the USA, which did not work in the same part of the Punjab as did the United Presbyterians. The conversion movement did not reach their area until the 1890s and so I was largely unaware of its earlier development and dynamics when I wrote that book. I did not treat it as a movement, but instead discussed the Chuhra converts in separate analyses of motives and consequences of conversion, Christian efforts to change religious beliefs, and the conflicts with members of other religious communities this led to.[5] While offering important insights that remain valid, this approach proved to be too fragmenting to be useful for a fuller study of the movement as a whole.

I took a very different approach in my *The Dalit Christians: A History*, first published in 1992. This study, covering all of India and not just the Punjab, was deliberately set within the context primarily of Dalit rather than of Christian history. In it I treated the phenomena of large-scale conversions as movements and set the Chuhra movement alongside other Dalit conversion movements elsewhere in India studied by other historians. Like them I used a basically chronological, narrative approach, starting with the founder and limiting the study to the sources provided by a single mission. A particular concern was to test J.W. Pickett's claim that these large conversion movements were characterized by group rather than individual decisions to convert, a claim that did not stand up very well.[6] I concentrated on the United Presbyterians up through the 1890s and only devoted a paragraph to the movement's expansion into other mission areas prior to World War I, by which time the Indian Christian population of the Punjab had grown from just under 4,000 in 1881 to almost

200,000, mostly because of Chuhra conversions.[7] In the process of comparing these movements I saw what appeared to be a pattern to them all, which I could not have seen had I, and the other historians whose works I drew upon, used the more topical approach that I had employed earlier.[8]

Since then I have published four major articles on the Chuhra conversion movement in the Punjab, none of which tells the story of the movement as a whole but each does presuppose that it was a movement. The first, 'Leadership in a Rural Dalit Conversion Movement', looked at the changing roles of the village catechist-teacher-pastor not as initiator so much as nurturer and organizer of the Dalit conversion movement prior to World War I, then between the wars, and finally since Independence.[9] The next, 'Dalits and Christianity in Colonial Punjab: Cultural Interactions', focuses upon the kinds of images, expectations, and even requirements that missionaries and Chuhra converts brought to their interactions during the movement's first (pre-World War I) and second (inter-war) generations.[10] 'Christian Conversion in the Punjab: What Has Changed?' again traces the development of the movement but compares the United Presbyterian experience with that of the Anglican Church Missionary Society (CMS) into whose 'territories' the movement spread in the early 1880s. As in the previous study I also compared the experiences of the first and second generation of converts.[11] Finally, 'The Quest for the Historical Ditt' is a study of the historiography of Ditt and thus of the evolution of a 'Ditt tradition', in which Ditt the symbol often became detached from Ditt the person.[12] In all four essays, I sought greater understanding of the Dalits involved; the missionaries were secondary.

Jeffrey Cox devotes a chapter of his *Imperial Fault Lines: Christianity and Colonial Power in India, 1818–1940* to 'Village Christians/Songs of Deliverance'. Cox's work, which concentrates on the Punjab, is not, as he himself points out, a connected history, but a series of probes designed (successfully in my opinion) to undermine confidence in the 'providentialist master narrative of progress toward a multiracial Christian community'.[13] He focuses upon missionaries and their interactions, as the imperial fault lines appear over and over again in their struggles 'with the conflict between universalistic Christian religious values and the imperial context of those values'.[14] His chapter on village Christians also consists of a series of probes, the first four of which (the ones that concern this study) he labels 'the crisis of village conversion', 'indigenous initiative', 'conversion and dignity', and 'patterns of conversion'. In all of these his major emphasis is on how the missionaries involved viewed, analysed, defined and responded to rural Dalit conversions rather than upon the Dalits themselves.[15] However, this topical approach, like my earlier one, while offering some insight, does not help us test our hypothesis about these being a conversion *movement*.

The most recent study of this subject, Christopher Harding's doctoral thesis 'The Dynamics of Low Caste Conversion Movements: Rural Punjab, *c.* 1880–1935', uses a comparison between the Protestant Punjab Mission of the Church Missionary Society and the Roman Catholic Belgian Capuchin mission, both of which came into contact with the conversion movement over a decade after it had begun. Like Cox, he does not provide a connected history of a Dalit conversion movement in the areas where those two missions worked, but instead examines several aspects of the dynamics involved topically. His chapter on 'The Communication of Christianity' sees these dynamics shaped by the contrasting cultural and intellectual assumptions of both missionaries and Dalits. It begins by making the important point that 'the communication of Christianity throughout rural Punjab was largely the business of Punjabis themselves'[16] and then examines the assumptions, views and roles in this communication process, first of 'informal agents' acting independently of the missions and then of those who were mission employees. He sees in low-caste culture 'a bold receptivity to new ideas and tools for self-advancement',[17] but finds that 'informal evangelisation was limited both in scope and content to the relatively small world of key individuals' personal contacts and spheres of influence. No notions of caste- or class-consciousness, or of broader social rebellion through conversion seem to have emerged at this time'.[18] Further, that while converts accepted Christian beliefs, they resisted 'unexpectedly invasive dimensions' of Christian obligations in their family life and life-cycle rituals.[19] These are important insights into and conclusions about what was going on, but they do not offer descriptions or analyses of overall development over time which would enable us to determine whether or not this was a movement.

This brief review of the literature begs a crucial question. Does the evidence warrant viewing all these Dalit conversions as part of a movement or movements of Dalits? Would it be more accurate to see the large number of Dalit conversions in the Punjab during the late nineteenth and early twentieth centuries instead as a trend, or as an accumulated consequence of 'mission work' or simply as locations of inter-faith or inter-cultural encounters? The historian who considers these questions important enough to pursue further must do two things: first, focus attention primarily on the Dalits who were (or were not) converting, rather than on the missionaries, and second, take a chronological narrative approach to find out how this 'conversion phenomenon' unfolded over time. My own research has convinced me that Dalit conversions in the Punjab at that time are best understood not only in movement terms but also as initiated and led by Dalits. Moreover, I found that this movement, like other Dalit conversion movements to Christianity elsewhere in India, passed through several stages, each of which had its own motivations and dynamics.

Missionary contemporaries and subsequent historians of large-scale conversion movements have been hard-pressed to explain why they occurred within one caste but not in another facing similar circumstances in the same locale, or why they occurred within that caste in one district but not in others. In comparing accounts of the origins of these movements I noticed that the person credited with starting the movement was already a leader among his caste fellows. This led me to posit an initial leader stage to these movements during which an individual, who was already respected and enjoyed a good degree of local influence among his caste members, decided, for reasons worth sharing, to convert to Christianity. If this initial or early convert was not a leader, then a movement would not occur; if he was a leader, then a movement became possible.

Ditt was not the first Chuhra convert to Christianity but he seems to have already been a leader. He was not a field labourer but a dealer in hides and skins who did business in a number of villages and thus had a wider experience of the outside world than did his caste fellows in the villages he visited. He was one of six brothers with large families and numerous acquaintances. Gordon says nothing about Ditt's motives for conversion, or what he found so attractive in the Christian message or even what presentation of Christianity Ditt shared with his family and neighbours. Gordon did report, however, that as Ditt went about his business from village to village, he told others that he was a Christian and invited them to believe in 'his newly-found Saviour'.[20] He also said of Ditt that 'whenever he detected worldly motives in persons professing religious inquiry, he refused to bring such people to the missionaries'.[21] Whatever influence Ditt had before his conversion seems to have been considerably enhanced in the years afterwards, as his counsel was sought in matters of business and marriage, as well as of religion.[22]

Gordon had much more to say about Chaughatta's religious quest and conversion. For over twenty years this atypical Chuhra had visited a great number of gurus and *faqir*s in search of someone who could give him knowledge of the one true God. In the course of his travels he had heard of Jesus and of missionaries, but had not met one until he heard a *padri* named Aziz-ul-Hakk preaching in Dinanagar. According to Gordon's account, the story of the 'sinless Saviour who was dead and is alive' fully satisfied the longing in Chaughatta's soul, which had sought rest from the burden of sin.[23] Chaughatta was given further instruction and then baptized in 1878 or 1879 at the age of about fifty. Like Ditt, he shared his new faith with friends and neighbours, one of whom, Prem Masih, a disillusioned former *faqir*, became an ardent evangelist along with Chaughatta. Like Ditt, both Chaughatta and Prem Masih had had a lengthy exposure to the wider world beyond their own village, but unlike Ditt they had reputations as religious seekers rather than as well-connected businessmen.

The second stage of the conversion movement really belonged to people like Ditt, his friend Kaka, Chaughatta and Prem Masih. Gordon wrote of them that, 'Going from house to house, from village to village, and seating themselves at the firesides of those who may be emphatically styled the poor of the land, these zealous labourers tell the story of Jesus the Son of God, who became a poor man, wrought miracles, died for sinners, arose from the dead, and ascended into heaven.'[24]

He also refers to the word about Jesus (Saviour of sinners, Friend of the poor) spreading like gossip among rural Chuhras. Indeed, Jesus and Christianity became important topics of conversation when Chuhras gathered together for weddings, funerals, melas and business.[25] In Chaughatta and Prem Masih's village of Awanka, five men were baptized in 1881. A short time later eighteen more men as well as eleven children were baptized and soon after that twenty-one more people, the wives and daughters of the earlier converts, joined them in being baptized.[26] At about the same time two men from the village of Subzkote visited a missionary, who baptized one of them. A year later that man returned with two others, one of whom was his former guru who said he would come back with all his followers. They had heard about Christianity from some village Christians, not from mission employees.[27] In 1882 Rev. Samuel Martin received a deputation of rural Chuhras who wished to be baptized. Martin sent a mission worker to investigate, who found in eight villages about one hundred people 'ready to profess their faith in Christ'. Martin went on to say that 'It appears that they had heard the gospel at some mela, and, after discussing the matter among themselves, had formed the resolution to become Christians and had sent the men who came here as pioneers. They have connections, also, with others who have already embraced Christianity.'[28]

While these Chuhras were actively evangelizing their friends and relatives, the mission held back. In 1875 they reported:

> It is now over two years and a half since this movement commenced among the lower classes in that part of the district. As it was something out of our usual experience, we felt it necessary to proceed cautiously until we understood the nature of the movement. We could perhaps by greater effort have increased the number making profession, but we have confined our labors more to the instruction of those who have already made profession, and left them to operate upon their friends and neighbors.[29]

A year later they still maintained this cautious approach.

No special effort was made to extend the work among these people, it being our aim to impart more thorough instruction to those already baptized; and as this movement was something out of our ordinary experience, we thought it well to see whether those already received stood firm, and were consistent with their profession, before making special effort to extend the work.[30]

Another concern expressed in later reports was whether the conversion of large numbers of Chuhras would alienate Hindus and Muslims who 'think it beneath their dignity to care for a religion in which *even* low caste people are received',[31] but the missionaries believed, based on their reading of the Bible, that 'a true work of the Spirit should commence and make its most marked progress among the lower classes is clearly in accordance with the word of God' (I Cor. I, 26–29).[32]

If Gordon's account is to be trusted, Ditt, Chaughatta and other Dalits were spreading a message essentially of divine affirmation and hope to those at the bottom of rural Punjabi society. That this message, as well as the invitation to live this life of affirmation and hope, which had a certain discipline built into it, aroused considerable interest among rural Chuhras seems to be beyond dispute. What is also clear from the mission's annual reports and correspondence is that those Chuhras who became interested saw in the message, and in those who were spreading it, a possible solution to some of their more immediate problems. Others found that the social cost of baptism was simply too high for them, either because the inevitable persecution was too severe or because they themselves could not give up some of their habits and customs which would now become forbidden. During this stage there were converts who either left the church or were excommunicated for these reasons. The result was that growth was slow in the early years; only in 1882 did the number of baptisms per year exceed one hundred. Yet, in 1884 one United Presbyterian missionary had this to say: 'The progress of converts from among [the Chuhras] I think is quite as satisfactory as the progress of converts from among any other class. They started on the race behind some others, but the comparative progress they have made on the Christian course is quite as marked.'[33]

It is difficult to pinpoint the date of the movement's entrance into a third stage of development, which had three important characteristics. The first and most definitive was that the mission, now convinced that the movement was 'God's doing', dropped its 'wait and see' attitude and began to actively supplement what the volunteer evangelists (some of Harding's 'informal agents') were doing to spread it. Not only did the mission give greater priority to rural than to urban work, it also began to seek out and preach to the Chuhras when touring the villages. The mission also played a major role in resourcing and organizing the movement, first by training and supplying village catechists-teachers in response to increasing requests for Christian instruction, and then by organizing local believers into interconnected congregations with their own elected leaders. The mission also established village primary schools where the number of converts warranted it and supplied the teacher-catechists to run them. This in turn led to a third important feature of this stage of the movement's development. There was now available to rural Chuhras some visible public evidence of what the consequences of conversion to Christianity might be. This 'demonstration effect' created additional interest in, and lent greater credibility to, the Christian message being preached. Chuhras could see among friends, relatives and acquaintances the difference that Christianity had made in individual, family and community lives. (The changes missionaries noted were a new confidence, status-enhancing lifestyle changes and the possibility of literacy.) This 'demonstration effect' influenced not only the numerical growth rate of the Punjabi Christian community but also the motivations of subsequent inquirers.

It was during this stage that the movement spread widely and the number of conversions grew dramatically.[34] It no longer remained within the confines of the United Presbyterian 'fold' but spread into the 'territories' of other missions,[35] initially those of the Church of Scotland and the Church Missionary Society. These and later missions – the American Presbyterians, Roman Catholics, Salvation Army, and Methodists – thus experienced the movement when it was at this stage of development and Chuhras were more aware of the 'demonstration effect' of conversion to Christianity than their predecessors had been.

It was perhaps no accident that the CMS had its first contact with the movement in 1885, when a deputation of Chuhras approached its missionaries in Batala with a proposal from the village of Fatehgarh. The deputation wanted both Christian instruction and a school, the costs of which they were prepared to share with the mission. Their proposal was accepted and within a year there were sixty-five Christians and a school in Fatehgarh.[36] Neither the CMS missionaries nor those of other societies had to spend much time in soul-searching about the movement and how best to respond to it; they already had the United Presbyterian experience to draw upon and learn from.

The involvement of additional missions altered the dynamics of the conversion movement in at least three ways. Not all the missions had the same policies with regard to intervening in conflicts between converts and their landlord employers, whether the latter were engaged in religious persecution or using excessive punitive powers to resolve disputes over wages and the like. The United Presbyterians, in their desire to encourage 'independence' and discourage *ma-bapism* with a 'hands-off' policy were at one end of the spectrum, while the CMS, seeking to redress local power imbalances by interceding with district officials was at the other.[37] Secondly, the presence of Christian alternatives, especially the Roman Catholic alternative from 1888 onwards, gave Chuhra converts and catechists some leverage in dealing with their own missions. If they felt that they were being neglected or treated unfairly, they could leave one mission and join another working in the same vicinity. Initial Roman Catholic contact with the movement had come when they were approached by some disgruntled Protestants and this became a major source of tension between the two missions from that time onwards.[38] Finally, with the opening up of the canal colonies in 1892, some of the missions acquired land on which to establish Christian villages. As it turned out, these were virtually the only villages where a Chuhra could expect to own land, especially after the Land Alienation Act of 1900, because the British were determined not to upset the rural social structure in any way.[39] All three developments altered perceptions of conversion and of the benefits to be derived from it.

As this description suggests, during this stage the movement seems to have moved a long way from the simple message of divine affirmation and hope with which it had begun. Missionaries from the start had tried to separate those Chuhra inquirers whose motivations were 'worldly' from those whose motivations were 'spiritual', rejecting the former and welcoming the latter. This, however, became increasingly difficult to do because they found the motivations to be far more complex. Was the desire for greater dignity and respect 'spiritual' or 'worldly'? Moreover, the missionaries themselves were subject to mood swings regarding the movement itself. These ranged from considerable degrees of optimism to equal degrees of pessimism and affected their assessments of the motivations driving it forward. Pandit Harikishan Kaul, the Punjab Census Commissioner in 1911 when the movement was well into this third stage and most of its complexities had become fairly obvious to close observers, was probably right in seeing it driven primarily by a desire for enhanced social status.[40]

At some point, and that point varied from mission to mission, the demands of the inquirers for Christian instruction exceeded the capacity of the missions to respond. They simply had no more catechist-teachers to send. Thus a fourth stage began in which the missions' desire to consolidate and nurture converts already baptized took priority over their desire to expand. Requests for instruction were turned down till new converts could be trained as catechists to meet the demands from inside and outside the baptized community. This crisis was augmented when the canal colonies opened up and Chuhra converts migrated to them seeking employment at higher wages. The missions had to either follow them, and thus further extend themselves, or lose these Christians permanently. Thus, there were intermittent periods of consolidation within periods of overall growth. For example, the Stocks noted a period of retarded United Presbyterian growth from 1891 to 1899, between two periods of considerable growth (1881–91 and 1900–30).[41] However, during the 1920s it was plain that the movement had lost its momentum. Conversions decreased significantly as rural missionaries became more involved in visiting villages where there already were converts to be encouraged, instructed and worshipped with, than in preaching to the unconverted.

The preceding pages give an overview of the nineteenth-century Dalit conversion movement to Christianity in the Punjab. What made it a Dalit *movement* was Dalit initiative and Dalit agency not only in seeking Christian instruction and baptism but also in 'spreading the word' and recruiting new members. (In this respect it stood in marked contrast, both in style and substance, to what nineteenth-century observers noted as a common tendency among members of the menial castes simply to accommodate to the religion of their landlords.)[42] While Dalit perceptions of Christianity and motivations for conversion were certainly varied and complex, it did seem to offer them ways of dealing with the profound social alienation they experienced at the bottom of the rural social hierarchy.[43] The desire for affirmation, human and divine, as well as for dignity and respect in this life, rather than just in some life to come, drove the movement forward. The Christian missions were responders, resourcers and, in a minimal sense, organizers of what remained throughout a Dalit-led movement. When the missions could no longer respond adequately, and when other alternatives appeared on the Punjabi horizon, the movement lost its attractiveness and momentum.

The movement remained rural and decentralized throughout its life span. Unlike Ambedkar's and Mangoo Ram's later movements, it never had a single leader or organization, but, as Harding has rightly pointed out, remained very localized within the realms of the personal contacts and influence of many separate local leaders. Moreover, its objectives were very limited. It did not aim at the transformation of a caste-based rural society, or even at the acquisition of power; those were not historical possibilities for Dalits in late-nineteenth-century Punjab. Instead, it aimed at status enhancement through an alternative self-understanding, concomitant lifestyle changes, possible occupational mobility and access to at least some help from sympathetic outsiders in dealing with the local power structure.

It is important for those interested in Dalit as well as Punjabi history to recognize this conversion movement as a Dalit movement. It was earlier than other modern Dalit movements in the Punjab and certainly larger than any of its contemporaries. As such, it not only set precedents from which subsequent Dalit movements might learn, but also, and perhaps more importantly, helped to set the stage that made possible other kinds of Dalit movements in the Punjab, such as the Ad Dharm movement. This conversion movement to Christianity provoked the Arya Samaj in particular to become concerned about the Dalits and engage in modest forms of Dalit uplift work. In 1906 the Aga Khan deputation asked the Viceroy not only for separate electorates for Muslims but also that Dalits not be included in the Hindu population totals because they were not accepted as fellow Hindus. This made conversion a political as well as a religious issue, since it would affect the communal balance of power in provincial politics, as became very evident first when the 1909 constitution granted separate electorates to Muslims, and then after the 1919 constitution gave them to Sikhs as well. Dalit leaders like Ambedkar and Mangoo Ram later were able to use the resulting 'politics of numbers' to begin the political empowerment of the Dalits. Although Ditt could not have foreseen this when he walked into Sialkot back in 1873, Dalits and their religious choices would come to matter politically in no small measure because of a movement that he had helped to launch.

NOTES

1. Andrew Gordon, *Our India Mission: A Thirty Years' History of the India Mission of the United Presbyterian Church of North America Together with Personal Reminiscences*, Philadelphia: Andrew Gordon, 1886, p. 425.
2. Ibid., p. 428.
3. Ibid., pp. 440–6.
4. Frederick and Margaret Stock, *People Movements in the Punjab with Special Reference to the United Presbyterian Church*, South Pasadena: William Carey Library, 1975.
5. John C.B. Webster, *The Christian Community and Change in Nineteenth Century North India*, New Delhi: Macmillan, 1976, pp. 58–64, 71–2, 125–31, 145–50.
6. J. Waskom Pickett, *Christian Mass Movements in India*, New York: The Abingdon Press, 1932, p. 22. Group decisions did occur, but individual and family decisions seem to have been more common. John C.B. Webster, *The Dalit Christians: A History*, 2nd edn.; Delhi: ISPCK, 1994, pp. 33, 49–50, 58.

7. According to the *Census of India*, the Indian Christian population of the Punjab and its Dependencies in 1881 was 3,912. The corresponding figures in the 1911 and 1921 census were 163,994 and 315,031.
8. Ibid., pp. 52–9.
9. John C.B. Webster 'Leadership in a Rural Dalit Conversion Movement', in Joseph T. O'Connell (ed)., *Organizational and Institutional Aspects of Indian Religious Movements*, Shimla: Indian Institute of Advanced Study, 1999, pp. 96–112.
10. John C.B. Webster, 'Dalits and Christianity in Colonial Punjab: Cultural Interactions', in Judith M. Brown and Robert Eric Frykenberg, eds., *Christians, Cultural Interactions, and India's Religious Traditions*, Grand Rapids: William B. Eerdmans, 2002, pp. 92–118.
11. John C.B. Webster, 'Christian Conversion in the Punjab: What has Changed?' in Rowena Robinson and Sathianathan Clarke, eds., *Religious Conversion in India: Modes, Motivations, and Meanings*, New Delhi: Oxford University Press, 2003, pp. 357–80.
12. John C.B. Webster, 'A Quest for the Historical Ditt', *Indian Church History Review*, XXXVII (June 2003), pp. 53–68.
13. Jeffrey Cox, *Imperial Fault Lines: Christianity and Colonial Power in India, 1818–1940*, Stanford: Stanford University Press, 2002, p. 12.
14. Ibid., pp. 6.
15. Ibid., pp. 116–33.
16. Christopher Harding, 'The Dynamics of Low-Caste Conversion Movements: Rural Punjab, *c.* 1880–1935', unpublished D. Phil. dissertation, Oxford University, 2004, p. 170.
17. Ibid., p. 331.
18. Ibid., p. 332.
19. Ibid., p. 334.
20. Andrew Gordon, *Our India Mission*, p. 424.
21. Ibid., pp. 426–7.
22. Ibid., p. 427.
23. Ibid., p. 442.
24. Ibid., pp. 445–6.
25. *The Twenty-Sixth Annual Report of the Board of Foreign Missions of the United Presbyterian Church of North America Presented to the General Assembly in May 1885*, p. 19. [Hereafter *UP Mission Annual Report* with the year added.]
26. Ibid., p. 444.
27. *UP Mission Annual Report* 1882, p. 41.
28. 'India Mission: Official Correspondence', *The United Presbyterian* (21 June 1883), p. 406.
29. *UP Mission Annual Report*, 1876, p. 19.
30. Ibid., 1877, p. 15.
31. Ibid., 1884, p. 50.

32. Ibid., p. 85. See also *UP Mission Annual Report*, 1885, pp. 25–7.
33. Ibid., p. 25.
34. This is reflected in the census figures for the Indian Christian population of the Punjab during this stage of the movement: 3,912 in 1881; 19,750 in 1891; 38,513 in 1901; and 1,63,994 in 1911.
35. The early Protestant missions had worked out an understanding according to which they divided up the region among themselves and agreed not to encroach upon another mission's territory without their prior permission. Neither the Roman Catholics nor the Salvation Army were parties to this understanding and so did not abide by it.
36. *Proceedings of the Church Missionary Society for Africa and the East, Eighty-Seventh Year, 1885–86*, pp. 111–12.
37. See Webster, 'Christian Conversion in the Punjab: What has Changed?' p. 358. The Rev. Barakat Ullah with the Church Missionary Society was later to condemn their practice in this regard as increasingly dangerous. 'An Aspect of the Mass Movement Problem in the Punjab', *National Christian Council Review* (May 1927), pp. 291–300.
38. 'Pauperes Evangelizantur', *Collectanea Lahorensia* (October–December 1938), pp. 162–4.
39. See Imran Ali, 'Canal Colonization and Socio-Economic Change', in Indu Banga, ed., *Five Punjabi Centuries: Polity, Economy, Society and Culture, c. 1500–1990*, New Delhi: Manohar, 1997, p. 351.
40. *Punjab Census Report 1911*, I, p. 192.
41. Frederick and Margaret Stock, *People Movements in the Punjab*, pp. 102–8.
42. Denzil Ibbetson observed in the 1881 Census that 'As a fact it is curious how generally the observances, if not the actual religion of these lower menials, follow those of the villagers to whom they are attached.' *Punjab Census 1881*, I, p. 306.
43. Ibid. One notes this restlessness and striving among them in the comments in the census.

CHAPTER 12

Widows in North-Western India under Colonial Rule

REETA GREWAL

Widowhood is a universal phenomenon, but the proportion of widows is said to be the highest in India.[1] Apparently, this situation is due to historical reasons. Traditionally, in the Brahmanical system at least over the last millennium, a widow was regarded as a non-person who was physically alive but socially dead. Remarriage was out of the question for her, and to control and contain the sexuality especially of the young widow who chose not to become Sati, a stringent code of dress, food and behaviour was imposed on her. She was deprived, despised, excluded and exploited in various ways.[2] However, the low-caste and lower class widow probably was relatively free from the severity of these social codes. Variations in the widow's position by religious systems and regional matrices have also been noticed.[3]

The Brahmanical tradition appears to have continued in north-western India broadly down to the beginning of the twentieth century, as evident from the following comment of the Superintendent of the 1911 census of the Punjab:

> The practice of Sati has long ceased to exist . . . but a large number of widows are seriously affected by the shock and shorten their span of life by deliberate exposure to privations of all kinds. This usually happens to the piously inclined childless widows. Others are harshly treated by their mothers-in-law or female relations. They are supposed to be practically dead to the world and are expected not only to eschew all luxuries, but to lead a life of absolute self-denial in respect of dress, ornaments and even food. . . . The present day thought has

led to a widow being now looked upon as an un-productive encumbrance and even a scourge to the family. Her presence at certain occasions of rejoicing and at the celebration of certain ceremonies has come to be looked upon as ominous and her lot is altogether a hard one. . . . Every now and then one hears of attempts to quietly put a young widow out of the way.[4]

Despite the normative sanction for compulsory widowhood in the Brahmanical social order, the lower classes generally allowed the remarriage of widows. Conversely, some Muslim and Sikh social groups in the region tended to emulate the Brahmanical custom and looked upon widow remarriage with disfavour.[5] However, the ground situation appears to be even more complex than what is visualized here.

The present chapter approaches the question of the nature and extent of social transformation in north-western India under colonial rule with reference to the demographic, legal and social position of widows in the rural and urban areas of its major subregions. It is well known that this frontier region, annexed last of all by the British, became the bulwark of the colonial defence system, and sent the largest number of recruits for the British Indian Army. This region had three major religious systems – Islam, Hinduism, and Sikhism – to which Christianity was added in the nineteenth century, giving impetus to the emergence of the movements for socio-religious reform. The Societies Registration Act of 1860 provided the framework for the hundreds of reformist associations that came up in the Punjab. The province had a rather large proportion of the depressed classes (later designated as the Scheduled Castes), and a substantial chunk of its population was seen by the colonial rulers as following the tribal customs. The decennial Census Reports afforded insights into the complexities and peculiarities of society in the region comprehended by the British province of the Punjab.[6]

WIDOWS IN THE CENSUS REPORTS

The existing studies of women in the colonial Punjab do not somehow look at the changing demographic profile of widows.[7] It is important to note first of all that the proportion of widows in the region was lower than in other parts of India. In 1881, 17.8 per cent of the female population in the country consisted of widows, their percentage in the Punjab was 14.8, but in other provinces it ranged from 15.8 in Assam to 22.3 in Bengal.[8] In the next fifty years, the percentage of widows in the female population continued to decrease throughout the subcontinent, including its north-western parts. In 1931, this percentage was 15.5 for India and 11.4 for the Punjab.[9] Ten years later, the percentage for the Punjab further came down to 10.[10] This trend appears to have continued into the post-independence period. It may be relevant to point out that in the Census of 1981, the percentage of widows in the total female population in the Punjab was 5.4 which remained the lowest in the country (Table 12.1).[11]

If the change in absolute numbers was less striking, it was only because the total population was on the increase in the second half of colonial rule in the Punjab as elsewhere in India. In 1881, the number of widows in the province was 15,03,300. It came down to 13,86,000 in 1901, but rose again to 15,51,000 in 1911, owing probably to the natural calamities like the plague, cholera and the earthquake. This apparent constancy in the numbers can be misleading if we do not keep in view the overall increase in population in the 1920s. In the Census of 1931, the total number of widows in the Punjab came down to 15,12,000.[12]

To explain the relatively low proportion of widows in the region, we may first concede that the factors considered responsible for the large numerical proportion of widows in the country were generally operative in this region too, like the prevalence of certain degree of polygamy, prohibition of widow remarriage, and the effect of scarcities, famines and epidemics. While the natural calamities affected both men and women, in all probability more women fell to these. At any rate, as noticed already, there was a general improvement in this situation in India by the 1920s when the plague, influenza, small pox and cholera epidemics had ceased to cause havoc, and fever was being dealt with more effectively.[13] One may assume in this context that the lower numerical proportion of widows in the Punjab was in broad correspondence with the comparatively low sex ratio in the region.[14] More importantly, as shown later in this essay, the practice of widow remarriage was generally upheld in the Customary Law operative among the peasant communities in the different subregions of the province. Furthermore, there was no normative prohibition against it among Muslims, Sikhs and the depressed classes who, together, vastly outnumbered the *dwija*s (higher caste Hindus).[15] At any rate, the socio-religious reform movements among Hindus, like the Brahmo Samaj, Arya Samaj and Dev Samaj, and the spread of education and awareness appear to have weakened the hold of the Brahmanical tradition over the life and attitudes of the *dwija*s in urban areas.

An analysis of the available census data in terms of religious affiliation may elucidate the situation further. In 1881, the relative proportions of Hindu and Muslim widows in the total number of widows was 46 per cent in each case. The widows among Sikhs constituted about 7 per cent at that time.[16] In 1911, the proportion of Hindu widows in the total number of widows decreased to 42.7 per cent, that of the Muslim widows came down to 44, while the Sikh widows recorded an increase to 12 per cent.[17] By 1931, this proportion came down to 37 per cent in case of the Hindu widows, but rose to 47 for Muslims, and 13.6 for widows among the Sikhs. In terms of their percentage in the total population of the community, it was 14.2 for Hindu widows, 10.4 for Muslim widows and 11.4 for widows among the Sikhs. Incidentally, at 15.8, the highest percentage of widows in a community was recorded among the Jains who rigorously upheld the notion of ascetic widowhood for all ages.[18] As regards the intercensal decrease and increase in the percentage of widows among the Hindus and Sikhs, this was in broad correspondence with their population figures: between 1901 and 1931, there was a decrease of 4 per cent among the Hindus, while an increase of 7 per cent was recorded in the case of the Sikhs.[19]

As regards the age-wise break up of the figures for widows, the Census of 1881 does not record any child widows up to the age of 5, but it does tell us that child marriage was prevalent in the region. The Census of 1911 reports its prevalence in all the subregions and among all the major castes and tribes.[20] In terms of absolute numbers, the married female infants in the age group of 0-5 numbered 2,077 in 1911, 2,677 in 1921, and 9,730 in 1931.[21] From 1881 to 1931, the percentage of married children below the age of 15 ranged between 6 and 8, and over 70 per cent of them happened to be females. Consequently, in the figures available for the widowed children, the proportion of the females was higher.[22] Their proportion in the total widowed population was reported to be .02 per cent in 1931. In the 5-10 years group, this percentage ranged from .08 in 1881 to .11 in 1931. In the 10-15 years group, there was a marginal decline in the percentage of widows, from .4 to .3 per cent. On the other hand, the figures for India show that there was an increase in the percentage of widows in the 5-10 age group, from .3 per cent in 1881 to .5 in 1931, while the 10-15 years category remained the same at 1 per cent.[23] As a whole, these figures indicate a smaller proportion of child widows in the Punjab. There is evidence pointing towards the norm of higher age of marriage at least among the Muslims and Sikhs in the Punjab even before its advocacy by the reformers and the caste associations under colonial rule.[24]

In terms of absolute numbers, however, child widows up to the age of 9 doubled in the Punjab between 1881 and 1931, rising from 1,208 to 2,444. In the age group of 10-15, the number decreased from 6,778 to 4,987. The 15-20 years group remained static at about 19,000, while in the 20-25 age group the number decreased from 41,000 to 34,000. The other age groups show minor variations with time. The number of widows in the 50-60 years group increased by 22,000, whereas the number in the 60 plus group decreased by a little over 15,000 by 1931.[25]

This analysis of the census data suggests so far that the total number of widows in the Punjab was lower than that of the country as a whole and decreased further with time. The region had a larger proportion of Muslim widows compared to the Indian average, and also an increased number of Sikh widows by the 1930s. In the age wise break-up, the number of child widows increased marginally, and the 30 to 60 years segment also showed a small increase. Among child widows, there was a higher proportion of Hindus; there were more Muslim widows in the 45 years plus category which corresponded to the higher proportion of Muslims in the total population of the region.

It may be of some interest to have a look at the numerical proportions of widows in the urban centres of the region as evident from the Census of 1931. Compared with the Punjab as a whole, some cities and towns had a lower proportion of widows. For example, in Lahore only 9.2 per cent of the female population consisted of widows. In Amritsar and Ludhiana this percentage was 10.7 each. In Jalandhar and Ambala, the proportion of widows was the same as in the region, that is 11.4 per cent, while in Ferozepur it was higher, at 11.9.[26] This seems to suggest that the larger centres had a relatively smaller proportion of widows, because these attracted a larger proportion of men in pursuit of jobs and opportunities.

The relative proportions of widows in the major communities of the urban population also varied. Compared to the average for the Hindu widows in the province, Lahore had a smaller proportion of Hindu widows, at 34.5 per cent, while their proportion was higher in Amritsar, Jalandhar, Ambala and Ludhiana. The number of widows among Sikhs was higher in Amritsar, their religious and cultural centre, than the provincial average for the Sikhs, but rather low in other cities and towns. In the case of Muslims, some cities like Lahore, Jalandhar and Ludhiana, had a higher proportion in comparison to the average, while the other centres like Ferozepur, Ambala and Amritsar had a lower proportion of widows (Table 12.2).[27] This variation seems to be related to the composition of population in the urban units and the dominant groups in them.

Variations in the numerical proportions of widows in the urban centres of different sizes was accompanied by variations in their position in the urban and rural areas of the region. Between the two extremes of compulsory widowhood and compulsory remarriage there were shifts arising at least partly from the circumstances of colonial rule.

WIDOWS IN THE CUSTOMARY LAW

The Hindu Widow Remarriage Act XV of 1856, which enabled a widow of 'full age' to remarry, 'produced meagre returns' all over India, because the widow's consent alone could not go far 'in the absence of a social milieu willing to carry it forward'.[28] In the north-western region, at any rate, this Act was ignored in favour of custom which recognized the remarriage of widows. The need to pacify the warlike tribes in the newly conquered region had obliged Governor-General Dalhousie to expressly give precedence to 'native institutions and practices' and maintain the village communities 'in all their integrity'. The 'popular institutions' were seen to differ 'widely from the prescriptions of Hindu and Muhammadan law'.[29]

The Punjab Laws Act of 1872 laid down that custom should be the primary rule of decision 'in questions regarding inheritance, special property of females, betrothal, marriage, dower, adoption, guardianship' and the like.[30] The *wajib-ul-arz* or village administration papers, combined with consultation with the village headmen, became the bases for preparing the *rivaj-i-am* or the general record of customs for tribes or groups of villages in a district. However, there reportedly was neither clarity nor agreement among the landowners regarding the existing usage. It often included what the influential among the landowners wanted to be followed for the future.[31] There is no evidence that the women of the locality were ever consulted about these issues that concerned them directly. The widow at any rate was found to be missing from the early records of rights prepared by the British.[32] Through the Land Revenue Act, however, a widow without any male lineal descendants succeeded for life to her deceased husband's property as a 'turstee' responsible for the payment of the revenues.[33]

The reports on the *rivaj-i-am* prepared in the tahsils and districts of the Punjab, and translated and periodically revised as the Customary Law between the 1890s and 1940s, record not only the variations of customs among the different groups of people in various subregions of north-western India, but also reflect changes in the widow's position over time.[34] The issues related to widowhood taken up in these reports include guardianship over and by her, inheritance and succession, alienation of property, and unchastity and remarriage.

Almost all social groups in the region took for granted that the widow would remain under the guardianship of her deceased husband's nearest kin and heirs. It was believed that let alone widows, women were never 'out of tutelage'.[35] The reporting for the Delhi district that the widow could manage her life herself, without a guardian,[36] is doubtful, because the records do not indicate the caste or class of the widows who were not dependant. As regards the widow's own right to be the guardian of her children, she could remain their guardian so long as she did not remarry outside the deceased husband's family.[37] However, in the Ferozepur district as well as among the Jats, Bhattis, Chohans and Kamins in the Jhelum area, she could retain guardianship over minor children from a former marriage, provided she was of 'good character'.[38]

The widow was usually not permitted to adopt a child except with the written consent of her deceased husband obtained in his lifetime, or of his kinsmen.[39] In that case too, only a child of a male relative of the husband could be adopted. This position seems to have continued throughout the colonial period as it was invoked even in the 1940s. A widower, on the other hand, could adopt a child without any such restriction in the Customary Law.[40]

As noticed already, a sonless widow was customarily allowed to inherit a share of her deceased husband's property for her lifetime only. This share was equal to that of one son's in Moga, Ludhiana, Kaithal and Delhi; in Gujranwala, she shared equally with the other widow of her husband who had sons.[41] The Sayyads allowed a half share to widows till remarriage or death.[42] This custom was followed by the Rairhs and Gujars in Ambala as well.[43] Among some groups, in case of more than one widow, no distinction was made in their shares.[44] At the same time, in several cases, as in the case of the Brahmans in Delhi, Hindu Jats in Gurdaspur and several tribes in the Attock district, the widow's right only to maintenance was recognized.[45] Another set of variations, for example, were noticeable in Ludhiana, where the Dogars did not permit inheritance if the widow was not a Dogar; the Hindu Jats allowed her a share only if she belonged to the same *got*; the Rajputs allowed a share if she belonged to the same tribe; and the Sidhu Jats recognized the widow's right to demand partition.[46] The widow's right to partition was supported by some in other areas as well but this remained exceptional.[47] On the other hand, all tribes in Jalandhar tahsil favoured maintenance only for the widow from outside the tribe.[48] The Indri tribe in Delhi and Kaithal allowed inheritance only of movable property by widows.[49] There were, thus, several variations in the widow's right to inheritance. These variations seem to be determined less by the subregion or religion and more by the custom of a particular social group in a locality.

When there were several widows in the same family – mother, wife, daughter-in-law – some conflict over succession did arise. In most cases they succeeded jointly and equally.[50] In case the widowed daughter-in-law had a daughter, there could be some conflict over whose right was superior. The widowed mother at times waived her share in favour of the widowed daughter-in law, but not always.[51] The widow's inheritance was contested by other descendants and kinsmen and it was generally believed also by the British revenue officials that a widow 'wasted' property since she was unable to enforce rights and manage lands effectively. The officials were therefore reluctant to permit partition of holdings, and actually refused division in some cases.[52]

If and when the widow inherited, her rights to succession were further restricted by a limited right to alienate the inherited property. It was generally recognized that the widow could not sell, gift or bequeath but could only mortgage in certain situations.[53] Dalip Singh, the compiler of the Customary Law in the Gujranwala district, emphatically states that, widows 'have no right to alienate any kind of property . . . except under special circumstances, for special objects, for necessary purposes, or with the consent of the collaterals', which appears to be the general situation. Several examples of mortgage of immovable property are then cited.[54] Among the reasons considered valid for mortgage are the last rites of the deceased husband, repayment of his debts, children's marriage, sickness, agricultural improvements and payment of land revenue. The widow could alienate property only if kinsmen refused to help, and generally for the payment of revenues alone.[55] Such restrictions did not apply to movable property, although the assumption was that all property alienations should be only for necessity.[56] In Ambala, it was believed that the widow could make small charities (*punarth*) and gifts to daughters and descendants from the ancestral property with the consent of the collaterals.[57]

As regards the self acquired property of the widow, referred to often as her 'special property' or her *stridhan*, a Brahman widow in the Delhi area could alienate it.[58] In Jalandhar and Gurdaspur also, a widow could alienate her *stridhan* in terms of her ornaments through sale, gift and mortgage.[59] The Hindus in Gurdaspur and Batala tahsils permitted alienation of *stridhan* only for religious purposes. A note in the report on the Customary Law of Gurdaspur district states that in the southern part of the district there was no custom of *stridhan*, while in the north some vestiges had remained but no 'real power'.[60] This would probably be true of some other parts too. In the south-western and the north-western areas, the term *stridhan* was 'unknown'; though the Hindus admitted to the widow's right to alienate her self-acquired property. As regards a Muslim widow's right over her 'special property,' which consisted of her *haq mehar* (dower), *jahez* (dowry), gifts received from relations, and property acquired by herself, it was recognized by most tribes, but the general opinion was in favour of restricting its use and disposal.[61]

The issue of the chastity of the widows was given crucial importance by nearly all groups. In theory, a widow was deprived of property if she was 'unchaste'.[62] Even if she acquired the reputation of unchastity she had to give up all claims according to the Sayyids, Dogars and Shaikhs of Gurdaspur.[63] Some Jats and Gujars in the Delhi district and some Hindu Jats in Ludhiana were of the view that an unchaste widow could continue to hold property so long as she remained in her deceased husband's house.[64] The Gujars, Sainis, Arains, Kalals, Labanas and the Mallahs of Shakargarh tahsil of Gurdaspur claimed that if a widow was pregnant through 'illicit relations' or married to another, her inheritance was forfeited.[65] According to the custom for Amritsar, revised and recorded in the 1940s, a widow lost claim to her deceased husband's property if she had left home during his lifetime to live in adultery, or had an illegitimate child on becoming widow, or remarried.[66] Towards the end of the colonial period, thus, 'unchastity' came to be more clearly defined or spelt out than in the late nineteenth century when the term was used as a blanket for various situations.

Widow remarriage was a valid and well established practice in the colonial Punjab. The well-known ethnographer, Ibbetson, regards this practice as an important marker of social distinction in the region. He notices its prevalence among the Jats, Gujars, Ahirs and Rors, who stood at the head of the castes who practised widow remarriage through *karewa*.[67] Socially and legally, it was as 'binding' as the *nikah*, *phera* or *anand* marriage.[68] The other social groups practising widow-remarriage included the Kalals, Arains, Labanas, Sainis, and Chhangs.[69] On the other hand, Brahmans, Rajputs, Khatris, including Bedis and Sodhis, Tagas, Kayasths, Banias, Sayyids, Pathans and Shaikhs did not consider it lawful, but there is evidence of its practice among them in the countryside.[70] Apparently, widow remarriage was not a question of caste but of agrarian necessity, socio-economic status, regulation of the widow's sexuality, and retention of control over family property.

Therefore, though considered inferior, the widow's 'lifetime interest' in her deceased husband's property was jealously watched by his family who strongly disapproved of the widow remarrying a stranger. They increasingly approached the revenue administrators and district officials, and even appealed to the courts against the widow's stance of independence. Although the courts occasionally upheld the widow's position, the colonial administrators were actually instructed to disallow her marriage to an outsider. The 'only satisfactory arrangement against which she had no appeal' was believed to be 'a firm anchoring of the widow in marriage' within the marital family.[71] After remarriage, in any case, the widow lost all her rights to her late husband's property.[72]

In her perceptive study of widow remarriage in terms of the custom of *karewa* in the Haryana subregion of the colonial Punjab, Prem Chowdhry describes it as 'social consent for co-habitation', sanctified by the agrarian needs. As a rule, *karewa*, *karao*, *chadar andazi* or *chadar dalna* was levirate marriage in which the widow was accepted as wife by one of the younger brothers of the deceased husband; failing him the husband's elder brother; failing him his agnatic first cousins. The difference of age did not matter and sometimes the widow was married to an infant in the family. Thus, the widow's right as to whom she could marry was severely restricted, and it could be settled only by her late husband's family. There were some instances even of the father-in-law marrying his widowed daughter-in-law through *karewa*, and the brotherhood recognizing it and the court upholding it.[73] *Karewa* gave equal status to the widow of the deceased and the wife of the second husband, and equal rights to children born of the *karewa* union.[74] Among some groups mere cohabitation of the widow with the brother of the deceased husband was presumed binding.[75]

Karewa covered a range of situations in the Punjab, both in terms of the ceremony and practice. It was essentially a simple procedure, with some sub-regional and local variations, and variations also according to religious affiliations. Since no Hindu woman could be married twice through the ceremony of a religious wedding (*vidhi* or *biah*), the remarriage of a widow did not generally entail *neota*, betrothal, *barat, phera* or *pandit*. In the *karewa* or *karao* ceremony in the south-eastern Punjab or the Haryana area, glass bangles (*churis*) were placed on the widow's wrists as a symbol of her *suhagan* status in the presence of the men of the community; sometimes, this was combined with a gold nosering (*nath*) in her nose and a red sheet over her head, with a rupee tied in one of its corners.[76] In central and western Punjab, in the presence generally of relatives and neighbours, a white *chadar* or sheet, which was coloured at the corners, preferably with saffron, was thrown by the man over the widow's head and a rupee was put by him in her hand, signifying his acceptance of her as his wife.[77] This ceremony was followed by distribution of sweets, *halwa* or jaggery (*gur*). The widow now simply resumed wearing her coloured clothes and jewels which she had stopped wearing on her husband's death. Among the Jats and Rors, *karewa* ceremony was only for widows of the family. In the other cases no ceremony was required.[78]

There were some variations according to religious affiliations. Among Hindus and Sikhs there was no fixed interval for remarriage. The Hindus generally followed a gap of a month and a quarter, or 40 days, though in some cases it was a year. At places, *chaunk* was worshipped by the priest in case of the

Hindus. By the early twentieth century, the Singh Sabhas in Jalandhar and Amritsar were performing *karewa* of the Sikh widows with *anand* rites. By the 1940s, *anand* marriage with its essential features had become common for the remarriage of widows among the Sikhs. The Muslim widows were remarried only through *nikah* and were not, in theory, restricted to the first husband's family. It was performed after *iddat* or the period of mourning, which was 4 months and 10 days from the death of the first husband. The second marriage (*nikah sani*) was devoid of the pomp and festivities of the first marriage.[79]

As regards the social groups practising widow remarriage, even those who had earlier denied its existence among their customs gradually began practising it during our period of study. By the early twentieth century, Bedis and Sodhis and some other Khatris in Gurdaspur accepted *karewa* as lawful when it was with the brother's widow.[80] The Brahmans and Rajputs, who had earlier declined to recognize *karewa*, now censured it but no longer penalized 'offenders' with excommunication.[81] Many Sayyads, Kanets and Brahmans as well as Manj and Ghorewala Rajputs began to allow widow remarriage by this time. Instances of *karewa* between the Jat males and the women of the Bania, Kumhar, Tarkhan, Bazigar, Jhiwar, Nai and Labana castes were gradually becoming acceptable. But the remarriage of Jats with the socially 'low' groups like the Chamars and Chuhras remained unacceptable. Such alliances were considered invalid even after many years of cohabitation, and such 'widows' were turned out after their social affiliations became known. Intercaste *karewa* was socially recognized but not upheld in court in all cases.[82]

Prem Chowdhry discusses at length the factors that appear to have sustained and even promoted *karewa* as it came to be followed by all the agriculturist castes in Haryana except the Rajputs. She sees a connection between the practice of bride price and *karewa* as both were practised in the same milieu. The wife was seen as an 'agricultural-cum-labour-cum-reproductive asset'.[83] As a potential wife and mother, as well as domestic and field labourer, a widow in Haryana was an asset and, therefore, not considered inauspicious. The one reason why the Arya Samaj became popular in the rural Haryana was that it advocated the *karewa* form of widow remarriage.[84] Favourable stance of the colonial administrators appears to have played a significant role in this situation. Chowdhry attributes this partly to their cultural predilections against the 'independent woman', but more to the economic backwardness of Haryana which sent a large number of recruits for their Army. *Karewa*, as it was practised in the area, was seen to help in the normal functioning of an agriculturist family, check fragmentation of holdings, safeguard the payment of land revenue, and ensure demographic equilibrium despite out-migration for work and large scale casualties in war. In the context of the agriculturist tribes of the Punjab as a whole, the British upheld remarrige on the assumption that it contributed towards the 'preservation of village community' and imposition of 'a unified tribal authority'.[85]

WIDOWS IN THE HINDU SOCIAL REFORM MOVEMENTS

The option of remarriage, though conceded in custom and law, was not available in practice to the widows of the urban based higher castes, especially among Hindus. Ideally, according to the orthodox view, the proper *dharma* for a widow amongst the *dwija*s was to live a simple life by renouncing good food, clothes, ornaments and all pleasures; to remain immersed in fasting and prayer, and undertake pilgrimage; never talk to men, or be present alone among them; to be *sannyasin* in fact in the memory of her late husband.[86] This prescription was the obverse of a lurking fear of her getting out of control and destroying family honour and happiness.

Writing in 1876, Shraddha Ram Phillauri, the first ideologue of Sanatan Dharm in colonial Punjab, expresses concern about the newspaper reports of the incidents of sexual exploitation, abortions, elopement, prostitution, and suicides of the Hindu widows from well-placed families in urban areas. He regards remarriage of widows as 'a thousand times' better alternative to these fallen levels of morality, and cites Parashar and Vashisht as permitting remarriage in certain situations, like the husband's death or prolonged absence or his physical, social and cultural disabilities. Phillauri is apprehensive, however, that once the possibility of a second marriage was conceded, it could encourage the wife to become bold in her attitude, and irresponsible in her *dharma*, towards her existing husband, especially if he happened to be wayward, disabled, terminally ill, poor, ignorant or foolish. As a safeguard against this situation, raising the age of marriage is suggested so that the qualities and defects of the prospective groom (and bride) could become known before the knot was tied. An unsuitable alliance could be obviated also by the close relations of the girl ascertaining the suitability of the bridegroom rather than leaving it to the self-interested *nai* or *pandit*.[87] Phillauri's prescriptions had no takers yet.

Meanwhile, the missionaries, who were based in urban areas and who had been aggressively trying to win the Punjab for Christianity,[88] saw the long suffering Hindu widows as potential converts who could give them points of entry into the high caste Hindu households. In order to 'improve' their condition, the Zenana Mission of the Church of England gave work to widows in the Amritsar area. The American Presbyterian Mission at Ludhiana opened a school for widows and gave scholarships and sewing machines to help widows earn a 'respectable living'.[89] Though not much could be done by the missionaries specifically for widows, the activities of the Zenana workers were seen as posing 'a great threat to the sanctity of the Hindu home'.[90]

This perceived threat evoked responses from the middle class reformers, particularly from the Arya Samaj. Anshu Malhotra sensitively captures their dilemma in dealing with the problem of higher caste widows. They had to be saved from conversion by the missionaries and sexual exploitation by the people around them. Remarriage could protect them against these pitfalls, harness their reproductive potential, and ensure their economic security, but it was widely seen as the negation of *pativrata dharma* and violation of caste and religion. Marrying the widows among the lower castes was even more unacceptable, as it jeopardized the purity of lineage. While the Aryas were divided amongst themselves about the course to be adopted with regard to the widow, they had to also counteract the general criticism of Swami Dayanand's idea of *niyog*, or temporary marriage contrived for offspring, as the solution of the problem of widows.[91]

As an alternative to their founder's prescription, the more radical among the Aryas chose to promote widow remarriage. They invoked the scriptures and launched societies in cities and towns to support such marriages. Their emphasis, however, was on remarriage of child widows whose *muklawa* had not taken place. By the turn of the twentieth century, this idea appears to have become more acceptable among Hindus cutting across castes and ideological affiliations.[92] It was in this context that Sir Ganga Ram, a social activist, set up the Vidhva Vivah Sahayak Sabha or Widow Remarriage Association at Lahore in 1914. At the risk of being ostracized, he also published pamphlets in Gurmukhi and Urdu in support of widow remarriage. The Sabha arranged 12 marriages in the first year, and the number gradually increased, going up to 453 in 1922, and 5,466 in 1931. They claimed to have remarried 44,500 widows between 1914 and 1931.[93] in view of the rather large number of widows of marriageable age, this was a small beginning, indeed.

Malhotra regards the programme of widow remarriage more as a 'posture' and 'the official propaganda line favoured by the reformers' who were 'deeply discomfited' with the built in contradiction between the *pativrata* ideal and remarriage. Therefore, many of them 'began to espouse a reworked notion of' ascetic widowhood', or 'the widow devoting her life to public service, especially as a teacher'.[94] Teaching could give the widow a meaningful existence and make her financially self-supporting. Incidentally, the high caste Hindu widow taking to teaching also suited the government as she could lend dignity to their schools, and provide a 'cheap alternative' to the problem of shortage of women teachers. Normal schools were opened to train the widows as teachers and stipends were given to them till the second decade of the twentieth century, when the number of widows receiving training became sufficiently large.[95]

However, the concern of the reformers was equally to ensure that the widow perpetuated the *pativrata* ideal, for which she had to be controlled and guided while being educated. At the Kanya Mahavidyalaya, Jalandhar which took initiative in providing education and scholarships to the deserving widows, an austere social and physical code was prescribed for them. They were moulded not only to become self-effacing teachers, but also serve the cause of the Arya Samaj in various ways. By the beginning of the third decade of the twentieth century, this 'new model for a widow' became widely acceptable. Sir Ganga Ram who had taken initiative in remarrying widows, now became instrumental in opening the Hindu Widow's Home in 1921, to house the ascetical widow pursuing education; she had become 'a powerful symbol of patriarchal imagination'.[96]

It would be unrealistic to assume that these cautious initiatives were acceptable to the Hindus at large. The Hindu orthodox opinion, broadly labelled as Sanatan Dharm, which had become organized and institutionalized in the Punjab by the 1920s, condemned remarriage and did not favour the Arya notion of ascetical widowhood combined with higher education for the widow. In fact, the Sanatanists supported child marriage as prescribed in the Shastras; their Putri Pathshalas provided 'elementary' education to girls to prepare them 'only for the role of a wife and mother'.[97] In this world-view, there apparently was no room for the rehabilitation of widows through education. The widow homes set up by the Sanatan Dharm Pratinidhi Sabha taught the widows how to sew and stitch to become self-supporting.[98]

An insight into the general attitude of the orthodox Hindus towards widowhood can be had from their writings produced in the region apparently in response to the changing circumstances of colonial rule. For example, writing in 1911, Pandit Bhanu Datt Pushkaran emphasizes that a girl (*kanya*) is married only once through the sacrament (*sanskar*) of marriage. There is no provision for a second marriage in the *vivah sutras*, for only the word kanya (*virgin*) is used in these which can not be stretched to cover the widow. Since she can neither be given away (*kanya dan*) by her parents, nor by her husband's family, the widow alone could give her own self away to another man as her second husband. However, in the case of the higher caste (*dwija*) widows, any form of remarriage or *niyog* is not permissible, underlines Pushkaran.[99]

By the third decade of the twentieth century, the Sanatanists appear to have become more responsive to the changing social environment. Writing in 1922, Pandit Mul Raj Sharma Nagar invokes Manu and Yajnavalkya in support of the remarriage of a virgin widow. With regard to the other widows the ideal of devoting the remainder of their life in prayers is reiterated. If the widow found it difficult she could take refuge with her late husband's brother or his agnates through *chadar dalna*, or a similar ceremony which was comparable to the *gandharva* form of marriage mentioned in the *Manusmriti*. Its offsprings should be allowed to inherit property, but a *dwija* marrying a widow would be deemed as Shudra. Nagar's emphasis, therefore, is on the opening of Vidhva Ashrams to provide economic security to the hapless Hindu widow and save her from bad company or the influence of another religion by which he meant Christianity. In such an institution she could learn stitching or weaving, or elementary treatment of women and children, or any other skill to make both ends meet. This, he emphasizes, is far more urgent than any other act of piety, or debating on the merits or demerits of widow remarriage![100]

Despite the plurality of visions about the widow in the north-western region, what was common to all the prescriptions – whether of the Sanatanists or the Aryas or of the colonial administrators – was the reassertion and reinforcement of the patriarchal controls over her. She lost the relative personal freedom available to her before the colonial administrators and law officers froze a fluid situation into the Customary Law and assiduously applied it to her disadvantage. At the same time, the tendencies noticeable during the first half of the twentieth century – the lower numerical proportions of widows, recognition of their right in property, growing social acceptance of their remarriage, and their increasing access to education and gainful employment – fructified and expanded in independent India in the later half of the twentieth century.

NOTES

1. A. Suryakumari, 'The Institution of Widowhood in Historical Perspective', in P.K.B. Nayar, ed., *Widowhood in Modern India*, Delhi: The Women Press, 2006, p. 9.
2. Ibid., pp. 10-16; Bharati Ray, ed., *From the Seams of History: Essays on Indian Women*, New Delhi: Oxford University Press, 1995, p. 4.
3. For example, the essays in a recently published collection deal with the problem of widowhood in Punjab, Bengal, Maharashtra, Gujarat, Andhra Pradesh, Karnataka, Tamil Nadu and Kerala, and also among

Muslims and Christians and in tribal, rural and urban areas. See P.K.B. Nayar, ed., *Widowhood in Modern India*, pp. v–xvi.

4. Pandit Harikishan Kaul (compl.), *Census of India 1911*, vol. XIV: *Punjab*, Pt. I, Lahore, 1912, p. 234.
5. Ibid., p. 233.
6. The British province of the Punjab broadly covered the north-western region between the rivers Yamuna and the Indus, besides a large part of the Western Himalayas and plains and hills across the Indus. The Delhi territory and the present Haryana area were added in 1858; the North West Frontier Province (NWFP) was carved out in 1901; and the city of Delhi and its environs were separated from the Punjab in 1911. Nearly 40 princely states of different sizes were politically attached to the province. The present chapter focuses mainly on the plain areas of the British Punjab. For the colonial context, see Reeta Grewal, *Colonialism and Urbanization in India: The Punjab Region*, New Delhi: Manohar, 2009, pp. 39–53.
7. There is only a passing reference to the numerical proportion of widows in the Punjab in Anshu Malhotra, *Gender, Caste, and Religious Identities: Restructuring Class in Colonial Punjab*, New Delhi: Oxford University Press, 2002, pp. 87–8.
8. Calculated from statistics in General Form VI: Distribution of Population by Civil Condition, Age and Sex arranged by Provinces or States, *Census of India 1881*, London, 1883. The proportions in other regions were as follows: Bengal 21.3 per cent, North Western Provinces 17.1 per cent, Madras 21.2 per cent, Bombay 17.9 per cent, Central Provinces 15.8 per cent, and Assam 15.8 per cent.
9. Calculated from Table VI: Age, Sex and Civil Condition, in Pt. II of the *Census of India 1931, vol. XVII: Punjab*, Lahore, 1933.
10. Calculated from Table V, *Census of the Punjab 1941*, Delhi, 1941. In 1941, the percentage of widows in Delhi was 10.7 and in the NWFP it was 10.9.
11. P.K.B. Nayar, 'Widowhood in India', in Nayar, ed., *Widowhood in Modern India*, p. 3, Nayar tabulates the relative position of the widows in Punjab and Haryana in the Census of 1981 as under:

TABLE 12.1: PERCENTAGE OF WIDOWS IN THE POPULATION OF INDIA BY MAJOR STATES (1981)

States	Widows in total female population	Widows among married females
Andhra Pradesh	10.2	17.7
Bihar	7.3	12.9
Gujarat	7.0	13.4

Haryana	*5.0*	*9.5*
Himachal Pradesh	7.6	14.6
Jammu & Kashmir	5.7	11.7
Karnataka	9.5	18.3
Kerala	9.1	18.5
Madhya Pradesh	7.8	13.8
Maharashtra	8.7	16.0
Orissa	9.0	17.3
Punjab	*5.4*	*10.9*
Rajasthan	7.1	12.7
Tamil Nadu	10.0	18.4
Uttar Pradesh	6.4	11.3
West Bengal	9.2	17.9
India	8.0	14.8

12. Calculated from the statistics on Age, Sex and Civil Condition in the Punjab Census Reports from 1881 to 1931.
13. See, for example, Sasha, 'The State, Society and Epidemics in Colonial Punjab, 1849–1947', Ph.D. thesis, Panjab University, Chandigarh, 2003, pp. 33–49.
14. From 1881 to 1931, the sex ratio in the Punjab region remained lower than the proportions for India as a whole. For detail, Reeta Grewal, *Colonialism and Urbanization in India*, p. 140.
15. Ibid., p. 126. For some idea of the demographic proportions of the depressed classes, see Harish C. Sharma, *Artisans of the Punjab: A Study of Social Change in Historical Perspective (1849–1947)*, New Delhi: Manohar, 1996, pp. 41–5.
16. Calculated from General Form VI: Statistics of Population, *Census of India 1881,* Pt. II, Calcutta, 1883.
17. Calculated from Table VII: Age, Sex and Civil Condition, *Census of Punjab 1911.*
18. Ibid., *Census of Punjab 1931.*
19. Ibid. For factors contributing towards the substantial increase in the number of Sikhs at the cost of Hindus, see Joginder Singh, 'The Sikh Community: Demography and Occupational Change, 1881–1931', in Indu Banga, ed., *Five Punjabi Centuries: Polity, Economy, Society and Culture, c. 1500–1990*, rpt., New Delhi: Manohar, 2000, pp. 470–5, 488.
20. Subsidiary Tables I–V on Civil Condition, *Census of Punjab 1911*, pp. 8–11.
21. Vijay Lakshmi, 'Children in the Colonial Punjab: A Social History', M.Phil. dissertation, Panjab University, Chandigarh, 2001, Table VII-B.
22. Ibid., pp. 39–41 and Tables VII A and VIII.

23. Calculated from Table VII: Age, Sex and Civil Condition, *Census of Punjab 1931*, Pt. II.
24. Amongst the Muhammadan tribes of the region, marriage was reported to be 'nearly always adult'. W.S. Talbot (compl.), *General Code of Tribal Customs in the Jhelum District*, vol. XIX, Lahore, 1901, p. 23. The age of the bride among Muslims ranged from 12 to 16 in different parts of the region. See, for example, E. Joseph, *Customary Law of the Rohtak District*, Lahore, 1911, p. 14. In case of the Sikhs also, the higher age of marriage probably was the norm as evident from an early manual of conduct (*rahitnama*) which lays down that 'both the boy and the girl should be atleast seventeen years of age'. J.S. Grewal, *The Sikhs: Ideology, Institutions and Identity*, New Delhi: Oxford University Press, 2009, p. 170. Among Hindus, marriage could be 'at any age', but the girl was generally given away (*muklawa*) before she was 13–14 years, that is on attaining puberty. *Customary Law of the Rohtak District*, p. 14. See also, H.C. Beadon (compl.), *Code of Tribal Custom in the Delhi District,* Delhi 1911, p. 6.
25. Based on Table VII: Age, Sex and Civil Condition, *Census of Punjab 1931*, Pt. II.
26. The religion-wise percentage of widows in urban areas is given below:

TABLE 12.2: PERCENTAGE OF WIDOWS BY MAJOR RELIGIONS

Urban Centre	Percentage in Population of Centre	Percentage by Religion		
		Hindu	Muslim	Sikh
Amritsar	10.7	42.50	40.9	15.5
Lahore	9.2	34.50	58.3	3.8
Jalandhar	11.4	40.20	54.3	1.2
Ludhiana	10.7	37.98	55.5	3.5
Ferozepur	11.9	51.10	39.1	4.9
Ambala	11.4	51.70	46.2	2.7
In the Punjab	11.4	37.00	47.0	13.6

Source: Table VII: Age, Sex and Civil Condition, *Census of Punjab* 1931, Pt. II.

27. Ibid.
28. Janaki Nair, *Women and Law in Colonial India: A Social History*, New Delhi: Kali for Women, 1996, pp. 62–3.
29. James M. Douie, *Punjab Settlement Manual*, 4th edn., Lahore, 1930, p. 266, para 560.
30. Ibid., pp. 266–7, paras 561–2.

31. Ibid., pp. 146–7, para 295.
32. Ibid., p. 134, para 271. This omission was among 'the principal errors' noticed in the early records of rights by Edward Prinsep, the Settlement Commissioner.
33. See, for example, *Customary Law of the Attock District* (compl. A.J.W. Kitchin), rev. edn., Lahore, 1911, p. 46.
34. For the process of revision of custom over time see, for example, *Abstract of Customary Law in the Amritsar District* (compl. A. Macfarquhar), Lahore, 1947, pp. 1–6; *Code of Tribal Custom in the Delhi District*, pp. 1–2; The other Reports on the Customary Law used in the present discussion are as follows: *Customary Law of the Ambala District*, Lahore, 1921; *Customary Laws in Gujranwala District*, Lahore, 1914; *Rivaj-i-am of the Jhang District*, Lahore, 1929; *General Code of Tribal Customs in the Jhelum District*, Lahore, 1901; *Customary Law of the Jullunder District*, Lahore, 1917; *Rivaj-i-am of Tahsil Kaithal of Pargana Indri in the Karnal District*, Lahore, 1892; *Customary Law of the Main Tribes in the Gurdaspur District*, Lahore, 1893; *Customary Law of the Gurdaspur District*, Lahore, 1913; *Customary Law of the Ludhiana District*, Lahore, 1911; *Customary Law of the Tahsils of Moga, Zira and Ferozepur*, Lahore, 1890; *Customary Law of the Pakpattan and Dipalpur Tahsils*, Lahore, 1925; *Customary Law of the Rohtak District*, Lahore, 1911. Henceforth, references to the Customary Law have been shortened and prefixed with *CL*.
35. For illustration, see *CL Moga, Zira and Ferozepur*, p. 12; *CL Ludhiana*, p. 49; *CL Amritsar*, p. 21; *Code Delhi*, p. 5; *CL Rohtak*, p. 21.
36. *Code Delhi*, p. 27.
37. *Rivaj-i-am Kaithal*, p. 8; *CL Gurdaspur*, 1893, p. 11; *CL Ambala*, p. 15; *CL Jullundur*, p. 27.
38. *CL Moga, Zira and Ferozepur*, p. 11; *CL Jhelum*, p. 31.
39. As mentioned, for instance, in *Code Delhi*, p. 40; *CL Gurdaspur*, 1913, p. 38; *CL Amritsar*, p. 58.
40. For example, *CL Jullundur*, p. 38.
41. *CL Moga, Zira and Ferozepur*, p. 13; *Rivaj-i-am Kaithal*, p. 11; *Code Delhi*, p. 7; *CL Ludhiana*, pp. 50–4; *CL Gujranwala*, pp. 18–19.
42. *CL Gurdaspur*, 1913, p. 15.
43. *CL Ambala*, p. 18.
44. *CL Gurdaspur*, 1893, p. 29; *Code Delhi*, p. 33; *CL Gujranwala*, p. 29.
45. *Code Delhi*, p. 30; *CL Gurdaspur*, 1913, p. 26; *CL Attock*, pp. 23–5.
46. *CL Ludhiana*, p. 70.
47. *CL Attock*, p. 56; *CL Gurdaspur*, 1913, p. 61; *CL Gujranwala*, p. 81.
48. *CL Jullundur*, p. 37.
49. *Rivaj-i-am Kaithal*, p. 10; *Code Delhi*, p. 8.

50. As in the case of both Hindu and Muslim Jats, Rajputs, Gujars and Arains in Amritsar district: *CL Amritsar*, p. 46.
51. *CL Jhelum*, p. 42; *CL Pakpattan and Dipalpur*, p. 25.
52. *CL Ambala*, p. 38.
53. *Rivaj-i-am Kaithal*, p. 10; *CL Ludhiana*, pp. 74–5; *CL Gurdaspur*, 1913, pp. 28–9; *CL Ambala*, p. 19; *CL Amritsar*, p. 46.
54. *CL Gujranwala*, pp. 25, 26–8.
55. Ibid., p. 25; *CL Gurdaspur*, 1893, p. 17; *CL Gurdaspur*, 1913, p. 29; *CL Jhelum*, p. 44.
56. *Rivaj-i-am Kaithal*, p. 10; *Code Delhi*, p. 8; *CL Jhelum*, p. 44; *CL Ambala*, p. 19; *CL Amritsar*, p. 46.
57. *CL Ambala*, p. 19.
58. *Code Delhi*, p. 46.
59. *CL Gurdaspur*, 1913, p. 46; *CL Jullundur*, p. 60.
60. *CL Gurdaspur*, 1893, p. 27. See also, *Code Delhi*, p. 46; *CL Rohtak*, p. 44.
61. *CL Jhelum*, p. 55; *CL Jhang*, p. 53; *CL Pakpattan and Dipalpur*, p. 41. Cf. *CL Attock*, pp. 29–30, 46.
62. For example, *CL Tahsils Moga, Zira and Ferozepur*, p. 16; *CL Gurdaspur*, 1893, p. 18; *Code Delhi*, p. 33; *CL Ludhiana*, p. 76; *CL Ambala*, p. 20.
63. *CL Gurdaspur*, 1893, p. 18. The Settlement Officer, Louis W. Dane, goes on to add that, in the absence of any concrete examples cited in support of forfeiture on unchastity, the tribes have generally stated 'what ought to be rather than what is the custom'.
64. *Code Delhi*, p. 33; *CL Ludhiana*, p. 64.
65. *CL Gurdaspur*, 1893, p. 18.
66. *CL Amritsar*, p. 46.
67. Denzil Ibbetson, *Panjab Castes*, 1st pub. 1883, rpt., Patiala: Languages Department Punjab, 1970, p. 35.
68. *CL Ludhiana*, p. 35.
69. *CL Gurdaspur*, 1893, p. 9; *CL Ludhiana*, pp. 39–40.
70. *Code Delhi*, p. 24; *CL Jullundur*, p. 22–3.
71. James M. Douie, *The Punjab Law Administration Manual*, 2nd edn. of 1908, rpt., Chandigarh: Government of Punjab, 1971, pp. 270–1.
72. See, for example, *CL Jhelum*, p. 43; *CL Rohtak*, p. 30; *CL Ludhiana*, p. 76; *CL Gurdaspur*, 1913, pp. 30, 31; *CL Gujranwala*, p. 25; *CL Pakpattan and Dipalpur*, p. 24.
73. Prem Chowdhry, *The Veiled Women: Shifting Gender Equations in Haryana*, rpt. with new Preface; New Delhi: Oxford India Paperbacks, 2004, pp. 74–5.
74. For example, *Rivaj-i-am Kaithal*, p. 18; *CL Gurdaspur*, 1893, p. 9; *Code Delhi*, p. 7.
75. *CL Ludhiana*, p. 41; *CL Gurdaspur*, 1913, p. 15; *CL Gujranwala*,

p. 11. This was not accepted in Delhi: *Code Delhi*, 1910, p. 24. Nor was it acceptable among Muslims who insisted on the *nikah* ceremony.

76. *Rivaj-i-am Kaithal*, p. 6; *Code Delhi*, pp. 7, 24; *CL Rohtak*, p. 17.
77. *CL Ludhiana*, p. 35; *CL Gurdaspur*, 1913, p. 15; *CL Jullundur*, p. 22; *CL Ambala*, p. 12; *CL Jhelum,* p. 27; *CL Pakpattan* and *Dipalpur,* p. 14.
78. *CL Ludhiana*, p. 40; *CL Rohtak*, p. 17; *CL Jullundur*, p. 22.
79. *CL Ludhiana*, p. 39; *CL Jullundur*, pp. 23, 24; *CL Gujranwala*, pp. 11–12; *CL Amritsar*, pp. 30, 32.
80. *CL Gurdaspur*, 1913, p. 15.
81. *CL Ludhiana*, p. 41; *CL Gujranwala*, p. 12.
82. *CL Ludhiana*, p. 27.
83. Chowdhry, *The Veiled Women*, p. 111.
84. Ibid., pp. 100–2.
85. Ibid., pp. 93-100 and passim.
86. Giridhar Sharma Chaturvedi, *Vidhvadharma* (Hindi), Moradabad: Sanatan Dharm Press, 1915, pp. 25–6. In this booklet published at the behest of the Secretary, Rishikul, Hardwar, Chaturvedi outrightly rejects the reformers' arguments for widow remarriage, and attributes the misery of lakhs of widows to their misdeeds in their previous lives, which could be helped only by *dharma shiksha*. Ibid., pp. 3–4. I am thankful to my colleague, Dr Sheena Pall, for lending the Sanatanist texts used in this essay.
87. 'Dharm Samvad' (Hindi), in *Shraddha Ram Phillauri Granthavali*, (ed. Harmahendra Singh Bedi), Delhi: Nirmal Publications, 1997, vol. II, pp. 97–9.
88. Reeta Grewal, *Colonialism and Urbanization*, pp. 50, 52, 164–5. See also, J.S. Grewal, 'Christian Presence and Cultural Reorientation: The Case of the Colonial Punjab', *Proceedings Indian History Congress*, Calcutta, 1990, pp. 535–42.
89. Malhotra, *Gender, Caste and Religious Identities*, p. 86.
90. John C.B. Webster, *The Christian Community and Change in Nineteenth Century North India*, New Delhi: Macmillian, 1976, pp. 142, 144.
91. Malhotra, *Gender, Caste and Religious Identities*, pp. 86–97.
92. Kenneth W. Jones, *Arya Dharm: Hindu Consciousness in 19th Century Punjab*, rpt., New Delhi: Manohar, 1989, pp. 218–19.
93. B.S. Saini, *The Social & Economic History of the Punjab 1901–1939*, Delhi: ESS ESS Publications, 1975, p. 69.
94. Malhotra, *Gender, Caste and Religious Identities*, p. 105.
95. Ibid., p. 106.
96. Ibid., pp. 107–9, 115.
97. Sheena Pall, 'The Sanatan Dharm Movement in the Colonial Punjab:

Religious, Social and Political Dimensions', Ph.D. thesis, Panjab University, Chandigarh, 2008, pp. 203–9.

98. Ibid., p. 151.
99. Pandit Bhanu Datt Pushkaran, *Hindu-Dharm-Marm* (Hindi), Lahore: Punjab Economical Yantralaya, 1911, pp. 129–31.
100. Pandit Mul Raj Sharma Nagar (of Sialkot), *Hindu Dharma Darpanam* (Hindi), Lahore: Vidya Prakash Press, 1979 Bikrami [1922], vol. II, pp. 212–14.

CHAPTER 13

Socio-Economic Transformation of the Scheduled Castes in North-Western India

A Study of Inter- and Intra-Regional Differentials

SURYA KANT

INTRODUCTION

The State in independent India took various constitutional and administrative measures to safeguard the interests of the former oppressed groups of Indian society, who are presently 'officially' termed as 'Scheduled' Castes and Tribes. The abolition of untouchability and the reservation of seats in educational institutions and public sector enterprises have contributed substantially to their upward socio-economic mobility. This has resulted in higher educational attainments, occupational diversification, and rural-urban migration amongst them. Upper-caste dominance has also become weaker.

Nevertheless, this has also exposed the internal differentials emanating from caste, sub-caste, clan and class identities. For example, the relatively well-off and politically articulate ones among the Scheduled Castes (SC) have cornered the major share of government largesse. This has eventually consolidated the position of the elite groups or individuals within the Dalits. Moreover, rivalries among the lower castes such as the Mahars and Mangs in Maharashtra, the Malas and Madigas in Andhra Pradesh, the Chamars and Chuhras in the north Indian states have emerged as an impediment to political mobilization, further reinforcing cleavages.

In fact, these castes and tribes have never been a homogeneous group. Given the wide differences in the historical backgrounds across regions and subregions in the country, some states have done better than others. It is generally stated that not only has a creamy layer emerged within the 'scheduled' population, but inter-regional and subregional differentials in their socio-economic development have also widened further.

This chapter attempts to study regional and subregional differentials in the socio-economic development of the SC population in the context of the north-western region comprising Punjab, Haryana, Himachal Pradesh, Jammu & Kashmir and the union territory of Chandigarh. The region contains 8 per cent of the total SC population against its share of 6 per cent in the total population of India. Further, 22 per cent of the total population of north-western India, as a region, is comprised of SC against the national average of 16.3 per cent. Obviously there is a higher concentration of SCs in this region.

It is hoped that an understanding of the regional pattern of the socio-economic transformation of the SCs will help state governments to evolve programmes and strategies for the socio-economic uplift of this segment of the Indian population, which historically has remained deprived of its rights.

For measuring the socio-economic transformation of the SCs three broad indicators of literacy, urbanization and occupational diversification have been taken up. Increased literacy among such castes has not only created greater awareness, but also opened up new avenues of employment, especially in public sector jobs, concentrated mainly in urban areas. All the indicators are inextricably intertwined.

Data on these indicators have been collected from the *Census of India*, published by the Registrar General and Census Commissioner of India, New Delhi. According to the 2001 census data, twenty-one states and three union territories, taken together, have 99.9 per cent of the total SC population in the country. To study changes in the socio-economic conditions of SCs, a period spanning over four decades, from 1961 to 2001, has been selected. This has been done for two reasons. Firstly, a period of four decades is long enough to assess the impact of change in the socio-economic conditions of the SCs. Secondly, it was during the 1961 census that, for the first time, detailed information about this segment of the population was collected. The 2001 census is the latest in the series. For a composite index of socio-economic transformation, the methodology evolved by the United Nations Development Programme for the construction of the human development index has been pressed into service.[1] Minimum and maximum limits for each indicator are 0 and 100, respectively.

The chapter is divided into two sections. In the first section, the demography of the SCs population in north-western India has been examined within the broad frame of the country as a whole, followed by inter- and intra-state comparison in the region under study. The second section examines inter- and intra-regional disparities in the socio-economic development of SCs and changes therein in north-western India.

SCHEDULED CASTES: A DEMOGRAPHIC PROFILE

The term 'Dalit', which stands literally for the oppressed, came into wider currency in the later part of nineteenth century through the writings and speeches of Jyotiba Phule. He was the first reformer of the modern period to take up the cause of the untouchables in Maharashtra state.[2] Castes which have neither power nor privileges are equated with Dalits. Both 'touchable' and 'untouchable' castes are included in this group. Such castes are officially termed as 'Scheduled Castes' in modern India.[3]

According to the 2001 census, 251 million, or more than 24 per cent of the total population of India, belong to the scheduled (castes and tribes) population. In other words, almost every fourth person in Indian society belongs either to a SC or to a Scheduled Tribe (ST). Separately, two-thirds or 166.6 million are SCs and the remaining one-third or 84.3 million are ST. In a way, every sixth person in India is a SC. With the exception of Nagaland and the union territories of Andaman & Nicobar Islands and Lakshadweep, SCs are notified in all the states and Union territories of India. However, they have a highly uneven zonal and inter-state distribution.

They are highly concentrated in some states, whereas in others they make up only a small fraction of the total population. In Uttar Pradesh alone, there are 35 million or more than one-fifth (21.1 per cent) of the total SCs in the country. West Bengal follows, accounting for another 18.4 million or 11 per cent of the total SC population in India. These two states together share about one-third of India's SC population. More strikingly, five states, namely, Uttar Pradesh, West Bengal, Bihar, Tamil Nadu and Andhra Pradesh, each with a population of more than 10 million SCs, account for more than half (54.5 per cent) the SCs population of the country. In fact, 85 per cent of the total SCs population resides in only eleven states, namely, Uttar Pradesh, West Bengal, Bihar, Tamil Nadu, Andhra Pradesh, Maharashtra, Rajasthan, Madhya Pradesh, Karnataka, Punjab and Orissa. A majority of these states fall in north India. In comparative terms, four southern states (i.e. Andhra Pradesh, Tamil Nadu, Karnataka and Kerala) together have only about 22 per cent of the total SC population of India, whereas the share of the four northern states (Uttar Pradesh, West Bengal, Bihar and Rajasthan) tends to be as high as about 46 per cent. Evidently the inter-state distribution of the SC population in India is highly uneven, as there is a greater concentration of these castes in the north Indian states.

In north-western India, Jammu & Kashmir, Punjab, Haryana, and Himachal Pradesh and Chandigarh (UT), taken together, had a population of 14.9 million SC making about 6 per cent of the total scheduled (caste and tribe) population in the country in 2001. The proportional shares of the north-western region in the scheduled and non-scheduled population of the country were almost the same. However, matters were quite different in the case of the SC population. The north-western region shared 13.5 million or 8 per cent of the total SC population of the country against only a 6 per cent share in the total population of the country. Obviously SCs are concentrated more in the north-western region in comparison to other regions of the country. For example, according to the 2001 census figures, SCs made up about 22 per cent of the total population of the north-western region against only 6.42 per cent in north-eastern India, 11 per cent in western India, 16 per cent of southern

India, 18 per cent in eastern India and 19 per cent in central India, the national average being 16.2 per cent.

There are, however, wide inter-state and inter-district variations in the distributional pattern of the SCs population in the country. It varies from a high of 29 per cent in Punjab, in north-western India, to a low of 0.03 per cent in Mizoram in north-eastern India. In each of the four states of Punjab, Himachal Pradesh, West Bengal and Uttar Pradesh, SCs constitute more than 20 per cent of the total population of the respective states. In comparison, SCs make up only about 1 per cent or less of the total population of the tribal population dominated states of Meghalaya, Sikkim and Mizoram. In fact, in areas dominated by the Christian, the Buddhist and the Muslim population, the SC population is conspicuously low. The conversion of the low-caste Hindus to Christianity, Buddhism and Islam in such areas in the past is mainly responsible for the marginal distribution of SCs in these states.

Uttar Pradesh, West Bengal, Tamil Nadu, and Himachal Pradesh have a higher share of the total SC population in comparison to their share in the total population of the country. For example, Uttar Pradesh accounted for only 16.1 per cent of India's total population against 21.2 per cent of the total SC population. Similarly, the respective shares of West Bengal are 7.8 per cent and 11 per cent. Such inter-state variations in the distribution of SC are full of implications in the context of political mobilization in a democratic set-up based on adult franchise.

Within north-western India, in 2001, more than a half (52 per cent) or 7 million of the total 13.6 million SC population in the region was in Punjab (Table 13.1). Another 30 per cent resided in Haryana. Both states together had 82 per cent of the total SC population against their share of 72 per cent of the total regional population. Earlier, in 1961, the share of Punjab in the total SC population in the region was as high as 55 per cent, but Haryana shared only about 26 per cent. Hence, their combined share in 1961 was about 81 per cent against 82 per cent in 2001. This indicates a faster growth of the SC population in Haryana as compared to Punjab during 1961–2001. Interestingly, unlike Haryana, the share of Himachal Pradesh in the regional total of the SC population declined during the same period, from 12.7 per cent in 1961 to 11 per cent in 2001.

However, the remarkable increase in the proportional share of Chandigarh (UT) is to be noted. Its share of 0.3 per cent in 1961 rose to 1.3 per cent in 2001. The same is very well reflected in the phenomenal growth of the SC population in Chandigarh (UT) during 1961–2001: 6.44 per cent against the average annual growth rate of 2.63 per cent for the region. The share of Jammu & Kashmir in the regional total of SC population remained almost the same in both 1961 and 2001. Nevertheless, the annual growth rate of the SC population in Jammu & Kashmir (2.66 per cent) was higher than the regional average (2.63 per cent). In comparative terms, the growth rate of SC population had been the slowest in Himachal Pradesh and the fastest in Chandigarh (UT) in the whole region during 1961–2001 (Table 13.1). Chandigarh (UT) attracts SCs in the lower categories of jobs pertaining to sanitation, garbage disposal and other menial activities. However, there is no evidence of heavy out-migration of SCs from Himachal Pradesh to explain the slow growth of the SC population in the state. It is because of the fact that the STs in Kinnaur and Lahul & Spiti districts of Himachal Pradesh reported themselves in substantial number as SCs before the census enumerators in 2001 instead of STs as at the time of the 1991 census enumeration. Notably, the SC population in the north-western region grew at a faster rate than the national average during 1961–2001. The annual compound growth rate of the SC population in the north-west was 2.63 per cent in comparison to 2.40 per cent at the national level. Secondly, the SC population in the north-western region grew at a much higher rate (2.63 per cent) than the non-SC population (1.68 per cent) in the region.

All the sixty-three districts in north-western India recorded SC population in the 2001 census. There were, however, wide variations in the distribution of the SC population at the district level, from a high of 8.91 lakh in Amritsar district (Punjab) to a low of only 75 persons in Kupwara district (Jammu & Kashmir). In all, there were twelve districts, making up only about one-fifth (19 per cent) of the total districts in north-western India, and when taken together, more than two-fifths

TABLE 13.1: NW INDIA: SOME DEMOGRAPHIC CHARACTERISTICS OF SCHEDULED CASTES POPULATION

States / U.T.	SC population (000 person)		% in total population	% share in all India	Annual growth rate	Urban population in (000 persons)		Annual urban growth rate (%)
	2001	1961	2001	2001	1961–2001	2001	1961	1961–2001
Punjab	7,029 (52)	2,632 (55)	28.9	4.2	2.49	1710	341	4.11
Haryana	4,091 (30)	1,268 (26.4)	19.4	2.5	2.97	880	350	2.33
Himachal Pradesh	1,502 (11)	610 (12.7)	24.7	0.9	2.28	99	9.5	6.03
Jammu & Kashmir	770 (5.7)	269 (5.6)	7.7	0.5	2.66	134	21	4.74
Chandigarh	158 (1.3)	13 (0.3)	17.5	0.1	6.44	143	3.7	9.57
Regional Total	13,550 (100)	4,792 (100)	21.6	8.2	2.63	2966	725.2	3.58
All India	1,66,636	64,511	16.2	100.0	2.40	33,625	6,899	4.06

Source: (1) *Census of India* (1961), *Special Tables on Scheduled Castes*, Part V, Registrar General and Census Commissioners of India, New Delhi; (2) *Census of India* (2001), *Special Table on Scheduled Castes and Scheduled Tribes*, on CD, Registrar General and Census Commissioner of India, New Delhi.

Note: Figures in parentheses indicate the percentage share of individual States/UTs in the total SC population in the north-western region.

(46 per cent) of the total SC population in the region. Each of these districts had a population of more than three lakh SCs in 2001. Among these districts, the dominant majority was from Punjab, where nine of the twelve districts fell in this category – the state of Punjab itself having a total of seventeen districts. Of the remaining three districts, two were from Haryana and one from Jammu & Kashmir. Another seventeen districts, each with a population of more than two lakh SCs had another one-third of the total SC population in the region. These districts were mainly from Haryana and Punjab. In this way, less than a half or 46 per cent of the total districts in the north-western region had more than three-fourths (78 per cent) of the total population. On the other side of the scale, seventeen districts, making up about 27 per cent of the total districts in the region, had only about one-fifth or the remaining 22 per cent of the total SC population of the region. Except for one district (Panchkula in Haryana), all were either in Himachal Pradesh or in Jammu & Kashmir.

In proportional terms, Nawanshahr district (Punjab) recorded as high as a 40.5 per cent share of the SC population in its total population, against the regional average of about 22 per cent. This was the highest share among all the districts in the north-western region and the third highest, after Kooch Bihar (50.1 per cent) in West Bengal and Sonabhadra (41.9 per cent) in Uttar Pradesh, in the whole country. At least five districts in the region had more than a one-third share of the SC population in their total population. All of them belonged to Punjab. In the country as a whole, there are 149 districts where the SC population made up one-fifth or more of the total population at the 2001 census. Thirty-five of their districts are distributed in the following manner: all the 17 districts in Punjab, 10 of 12 in Himachal Pradesh, and 8 of 19 in Haryana. At the level of individual states, Nawanshahr (40.5 per cent), Sirmaur (29.6 per cent), Faridabad (27.4 per cent), and Kathua (23.2 per cent) had the highest share of the SC population in Punjab, Himachal Pradesh, Haryana and Jammu & Kashmir, respectively. Chandigarh (UT) had a 17.5 per cent share of the SC population. On the opposite side of the scale, Kupwara (0.01 per cent) in Jammu & Kashmir, Lahul & Spiti (0.7 per cent) in Himachal

Pradesh, Gurgaon (11.3 per cent) in Haryana, and Firozepur (22.8 per cent) in Punjab recorded the lowest shares of SC population in the region. It has been observed at the national level, that the SC population is highly concentrated in a few districts of the north Indian plains and coastal Tamil Nadu. Out of the twenty districts with the highest SC population, seven districts are in Punjab, five in Uttar Pradesh, four in West Bengal, two in Tamil Nadu and one each in Rajasthan and Jharkhand.[4]

Another peculiarity of the SC population distribution is the high degree of heterogeneity in terms of castes and sub-castes. In 2001, there were as many as 1221 sub-castes of SCs. Earlier, in 1951, the number of sub-castes was only 779. Obviously, over the years, more castes have been added to the SC list, mainly due to populist considerations, influenced by the attractive benefits, including reservation in legislative bodies, government jobs and educational institutions. The number of castes varies from a minimum of 4 in Sikkim to a maximum of 101 in Karnataka. In other words, the SC population is most homogeneous in Sikkim and the least in Karnataka.

However, in 1971 the 10 largest sub-castes of the SCs constituted more than 50 per cent of the total SC population in India. Specifically, Chamars make up more than half of this 50 per cent. In other words, Chamars constitute one-fourth of the total SC population in the country. In their spatial distribution, Chamars are highly concentrated in a few north Indian states. Notably, according to the 1931 census, which last collected detailed information on castes, 6.3 million or 24.4 per cent of the total 25.8 million Chamars in India were in Uttar Pradesh (then known as United Provinces of Agra and Oudh). Adi Dravida, Pasi, Madiga, Dusadh, Mala, Dhobi, Paraiya, Mahar, and Adi Karnataka made up the remaining half. Chamars dominated particularly in Punjab, Haryana, Uttar Pradesh, Rajasthan, Madhya Pradesh and Bihar; Adi Dravida and Paraiyan in Tamil Nadu; Madigas and Malas in Andhra Pradesh; Dusadhs in north Bihar; Dhobis in parts of Uttar Pradesh and Orissa; Mahars in Maharashtra; and Adi Karnataka in southern Karnataka.

Within north-western India, the number of SC sub-castes varied from a high of 56 in Himachal Pradesh to a low of 13 in Jammu

& Kashmir in 2001. The number of sub-castes was 37 each in Haryana and Punjab and 36 in the union territory of Chandigarh (Table 13.2). However, there are several sub-castes that are common to all the states in north-western India. For example, Batwal, Chamar/Ramdasi/Ravidasi, Doom, Megh/Julaha/Kabir-panthi, and Chuhra/Bhangi are common to all the 4 states and the union territory of Chandigarh in the region. Further, as many as 30 sub-castes are common in Haryana, Punjab, Himachal Pradesh and Chandigarh (UT). Against this, there are as many as 19 sub-castes which are found exclusively in Himachal Pradesh. Another, 8 sub-castes are found exclusively in Jammu & Kashmir (see Appendix 1). Overall, despite a high homogeneity of SC sub-castes in north-western India, and that too for historical reasons, there are well-marked inter-state differentials. In fact, even inclusion or exclusion of different castes in the 'scheduled' category of castes makes an interesting story. As an illustration, castes, namely, Jogi, Lohar and Teli, are generally categorized as 'Other Backward Castes' (OBC) in the majority of north Indian states, but these castes find a place in the category of 'Scheduled Castes' in Himachal Pradesh.

It is to be noted here that, other than demographic implications, the concentration of a particular caste in a state, or part of it, carries significance for political mobilization and climbing the ladder of political power. For example, in 1971 the Chamars

TABLE 13.2 NORTH-WESTERN REGION: DISTRIBUTION OF SC SUB-CASTES BY STATE/UT, 2001

Name of State/UT	No. of SC Sub-Castes
1 Jammu & Kashmir	13
2. Punjab	37
3. Haryana	37
4. Himachal Pradesh	56
5. Chandigarh (UT)	36
NW Region	169 (63 excluding common sub-castes – see Appendix 1)
All-India	1,226

Source: *Census of India* (2001), *Special Tables on Scheduled Castes and Scheduled Tribes*, on CD, Registrar General and Census Commissioner of India, New Delhi.

constituted between 40 and 90 per cent of all the SCs in areas of their concentrations. Numerically, they dominate in the whole of Haryana and north-eastern Punjab in the districts of Gurdaspur, Nawanshahr, Kapurthala, Jalandhar, and Hoshiarpur districts of Punjab. Such a geographical distribution of castes carries great significance in political mobility and gaining power. Nevertheless, relations among the different sub-castes also plays an important role.

The SC population is predominantly rural. In 2001, 80 per cent or four-fifths were living in rural areas. This proportion was 72 per cent for the country as a whole and only 69 per cent for the non-SC population. In 1961, about nine out of ten SCs (or 89.3 per cent) were rural by residence. This ratio was two out of ten for the non-SC population. There have been wide inter-state variations in the urban-rural distribution of SCs. In general, states and union territories that have a high degree of urban-industrialization have a higher proportion of SCs in urban areas.

In north-western India, 22 per cent, or more than one-fifths of the SC population resides in urban areas. Although this proportion is higher than the national average (20 per cent), it is lower than the share of the non-SC population (31.2 per cent) living in urban areas of the region. There are wide inter- and intra-state variations within the region. It varies from a high of 24 per cent in Punjab to a low of about 7 per cent in Himachal Pradesh. In Jammu & Kashmir also the share of urban SC is quite low (17. 4 per cent). However, in Chandigarh (UT) more than nine-tenths (90.5 per cent) of the SC population lives in urban areas.

In 1961, in north-western India only about 16 per cent of the SC population was urban by residence. This share was only about 11 per cent for the country as a whole. Within the region, the share of urban SCs in Himachal Pradesh was only about 4 per cent. This share was 8 per cent in Jammu & Kashmir and 9 per cent in Haryana. Of the four states in the region, it was only Punjab where the share of urban SC population was higher (13 per cent) than the national average. Notwithstanding the low proportion of the SC population in urban centres in Himachal Pradesh, the urban SC population in the state grew at an annual compound rate of 6 per cent during 1961–2001. Against this, the annual growth rate of the urban SC population was only 2.3 per cent in Haryana, 4 per cent the Punjab and about 5 per cent in Jammu & Kashmir. In the case of Chandigarh (UT), it was as high as about 10 per cent.

At the district level, among the sixty-three districts in north-western India, the share of the urban SC population in 2001 varied from a high of 98 per cent in Srinagar district to only about 2 per cent in Doda district, both in Jammu & Kashmir. Within Punjab, Jalandhar district recorded the highest percentage (36 per cent) of SC population in urban areas, against the lowest (11 per cent) share in Nawanshahr district. The more urbanized and industrialized districts of Ludhiana, Jalandhar and Amritsar recorded a higher share of SC population in urban areas, against the economically backward and low-urbanized districts of Mansa, Moga, Muktsar, Nawanshahr and Hoshiarpur which recorded a low proportion of SC population in urban areas. Nine of the seventeen districts in the state had a proportion lower than the regional average. In Himachal Pradesh, it was only in one district – Shimla – that the share of the urban SC population was in double digits (14 per cent). All others recorded an urban SC population which was less than the regional average. In Jammu & Kashmir, there were the sharpest inter-district variations in the share of the urban SC population in the region. The share ranged from a high of 98 per cent in Srinagar district to only 2 per cent in Doda district. Here, 8 of total 14 districts in the state had a share of urban SC population which was higher than the regional average. In contrast, three districts of Doda (2.1 per cent), Udhampur (10.4 per cent) and Rajauri (4.7 per cent) had a proportion which was less than half of the regional average. In Haryana, Faridabad district was at the top with 41.4 per cent and Mahendragarh at the bottom with only 11.5 per cent share; 13 of the total 19 districts in the state had shares of urban SC population lower than the region average.

Evidently the SC population is still predominantly rural by residence. Some sub-castes are, however, highly urbanized. Nearly a half of the urban SCs come from the Chamar, Chuhra, Adi Dravida and Bauri communities. Urban living and employment in the tertiary sector have made them aware of their rights and induced an awareness to fight against injustice. Being literate, they are easy to organize politically. Hence, numerically large and urbanized sub-castes enjoy an advantage over the others in the context of political mobilization. Chamars, who are relatively more urbanized and numerically larger in the north Indian states including Punjab and Haryana, are also placed in an advantageous position in comparison to the other SC sub-castes in the region. Other such states in north India include Uttar Pradesh, Rajasthan, Bihar and Madhya Pradesh. The same applies to the Adi Dravida in Tamil Nadu and Bauris in parts of Orissa, Bihar and West Bengal.

Briefly, the SC population has, numerically as well as proportionally, a relatively higher concentration in the states of north-western India. In 2001, the north-western region had 13.5 million or 8 per cent of the total SC population of the country against only a 6 per cent share of the total population of the country. SCs made up about 22 per cent of the total population of north-western India, which was not only the highest share among all the regions in the country but also much higher than the national average of 16.2 per cent. Within north-western India, Punjab and Haryana taken together shared 82 per cent of the total SC population, against their share of 72 per cent of the total regional population in 2001. At the district level, Nawanshahr district (Punjab) recorded a 40.5 per cent share of the SC population in its total population, which was the third highest share in the country as a whole. Twelve districts with the highest SC population, making up only about one-fifth of the total districts in north-western India, had, collectively, more than two-fifths of the total SC population in the region.

SOCIO-ECONOMIC TRANSFORMATION OF SCs

In this section an attempt has been made to analyse inter- and intra-state variations in the level of the socio-economic development of the SC population and the change therein. To measure the level of socio-economic development an index of development based on the concept of the human development index has been evolved. The index value varies from 0 to 1, in which 0 stands for no development and 1 stands for the maximum of the range. A period of forty years – 1961 to 2001 – has been taken to examine the changes in socio-economic conditions.

Literacy and education play a pivotal role in awakening an individual against socio-economic and political prejudices. Not only is the literacy level of the SC population much lower than that of the non-SC population, it also varies widely from state to state. In 2001, the SCs' literacy rate was only about two-thirds that of the non-SCs. In 1961 it was only about one-third of the non-SCs' literacy rate. Evidently the literacy rate of SCs has been growing fast in the post-Independence period. But it was still low in comparison to the non-SCs. Further, the national average being 55 per cent, it varied from a high of 73 per cent in Kerala to a low of 22 per cent in Bihar in 2001.

Fortunately, all the states in north-western India had a higher rate than the national average. Within the region, Himachal Pradesh was at the top with the SC literacy rate of more than 70 per cent in 2001. Against this, Haryana was at the bottom with a 55 per cent literacy rate of the SC population. Accordingly, the literacy index varied from a high of 0.703 (Himachal Pradesh) to a low of 0.554 (Haryana). While none of the states had an index value lower than the national average (0.547), Punjab and Haryana had a lower than the regional average of 0.575. Earlier, in 1961, except for Haryana all the other states in north-western India had literacy rates lower than the national average of 10.3 per cent (Table 13.3).

At the district level, variations in SC literacy rates were quite sharp. They varied from a high of 99.4 per cent in Badgam district (Jammu & Kashmir) to a low of about 35 per cent in Mansa district (Punjab). Most of the districts (eight out of fourteen) in Jammu & Kashmir recorded, a literacy rate of 90 per cent or higher for the SC population. However, it is to be noted here that numerically the SC population was quite low in all such districts. For example, the SC population was only 75 persons in Pulwama district, which had a SC literacy rate of 99 per cent in 2001. One of the possibilities is that all such persons were employees in paramilitary/armed forces, stationed there for security reasons. The majority of the districts in Himachal Pradesh also recorded high literacy rates for SCs. Eight of its twelve districts in 2001 had an SC literacy rate which was between 70

TABLE 13.3: NORTH-WESTERN INDIA: INDICATORS OF SOCIO-ECONOMIC TRANSFORMATION OF SCs BY STATES/UTs, 1961–2001 (*Figures in Percentage*)

State/UT	Literacy rate		Urbanization		Non-agricultural workers	
	1961	2001	1961	2001	1971	2001
Punjab	8.9	56.2	13.0	24.3	29.6	60.8
Haryana	11.0	55.4	9.0	21.5	17.7	58.8
Himachal Pradesh	9.2	70.3	3.9	6.6	13.0	38.2
Jammu & Kashmir	6.3	59.0	7.8	17.4	24.5	50.4
Chandigarh	24.4*	67.7	81.9*	90.5	93.6*	99.8
N-W India	–	57.9	–	21.9	–	57.5
All India (SC population)	10.3	54.7	10.7	20.2	17.5	38.8
All India (non-SC population)	27.8	68.8	20.6	31.6	35.3	51.4

Source: Calculated from *Census of India*, Special Tables on Scheduled Castes, Part V, Registrar General and Census Commissioner of India, New Delhi.

Notes: Census data on Industrial classification of workers for 1961 and 2001 are not comparable due to definitional change, data for the third indicator relates to 1971 and 2001. It has been done to maintain comparability. Further, literacy figures for 1961 and 2001 are not strictly comparable, due to definitional change.

* For Chandigarh (UT), figures relates to 1971 census, as figures for 1961 were not available.

and 80 per cent. On the other hand, only four districts in Punjab – Hoshiarpur, Nawanshahr, Jalandhar and Rupnagar – attained such a distinction and none from Haryana. Within Punjab, Hoshiarpur ranked first with an SC literacy rate of about 78 per cent and Mansa district was at the bottom with about 35 per cent. Within Haryana, Rewari district topped with about 69 per cent and Fatehabad district ranked lowest with 41 per cent. Quite interestingly, the three lowest-ranking districts – Firozepur, Muktsar and Mansa, each with a 40 per cent or lower SC literacy rate – belonged to Punjab, the most economically developed state in the region. Geographically speaking, most of the districts with low SC literacy rates are located in the south-western parts of Punjab and Haryana.

Urbanization varies widely among states. In 2001, the proportion of SCs in urban areas varied from a high of 24.3 per cent in Punjab to a low of 6.6 per cent in Himachal Pradesh. In the case of Chandigarh (UT), the proportional share was as high as 90.5 per cent. Accordingly, the urbanization index ranged from 0.905 in Chandigarh to only 0.066 in Himachal Pradesh. The average index value for the country as a whole was 0.202, against which Himachal Pradesh and Jammu & Kashmir faired quite badly.

Early in 1961, inter-state variations in this regard were even wider. At that time the index value varied from a high of 0.130 in Punjab to a low of 0.039 in Himachal Pradesh. Again, Chandigarh (UT) recorded a very high index value of 0.819. Punjab was the only state in the region that faired better than the national average. In terms of change in the urbanization index for the SC population, the north-western region as a whole did better than the country as a whole during 1961–2001.

Of the 63 districts in the region, Srinagar district (Jammu & Kashmir) had the highest proportion of SC population (97.6 per cent) residing in urban areas and Doda district, in the same state, had the lowest (2.1 per cent) in 2001. In the districts of Lahul & Spiti and Kinnaur in Himachal, urban centres were yet to emerge. Chandigarh had the second highest share of about 91 per cent in this context. On the whole, the majority of the districts in the region, i.e. 40, or two-thirds of the districts, had a share of the SC population in urban areas which was lower than the regional average (22 per cent). In fact, in about one-fourth of the districts this share was less than 10 per cent or less than half of the regional average. Obviously there were wide inter-district variations in this context. Among the states in the region, Jammu & Kashmir had the widest inter-district variations in terms of the share of SC population residing in urban areas, while the reverse was true of Himachal Pradesh. At the level of individual states, Srinagar (97.6 per cent) and Doda (2.1 per cent) in Jammu & Kashmir, Faridabad (41.4 per cent) and Mahendragarh (11.5 per cent) in Haryana, Jalandhar (36.2 per cent) and Nawanshahr (11.3 per cent) in Punjab and Shimla (14 per cent) and Kangra (4 per cent) in Himachal Pradesh recorded the highest and lowest shares of SC urban population, respectively.

Occupational diversification plays an important role in raising the income level and social status of those working in non-farm occupations. In this context, SCs are lagging far behind the non-SCs. In 2001, only about 39 per cent of the total SC workers in the country were engaged in non-farm occupations, against more than 51 per cent of non-SC workers. However, the situation in the north-western region was much better, as about 58 per cent of total SC workers in the region as a whole were engaged in non-farm occupations. Nevertheless, this share was much lower than the share of non-scheduled workers in the region engaged in non-farm activities. Evidently, the SC population was still predominantly agricultural, working mainly as agricultural labourers and casual workers. In 2001, the occupational diversification index varied from a high of 0.608 in Punjab to a low of 0.382 in Himachal Pradesh, with the average value being 0.575. In Chandigarh (UT), the index value was as high as 0.998.

At the district level, the share of SC workers engaged in non-farm activities varied from a high of 100 per cent in Kupwara district (Jammu & Kashmir) to a low of 16 per cent in Kullu district (Himachal Pradesh). Of the top ten districts, each having more than 75 per cent of SC workers in non-farm occupations, eight were from Jammu & Kashmir. Of the remaining two, one each was from Haryana and Chandigarh (UT). On the whole, in about half, or 31, of the 63 districts in north-western India, 50 per cent or more of SC workers were engaged in non-farm activities. At the other end of the scale, there were 6 districts, all from Himachal Pradesh, where less than 30 per cent of SC workers were engaged in non-farm activities. Districts with a higher proportional share of SC workers in non-farm activities were either urban-industrialized or had border location, especially in Jammu & Kashmir. In the districts of Jammu & Kashmir, where a high proportion of SC workers was engaged in non-farm activities, the SC population was small. Secondly, almost all the workers from the SC population in such districts were engaged in the category of 'other services' as per the census method of classifying workers into industrial categories. This means that most of the SC workers in such districts of Jammu & Kashmir were engaged in government services – either stationed as paramilitary/armed forces personnel to guard the international border with Pakistan or working in administrative services provided by the state/union government.

A composite index of the socio-economic development of SC population, evolved by averaging indices of literacy, urbanization and occupational diversification, both for 1961 and 2001, is highly revealing. The level of socio-economic development of the SC population is quite low in comparison to the non-SC population. In 2001, the index of socio-economic development for the SC population was less than two-thirds of the non-SC population. Earlier in 1961, it was only about half of the index for non-SC population (Table 13.4). Evidently, even though the

TABLE 13.4: NORTH-WESTERN INDIA: INDICES OF DIFFERENT INDICATORS OF SOCIO-ECONOMIC TRANSFORMATION OF SCs BY STATES/UTs, 1961 AND 2001

State/UT	Literacy rate		Urbanization		Non-agricultural workers	
	1961	2001	1961	2001	1961	2001
Punjab	0.089	0.562	0.130	0.243	0.296	0.608
Haryana	0.110	0.554	0.090	0.215	0.177	0.588
Himachal Pradesh	0.092	0.703	0.039	0.066	0.130	0.382
Jammu & Kashmir	0.063	0.590	0.078	0.174	0.245	0.504
Chandigarh	0.244	0.677	0.819	0.905	0.936	0.998
Regional Average	–	0.579	–	0.219	–	0.575
All India (SC population)	0.103	0.547	0.107	0.202	0.175	0.388
Non-SC population in Region	0.278	0.688	0.206	0.316	0.353	0.514

Source: (1) *Census of India* (1961), *Special Tables on Scheduled Castes*, Part V, Registrar General and Census Commissioner of India, New Delhi; (2) *Census of India* (2001), *Special Tables on Scheduled Castes and Scheduled Tribes*, on CD, Registrar General and Census Commissioner of India, New Delhi.

development gap between the SCs and non-SCs has remained wide, it has reduced considerably during 1961–2001.[5]

Moreover, there are inter-state variations in the socio-economic development of SCs. Within north-western India, the index value for Himachal Pradesh (0.384) was less than half or 45 per cent of Chandigarh UT (0.857) in 2001. Punjab recorded the second highest index value of 0.471 after Chandigarh (UT). The index value for Haryana was much lower than Punjab's. In other words, the SC population was much better off in Punjab than in the neighbouring state of Haryana. Nevertheless, the SC population in north-western India was enjoying a much better level of socio-economic development than the SC population in the country as a whole (Table 13.5).

For the country as a whole, the socio-economic index value rose from 0.128 in 1961 to 0.379 in 2001, suggesting a fast change in the socio-economic life of the SCs in post-independent India. During 1961–2001, the socio-economic development index value for the SC population increased by about three times. Against this, the change in the index value for the non-SC

TABLE 13.5: N-W INDIA: COMPOSITE INDEX OF SOCIO-ECONOMIC TRANSFORMATION OF SCs AND CHANGE IN INDEX DURING 1961–2001

States	1961	2001	Change, 1961–2001
Punjab	0.172(2)	0.471(2)	0.299(2)
Haryana	0.126(4)	0.452(3)	0.326(1)
Himachal Pradesh	0.087(5)	0.384(5)	0.297(3)
Jammu & Kashmir	0.137(3)	0.423(4)	0.286(4)
Chandigarh	0.666(1)	0.857(1)	0.191(5)
All-India (SC population)	0.128	0.379	0.251
All-India (non-SC population)	0.279	0.506	0.227

Sources: (1) *Census of India* (1961), *Special Tables on Scheduled Castes*, Part V, Registrar General and Census Commissioner of India, New Delhi; (2) *Census of India* (2001), *Special Tables on Scheduled Castes and Scheduled Tribes*, on CD, Registrar General and Census Commissioner of India, New Delhi.

Note: Figures in parentheses indicates rank of the State/UT in the region.

population has been only half: from 0.279 in 1961 to 0.506 in 2001. Evidently, the socio-economic transformation of the SCs has been faster than that of the non-SCs in India. This clearly indicates the success of government programmes and policies initiated for the uplift of the downtrodden sections of society in Indian. Within north-western India, Haryana was at the top with an index value of 0.326 in the socio-economic transformation of the SC population; against this Chandigarh (UT) was at the bottom with a change index value of only 0.191. With a change in index value of 0.299, Punjab was next only to Haryana. Notably, the change in index value for Himachal Pradesh, having the lowest index value for socio-economic development of the SC population in the whole region, recorded a change in index value almost similar to that of Punjab's. On the other side, Chandigarh, which had the highest index value of socio-economic development for the SC population in 1961 and 2001 both, recorded the lowest change in index value of 0.191. In other words, states where the level of socio-economic development for the SC population was high recorded a relatively low level of change during 1961–2001.

At the district level, variations in the socio-economic development level of the SC population were quite sharp. In 2001, the index value varied from a high of 0.983 for Srinagar district (Jammu & Kashmir) to a low of only 0.275 for Doda district in the same state. In other words, socio-economic conditions of SC population were nearly four times better in Srinagar district than in Doda district. Of the twenty-one districts (one-third) in north-western India, where the index value of socio-economic development was higher than 0.5, nine districts were in Jammu & Kashmir, another eight in Punjab, three in Haryana and the remaining one was in Chandigarh (UT). In their geographical distribution, most such districts are located along the Indo-Pak border in Jammu & Kashmir, in the Beas-Sutlej doab of Punjab and in the Haryana subregion of the National Capital Region, Delhi. In Punjab and Haryana, all such districts come under the category of urban-industrialized districts – where a variety of low-paid jobs in the informal sector and health and sanitation services provided by the civic bodies attract SC workers. In Jammu & Kashmir, all such districts have SC population relatively in small numbers, most of them working as employees of the state government or of the Indian armed forces to guard the international border with Pakistan.

At the other end of the scale, there are seven districts where the index of socio-economic development for the SC population was less than 0.3. These include Sirmaur (0.299), Chamba (0.294) and Kullu (0.285) districts in Himachal Pradesh; Udhampur (0.287) and Doda (0.275) districts in Jammu & Kashmir; Fatehabad (0.290) district in Haryana and Mansa (0.289) district in Punjab. In fourteen, or about one-fourth of the districts in the region, the index value of socio-economic development for the SC population ranged between 0.5 and 0.4. These were mainly located in Haryana state. They included Ambala, Rohtak, Yamunanagar, Panipat, Rewari, Jhajjar, Sonepat, Mahendragarh, Kurukshetra and Bhiwani districts in Haryana; Amritsar and Patiala districts in Punjab, Una district in Himachal Pradesh and Punch district in Jammu & Kashmir. There were twenty, or one-third of the total districts in the region, where the index of socio-economic development for the SC population was less than the national average of 0.379. Seven of twelve districts in Himachal Pradesh, five of nineteen districts in Haryana, five of seventeen districts in Punjab and three of fourteen districts in Jammu & Kashmir fall in this category. On the whole, twenty-one, or one-third, of the total districts in the region – where the index value of socio-economic development of the SC population was higher than 0.5 – are categorized as 'high'; another fourteen or more than one-fifth of the districts are categorized as 'moderate'; and the remaining twenty-eight, or more than two-fifths of the districts are in the category of 'low' in the level of socio-economic development of the SC population in 2001 (Table 13.6).

Within the states of north-western India, Srinagar district (0.983) was at the top and Doda district (0.275) at the bottom in Jammu & Kashmir state. Jalandhar (0.609) and Mansa (0.289) districts in Punjab, Ambala (0.497) and Fatehabad (0.290) districts in Haryana and Una (0.408) and Kullu (0.285) districts in Himachal Pradesh fell between. It is interesting to note that

TABLE 13.6: N-W INDIA: CLASSIFICATION OF DISTRICTS BY LEVEL OF SOCIO-ECONOMIC DEVELOPMENT OF SC POPULATION, 2001

Index Value/Level	Name of the district
More than 0.500 (High)	Srinagar, Badgam, Anantnag, Leh (Ladakh), Pulwama, Chandigarh, Baramulla, Kupwara, Kargil, Jalandhar, Ludhiana, Panchkula, Rupnagar, Faridabad, Gurgoan, Nawanshahr, Hoshiarpur, Jammu, Kapurthala, Gurdaspur, Fatehgarh Sahib (Total = 21)
0.500–0.400 (Moderate)	Ambala, Rohtak, Yamunanagar, Panipat, Rewari, Jhajjar, Sonepat, Punch, Amritsar, Mahendragarh, Patiala, Una, Kurukshetra, Bhiwani (Total = 14)
Less than 0.400 (Low)	Kangra, Hamirpur, Karnal, Sangrur, Faridkot, Lahul & Spiti, Solan, Kathua, Hisar, Shimla, Bilaspur, Rajauri, Jind, Bathinda, Firozepur, Kinnaur, Mandi, Kaithal, Sirsa, Moga, Muktsar, Sirmaur, Chamba, Fatehabad, Mansa, Udhampur, Kullu, Doda (Total = 28)

Source: (1) *Census of India* (1961), *Special Tables on Scheduled Castes*, Part V, Registrar General and Census Commissioner of India, New Delhi; (2) *Census of India* (2001), *Special Tables on Scheduled Castes and Scheduled Tribes*, on CD, Registrar General and Census Commissioner of India, New Delhi.

the index value of the top-ranking district in Himachal Pradesh was only about two-fifths of the top-ranking district in Jammu & Kashmir. At the other end of the scale, the index value of the lowest-ranking district in Himachal Pradesh was higher than that of the lowest-ranking district in Jammu & Kashmir.

Briefly, the socio-economic development of the SC population is not only lower than that of the non-SC population in the country as a whole and as well as in the north-western region, but it also displays wide inter- and intra-state variations. However, there has been a rapid transformation in the socio-economic conditions of the SCs, population during the post-Independence period. It has been, in fact, faster than that of non-SC population. This speaks of the positive impact of government policies and programmes initiated for the socio-economic development of the SCs in the post-independence period. However, some states have done better than other states. Union territories, on the whole, have done very well in this regard.

Within north-western India, Punjab and Chandigarh (UT) recorded high levels of socio-economic development for the SC population in the whole region, both in 1961 and in 2001. But in terms of change in socio-economic conditions of the SC population during 1961–2001, Haryana and Himachal Pradesh have done much better in the whole region. At the district level, with an index value of 0.983, Srinagar district was at the top and Doda district, both in Jammu & Kashmir state, with an index value only of 0.275, at the bottom in terms of the socio-economic development of the SC population in the region. There were twenty districts or one-third of the total, in the region where the index of the socio-economic development for the SC population was less than the national average of 0.379.

CONCLUSION

In north-western India, where more than 13 million or 8 per cent of the total SC population of the country resides, every fifth person belongs to the 'SC' category. This ratio is one in six for the country as a whole. SCs make up about 22 per cent of the total population of north-western India, which is not only the highest share among all the regions in the country but also much higher than the national average of 16.2 per cent. Within north-western India, the proportional share of the SC population in Punjab is not only the highest in the region but also the highest among all the states in the country. Punjab, together with Haryana, shared 82 per cent of the total SC population, against their share of 72 per cent total population in north-western India in the 2001 census. Of sixty-three districts in north-western India, Nawanshahr district of Punjab recorded an SC population of about 41 per cent. This was the third highest share in the country as a whole after Kooch Bihar district

(50.1 per cent) in West Bengal and Sonabhadra district (41.9 per cent) in Uttar Pradesh. The twelve top-ranking districts in SC population, constituting only about one-fifth of the total districts in north-western India, had, collectively, more than two-fifths of the total SC population in the region.

There is a large heterogeneity of sub-castes within the SCs. There were at least 1,221 sub-castes of SCs in India during the 2001 census. The number varied from a maximum of 101 in Karnataka to a minimum of 4 in Sikkim. Within north-western India, the number of SC sub-castes varied from a high of 56 in Himachal Pradesh to a low of 13 in Jammu & Kashmir. The number of SC sub-castes was 37 each in Haryana and Punjab and thirty-six in Chandigarh (UT). Sub-castes, such as Batwal, Chamar/Ramdasi/Ravidasi, Doom, Megh/Julaha/Kabirpanthi, and Chuhra/Bhangi are common to all the four states and the union territory of Chandigarh. Further, as many as 30 sub-castes are common in Haryana, Punjab, Himachal Pradesh and Chandigarh (UT). Against this, 19 sub-castes are found exclusively in Himachal Pradesh and another 8 in Jammu & Kashmir. Overall, despite a degree of homogeneity of SC sub-castes in north-western India, there are well-marked inter-state differentials. Sub-castes like Jogi, Lohar and Teli are generally categorized as OBCs in a majority of north Indian states, but categorized as 'scheduled castes' in the Himachal Pradesh.

Finally, it is satisfying to note that the pace of change in the socio-economic conditions of SCs has accelerated during the post-independence era, narrowing the wide gap in well-being between the SC and non-SCs. In fact, former Dalit castes are now more aware in social, political and economical terms. This trend is likely to continue in the future as well, but with greater benefits to the newly emerged elite within the Dalits. The focus of government programmes and policies formulated in the future, for socio-economic development of the SC population, should remain on the minimization of existing inter- and intra-regional disparities. They should also be directed towards reducing the disparity between the 'scheduled' and 'non-scheduled' castes, as well as between the 'creamy' and 'non-creamy' layers within the 'SCs'.

NOTES

1. *Human Development Report*, UNDP, New Delhi: Oxford University Press, 1999, p. 134.
2. M.S. Gore, *The Social Context of an Ideology: Ambedkar's Political and Social Thought*, New Delhi: Sage, 1993, p. 211.
3. However, some scholars prefer to use this term in an ideological and political sense. According to K.L. Sharma, 'the word dalit refers to ideological transformation of the scheduled castes indicating their heightened protests against the upper caste domination by way of rejection of the upper caste cognitive paradigms and creation of their own cultural idioms, literature and ethnic harmony'. 'Caste and class in the emergence of dalit identity and movement', in *Sociology of Rural Development*, ed. U.R. Nahar, Jaipur: Rawat Publication, 1995, p. 88. He further adds, 'the process of the emergence of the word dalit is a part of journey which starts from *harijan* to "scheduled castes" and from scheduled castes to dalit' (p. 93).
4. Surya Kant, 'Socio-economic Transformation and Political Mobilization of Dalits in India', *Journal of Gandhian Studies* (*A Journal of Indian Society of Gandhian Studies*), vol. 3, no. 3, 2005, pp. 47–83. See also p. 52.
5. Ibid., p. 60.

APPENDIX 1

N-W REGION: DISTRIBUTION OF SUB-CASTES OF SCHEDULED CASTES, 2001

SC Castes Found in all the Five States and UT	
Batwal, Chamar/Ramdasia/Ravidasi, Doom, Megh/ Julaha/Kabirpanthi, Chuhra/Bhangi	(5)
SC Castes Found in Punjab, Haryana, Himachal Pradesh, and Chandigarh	
Ad Dharmi, Bangali, Barar, Bauri, Bazigar, Bhanjara, Chanal, Dagi, Darain, Dhanak, Dhogri/Sigi, Gagra, Gandhila, Gandel, Khatil, Kori/Koli, Mariya, Mazhabi, Nat, Od, Pasi, Perna, Pherera, Sanhai, Sanhal, Sansi, Sansio, Sapela, Sarera, Sikligar, Sirkibana	(30)
SC Castes Found only in Punjab and Haryana	
Deha	(1)
SC Castes Found only in Jammu & Kashmir	
Barwala, Basith, Gardi, Jolaha, Ratal, Saryara, Watal, Dhyar	(8)
SC Castes Found only in Himachal Pradesh	
Badhi, Bandhela, Bansi, Barad, Chhimba, Darai, Daula, Dhaki, Dhaogri, Hali, Hesi, Jogi, Kamoh, Karoach, Lohar, Rehar, Sipi, Teli, Thathiar	(19)
Total	= 63

CHAPTER 14

Sociocultural Transformation in Rural Punjab: Some Case Studies

RAJESH GILL

Any discussion on sociocultural transformation in rural Punjab implies that, foremost there are changes in its economy, i.e. a perceptible shift from the agricultural to the non-agricultural sector coupled with a high indebtedness of the State. Next, considerable emphasis is generally laid upon the growing disenchantment of the peasantry with farming as an occupation due to an increased cost of production, shortage of water and power and withdrawal of subsidies, along with an increasing level of conspicuous consumption. At the sociocultural front, the declining sex ratio has often been cited as a case of resilience of patriarchy in the state. Empirical studies have attributed the high incidence of female foeticide and a re-strengthened patriarchy in the state to economic prosperity, urbanization and easy access to the sex determination tests, especially in the cities and towns.

The question that arises from this description of contemporary rural Punjab is: whether it is possible to make generalizations for the whole of rural Punjab on the basis of these observations. For instance, has patriarchy tightened its hold in the villages of Punjab so that the people in these villages do not want girl children? Has the youth in the villages of Punjab become addicted to liquor, opium, *bhang* and so on? Have the parents of marriageable sons lost all inhibitions and feel no shame in asking for large dowries in the shape of endless lists comprising cars, electronic goods and so on? Too much talk on issues such as female foeticide, fraudulent NRI marriages and dowry harassment in the state also gives an impression that all over Punjab things have gone from bad to worse.

Actually, the problem lies in the fact that while statistical figures are available – district-wise, town-wise and to some extent village-wise – depicting the demographic, economic and even political change in the state, there is absolutely no authentic source of information for gauging the contours of sociocultural transformation. What normally happens is that one makes generalizations on the basis of some isolated studies or journalistic accounts of emerging social patterns in print or the electronic media. What is lost in the process are the historicity, contextuality and peculiarity of various situations, pertinent for understanding how the lifestyle, attitudes and behaviour patterns of the common people in villages have changed. Also, most of the explanations offered for the statistical trends come from the so-called experts and observers giving an outsider's viewpoint. What needs to be traced is what the people themselves think about their changing environment. What do they compare their present with? The reference point of the observer may be totally different from that of the people themselves.

These questions would be taken up here for analysis. The main objective in this study was to gauge the sociocultural transformation in rural Punjab. In sociocultural transformation and included the changes in inter-caste relations within the village, occupational changes in terms of caste status, the emerging role of panchayats in the development of the village and the changed gender equations within the households; all from the perspective of the villagers themselves. Of course, in the end some conclusions have been drawn on the basis of personal observations and fieldwork experience. The study was conducted in a qualitative manner, with a consistent effort to procure an ethnographic account of the change in the rural set-up as experienced and reported by the people themselves. Prolonged discussions were held with the villagers, especially the elderly men and women, to see how they view the contemporary reality in comparison with the past. Do they endorse the view that things have gone from bad to worse? Finally, the objective was also to identify the factors that intervene in the process of sociocultural change in the rural set-up, particularly in the context of Punjab.

The present analysis as well as the tables given below are based upon fieldwork conducted in two villages of Punjab, Devinagar and Janetpur, located in district Patiala, about 20 km from Chandigarh, close to the national highway. Both these villages are very close to the town of Dera Bassi (about 2 or 3 km). Both are small, with a population of less than 1,000 each. Case studies of both these villages were conducted and a comparison was made between the two with regard to the dimensions mentioned above.

However, before going into the sociocultural transformation in the sample villages, it would be meaningful first to get an idea of their demographic profile based upon the census of 2001. Table 14.1 gives information regarding population statistics.

The two villages have a small population with less than 1,000 persons and 200 households each.

Table 14.2 gives the caste composition of the two villages. It indicates that in both villages under study Scheduled Castes (SC) constitute slightly less than 40 per cent of the total population.

TABLE 14.1: TOTAL MALE AND FEMALE POPULATION AND NUMBER OF HOUSEHOLDS

Village	Total Households	Total Pop.	Male Pop.	Female Pop.
Janetpur	125	782	425	357
Devinagar	186	908	498	410

TABLE 14.2: TOTAL SCHEDULED CASTE POPULATION (MALE AND FEMALE)

Village	SC (Persons)	SC (Male)	SC (Female)	% of Total Pop.
Janetpur	309	176	133	39.5
Devinagar	354	198	156	38.9

The two villages differ greatly as far as literacy rate is concerned. The level of female literacy is lower than that of male literacy in both villages, although the gender gap in literacy is much higher in Devinagar as compared to Janetpur, as indicated in Table 14.3. Interestingly, the literacy rate is quite high in Dera Bassi tahsil, in which the villages under study are located. While the literacy rate is 69.90 per cent in Patiala as well as Punjab, it is as high as 75.50 per cent in Janetpur and as low as 66.10 per cent in Devinagar. Actually, while the total literacy level in Janetpur is higher than in the State of Punjab, in Devinagar it is consistently lower as compared to the state average.

The sex ratio in the two villages varies in that Janetpur has 840 females per 1,000 males, while Devinagar has only 823 females per 1,000 males. Interestingly, the sex ratio for the 0–6 years age group is very low in Janetpur, i.e. 645, while it is certainly better in Devinagar, i.e. 814. This is quite strange since Janetpur has a very high level of literacy, both male and female, and thus such a low child sex ratio indicates a serious inconsistency in the demographic pattern (Table 14.4).

TABLE 14.3: LITERATES TOTAL: MALE, FEMALE AND LITERACY RATE, MALE AND FEMALE

Settlement	Person	Male	Female	Lit.R. (P)	Lit.R. (M)	Lit.R. (F)
Janetpur	592	336	256	75.7	79.0	71.7
Devinagar	600	359	241	66.1	72.1	58.8
Dera Bassi	–	–	–	76.2	79.8	72.1
Patiala	–	–	–	69.9	76.1	62.9
Punjab	–	–	–	69.9	75.6	63.5

TABLE 14.4: SEX RATIO (FEMALES PER THOUSAND MALES)

Settlement	Sex Ratio	Sex Ratio (0–6 yrs.)
Janetpur	840	645
Devinagar	823	814
Dera Bassi	819	774
Patiala	864	770
Punjab	874	793

Having had a quick glance at the basic statistics on population composition in the villages under study, how the above demographic features have been influencing the pace and nature of sociocultural transformation in these settlements, will be examined in the following discussion.

WHAT HAS HAPPENED TO CASTE IN THESE VILLAGES?

Both villages have one thing in common: not too many caste groups live there. Janetpur has mainly Jat Sikhs and Ramdasias as the two most preponderant caste groups, while Devinagar has a dominance of Sainis – both numerically and socially – the other major caste group being the Balmikis. In both villages, the two caste groups are located in residential segregation, although it was interesting to note that an outsider cannot distinguish the residential area of the upper castes from that of the lower castes. There are no *kutcha* houses in either of the two villages and well-constructed houses could be seen in both areas, with no perceptible difference in terms of the material used or type of construction. In both villages, it was a repeated refrain especially by the upper-caste respondents, that economically, the Balmikis and Ramdasias were better than the upper castes since most of them are engaged in regular jobs in government offices, private firms, factories, etc. Most of the Ramdasias in Janetpur are engaged in boring wells for irrigation and are making good money in their business.

Children of both upper and lower castes go to the same schools. In fact, teachers in some private and village government schools reported that parents of Harijan children take greater pains to monitor their wards' academic progress. They are also more regular in paying the monthly school fees and ensure that their wards come to school in proper uniform, whereas upper-caste agricultural families hardly take time out to monitor their wards' educational training. On the whole, it was found that parents in jobs, either government or private, were more watchful of their children's education, while those engaged in agriculture were very irregular in paying the school fees, always waiting for the harvesting season. Because of this, they frequently shift their child from one school to another, unconcerned about the damage this causes.

INTER-CASTE RELATIONS

As mentioned above, the two broad caste groups reside in complete residential segregation. Therefore, diachronically speaking, they hardly interact with each other socially. But if one compares the present with the past, today things are much better. Earlier, upper castes, especially the Jats, as narrated by the villagers, would serve tea to the lower castes in glass utensils. If steel glasses were used, they would be purified by putting fire into them a number of times. The aged women said that they had seen their mothers-in-law doing that, but now such inhibitions were hardly visible. Upper-caste women and men visit Harijans on social occasions, although regular visits to their houses without any occasion were rare. Young girls belonging to upper castes, however, rarely visit lower-caste families in the village.

Although it was emphasized, time and again, by upper-caste male respondents that no caste distinctions exist in the village, especially in terms of social and religious activities, it was interesting to observe that there were two gurdwaras in each of the two villages – one for upper-caste Sikhs and the other one for the Harijans. In both the villages, the upper-caste male respondents said that at first there used to be only one gurdwara for members of all castes. Some politically motivated people from the lower castes, wanting to establish a distinct place for themselves, had another gurdwara built. But in both the cases, members of both upper- and lower-caste groups have been visiting both gurdwaras. For religious celebrations, the lower-caste people come to the upper-caste gurdwara, have *langar* there, while upper-caste people visit the other gurdwara to celebrate the birthday of Guru Ravi Dass. Usually more men than women from upper-caste groups join the lower-caste villagers in such activities. However, the very fact that there is a separate gurdwara for the Harijans in each of the two villages substantiates the observance of caste distinctions by villagers. Actually, it came out during informal conversations with the respondents that caste distinctions normally were at a minimum near and during elections – both panchayat and others – but in normal times things were entirely different.

Compared with the traditional pattern, therefore, social and political distance between the upper and lower castes has certainly diminished though it varies with the elections. Inter-caste relations therefore, though not absolutely egalitarian, have improved considerably. This is also due to another interesting development. In conversations with the members of the two panchayats, it was noticed that the upper-caste members showed a lot of consideration for the Harijan families, because they had now been incorporated into the village mainstream due to caste reservation in panchayats. At the time of the fieldwork, preparations were under way to celebrate the birthday of a local MLA. The woman *panch* who was organizing the show when asked if she would include the Harijan women, answered argued forcefully, 'Of course, yes! How can we exclude them? They are as much a part of the village as all of us.' This woman happened to be a very successful *panch* for three terms and was quite politically ambitious. Hence, it seems that it has become a political compulsion for the upper castes of the village to enfold the lower castes in their socio-political lives for fear of losing of votes. Whether they like it or not, upper-caste members of the villages have no choice but to at least publically show as much concern and respect for the Harijans as they show to their own caste members. This is perhaps the most influential indirect implication of the electoral democracy being implemented in the rural areas with the introduction of the coming Seventy-third Constitutional Amendment Act.

CASTE AND OCCUPATION: THE CHANGING ASSOCIATION

The two villages under study have been quite backward, with no water sources till about twenty years back. In each village, as narrated by almost every respondent, especially the elderly women, there used to be a single well from which all households had to draw water for domestic use, i.e. bathing, washing, cooking, etc. People did not wash their clothes daily, and would try to save water by restricting the frequency of bathing. No major crops could be cultivated except for some vegetables which were grown during the monsoon season with the help of rainwater. The villagers were poor and unable to make both ends meet. It was with the intervention of the late Capt. Kanwaljit Singh that lakhs of rupees were spent on two tube wells, which ultimately succeeded in bringing water to these two villages. At present, most of the Jats and Sainis, traditionally agricultural castes, are continuing with farming as their main occupation, although there are no big landlords here.

The Ramdasias, Balmikis and other Harijan castes residing in these villages do not own any land. But many of them are employed in government jobs and factories nearby. Very few of them are now opting for agricultural labour. One reason is that farmers prefer migrant labourers to the local ones for cultivation and harvesting because the former prove to be much cheaper, at almost half the wage. Thus, while there is not too much of affluence in the villages, there is not much poverty either. There has not been much migration into the villages because of which the traditional flavour and texture have been retained.

HOW EFFECTIVE ARE THE PANCHAYATS?

Normally there is a tendency among academics to make broad generalizations about the effectiveness of village panchayats since the implementation of the Seventy-third Constitutional Amendment Act. There is a need for caution here. Fieldwork for the present study revealed that it may not always be feasible to arrive at uniformity in terms of the working of the village panchayats, which depends upon a number of factors, discussed below. The field survey resulted in altogether different experiences in the two villages, in terms of the effectiveness of the panchayats, for very interesting reasons which I will be elaborated in the following discussion. In both villages, *sarpanch*es belonged to the upper castes: a Jat in Janetpur and Saini in Devinagar, though the former was a woman *sarpanch*. Since the inception of the Congress government in Punjab in 2002, no grant has been received by village Janetpur despite the fact that a fixed amount is sanctioned to each panchayat. As revealed by the *sarpanch* and the *panch*es, in this village political reasons are responsible for this sorry state of affairs. Consequently, no developmental work has been undertaken. Also, the village panchayat has no source of income since it has no land of its own. It was discovered during the study that for any panchayat to be effective, it is important that, apart from the government grants, a village must have some land, or *shamlat* or other resources of its own which, bring a regular income to the panchayat. The panchayat of Janetpur had neither any such income, nor received any grants. The reason for not getting government grants even after three years of tenure was that the village, traditionally, had been closely affiliated to the late Capt. Kanwaljit and the villagers swore by his name. This was because his efforts had brought them prosperity. But the villagers had failed to change, their loyalties with the change in government and thus had failed to garner any financial support. According to the husband of the *sarpanch* (who was actually conducting the duties), 'A *sarpanch* in any panchayat has to be economically affluent, with at least four or five thousand rupees in his pocket for any emergency. With our kind of bankrupt panchayat, the *sarpanch* has to spend money even for the tea and other things served at the meetings out of his/her own pocket. How is it then possible for a poor scheduled caste *sarpanch* to conduct even a meeting at his place?'

The other village by contrast had been smarter. The woman *panch* who had a long association with the panchayat narrated, 'From inside, madam, we are with Capt. Kanwaljit. But we have to think about the welfare of the village also. Therefore, now we have got aligned to the Congress party and have received handsome amount of government grants.' The village lanes had been concretized and a platform with cement slabs constructed for holding panchayats and other village meetings. Also, this panchayat had its own land which brought in a good income.

Based in fieldwork in other villages around Chandigarh and elsewhere, one expected to find some liquor shops in these villages too, apart from a high rate of addiction among young and old males to alcohol, opium, bhang, injectibles, cough syrups, pain killers, etc. But surprisingly in both villages there was no *theka*, or liquor shop. Villagers said that they worked unitedly in this regard and had not allowed it to happen. They were sure that in future too they would not allow any liquor shop in the village. One reason for this is that in Devinagar there is a huge following of the Radha Soami sect, which imposes restrictions on eating meat and taking intoxicants. In Janetpur on the other hand, Sikhism had a strong influence. During visits to the village, large groups of men could be seen in the gurdwara, irrespective of the time of day. Very frequently announcements were made on a loud speaker in the gurdwara giving various kinds of information to the villagers. An announcement to the effect that the researcher wanted to talk to the aged men in the village, was made and within ten minutes a number of men gathered there, ready with all the information. This type of togetherness goes a long way in preserving the traditional values in the village. One of the reasons why there are not many young boys addicted to drugs is that people there are not wealthy and have limited resources. In all the households where farming is being followed, young boys have to help their fathers in cultivation and other related activities, due to which they are left with little time to loiter. People in both villages ascribed the near absence of addiction among the youth to the limited economic resources of the households. During visits to the villages one did not find even a single *amli* (opium addict) in the villages something that is so common in many of the villages in Punjab.

It is therefore, safe to conclude that it is inadequate to draw general conclusions about village panchayats, disregarding the differences between the villages in terms of political affiliations, the political shrewdness of the village panchayat members, the resources owned by the panchayats and so on.

CHANGING GENDER EQUATIONS WITHIN THE VILLAGE HOUSEHOLDS

Rural Punjab has generally, been treated basically as an agrarian society, with a very strong patriarchy, in both the private and public domains. The cultural history of Punjab provides enough indications of the extremely discriminatory attitude of society in general towards daughters, daughters-in-law, widows and so on. While the agriculturally prosperous state with a high per capita income was, some decades ago, expected to usher in a society which would give a dominating role to its women, the reality is quite different as the statistics of the census of 2001 suggest. The sharp decline in the sex ratio, especially in the 0–6 years age group, has once again proclaimed Punjab as a highly patriarchal society despite the significant strides made by it in the agricultural and agro-industrial arenas.

There is, however, a need to verify the ground reality as it exists today. It seems wrong to make a single judgement for the whole of Punjab, which includes large and small villages, rich and poor villages, fertile and thirsty villages, villages in close proximity to cities and very remote villages. Is it possible to make broad generalizations for all these villages? Further, the question is, do all these rural settlements share common points of reference, with which one can compare the contemporary situation? Certainly not. For any in-depth understanding of present-day gender relations, one cannot do without tracing the past and then making a comparison. This is what has been attempted in this study.

In detailed discussions with the aged women of the two villages, both in isolation as well as in groups, they came out with some very interesting observations often exchanging their experiences with each other. When asked to reveal their experiences about when they first entered the village after marriage, all of them gave a similar response: 'It is much much better today. There was no water in the village, roads were not there and it was difficult to walk through the village lanes during monsoons.' Because of the shortage of water and lack of cultivation, women's life was very strenuous and tiring. They had to fetch water from the well, manage the household and observe *purdah* from the male members in the family.

These women in their 70s and 80s said that when a girl was to enter the village for the first time after marriage, the bridegroom would leave her outside the village, come home and pick up his sister who would take along a long skirt (nine or more yards) for the bride to wear and only then could she be brought home. Whenever she had to go outside her home, she would have to wear that long skirt. Since there were no lavatories in the houses, women had to go out in the open to ease themselves very early in the morning. The daughters-in-law would have to wear the skirts covering the whole body even when they had to ease themselves. When both mother-in-law and daughter-in-law had to go out in the village, both would wear the *ghagra*, the latter following the former. The women gave two reasons for this dress code. First, this was primarily done in order to distinguish the daughter from the daughter-in-law and secondly, the *ghagra* could conceal the body contours, thus acting as a *purdah* for the girl.

The young girls, mainly daughters-in-law, laughed saying that they had been saved the trouble of wearing the heavy *ghagra*. The women also said that the domestic work in the old days had been extremely tiring. They would grind the wheat to get flour, even grind the pulses for domestic use, and would daily apply mud to the *kutcha* floor. Cooking itself was an extremely strenuous exercise. The introduction of cooking gas, washing machines, refrigerators, food processors, etc., has significantly lessened the burden of domestic work for the women in the villages. These women also said that unlike the earlier generations, they no longer wait endlessly for their husbands to come home before they eat it. Now they wait if the husband is expected to come home on time, but if his working hours are irregular, they have their meals and serve the men as and when they come home. This is a very significant change in view of an observation made by Malcolm Lyall Darling (1934: 287) in a study on Punjabi villages. He comments:

> If a wife is free from other duties and has a house of her own, with no mother-in-law about, she may sit with her husband while he eats; but if she does this, it is probably to keep off the flies, and more often she is too busy serving him or feeding the children. It is only when both husband and children are satisfied that she can eat herself, and she must then be content with whatever scraps remain, and if unexpected guests come in, there may not be even this. In other ways her inferiority is marked.

Women in these villages of Punjab have thus come a long way in the process of social transformation.

As daughters-in-law, women are in a much more comfortable position in these villages as compared to the earlier generations. In most homes, they do not cover their head in front of the male members. They sat with all other members of the family chatting with me and intervening occasionally. Their mothers-in-law did not enjoy this type of liberty when they were young and had to observe strict norms in front of male elders. For instance, they could not sit on the cot or chair if the father-in-law or elder brother-in-law or other male relatives of the husband were sitting there. Instead, they would immediately sit on the floor, and even when they had to leave the room, they would move in the sitting position, almost crawling. In other words, they were not supposed to stand in front of the male relatives.

Questions relating to how marriages were being conducted in these villages, especially in view of the increasing demands of dowry, misbehaviour indulged in by the bridegroom's family, exorbitant expenditure on the ceremony of marriage and so on, in other parts of Punjab brought surprising answers. In neither village had a single case of dowry demand or dowry harassment occurred. This was corroborated by the fact that till date, the villagers have been conducting marriage ceremonies within the village, in the school, *dharamshala* or in the open space, rather than in the marriage palaces. Unlike the villages near Jalandhar, Ludhiana, Faridkot and other relatively affluent districts of Punjab, there are no marriage palaces near these villages. At the time of the survey, however, one marriage palace was being built on the outskirts of Janetpur.

An interesting case was narrated by a resident of Devinagar: While fixing the match of a girl in the village, the boy's family visited the girl's house and started talking of dowry items. The people of the village gathered there immediately, told them to leave the place and look for a match somewhere else. It was difficult to believe this since an altogether different kind of picture had been projected of contemporary Punjab. On further probing it was revealed that the reason why these problems relating to marriages have not polluted these villages is that people are not very rich here. Those engaged in farming have small landholdings, the largest landholding in both the villages being of not more than 15–16 acres. Villagers also pointed out that while looking for matches for their sons and daughters, they avoid contacting very rich and big landlords. Instead, they looked for average kinds of families. A second very interesting reason is that the marriages, even by the so-called better-off families of the villages, are conducted in a relatively simple manner, very unlike the way they are conducted in Malwa and

Majha regions. Therefore, people have so far avoided practices that could have left the families bankrupt after a daughter's marriage.

Another extremely interesting comment that came from a woman who had married off three of her sons was that these days it is equally expensive to marry off a son as it was a daughter. She said that earlier all the sons could be married off with a single gold ring and a set of bangles. These would be taken back from the older daughter-in-law and given to the new one and so on. But now no daughter-in-law will give back her jewellery to her mother-in-law. In fact, earlier, a daughter-in-law hardly possessed anything of her own, for example, cosmetics, jewellery and even clothes. These things were taken away by the mother-in-law, and the daughter-in-law had no private space of her own to keep her belongings under lock and key. But now daughters-in-law will not give their belongings to anybody else and have complete control over them. This, according to the mothers-in-law, has made a son's marriage much more costly. Also, nowadays, the boy's family has to make proper arrangements for the welcome of the bride's family too, something that could never have been imagined before.

The elderly women, now grandmothers, presented beautiful narratives of how they had to beg their mothers-in-law for every small thing of daily use. For instance, one woman said, 'When I used to ask for soap, my mother-in-law would get furious and would say, 'I gave you one two days back, how could you finish it so quickly?' Other women nodded their heads and affirmed that they had all had similar experiences. They had to face objections from their mothers-in-law even if they bathed their children twice because that led to a greater consumption of soap and water. These women also said that when the mother-in-law would leave the house, she would leave one glass of milk outside and lock everything else in the kitchen. So one can conclude that having a good supply of livestock in the household did not necessarily imply more milk for the younger women. On a lighter note these women also revealed how they, along with other daughters-in-law in the village, would ridicule their mothers-in-law for all this and would often teased them by showing them duplicate keys to the locks.

CONCLUSION

The above analysis, based upon the fieldwork conducted in two villages of Punjab during 2002–4, indicates sociocultural transformation whereby the caste and gender relations within the villages have undergone considerable change towards a flexibility which today characterizes the husband-wife, mother-in-law daughter-in-law and inter-caste relationships. This change, measured in a qualitative manner in terms of how relationships existed in the past, indicates a weakening of patriarchy at least in the dimensions discussed in the chapter. Similarly, while the social distance between castes, the highest and the lowest, has declined, at least for political purposes, it in no way means that caste has lost its relevance in other dimensions too. That would certainly be an oversimplification.

It would be appropriate here to bring in the very important concept of 'dominant caste' used by M.N. Srinivas for the first time in 1955 in his essay 'The Social System of a Mysore Village'. Elaborating it later in 'The Dominant Caste in Rampura', Srinivas (1955: 18) defined the 'dominant caste' thus:

> A caste may be said to be 'dominant' when it preponderates numerically over the other castes, and when it also wields preponderant economic and political power. A large and powerful caste group can more easily be dominant if its position in the local caste hierarchy is not too low.

Today the concept of dominant caste seems to be even more relevant in the light of the present study, since in village politics, a larger number also means a larger vote-bank. During the fieldwork, one came across members of upper castes often bickering about the growing economic, occupational and even social status of Harijans in their private conversation; however, they used extreme self-restraint while talking about them in public. Those actively engaged in politics took special care while discussing the low-caste residents of the village, exuding a very sympathetic and patronizing atttitude towards them, at least in public. In this context, therefore, if Balmikis or Harijans constitute a numerically strong group in the village, one would naturally expect an altogether different attitude from the politically ambitious upper castes, whose political careers depend upon numbers.

One should, of course, not call these two cases unique or

peculiar. It is possible that many such villages exist in the different districts of Punjab. But certainly, one can conclude here that sociocultural transformation in rural Punjab cannot be understood without contextualizing the settlement under study. Of course, urbanization, commercialization and information technology have eroded the traditional rural social structure, value system and caste equations, but the change is not unidirectional and all the transformation cannot be explained in terms of these processes alone. While religion may divide people with its parochial appeal in a few cases, it also has the potential to effectively avoid serious social problems haunting a sizeable rural population. Further, while the modern panchayats have decentralized power and resources within the different groups in the villages, they have also forced the upper caste people to enfold the lower castes in the mainstream, to get both votes as well as funds and grants from the respective authorities.

Finally, one factor that seems to have boosted patriarchy in Punjab appears to be the excess of money and the consequent urge to display it through social ceremonies amongst which marriage tends to be the most prominent. Secondly, women in the villages of Punjab may seem to be restricted within the homes, far less empowered as compared to their sisters in the cities and towns; but when compared to their mothers and grandmothers within the same contexts, they are certainly placed today in a much more liberal, dominant and advantageous position.

The villages under study did not have many migrants, as is the case in many of the villages close to the periphery of large cities. Therefore, they had a relatively effective panchayat system. The problems are very different in villages which have on the one hand a very diverse composition in terms of caste groups, and on the other a predominant section of population consisting of migrants from other states of India. In many villages of Punjab, entire panchayats, including the post of *sarpanch*, have been hijacked by the migrant labourers, much to the discomfort of the local residents. Although it is another thing that in some cases, with a view to monopolizing power within their households, prominent persons have got their own SC servants appointed as *sarpanches* so that the real centre of power remains where it has always been.

To conclude, it must be reiterated that more studies of a comparative nature are required in different areas of rural Punjab in order to obtain a realistic picture of the ground reality and to frame generalizations. The forces of agricultural and industrial development, urbanization, commercialization, etc., cannot be expected to rule out the important role played by the peculiar traits of the rural community under observation. Moreover, attempts to homogenize the whole of rural Punjab may conceal rather than reveal the emerging patterns of change that are so dependent upon contextual attributes.

BIBLIOGRAPHY

Darling, Malcolm Lyall, *Wisdom and Waste in the Punjab Village*, London: Oxford University Press, 1934.

Dumont, Louis, *Homo Hierchicus*, Chicago: University of Chicago Press, 1980.

Gill, M.S., *Punjab Society, Perspectives and Challenges*, New Delhi: Concept Publishing Company, 2003.

Gill, Rajesh, 'Market, Media and Gender in Globalized Punjab', in *State, Market and Civil Society-Issues and Interface*, ed. Rajesh Gill, Jaipur: Rawat Publications, 2005.

Sharma, Ursula, *Concepts in the Social Sciences: Caste*, Buckingham: Open University Press, 1999.

Singh, Pritam, *Punjab Economy: The Emerging Pattern*, New Delhi: Enkay Publishers Pvt. Ltd., 1995.

Srinivas, M.N., *India's Villages*, Calcutta: Government of West Bengal, 1955.

———, *The Dominant Caste and Other Essays*, New Delhi: Oxford University Press, 1987.

CHAPTER 15

Social Transformation and *Khaps* in Haryana

P.S. VERMA

The process of modernization has brought about far-reaching changes in the Indian society. The classical type of patron–client relation has become less sacrosanct, resulting in the breakdown of the traditional system of ritual hierarchy. The occupational structure is no longer conditioned by caste or *varna* norms, according to which caste was a group of people who practised a particular occupation. If state-induced transformation in the agrarian sector has benefited the intermediary agriculturist castes, the constitutional measures pertaining to social justice and 'affirmative action' have raised the socio-economic and political status of the weaker sections, resulting in the 'melting away of the unjust *jajmani* system' in contemporary times. According to D.L. Seth:

> The stratificatory system as it functions in India today, can, therefore, no longer be characterized as a hierarchy of ritual statuses. Put in stronger terms, the Indian caste system, for long conceived of as a ritual status system has disintegrated, although castes as individual self-conscious communities continue to survive. But by organizing themselves horizontally into larger conglomerates and coalitions, they are now entering new social formations which have emerged in India's stratificatory system.[1]

The old vertical relations have been replaced by the horizontal ones, and the caste is changing rapidly, finding a place for itself in non-conventional and secular domains of social, political, and economic life.[2] Moreover, the constituents of different caste identities tend to aspire to new professions instead of sticking to hereditary or ancestral occupations. Better education, white-collar jobs, middle-class lifestyles, power sharing, non-farm sources of income, etc., have become the new symbols of status. The ritual-based cultural system, enshrined in a system of normative principles, is getting relegated and replaced by an open society in which even inter-community marriages, more particularly in urban areas, are not opposed. Mention may be made here that present-day villages are much different from the villages of 1947 or so. In fact, the lifestyles and behavioural patterns of people have altered considerably. The new generation has become indifferent to the notions of purity and pollution. Even customary marriage practices of caste endogamy and *gotra* (clan) exogamy have started eroding. As a result, the validity of restrictions on marrying into the *gotra*s of one's mother, paternal grandmother, maternal grandmother, etc., has been questioned and resisted. Likewise, the norm of disallowing marriages within the same, or adjacent, villages has also been violated. It is against this background, that a study about the nature, history, organization, support structure and functions of the single or multi-village *khap* panchayats becomes relevant.

Though the legal-rational framework of the modern state has considerably weakened the kinship-based *khap* panchayats, they still play a vital role in the social life of the countryside, where each caste maintains its own identity and pattern of interaction with other castes. Further, the politicization of caste has not only kept the caste system alive in a 'rapidly changed historical setting', but also helped the conservative tendencies of castes to coexist with the legal-rational framework of the existing system of governance. Each caste is further divided into numerous *gotra*s, which, while serving the caste system as its parts, also safeguard and strengthen their own sub-structural identity. The caste as an endogamous structure thus consists of *gotra* exogamous substructures which operate through associations or panchayats of their own. The role of such groups or panchayats has been more pronounced in the peasant castes, particularly amongst the Jats in Haryana and the neighbouring states. According to some:

Village panchayat is a common feature in other communities also, but the conventional *khap* or area and tribal as well as the *sarva khap* panchayat are unique with the Jats in Haryana, Delhi and western Uttar Pradesh. Historically, these panchayats represent today the ancient *gana*, *samgha*, and *sarva samgha* or *deshiye* panchayats or assemblies in which the selected or elected decision-making body was known as *simiti* and the rest as *sabha*.[3]

Since the *khap* panchayats in the past enjoyed the force of tradition, homogeneous belief systems, consent of caste or *gotra* men, dominating leadership and 'normative principles of social intercourse permitted within and between the castes and *gotras*', it had been possible for them to decide the complicated matters of inter- or intra-caste disputes without difficulty. Even in present times, though the society has undergone change and the statutory three-tier system of panchayati raj has come into existence, the conventional panchayats still make their presence felt in the countryside. They frequently intervene in matters relating to marriage, engagements, inter-caste disputes, etc., and their diktats have been carried out successfully, though they do not enjoy any legal status. In terms of their origins, some believe that the *khap* panchayats originated in the seventh century AD during the reign of King Harshvardhan. Likewise, others have traced their origins to periods ranging from the twelfth to the fourteenth century. As an example, the Benain *khap* claimed to have been founded in the fourteenth century.[4] Some writers, while emphasizing that the *khaps* originated in pre-industrial society and also in times prior to the colonial intervention in India, have observed:

> *Khap* panchayats came to occupy a centrality in the emergent small agricultural and cattle-rearing society that developed with the long-drawn habitation and settling into the village based productive agriculture in the plains around the Ghaggar, the Yamuna, and beyond, of the peoples now identified, based on their respective places of displacement and migration, or the modes of living adopted, as Jats, and also, to a greater or less degree, Gujars, Ahirs, Meos, Rajputs, Rors et al.[5]

Generally it is believed that these institutions were the product of the 'political economy of medieval communal agriculture'.

They came into being 'as an outgrowth of clannish formations in the tribal era' and played an important role in fostering a sense of brotherhood among members of a *khap*, thus creating an instrument of social security in an age when the modern concept of law and order was unheard of, and might as a right largely prevailed.[6] However, the *khap*s are mainly prevalent in the land of Jats, roughly comprising Haryana, western UP, Punjab and some parts of Rajasthan and Madhya Pradesh.[7] Since the Jats are 'organized into exogamous patri-clans', the clan councils as 'corporate group structures' play a vital role in their socio-economic and political life. According to Pradhan:

> In Meerut division each Jat clan has a compact geographical area of its own. The villages in which a clan is settled are organized into a clan council, and the area under its jurisdiction is called the *Khap*. Each clan has a hereditary headman called the *Chaudhary*, also the headman of the *Khap* council.[8]

In Haryana, besides some hereditary headmen, there are several *khap*s that are headed by elected *pradhan*s. However, these headmen/*pradhan*s are elected by *khap* members on the basis of consensus, not through ballot. Moreover, they are elected only from the head (original) village connected with the ancestors of a *khap*. For example, if the *pradhan* of the Sangwan *khap* is elected only from Charkhi village, the Benain *khap* is headed by a man from Danoda Kalan village. Anyway, the *khap pradhan*s, whether hereditary or elected, do not enjoy any material perks or privileges like salary and allowances. But they play a decisive role in the decision-making process of the *khap* panchayats. Most of the *khap pradhan*s are elderly persons belonging to relatively better-off agricultural families. They are also elected on a permanent basis. Moreover, they enjoy prestige and have a better understanding of the traditions and customs that guide the affairs of the *khap* panchayats. Most of the *khap*s are multi-village organizations which wield considerable political clout and act as 'instruments of social control' in their respective areas. They are based on the principles of local contiguity and *khap bhaichara* and exogamy. Most of the *khap* panchayats in Haryana are named after the dominant clans but also contain various other minor clans and castes residing within the area of the *khap*. The minor clans and castes also acknowledge the leadership, or dominance, of the clan that controls the bulk of the agricultural land and the maximum number of villages within the territorial limits of the *khap*. For example, a twelve-village Saroha *khap*, consisting of the seven villages of the Saroha clan, two of Rana and one each of Jhajria, Joshi and Hooda *gotra* is named after the dominant clan, i.e. Saroha. All the clans and castes residing in the twelve villages accept its leadership.

Apart from the internal affairs of the dominant clan, the *khap* panchayats also decide inter-clan and inter-caste disputes and other matters of common interest.[9] Occasionally, even matters relating to development, such as roads, bridges, schools, or for that matter the liquor menace, etc., have been taken up and articulated by the *khap* panchayats. In 1993, *khap* panchayats opposed the state government's scheme to allow the official village panchayats to start *theka*s of wine in their villages. Consequently, this scheme was a failure.[10] This apart, during the days of the Punjabi Suba Movement, the Naujawan Sabha of the Choubisi Khap Panchayat presented a memorandum to the parliamentary committee for reinstating old Haryana by including areas of Abohar–Fazilka, Nalagarh, Kunolaghat tahsil, Ropar and Chandigarh besides some districts of western UP, Delhi and Rajasthan.[11] It was claimed that these areas were culturally similar to Haryana.

There are various types of *khap* panchayats in different parts of the state. Some of them are single *gotra khap*s, while some are multi-caste in nature. There are over two hundred *gotra*s (major or minor) of Jats in Haryana, and a number of them enjoy the privilege of having their own *khap*. However, regarding variations, if the Dahiya *khap* – or for that matter the Gathwala *khap* or the Hooda or Antil *khap* – illustrates the single *gotra* dominated multi-village *khap*, the *khap* panchayat of Meham, popularly known as a *chaubisi* (a group of twenty-four villages), is a multi-*gotra* and multi-caste *khap* panchayat.[12] Organizations like the Ghirai *chalisa* (forty villages); Satrol *khap* (a group of seventy villages); *chaurasi* (eighty-four villages), etc., also represent the multi-*gotra* and multi-caste *khap* panchayats. The multi-*gotra khap*s have, on occasion, played an important role in matters relating to intra-*khap* and inter-caste or community conflicts. Likewise, there are *sarva-khap*s that act as political organizations of various clans or castes in the geographical area inhabited by them. They comprise different *khap*s of the area. 'Though the *sarva-khap* council as an institution is not based upon kinship affinity, it is an extension of the principle which acts as a charter for the *khap*, clan and caste councils'.[13] Matters relating to inter-caste disputes, or the issues involving various *khap*s, may be referred to the *sarva-khap* panchayats in which the representatives of the concerned *khap*s participate and settle the dispute. On occasion, *sarva-jatiya khap* panchayats have been held on matters like reduction of expenditure at marriages and lack of development works like roads, schools, irrigation, etc. Incidentally, unlike the dominant clan-led *khap* panchayats, the *pradhan* or chairman of the *sarva-khap* is not permanent but elected only for the meeting. Moreover, decisions of the *sarva-khap* panchayats are implemented by the concerned *khap* panchayats. They may disagree with the decisions of the *sarva-khap*. The clan-conscious farmers generally go along with the decisions taken by their own *khap* panchayats.

Structurally, the *khap*s are made up of various socio-political units spread all over the area of the *khap*. For example, the *chaubisi khap* consists of five *tappa* councils (a group or cluster of neighbouring villages) and twenty-four villages or *majra*s (divided into *pana*s, *thok*s or *thola*s).[14] Since the Meham *chaubisi* is not dominated by a single clan, the *tappa*s are not purely kinship-based units. In terms of their role, the *tappa*s, *panna*s, *thok*s or *thola*s tend to settle disputes at the grass-roots level. However, when they fail to resolve the matter, then the concerned group would approach either the *khap* panchayat or the judicial bodies. Many village people avoid the judiciary because of the expense, delays in court cases and other problems. The *khap* panchayats on the other hand take immediate action, and both the guilty and the victim are spared of exploitation by the professionals, police, etc. Even a critic of the *khap* panchayats, while pointing out that the lack of faith in the legal system and the fear of being humiliated by the police have turned illegal caste panchayats into law-enforcing agencies, observed: 'The victims have gone on record to state that even if they manage to fight it out in court, the rapist will ultimately go scot free and return to avenge the fact that he was pulled to court. Panchayats, they felt, settled the matter not only once for all but "right there and then", besides saving them from the humiliation of insensitive police handling'.[15]

Like the Meham *chaubisi*, every *khap* is made up of various socio-political units. The Benain *khap* has three *tappa* councils headed by *pradhans* chosen from the head-villages of Danoda, Dhamtahn and Kalwan. The Danoda *tappa* has fifteen villages; Dhamtahn twenty-nine and Kalwan twelve. Below the *tappas*, are the *pattis*, *panas*, etc., which work at the village level.

The nomenclature of the constituent units may differ from one *khap* to another. For example, the Sangwan *khap*, which has over forty villages under its jurisdiction, operates through *kannis* instead of *tappas*. This *khap* is dominated by the Sangwan clan and has three *kannis* (a cluster of villages) and eight sub-*kannis*. Both the *kannis* and the sub-*kannis* are a cluster of villages based on principles of local contiguity and kinship bonds. The number of villages under a *kanni* and sub-*kanni* varies from five to twenty-two. If the Bhiri Kalan *kanni* consisted of twenty-two villages, the Jhoju Kalan and the Charakhi *kanni* comprised thirteen and five villages, respectively. Each *kanni* is headed by a *pradhan* elected only from the major village of the *kanni*. The major villages of the three *kannis* are Jhoju Kalan, Bhiri Kalan and Charakhi. The three *kannis* are further divided into eight sub-*kannis*, each headed by a *pradhan* elected from the major village of the sub-*kanni*. The neighbouring Sheoran *khap-84* also operates through the *kannis*. When the *kannis* and sub-*kannis* fail to resolve a dispute in their respective area, they may refer it to the *pradhan* of the *khap*. He in turn may either invite a meeting of the *khap* panchayat or resolve the problem through discussion with the leaders of the concerned *kannis* or sub-*kannis* of the clan. A meeting of the *khap* panchayat is held only when the efforts of the concerned *kannis*, sub-*kannis* or village panchayats fail to resolve the matter. Resolutions passed by the *khap* panchayat are considered as binding on the people, clans or castes involved. However, if the dispute relates to castes other than the Jats, it is resolved either by the panchayats of the respective castes or by the *pradhan* of the dominant *khap* along with the other influential people of the *khap* and the leaders of the concerned castes.

The activities of *khap* panchayats have focused upon issues such as the preservation of time-honoured traditions and social norms, retention of customary norms regarding marriage, prevention of dowry and divorce, settlement of factional fights between various social groups within the jurisdiction of the *khap*, etc. A meeting of a *khap* panchayat is convened by the *pradhan* when a problem arises. Matters pertaining to problems, offences and disputes are decided on the basis of the considered opinion of the members and office-bearers present at the *khap* meeting. They are basically guided by conventional wisdom. Most of the *khap*s have their *chaupal*s (meeting places) or halls where the *khap* members assemble and hold discussions. In addition, some have *chabutra*s (platforms or open meeting places) what are regarded as sacrosanct by the lineage groups. The hall and platform of certain *khap*s, like the Benain *khap*, are worth crores of rupees. The decisions of *khap*s are taken on the basis of general consensus and a 'spirit of compromise'. Once a decision is taken, it becomes morally binding upon the person or group concerned. Defiance of its decisions is never regarded kindly by the *khap* and its constituents. The decisions 'can be broken only at the expense of incurring a curse by the (*khap*) panchayat which is considered as infallible'.[16] Many times certain *khap*s have taken very harsh and regressive decisions on the pretext of honouring *biradari* traditions.

Since the existence of *khap*s is customary in nature – without any formal legal status – their decisions are mainly backed by the traditional norms and customs. However, their decisions receive considerable support from people in the villages. The mindset of the Jat farmers itself is a great source of support and strength to *khap* panchayats. Jats attach considerable importance to the notion of *bhaichara* and to clan or lineal affinities. They generally tend to behave more as members of a collective body or clan or caste than as individuals having a personal identity. In fact, considerations of descent, clan, caste, etc., take precedence over notions of individualism. Some scholars, while commenting on the Jats, observed: 'For the traditional Jats in the villages of west UP, freedom means the liberty to follow their traditions, lifestyles and customs without hindrance from outside. Many of them still believe that they would be better off if they could settle disputes at the village or at the *khap* panchayat level.'[17] It is mainly because of such factors that, in certain villages of western UP, caste panchayats have undertaken the responsibility of settling all sorts of cases – including murder, rape, property, marriages, etc. According to the *pradhan* of a caste panchayat, 'It is five years since the police last entered Johri village'.[18] Even the Bhartiya Kisan Union (BKU) chief, Mahender Singh Tikait, once emphasized that, 'A time will come when the *kisans* will no longer have to go to the courts for anything. They would have an executive and judicial wing to their BKU panchayat that would adjudicate on all matters.'[19] Incidentally, even the agitations by *kisans* in UP were often successful because of the support of *khap* panchayats. Regarding this, a BKU leader said that the *khap* pride was very crucial in encouraging the people to participate in BKU-sponsored agitations.[20] Almost the same holds true of Jat-dominated areas in other states, including Haryana. For example, the *khap* leaders have often contributed to the mobilization of farmers during the course of agitations regarding prices, irregular supply and rates of electricity and power dues.

Khap panchayats also gather support from past events wherein dominant *khaps* have acted quite positively at critical times. For example, the Meham *chaubisi* and various other *khaps* of Haryana had vigorously participated in the 1857 revolt. In UP too the major *khaps* had revolted against British rule. 'Various *khaps* including Baliyan, Salaklain (or Desh), Gathwala and Kalaslain took a notable part in the revolt under the leadership of Nana Sahib, Begum Samru of Budhana and their own *khap* leaders'.[21] The Jats, who claim martial status, also praise *khaps* for their role against invaders in the past. 'Their *sarva-khap* records supposedly give details of many agreements between *khap chaudhris* and indigenous rulers to join hands and repulse foreigners'.[22] Many *khaps* are known among their followers for having protected their constituents in the past. The *khap* militia, depending on the situation, used to cooperate and confront the rulers of the time. Some major *khaps* had also fought against the imposition of religious taxes like *jizya*. According to M.C.

Pradhan, the exemption from *jizya* allowed by Emperor Akbar was taken as a victory for the *khaps* and *sarva-khap* councils.[23] In the Rohtak belt, the *chaubisi*, along with other major *khaps* (Malik, Dahiya, Hooda, etc.), had also fought against the oppression and immoral acts of some *nawabs* in the seventeenth century.[24] Influential people amongst the Jats to this day appreciate what the *khaps* did in the distant past. It is claimed that *khaps* have enjoyed great social sanction on account of their historic role in the past.

Apart from shielding traditions, territory and people, issues like reduction of expenditure on marriages had also engaged the attention of the *khap* panchayats. Some believe that in Haryana, the first decision on the reduction of expenditure on marriage ceremonies was taken as early as AD 1197 in Hisar, where a *khap* was organized under the leadership of Raja Bhimdeva. The second decision regarding non-interference in marriage was taken at the second meeting of the *khap* panchayat held at Shikarpur village in AD 1286.[25] Even in modern times *khaps* have invariably focused on preventing extravagance during marriages. Some of the decisions taken by a *khap* panchayat held on 8–9 March 1950 were reduction in expenditure on entertaining *baraat*, ban on the display of ornaments, *shagun* of Re. 1 only at the time of betrothal, ban on child marriages, no *Kothali* on *Teej* and fixing a ceiling on the number of utensils and clothes to be given in a dowry.[26] Almost similar decisions were taken by the Benain *khap* on 28 March 1976. Even as late as 21 March 1993, the *sarva-khap* panchayats at village Sisana (Sonepat) passed almost similar resolutions. Besides this, the *khap* panchayats have, on occasion, aided their helpless clansmen in times of crisis. Those who have sought help at the *khap chabutra* or *chaupal* have never returned disappointed. Such factors have helped *khap* panchayats to maintain their identity and support structure in a changed milieu.

In the past the *khaps* frequently faced threats, particularly during British rule, but had shown great resilience. In fact, the British judicial system and the law and order mechanism deprived the *khaps* of many of their traditional powers and rights. In present times, even the current statutory panchayati raj system has divested the *khaps* of most of their functions and powers.

In addition, with the expansion of the activities of the state in the day-to-day life, the sanctity of *khap* panchayats has been considerably diluted. Nonetheless, they still hit the headlines in the wake of contentious marriages, local disputes and periodic elections. Since the caste factor has become a central consideration in the electoral politics in Haryana, *khap* panchayats are mobilized by ticket-seekers in order to strengthen their claim. As in the earlier elections, in the recent assembly polls (February 2005) too some candidates mobilized the support of *khap*s in their area to win their seats. Moreover, some *khap* panchayats like the Meham *chaubisi*, have invariably sponsored or adopted candidates who, barring a few exceptions, have always been successful in getting elected. In fact, the support pledged by a major *khap* has invariably ensured victory. On occasion, even lightweight politicians supported by *khap*s have won against powerful leaders. Interestingly, a candidate who had lost an election to the office of *sarpanch* of a village panchayat won the assembly polls mainly because of the support extended to him by the *khap* panchayats, including his own *gotra-khap*, which commanded influence in as many as twenty-four villages.[27] According to the *pradhan* (a retired colonel) of a major *khap* representing over fifty villages in the mid-1960s, when a powerful political leader was denied the Congress ticket, he came to the holy place of the *khap* to seek its blessing and consequently won the election with a considerable margin.

Keeping in view the vitality of *khap* panchayats, the major political parties and their leaders have never intervened in the affairs or controversial decisions of these bodies. In August 2005, the union panchayati raj minister, Mani Shankar Aiyar, said that there was no scope for such caste panchayats in a civilized society, and that these should not be permitted to exercise any extra-constitutional power.[28] But his ideas did not receive a positive response in Haryana and elsewhere. Some senior politicians, on the other hand, said that these *khap*s had been part of the social system for long and cannot be banned. Further, it was said that 'people have faith in them'.[29] As a matter of fact, no powerful politician from the state would like to say anything against the *khap* panchayats in the existing situation. Recently, when the district magistrate of Bijnor (UP) took the unprecedented step of actually banning the caste panchayats and declaring them illegal, his counterparts in other districts did not follow suit. The Bijnore magistrate's 'logic was that caste panchayats were exceeding their brief and taking the law into their hands. The others have, however, steered clear because of public support these panchayats apparently enjoy'.[30] The *khap* leaders believe that disputes in villages can be better resolved through conventional wisdom and face-to-face interaction rather than by an impersonal judicial system. During the course of discussions with some *khap pradhan*s and other influential Jats, it was found that they were against the system of inter-caste and love marriages. Influential people of the *khap* also held the view that it would have been better had the inheritance rights been confined to sons or male members of the family. This, according to them, would have saved families from factional fights. However, they supported the cause of education for women and their increasing participation in public life. Similarly, they have no clash with the statutory panchayats. In fact, two out of the four *khap pradhan*s, interviewed for this study were also elected as *sarpanch*es of their respective village panchayats.

The *khap* panchayats do not relent on matters relating to *biradari* traditions. Hence, there is no fusion of tradition and modernity. They operate as caste or clan-based systems and articulate paternalism, male-dominance, hierarchy and *status quo*. Recently, some *khap* panchayats issued decrees in matters relating to marriages which were not in conformity with customs and traditions. This can be illustrated by some cases which, among others, also attracted the attention of the press and media.

1. Recently, in Bhiwani district, a man of Maan *gotra* solemnized his son's marriage with a girl belonging to the Bhambhu *gotra*, which made her the maternal niece (*bhanji*) of the Sheorans, a large number of whom lived in the groom's village.[31] The panchayat of the Sheoran *gotra* objected to this match. In fact, on 13 December 2004, it asked the Maan family to break off the engagement. The Maan family, however, went ahead with the wedding which was solemnized on 14 December 2004. This provoked the Sheorans to hold a *chaugama* (four-villages) mahapanchayat – a constituent of the Sheoran *Khap*-84 (Sheoran

chaurasi) – on 22 December 2004, which not only ordered the couple out of the village but also evicted them from all the movable and immovable property of the Maan family. In one of the meetings of the *chaugama*, it was also declared that if any person, including members of the family, continued relations with the couple, he or she would be fined Rs. 1,100.[32] All this clearly shows that the major *khap*s have maintained social control and dominance, and have never allowed the social 'equilibrium' to change.

2. Apart from the above case, in 2004, a man of the Lohan *gotra* decided to marry his daughter to a family of the Kadian *gotra* in Kaithal district. But the Lohans opposed this because around twenty to twenty-five families of the Lohan *gotra* lived in the groom's village. In fact, the Lohans sought termination of the engagement on the plea that in 1978, a Lohan *khap* panchayat had prohibited the members of the community from marrying their girls in those villages in which Lohan families were settled.[33] Some members of the *khap* maintained that they would not marry their daughter in a village where even two families of Lohans resided. Since the dominant Kadians in the bridegroom's village did not oppose the proposed marriage, the dispute was primarily amongst members of the Lohan community.[34] However, since the Lohan *khap* refused to consent to an engagement of a Lohan girl with a Kadian boy, the ego of the dominant Kadians was hurt. This resulted in a boycott of the Lohans by the Kadians in the village. The other eighteen castes in the village soon followed suit. This spelt trouble for the Lohans as their shops, STD booths-cum-photography shops, etc., were deserted. Even labourers reportedly refused to harvest their paddy crop. While justifying the social boycott of Lohans, an elderly Kadian remarked: 'Had Lohans' opposition to the match been allowed to be enforced, it would have meant that girls from any caste could not marry boys of this village'.[35] Further, he emphasized that they should have followed the decision taken by the *sarva-jatiya* panchayat that the Lohans of this village would not interfere in the affairs of the two families.[36] However, the Lohans maintained that the Kadians had been able to impose a social boycott because they commanded dominance in the village, so

much so, a meeting of the *sarva-jatiya* panchayat of the groom's village and representatives of the Lohan *khap* to resolve the imbroglio also ended in a deadlock on 2 November 2004. If the *sarva-jatiya* panchayat insisted that the Lohans first withdraw their objection to the proposed marriage, the Lohans demanded that the *sarva-jatiya* panchayat end the boycott of their *gotra* in the village.[37] The dominant Kadians even walked out of the meeting, held in their own village. This was taken as an insult to the Lohans. Consequently, the Lohan *khap* mahapanchayat of seventeen villages, in its meeting held on 23 November 2004, asked the girl's father, a Lohan, to cancel the proposed marriage of his daughter. However, he refused to do so. He said, that if the *khap* panchayat had objections to the marriage of his daughter in the bridegroom's village, he would organize the marriage ceremony in the city as the groom's family had a house there too.

3. Sometimes the diktats of one or more *khaps* have encouraged other *khaps* even in distant areas to impose similar restrictions on their constituents. For example, on 10 October 2004, the Rathee *khap* annulled the eighteen-month-old marriage of a couple in Jhajjar district. The *khaps* of three villages asked the couple to dissolve their marriage and live as siblings. When the father of the girl said that he belonged to the Hooda *gotra*, not the Rathee *gotra*, the *khap* panchayat on 14 October 2004 reportedly asked him to produce documentary evidence of his Hooda origins.[38] In a meeting of the Rathee *khap* held on 28 October 2004, he convinced the members that he belonged to the Hooda *gotra*, upon which the *khap* accepted the marital status of the couple. The *pradhan* of the *khap* announced that no one would oppose the girl's return to her in-laws' house. Though the *pradhan* assured the couple and the family of their safety, the superintendent of police said that they would be provided police protection for 'as long as necessary'.[39] The state had to intervene as the All India Democratic Women's Association (AIDWA) approached the National Human Rights Commission (NHRC). The Haryana branch of Peoples Union for Civil Liberties (PUCL) also filed a Public Interest Litigation (PIL) in the Punjab and Haryana High Court. The court restrained the

khap panchayat from interfering in the marital life of the couple. The high court bench also directed the authorities to ensure that no one could coerce the couple to change the status of their marriage. Moreover, the NHRC even directed the Haryana government to submit a report on the case within a week. This apart, various other associations like the Janwadi Mahila Samiti, Samajik Nyaya Manch, Sampuran Kranti Manch, etc., also put pressure on the administration and related bodies. The girl, relieved at the decision of the *khap* panchayat, thanked the media, judiciary, social and women's organizations and members of her family for their support. The involvement of these various civil society groups had a positive impact on the situation.

4. As recently as 19 January 2006, the Sheoran-25 panchayat of the larger Sheoran-84 *khap* panchayat expelled two families belonging to two different villages of Bhiwani district for marrying their children despite the panchayat's objections. The panchayat's version was that, since both villages are part of the Sheoran-25 *kanni*, the marriage could not be accorded social sanction as per the *bhaichara* norms. The brides belonged to the dominant Sheoran *gotra* and the bridegrooms to a Gill family of another village of the district. Since both villages are part of the same *kanni*, such marriages are considered objectionable as per a resolution of the Sheoran-84 *khap* panchayat. This resolution prohibits matrimonial alliances between families in villages falling in a particular *kanni*.[40] The presence of some Sheoran families in the grooms' village was another irritant for the panchayat, which insisted that as per tradition girls of Sheoran *gotra* could not marry boys of Gill *gotra*. The Sheoran-25 panchayat thus ordered the two families to leave their villages within fifteen days, besides imposing a token fine of 1 *dhela*. The panchayat took this decision despite the fact that the high court had recently asked the home secretary of Haryana to file an affidavit specifying the government's stand on the *khap* panchayats in the state. The panchayat also ordered a social boycott of the two families, saying that any family maintaining any kind of relations with them would also meet the same fate.[41] Further, it ordered that the respective villages would be responsible for the implementation of the *khap's* decision. Surprisingly, the panchayat of

the grooms' village, on 21 January 2006, refused to abide by the *khap*'s decision. In fact, it accorded social sanction to the marriage and resolved not to accept the Sheoran-25 panchayat's decision to expel the grooms' family from their village. This apart, the *khap*'s decision was termed as one-sided and irresponsible. Further, it was declared that if necessary, the panchayat would approach the high court.[42] This was soon followed by a PIL filed in the high court by the PUCL through its advocate and the fathers of the brides and bridegrooms. The petition sought the registration of a criminal case against the office-bearers of the *khap* for issuing unconstitutional diktats.[43] The high court directed the deputy commissioner and the superintendent of police (Bhiwani) to ensure that no harm came to the life and liberty of the two newly married couples and their family members. In addition, the court directed the home secretary, Haryana, to file a detailed report within four weeks regarding the controversy.[44] On 27 January 2006, members of the Jana Sangharsh Samiti also protested against the *khap*'s decision and threatened to launch an agitation if action was not taken against the *khap* leaders. However, the major political parties in the state as usual remained silent on the issue. Anyway, the dissenters and the aggrieved moved the court against the panchayat's verdict. Incidentally, earlier in two such cases, the court's intervention gave considerable relief to the aggrieved families, 'But in neither case could the Court intervene to set aside the social boycott of the families.'[45]

In brief, the foregoing discussion shows that in spite of a great deal of churning, especially after Independence, the traditional authority structures of caste, clan and kinship still dominate the social ethos and command considerable influence in the countryside. Caste leaders extol the virtues of established customs and resist the pressures unleashed by the forces of modernization and change. Caste panchayats, as a mechanism of social control and dominance, emphasize the individual's sense of social belonging. The structuring of society along universalistic principles and in accordance with the process of modernization, particularly in the social sphere, have hardly impressed them. Recently, a powerful *sarva-khap* mahapanchayat on 19 December 2004 even decided to ban love marriages. To resist change, tough measures like the annulment of marriages or engagements, ostracization, ban on love marriages, etc., have been enforced.

However, of late, caste panchayats have started losing out to changing times[46] due to a growing awareness brought about by education, press and the electronic media, etc. Civil liberty groups, the feminist movement, judicial activism and human rights organizations have also played an important role. Enlightened people have started opposing *khap* diktats. Some families of politicians and bureaucrats in Haryana have also entered into inter-caste marriages. Similarly affected couples have started approaching the judiciary and the Human Rights Commission for redressal of their grievances. The scenario is thus changing. Affected couples and their families, who used to earlier accept the verdicts of *khap*s because of community pressures and expensive court proceedings, can now be helped by a number of organizations. Moreover, there is a greater assertion of the right to choice that cannot be checked by antiquated criteria. Kinship-based organizations, therefore, need to come to grips with the reality that is manifesting itself through the fast pace of socio-economic and political change in the countryside. Certain other critical matters, like the falling sex ratio and female foeticide, subordination of women, ecological imbalances, liquor menace, atrocities on weaker sections, etc., need to be given more attention so as to facilitate proper development in the fast-growing state of Haryana.

NOTES

1. D.L. Seth, 'Caste and Class: Social Reality in Political Representation', in *Caste and Democratic Politics in India*, ed. Ghanshyam Shah, Delhi: Permanent Black, 2002, pp. 214–15.
2. K.L. Sharma, ed., *Caste and Class in India*, Jaipur: Rawat Publications, 1994, p. 5.
3. Hukam Singh, 'Jat', in *People of India – Haryana*, vol. XXIII, ed. K.S. Singh, M.L. Sharma and A.K. Bhatia, New Delhi: ASI and Manohar, 1994, p. 241.
4. Ch. Albel Singh, *Bhirahani to Benain: Benain Khap Ka Itihas*, Jind, 1985, p. 13.

5. Pradeep Kasni, '*Khap* Panchayats Staging a Comeback', *The Tribune*, 9 May 2003.
6. D.R. Chaudhry, 'Khap Panchayats: Out of Tune with the Times', *The Tribune*, 28 January 2006.
7. Dharam Pal S. Mor, 'Signs of Tribal Culture', *The Tribune*, 9 May 2003.
8. M.C. Pradhan, *The Political System of the Jats of Northern India*, London: Oxford University Press, 1966, p. 1.
9. Ibid., p. 115.
10. Hukam Singh, 'Jat', p. 241.
11. For a detailed analysis of *khap* panchayats see, K.S. Sangwan, 'The Rural Elite and Multi-village Panchayat in Haryana: The Case of Chaubisi in District Rohtak', Chandigarh: Panjab University, Ph.D. thesis, 1986, p. 262.
12. Ibid. p. 27.
13. Pradhan, *Political System of the Jats*, p. 134.
14. Sangwan, 'The Rural Elite and Multi-village Panchayat in Haryana', p. 203.
15. Kum Kum Chadha, 'Caste Beyond the Law', *The Hindustan Times*, Chandigarh, 12 October 2005.
16. Pradhan, *Political System of the Jats*, p. 183.
17. Dipankar Gupta, *Rivalry and Brotherhood: Politics in the Life of Farmers in Northern India*, New Delhi: Oxford University Press, 1997, p. 8.
18. Kum Kum Chadha, 'Law is an Ass for this Panchayat', *The Hindustan Times*, Chandigarh, 8 August 2005.
19. Gupta, *Rivalry and Brotherhood*, p. 89.
20. Ibid., p. 158.
21. Pradhan, *Political System of the Jats*, pp. 108–9.
22. Gupta, *Rivalry and Brotherhood*, p. 101.
23. Pradhan, *Political System of the Jats*, p. 98.
24. Sangwan, 'The Rural Elite and Multi-village Panchayat in Haryana', p. 251.
25. Raman Mohan, 'No Longer Relevant', *The Tribune*, Chandigarh, 17 April 2003.
26. Shamim Sharma, 'Social Requirement: Are Khap Panchayats Necessary', *The Tribune*, Chandigarh, 17 April 2003.
27. Narender Singh Akela, 'Khaapon ke Faisle per Hogi Nazar', *Dainik Bhaskar*, Chandigarh, January 2005.
28. *The Hindustan Times*, Chandigarh, 23 August 2005.
29. Ibid., 24 August 2005.
30. Chadha, 'Caste Beyond the Law'.
31. *The Hindustan Times*, Chandigarh, 23 December 2004.

32. Shiv Sharma, 'Gotra Trouble: Couple Asked to Leave Village', *The Hindustan Times*, Chandigarh, 7 February 2005.
33. Sumit Dhawan, 'Lohan Khaap Proposes Talks, Reforms', *The Tribune*, Chandigarh, 1 November 2004.
34. Devendra Uppal, 'Lohans to Meet Kadiyans to End Jakholi Boycott', *The Hindustan Times*, Chandigarh, 2 November 2004.
35. Surendra Miglani, 'Lohans Turn to Govt. to Fight Khaap Diktat', *The Hindustan Times*, Chandigarh, 27 October 2004.
36. Satish Sethi, 'Uneasy Calm at Jakholi Village', *The Tribune*, Chandigarh, 27 October 2004.
37. Surendra Miglani, 'Meet on Jakholi Gotra Row Ends in Deadlock', *The Hindustan Times*, Chandigarh, 3 November 2004.
38. Raman Mohan, 'Villagers to Validate Her Marriage', *The Tribune*, Chandigarh, 29 October 2004.
39. *The Hindustan Times*, Chandigarh, 29 October 2004.
40. Raman Mohan, 'Khap Panchayat at it Again', *The Tribune*, Chandigarh, 20 January 2006.
41. Ibid.
42. See Raman Mohan, 'Couples Returned to Village', *The Tribune*, Chandigarh, 22 January 2006.
43. *The Tribune*, Chandigarh, 25 January 2006.
44. Ibid., 26 January 2006.
45. See Prem Chowdhry, 'Caste Panchayats and the Policing of Marriage in Haryana: Enforcing Kinship and Territorial Exogamy', in *Caste in Question: Identity or Hierarchy*, ed. Dipankar Gupta, New Delhi: Sage, 2004, pp. 32–4.
46. Navneet Sharma, 'Gotra Khaaps Losing Out to Times, Awareness', *The Hindustan Times*, Chandigarh, 27 October 2004.

CHATPER 16

Literacy and Social Transformation in North-West India

SWARNJIT MEHTA AND SIMRIT KAHLON

PROBLEMATIZING THE ISSUE

The hypothesis for exploring the inter-linkages between literacy and social transformation is that there are dialectical – rather than linear/cause-effect – relationships between the two. The underlying logic is that literacy is both an indicator as well as one of the most important instruments in the process of social transformation. The present study follows the internationally accepted definition of literacy, viz., the ability to read or write a simple postcard with understanding. As for social transformation, the dictionary meaning of the term is followed, which emphasizes a complete change in the form, appearance or character of society. It encompasses social change and social development. Literacy levels, and inequities therein, are impacted by the process of social and economic transformation. At the same time these also engineer, encourage and are instrumental in shaping the dynamics of social transformation. The dialectical relationships underscore that neither literacy nor social transformation is monocausal. They mutually reinforce each other and are interdependent. One cannot happen without the other.

Global experience, development levels notwithstanding, shows that social transformations and literacy transitions (from total illiteracy to universal literacy) have gone hand in hand. One cannot envisage a universally literate society without social development and vice versa. Of course, once the illiteracy barrier is broken and a society is initiated into the process of transformation, it follows a path towards progressively higher and varied levels of education.

A society develops, or is transformed as a whole, through its various constituents: the rural and the urban; the males and the females; caste-, class-, or religion-based groups. Responses to policy initiatives and other inputs are differentiated. Equally uneven are the outcomes, which include, among others, improvements in literacy levels and greater equity across gender, regions and other differentiations.

OPERATIONALIZING AND CONTEXTUALIZING THE PROBLEM

To examine the propositions presented in this chapter the three states constituting the north-west region have been selected. These states largely coincide with the boundaries of undivided Punjab in 1947. One part of Punjab, on transfer to Pakistan, became the Punjab province. In a way the whole of this region shared a common history, economy, society and polity. Indian Punjab was reorganized into the three states in 1966 (Himachal Pradesh was a union territory to begin with but attained statehood in 1971). The chapter traces the trajectory of the progress of literacy in the three states for a period spanning over four decades (1961 to 2001). These trends in literacy, when placed against the all-India experience for the same period, acquaint one with the experience of the individual states. Education of females in particular, in the process of social transformation, has been brought under special focus. The chapter also traces the trends in rural-urban, male-female literacy rates to focus sharply on the question of inequities. Similarly, trends in the progress of literacy among the Scheduled Castes and Scheduled Tribes (applicable only in the case of Himachal Pradesh) assume importance in understanding the overall literacy scenario. The literacy trajectories have been placed in the context of state policy and spending on education, with the broad assumption that these reflect the priority accorded to education in the planning and allocation of resources for improving the human capital that is crucial in the process of social transformation. Without working out statistical correlations, an attempt has been made here to address the issues more in the qualitative mode.

BROAD TRENDS IN LITERACY LEVELS IN THE NORTH-WEST REGION

With nearly one half (55.18 per cent) of the total population of India as literate in 2001, the progress since 1961 (24 per cent) has by no means been tardy. It was indeed slow to begin with (5.46 per cent points) during 1961–71; it improved by 6.77 in the subsequent decade of 1971–81; there was a slight dip to 6.61 in 1981–91, only to pick up during 1991–2001 by 12.24 percentage points (Table 16.1). In less than half a century the overall literacy rate of India's population more than doubled, but despite this nearly half the population remains illiterate.

Of the three states under review Punjab had a somewhat better start with 26.74 per cent of its population recorded as literate in 1961 which improved by 6.93 percentage points in 1961–71; and by 7.19, 9.53 and 12.18 percentage points during the successive decades. Haryana's literacy rate stood at 19.93 per cent in 1961 and progressively improved by 6.96, 9.25, 9.10 and 12.75 per cent in the successive decades. In the case of HP, a literacy rate of 21.26 in 1961 registered an increase of 10.70 per cent during 1961–71 (higher than both Punjab and Haryana); 10.52 in 1971–81; 11.00 in 1981–91; and 12.82 per cent during 1991–2001. Clearly HP stands out with faster and bigger gains on the literacy front with the literacy rate for the total population increasing more than three lines during this period. HP also improved its all-India ranking out-performing the neighbouring states of Punjab and Haryana (Table 16.2). Particularly notable

TABLE 16.1: PROGRESS IN LITERACY, 1961–2001

Year	India	Punjab	Haryana	Himachal Pradesh
1961–71	5.46	6.93	6.96	10.70
1971–81	6.77	7.19	9.25	10.52
1981–91	6.61	9.53	9.10	11.00
1991–01	12.24	12.18	12.75	12.82

Source: Census of India, 1961, 1971, 1981, 1991, 2001.

TABLE 16.2: LITERACY RATES: THE NORTH-WESTERN REGION

Year	Sex	India	Punjab	Haryana	Himachal Pradesh
1971	Persons	29.46	33.67	26.89	31.96
	Males	39.45	40.38	37.29	43.19
	Females	18.70	25.90	14.89	20.23
1981	Persons	36.23	40.86	36.14	42.48
	Males	46.89	47.16	48.20	53.19
	Females	24.82	33.69	22.27	31.46
1991	Persons	42.84	48.97	45.24	53.48
	Males	52.74	54.91	56.10	62.96
	Females	32.17	42.22	32.72	43.76
2001	Persons	55.18	61.15	57.99	66.30
	Males	63.99	65.69	66.73	73,45
	Females	45.74	55.96	47.84	58.92

Source: Census of India.

has been the progress since 1981. Why? This question will be answered after considering some other dimensions, i.e. gender and other differences in this regard.

PROGRESS OF FEMALE EDUCATION AND TRENDS IN MALE–FEMALE LITERACY RATES AND GENDER GAPS

The social benefits of education in general and of females in particular are all too well known. Several studies have brought out the close relationship between the education of parents and infant mortality. An increase in child immunization rates and a fall in infant mortality rates are associated with education of parents – especially that of mothers. Studies have also brought out the close link between female education and family planning.[1] In the context of social transformation female literacy thus occupies a central position.

For India as a whole, the trends in female literacy have been sketched at length.[2] The path of female literacy has been charted not only for the last four decades but also for different historical periods beginning with the ancient through medieval, colonial and modern.[3]

The 1961 census returned only 16 per cent of females in India as literate. Subsequent decades recorded progressive improvements in this regard (Table 16.3). By 2001, a female literacy rate of 45.7 per cent had been reached. Of the three states of the north-west region, Punjab had a head-start with 17.41 per cent as compared to Haryana (9.21 per cent) and Himachal Pradesh (9.49 per cent). Through 1961–2001, Punjab recorded slower increases and was surpassed by HP in 1991 when the hill state registered a literacy rate of 43.76 per cent for its females compared with 42.22 per cent for females in Punjab. The tempo was maintained and in 2001 it was 58.92 per cent in HP compared with 55.96 per cent in Punjab. The rates have been looking up in Haryana too, though they were invariably lower than those for both Punjab and HP. In order to capture the male-female differences in improvements in literacy rates, male-female literacy ratios were worked out for the purpose of this study which revealed some interesting features.

For every 100 literate males there were 38 literate females in India, a ratio which improved through the decades ending up with 100:72 in 2001 (Table 16.4). The corresponding ratios for Punjab are 100:48 and 100:85; for Haryana 100:31 and 100:71; for HP 100:31 and 100:77. Thus, despite a faster pace of improvement in female literacy in HP the male-female ratio in

TABLE 16.3: PROGRESS OF FEMALE LITERACY

Year	1961	1971	1981	1991	2001
India	16.0	18.7	24.8	32.27	45.7
Punjab	17.4	25.9	33.7	42.2	56.0
Haryana	9.2	14.9	22.3	32.7	47.8
Himachal Pradesh	9.5	20.3	31.5	43.8	58.9

Source: Census of India.

TABLE 16.4. LITERACY: MALE–FEMALE RATIOS

Year	1961	1971	1981	1991	2001
India	100:38	100:48	100:53	100:61	100:72
Punjab	100:48	100:65	100:72	100:76	100:85
Haryana	100:31	100:40	100:42	100:59	100:71
Himachal Pradesh	100:31	100:40	100:46	100:69	100:77

Source: Census of India.

TABLE 16.5: MALE–FEMALE DIFFERENTIALS IN LITERACY, 1961–2001

Year	1961	1971	1981	1991	2001
India	18.00	20.75	20.57	20.57	18.25
Punjab	17.29	14.48	13.47	12.69	9.73
Haryana	20.02	22.40	25.93	23.38	18.89
Himachal Pradesh	22.82	22.91	21.73	19.20	14.53

Source: Census of India.

Punjab is still better though male–female gaps in literacy are a reality for all the three states as well as for India as a whole. However, individual state experiences are quite at variance with the all-India trend wherein the male–female literacy gap was almost as wide in 2001 as it was in 1961 (see Table 16.5). In Punjab the gap has been narrowing over the decades. In Haryana it hovers at around 20 while in HP the gap in the male–female literacy rates is also narrowing, the process having accelerated since the 1980s.

These trends clearly indicate the persistence of literacy differentials by gender, though happily these are becoming less sharp. A frontal attack on illiteracy among females is nevertheless highly desirable.[4]

THE RURAL–URBAN DIVIDE IN LITERACY

Glaring gaps in literacy levels in the rural and urban areas prompted the use of the term 'divide' in this context. At the all-India level, from 1971 awards, the rural and urban areas for the total – as well as the male – population have moved closer, but in the case of females the rural–urban gap is still 'wide' (Table 16.6). This indicates that women in the rural areas still need to be targeted with more serious efforts to improve literacy rates among them so as to enable them to play their role more effectively in the process of social transformation.

As for the constituent states, the rural–urban gap was the widest in HP in 1961 (40.03 per cent), followed by Haryana (30 per cent) with Punjab closely following with 27.9. During 1961–2001, the position changed drastically with HP recording the minimum gap (13.8 per cent), with Haryana and Punjab at

TABLE 16.6:. RURAL–URBAN DIFFERENCE IN LITERACY RATES, 1961–2001

Year	Sex	1961	1971	1981	1991	2001
India	Persons	N.A	28.7	27.7	28.4	21.2
	Males	N.A	27.5	25.0	23.2	15.6
	Females	N.A	29.0	29.9	33.4	26.8
Punjab	Persons	27.9	24.7	20.4	19.3	24.4
	Males	28.0	23.9	18.8	16.5	12.0
	Females	26.2	25.5	22.1	22.3	16.8
Haryana	Persons	30.0	29.3	26.5	23.8	16.0
	Males	31.5	26.5	21.5	17.2	10.4
	Females	27.7	32.2	32.0	31.5	22.0
Himachal Pradesh	Persons	40.0	30.7	27.0	22.3	13.8
	Males	38.0	25.6	22.0	15.1	7.5
	Females	37.8	34.1	30.7	28.5	19.3

Source: Census of India.

16.0 and 24.4 respectively. However, male literacy rates recorded narrow gaps in 2001 for HP (7.5) when compared to Haryana (10.4) and Punjab (12.0). Rural–urban areas are wide apart as far as female literacy is concerned. This applies more to Haryana (22.0), but the distortion exists in Punjab as well (16.8), and even in Himachal Pradesh (19.3).

It emerges from the data that the rural areas still have to cover a long road in order to touch the high point of a totally literate society. Women in the rural areas in particular have to be drawn into the literacy stream on a large scale to enhance their involvement in the transformation process.

It needs examination as to why rural female literacy follows a reverse pattern compared to rural literacy as a whole in the three states of Punjab, Haryana and Himachal Pradesh. Perhaps the higher rural prosperity of Punjab compared to that of Haryana and Himachal Pradesh has something to do with it.

LITERACY AND THE SCHEDULED CASTES AND TRIBES: LEVELS AND TRENDS, 1971–2001

Like women and rural areas, the Scheduled Castes (SC) constitute the disadvantaged sections of society in any region of India. In the north-west region, in all its three states, the SC population recorded literacy rates that were nearly half that of the total population. The gap kept on narrowing over the decades, though the pace varied over decades and for individual states. A comparison of data suggests that the progress has been faster in the case of HP, from 18.8 per cent in 1971, the rate shot up to 70.3 per cent (Table 16.7) in 2001. For Punjab and Haryana the respective figures are 16.1 to 56.2, and 12.6 to 55.4. SC women were the most deprived in this respect in 1971. Literacy rates for them in 1971 in all three states were below 10 per cent. The male-female gaps in literacy among the SC have consistently widened between 1971 to 1991, narrowing during 1991–2001 with female literacy rates picking up faster during that decade. In the case of Punjab the gap has come down from 18.8 to 15.1 per cent, while in the case of Haryana (with a very low literacy rate among the SCs even in 1971 [12.6 per cent only] the gap widened till 1991 with some closure in 1991–2001. In HP the gap widened further till 1991 but showed a reverse trend in 1991–2001. The SCs constitute a sizeable section of the population in the north-west section.

In HP the Scheduled Tribe (ST) population is sizeable, and it recorded a literacy rate of 47.09 per cent in 1991, which was still lower than the corresponding rate for the SCs, i.e. 53.2.

TABLE 16.7: LITERACY LEVELS OF THE SCHEDULED CASTE POPULATION, 1971–2001

Year	Sex	1971	1981	1991	2001
India	Persons	14.6	21.4	37.4	54.7
	Males	23.4	31.1	49.9	66.6
	Females	6.4	10.9	23.8	41.9
Punjab	Persons	16.1	23.9	40.1	56.2
	Males	22.9	31.0	49.8	63.4
	Females	8.2	16.7	31.0	48.3
Haryana	Persons	12.6	20.2	39.2	55.4
	Males	20.9	31.5	52.1	66.9
	Females	3.1	7.1	24.2	42.3
Himachal Pradesh	Persons	18.8	31.5	53.2	70.3
	Males	27.4	41.9	65.0	80.0
	Females	9.7	20.6	41.0	60.4

Source: Census of India.

It emerges that the transformation process has been slow, and among the SCs the literacy levels, despite improvements, are still low. Gender differences in this regard are wide and persisting.

EXPLORING THE DIALECTICAL RELATIONSHIPS BETWEEN LITERACY AND SOCIAL TRANSFORMATION: SOME EXPLANATIONS

As noted earlier:

(i) HP has performed better than Punjab and Haryana on the overall literacy front;
(ii) gender gaps in literacy are narrowing, faster in HP than in the other two states;
(iii) the rural–urban gap is moving closer in all the three states, with the pace being faster for males, and female literacy rates are still showing wider rural–urban gaps; and
(iv) SCs (in the case the of Himachal Pradesh, STs as well) are still way behind the rest on the literacy scale.

We restate our proposition that literacy trends simultaneously reflect the processes of social transformation, which are themselves either strengthened or weakened by these trends.[5] Additionally, inputs having a bearing on literacy trends – which include government and private spending on education through the provision of facilities and facilitating access to them through the education policy and a commitment to create a literate, educated and equitous society – play a crucial role in sustaining complex relationships.[6]

What are the inputs for the spread of literacy and education? Immediately, one thinks of public spending on the opening and maintenance of educational institutions, particularly primary schools, on the one hand, and a strong politico-social commitment (not just on paper but a clear manifestation of it) to education as an important instrument of empowerment on the other.

Another look at the literacy levels and trends in the three states against the parameters of public spending, and policies and strategies for education is necessary. According to the *National Human Development Report*, Planning Commission,

2000, Punjab, Haryana and Himachal Pradesh spent 2.87, 2.57 and 7.08 per cent, respectively, of Gross State Domestic Product on education. Expenditure on education within the state budget does reflect the priority accorded to this catalyst of social change. Both Punjab and Haryana spend much less on education. For Punjab, a detailed multilevel study noted significant relationships between budget and enrolment and budget and scholastic achievement, among other findings (IDC 2003).[7] Himachal Pradesh is way ahead of both Punjab and Haryana in age-specific enrolment ratios,[8] and much better, though not ideal, teacher–pupil ratios at primary level education.[9] The situation in Punjab is pathetic,[10] where a very thin slice of the state budget is allocated for education. There are schools without teachers and many single teacher schools without even the basic facilities (35,000 vacancies of schoolteachers are reported).[11] Comparable figures for Haryana are not available.[12] So even a state with a high per capita income cannot become more literate if it does not spend adequately on education. Sustained efforts to expand both the quantity and quality of schooling facilities yield results in the long run. HP started with a very low crude literacy rate of 21 per cent for males and 9 per cent for females in 1961. Within two decades, the literacy rates in the 10–14 age group shot up to 95 per cent for males and 87 per cent for females, and that too in the rural areas. For urban areas the rates increased to 96 per cent and 97 per cent for males and females respectively.[13] Much better school attendance in HP in the age group of 10–14 was revealed in the NSS data.[14] These comments on HP find support in other studies.[15]

The issue of public policy on education and the strategy to achieve certain goals – including bridging of gender gaps and promoting education of women – are interconnected. School enrolments are linked with the success or failure of government initiatives, such as the District Primary Education Programme (DPEP), Midday Meals, Total Literacy Campaign (TLC) and the like. These find a reflection in the trends in literacy, especially among females, SCs and STs and in the rural areas. More serious focus on these deprived groups in the implementation of various programmes seems to have had a positive fallout. This needs to be sustained in HP, and the other two states need to learn some lessons from it. Social and political mass movements with a commitment to creating an educated society need to pursue their agenda in this direction. Something can be learnt from the Latin American experience too.[16]

NOTES

1. A 1980 study revealed that fertility among educated females (primary level) was 4.5 per cent and for those without any education, was 5.1 per cent. As education levels increase to upper primary and secondary levels, the fertility rate declined: 4.0; 3.1; 2.2 respectively. Ashish Bose, 'Demographic Zones and Sub-Zones of India: Policy Implications', *Geographical Review of India*, vol. 54 (1), 1992, pp. 1–16, see p. 6.
2. Malini Karkal, 'Progress in Literacy in India: A Statistical Analysis', *Indian Journal of Social Work*, vol. 52 (2), 1991.
3. Nina Singh, 'Female Literacy in India: The Emerging Trends', *Population Geography*, vol. 20, 1988, pp. 23–36, Table I.
4. Very perceptive messages aired in the media help in breaking the barrier. Recent announcements regarding scholarships to girl students by the CBSE are a case in point.
5. V.R. Ramachandran, 'Kerala's Development Achievements', in *Indian Development: Selected Regional Perspectives*, J. Dreze and Amartya Sen, Oxford and New Delhi: Oxford University Press, 1996.
6. Ibid. The dialectical relationship between educational progress and social change has been highlighted in a case study of Kerala. Ramachandran describes how education helps in overcoming the traditionally deep-rooted inequalities of caste, class, and gender, and how the removal of these inequalities contributes positively to the spread of education.
7. 'Cost Benefit Analysis of Primary Education', project sponsored by the department of Planning, Punjab: Institute for Development and Communication, Mimeographed, 2003.
8. *Himachal Pradesh Development Report*, 2005, Table 7.10.
9. Ibid., Table 7.13.
10. Thousands of teaching posts in Punjab schools in rural areas are lying vacant. It is not that qualified teachers are not available, but that political will is lacking.
11. *Fifth All-India Educational Survey*, New Delhi: National Council for Educational Research and Training, 2 vols., 1992, p. 895.
12. Haryana's chief minister has repeatedly announced that his government is serious about education and will initiate the process of recruitment of schoolteachers thus admitting to a lacuma on this account.

13. Karkal, 'Progress in Literacy in India'.
14. Pravin Visaria, A. Gumber and L. Visaria, 'Literacy and Primary Education in India, 1980–81 to 1991', *Journal of Educational Planning and Administration*, vol. 7 (1), 1993.
15. P.D. Bhardwaj, 'Literacy in Himachal Pradesh', *Population Geography*, vol. 21, 1999, pp. 31–42.
16. David Archer and Patrick Costello, *Literacy and Power: The Latin American Battleground*, London: Earthscan Publications, 1990.

CHAPTER 17

Ethnography of Gender, Property and Reform in Himachal Pradesh*

RAJ MOHINI SETHI

Indigenous folk cultural practices provide a repertoire of socially constructed, historically situated frames of production and interpretation. An ethnographic analysis of customary cultural practices can help in identifying common threads between gender, property and reform within, and across, religious groupings. It would also help to enrich the existing repertoire of knowledge and provide a critical evaluation of the local in relation to the other, that is, the pan-Indian tradition. Further, local traditions with distinct historical and cultural background which have for long been associated with certain geographical regions are today in the process of being replaced, or juxtaposed against the pan-Indian cultural practices. Such interactions affect not only the shape of existing frames and meanings generated through these processes, but also give rise to new forms which depict several shades of global and local identities. Within this framework, the main concern of this chapter is to focus on the ethno-historical and cultural reality of Himachal Pradesh, and lay bare the intricate relationship between gender, property and reform. While doing so, it attempts to render visible the historical and institutional structures governing the representative spaces of women and men within different gender and property regimes.

* This is a revised version of the essay originally written for the Centre of Rural Studies, Lal Bahadur Shastri National Academy of Administration, Mussourie.

The present study involved collection and analysis of secondary data such as documentary evidence consisting of digests, documents, literary, legal and sociological texts and travelogues referring to the past of existing customary practices guiding women's and men's access to and control over property and other resources. Information gathered from these sources was substituted with personal observations and information gathered from different sections of the community. All these put together form the basis of this study. Most ethnographies combine elements of etic and emic analyses, but the practicalities of data collection in this study gave precedence to the emic although the etic perspective was not totally ignored.

SOCIAL DEVELOPMENT PROFILE

The state of Himachal Pradesh came into being on 15 April 1948 through the integration of thirty princely Punjab Hill States, with other areas being merged later. The state was accorded full statehood in 1971. The state's land use patterns reflect the social, cultural and economic development of the society. Agriculture and related activities such as horticulture and floriculture represent the main occupations of the people of Himachal Pradesh. Around 64.4 per cent of the total holdings of the state are of marginal farmers who owned less than one hectare covering 23 per cent of the total area in 1995–6.[1] If the small and marginal farmers owning one or two hectares of land are added to this proportion then the proportion of holdings comes to 84.5 per cent. When all categories of holdings are taken into consideration, the average size of the holdings in the state comes to 1.2 hectares.[2]

Analysis of district-wise land-use patterns reveals that the districts with a large spatial expanse, such as those of Lahul & Spiti, which are snowbound throughout the year are sparsely populated and cover around 25 per cent of the state's area. Low-lying districts such as Hamirpur, Bilaspur, Una and Solan have a relatively much smaller spatial expanse but are heavily populated. These districts together account for, only 10 per cent of the state's geographical area but each individually has an area of less than 5 per cent. The middle range districts of the state have a spatial expanse ranging between 5 and 12 per cent of the total geographical area.[3]

The state of Himachal Pradesh, like the other states of India, represents a multicultural social organization consisting of a wide range of religious and ethnic groups. The majority of the population of the state is comprised of Hindus. The state also has a fairly large population of Sikhs, Buddhists and Muslims; apart from a fair sprinkling of Christians. Its share of STs is 4.22 per cent of the total population of the state. The districts of Chamba, Kinnaur, Lahul & Spiti, Kullu and Mandi have high proportions of STs residing in them. Around 25.34 per cent of the total population of the state consists of the SCs.

The gender profile of Himachal Pradesh looks very different from many other states of India. Its performance on the gender-related development index (GDI) has a much better ranking of 94th in a group of 130 countries and in relation to other states of India. Even the economically advanced states of Punjab and Haryana have lower ranks. The state of Himachal Pradesh also shows the lowest differential of 4.7 per cent in the values of Human Development Index (HDI) and Gender Development Index (GDI), while the corresponding differentials for the states of Punjab and Haryana are very high, that is, 19.8 for Punjab and 24.3 for Haryana. A look at a few individual development indices shows that the overall performance of the state of Himachal Pradesh has been quite encouraging. The sex ratio of the state is much higher. It stood at 970 females to 1,000 males in 2001 although it was 976 in 1991. The sex ratios of Punjab and Haryana are 874 and 861 respectively. The female literacy rate of Himachal Pradesh is 68.08 per cent which again is much higher than that of the adjoining states of Haryana and Punjab which is 56.31 and 63.55 per cent respectively. The state work participation rates are very high compared to the country as a whole. In 2001, women constituted 46.47 per cent of the total working population. Similarly, Himachal's share of the earned income for women is 0.375 while that of men is 0.625; and the state's economically active population is 0.401 per cent women and 0.599 per cent men.[4] The proportions of earned income and economically active population of women in Himachal Pradesh are much higher than those of Punjab and Haryana. The share of earned income of men in Haryana is 0.930 and of women 0.070. These proportions for the state of Punjab are 0.941 for men and 0.050 for women. Again, the share of economically active women in Haryana is only 0.161 against 0.839 per cent men, while the corresponding figures for Punjab are 0.067 for women and 0.933 for men. However, Himachal Pradesh has a much lower GDP as compared to the other two states. In 1992, the GDP of Himachal Pradesh was Rs. 1,180 crore while that of Haryana and Punjab was Rs. 1,915 crore and Rs. 2,124 crore respectively. The per capita income of the people of Himachal Pradesh was Rs. 12,692 in 1998–9 while that of Haryana and Punjab was Rs. 19,773 and Rs. 21,863 respectively.

The above data clearly shows that the gender profile of Himachal Pradesh is far better than that of Haryana and Punjab, even though the state is economically poorer than the other two states. On the face of it, it appears that the gender question is not as acute in Himachal Pradesh as it is in other states of India. It would therefore be worthwhile to investigate how gender relations have shaped themselves around the issues of ownership of property and its control, and find out how far the different constructions of the 'feminine' and 'masculine' help in the resolution of issues related to gender equity.

ETHNO-HISTORY AND CULTURAL REALITY

Prior to 1948, the state of Himachal Pradesh was part of the area called Punjab Hill States which was formed through the amalgamation of around thirty princely states. All these states came within the ambit of the Punjab Customary Law. Each of these states had its own custom with regard to succession, inheritance, ownership and control of land. The Punjab Laws Act, 1872 specifically states that the province was to be guided by custom in matters of succession, special property of females, betrothal, marriage, divorce, dower, adoption, guardianship, minority, family relations, wills, legacies and partitions. The primary rule of decision in all these matters was custom. Hindu and Muslim laws were applicable only where no customary law applied.[5] It is evident from the above that customary practices differed between, and within, the different princely states. The prominent customary practices of these hill states with regard to gender and property are described below.

Throughout the Shimla Hills, Kangra, Chamba, Kullu, Sirmaur and Lahul & Spiti areas of Himachal Pradesh polygamy, monogamy and polyandry were a widespread phenomenon. The practice of polygamy was common among the princely households and among the other ruling elites. However, the general rule was that of monogamy, especially among the non-landed households. Polyandry prevailed in large parts of Kullu, Saraj, Bashahr, Shimla Hills, Sirmaur, Kinnaur, Lahul & Spiti. The practice of polyandry was a recognized institution and was widespread. Two forms of polyandrous marriages were practised in these areas: one, where the joint husbands were brothers; and second where they were unrelated. The former was a more common practice among the Kanets who are primarily agriculturists, as well as among some categories of Brahmins and Rajputs. All the lower social classes also followed the custom. In the other form of polyandry, two men who were unrelated became *dharma bhai* (brothers by religion) and shared a wife. In these marriages, the children were not admitted into the brotherhood of the father. Cousins or half-brothers usually entered into this form of marriage. However, the more common pattern was the sharing of the joint wife by uterine brothers (from the same mother).[6]

The explanation given by the practitioners of polyandry was that the day-to-day life in the region is difficult, even for sustaining the existing population because of the acute scarcity of cultivable land within a harsh geo-physical environment, therefore, keeping population growth rate under control was a challenge which was met through this practice. Moreover, it was believed that a household of brothers could derive the maximum benefit from their engagement in different sources of livelihood such as cultivation of joint land, cattle-rearing, trade and commerce. In relation to gender the common belief was that it was easier for brothers to live together than for sisters-in-law. In the princely states the practice of polyandry was encouraged by the rulers who exacted penalties if the land-holdings were partitioned.[7] A polyandrous marriage 'enabled a balance to be struck between a family's need for labour in the fields and the danger of producing more children than what the fields could support'.[8] On the face of it, polyandry appeared as the most striking feature of traditional family life, but in essence, it was based on a monomarital principle where only one marriage per household was allowed in one generation. Actual practice, however, varied from strict adherence to the principle in Kinnaur, Lahul & Spiti. Custom also differed with regard to the conferment of paternity in polyandrous marriages. Usually all the husbands were recognized as fathers of each child. The eldest father was the *teg babach* (elder father) and the others were *gato babach* (younger fathers). If for any reason, the joint family broke up, the wife named the fathers of her children. Among the lower castes, a draw of lots was sometimes resorted to for the allotment of children, if one of the brothers wanted a partition of the family property because he wanted to marry another woman. In some areas, the woman was considered as the wife of the eldest brother and all the children were considered to be his children.

The division of property and inheritance among the polyandrous households gave preference to the male line and in no way indicated any closeness to the matriarchal or matrilineal system. The essential feature of the system is the patriarchal form of inheritance based on the monomarital principle. The most commonly accepted rule of inheritance was where three or four brothers shared one wife, the eldest brother was deemed the father of the first-born son, the second brother the father of the next born and so on. The rule of collateral inheritance in Kullu district was guided by the rule of *pagvand*, that is, all legitimate sons of a father got equal shares without reference to the number of sons born. Among the Kanets of Himachal Pradesh and other lower castes, custom treated all sons as legitimate even where a formal marriage ceremony had not been enacted. Even a *pichlag*, or a posthumous son born to a widow in the house of the second husband, was considered the son of the second husband and would inherit in the same manner as other sons. The polygamous households in the higher reaches of the old Kangra district determined inheritance and succession on the basis of the rule of *jathong* and *kanchong*. *Jathong* refers to the rights of the eldest and *kanchong* to the rights of the youngest.

The monogamous households of Lahul & Spiti were governed by the rule of primogeniture in matters of inheritance.[9]

In Lahul, there are three categories of Lahulis. These are Buddhists, Hindus, and a social category which professes both Budhhism and Hinduism. Almost all the Hindus migrated from Kangra, Kullu and Chamba districts around two centuries ago. Monogamy was the general rule in this region. However, polygamy was not quite uncommon among the rich landowning households. Polyandry was also a recognized institution and widely practised by the landowning households. Among the Thakur households, the rule of primogeniture in inheritance was strictly observed, especially among the Buddhists. As long as the younger brothers lived with the elder brother they had the right to maintenance and were given the title of 'little Thakurs', but if they decided to separate and set up their own establishments they were entitled to a small piece of land known as the younger son's land (*dotoenzing*) on which they had to sustain themselves. The descendants of the younger sons were supposed to perform services for or pay rent to the Thakur (the eldest son and head of the household). Among small landholders, all sons were entitled to equal shares of their father's holding but although the division of the family property took place, they continued to live together with wife, land, house and cattle in common. In some parts of Lahaul such as Pattan, and the valley of Chandra-Bhaga, where there was a sizeable section of the Hindu population and where landholdings were relatively larger and also where the productivity of the land was higher, quite a large number of brothers married separate wives and resorted to the division of the family house and land according to Hindu law.[10]

In Spiti as well, the rule of primogeniture applied to inheritance. Soon after marriage, the eldest son succeeded to the family estate and the ancestral dwelling unit or the big house known as *khang-chhen,* during the lifetime of his father. On the son's succession, the father retired to a smaller dwelling unit with a small plot of land for his maintenance. He thereafter absolved himself of the family estate and its responsibilities. The younger sons and brothers of the *khang-chheng-pa* (father) were sent to Buddhist monasteries in their childhood where they spent the rest of their lives. The larger holding was transferred in the same shape and size from one eldest son to another. If the *khang-chheng-pa* failed to beget a child, one of his brothers would abandon the monastery and take the eldest brother's place in the family. These households were based on the monomarital principle, i.e. only one marriage per household in each generation. The younger sons of the landholding households had to seek refuge in the monastery. Only the second son was entitled to become a Lama (*da-ching*). The younger ones were given a subsistence allowance by the elder brother in return for which they provided their services for his household. The *Gazetteer of the Kangra District* also mentions that monogamy was the rule in Spiti and a second wife was brought home only under exceptional circumstances.[11] Polyandry was common among the lower social classes known as *dutalpa*s and *buzhan*s, who were wage workers with very small landholdings, sometimes only a small dwelling unit. They were believed to be the descendants of monks of the Pin monastery. The younger sons in these households had to fend for themselves.

WIDOWS' RIGHT TO INHERITANCE

The right to inheritance of ancestral property also extended to the widow of the deceased agnate without sons. The widow had the usual life-interest in the share of the estate that would have fallen to her husband. This life interest in the estate of her husband gave the wife more space within an overall agnatic principle of inheritance. The widow's right to life tenure originated in her right to maintenance. In due course of time, it became her right to the enjoyment of the whole estate. She derived this right from her marriage, as her husband's representative. A widow's right to inherit the estate of her husband for her lifetime among the upper castes of Kangra district was subject to her remaining chaste, and the fear of forfeiture of their property prevented widows from marrying again. In Kullu and other areas where *jhanjrara* marriages were prevalent, the widow could not be deprived of her life tenure in her late husband's estate for not remaining chaste as long as she lived in the deceased husband's homestead. In Lahaul and Spiti, a widow could remarry if the brother-in-law did not wish to leave the monastery and live with her. By remarrying she would not forfeit her interest in the estate as long as she resided on it and looked after it. The *karewa* form of widow remarriage was recognized by almost all castes in the upper hills, especially the Kanets, Brahmins and Rajputs and all other low castes. No special ceremony existed for these marriages. In these marriages, the second husband was most commonly the younger brother of the first. The Kanets also allowed the widow to marry her late husband's elder brother. If the second husband was a stranger he paid some *reet* (bride price) amount to the first husband's family, popularly known as *makhtal*. On remarriage, a widow would forfeit all her rights to the first husband's property which belonged to his sons whether by her or by other wives. In such cases, her children by the first husband were supported by his brothers.[12]

Divorce and remarriage were common practices in Shimla, Sirmaur and Kangra Hill areas. A woman would agree to stay with her husband only as long as things were agreeable, and the slightest provocation would induce her to leave him. She would then go back to her parents and return the *reet* (bride price) amount to her husband. Thereafter, she was free to marry another man. If the husband or his relatives refused to accept the *reet* amount, the woman would then behave in such a manner that the husband was forced to divorce her.[13] In *karewa* or *reet* marriages, a child born in the new husband's house, succeeded to his property if he was an heir. Contrarily, if the wife left her husband and returned to her father's house and gave birth to a child, the child was said to be the husband's if he had not already taken back the *reet* amount from her. The *reet* system of divorce, which was applicable to *jhanjrara* or *gaadar* marriages, was prevalent in these areas. The term *reet* was applied to the value of clothes, ornaments, cash and money spent on the marriage arrangements. All these were given by the husband and his family to the bride and her father. If a wife wished to leave her husband, the divorce became effective through the return of the *reet* articles and money. If a husband decided to divorce his wife, he had to forego the *reet* money.[14]

DAUGHTERS' RIGHT TO INHERITANCE

Daughters, especially orphan daughters, had the same right to the father's property as the widow, as long as they remained unmarried. The daughter, or her children, could never succeed by simple inheritance to landed estate in preference to kinsmen, however, remote. In actual practice, however, some daughters were allowed to inherit. In some areas such as Kullu, a father could, by a formal deed of gift executed during his lifetime, give his estate to a daughter in the absence of sons without the consent of the next of kin. A distant kin, three or four times removed, would sometimes lay claim to the land inherited by the daughter if it had not been gifted to her by her father. A form of property inheritance which allowed a *ghar-jamai* (a husband who chose to stay in the wife's house), who was treated as an adopted son, was also resorted to. The most important customary practice with regard to inheritance in Lahaul and Spiti was that in the absence of sons, a daughter would succeed to her father's whole estate in preference to nephews or other male kinsmen. However, she had to fulfil certain conditions: (a) before her father's death she should not have married and settled with her husband away from the father's house; (b) if she was unmarried she could hold the estate for life as an unmarried person or marry and make her husband live with her in her father's homestead.

Daughters had some property rights in the form of *stridhan* which was the sum total of gifts of movables that a woman received from her parental family, relatives and friends and the husband's family at the time of marriage. In theory, she was supposed to have absolute control over this property. In actual practice, however, she was allowed only limited control over such property. In most parts of Punjab and Himachal, wherever the custom is prevalent, substantial portions of the dowry are customarily appropriated by the parents-in-law. Moreover, the giving of dowry is dependent on the discretion and social status of the parents and brothers. The total value of goods and cash received in dowry is far less than the son's share of inheritance. The Punjabi agrarian society considered the wife and anything associated with her, such as her ornaments, her other movable and immovable property and also her earnings, as the property of her husband. In areas where dowry-giving and receiving is extensively practised, a daughter's worth is equated with the social and economic status of her parental family. In Himachal, this practice was found largely in the low-lying hill areas of the state. Communities practising dowry-giving and receiving were the high-ranking castes who practised hypergamy. When the customary laws lost their validity because of the universal application of the Hindu Personal Law, many communities who used to give bride price have now shifted to giving dowry. The practice of giving and receiving dowry continues unabated and the quantum of dowry has increased manifold. Women face violence, torture and humiliation for bringing inadequate dowry. The graph of dowry deaths and other related crimes has shown an exponential growth.[15]

Unmarried daughters of a landholder were entitled to maintenance from their father, brother, nephew or whoever was the head of the family. They had to be either provided for within the same house, in the same way as were his family members, or given a separate house and plot of land. They forfeited this claim if they went to live in another man's house. Under no other circumstances could they be deprived of the house, or plot allotted to them during their lifetime. Many women never married and continued to live in their father's/brother's house until their death.

From the above analysis of customary practices in Himachal Pradesh, it is apparent that in the hill areas the important components of social structure were an agrarian pastoral society where there was limited availability of cultivable land and where the average size of the holding was 1.2 hectares. Scarcity of cultivable land gave rise to a moral ideology that favoured the prevention of fragmentation of hereditary estates into uneconomic holdings. This moral ideology assured the continuity of male agnatic kinship, and maximization of the productivity of land through the pooling of family resources within an ecology of low-carrying capacity. The practice of polyandry and polygyny ensured a sufficient supply of family labour for agricultural and other activities and acted as a barrier against population explosion. There existed a symbiotic relationship between the land, the people and the physical characteristics of the environment. However, women within this system were the main losers, especially those who could not be married and whose reproductive capacities were abnegated in the name of social and economic stability. In Lahul & Spiti, some of them became nuns, the rest provided family labour in lieu of maintenance. The higher castes in the lower hill areas, especially the Rajputs, practised hypergamy. Exorbitant marriage expenses and increasing debts resulted in a lower valuation of the girl child, which gave female infanticide tacit sanction and which has been recorded as a common practice.[16] Though, by and large, women undergoing multi-partner marriages were subjected to various types of indignities, the practice of *reet*, *karewa* or *jhanjrar* customs provided women with relatively more space than was available to them under the Hindu Law.[17]

WOMEN, LAW AND ACCESS TO LAND

In areas of Himachal Pradesh where the landholdings were relatively large and people followed the Hindu religion, brothers married separate women and divided the house and land in equal shares as prescribed by Hindu Law. Thus, prior to 1956, the Mitakshara school of Hindu Law was the main guiding force among the people who were not guided by local customary laws. The Mitakshara law of inheritance recognized the Hindu male as a member of the joint/undivided family known as coparcenary. His undivided interest in the said coparcenary devolved on his coparceners through survivorship. The self-acquired or separate property went to his heirs by succession in accordance with Section 43. Women under this law could not inherit coparcenary property, as they were outside its ambit. However, a daughter could inherit the self-acquired or separate property of the father if he so willed it. Important changes were, however, introduced in the law of succession by the passage of the Hindu Women's Right to Property Act (XVIII of 1937 amended by XI of 1938). This Act gave women better rights in respect of property. The Act stated that where a Hindu died intestate leaving separate property, his widow was entitled to succeed to that property to the same share as a son. This law further stated that when a Hindu died having an interest in the Hindu joint family property, his widow had in the property the same interest as he himself. Any interest that devolved on a Hindu widow in this manner was to be considered as the limited interest to a Hindu woman's estate. It provided her with the same right of claiming partition as a male heir. This Act was later repealed by Section 31 of the Hindu Succession Act, 1956. Rights acquired and liabilities incurred under the earlier Act, however, remained the same. This Act (Hindu Woman's Right to Property Act, 1937) introduced far-reaching changes in the law of succession and its intention was partially to give fair and equitable treatment to women in matters of succession. Under the Hindu Women's Rights to Property Act, 1937, the widow could take over only a limited interest in the 'widow's estate' in the estate of her husband. This estate went back to the heirs of her husband on her death. She was only entitled to the income of the property inherited by her. She had no power to dispose of the corpus of the property. It was only after the passage of Hindu Succession Act, 1956 that a woman has been conferred full heritable rights in all property acquired by her. Again, under the Hindu law, daughters do not inherit until all the widows are dead. The inheritance goes first to unmarried daughters, thereafter to married daughters who are married and 'enriched', that is, possessed of means. However, under the 1937 Act, the rules of devolution were quite vague and the legislation was enacted in a piecemeal manner. It gave rise to several anomalies in the interpretation and implementation of the law. Some of these conundrums were (a) the Act touched many branches of Hindu Law such as partition of the joint family adoption, maintenance, and disqualification from inheritance. Thus the contradictions arising out of these could not be handled by the logic and provisions of the Act; (b) various judgements refer to the difficulties encountered in the interpretation of this Act; (c) the Act was not a codified enactment, nor even a general amendment of the law of inheritance. It remained outside the main body of the existing law and its expressed intention of giving better rights to women and ameliorating their status remained unresolved.

It is clear from the preamble of the Hindu Succession Act, 1956 that its intention was to amend and codify the law relating to intestate succession. The Act has brought about some fundamental changes in the law of succession. All prior laws ceased to have effect after the passage of this Act. The Act provides equal opportunity to women in the acquisition of proprietary rights in their father's estate. According to the provisions of this Act, daughters have equal rights with the sons in matters of inheritance. It eliminates the distinction between the married daughter who is provided for and the unmarried daughter not provided for. It also obliterates the distinction between a woman with or without children for the purpose of succession. It also eliminates the popular conception of 'the limited estate of women'. The Act makes the woman absolute owner of her share of the property as a man becomes of his. The main purpose of this Act was to provide equity and financial security to women and to prevent their destitution.

The overriding effect of the Act was that it superseded the Punjab Customary Law. All matters of succession are now governed by the provisions of the Hindu Succession Act. Some matters have, however, been expressly removed from the operation of the Act. Thus, the Act does no hold sway under the following conditions: (a) where property succession is regulated by the Indian Succession Act, 1925 under the provisions of Section 21 of the Special Marriage Act, 1954; (b) where the estate descends to a single heir by the terms of agreement entered into by the ruler of any Indian state; (c) the Valiamma Thampuran Kovilagam Estate; (d) and when a Hindu male dies leaving an interest in the Mitakshara coparcenary property, his interest in the property shall devolve on the surviving members of the coparcenary and not in accordance with the Act. This last provision deals with the question of a coparcener dying without making any testamentary disposition of his undivided share in joint family property. Section 30 of this Act empowers a Hindu male to dispose of by will his interest in the coparcenary property. The Mitakshara School recognizes two modes of devolution of property: survivorship and succession. The rules of succession apply to property held in absolute severalty.

One important feature of coparcenary under the Mitakshara Law is that it excludes women from its ambit. Even a wife who is entitled to maintenance out of the husband's property is not a coparcener of her husband. Neither is the mother a coparcener with her sons. Persons included in the joint or coparcenary property are those who acquire the right by birth, usually the sons and grandsons of the joint property holder. In view of all these factors, the main purpose of the Hindu Succession Act, which was to provide equal rights and opportunity to women in the acquisition of proprietary rights in the father's estate, has got diluted. For self-acquired property, fathers generally make a testament in favour of their sons depriving their daughters, and ancestral property, till recently, came within the ambit of coparcenary. Moreover, the principal of agnatic kinship in the male line – which has been the customary law guiding the lives of the people of Himachal for centuries – still holds sway and has considerable sentimental value for them. The net result of all these factors is that a very small proportion of women have acquired proprietary rights to agricultural land in the state. Most of the women who have acquired these rights are either widows or mothers of minor children. A very small proportion of daughters and wives today, mostly belonging to the well-to-do households with large landholdings, have also acquired proprietary rights in land through gifts or through inheritance and division due to ceiling on holdings.

The Dowry Prohibition Act, 1961 and 1984 legally apply to all socially approved practices which allow for the exchange of money as a prerequisite for arranging a marriage. It defines dowry as any property or valuable security, given or agreed to be given, either directly or indirectly, by one party to a marriage to the other party to the marriage; or by the parents of either party to a marriage; or by any other person to either party to a marriage or to any other person; at or before, or after the marriage as a consideration for the marriage of the said parties. It excludes dower, or *meher*, in the case of persons governed by the Muslim Personal Law.

When dowry is given voluntarily, it is not regarded as a social evil. But when dowry is interpreted as a 'pre-nuptial contract of payments made by the bride's father with the bridegroom or his guardian', it becomes a social evil. Under the Act, the giving or taking or abetting the giving or taking of dowry, shall be punishable by imprisonment or a fine or both. Further, dowry is for the benefit of the wife or her heirs. It also states that when dowry is received by any person other than the woman in connection with whose marriage it is given, that person shall transfer it to the woman within one year after the date of marriage or after its receipt. If any person fails to transfer such property to the woman concerned within the prescribed time limit, he shall be punished with imprisonment or fine.

The Act excludes cash, ornaments, clothes or other articles given as marriage presents from the definition of dowry. This provision has been recently interpreted differently by the Supreme Court of India.

The Dowry Prohibition Act, 1961 was amended again by Act No. 63 of 1984. The new Act substitutes the words 'in connection with the marriage of the said parties' with the words 'in consideration of the marriage of the said parties' in Section 2 of the Act. It further introduces changes in the rules regarding punishment (from not less than six months to two years and the amount of Rs. 5,000 to 10,000). Further, the offences committed under the Act are cognizable for certain purposes and non-cognizable for other purposes such as Section 42 of CPC (2 of 1974). However, the offences are bailable and non-compoundable, Section 498 A of the IPC allows for three years imprisonment in cases of dowry harassment. This clause was added in 1983 after women's groups agitated against the growing violence against women. The main aim of the Dowry Prohibition Act, along with the Hindu Succession Act, was to ameliorate the position of women within the family.

GENDER IDEOLOGIES

The above analysis of cultural practices and Hindu law shows that in Himachal Pradesh a woman's relationship to land falls within a very ambiguous zone. On the one hand, she is excluded from ownership and control of land and on the other, her labour for cultivating the land is considered invaluable. Her exclusion from ownership and control of land occurs because the prevalent gender ideologies privilege the elite male and revolve around androcentric notions surrounding issues of succession, inheritance and ownership of property. Concrete expressions of this androcentric ideology can be seen in the widespread belief and practice of the agnatic principle among the peasant communities of Himachal Pradesh. The privileging of the agnatic principle helps in the treatment of all male lineal descendants as first-order descendants, and the woman – i.e. the widow – as the second-order descendant who is only entitled to a life estate in the property. The prevailing gender discourse further emphasizes the exclusion of daughters and sisters from the inheritance, ownership and control of property. The oft-repeated justification provided for their exclusion from inheritance and ownership of property refers to their temporary and transitory connection with the lineage of the natal family. Thus, the female need to own and control land and property is 'othered' because of her temporary association with the natal lineage and because of her 'femininity'.

The mechanism of the bride price helps to seal a contract which transfers the valued labour of wives to husbands; while the wives (women) experience the status of outsiders in the lineage of their husbands and have only use, rights to land or property. In this manner, the biological-economic woman's valued production has to be deeded in favour of the privileged gender person, the man. The message conveyed is that the powerful identity of women must be controlled by men. This multifaceted gender regime permeates all aspects of social life in Himachal Pradesh.

REFORMS AND WOMEN

The nineteenth century saw the arrival of social reforms. Social reformers of this century had considerable faith in the power of law in eliminating dehumanizing social practices, especially in relation to women. However, the discourse of equality was missing from this discourse of reforms. In the twentieth century, the emphasis shifted to the reform of personal laws and the issues of equality. The oppositional discourse on the reform of personal laws was embedded in the belief that granting of property rights to women would increase litigation, lead to fragmentation of holdings and escalate violence among family members, all of which would lead to the breakdown of the joint family. It further considered the reform of marriage laws as spoilers of the 'ideal of chastity' and 'purity of family life' within the received notions of femininity. Though this discourse sanctioned partial gender equality in the public sphere, it opposed all notions of equality in the private sphere.

Currently all issues of property concerning succession come under the ambit of the Hindu Succession Act, 1956 and those related to marriage under the Hindu Marriage Act. The reach of Hindu Personal Law extends to all Indian states except Jammu & Kashmir. The overriding effect of these Acts was that they superceded the existing customary laws. The STs, however, continued to be guided by their own customary laws. Since the discourse on the reform of personal laws was enwrapped in dissent and debate, the passage of legislative enactments failed to achieve their desired purpose. Instead the ideological construction of women as wives and mothers has persisted till date. Familial ideology continues to construct women as an economically dependent category. Because of the persistence of this ideology, legal regulations operate in such a way that women remain delegated to positions of economic dependence. In many areas of Himachal Pradesh customary practices such as polyandry are still being practised and the related issues of inheritance, succession, ownership and control of property continue to be guided by the local customary practices.[18]

Whereas the discourse on social reform such as the reform of Hindu personal laws was mired in dissent and debate, there seems to have been complete unanimity among the colonial administrators, social reformers, ruling elite and the press. On the reform of local customary traditions and bringing them into the fold of Hindu law. Certain customary practices that were not in strict conformity with the colonial and orthodox Hindu sensibilities came in for criticism. It was the freedom enjoyed by women that represented the actual grievance against the custom of *reet*. The practice of *reet* gave women the freedom to leave one set of husbands for another when everyday life became tough for them within the existing system. A woman had only to ensure that her parents returned the bride price to the former husband. It was this freedom enjoyed by women that represented the actual grievance against the custom of polyandry than any humanitarian consideration of making woman equal to man. The following excerpts make the point clear. In his *Digest of Customary Law* W.H. Rattigan makes the following statement:

A caste custom which permits a woman to desert her husband as her pleasure and marry again without his consent is void for immorality.

Rattigan made the statement in a case of repudiation of marriage by the wife wherein the Bombay High Court had observed, 'If a wife could leave her husband whenever she pleased, and without any forms whatever, the marriage tie would have no force at all. . . . A caste in which such a state of society was allowed, would reduce its members to the level of the beasts of the field.'[19]

Social reformers felt that the custom of *reet* gave women a ready and effective weapon to use to their advantage in whatever manner they desired. Therefore, attempts were made by various social reform organizations and people's groups such as the Rajput Sthaniya Sabha, the Prabandhini Sabha and the Hindu Conference for the elimination and suppression of this custom through legislation. In pursuance of this movement, the Patiala State was the first to legislate upon it in 1912 and declared *reet* as an invalid form of marriage. However, this judgement had no substantial effect. Thereafter, the ruler of Bhagat State passed a legislation to abolish *reet* in 1917. Again, in 1925, a news item in the *Hindustan Times* expressed dissatisfaction at the continuity of *reet* and made a plea to all concerned (except the women who practised it), such as the Indian State, the social reformers and the rulers of the Hill States and other elites, to make a combined effort to weed out this customary practice altogether.[20] This contextual reality provided the rationale for superceding existing customary traditions, and bringing them within the fold of the Hindu Marriage Act and the Hindu Succession Act. As a result, the custom of *reet* has almost disappeared to be replaced by the dowry system. Along with it, the freedom, women enjoyed to divorce a husband has disappeared. However, the practice of polyandry persists and is even being forced on women to ensure that their share of the property remains within the brotherhood of the male members of the household.

Enhancing gender equality in matters of property and personal laws requires that reforms become a legal possibility and an administrative viability. It also requires social acceptability and moral legitimacy. On all these counts the Indian state and society have failed. They have failed to dislodge the dominant familial ideology that has been persistently creating and sustaining the ideology of 'dependence of women', and where under customary practices women were enabled to take 'independent decisions' the orthodox male consensus on forms of morality saw to it that it was undone.

LAND REFORMS AND WOMEN

The history of land reforms in Himachal Pradesh started with the passage of the Punjab Tenancy Act, 1887b, when the state was part of the erstwhile state of Punjab. The purpose of this Act was to confer occupancy rights on the tenants who had been cultivating a piece of land for two or more generations, or who had earlier been the owner-cultivators of the said land and had continued to occupy it in spite of the fact that they had ceased to be landowners. The Act recognized the custom in particular parts of the country, such as Himachal Pradesh, where certain persons made improvements by bringing waste land (*nautor* land) under cultivation. However, under the Punjab Tenancy Act, 1887, a tenant could not acquire a status higher than what was claimed by him. The main object of the Act was to prevent the wrongful dispossession of a tenant by the landlord or any other person. The (Land Acquisition Act, 1894) regulated the acquisition of land for public purposes or for companies. It dwelt on the method of fixing compensation on the acquisition of land. The valuation of lands, which was earlier subject to arbitration with no right to appeal, was now given the right to appeal. This helped the landowner to save his land. Under this Act a married woman was treated as if she were unmarried for the purposes of determining the rights of the landholder. This Act was later superseded by the Land Acquisition (H.P. Amendment) Act, 1986 (Act 17 of 1986). The Act amended Sections 18 and 31 of the earlier Act and introduced a new Section 52A in it.

The Himachal Pradesh Big Landed Estates and Land Reforms Act, 1953 (15 of 1954) was enacted with the object of imposing a ceiling on very large holdings and allow for the purchase of surplus land. Small landowners were kept out of the ambit of this Act. This agrarian reform measure was saved from the operation of Articles 14, 19 and 31 of the Constitution. The permissible area under this Act was 30 standard acres. However, the permissible limit was not applicable to areas under orchards or land owned by displaced persons. One salutary effect of this legislation was that the number of large estates was considerably reduced and the number of intermediaries was also reduced because of the acquisition of proprietary rights by the tenants.

The real elimination of the class of intermediaries occurred after the introduction of the (Himachal Pradesh Tenancy and Land Reforms Act, 1972). The Act protects the right of tenants, other than occupancy tenants, to acquire the interests of landowner under Section 104. The Act gives the right of resumption to the landowner for personal cultivation of one and half acres of irrigated land or three acres of unirrigated land under tenancy. It gives the tenants proprietary rights automatically. Again, if the landowner does not personally cultivate the land resumed by him under Sub-section (1), then such land is vested with the state government. However, the first right to own the land remains with the tenant. Again, under Section 8 of the Act, some categories of landowners are allowed to have their land cultivated by the tenants. These categories are:

a. Minor children or unmarried women, if a woman is married, then widowed, divorced or separated women can get their land cultivated by a tenant;
b. If the landowner is permanently incapacitated because of physical or mental infirmity;
c. Landowners who are members of the armed forces;
d. Landowners who have an offspring serving in the armed forces.

Section 113 of the Act specifies that no land over which proprietary rights have been acquired can be transferred by sale, mortgage and gift or otherwise for a period of ten years from the date of acquisition or proprietary rights. Section 118 of the Act puts a bar on the transfer of land to non-agriculturists, but allows the transfer of land to landless agricultural labourers. Preference is given to landless persons of SCs and STs, village artisans or landless persons following agriculture-related vocations or to the state government, cooperative societies or banks. With the commencement of this Act, all existing Acts and their amendments stood repealed in all areas of Himachal Pradesh under Section 126 and 127 and a large number of tenants acquired proprietary rights after the implementation of the provisions of this Act. Only a few protected categories of landowners can give their lands to tenants for cultivation on tenancy basis. These categories include single women such as unmarried, widowed or divorced, and minors and persons employed with the armed forces. The Act also provides various safeguards to tenants. It confers proprietary rights on *kismi* and occupancy tenants. Non-occupancy tenants can only be ejected from the land if they fail to pay the rent regularly or cultivate the land according to the customary practices of the locality, or if the land was sublet or used for any other purpose than what was prescribed. If there is a rent decree against the tenant, he is given six months to clear the arrears or else the land is relinquished to the government.[21]

The Himachal Pradesh Ceiling on Landholdings Act, 1972 (Act no. 19 of 1973) consolidated and amended laws relating to ceiling on landholdings and acquisition and disposal of surplus areas. It was an improvement over the Himachal Pradesh Big Landed Estates Act. According to this Act, the permissible area of a landowner or a tenant or a mortgagee or a family consisting of husband, wife and three minor children is (a) land under assured irrigation capable of growing two crops in a year – 10 acres; (b) land under assured irrigation capable of growing one crop in a year – 15 acres; and (c) land of classes other than those described in (a) and (b) above including land under orchards – 30 acres. The permissible area for the hill areas of Kinnaur, Lahul & Spiti, Pangi, Bharmour, Chhota Bhangal and Bara Bhangal and the areas of Dodra Kawar Patwar is 70 acres.

An important clause under Section 4.4 of the Act provides that every adult son (of a person) shall be treated as a separate unit and he shall be entitled to land up to the permissible limit allowed to a family under Sub-sections (1) and (2); subject to the condition that the aggregate land of the family along with the separate units does not exceed twice the permissible area. The term 'adult son' has been substituted for the words 'or daughter of landowner' in Section 3 of H.P. Act 1 of 1974. Lands owned by the government or cooperative farming societies are exempted from this limit. The Ceiling on Land Holdings Act forbade all persons falling within its ambit in the State of Himachal Pradesh from holding any land above the permissible area after a particular date. It also prevented all transfers of surplus lands after the passage of the Act. The substitution of the term 'adult son' as against 'or daughter of landowner' under Section 3 of H.P. Act 1 of 1974 appears as a retrograde step as far as the rights of women to inherit, own and control the land are concerned. This clause has been disputed time and again in the Himachal Pradesh High Court but the Court refuses to allow the adult daughter a separate permissible area under the protection of the axiom 'settled principle of Law'.[22] The rule relating to Himachal Pradesh's grant of *nautor* land to landless persons and other eligible persons gives grant of *nautor* land (wasteland owned by the government) up to 1 acre to landless persons for the purpose of agriculture or horticulture.

The series of land reform measures undertaken by the state government in Himachal Pradesh have given rise to various anomalous situations. The Himachal Pradesh Abolition of Big Landed Estates and Land Reforms Act, 1953 was the first Act of independent India which put a ceiling on large landholdings and distributed surplus lands to the tiller. The landlords who lost their lands as a result of this Act waged a political and legal battle to forestal and circumvent the implementation of the Act by taking shelter under various flaws and loopholes in the Act. When certain areas of Punjab were merged with the states of Himachal Pradesh in 1966, the poor tenants and agricultural labourers in the erstwhile Punjab areas had no protection. Therefore, three important laws were enacted to benefit the landless agricultural labourers, tenants and marginal and small farmers in these areas. The three landmark pieces of legislation were the Himachal Pradesh Tenant's Act, 1971 (applicable to transferred territories only), The Himachal Pradesh Ceiling on Landholdings Act, 1972 and the Himachal Pradesh Tenancy and Land Reforms Act, 1972.[23]

The passage of these Acts was accompanied by large-scale programmes of land allotment to landless families. The whole exercise was undertaken by the state government in the 1970s. The aim of the government was to answer that no landless people were left under its jurisdiction. The state legislature and the bureaucracy were earnest in implementing the slogan given to the exercise by Jyoti Basu in 1970, that by the time they reach Bengal, all agricultural workers should have become landowners.[24] As a result, when the state government found the surplus lands insufficient to make every landless labourer a landowner, it introduced the Himachal Pradesh Nautor Land Rules, 1968 whereby 20 *bigha*s of *nautor* (wasteland or forest land) could be granted for purposes of horticulture or agriculture.[25] Later in 1971, according to government instructions, the grant of *nautor* land was specifically limited to tenants who had to be ejected in the process of resumptions under Section 104 of the Himachal Pradesh Tenancy and Land Reforms Act, 1972. The grant of *nautor* land was to continue only for 'Harijans' and landless agricultural labourers under this ruling. In view of the strong will displayed by the state government, and armed with these laws and rules by 1981, the state of Himachal Pradesh was left with little or no landless agricultural labour. Today it is only 2.72 per cent of the total rural work force. In 1991, the total population of landless agricultural labourers in the state stood at 58,668 out of which 48,891 were men and 9,777 were women.[26] A few protected categories of landowners such as widows, minors, disabled persons and army personnel were allowed to lease in and lease out land on a tenancy basis. This process of conferment of proprietary rights continues even today.[27] The government has also made provisions for legal aid to the small and marginal farmers in case of violations of the law.

In spite of a very progressive legislation and a high level of political will to implement it, all is not well with the state of Himachal Pradesh. Most of the land allotted to the landless and small farmers has remained uncultivated. These lands are uncultivable and require large-scale investments in the form of capital, labour technology and technical know-how, all of which are hardly accessible to the small landholders. Hence, these lands are lying uncultivated. A majority of the new landholders was from the artisan castes, which had neither technical knowledge of agriculture nor the inclination to pursue it as a whole-time occupation. Most of the surplus agricultural lands in the state are located in rain-fed areas. The beneficiaries of land reform consider the land allotted land too small (5 *bigha*s or 0.4 hectares), which is a very uneconomical size for cultivation. Therefore, most beneficiaries have either sold the lands in spite of a provision against it, or let it remain uncultivated for the last twenty years.

Another class of landholders that has benefited from legislation on ceiling of landholdings is the present-day orchard owners who earlier had barren *ghasni* (grasslands) lands and who now have converted them into orchards. Every adult son could claim 30 standard acres of land as his permissible limit. These orchard owners of Himachal Pradesh are believed to be minting money today. The apple growers lobby in the state also has considerable political clout.

Another fallout of the land reform measures has been that today agricultural labour is not available. An average medium-size holding of 10 acres has become uneconomical because mechanized farming, such as small tractors, cannot be used on these lands. Resultantly, large numbers of medium landowners have become disillusioned with the land reform policy and have been asking for a higher ceiling on holdings. It was for these very reasons that in Kangra district, where the land reform policy showed its results, the ruling Congress government lost in the 1977 elections. Thereafter, in 1977, a committee on land reforms was set up under the chairmanship of Mian Bhag Singh, but the report of the committee has not seen the light of the day. The medium and large farmers lobby has been agitating for the introduction of fixed-term tenancy in the rural areas as in the urban areas. They also suggest measures to stop the exploitation of tenants. For this purpose, they suggest that the landowner give a two-third share to the tenant. If the government fails to implement these suggestions, the money-order economy and the out-migration of the educated social classes will continue in the state.

In Kangra district, the tenants-turned-landowners and beneficiaries of *nautor* lands sold their land in spite of the provision against it. In Mandi district, the tenants were quite happy to acquire the status of landowners because the big landed estates belonged to the Khatris and not the local inhabitants. In other states of India, the ruling classes did not have the will to destroy and diminish the power of the peasantry.[28]

The different laws discussed earlier have only two important provisions relating to women. These provisions either confer the right of ownership on women or deprive them of it. The first provision is that under the Himachal Pradesh Tenancy and Land Reform Act, 1972, an unmarried, divorced, separated or widowed woman cannot be ejected from the land if she sublets the holding, or part thereof, without the consent of the landowners. The second provision allows unmarried, divorced, separated and widowed women landowners to lease out their lands on tenancy basis. Taking shelter under the latter provision many persons have recorded the women of their households (especially unmarried daughters) as landowners in the revenue records. The former provision relates to permissible area under the Ceiling on Landholdings Act. As mentioned earlier, Section 4 of the Act holds that every adult son of a person shall be treated as a separate unit of permissible area. In this clause, the substitution of the words 'every son or daughter of landowner' with the words 'every adult son' was clearly a retrograde step as far as women were concerned. Three provisions of Section 4 of this Act were challenged in the High Court of Himachal Pradesh through a Civil Writ Petition No. 4 of 1974, Raj Kumar Rajindra Singh *vs.* the Union of India. The full bench decided the case on 23 June 1976, upholding the validity of the Act and repelling the different contentions of the petitioners. The bench held that Section 4 of the Act was violative of Articles 14, 15, 19, 26 and 31 of the Constitution. It also held that Section 4 of the Act only provided criteria for computing the permissible area of the landholder. The entire permissible area that the landholder could retain was based on a fictional notion of the required permissible area or upper limit in respect of adult son or sons. It did not create a right to a share in favour of the son in the landholding of the landholder. Therefore, there was no question of discrimination between a son and a daughter. The judges further held that the wife has not been specifically denied permissible area.

The wife is specifically included within the definition of the family or the landholding unit of the person if she has an independent holding. However, it would have been better if the state had not substituted the term 'adult son or daughter' with 'adult son'. It would have given more teeth to the Hindu Succession Act which has, by and large, failed to provide de facto rights of inheritance, especially land, to women.

CURRENT SCENARIO

Many of the sociocultural customary practices of Himachal Pradesh have survived from the pre-colonial through the colonial to the present day. More importantly, the normative structures regulating the institutions of marriage, family and kinship have remained the same. After the passage of the Hindu Marriage Act, 1955 and the Hindu Succession Act, 1956, all prior laws (customary as well as Hindu law) ceased to be effective. However, the practice of polyandry, in its various forms, continues – though its practitioners are reluctant to admit its continuity for fear of legal action against them. Moreover, the STs are outside the ambit of these Acts and have the choice to be governed by their own customary laws or the provisions of Hindu law. However, because of social contacts with people outside the region, and the influence of Western culture, and also because of the modernization of Indian society as a whole, certain customary practices have been remodelled over a period of time. Greater change can be observed in the food and dress habits of the people. Although the practice of polyandry in its various forms continues to some extent even today, the people's attitudes have undergone a change over time. Educated people are apologetic about the practice and believe that the institution lowers their prestige in relation to the 'others' who are governed by Hindu personal laws. Given an opportunity, especially in situations where the brothers are forced to live separately because of different occupations and migration, people have discarded the practice of polyandry in favour of monogamy. With monogamy becoming the preferred type of marriage practice, and the emphasis on nuclear families becoming the norm of the day, as well as the two-child norm propagated by the state, younger women who have gone in for monogamous marriages find that the burden of work has increased rather than decreased under the new arrangements. They further experience a loss of autonomy which their mothers and grandmothers enjoyed within the polyandrous system, despite certain other indignities attached to the system. Although the issues of ownership and control of property are based on the agnatic principle even in polyandrous families as under Hindu law, the ready acceptance and simpler processes of divorce and remarriage, and the sexual, social and economic freedom that formed part of the package of these customary practices, provided women greater space because of the monomarital principle.

The prevalence of monogamy under Hindu law was always there in the outer Himalayas, especially the Kangra and Chamba regions. Today, the Hindu Marriage Act finds wide acceptance in the moderate hill areas as well. The acceptance and practice of Hindu law has brought all the retrograde practices associated with it, such as dowry, leading to the devaluation of women, to areas where customary practices held sway earlier. The spread of dowry and its increasing demands and expenses have devalued women's status. Dowry-related violence has also become part of everyday life situations. Although sons were valued under the customary practices, their value has increased far more under the new arrangements where they command huge dowries, and also because of the propagation of the two-child norm. As a result, child sex ratios have been declining in Himachal Pradesh during the last two decades. In the 1991 census, the sex ratio of the state stood at 976, but in 2001, it went down to 970. Again, instances of female foeticide have increased considerably. Legislative reform of the personal laws seems to have achieved little in terms of providing gender justice to the people.

The agrarian social structure of Himachal Pradesh differs considerably from other areas in India. The backbone of this structure comprises a large mass of self-cultivating peasant proprietors with an almost virtual absence of wage labour. This peculiar characteristic of the agrarian social structure of the state can be attributed to the scarcity of cultivable land and the effective implementation of land reform measures in the state.

Resultantly, the majority of the cultivators today can be lumped together in the categories of medium, small or marginal self-cultivating farmers with a fair sprinkling of big landholders. The distribution of surplus land among the landless agricultural labourers has helped to drastically reduce their proportion in the agrarian social hierarchy, and the conferment of ownership rights on the tenants has made them join the ranks of the medium and small farmers. However, it is debatable whether women and men in Himachal Pradesh occupy the same space within the rural normative structure of ownership, control and distribution of land and other resources. The following analysis elaborates this point.

The figures of the provisional population census analysis of 2001 show that main and marginal workers constitute 49.28 per cent of the total population of the state, and the state occupies the third position in the country in terms of work participation rates, next only to Mizoram and Dadra, Haveli and Nagar. The rest of the 50.72 per cent can be located in the different categories of non-workers. Within the total population of workers 56.34 per cent are men and 43.66 per cent women. When one looks at the rural areas of Himachal Pradesh, one will find that 50.63 per cent of the total population has been recorded as workers. The working population of the state consists of 32.14 per cent main workers and 18.49 per cent marginal workers. The proportion of rural male workers to total rural males is 54.74 per cent, comprising 42.30 per cent of the main workers and 12.44 per cent of the marginal workers. Correspondingly, the proportion of women workers in the total female population in rural areas is around 46.67 per cent. This proportion of women workers consists of 21.88 per cent main workers and 24.59 per cent marginal workers. The data clearly shows that the proportion of women marginal workers is almost double the proportion of men marginal workers while their proportion in the population of main workers is almost half that of male workers. The data also highlights the significant contribution of women to agricultural in Himachal Pradesh.

The data in Table 17.1 gives a fair idea of the decadal variations in the proportions of workers in Himachal Pradesh. In 1971,

TABLE 17.1: DECADAL VARIATIONS IN WORK PARTICIPATION RATES IN HIMACHAL PRADESH (RURAL)

Year	Total workers		Main workers		Marginal workers	
	Men	Women	Men	Women	Men	Women
1961	56.79	43.21	–	–	–	–
1971	72.46	27.54	–	–	–	–
1981	73.15	26.85	–	–	–	–
1991	50.46	36.61	48.79	20.08	01.67	16.53
2001	54.74	46.47	42.30	21.88	12.44	24.59

Sources: 1. *Census of India* 1981, Series 7 H.P. Part II B Primary Census Abstract;
2. *Census of India* 1971, Series 7 H.P. Part I B, General Report;
3. *Census of India* 2001, Series 3 H.P. Provisional Population Paper 3 of 2001.

the proportion of women workers in the state showed a notable decline from 43.21 per cent in 1961 to 27.54 per cent in 1971, and the proportion of men workers registered a corresponding upswing from 56.79 to 72.46 per cent. The main reason for this upswing was the change in the definition of the worker, which ignored all seasonal or part-time workers from the category of workers. The reorganization of the state and the amalgamation of areas of erstwhile Punjab – and also mechanized farming – was another reason for the increase in the population of male workers. Between 1971 and 1981, the data shows no variations in the proportions of workers. However, the 1991 census once again shows a considerable upswing in the proportion of women workers from 26.85 per cent in 1981 to 36.61 per cent in 1991. The reason is the change in the definition of worker and the division between main and marginal workers. The 1991 census data also shows a substantial decline in the proportion of men workers in the state. The 2001 census data maintains the overall pattern of the 1991 census but shows a substantial increase in the proportions of both men and women workers, specifically the category of marginal workers. In the case of men workers, the data suggests that for a substantial proportion of men, agriculture is now a marginal occupation, and the activity is under the care of the womenfolk.

The data on cultivators and agricultural labourers in Table 17.2 is quite revealing. It shows that in 1961 the proportions of both women and men cultivators in the state were very high (92.74 and 71.50 per cent respectively), whereas the proportion of landless agricultural labourers in the state was only 1.41. The main reason for this was the distribution of surplus lands under the Himachal Pradesh Abolition of Big Landed Estates and Land Reforms Act, 1953 and the Himachal Pradesh Ceiling on Land Holdings Act, 1972. The former helped to increase the proportions of cultivators in the state and the latter contributed to the decline in the proportions of agricultural labourers. However, in 1991 the proportion of men and women agricultural labourers showed an almost fourfold increase (4.17 per cent of the total workers), because they had sold their uneconomic holdings and had become landless workers once again. Overall, Table 17.2 shows that the proportion of women cultivators in the state was initially very high but between 1961 and 1971, there was a substantial decline from 92.74 per cent to 89.09 per cent, and a corresponding increase in the proportion of women agricultural labourers from 1.01 to 4.09 per cent. Again, between 1981 and 1991, the proportion of women cultivators came down to 86.91 per cent from 89.57 per cent, and the proportion

TABLE 17.2: DECADAL VARIATIONS IN THE PROPORTIONS OF CULTIVATORS AND AGRICULTURAL LABOURERS BY GENDER IN HIMACHAL PRADESH

Year	Cultivators			Agricultural Labour		
	Total	Men	Women	Total	Men	Women
1961	80.68	71.50	92.74	1.41	1.72	1.01
1971	70.64	63.63	89.09	4.17	4.20	4.09
1981	68.08	60.19	89.57	2.72	3.09	1.71
1991	63.29	54.15	86.91	3.30	3.81	1.98
2001	70.43	55.24	88.48	3.29	3.59	2.94

Sources: 1. *Census of India* 1981, Series 7 H.P. Part II B Primary Census Abstract;
2. *Census of India* 1971, Series 7 H.P. Part I B, General Report;
3. *Census of India* 2001, Series 3 H.P. Provisional Population Paper 3 of 2001.

of women agricultural labourers rose only marginally from 1.71 to 1.98 per cent. This shows a shift from agriculture to other occupations or withdrawal from the workforce. In 2001, the increase in the proportion of women cultivators could be attributed to the government notification of 1986 conferring joint titles to husband and wife in cases of land allotment to the landless and other eligible persons. The figures for the proportions of women and men agricultural workers indicate that in Himachal Pradesh agriculture is mainly a women's activity.

The average size and number of operational holdings in the state reduced from 1.62 to 1.16 hectares between 1976–7 and 1995–6 (Table 17.3). The proportion of marginal holdings

TABLE 17.3: LAND SIZE AND SIZE OF THE OPERATIONAL HOLDINGS IN HIMACHAL PRADESH

	1976–7			1995–6		
Land size (in hectares)	Per cent total holdings	Average size of holdings	Per cent	Per cent total holdings	Average size of holdings	Per cent
Marginal						
Below 0.5	34.36	0.24	5.04	41.90	–	9.00
Very Small						
0.5–1.0	20.32	0.73	9.12	22.50	0.40	14.10
1.0–2.0	21.96	1.44	19.46	20.10	1.40	24.10
Small						
2.0–3.0	10.60	2.44	15.24	7.60	2.70	15.60
3.0–4.0	5.11	3.44	10.82	3.40	–	9.90
Medium						
4.0–5.0	2.80	4.48	7.72	1.70	–	6.60
5.0–10.0	4.04	6.74	16.79	2.30	5.70	12.90
Large						
10.0–20.0	0.98	13.07	7.86	0.40	15.60	5.20
20.0+	0.27	58.02	7.95	0.10	–	2.60
Total	100.00	1.62	100.00	100.00	1.16	100.00

Sources: 1. Directorate of Agricultural Census Himachal Pradesh;
2. Directorate of Land Records;
3. Himachal Pradesh Statistical Outline H.P., 2000–1.

(less than 1 hectare) increased during the same period. The proportion of holdings between 1 and 2 hectares also increased. However, there was appreciable change in holdings of 2 to 4 hectares, but the proportion of holdings varying from 4 to 10 hectares and of more than 10 hectares recorded a considerable decrease. The cultivator's relationship to the size of the landholding in Himachal Pradesh is such that it deters him/her from investing money, labour and technology to raise its productivity and income from it. It is believed that a good land tenure system helps to encourage productive investments and also in improving the efficiency of land. In Himachal Pradesh the harsh geophysical environment, the incapacity of the poor farmer to invest in land and the ridiculously small size of the holdings act as deterrents to increasing the productivity of the land.[29]

The above analysis of ownership and control of land signifies power equations among agricultural communities. Every society develops its own norms of inclusion and exclusion for the determination of nodal points of power, authority and the control of resources. Societies in which the principle of agnatic kinship forms the guiding principle in inheritance bestow land resources, power and authority on men and put the womenfolk at a great disadvantage. This exclusion of women from the line of inheritance, ownership and control of resources confers on them a secondary status in the agrarian social structure and contributes to their overall subordination in society in spite of their economic contributions and advantage. Women's participation in agricultural activities has increased during the last fifty years, creating a situation where there has occurred large-scale 'feminization of the agricultural labour force' without the corresponding authority of decision-making in the sale, mortgage, purchase of land or other instruments of production necessary for innovative farming. Non-ownership of titles to land has been a major factor in hindering rural development in the state. Women's lack of independent access and control of land has been one of the main hurdles in the effective implementation of developmental activities. In Himachal, the tiller of land very often is the woman; agricultural knowledge and experience is also hers but the capital, managerial and risk-bearing capacity is centralized by men at the household level. Since the men work outside the village in the cash economy, they lack the desire to adopt new farm technology or make investments in it. It is for these reasons that even under irrigated conditions, the majority of the farmers who have been given land have not adopted new technology or the IRDP package of services for their farmlands. Overall, there exists a complacency among the small and marginal landholders of today. They lack the urge, interest and capacity to improve their agricultural productivity and their economic condition. It seems that the underlying logic of land reforms, that is, land to tiller, which should have had a positive multiplex effect on cultivators in improving the productivity of land has not happened in the state of Himachal Pradesh. Thus, land reforms may be a necessary condition for effecting development in agriculture, but it is not a sufficient condition for development.[30]

The 'feminization of subsistence farming' and the 'masculinization of commercial agriculture' have helped to promote the skewed distribution of power and authority in Himachal Pradesh. Men as heads of the household successfully exercise their authority in retaining ownership and control of land and other resources and at the same time make extensive use of women's labour for subsistence as well as commercial agriculture. The coexistence of various customary practices, along with Hindu law in its present form, has created more conundrums in the creation of a gender-just society even in a state where women's contribution to agriculture is valued by tradition and custom. The issues of power and authority continue to be guided by the agnatic principle that privileges the male. The provisions of the Hindu Succession Act treating women as equals have been rendered toothless. This is apparent from the following existential reality.

The women who have been recorded as cultivators in the land records of the state, are widows, unmarried daughters or daughters without brothers.[31] Around 25 to 30 per cent of women are believed to be de facto landowners. The practice of village exogamy within a radius of 8 to 10 km makes conditions difficult for married daughters to be effective owners and controllers of their lands. Consequently, only 50 per cent of women landowners cultivate the land themselves, the rest have given their lands for cultivation on tenancy or remain nominal owners of land while effective control remains with male kinsmen. Widows who earlier enjoyed the right of 'limited estate' to inheritance of their husband's property now can use it as an absolute right, but rarely exercise it.

Women who cultivate the lands themselves encountered many hurdles in their effective management. One informant said:

> Even if women cultivate their lands themselves, ploughing of the fields has to be done by men. For this purpose, women have to seek the help of men for ploughing the land for them or helping to arrange for agricultural labour. Moreover, the cultural barriers to women's participation in public life restrict their movements in public spaces. Therefore, their dependence on men is inevitable.

A *patwari* posted near Totu said that four daughters who inherited the land of their father cultivate it themselves, even ploughing the fields. However, such instances of women managing their own farmlands are rare and not the rule. Only 5 per cent of women owners of land are also self-cultivators. Women farm owners face two major problems. One, kinspersons and others owning the adjoining lands create problems of boundary maintenance such as encroachments by male neighbours or kinsmen on the *meind* (boundary) separating the lands of two owners. The second major problem encountered by women cultivators is of marketing the produce. They find it difficult to get a good price for their produce because they lack mobility and knowledge of existing market rates. Hence the agricultural incomes of women cultivators are smaller as compared to those of men. Since most of the landholdings in Himachal Pradesh are ridiculously small and uneconomical, they even fail to provide subsistence to the women who own it. The following example illustrates this point:

> Shanti Devi inherited twelve biswas of land from her father as she had no brother. She has four grown up sons and a widowed daughter. The youngest son, and his family of four, and the widowed daughter live with Shanti Devi in her joint household. The income or produce from

land is not sufficient for the survival of the family. The earnings (Rs. 4,000 per month) of her younger son, who is employed as a technician, help in the survival of her household.

Again, an oft-repeated comment of women cultivators was that for the effective control of land it is necessary for them to live in the village where their lands are situated. Some women had surmounted all hurdles of land management and control. These women are largely orchard owners or florists who have large estates which require less labour throughout the year. Intensive management and labour inputs are required only during the fruit or flower-picking season. Women orchard owners access markets which fetch higher prices for their produce. For such women farming is a vocation. They belong to the upper crust of the social hierarchy.

Another category of women cultivators is of wives whose husbands are employed outside the village. For all practical purposes, these women cultivate and manage the farmland, but the ownership rights remain with the husband. The husband pockets the income after the sale of the produce at the time of his periodical home visits. This category of women cultivators is found in abundance in Himachal Pradesh among all categories of cultivating households.

A few wives of rich households have also been shown on the revenue records as landowners. These women acquired ownership rights because the land was gifted to them by their parents or husbands. The husbands of these women are employed away from the village and this helps them to lease out land on tenancy or hire labour for cultivation.

Many informants said that educated daughters have started asking for their share of land and property under the Hindu Succession Act, but their number is very small. In cases where parents had gifted land to their daughters and the title to land stood in the daughter's name, the real control and management remained with the father or brothers in whose favour the daughters had relinquished their right to property.

In the end, it may be summarized that in spite of their large-scale participation in agricultural activities and their economic value for the people of Himachal Pradesh, women in the state are being denied the actual ownership and control rights to land or the right to be effective decision-makers. One positive feature is the relatively high rates of female literacy and sex ratio, and the high participation of rural women in non-governmental organizations. Women's role in the local bodies such as panchayats is significant. Some NGOs, such as SUTRA have for a long time been raising demands for joint *patta*s and creating awareness about effective ownership, control and management of land. This demand has been partially incorporated in the Himachal Pradesh Government Notification of January 1987 conferring joint titles when the allotment of land and house sites is made to the landless and other eligible persons.

CONCLUSION

It appears that custom, law and the state have all joined hands to regulate conjugality for the perpetuation of patrilineal agnatic inheritance within a wide spectrum of the social life in north India. While codifying the personal laws of the land, the colonial administrators looked at existing customary or Hindu practices as 'criminal and primitive' while maintaining a semblance of non-intervention. Perhaps they were applying the rationality of the 'post-enlightenment Western Law' to these practices; but their real intention was to involve the Indian public in this (rational) discourse, to which extent they were quite successful.[32] Social reformers talked about equality, but at the abstract level. The lawmaking processes of the independent Indian state accommodated the voices of orthodox Hindu discourse and made room for spaces which legitimized skewed distributions. Gender justice became a casualty through legislation enacted in a piecemeal manner. Local traditions which provided more space to women within existing patriarchal packages were ignored and carried the imprint 'derogatory' within the prevailing Hindu psyche. The state programmes of development were initiated without providing ownership titles to women even in areas where women's contribution to agricultural activities was substantial, thus rendering the implementation of development programmes ineffective and deepening the gender hiatus through the creation of two different levels of agriculture, that is, 'feminization of subsistence agriculture' and 'masculinization of commercial agriculture'. Modern development models also seem to be lopsided; policies have been framed and implemented as if they had a universal applicability over the Indian state, without taking into account existing local requirements.

NOTES

1. *State Statistical Abstract of Himachal Pradesh*, Shimla: Government of Himachal Pradesh Department of Economics & Statistics, 1999, p. 9.
2. *Himachal in Figures 2002*, Shimla: Department of Economics and Statistics, Government of Himachal Pradesh, 2002, p. 21.
3. *State Statistical Abstract of Himachal Pradesh*, 1999; *State of The Environment Report*, Government of Himachal Pradesh, 2000, pp. 34–50.
4. *Census of India, Economic Tables*, part III B Series, Himachal Pradesh, 1991; *Census of India*, 1991; A.K. Shiva Kumar, 'UNDP Gender-Related Development Index: A Computation for Indian States', *Economic and Political Weekly*, special article, vol. 2, 1996, pp. i-vii.
5. W.H. Rattigan, *A Digest of Civil Law for the Punjab Chiefly Based on Customary Law*, 14th edn., revised by H.L. Sarin and K.L. Pandit, Allahabad: University Book Agency, 1966, pp. 1–9.
6. Alexander Cunningham, *Ladak, Physical Statistical and Historical: With Notices of the Surrounding Countries*, New Delhi, 1970 (1st pub. in London, 1854), pp. 289–90; *Gazetteer of the Kangra District*, parts II to V Kullu, Lahul & Spiti (Punjab Government, 1897), New Delhi: Indus Publishing Co., rpt 1994, pp. 82–4; *Gazetteer of the Simla Hill States* (District Gazetteer of Punjab), 1910, vol. VIII New Delhi: Indus Publishing Co., rpt 1995, pp. 12–18; Y.S. Parmar, *Polyandry in the Himalayas,* Delhi: Vikas Publishing, 1975, pp. 80–99; Janet Rizvi, *Ladakh: Crossroads of High Asia*, New Delhi: Oxford University Press, 2nd edn., 1996, pp. 129–44.
7. *Gazetteer of Simla Hill States*, 1910, pp. 12–18.
8. Janet Rizvi, *Ladakh: Crossroads of High Asia*, p. 134.
9. *Gazetteer of the Kangra District*, part I, Kangra (Punjab Government, 1883–84), New Delhi: Indus Publishing Co., rpt 1994, pp. 63–5; *Gazetteer of the Kangra District,* 1897, part III, pp. 82–4.
10. *Gazetteer of Kangra District* 1897, part III, pp. 10–13.
11. *Gazetteer of the Kangra District*, 1897, part IV, pp. 82–3.
12. K.C. Rattigan, *A Digest of Civil Law*, pp. 116; *Gazetteer of the*

Kangra District, 1883–4: part I, p. 65; and also *Gazetteer of the Kangra District,* 1897, part III, pp. 13–14, for Lahaul.

13. Parmar, *Polyandry in the Himalayas,* p. 77.
14. *Gazetteer of the Kangra District*, 1883–84, part I, Kangra, pp. 63–65; *Gazetteer of the Simla Hill States* (*District Gazetteer of Punjab*, 1910, vol. 8) New Delhi: Indus Publishing Co., rpt 1995, part A, p. 36.
15. W.H. Rattigan, *A Digest of Customary Law*, 15th edn. Allahabad: University Book Agency, 1995, pp. 843–7, 550–4; Rattigan, *A Digest of Civil Law*, pp. 482; and personal information.
16. *Gazetteer of Chamba State*, 1904, pp. 129; *Gazetteer of Kangra District*, 1883–4, part I, pp. 72–3.
17. Rizvi, *Ladakh*, p. 134; Parmar, *Polyandry in the Himalayas*, pp. 68–9; Raj Mohini Sethi, 'Women and Development: A Profile of Active Agricultural Producers', in *Sociological Bulletin*, vol. 3 (2) 1989 2: 217–33, September, p. 231.
18. Ratna Kapur and Brenda Cossman, *Subversive Sites: Feminist Engagements with Law in India*; New Delhi: Sage, 1996, pp. 55–6; Prem Chowdhry, 'Conjugality, Law and the State: Inheritance Rights as Pivot of Control in North India', in *National School of Law Journal*, vol. 1, 1993, pp. 95–116; Parmar, *Polyandry in the Himalayas*, p. 168.
19. Bombay High Court Reports (Crown Cases), 1864, 2, 117: 121, cited in K.C. Rattigan, *A Digest of Customary Law*, pp. 541–2.
20. Parmar, *Polyandry in the Himalayas,* pp. 170–4.
21. Raj Mohini Sethi, *Women in Agriculture*, Jaipur: Rawat, 1991; *Census of India*, 1981, Series 7, Himachal Pradesh; *Himachal Pradesh Land Code*, 1991.
22. Bina Aggarwal et al., 'Report of the Committee on Gender Equality in Land Tenurial laws', submitted to Ministry of Rural Development, Government of India, New Delhi, 2000.
23. D.S. Thakur, H.R. Sharma and K.D. Sharma, 'Demise of Land Reforms and the Next Step', in *Land Reforms in India*, ed. M.L. Sharma and R.K. Punia, Delhi: Ajanta Publications, 1989.
24. Personal interview with Rana Kultar Chand, former Speaker of Himachal Pradesh Legislative Assembly.
25. Personal interview.
26. *Statistical Outline Himachal Pradesh*, Shimla: Government of Himachal Pradesh, 2000–1.
27. Personal interviews; D.S. Thakur, H.R. Sharma and K.D. Sharma. 'Demise of Land Reforms and the Next Step'.
28. Personal interviews.
29. D.V. Singh et al., 'Impact of Land Reforms on the Socio-Economic

Structure of Farming Families: A Case Study in Himachal Pradesh', in *Land Reforms in India*, ed. M.L. Sharma and R.K. Punia, Delhi: Ajanta Publications, 1989.

30. D.S. Thakur, H.R. Sharma and K.D. Sharma, 'Demise of Land Reforms and the next Step'; D.S. Thakur and K.D. Sharma, 'Weaklings of Agriculture in Himachal Pradesh', *Him. J. Agric. Research*, 10 (2). 1984; D.V. Singh et al., 'Impact of Land Reforms on the Socio-Economic Structure of Farming Families'.
31. As revealed by the *patwaris* and *kanungos* in personal interviews.
32. Srimati Basu, *She Comes To Take Her Rights: Indian Women, Property and Propriety*, New Delhi: Kali for Women, 2001, p. 196.

BIBLIOGRAPHY

Aggarwal, Bina, *A Field of One's Own: Gender and Land Rights in South Asia*, Cambridge: Cambridge University, 1994.

Aggarwal, Bina, et al., 'Report of the Committee on Gender Equality in Land Tenurial laws', submitted to Ministry of Rural Development, Government of India, New Delhi, 2000.

Aggarwal, O.P., *Customary Law in the Punjab Report, Himachal Pradesh*, Lahore: Lahore Law Publishers.

Basu, Srimati, *She Comes to Take Her Rights: Indian Women, Property and Propriety*, New Delhi: Kali for Women, 2001.

Anonymous, *Brief Facts*, Shimla: Economics & Statistical Department, Government of Himachal Pradesh, 2000.

Census of India, *Provisional Population Totals*, 2001, Paper 1 of 2001, Series 3, Himachal Pradesh.

———, *Provisional Population Totals*, Rural Urban Distribution, Paper 2 of 2001 Himachal Pradesh Series 3.

———, *Economic Tables*, part III B Series, Himachal Pradesh, 1991.

———, *Provisional Population Totals, Himachal Pradesh*, Series 3, Paper 3 of 2001.

Chowdhry, Prem, 'Conjugality, Law and the State: Inheritance Rights as Pivot of Control in North India', in *National School of Law Journal*, vol. 1, 1993: 95–116.

Cunningham, Alexander, *Ladak, Physical Statistical and Historical: With Notices of the Surrounding Countries*, New Delhi, 1970 (1st pub. in London 1854).

Districts in Figures, Himachal Pradesh, Shimla: Department of Economics and Statistics, Government of Himachal Pradesh, 2001.

Gazetteer of the Chamba State, Punjab States Gazetteer (Punjab Government 1904, vol. XXI A), New Delhi: Indus Publishing Co., rpt. 1996.

Gazetteer of the Kangra District, part I Kangra (Punjab Government, 1883–4), New Delhi: Indus Publishing Co., rpt. 1994.

———, parts II to V, Kullu, Lahaul & Spiti (Punjab Government, 1897), New Delhi: Indus Publishing Co., rpt. 1994.

Gazetteer of the Simla District, District Gazetteer of Punjab (Punjab Government, 1904), New Delhi: Indus Publishing Co., rpt. 1997.

Gazetteer of the Simla Hill States (District Gazetteer of Punjab, 1910, vol. VIII), New Delhi: Indus Publishing Co., rpt. 1995.

Himachal in Figures 2002, Shimla: Department of Economics and Statistics, Government of Himachal Pradesh, 2002.

Hutchison, J. and J.P. Vogel, *History of the Punjab Hill States*, vol. I, Shimla: Department of Languages and Culture, Himachal Pradesh, 1982.

Indian Law Reports, 'Raj Kumar Rajindra Singh V. The Union of India' Civil Writ Petition No. 4 of 1974, 1976.

Jain, J.L., *Commentary on the PEPSU Tenancy and Agricultural Lands Act,* Chandigarh: Jain Law Agency, 1970.

Kapur, Ratna and Brenda Cossman, *Subversive Sites: Feminist Engagements with Law in India*, New Delhi: Sage, 1996.

Kaul, Neeta, *Land Laws in Punjab and Haryana*, Chandigarh: Chawla Publications, 2000.

Mahajan, K.C., *Interpretation of Revenue Terms*, Ludhiana: Khera Publishers, 1993.

Mann, B.S., *Commentary on the Punjab Land Reforms Act, 1972*, Chandigarh: Singla Law Agency, 1987.

Parmar, Y.S., *Polyandry in the Himalayas,* Delhi: Vikas Publishing, 1975.

Punia, R.K. and Malkit Kaur, 'Access of Women to Land and its Use', in *Land Reforms in India*, ed. M.L. Sharma and R.K. Punia, Delhi: Ajanta Publications, 1989.

Raghunath, Usha, 'Land Reforms and Women Agricultural Labourers: Case Studies in Nellore District', in *Land Reforms in India*, ed. B.N. Yugandher, New Delhi: Sage, 1996.

Rajput, Pam and Satnam Kaur, 'Land Reforms and Women Some Dimensions', in *Land Reforms in India*, ed. M.L. Sharma and R.K. Punia, Delhi: Ajanta Publications, 1989.

Rattigan, K.C., *A Digest of Civil Law for the Punjab Chiefly Based on Customary Law* 14th edn, revised by H.L. Sarin and K.L. Pandit, Allahabad: University Book Agency, 1966.

———, *A Digest of Customary Law*, 15th edn, Allahabad: University Book Agency, 1995.

Rizvi, Janet, *Ladakh: Crossroads of High Asia*, New Delhi: Oxford University Press, 2nd edn, 1996.

Rose, H.A., *A Glossary of the Tribes and Castes of the Punjab and North-West Frontier Province*, vols. I, II and III, New Delhi: Asian Educational Services, 1990.

Sethi, Raj Mohini, 'Implementation Completion Report on Kandi Areas (Hills)', Appendix E for World Bank Project G. 2100–IN/Ln.3175–in), 1999.

———, 'Women and Development: A Profile of Active Agricultural Producers', in *Sociological Bulletin*, vol. 3, September 1989, 2, 217–33.

———, 'Women and Hindu Personal Laws' *Journal of Sociological Studies*, vol. 6, January, University of Jodhpur, Jodhpur, 1987.

———, *Female Labour in Agriculture*, Monograph Series, Chandigarh: Department of Sociology, Panjab University, 1982.

———, *Women in Agriculture*, Jaipur: Rawat, 1991.

Sharma, H.R. and D.S. Thakur, 'Impact of Transfer of Improved Technology', *Him. J. Agric. Research* 11 (i).

Shiva Kumar, A.K., 'UNDP Gender-Related Development Index: A Computation for Indian States', *Economic and Political Weekly*, Special article, vol. 2, 1996.

Singh, D.V. et al., 'Impact of Land Reforms on the Socio-Economic Structure of Farming Families: A Case Study in Himachal Pradesh', in *Land Reforms in India*, ed. M.L. Sharma and R.K. Punia, Delhi: Ajanta Publications, 1989.

Singh, B.P. and P.S. Dutta. 'Marginal Farmers and Land Reforms', in *Land Reforms in India*, Sage: New Delhi, 1995.

State of The Environment Report, Shimla: State Council for Science, Technology and Environment, Government of Himachal Pradesh, 2000.

State Statistical Abstract of Himachal Pradesh, Shimla: Government of Himachal Pradesh Department of Economics & Statistics, 1999.

Statistical Outline Himachal Pradesh, Shimla: Government of Himachal Pradesh, 2000–1.

Thakur, D.S. and K.D. Sharma, 'Economics of Vegetable Production and Diversification of Farming in Himachal Pradesh' *Him. J. Agric. Research*, 11 (2), 1985.

———, 'Economics of Agriculture in Himachal Pradesh' *Him. J. Agric. Research*, 10 (2), 1984.

Thakur, D.S., H.R. Sharma and K.D. Sharma, 'Demise of Land Reforms and the next Step', in *Land Reforms in India*, ed. M.L. Sharma and R.K. Punia, Delhi: Ajanta Publications, 1989.

Glossary

arhat: a Persian wheel (for lifting water from a well).

aarti: offering worship to a deity with incense, flowers, milk, fruit and the like, together with the singing of praises.

aarhtiyas: middlemen.

adalati: a judicial officer.

Adi Granth: the Sikh scripture, compiled by Guru Arjan in 1604 (containing the compositions of the first five Gurus and of a number of *bhagat*s, *sant*s and *sufi*s) and authenticated by Guru Gobind Singh with the compositions of Guru Tegh Bahadur. Now known as the *Guru Granth Sahib*.

ak: a wild plant in a sandy tract known for its poisonous juice; *Calotropis procera*.

Akal Takht: the platform constructed in front of the Harmandir by Guru Hargobind to preside over the temporal affairs of his followers. A structure raised on the spot came to be known as the Akal Bunga. It served as the headquarters of the Akalis or Nihangs till the early nineteenth century.

Akali: a protagonist of gurdwara reform around the 1920s; now a member of the Shiromani Akali Dal.

akhand-path: an uninterrupted reading of the *Guru Granth Sahib*.

akhara: a wrestling ground.

alwan: a shawl made of wool.

amaldari: administration.

amli: an opium addict.

anand marriage: Sikh marriage ceremony in which the *Guru Granth Sahib*, and not fire, is used for circumambulation and in which a Brahman has no role.

ardas: a formal, collective prayer of the Sikhs, probably going back to the time of Guru Nanak.

atta: flour.

avtar: incarnations of Lord Vishnu, particularly Rama and Krishna.

bahi khatas: old style account books.
bahu: a daughter-in-law.
bani: literally speech; the utterances of the Gurus and the *bhagats* recorded in the *Adi Granth*; the amplified form *gurbani* or *bhagat-bani* is commonly used.
banjaras: carriers of goods by profession, moving in small or large caravans.
baraat: a marriage procession.
begane put: strangers.
bhagat: a devotee of the human incarnations of Vishnu, that is, Rama and Krishna; generally a non-Muslim devotee of God.
bhaichara: a caste or clan Brotherhood.
bhajan: a way of remembering God, or praising Him; a composition in praise of God or expressing devotion to God.
bhajan mandalis: a group of people singing hymns in prais of God.
bhajnik: one who sings *bhajans*.
bhang: hemp, cannabis; its leaves and pistils; hashish.
bigha: a measure of land about 4 *kanals* or 2,000 yards.
biradari: brotherhood.
bhet: offering; an offering made to the Guru or *Guru Granth Sahib*.
bhog: mortuary rites.
brahmacharya: celibacy.
bunga: a structure, a building; used for each of the many structures raised around the sacred tank in Amritsar.
chacha: the father's younger brother.
chadar: a sheet used as a veil; also used in levirate marriage.
chaliha: a form of offering sent by the Sikhs to their Guru in the late seventeenth and early eighteenth century.
chaprasi: a peon.
char lands: river banks.
charan-pahul: literally, nectar of the foot; the practice of drinking the water in which the toe of the Guru has been dipped, symbolizing humility and dedication on the part of the initiate; also called *charanamrit*.
chari: fodder.
Chaudhriat: the office or remuneration of a Chaudhari.
chaukidar: a watchman.
chaunk: the square as a symbol of purity and sacredness.
chaupal: an assembly (in a village); a verandah.

chautahi: a twofold cotton thick sheet spread under the bed sheet.

chhole: gram.

chilm: a clay bowl with or without stem in which tobacco is smoked.

choti: top-knot.

chulah: a stove; hearth.

churis: glass bangles.

dan: charity; emphasis in the Sikh tradition is on giving something to others rather than receiving anything from them.

dan patar: a donation box.

darbar: royal court; used for the Harmandir, and also for the *Guru Granth Sahib* installed therein.

darogha: a superintendent of police; head of an organization.

Darwan (darban): a security personnel.

Dasam Granth: the term used for the compilation earlier called the Book of the Tenth King (*Dasan Patshah ka Granth*); its compilation is commonly attributed to Bhai Mani Singh; the authorship of its contents (a number of independent compositions) and the date of its compilation have been the subject of debate.

daswand: literally, one-tenth; the contribution which a Sikh was expected to make towards the funds of the Guru and the community; traced to Guru Arjan; made popular by the Khalsa.

devar: brother-in-law.

dhai: midwife; a wet nurse.

dharamshala: a halting place run charitably and generally attached to a temple.

dharm: duty in the broadest sense; includes a Hindu's religious, social and occupational obligations as defined by his place in the social system; also used to denote 'religion'.

dharma bhai: brother by religion.

dharmarth: land revenue alienated for charitable or religious purposes.

dharmsal: literally, place for earning merit; Sikh sacred space or place of worship in early Sikh history; now generally called *gurdwara*.

diwan: the keeper of a treasury; the head of the finance dept. in a province or state; religious meeting.

dolu:	a bucket.
durries:	carpets or matting made of cotton.
dwijas:	higher caste Hindus, consisting of the Brahmans, Kshatriyas and Vaishyas, entitled to wear the scared thread.
fakir:	a pious person; a devotee of God; used generally for a Muslim mendicant.
faujdar:	literally, one who kept troops; a military officer under the Mughals to maintain law and order and to assist civil authorities; the office survived into the early nineteenth century.
gabrun:	rich silk cloth.
gaddi:	a throne; the seat of the head of a religious fraternity.
gadela:	a cushion.
gali:	a lane.
gana, samgha, sarva samgha:	denoting assemblies through which collectivities functioned in ancient India.
ghagra:	an ankle length skirt.
ghalari:	a sugar cane crusher.
ghar-jamai:	a husband who stay in the house of the wife's parents.
ghasni:	grasslands.
ghat:	a landing-place; wharf; a river bank; a flight of steps to water; a place (as at a river bank) for washing clothes.
golak:	literally, a box to receive cash offerings or for family saving; Gurdwara funds.
gotra:	a sub-caste; sub-division of a caste.
granthi:	a professional reader of the Granth; the functionary incharge of a *gurdwara*.
gumashta:	an assistant or subordinate, generally of a revenue collector.
gur:	jaggery.
gurdwara:	literally, the door of the Guru; a Sikh place of worship, and generally a centre of social activity too.
gurmata:	the collective decision taken before *Guru Granth Sahib*.
gurpurab:	celebration of an event connected with the Guru, generally birth or death.
guru:	a preceptor; a religious teacher; an epithet used for the founder of Sikhism and each of his nine successors.
hakim:	a practitioner of Unani medicine.

halimi-raj:	literally, rule of moderation in which there is no oppression or coercion; an expression used by Guru Arjan for the entire dispensation of Guru Nanak and his successors.
halwa:	a sweet made of flour, *ghee* and sugar.
harami:	born out of an illicit relation; a bastard.
haq mehar:	dower.
holan:	barbecued green grass pods.
hookah:	a device for smoking tobacco through water.
hukamnama:	literally, a 'written order'; used generally for the letters of the Sikh Gurus to their followers.
iddat:	period of mourning.
ishtihar:	advertisement.
izarband:	latticed string to tie pyjamas.
izzat:	honour; good name; esteem.
jagir:	an assignment of land revenue in lieu of salary for performing service for the state; *jagirdar:* the holder of a *jagir.*
jahez:	dowry.
jajmani system:	reciprocal obligations of the landholders and the village servants.
Jat:	an important agricultural caste/tribe in the Punjab; used also for the cultivators in general.
jatha:	a group or a band.
jhatka:	meat of an animal which has been killed by a swift blow on the back of the neck.
jhoothi:	leftover food.
jhoti:	a young female buffalo.
jizya:	the tax imposed on non-Muslim subjects under a Muslim ruler; it was formally abolished by Akbar, reimposed by Aurangzeb, and abolished again by his successors.
Jogi:	a renunciant, generally belonging to one of the twelve Gorakhnathi orders.
jutti:	a shoe
kachh:	short drawers of a special kind meant to be worn by those Sikhs who have been initiated through baptism of the double-edged sword.
kaddu:	pumpkin.
kameez:	a shirt.
kamin:	a village menial.
kanat:	a thick cloth used to form a temporary enclosure.
kangha:	the comb supposed to be kept by a baptized Singh as one of the 5 'k's.
kanya:	an unmarried girl.

kanya dan: giving away of a daughter in marriage.
kar: literally a tax; an offering.
kara: iron bracelet meant to be worn by the baptized Khalsa.
karah parshad: the sacred food prepared in a cauldron (*karaha*) was called *karah parshad*, its three ingredients being wheat flour, sugar and *ghee*.
karewa: the custom of marrying a widow generally to the younger brother of the deceased; the other terms used for this practice were *karao, chadar-andazi* and *chadar dalna*.
karkhana: a factory.
katcha: temporary; raw, unripe, unbaked.
katha: a narrative; an exposition; *katha vachak* or *kathavala:* one who renders a *katha*.
katra: an enclosed market-cum-residential locality, with a separate entrance and management.
kesh: uncut hair along with unshaven beard.
Khalsa: the Sikh brotherhood instituted by Guru Gobind Singh; used for an individual as well as the collective body.
khandani: belonging to a well placed family; respectable.
khes: a kind of heavy patterned cloth.
kinari: an embroidered strip stitched on to the border of a cloth.
kirpan: a sword.
kirtan: corporate singing of divine praises, both in the morning and the evening.
kisan: a farmer.
kismi: a form of tenancy in Himachal Pradesh.
Kothali: the goldsmith's crucible.
kothri: a small or dark room (of a house); a store room.
kudrat: nature.
kuks: shrieks.
kurta: a collarless shirt, generally of knee length.
lambardar: a village headman.
langar: a community meal; the kitchen attached to a gurdwara from which food is served to all, regardless of caste or creed.
lathi: a staff; a club, prop, support.
lingam: a phallus image (idol) or the form in which Shiva is worshipped.
Lohar: an ironsmith.
loi: a woollen shawl.

ludhrak: a plant, the root of which was believed to have medicinal value.
madi: a mansion.
mahant: the head of a religious establishment; the Udasi custodian of a gurdwara.
majra: a village.
makki: corn.
mandal: a circle, zone, territory, subdivision.
mandi: a market, specially a wholesale market for a particular commodity (as grain or vegetables).
mandir: a temple.
manja: a cot.
mantra: a hymn or a formula purportedly with magical powers.
mantri: the secretary.
mash, moong: pulses.
masool phatak: duty charged on releasing a stray animal from official custody.
mastana: intoxicated.
mauli: a coloured cotton thread worn as a part of Brahmanical rites.
meind: a boundry.
mela: a fair.
mistri: a mason.
mohalla: a residential locality in a town.
moorha: a chair made of cane and jute.
morcha: the non-violent mode of agitation by the Akali Jathas.
mukhia: the village headman.
muklawa: the ceremony of sending away the young bride on attaining puberty to the house of her husband.
mullah: a Muslim priest and teacher, generally in-charge of the village mosque.
munaqqa: dry grapes.
murasila: a formal letter.
mutsaddi: an accountant or an official.
nagar kirtan: a moving procession singing God's praises.
naib: a deputy.
nam, dan, isnan: the phrase used by Guru Nanak for the essential features of the Sikh way of life, that is meditation on God, charity, and physical and moral purity.
namda: a thick felt.
nath: a nosering, generally made of gold.
nautor: wasteland or forest land.

nawab: a title used generally for provincial governors under the Mughals; used also for a subordinate ruler.

nazim: an administrator; the governor of a province.

nazool: the evacuee property.

neota: an invitation.

nikah: marriage ceremony among the Muslims.

niyog: a temporary marriage contracted for offspring prescribed by Manu, and recommended by Swami Dayanand as a solution to the widow problem of his day.

padri: a Christian priest or minister.

pagri: the turban.

pagvand: derived from *pag* (a turban), to signify equal division of an estate amongst all the sons from different wives.

paisa: the copper coin valued at 64th of a rupee.

pandal: a temporary arrangement under a canopy made of cloth for seating a large number of people.

panchayat: the assembly of the representatives of a caste or brotherhood in a village; *panch:* an individual member; *sarpanch:* head of the panchayat.

Panth: literally, the people following a particular path; collectively, the followers of the Gurus; the Sikh community.

parkarma/parikrama: the circumambulatory path around the Harmandir and the tank.

pashm: wool of a fine quality.

pathshala: an elementary school.

pativrata dharma: a wife's total devotion to her husband.

patta: the document stating the revenue demand assessed upon an individual owner of land.

pattu: a hand-woven light woollen blanket.

patwari: the keeper of revenue records of a village.

phera: the rounds taken in the ceremony of marriage generally around sacred fire, and conducted by a priest.

phulkari: an embroidered sheet of rough cotton cloth.

pinjrapole: a shelter for infirm and sterile cattle.

pipal: a shady tree held sacred; *Ficus religiosa*.

prachar: preaching; *pracharak:* a preacher.

pradhan: the headman.

puja: worship of a deity; idolatry.

pujari: the attendant of a shrine; a Brahman priest.

pukka: a house made of bricks or stone.
punarth: in charity.
pundit: literally, a learned person; generally used for a Brahman.
purdah: veiling; seclusion of women, particularly among high class Muslims, and adopted by some non-Muslims as a mark of social respectability.
qanungo: the hereditary keeper of the revenue records and practices.
qasba: a small town.
rababi: one who plays on the *rabab*, a kind of violin with three strings.
rabi: the spring crops generally sown in October-November and reaped in April-May.
ragi: a professional singer of the compositions of the Sikh scripture.
rahit: a way of life, used specially for the Sikh way of life in accordance with the ethical principles enunciated by the Gurus.
Rahitnama: a written manual of the Sikh way of life.
rais: an aristocrat.
raj tilak: the coronation ceremony.
rayatwari system: a system of assessment of revenue directly on the cultivator.
reet: bride price.
roti: a cake made of flour.
rumala: a piece of cloth used for covering the *Guru Granth Sahib*.
saag: a leafy vegetable, generally *sarson*.
sabha: a society or an association.
sadhu: a religious person, generally a renunciant not affiliated to the Brahmanical system.
Sahajdhari: a Sikh who is not baptized as a Singh and does not observe the Khalsa code of discipline; a non-Khalsa Sikh.
sahukar: a wealthy merchant; a moneylender.
Saligram: symbol of Lord Vishnu in black stone.
sanad: a written document possessing legal validity.
sangat: an assembly; a congregation of Sikhs; the collective body of Sikhs at one place.
sankalp: the vow to make an offering after a particular wish is fulfilled or for the fulfilment of a particular wish.
sannyasin: literally, a renunciant.

sanskar: a sacrament.
sant: literally, a saint; generally used for Namdev, Kabir, Ravidas and Dadu who worshipped formless God.
Sarbarah: literally, a head; manager of the Golden Temple.
sardar: a leader; a Sikh ruler; any Khalsa Sikh.
sarkar: government.
sarovar: a tank, pool of water.
sarson ka tel: mustard oil.
sarva-khaps: the political organization of various clans or castes in the geographical area inhabited by them.
satsang: literally, true association; singing hymns in praise of God in congregation.
satyagrahis: those who adopted Mahatma Gandhi's ideology of non-violence as a strategy for attaining freedom.
seree/siri/sanjhi: a sharecropper, an attached agricultural labourer.
sevak: literally, a servant; a worker.
shabad: literally, a word; a hymn; verses from *Guru Granth Sahib*.
shagun: a formal gift offered generally on a happy occasion, especially marriage.
shahidi: martyrdom.
shamlat: the common land of a village.
shastrarth: religious debate.
Shastras: religious treatises in the Brahmanical system regarded as authoritative.
shraddha: the rite in which the dead ancestors are fed through the mediacy of Brahmans.
shuddhi: literally, purification the rite evolved by the Arya Samaj for reconversion as well as purification of the low castes.
sipahi: a soldier.
siropa: a piece of cloth symbolic of honour.
solah sanskar: sixteen sacraments, from pre-natal stage to death.
stridhan: personal property of a woman, consisting of ornaments, clothes, and sometimes, property received from her parental family and after marriage.
surahi: an earthen water vessel with a long narrow neck.
susi: a kind of cotton cloth, used generally by women.
tahsil: the sub-division of a district in the British and post-independence period; *tahsildar*: the officer-in-charge of a *tahsil*.
takhmina: individual assessment.
tarameera: an oil seed.
tarpan: a ritual offering.

Teli:	an oil-presser.
tilak:	the sacred mark on the forehead of a Brahman, an upper caste Hindu, or the member of a religious sect.
thana:	a police station.
thanadar:	commandant of a garrison or a fort.
theka:	a liquor shop, generally selling country liquor.
thekedar:	a contractor.
tulsi:	the basil plant which is considered sacred.
updesh:	sermon.
updeshak:	a male Hindu preacher or missionary.
vaid:	a practitioner of indigenous medicine.
vakil:	an agent or a deputy; an envoy.
vanaspati:	artificial *ghi* or clarified butter.
varna:	literally colour; rendered as 'caste' in English.
varnashrama-dharma:	the concept of the fourfold division of the social order (Brahman, Kshatriya, Vaishya, Shudra), and of individual lifespan (Brahmacharya, Grihastha, Sannyas and Vanprasta).
Vars:	a literary genre, generally used for heroic poetry.
vehra:	a courtyard.
Vilayat:	a foreign country.
vidhi or biah:	the ceremony of a religious wedding conducted by a Brahman priest.
zaildar:	the officer of a group of villages.
zulm:	torture; oppression.

Foreign Friends of the Institute

CANADA

Harmohinder Singh Bains, Lakhwinder Singh Bains, Manga Bassi, Jugraj Bath, Sarbjit Singh Bathal, Sadhu Binning, Piara Singh Beesla, Bachan Singh Buttar, Harcharan Singh Daliwal, Paramjit Singh Dhaliwal, Pritpal Singh Dhaliwal, Ujjal Dev Singh Dosanjh, Niranjan Singh Gill, Paramjit Singh Gill, Sarwan Singh Gill, Zora Singh Gill, Hardial Singh Grewal, Harnek Singh Grewal, Rajinder Singh Hans, Sukhwant Hundal, Jaswant Singh, Kulwant Singh Khatra, Raghbir Singh Mangat, Sohan Punni, Gurmail Ria, Gurpal Singh Sahota, Jasbir Singh Sahota, Ranbir Singh Sahota, Harbhajan Singh Sandhu, Surjit Singh Sandhu, K.S. Sekhon, Dharampal Sharma, Amrik Sull and Gulzar Singh Willing, Vedic Hindu Society of British Columbia.

UNITED KINGDOM

Hardev Singh Brar, Hari Singh Chahal, Tejinder Singh Dhaliwal, Gurcharan Singh Grewal, Gurdev Singh Grewal, Hardeep Singh Grewal, Jagdev Singh Grewal and Malkiat Singh Grewal.

UNITED STATE OF AMERICA

Karam Singh Burn, Bhupinder Singh Gill, Rahuldeep Gill, Harjit Singh Mangat and Jasbir Kaur Saluja.

Contributors

KUMOOL ABBI, Reader in Sociology, Panjab University, Chandigarh.

HIMADRI BANERJEE, Professor of History, Jadavpur University, Kolkata.

KUSUM CHOPRA, formerly Professor of Economics at the Centre for the Study of Regional Development, Jawaharlal Nehru University, New Delhi.

J.S. GREWAL, formerly Professor of History and Vice-Chancellor, Guru Nanak Dev University, Amritsar, and Director, Indian Institute of Advanced Study, Shimla.

REETA GREWAL, Reader in History, Panjab University, Chandigarh.

RAJESH GILL, Professor of Sociology, Panjab University, Chandigarh.

SUCHA SINGH GILL, Professor of Economics, Punjabi University, Patiala.

SIMRIT KAHLON, Lecturer in Geography, DAV College, Chandigarh.

SURYA KANT, Professor of Geography, Panjab University, Chandigarh.

ATIYA HABEEB KIDWAI, Professor of Geography, Centre for the Study of Regional Development, Jawaharlal Nehru University, New Delhi.

SWARNJIT MEHTA, formerly Professor of Geography, Panjab University, Chandigarh.

SHEENA PALL, Senior Lecturer in History, Panjab University, Chandigarh.

VEENA SACHDEVA, Reader in History, Panjab University, Chandigarh.

SASHA, Senior Lecturer in History, Panjab University, Chandigarh.

HARISH C. SHARMA, Professor of History, Guru Nanak Dev University, Amritsar.

RADHA SHARMA, Professor of History, Guru Nanak Dev University, Amritsar.

RAJ MOHINI SETHI, formerly Professor of Sociology, Panjab University, Chandigarh.

CHETAN SINGH, Professor of History, Himachal Pradesh University, Shimla.

MANJIT SINGH, Professor of Sociology, Panjab University, Chandigarh.

P.S. VERMA, formerly Professor of Political Science, Panjab University, Chandigarh.

JOHN C.B. WEBSTER, taught at Baring Union Christian College and worked as Director of the Christian Institute of Sikh Studies, Batala.

Index